Learning Java™

Patrick Niemeyer and Jonathan Knudsen

Beijing · Cambridge · Farnham · Köln · Paris · Sebastopol · Taipei · Tokyo

THE JAVA™ SERIES

Learning Java™

Learning Java™

by Patrick Niemeyer and Jonathan Knudsen

Copyright © 2000 O'Reilly & Associates, Inc. All rights reserved.
Portions of this book previously appeared in *Exploring Java*, Copyright © 1997, 1996 O'Reilly & Associates, Inc. All rights reserved.
Printed in the United States of America.

Published by O'Reilly & Associates, Inc., 101 Morris Street, Sebastopol, CA 95472.

Editors: John Posner and Mike Loukides

Production Editor: Nicole Arigo

Cover Designer: Edie Freedman

Printing History:

> May 2000:   First Edition

Library of Congress Cataloging-in-Publication Data

Niemeyer, Patrick.
  Learning Java / Patrick Niemeyer & Jonathan Knudsen.
    p. cm.
  ISBN 1-56592-718-4
    1. Java (Computer program language) I. Knudsen, Jonathan. II. Title.

QA76.73.J38 N545 2000
005.13'3–dc21

                                                        00-039961

ISBN: 1-56592-718-4
[M]

Table of Contents

Preface

This book is about the Java™ language and programming environment. If you've been at all active on the Internet in the past few years, you've heard a lot about Java. It's one of the most exciting developments in the history of the Internet, rivaling the creation of the World Wide Web. Java became the darling of the Internet programming community as soon as the alpha version was released. Immediately, thousands of people were writing Java applets to add to their web pages. Interest in Java only grew with time, and support for Java in Netscape Navigator guaranteed it would be a permanent part of the Net scene.

What, then, is Java? Java is a network programming language that was developed by Sun Microsystems. It's already in widespread use for creating animated and interactive web pages. However, this is only the start. The Java language and environment are rich enough to support entirely new kinds of applications, like dynamically extensible browsers and mobile agents. There are entirely new kinds of computer platforms being developed around Java (handheld devices and network computers) that download all their software over the network. In the coming years, we'll see what Java is capable of doing; fancy web pages are fun and interesting, but they certainly aren't the end of the story. If Java is successful (and that isn't a foregone conclusion), it could change the way we think about computing in fundamental ways.

This book gives you a head start on a lot of Java fundamentals. *Learning Java* attempts to live up to its name by mapping out the Java language, its class libraries, programming techniques, and idioms. We'll dig deep into interesting areas and at least scratch the surface of the rest. Other titles in the O'Reilly & Associates Java Series will pick up where we leave off and provide more comprehensive information on specific areas and applications of Java.

Whenever possible, we'll provide meaningful, realistic examples and avoid cataloging features. The examples are simple but hint at what can be done. We won't
be developing the next great "killer app" in these pages, but we hope to give you a
starting point for many hours of experimentation and tinkering that will lead you
to learn more on your own.

New Developments

This book, *Learning Java*, is actually the third edition—reworked and retitled—of
O'Reilly's popular *Exploring Java*. We've de-emphasized web-page applets this time
around, reflecting their diminishing role over the past couple of years in creating
"smart" web pages. Other technologies have filled in the gap: JavaScript on the client side, and Java servlets and Active Server Pages on the server side.

We cover the most interesting features of Sun's newest release of Java, officially
called *Java 2 SDK Version 1.3*. (In the old days, it would have been called "JDK," for
"Java development kit;" we use the newer, officially blessed "SDK," for "software
development kit," throughout this book.) These features include servlets, the Java
Media Framework (JMF), timers, the collections, 2D graphics, and image-
processing APIs, using the Java security manager, and using Java 2 signed applets.

Another important change, though not as recent as SDK 1.3, is the ascendancy of
Java Swing as the main API for graphical user interface programming. Much of the
material relating to AWT, Java's original GUI programming interface, has been
recast and updated to use Swing facilities.

Audience

This book is for computer professionals, students, technical people, and Finnish
hackers. It's for everyone who has a need for hands-on experience with the Java
language with an eye toward building real applications. This book could also be
considered a crash course in object-oriented programming; as you learn about
Java, you'll also learn a powerful and practical approach to object-oriented software development.

Superficially, Java looks like C or C++, so you'll be in the best position to use this
book if you've some experience with one of these languages. If you do not, you
might want to refer to books like O'Reilly's *Practical C Programming* for a more
thorough treatment of basic C syntax. However, don't make too much of the syntactic similarities between Java and C or C++. In many respects, Java acts like more
dynamic languages such as Smalltalk and Lisp. Knowledge of another object-
oriented programming language should certainly help, although you may have to
change some ideas and unlearn a few habits. Java is considerably simpler than languages like C++ and Smalltalk.

Although we encourage you to take a broad view, you would have every right to be disappointed if we ignored the Web. A substantial part of this book does discuss Java as a language for World Wide Web applications, so you should be familiar with the basic ideas behind web browsers, servers, and web documents.

Using This Book

This book is organized roughly as follows:

- Chapters 1 and 2 provide a basic introduction to Java concepts and a tutorial to give you a jump start on Java programming.

- Chapter 3 discusses tools for developing with Java (the compiler, the interpreter, the JAR file package). It also covers important concepts such as embedding Java code in HTML support and object signing.

- Chapters 4 through 8 describe the Java language itself. Chapter 8 covers the language's thread facilities, which should be of particular interest to advanced programmers.

- Chapters 9 and 10 cover much of the core API. Chapter 9 describes basic utilities, and Chapter 10 covers I/O facilities.

- Chapters 11 and 12 cover Java networking, including sockets, URLs, and remote method invocation (RMI).

- Chapters 13 through 18 cover the Abstract Window Toolkit (AWT) and Swing, which provide graphical user interface (GUI) and image support.

- Chapter 19 covers the JavaBeans™ component architecture.

- Chapter 20 covers applets, the area in which Java saw its initial success.

If you're like us, you don't read books from front to back. If you're really like us, you usually don't read the preface at all. However, on the off chance that you will see this in time, here are a few suggestions.

If you are an experienced programmer who has to learn Java in the next five minutes, you are probably looking for the examples. You might want to start by glancing at the tutorial in Chapter 2, *A First Application*. If that doesn't float your boat, you should at least look at the information in Chapter 3, *Tools of the Trade*, which tells you how to use the compiler and interpreter, and gives you the basics of a standalone Java application. This should get you started.

Chapters 11 and 12 are essential if you are interested in writing advanced networked applications. This is probably the most interesting and important part of Java.

Chapters 13 though 19 discuss Java's graphics features and component architecture. You should read this carefully if you are interested in Java applications for the Web.

Getting Wired

There are many online sources for information about Java. Sun Microsystem's official web site for Java topics is *http://java.sun.com*; look here for the latest news, updates, and Java releases. This is where you'll find the Java Software Development Kit (SDK), which includes the compiler, the interpreter, and other tools. Another good source of Java information, including free applets, utility classes, and applications, is the Gamelan site, run by EarthWeb; its URL is *http://www. gamelan.com*.

You should also visit O'Reilly & Associates' Java site at *http://java.oreilly.com*. There you'll find information about other books in O'Reilly's Java Series, and a pointer to the home page for *Learning Java*, *http://www.oreilly.com/catalog/learnjava/*, where you'll find the source code examples for this book.

The *comp.lang.java* newsgroup can be a good source of information and announcements, and a place to ask intelligent questions.

Conventions Used in This Book

The font conventions used in this book are quite simple.

Italic is used for:

- Unix pathnames, filenames, and program names
- Internet addresses, such as domain names and URLs
- New terms where they are defined

Boldface is used for:

- Names of GUI buttons and menus

`Constant width` is used for:

- Anything that might appear in a Java program, including method names, variable names, and class names
- Command lines and options that should be typed verbatim on the screen
- Tags that might appear in an HTML document

`Constant width bold` is used for:

- In code examples, text that is typed by the user

In the main body of text, we always use a pair of empty parentheses after a method name to distinguish methods from variables and other creatures.

In the Java source listings, we follow the coding conventions most frequently used in the Java community. Class names begin with capital letters; variable and method names begin with lowercase. All the letters in the names of constants are capitalized. We don't use underscores to separate words in a long name; following common practice, we capitalize individual words (after the first) and run the words together. For example: `thisIsAVariable`, `thisIsAMethod()`, `ThisIsAClass`, and `THISISACONSTANT`.

How to Contact Us

We have tested and verified all the information in this book to the best of our abilities, but you may find that features have changed or that we have let errors slip through the production of the book. Please let us know of any errors that you find, as well as suggestions for future editions, by writing to:

O'Reilly & Associates, Inc.
101 Morris St.
Sebastopol, CA 95472
1-800-998-9938 (in the U.S. or Canada)
1-707-829-0515 (international/local)
1-707-829-0104 (fax)

You can also send messages electronically. To be put on our mailing list or to request a catalog, send email to:

info@oreilly.com

To ask technical questions or to comment on the book, send email to:

bookquestions@oreilly.com

We have a web site for the book, where we'll list examples, errata, and any plans for future editions. You can access this page at:

http://www.oreilly.com/catalog/learnjava/

For more information about this book and others, see the O'Reilly web site:

http://www.oreilly.com

Acknowledgments

Many people have contributed to putting this book together, both in its *Exploring Java* incarnation and in its current form as *Learning Java*. Foremost we would like to thank Tim O'Reilly for giving us the opportunity to write this book. Special thanks to Mike Loukides, the series editor, whose endless patience and experience got us through the difficult parts. Paula Ferguson and John Posner contributed their organizational and editing abilities to get the material into final form. We could not have asked for a more skillful or responsive team of people with whom to work.

Particular thanks are due to our technical reviewers: Andrew Cohen, Eric Raymond, Lisa Farley, and Jim Farley (not related). All of them gave thorough reviews that were invaluable in assembling the final draft. Eric contributed many bits of text that eventually found their way into the book.

Speaking of borrowings, the original version of the glossary came from David Flanagan's book, *Java in a Nutshell*. We also borrowed the class hierarchy diagrams from David's book. These diagrams were based on similar diagrams by Charles L. Perkins. His original diagrams are available at *http://rendezvous.com/java/*.

Thanks also to Marc Wallace and Steven Burkett for reading the book in progress. As for the crowd in St. Louis, a special thanks to LeeAnn Langdon of the Library Ltd. and Kerri Bonasch. Deepest thanks to Victoria Doerr for her patience and love. Finally, thanks for the support of the "lunch" crowd: Karl "Gooch" Stiefvater, Bryan "Butter" O'Connor, Brian "Brian" Gottlieb, and the rest of the clan at Washington University.

Yet Another Language?

The greatest challenges and most exciting opportunities for software developers today lie in harnessing the power of networks. Applications created today, whatever their intended scope or audience, will almost certainly be run on machines linked by a global network of computing resources. The increasing importance of networks is placing new demands on existing tools and fueling the demand for a rapidly growing list of completely new kinds of applications.

We want software that works—consistently, anywhere, on any platform—and that plays well with other applications. We want dynamic applications that take advantage of a connected world, capable of accessing disparate and distributed information sources. We want truly distributed software that can be extended and upgraded seamlessly. We want intelligent applications—like autonomous agents that can roam the Net for us, ferreting out information and serving as electronic emissaries. We know, to some extent, what we want. So why don't we have it?

The problem has been that the tools for building these applications have fallen short. The requirements of speed and portability have been, for the most part, mutually exclusive, and security has been largely ignored or misunderstood. There are truly portable languages, but they are mostly bulky, interpreted, and slow. These languages are popular as much for their high-level functionality as for their portability. And there are fast languages, but they usually provide speed by binding themselves to particular platforms, so they can meet the portability issue only halfway. There are even a few recent safe languages, but they are primarily offshoots of the portable languages and suffer from the same problems.

Enter Java

The Java™ programming language, developed at Sun Microsystems under the guidance of Net luminaries James Gosling and Bill Joy, is designed to be a machine-independent programming language that is both safe enough to traverse networks and powerful enough to replace native executable code. Java addresses the issues raised here and may help us start building the kinds of applications we want.

Initially, most of the enthusiasm for Java centered around its capabilities for building embedded applications for the World Wide Web; these applications are called *applets*. Applets could be independent programs in themselves, or sophisticated frontends to programs running on a server. More recently, interest has shifted to other areas. With Java 2, Java has the most sophisticated toolkit for building graphical user interfaces; this development has allowed Java to become a popular platform for developing traditional application software. Java has also become an important platform for server-side applications, using the *servlet* interface, and for enterprise applications using technologies like Enterprise JavaBeans™. And Java is the platform of choice for modern distributed applications.

This book shows you how to use Java to accomplish real programming tasks, such as building networked applications and creating functional user interfaces. There's still a chapter devoted to applets; they may become more important again when the Java 2 (and subsequent) versions of the Java platform are more widely distributed in web browsers.

Java's Origins

The seeds of Java were planted in 1990 by Sun Microsystems patriarch and chief researcher, Bill Joy. Since Sun's inception in the early '80s, it has steadily pushed one idea: "The network is the computer." At the time though, Sun was competing in a relatively small workstation market, while Microsoft was beginning its domination of the more mainstream, Intel-based PC world. When Sun missed the boat on the PC revolution, Joy retreated to Aspen, Colorado, to work on advanced research. He was committed to accomplishing complex tasks with simple software, and founded the aptly named Sun Aspen Smallworks.

Of the original members of the small team of programmers assembled in Aspen, James Gosling is the one who will be remembered as the father of Java. Gosling first made a name for himself in the early '80s as the author of Gosling Emacs, the first version of the popular Emacs editor that was written in C and ran under Unix. Gosling Emacs became popular, but was soon eclipsed by a free version, GNU Emacs, written by Emacs's original designer. By that time, Gosling had moved on to design Sun's NeWS window system, which briefly contended with the X Window

System for control of the Unix graphical user interface (GUI) desktop in 1987. While some people would argue that NeWS was superior to X, NeWS lost out because Sun kept it proprietary and didn't publish source code, while the primary developers of X formed the X Consortium and took the opposite approach.

Designing NeWS taught Gosling the power of integrating an expressive language with a network-aware windowing GUI. It also taught Sun that the Internet programming community will refuse to accept proprietary standards, no matter how good they may be. The seeds of Java's remarkably permissive licensing scheme were sown by NeWS's failure. Gosling brought what he had learned to Bill Joy's nascent Aspen project, and in 1992, work on the project led to the founding of the Sun subsidiary, FirstPerson, Inc. Its mission was to lead Sun into the world of consumer electronics.

The FirstPerson team worked on developing software for information appliances, such as cellular phones and personal digital assistants (PDAs). The goal was to enable the transfer of information and real-time applications over cheap infrared and packet-based networks. Memory and bandwidth limitations dictated small and efficient code. The nature of the applications also demanded they be safe and robust. Gosling and his teammates began programming in C++, but they soon found themselves confounded by a language that was too complex, unwieldy, and insecure for the task. They decided to start from scratch, and Gosling began working on something he dubbed "C++ minus minus."

With the foundering of the Apple Newton, it became apparent that the PDA's ship had not yet come in, so Sun shifted FirstPerson's efforts to interactive TV (ITV). The programming language of choice for ITV set-top boxes was the near ancestor of Java, a language called Oak. Even with its elegance and ability to provide safe interactivity, Oak could not salvage the lost cause of ITV. Customers didn't want it, and Sun soon abandoned the concept.

At that time, Joy and Gosling got together to decide on a new strategy for their language. It was 1993, and the explosion of interest in the Internet, and the World Wide Web in particular, presented a new opportunity. Oak was small, robust, architecture-independent, and object-oriented. As it happens, these are also the requirements for a universal, network-savvy programming language. Sun quickly changed focus, and with a little retooling, Oak became Java.

Future Buzz?

It would not be overdoing it to say that Java has caught on like wildfire. Even before its first official release, while Java was still a non-product, nearly every major industry player jumped on the Java bandwagon. Java licensees included Microsoft, Intel, IBM, and virtually all major hardware and software vendors. (That's not to say that everything has been coming up roses. Even with all of this support Java has taken a lot of knocks and had some growing pains during its first few years.)

As we begin looking at the Java architecture, you'll see that much of what is exciting about Java comes from the self-contained, virtual machine environment in which Java applications run. Java has been carefully designed so that this supporting architecture can be implemented either in software, for existing computer platforms, or in customized hardware, for new kinds of devices. Sun and other industry giants are producing fast Java chips and microprocessors tailored to run media-rich Java applications. Hardware implementations of Java could power inexpensive network terminals, PDAs, and other information appliances, to take advantage of transportable Java applications. Software implementations of Java are available now for portable computing devices like the popular Palm™ PDA.

Many people see Java as part of a trend toward cheap, Internet-based, "operating system-less" appliances that will weave the Net into more and more consumer-related areas. The first attempts at marketing "network computers" as alternatives to the standard PC have not gone very well. (The combination of Windows and cheap PC hardware form a formidable barrier.) But the desktop is only one corner of the network. Only time will tell what people will do with Java, but it's probably worth at least a passing thought that the applet you write today might well be running on someone's wristwatch tomorrow. If that seems too futuristic, remember that you can already get "smart cards" and "wearable" devices like rings and dog tags that have Java interpreters embedded in them. These devices are capable of doing everything from financial transactions (paying a hotel bill) to unlocking a door (the door to your hotel room) to rerouting phone calls (so your hotel room receives your business calls). The hardware is already here; it can't be long before the rest of the software infrastructure begins to take advantage of it. A Java wristwatch is not a silly notion.

A Virtual Machine

Java is both a compiled and an interpreted language. Java source code is turned into simple binary instructions, much like ordinary microprocessor machine code. However, whereas C or C++ source is refined to native instructions for a particular model of processor, Java source is compiled into a universal format—instructions for a *virtual machine*.

Compiled Java *byte-code*, also called *J-code*, is executed by a Java runtime interpreter. The runtime system performs all the normal activities of a real processor, but it does so in a safe, virtual environment. It executes the stack-based instruction set and manages a storage heap. It creates and manipulates primitive datatypes, and loads and invokes newly referenced blocks of code. Most importantly, it does all this in accordance with a strictly defined open specification that can be implemented by anyone who wants to produce a Java-compliant virtual machine. Together, the virtual machine and language definition provide a complete specification. There are no features of Java left undefined or implementation-dependent. For example, Java specifies the sizes of all its primitive data types, rather than leave it up to each implementation.

The Java interpreter is relatively lightweight and small; it can be implemented in whatever form is desirable for a particular platform. On most systems, the interpreter is written in a fast, natively compiled language like C or C++. The interpreter can be run as a separate application, or it can be embedded in another piece of software, such as a web browser.

All of this means that Java code is implicitly portable. The same Java application byte-code can run on any platform that provides a Java runtime environment, as shown in Figure 1-1. You don't have to produce alternative versions of your application for different platforms, and you don't have to distribute source code to end users.

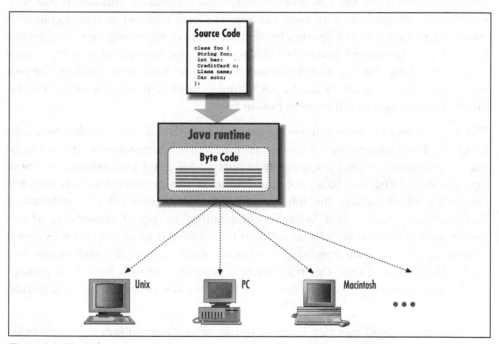

Figure 1-1. The Java runtime environment

The fundamental unit of Java code is the *class*. As in other object-oriented languages, classes are application components that hold executable code and data. Compiled Java classes are distributed in a universal binary format that contains Java byte-code and other class information. Classes can be maintained discretely and stored in files or archives on a local system or on a network server. Classes are located and loaded dynamically at runtime, as they are needed by an application.

In addition to the platform-specific runtime system, Java has a number of fundamental classes that contain architecture-dependent methods. These *native methods* serve as the gateway between the Java virtual machine and the real world. They are implemented in a natively compiled language on the host platform. They provide access to resources such as the network, the windowing system, and the host filesystem. The rest of Java is written entirely in Java, and is therefore portable. This includes fundamental Java utilities like the Java compiler and Sun's HotJava web browser, which are also Java applications and are therefore available on all Java platforms.

Historically, interpreters have been considered slow, but because the Java interpreter runs compiled byte-code, Java is a relatively fast interpreted language. More importantly, Java has also been designed so that software implementations of the runtime system can optimize their performance by compiling byte-code to native machine code on the fly. This is called *just-in-time compilation.* Sun claims that with just-in-time compilation, Java code can execute nearly as fast as native compiled code and maintain its transportability and security. There is only one true performance hit that compiled Java code will always suffer for the sake of security —array bounds checking. But on the other hand, some of the basic design features of Java place more information in the hands of the compiler, which allows for certain kinds of optimizations not possible in C or C++.

The latest twist in compilation techniques is a new virtual machine that Sun calls HotSpot. The problem with a traditional just-in-time compilation is that optimizing code takes time, and is extremely important for good performance on modern computer hardware. So a just-in-time compiler can produce decent results, but can never afford to take the time necessary to do a good job of optimization. HotSpot uses a trick called "adaptive compilation" to solve this problem. If you look at what programs actually spend their time doing, it turns out that they spend almost all of their time executing a relatively small part of the code again and again. The chunk of code that is executed repeatedly may only be a small percent of the total program, but its behavior determines the program's overall performance.

To take advantage of this fact, HotSpot starts out as a normal Java byte code interpreter, but with a difference: it measures (profiles) the code as it is executing, to see what parts are being executed repeatedly. Once it knows which parts of the code are crucial to the performance, HotSpot compiles those sections—and only those sections—into true machine code. Since it only compiles a small portion of the program into machine code, it can afford to take the time necessary to optimize those portions. The rest of the program may not need to be compiled at all— just interpreted—saving memory and time.

The technology for doing this is very complex, but the idea is essentially simple: optimize the parts of the program that need to go fast, and don't worry about the rest. Another advantage of using an adaptive compiler at runtime is that it can make novel kinds of optimizations that a static (compile time only) compiler cannot dream of.

Java Compared with Other Languages

Java is a new language, but it draws on many years of programming experience with other languages in its choice of features. So a lot can be said in comparing and contrasting Java with other languages. There are at least three pillars necessary to support a universal language for network programming today: portability, speed, and security. Figure 1-2 shows how Java compares to other languages.

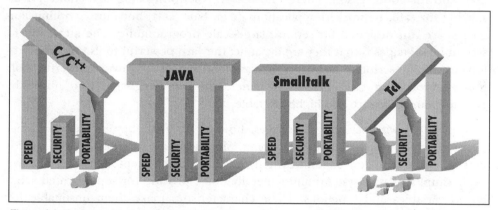

Figure 1-2. Programming languages compared

You may have heard that Java is a lot like C or C++, but that's really not true, except at a superficial level. When you first look at Java code, you'll see that the basic syntax looks a lot like C or C++. But that's where the similarities end. Java is by no means a direct descendant of C or a next-generation C++. If you compare language features, you'll see that Java actually has more in common with languages like Smalltalk and Lisp. In fact, Java's implementation is about as far from native C as you can imagine.

The surface-level similarities to C and C++ are worth noting, however. Java borrows heavily from C and C++ syntax, so you'll see lots of familiar language constructs, including an abundance of curly braces and semicolons. Java also subscribes to the C philosophy that a good language should be compact; in other words, it should be sufficiently small and regular so a programmer can hold all the language's capabilities in his or her head at once. Just as C is extensible with libraries, packages of Java classes can be added to the core language components.

C has been successful because it provides a reasonably featureful programming environment, with high performance and an acceptable degree of portability. Java also tries to balance functionality, speed, and portability, but it does so in a very different way. C trades functionality for portability; Java trades speed for portability. Java also addresses security issues, while C doesn't.

Java is an interpreted language, so it won't be as fast as a compiled language like C. But Java is fast enough, especially for interactive, network-based applications, where the application is often idle, waiting for the user to do something or waiting for data from the network. For situations where speed is critical, a Java implementation can optimize performance with just-in-time compilation to byte-code, as previously discussed.

Scripting languages, like Perl, Python, Tcl/Tk, and Wksh, are becoming very popular, and for good reason. There's no reason a scripting language could not be suitable for safe, networked applications (e.g., Safe Tcl), but most scripting languages are not designed for serious, large-scale programming. The attraction to scripting languages is that they are dynamic; they are powerful tools for rapid prototyping. Some scripting languages, like awk and Perl, also provide powerful tools for text-processing tasks that more general-purpose languages find unwieldy. Scripting languages are also highly portable.

One problem with scripting languages, however, is that they are rather casual about program structure and data typing. Most scripting languages (with a hesitant exception for Perl 5.0 and Python) are not object-oriented. They also have vastly simplified type systems and generally don't provide for sophisticated scoping of variables and functions. These characteristics make them unsuitable for building large, modular applications. Speed is another problem with scripting languages; the high-level, fully interpreted nature of these languages often makes them quite slow.

Java offers some of the essential advantages of a scripting language, along with the added benefits of a lower-level language.

Incremental development with object-oriented components, combined with Java's simplicity, make it possible to develop applications rapidly and change them easily, with a short concept-to-implementation time. Java also comes with a large base of core classes for common tasks such as building GUIs and doing network communications. But along with these features, Java has the scalability and software-engineering advantages of more static languages. It provides a safe structure on which to build higher-level networked tools and languages.

However, don't confuse Java with JavaScript! JavaScript is an object-based scripting language being developed by Netscape and others. It serves as a glue and an "in the document" language for dynamic, interactive HTML-based applications.

JavaScript draws its name from its intended integration with Java. You can currently interact with Java applets embedded in HTML using JavaScript. There have been a few portable implementations of JavaScript that would promote it to the level of a general scripting language. For more information on JavaScript, check out Netscape's web site (*http://home.netscape.com*).

As we've already said, Java is similar in design to languages like Smalltalk and Lisp. However, these languages are currently used mostly as research vehicles, rather than for developing large-scale systems. One reason is that they never developed a standard portable binding to operating-system services, like the C standard library or the Java core classes. Smalltalk is compiled to an interpreted byte-code format, and it can be dynamically compiled to native code on the fly, just like Java. But Java improves on the design by using a byte-code verifier to ensure the correctness of compiled Java code. This verifier gives Java a performance advantage over Smalltalk because Java code requires fewer runtime checks. Java's byte-code verifier also helps with security issues, something that Smalltalk doesn't address. Smalltalk is a mature language, though, and Java's designers took lessons from many of its features.

Throughout the rest of this chapter, we'll present a bird's-eye view of the Java language. We'll explain what's new and what's not-so-new about Java, how it differs from other languages, and why.

Safety of Design

You have no doubt heard a lot about the fact that Java is designed to be a safe language. But what do we mean by safe? Safe from what or whom? The security features that attract the most attention for Java are those features that make possible new types of dynamically portable software. Java provides several layers of protection from dangerously flawed code, as well as more mischievous things like viruses and Trojan horses. In the next section, we'll take a look at how the Java virtual machine architecture assesses the safety of code before it's run, and how the Java *class loader* (the byte-code loading mechanism of the Java interpreter) builds a wall around untrusted classes. These features provide the foundation for high-level security policies that allow or disallow various kinds of activities on an application-by-application basis.

In this section, though, we'll look at some general features of the Java programming language. Perhaps more important than the specific security features, although often overlooked in the security din, is the safety that Java provides by addressing common design and programming problems. Java is intended to be as safe as possible from the simple mistakes we make ourselves, as well as those we inherit from contractors and third-party software vendors. The goal with Java has been to keep the language simple, provide tools that have demonstrated their use-fulness, and let users build more complicated facilities on top of the language when needed.

Syntactic Sweet 'n' Low

Java is parsimonious in its features; simplicity rules. Compared to C, Java uses few automatic type coercions, and the ones that remain are simple and well-defined. Unlike C++, Java doesn't allow programmer-defined operator overloading. The string concatenation operator + is the only system-defined, overloaded operator in Java. All methods in Java are like C++ virtual methods, so overridden methods are dynamically selected at runtime.

Java doesn't have a preprocessor, so it doesn't have macros, #define statements, or conditional source compilation. These constructs exist in other languages pri-marily to support platform dependencies, so in that sense they should not be needed in Java. Conditional compilation is also commonly used for debugging purposes. Debugging code can be included directly in your Java source code by making it conditional on a constant (in Java, a variable declared to be static and final). The Java compiler is smart enough to remove this code when it deter-mines that it won't be called.

Java provides a well-defined *package* structure for organizing class files. The pack-age system allows the compiler to handle most of the functionality of the *make* util-ity (a sophisticated tool for building executables from source code). The compiler also works with compiled Java classes, because all type information is preserved; there is no need for header files. All of this means that Java code requires little context to read. Indeed, you may sometimes find it faster to look at the Java source code than to refer to class documentation.

Java replaces some features that have been troublesome in other languages. For example, Java supports only a single inheritance class hierarchy, but allows multi-ple inheritance of interfaces. An *interface*, like an abstract class in C++, specifies some of the behavior of an object without defining its implementation, a powerful mechanism borrowed from Objective C. It allows a class to implement the behav-ior of the interface, without needing to be a subclass of anything in particular. Interfaces in Java eliminate the need for multiple inheritance of classes, without causing the problems associated with multiple inheritance. As you'll see in Chapter 4, *The Java Language*, Java is a simple, yet elegant, programming language.

Type Safety and Method Binding

One attribute of a language is the kind of type checking it uses. When we catego-rize a language as *static* or *dynamic* we are referring to the amount of information about variable types that is known at compile time versus what is determined while the application is running.

In a strictly statically typed language like C or C++, data types are etched in stone when the source code is compiled. The compiler benefits from having enough information to enforce usage rules, so that it can catch many kinds of errors before the code is executed, such as storing a floating-point value in an integer variable. The code doesn't require runtime type checking, so it can be compiled to be small and fast. But statically typed languages are inflexible. They don't support high-level constructs like lists and collections as naturally as languages with dynamic type checking, and they make it impossible for an application to safely import new data types while it's running.

In contrast, a dynamic language such as Smalltalk or Lisp has a runtime system that manages the types of objects and performs necessary type checking while an application is executing. These kinds of languages allow for more complex behavior, and are in many respects more powerful. However, they are also generally slower, less safe, and harder to debug.

The differences in languages have been likened to the differences among kinds of automobiles.* Statically typed languages like C++ are analogous to a sports car—reasonably safe and fast—but useful only if you're driving on a nicely paved road. Highly dynamic languages like Smalltalk are more like an offroad vehicle: they afford you more freedom, but can be somewhat unwieldy. It can be fun (and sometimes faster) to go roaring through the back woods, but you might also get stuck in a ditch or mauled by bears.

Another attribute of a language is the way it binds method calls to their definitions. In an early-binding language like C or C++, the definitions of methods are normally bound at compile time, unless the programmer specifies otherwise. Smalltalk, on the other hand, is a late-binding language because it locates the definitions of methods dynamically at runtime. Early-binding is important for performance reasons; an application can run without the overhead incurred by searching method tables at runtime. But late-binding is more flexible. It's also necessary in an object-oriented language, where a subclass can override methods in its superclass, and only the runtime system can determine which method to run.

Java provides some of the benefits of both C++ and Smalltalk; it's a statically typed, late-binding language. Every object in Java has a well-defined type that is known at compile time. This means the Java compiler can do the same kind of static type checking and usage analysis as C++. As a result, you can't assign an object to the wrong type of variable or call nonexistent methods on an object. The Java

---

* The credit for the car analogy goes to Marshall P. Cline, author of the C++ FAQ.

compiler goes even further and prevents you from messing up and trying to use uninitialized variables.

However, Java is fully runtime typed as well. The Java runtime system keeps track of all objects and makes it possible to determine their types and relationships during execution. This means you can inspect an object at runtime to determine what it is. Unlike C or C++, casts from one type of object to another are checked by the runtime system, and it's even possible to use completely new kinds of dynamically loaded objects with a level of type safety.

Since Java is a late-binding language, all methods are like *virtual methods* in C++. This makes it possible for a subclass to override methods in its superclass. But Java also allows you to gain the performance benefits of early-binding by explicitly declaring (with the `final` modifier) that certain methods can't be overridden by subclassing, removing the need for runtime lookup. (Adaptive runtime compilers like HotSpot may be able to eliminate the need for you to worry about this though, as they can detect usage patterns and improve performance automatically, where possible.)

Incremental Development

Java carries all data-type and method-signature information with it from its source code to its compiled byte-code form. This means that Java classes can be developed incrementally. Your own Java classes can also be used safely with classes from other sources your compiler has never seen. In other words, you can write new code that references binary class files, without losing the type safety you gain from having the source code. The Java runtime system can load new classes while an application is running, thus providing the capabilities of a dynamic linker.

A common irritation with C++ is the "fragile base class" problem. In C++, the implementation of a base class can be effectively frozen by the fact that it has many derived classes; changing the base class may require recompilation of the derived classes. This is an especially difficult problem for developers of class libraries. Java avoids this problem by dynamically locating fields within classes. As long as a class maintains a valid form of its original structure, it can evolve without breaking other classes that are derived from it or that make use of it.

Dynamic Memory Management

Some of the most important differences between Java and C or C++ involve how Java manages memory. Java eliminates ad hoc pointers and adds garbage collection and true arrays to the language. These features eliminate many otherwise insurmountable problems with safety, portability, and optimization.

Garbage collection alone should save countless programmers from the single largest source of programming errors in C or C++: explicit memory allocation and deallocation. In addition to maintaining objects in memory, the Java runtime system keeps track of all references to those objects. When an object is no longer in use, Java automatically removes it from memory. You can simply ignore objects you no longer use, with confidence that the interpreter will clean them up at an appropriate time.

Sun's current implementation of Java uses a conservative mark-and-sweep garbage collector that runs intermittently in the background, which means that most garbage collecting takes place between I/O pauses, mouse clicks, and keyboard hits. Next generation runtime systems like HotSpot have more advanced garbage collection that can even differentiate the usage patterns of objects (such as short-lived versus long-lived) and optimize their collection. Once you get used to garbage collection, you won't go back. Being able to write air-tight C code that juggles memory without dropping any on the floor is an important skill, but once you become addicted to Java you can "realloc" some of those brain cells to new tasks.

You may hear people say that Java doesn't have pointers. Strictly speaking, this statement is true, but it's also misleading. What Java provides are references—a safe kind of pointer—and Java is rife with them. A reference is a strongly typed handle for an object. All objects in Java, with the exception of primitive numeric types, are accessed through references. If necessary, you can use references to build all the normal kinds of data structures you're accustomed to building with pointers, such as linked lists, trees, and so forth. The only difference is that with references you have to do so in a type-safe way.

Another important difference between a reference and a pointer is that you can't do pointer arithmetic with references (they can only point to specific objects or elements of an array). A reference is an atomic thing; you can't manipulate the value of a reference except by assigning it to an object. References are passed by value, and you can't reference an object through more than a single level of indirection. The protection of references is one of the most fundamental aspects of Java security. It means that Java code has to play by the rules; it can't peek into places it shouldn't.

Unlike C or C++ pointers, Java references can point only to class types. There are no pointers to methods. People often complain about this missing feature, but you will find that most tasks that call for pointers to methods, such as callbacks, can be accomplished using interfaces and anonymous adapter classes instead.* (We will

---

* As of Java 1.1, there is a Method class, which lets you have a reference to a method. This is part of the Java reflection API. You can use a Method object to construct a callback, but it's not the normal way of doing things.

discuss these in Chapter 6, *Relationships Among Classes*, and in the Swing-related chapters; they are heavily used in tying together graphical user interface components).

Finally, arrays in Java are true, first-class objects. They can be dynamically allocated and assigned like other objects. Arrays know their own size and type, and although you can't directly define or subclass array classes, they do have a well-defined inheritance relationship based on the relationship of their base types. Having true arrays in the language alleviates much of the need for pointer arithmetic like that in C or C++.

Error Handling

Java's roots are in networked devices and embedded systems. For these applications, it's important to have robust and intelligent error management. Java has a powerful exception-handling mechanism, somewhat like that in newer implementations of C++. Exceptions provide a more natural and elegant way to handle errors. Exceptions allow you to separate error-handling code from normal code, which makes for cleaner, more readable applications.

When an exception occurs, it causes the flow of program execution to be transferred to a predesignated "catcher" block of code. The exception carries with it an object that contains information about the situation that caused the exception. The Java compiler requires that a method either declare the exceptions it can generate or catch and deal with them itself. This promotes error information to the same level of importance as argument and return typing. As a Java programmer, you know precisely what exceptional conditions you must deal with, and you have help from the compiler in writing correct software that doesn't leave them unhandled.

Multithreading

Applications today require a high degree of parallelism. Even a very single-minded application can have a complex user interface—which requires concurrent activities. As machines get faster, users become more sensitive to waiting for unrelated tasks that seize control of their time. Threads provide efficient multiprocessing and distribution of tasks for both client and server applications. Java makes threads easy to use because support for them is built into the language.

Concurrency is nice, but there's more to programming with threads than just performing multiple tasks simultaneously. In many cases, threads need to be synchronized, which can be tricky without explicit language support. Java supports synchronization based on the monitor and condition model developed by C.A.R. Hoare—a sort of lock and key system for accessing resources. The keyword `synchronized` designates methods for safe, serialized access within an object. Only one synchronized method within the object may run at a given time. There are also simple, primitive methods for explicit waiting and signaling between threads interested in the same object.

Learning to program with threads is an important part of learning to program in Java. See Chapter 8, *Threads*, for a discussion of this topic. For complete coverage of threads, refer to *Java Threads*, by Scott Oaks and Henry Wong (O'Reilly & Associates).

Scalability

At the lowest level, Java programs consist of *classes*. Classes are intended to be small, modular components. They can be separated physically on different systems, retrieved dynamically, stored in a compressed format, and even cached in various distribution schemes. Over classes, Java provides packages, a layer of structure that groups classes into functional units. Packages provide a naming convention for organizing classes and a second level of organizational control over the visibility of variables and methods in Java applications.

Within a package, a class is either publicly visible or protected from outside access. Packages form another type of scope that is closer to the application level. This lends itself to building reusable components that work together in a system. Packages also help in designing a scalable application that can grow without becoming a bird's nest of tightly coupled code dependency.

Safety of Implementation

It's one thing to create a language that prevents you from shooting yourself in the foot; it's quite another to create one that prevents others from shooting you in the foot.

Encapsulation is a technique for hiding data and behavior within a class; it's an important part of object-oriented design. It helps you write clean, modular software. In most languages, however, the visibility of data items is simply part of the relationship between the programmer and the compiler. It's a matter of semantics, not an assertion about the actual security of the data in the context of the running program's environment.

When Bjarne Stroustrup chose the keyword `private` to designate hidden members of classes in C++, he was probably thinking about shielding you from the messy details of a class developer's code, not the issues of shielding that developer's classes and objects from the onslaught of someone else's viruses and Trojan horses. Arbitrary casting and pointer arithmetic in C or C++ make it trivial to violate access permissions on classes without breaking the rules of the language. Consider the following code:

```
// C++ code
class Finances {
    private:
        char creditCardNumber[16];
        ...
};

main() {
    Finances finances;

    // Forge a pointer to peek inside the class
    char *cardno = (char *)&finances;
    printf("Card Number = %s\n", cardno);
}
```

In this little C++ drama, we have written some code that violates the encapsulation of the Finances class and pulls out some secret information. This sort of shenanigan—abusing an untyped pointer—is not possible in Java. If this example seems unrealistic, consider how important it is to protect the foundation (system) classes of the runtime environment from similar kinds of attacks. If untrusted code can corrupt the components that provide access to real resources, such as the filesystem, the network, or the windowing system, it certainly has a chance at stealing your credit card numbers.

In Visual BASIC, it's also possible to compromise the system by peeking, poking, and, under DOS, installing interrupt handlers. Even some recent languages that have some commonalties with Java lack important security features. For example, the Apple Newton uses an object-oriented language called NewtonScript that is compiled into an interpreted byte-code format. However, NewtonScript has no concept of public and private members, so a Newton application has free reign to access any information it finds. General Magic's Telescript language is another example of a device-independent language that does not fully address security concerns. The list goes on ...

If a Java application is to dynamically download code from an untrusted source on the Internet and run it alongside applications that might contain confidential information, protection has to extend very deep. The Java security model wraps three layers of protection around imported classes, as shown in Figure 1-3.

At the outside, application-level security decisions are made by a security manager. A security manager controls access to system resources like the filesystem, network ports, and the windowing environment. A security manager relies on the ability of a class loader to protect basic system classes. A class loader handles

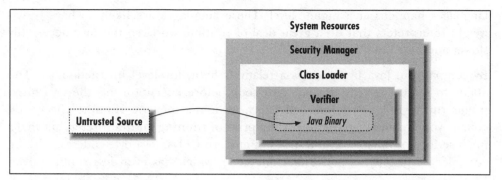

Figure 1-3. The Java security model

loading classes from the network. At the inner level, all system security ultimately rests on the Java verifier, which guarantees the integrity of incoming classes.

The Java byte-code verifier is a fixed part of the Java runtime system. Class loaders and the security managers (or *security policies* to be more precise), however, are components that may be implemented differently by different applications that load byte-code, such as applet viewers and web browsers. All three of these pieces need to be functioning properly to ensure security in the Java environment.*

The Verifier

Java's first line of defense is the *byte-code verifier*. The verifier reads byte-code modules before they are run and makes sure they are well-behaved and obey the basic rules of the Java language. A trusted Java compiler won't produce code that does otherwise. However, it's possible for a mischievous person to deliberately assemble bad code. It's the verifier's job to detect this.

Once code has been verified, it's considered safe from certain inadvertent or malicious errors. For example, verified code can't forge references or violate access permissions on objects. It can't perform illegal casts or use objects in unintended ways. It can't even cause certain types of internal errors, such as overflowing or underflowing the operand stack. These fundamental guarantees underlie all of Java's security.

You might be wondering, isn't this kind of safety implicit in lots of interpreted languages? Well, while it's true that you shouldn't be able to corrupt the interpreter with bogus BASIC code, remember that the protection in most interpreted

---

* You may have seen reports about various security flaws in Java. While these weaknesses are real, it's important to realize that they have been found in the implementations of various components, namely Sun's byte-code verifier and Netscape's class loader and security manager, not in the basic security model itself. One of the reasons Sun has released the source code for Java is to encourage people to search for weaknesses, so they can be removed.

languages happens at a higher level. Those languages are likely to have heavy-weight interpreters that do a great deal of runtime work, so they are necessarily slower and more cumbersome.

By comparison, Java byte-code is a relatively light, low-level instruction set. The ability to statically verify the Java byte-code before execution lets the Java inter-preter run at full speed with full safety, without expensive runtime checks. Of course, you are always going to pay the price of running an interpreter, but that's not a serious problem with the speed of modern CPUs. Java byte-code can also be compiled on the fly to native machine code, which has even less runtime over-head.

The verifier is a type of theorem prover. It steps through the Java byte-code and applies simple, inductive rules to determine certain aspects of how the byte-code will behave. This kind of analysis is possible because compiled Java byte-code con-tains a lot more type information than the object code of other languages of this kind. The byte-code also has to obey a few extra rules that simplify its behavior. First, most byte-code instructions operate only on individual data types. For exam-ple, with stack operations, there are separate instructions for object references and for each of the numeric types in Java. Similarly, there is a different instruction for moving each type of value into and out of a local variable.

Second, the type of object resulting from any operation is always known in advance. There are no byte-code operations that consume values and produce more than one possible type of value as output. As a result, it's always possible to look at the next instruction and its operands, and know the type of value that will result.

Because an operation always produces a known type, by looking at the starting state, it's possible to determine the types of all items on the stack and in local vari-ables at any point in the future. The collection of all this type information at any given time is called the *type state* of the stack; this is what Java tries to analyze before it runs an application. Java doesn't know anything about the actual values of stack and variable items at this time, just what kind of items they are. However, this is enough information to enforce the security rules and to ensure that objects are not manipulated illegally.

To make it feasible to analyze the type state of the stack, Java places an additional restriction on how Java byte-code instructions are executed: all paths to the same point in the code have to arrive with exactly the same type state.* This restriction

---

* The implications of this rule are of interest mainly to compiler writers. The rule means that Java byte-code can't perform certain types of iterative actions within a single frame of execution. A common example would be looping and pushing values onto the stack. This is not allowed because the path of execution would return to the top of the loop with a potentially different type state on each pass, and there is no way that a static analysis of the code can determine whether it obeys the security rules.

makes it possible for the verifier to trace each branch of the code just once and still know the type state at all points. Thus, the verifier can insure that instruction types and stack value types always correspond, without actually following the execution of the code. For a more thorough explanation of all of this, see *The Java Virtual Machine*, by Jon Meyer and Troy Downing (O'Reilly & Associates).

Class Loaders

Java adds a second layer of security with a class loader. A class loader is responsible for bringing the byte-code for one or more Java classes into the interpreter. Every application that loads classes from the network must use a class loader to handle this task.

After a class has been loaded and passed through the verifier, it remains associated with its class loader. As a result, classes are effectively partitioned into separate namespaces based on their origin. When a loaded class references another class name, the location of the new class is provided by the original class loader. This means that classes retrieved from a specific source can be restricted to interact only with other classes retrieved from that same location. For example, a Java-enabled web browser can use a class loader to build a separate space for all the classes loaded from a given uniform resource locator (URL).

The search for classes always begins with the built-in Java system classes. These classes are loaded from the locations specified by the Java interpreter's class path (see Chapter 3, *Tools of the Trade*). Classes in the class path are loaded by the system only once and can't be replaced. This means that it's impossible for an applet to replace fundamental system classes with its own versions that change their functionality.

Security Managers

Finally, a *security manager* is responsible for making application-level security decisions. A security manager is an object that can be installed by an application to restrict access to system resources. The security manager is consulted every time the application tries to access items like the filesystem, network ports, external processes, and the windowing environment, so the security manager can allow or deny the request.

A security manager is most useful for applications that run untrusted code as part of their normal operation. Since a Java-enabled web browser can run applets that may be retrieved from untrusted sources on the Net, such a browser needs to install a security manager as one of its first actions. This security manager then restricts the kinds of access allowed after that point. This lets the application impose an effective level of trust before running an arbitrary piece of code. And once a security manager is installed, it can't be replaced.

In Java 2, the security manager works in conjunction with an access controller that lets you implement security policies by editing a file. Access policies can be as simple or complex as a particular application warrants. Sometimes it's sufficient simply to deny access to all resources or to general categories of services such as the filesystem or network. But it's also possible to make sophisticated decisions based on high-level information. For example, a Java-enabled web browser could use an access policy that lets users specify how much an applet is to be trusted or that allows or denies access to specific resources on a case-by-case basis. Of course, this assumes that the browser can determine which applets it ought to trust. We'll see how this problem is solved shortly.

The integrity of a security manager is based on the protection afforded by the lower levels of the Java security model. Without the guarantees provided by the verifier and the class loader, high-level assertions about the safety of system resources are meaningless. The safety provided by the Java byte-code verifier means that the interpreter can't be corrupted or subverted, and that Java code has to use components as they are intended. This, in turn, means that a class loader can guarantee that an application is using the core Java system classes and that these classes are the only means of accessing basic system resources. With these restrictions in place, it's possible to centralize control over those resources with a security manager.

Application and User-Level Security

There's a fine line between having enough power to do something useful and having all the power to do anything you want. Java provides the foundation for a secure environment in which untrusted code can be quarantined, managed, and safely executed. However, unless you are content with keeping that code in a little black box and running it just for its own benefit, you will have to grant it access to at least some system resources so that it can be useful. Every kind of access carries with it certain risks and benefits. The advantages of granting an untrusted applet access to your windowing system, for example, are that it can display information and let you interact in a useful way. The associated risks are that the applet may instead display something worthless, annoying, or offensive. Since most people can accept that level of risk, graphical applets and the World Wide Web in general are possible.

At one extreme, the simple act of running an application gives it a resource, computation time, that it may put to good use or burn frivolously. It's difficult to prevent an untrusted application from wasting your time, or even attempting a "denial of service" attack. At the other extreme, a powerful, trusted application may justifiably deserve access to all sorts of system resources (e.g., the filesystem, process creation, network interfaces); a malicious application could wreak havoc with these resources. The message here is that important and sometimes complex security issues have to be addressed.

In some situations, it may be acceptable to simply ask the user to "okay" requests. Sun's HotJava web browser can pop up a dialog box and ask the user's permission for an applet to access an otherwise restricted file. However, we can put only so much burden on our users. An experienced person will quickly grow tired of answering questions; an inexperienced user may not be able to answer the questions correctly. Is it okay for me to grant an applet access to something if I don't understand what that is?

Making decisions about what is dangerous and what is not can be difficult. Even ostensibly harmless access, like displaying a window, can become a threat when paired with the ability for an untrusted application to communicate from your host. The Java Security Manager provides an option to flag windows created by an untrusted application with a special, recognizable border to prevent it from impersonating another application and perhaps tricking you into revealing your password or your secret recipe collection. There is also a grey area, in which an application can do devious things that aren't quite destructive. An applet that can mail a bug report can also mail-bomb your boss. The Java language provides the tools to implement whatever security policies you want. However, what these policies will be ultimately depends on who you are, what you are doing, and where you are doing it.

Signing Classes

Web browsers such as HotJava start by defining a few rules and some coarse levels of security that restrict where applets may come from and what system resources they may access. These rules are sufficient to keep the waving Duke applet from clutching your password file, but they aren't sufficient for applications you'd like to trust with sensitive information. To fully exploit the power of Java, we need to have some nontechnical basis on which to make reasonable decisions about what a program can be allowed to do. This nontechnical basis is *trust*; basically, you trust certain entities not to do anything that's harmful to you. For a home user, this may mean that you trust the "Bank of Boofa" to distribute applets that let you transfer funds between your accounts, or you may trust L.L. Bean to distribute an applet that debits your Visa account. For a company, that may mean that you trust applets originating behind your firewall, or perhaps applets from a few high-priority customers, to modify internal databases. In all of these cases, you don't need to know in detail what the program is going to do and give it permission for each operation. You only need to know that you trust your local bank.

This doesn't mean that there isn't a technical aspect to the problem of trust. Trusting your local bank when you walk up to the ATM means one thing; trusting some web page that claims to come from your local bank means something else entirely. It would be very difficult to impersonate the ATM two blocks down the street (though it has been known to happen), but, depending on your position on the Net, it's not all that difficult to impersonate a web site, or to intercept data coming from a legitimate web site and substitute your own.

That's where cryptography comes in. Digital signatures, together with certificates, are techniques for verifying that data truly comes from the source it claims to have come from and hasn't been modified en route. If the Bank of Boofa signs its checkbook applet, your browser can verify that the applet actually came from the bank, not an imposter, and hasn't been modified. Therefore, you can tell your browser to trust applets that have the Bank of Boofa's signature. Java supports digital signatures; the details are covered in Chapter 3.

Java and the World Wide Web

The application-level safety features of Java make it possible to develop new kinds of applications that were infeasible before now. A web browser that implements the Java runtime system can incorporate Java applets as executable content inside of documents. This means that web pages can contain not only static hypertext information but also full-fledged interactive applications. The added potential for use of the Web is enormous. A user can retrieve and use software simply by navigating with a web browser. Formerly static information can be paired with portable software for interpreting and using the information. Instead of just providing some data for a spreadsheet, for example, a web document might contain a fully functional spreadsheet application embedded within it that allows users to view and manipulate the information.

Applets

The term "applet" is used to mean a small, subordinate, or embeddable application. By "embeddable," we mean it's designed to be run and used within the context of a larger system. In that sense, most programs are embedded within a computer's operating system. An operating system manages its native applications in a variety of ways: it starts, stops, suspends, and synchronizes applications; it provides them with certain standard resources; and it protects them from one another by partitioning their environments.

As far as the web browser model is concerned, an applet is just another type of object to display; it's embedded into an HTML page with a special tag. Browsers make a distinction between items presented inline and items anchored via hypertext links and made available by external means, such as a viewer or helper application. If you download an MPEG video clip, for instance, and your browser doesn't natively understand MPEG, it will look for a helper application (an MPEG player) to pass the information to. Java-enabled web browsers generally execute applets inline, in the context of a particular document, as shown in Figure 1-4. However, less capable browsers could initially provide some support for Java applets through an external viewer.

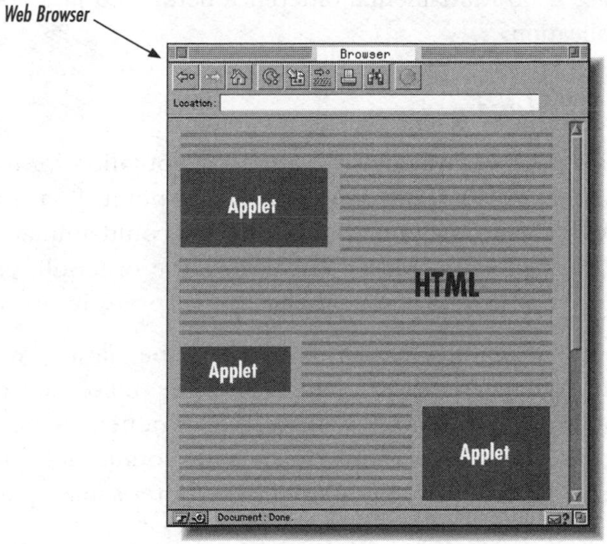

Figure 1-4. Applets in a web document

A Java applet is a compiled Java program, composed of classes just like any Java program. While a simple applet may consist of only a single class, most large applets should be broken into many classes. Each class is stored in a separate class file. The class files for an applet are retrieved from the network as they are needed. A large applet doesn't need to retrieve all its parts or all its data before beginning to interact with the user. Well-designed applets can take advantage of multithreading to wait for certain resources in the background, while performing other activities.

An applet has a four-part life cycle. When an applet is initially loaded by a web browser, it's asked to initialize itself. The applet is then informed each time it's displayed and each time it's no longer visible to the user. Finally, the applet is told when it's no longer needed, so that it can clean up after itself. During its lifetime, an applet may start and suspend itself, do work, communicate with other applications, and interact with the Web browser.

Applets are autonomous programs, but they are confined within the walls of a web browser or applet viewer, and have to play by its rules. We'll be discussing the details of what applets can and can't do as we explore features of the Java language. However, under the most conservative security policies, an applet can interact only with the user and can communicate only over the network with the host from which it originated. Other types of activities, like accessing files or interacting directly with outside applications, are typically prevented by the security manager that is part of the web browser or applet viewer. But aside from these restrictions, there is no fundamental difference between a Java applet and a standalone Java application.

New Kinds of Media

When it was first released, Java quickly achieved a reputation for multimedia capabilities. Frankly, this wasn't really deserved. At that point, Java provided facilities for doing simple animations and playing audio. You could animate and play audio simultaneously, though you couldn't synchronize the two. Still, this was a significant advance for the Web, and people thought it was pretty impressive.

Java's multimedia capabilities have now taken shape. Java now has CD-quality sound, 3D animation, media players that synchronize audio and video, speech synthesis and recognition, and more. The Java Media Framework now supports most common audio and video file formats; The Java Sound API (part of the core classes) has the ability to record sound from a computer's microphone.

New Software Development Models

For some time now, people have been using visual development environments to develop user interfaces. These environments let you generate applications by moving components around on the screen, connecting components to each other, and so on. In short, designing a user interface is a lot more like drawing a picture than like writing code.

For visual development environments to work well, you need to be able to create reusable software components. That's what the JavaBeans architecture is all about: it defines a way to package software as reusable building blocks. A graphical development tool can figure out a component's capabilities, customize the component, and connect it to other components to build applications. JavaBeans takes the idea of graphical development a step further. JavaBeans components, called Beans, aren't limited to visible, user interface components: you can have Beans that are entirely invisible and whose job is purely computational. For example, you could have a Bean that does database access; you could connect this to a Bean that lets the user request information from the database; and you could use another Bean to display the result. Or you could have a set of Beans that implement the functions in a mathematical library; you could then do numerical analysis by connecting different functions to each other. In either case, you could "write" programs without writing a single line of code. Granted, someone would have to write the Beans in the first place; but that's a much smaller task, and we expect markets to develop for "off the shelf" Bean collections.

Before it can use a Bean, an application builder must find out the Bean's capabilities. There are a few ways it can do this; the simplest is called *reflection*. To write a Bean that uses reflection, all you need to do is follow some well-defined conventions (design patterns) that let the graphical interface builder (or any other tool that wants to do the work) analyze the Bean.

If they need to, Beans can provide additional information using a process called *introspection*. But even without introspection, a graphical development tool can analyze a Bean, figure out what it can do, and let a user change the Bean's properties without writing any code.

Of course, once a development tool has customized a Bean and connected it to other Beans, it needs a way to save the result. A process called *serialization* lets a tool save the Bean's current state, along with any extra code it has written to stitch Beans together in an application.

Visual development tools that support Java Beans include IBM's VisualAge, Inprise's JBuilder (*http://www.inprise.com*), WebGain's Visual Cafe (*http://www. webgain.com*), and Sun's Forte for Java. By using a "bridge," Java Beans can function inside ActiveX.

Java as a General Application Language

The Java applet API is a framework that allows Java-enabled web browsers to manage and display embedded Java applications within web documents. However, Java is more than just a tool for building transportable multimedia applications. Java is a powerful, general-purpose programming language that just happens to be safe and architecture-independent. Standalone Java applications are not subject to the restrictions placed on applets; they can perform the same jobs as programs written in languages like C and C++ do.

Any software that implements the Java runtime system can run Java applications. Applications written in Java can be large or small, standalone or component-like, as in other languages. Java applets are different from other Java applications only in that they expect to be managed by a larger application. They are normally considered untrusted code. In this book, we will build examples of both applets and standalone Java applications. With the exception of the few things untrusted applets can't do, such as access files, all of the tools we examine in this book apply to both applets and standalone Java applications.

A Java Road Map

With everything that's going on, it's hard to keep track of what's available now, what's promised, and what has been around for some time. Here's a road map that imposes some order on Java's past, present, and future.

The Past: Java 1.0 and Java 1.1

Java 1.0 provided the basic framework for Java development: the language itself plus packages that let you write applets and simple applications. Although Java 1.0 is officially obsolete, it will be some time before vendors catch up with the newer releases.

Java 1.1 superseded Java 1.0. It incorporated major improvements in the AWT package (Java's original GUI facility) and many new features. Java 1.1 remains important, because it is supported natively by both the Netscape Navigator and Microsoft Internet Explorer browsers. For various political reasons, the future of the browser world is uncertain; to execute applets using any features of Java 2, you need to use the Java plug-in, which allows Netscape and IE to execute Java 2 code.

The Present: Java 2

Java 2 was released in December 1998, providing many improvements and additions. The most notable addition is Swing, which is a new user interface toolkit with capabilities far exceeding AWT's. (Swing, AWT, and some other packages are now called the JFC, or Java Foundation Classes.) Here's a brief overview of the most important features of the core Java 2 API:

JDBC (Java Database Connectivity)
> A general facility for interacting with databases. (Introduced with Java 1.1.)

RMI (Remote Method Invocation)
> Java's distributed objects system. RMI lets you call methods on objects hosted by a server running somewhere else on the network. (Introduced with Java 1.1.)

Java Security
> A facility for controlling access to system resources, combined with a uniform interface to cryptography. Java Security is the basis for signed classes, which were discussed earlier.

JFC (Java Foundation Classes)
> A catch-all for a number of new features, including the Swing user interface components; "pluggable look-and-feel," which means the ability of the user interface to adapt itself to the "look-and-feel" of the platform you're using; drag and drop; and accessibility, which means the ability to integrate with special software and hardware for people with disabilities.

Java 2D

Part of JFC; enables high-quality graphics, font manipulation, and printing.

Internationalization

The ability to write programs that adapt themselves to the language the user wants to use; the program automatically displays text in the appropriate language. (Introduced with Java 1.1.)

The following features aren't part of the core Java 2 definition; you may have to download them separately. Most of them are what Sun calls "standard extensions":

JNDI (Java Naming and Directory Interface)

A very general service for looking up resources. JNDI unifies access to directory services like LDAP, Novell's NDS, and others.

JavaMail

A uniform API for writing email software.

Java 3D

A facility for developing applications with 3D graphics.

Java Media

Another catch-all that includes Java 2D, Java 3D, the Java Media Framework (a framework for coordinating the display of many different kinds of media), Java Speech (for speech recognition and synthesis), Java Sound (high-quality audio), Java TV (for interactive television and similar applications), and others.

Java Servlets

A facility that lets you write custom Internet servers. It is most frequently used to write web server applications, but it's much more general.

Java Cryptography

Actual implementations of cryptographic algorithms. (This package was separated from Java Security for legal reasons.)

JavaHelp

A facility for writing help systems and incorporating them in Java programs.

Enterprise JavaBeans

A component architecture for building distributed server-side applications.

Jini

An extremely interesting catch-all that is designed to enable massively distributed computing, including computing on common household appliances. In a few years, your stereo may be able to execute Java programs.

Java Card

A version of Java for very small (i.e., credit card-sized) devices, which have severe limitations on speed and memory.

In this book, we'll try to give you a taste of as many features as possible; unfortunately for us (but fortunately for Java software developers), the Java environment has become so rich that it's impossible to cover everything in a single book.

The Future

You can think of the first four years of Java development as a "big bang," followed by an "inflationary" phase as Sun added new features, and improved old features, at an incredible rate. Things seem to be slowing down now: new APIs aren't being announced as often, and those that are announced tend to be more specialized. At least for the moment, the Java world is stabilizing.

But it's important to look into the new areas into which Java is headed. The most interesting of these is consumer devices. An interesting game to play is thinking of what an everyday appliance might be able to do if it had a Java processor in it. A common bread maker could download "breadlets" (applets that implement bread recipes) from the Internet; your stereo wouldn't just play CDs—it could find music sources on the Internet and perhaps even facilitate live, distributed jam sessions using technologies like Java Sound. These devices could probably be built without Java, but that's not saying much: after all, no software has yet been written that couldn't (in theory) be hand-coded in assembly language. More to the point, Java (and especially Jini) make it much easier to develop these kinds of applications in reliable, safe ways.

Until now, discussion of Java on consumer devices has been limited to visionary, hypothetical talk. However, this is changing. There is already a version of the Java Virtual Machine that runs on 3Com's Palm devices; JVMs for cell phones, pagers, and other personal communication devices are on the way. While this book can't go into the details of development for such devices, it's important to realize that the vision is becoming reality. The step from a Palm hand-held computer to a cell phone to your VCR or television is extremely small—much smaller than the leap from a personal computer to the Palm.

Availability

By the time you read this book, you should have several choices for Java development environments and runtime systems. Sun's Java 2 SDK* is available for Solaris, Linux, and Windows. Visit Sun's Java web site at *http://java.sun.com* for more information about the Java 2 SDK. There are also Java ports for other platforms,

---

* The Java 2 SDK used to be called the JDK. Sun's marketing group has an unfortunate tendency to change terminology for reasons that are no doubt clear to them, but only introduce confusion for everyone else. In this book, we'll use SDK, even for older versions of Java that were distributed as the JDK.

including NetWare, HP-UX, OSF/1 (including Digital Unix), Silicon Graphics' IRIX, and various IBM operating systems (including AIX and OS2). For more information, see the web pages maintained by the vendor you're interested in. Sun maintains a web page summarizing porting efforts at *http://java.sun.com/cgi-bin/java-ports.cgi*. Another good source for current information is the Java FAQ from the *comp.lang.java* newsgroup.

There are efforts under way to produce a free clone of Java, redistributable in source form. The Java Open Language Toolkit (JOLT) Project is working to assemble a high-quality Java implementation that will pass Sun's validation tests and earn a Java stamp. The JOLT Project web page is accessible from *http://www.redhat.com*.

Netscape Navigator and Microsoft Internet Explorer both come with their own Java runtime system that runs Java applets and supports SDK 1.1. Neither supports Java 2 at present, although the newest release of Navigator (6.0) is supposed to support Java 2 and future versions through a new "open Java" API. To ameliorate the problem in general, Sun has released a Java plug-in that supports Java 2; it is distributed with the Java SDK for Windows.

2

A First Application

Before getting into the details of the Java language, let's jump right into some working code. In this chapter, we'll build a friendly little application that illustrates a number of techniques we use throughout the book. We'll take this opportunity to introduce general features of the Java language and of Java applications. However, many details won't be fleshed out here, but in subsequent chapters.

This chapter also serves as a brief introduction to the object-oriented and multithreaded features of Java. If these concepts are new to you, you can take comfort in the knowledge that encountering them for the first time in Java should be a straightforward and pleasant experience. If you have worked with another object-oriented or multithreaded programming environment, clear your mind; you will especially appreciate Java's simplicity and elegance.

We can't stress enough the importance of experimentation as you learn new concepts. Don't just examine the examples—run them. Copy the source code from the accompanying CD-ROM, or from our web site at *http://www.oreilly.com/catalog/learnjava*. Compile the programs on your machine, and run them.

If you follow along with the online examples, be sure to take some time and compile them locally. Then, turn our examples into your example: play with them; change their behavior, break them, fix them, and, as Java architect Arthur van Hoff would say: "Have fun!"

HelloJava1

In the tradition of introductory programming texts, we begin with Java's equivalent of the archetypal "Hello World" application. In the spirit of our new world, we'll call it *HelloJava*.

We'll take four passes at this example (HelloJava1, HelloJava2, etc.), adding features and introducing new concepts along the way. Here's a minimalist version:*

```
//file: HelloJava1.java
public class HelloJava1 extends javax.swing.JComponent {

    public static void main(String[] args) {
        javax.swing.JFrame f = new javax.swing.JFrame("HelloJava1");
        f.setSize(300, 300);
        f.getContentPane().add(new HelloJava1());
        f.setVisible(true);
    }

    public void paintComponent(java.awt.Graphics g) {
        g.drawString("Hello, Java!", 125, 95);
    }
}
```

Place this text in a file called *HelloJava1.java*. Now compile this source:

```
% javac HelloJava1.java
```

This produces the Java byte-code binary class file *HelloJava1.class*.

You can run the application by starting the Java runtime system, specifying the class name (not the filename) as an argument:

```
% java HelloJava1
```

(The name of the Java interpreter varies among implementations. Microsoft's is named `jview`, not `java`.) You should see the proclamation shown in Figure 2-1. Now congratulate yourself: you have written your first application! Take a moment to bask in the glow of your monitor.

When you click on the window's close box, the window goes away, but your program will still be running. To stop the runtime system and return control to your command-line interpreter, type Ctrl-C or whatever key sequence stops a running application on your platform. We'll remedy this shortcoming in a later version of the example.

HelloJava1 may be a small program, but there is actually quite a bit going on behind the scenes. Those few lines represent the tip of an iceberg. What lies under the surface are layers of functionality provided by the Java language and its foundation class libraries. In this chapter, we'll cover a lot of ground quickly in an effort to show you the big picture. We'll try to offer enough detail for a firm understanding of what is happening in each example, deferring full explanations

---

* All of the ready-to-run examples in this book are included on the accompanying CD-ROM. The comment line `//file: ...` indicates the name of the source file.

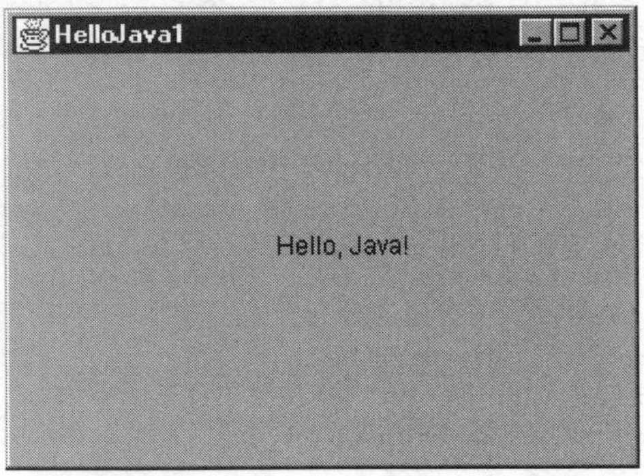

Figure 2-1. The HelloJava1 application

until the appropriate chapters. This holds for both elements of the Java language and the object-oriented concepts that apply to them. Later chapters will provide more detailed cataloging of Java's syntax, components, and object-oriented features.

Salutations, Java!

There are many ways to say "Hello, Java!" The simplest command-line version of HelloJava looks like this:

```
public class HelloJavaCommandLine {
  public static void main(String[] args) {
    System.out.println("Hello, Java!");
  }
}
```

Weighing in at just five lines, this program uses the System class to write some text to the console. The HelloJava examples in this chapter are a little lengthier; they are structured to show off Java's user interface toolkit, Swing, and to provide a quick fly-through of the Java language and libraries.

If we weren't concerned about the tutorial, we could create a graphic example that's just as pithy as the command-line version, using the JOptionPane class:

```
public class HelloJavaSimple {
  public static void main(String[] args) {
    javax.swing.JOptionPane.showMessageDialog(null, "Hello, Java!");
  }
}
```

Classes

The previous example defines a *class* named `HelloJava1`. Classes are the funda-mental building blocks of most object-oriented languages. A class in Java is very much like a class in C++, and somewhat like a `struct` in C. It's a group of data items, with associated functions that perform operations on this data. The data items in a class are called *fields* or *variables*; the functions are called *methods*. A class might represent something concrete, like a button on a screen or the information in a spreadsheet, or it could be something more abstract, such as a sorting algo-rithm or possibly the sense of ennui in your MUD character. A hypothetical spreadsheet class might, for example, have variables that represent the values of its individual cells and methods that perform operations on those cells, such as "clear a row" or "compute values." We'll talk more about this in a little while.

Our `HelloJava1` class contains an entire Java application. It holds two general types of variables and methods: those we need for our specific application's tasks and some special predesignated ones we provide to interact with the outside world. The Java runtime system, in this case the `java` command-line tool, calls methods in `HelloJava1` to pass us information and prod us to perform actions. Our simple `HelloJava1` class implements two important methods. The first, `main()`, is called when the application is first started. We'll talk more about it in the next section. The second method, `paintComponent()`, is called by Java when it's time for our application to draw itself on the screen.

The main( ) Method

When you run our example, what really happens? The `java` command looks in the `HelloJava1` class to see if it contains a special method called `main()`. If it does, this method is run. The `main()` method is simply an entry point for an application. It's a piece of code that you want to be run when the application first starts.

The `main()` method sets up a window (a `JFrame`) that will contain the visual out-put of the `HelloJava1` class. What really interests us here is not the `main()` method but the rest of the class. We'll go through several incarnations of this class, adding features and methods. But the `main()` method will remain largely unchanged, keeping its basic function of creating a window that holds the Hello-Java example.

Let's quickly walk through the `main()` method, just so you know what it does. First, `main()` creates a `JFrame`, a window that will hold our example:

```
javax.swing.JFrame f = new javax.swing.JFrame("HelloJava1");
```

The new word in this line of code is tremendously important: `javax.swing.`
`JFrame` (just `JFrame` for short) is the name of a class that represents a window you
can see on your screen. The class itself is just a template, like a building plan. The
new keyword tells Java to allocate memory and initialize a new `JFrame` object.

When frame windows are first created, they are very small. Our next task is to set
the size to something reasonable:

```
f.setSize(300, 300);
```

Then we create our actual example and put it inside the frame window:

```
f.getContentPane().add(new HelloJava1());
```

Here, we're actually creating a new `HelloJava1` object and placing it inside the
`JFrame` we just created.

`main()`'s final task is to show the frame window and its contents, which otherwise
would be invisible. An invisible window makes for a pretty boring application.

```
f.setVisible(true);
```

That's the whole `main()` method. As we progress through the examples in this
chapter, it will remain mostly unchanged as the `HelloJava` class evolves around it.
Let's get started!

Classes and Objects

A class is a blueprint for a part of an application; it lists methods and variables that
go into making up that part. Many individual working copies of a given class can
exist while an application is active. These individual incarnations are called
instances of the class, or *objects*. Two instances of a given class may contain different
data, but they always have the same methods.

As an example, consider a `Button` class. There is only one `Button` class, but an
application can create many different `Button` objects, each one an instance of the
same class. Furthermore, two `Button` instances might contain different data, perhaps giving each a different appearance and performing a different action. In this
sense, a class can be considered a mold for making the object it represents: something like a cookie cutter stamping out working instances of itself in the memory
of the computer. As you'll see later, there's a bit more to it than that—a class can
in fact share information among its instances—but this explanation suffices for
now. Chapter 5, *Objects in Java*, has the whole story on classes and objects.

The term *object* is very general and in some other contexts is used almost interchangeably with *class*. Objects are the abstract entities all object-oriented languages refer to in one form or another. We will use object as a generic term for an

instance of a class. We might, therefore, refer to an instance of the `Button` class as a Button, a `Button` object, or, indiscriminately, as an object.

The `main()` method in the previous example creates a single instance of the `HelloJava1` class and shows it in an instance of the `JFrame` class. You could modify `main()` to create many instances of `HelloJava1`, perhaps each in a separate window.

Variables and Class Types

In Java, every class defines a new *type* (data type). A variable can be of this type and then hold instances of that class. A variable could, for example, be of type `Button` and hold an instance of the `Button` class, or of type `SpreadSheetCell` and hold a `SpreadSheetCell` object, just as it could be any of the more familiar types such as `int` or `float`.

Ignoring the `main()` method for the moment, there is only one variable in our simple HelloJava example. It's found in the declaration of the `paintComponent()` method:

```
public void paintComponent(java.awt.Graphics g) {...}
```

Just like functions in C (and many other languages), a method in Java declares a list of variables that hold its arguments, and it specifies the types of those arguments. Our `paintComponent()` method takes one argument named (somewhat tersely) g, which is of type `Graphics`. When the `paintComponent()` method is invoked, a `Graphics` object is assigned to g, which we use in the body of the method. We'll say more about `paintComponent()` and the `Graphics` class in a moment.

But first, a few words about variables. We have loosely referred to variables as holding objects. In reality, variables that have class types don't so much contain objects as point to them. Class-type variables are references to objects. A reference is a pointer to or a name for an object.

If you declare a class-type variable without assigning it to an object, it doesn't point to anything. It's assigned the default value of `null`, meaning "no value." If you try to use a variable with a null value as if it were pointing to a real object, a runtime error (`NullPointerException`) occurs.

Where do you get an instance of a class to assign to a variable in the first place? The answer is through the use of the *new* operator. We'll examine object creation a little later in the chapter.

Inheritance

Java classes are arranged in a parent-child hierarchy, in which the parent and child are known as the *superclass* and *subclass*, respectively. We'll explore these concepts fully in Chapter 6, *Relationships Among Classes*. In Java, every class has exactly one superclass (a single parent), but possibly many subclasses. The only exception to this rule is the Object class, which sits atop the entire class hierarchy; it has no superclass.

The declaration of our class in the previous example uses the keyword extends to specify that HelloJava1 is a subclass of the JComponent class:

```
public class HelloJava1 extends javax.swing.JComponent {...}
```

A subclass may be allowed to inherit some or all of the variables and methods of its superclass. Through inheritance, the subclass can use those variables and methods as if it has declared them itself. A subclass can add variables and methods of its own, and it can also override the meaning of inherited variables and methods. When we use a subclass, overridden variables and methods are hidden (replaced) by the subclass's own versions of them. In this way, inheritance provides a powerful mechanism whereby a subclass can refine or extend its superclass.

For example, the hypothetical spreadsheet class might be subclassed to produce a new scientific spreadsheet class with extra mathematical functions and special built-in constants. In this case, the source code for the scientific spreadsheet might declare methods for the added mathematical functions and variables for the special constants, but the new class automatically has all the variables and methods that constitute the normal functionality of a spreadsheet; they are inherited from the parent spreadsheet class. This means the scientific spreadsheet maintains its identity as a spreadsheet, and we can use it anywhere the simpler spreadsheet is used.

Our HelloJava1 class is a subclass of the JComponent class and inherits many variables and methods not explicitly declared in our source code. These members operate in the same way as the ones we add or override.

The JComponent Class

The JComponent class provides the framework for building user interface components (called controls or widgets in other windowing systems). Particular components, such as buttons, labels, and list boxes, are implemented as subclasses of JComponent.

We override methods in such a subclass to implement the behavior of our particular component. This may sound restrictive, as if we are limited to some predefined set of routines, but that is not the case at all. Keep in mind that the methods we are talking about are means of interacting with the windowing system. A realistic application might involve hundreds or even thousands of classes, with legions of methods and variables and multiple threads of execution. The vast majority of these are related to the particulars of our job. The inherited methods of the JComponent class, and of other predefined classes, serve as a framework on which to hang code that handles certain types of events and performs special tasks.

The paintComponent() method is an important method of the JComponent class; we override it to implement the way our particular component displays itself on the screen. The default behavior of paintComponent() doesn't do any draw-ing at all; here, we're overriding paintComponent() to do something interesting. We don't override any of the other inherited members of JComponent because they provide basic functionality and reasonable defaults for this (trivial) example. As HelloJava grows, we'll delve deeper into the inherited members and use addi-tional methods. We will also add some application-specific methods and variables for the needs of HelloJava.

JComponent is really the tip of another iceberg called SwingSwing. Swing is Java's user interface toolkit; we'll discuss it in some detail in Chapters 13 through 18.

Relationships and Finger Pointing

We can correctly refer to HelloJava1 as a JComponent because subclassing can be thought of as creating an "is a" relationship, in which the subclass is a kind of its superclass. HelloJava1 is therefore a kind of JComponent. When we refer to a kind of object, we mean any instance of that object's class or any of its subclasses. Later, we will look more closely at the Java class hierarchy and see that JComponent is itself a subclass of the Container class, which is further derived from a class called Component, and so on, as shown in Figure 2-2.

In this sense, a HelloJava1 object is a kind of JComponent, which is a kind of Container, and each of these can ultimately be considered to be a kind of Component. It's from these classes that HelloJava1 inherits its basic graphical user interface functionality and the ability to have other graphical components embedded within it.

Component is a subclass of the top-level Object class, so all of these classes define kinds of Objects. Every other class in the Java API inherits behavior from Object, which defines a few basic methods, as you'll see in Chapter 7, *Working with Objects and Classes*. We'll continue to use the word object (lowercase o) in a generic way to refer to an instance of any class; we'll use Object to refer specifically to that class.

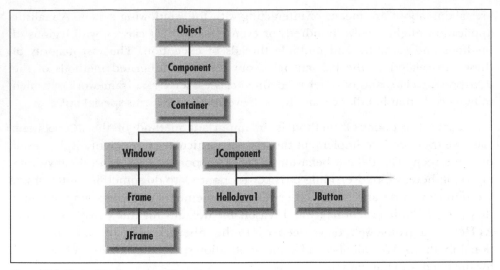

Figure 2-2. Part of the Java class hierarchy

Packages

In our previous example, the JComponent class is referenced by its fully qualified name javax.swing.JComponent:

```
public class HelloJava1 extends javax.swing.JComponent {...}
```

The prefix on the class name identifies it as belonging to the javax.swing package. Packages provide a means for organizing Java classes. A *package* is a group of Java classes that are related by purpose or by application. Classes in the same package have special access privileges with respect to one another and may be designed to work together. Package names are hierarchical and are used somewhat like Internet domain and host names, to distinguish groups of classes by organization and application. Classes may be dynamically loaded over networks from arbitrary locations; within this context, packages provide a crude namespace of Java classes.*

javax.swing identifies a particular package that contains classes related to Swing, Java 2's fancy graphical user interface toolkit. javax.swing.JComponent identifies a specific class, the JComponent class, within that package. The java. hierarchy is special. Any package that begins with java. is part of the core Java API and is available on any platform that supports Java. While javax normally denotes a

---

*   There are many efforts under way to find a general solution to the problem of locating resources in a globally distributed computing environment. The Uniform Resource Identifier Working Group of the IETF has proposed Uniform Resource Names (URNs). A URN would be a more abstract and persistent identifier that would be resolved to a URL through the use of a name service. We can imagine a day when there will exist a global namespace of trillions of persistent objects forming the infrastructure for all computing resources. Java provides an important evolutionary step in this direction.

standard extension to the core platform, javax.swing is an exception—it really is part of the core API. Figure 2-3 illustrates some of the core Java packages, showing a representative class or two from each.

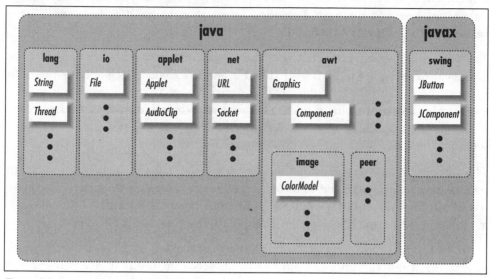

Figure 2-3. Some core Java packages

Some other notable core packages include: java.lang, which contains funda-mental classes needed by the Java language itself; java.awt, which contains classes of the pre-Java 2 Abstract Window Toolkit; and java.net, which contains the networking classes.

A few classes contain methods that are not written in Java, but are instead part of the native Java implementation on a particular platform. These are the only classes that have to be ported to a new platform. They form the basis for all interaction with the operating system. All other classes are built on or around these and are completely platform-independent.

The paintComponent( ) Method

The source for our HelloJava1 class defines a method, paintComponent(), that overrides the paintComponent() method from the JComponent class:

```
public void paintComponent(java.awt.Graphics g) {
    g.drawString("Hello, Java!", 125, 95);
}
```

The paintComponent() method is called when it's time for our example to draw itself on the screen. It takes a single argument, a Graphics object, and doesn't return any type of value (void) to its caller.

Modifiers are keywords placed before classes, variables, and methods to alter their accessibility, behavior, or semantics. `paintComponent()` is declared as `public`, which means it can be invoked (called) by methods in classes other than `HelloJava1`. In this case, it's the Java windowing environment that is calling our `paintComponent()` method. A method or variable declared as `private` is inaccessible from outside of its class.

The `Graphics` object, an instance of the `Graphics` class, represents a particular graphical drawing area. (It is also called a *graphics context*.) It contains methods that can be used to draw in this area, and variables that represent characteristics such as clipping or drawing modes. The particular `Graphics` object we are passed in the `paintComponent()` method corresponds to our component's area of the screen.

The `Graphics` class provides methods for rendering shapes, images, and text. In `HelloJava1`, we invoke the `drawString()` method of our `Graphics` object to scrawl our message at the specified coordinates. (For a description of the methods available in the `Graphics` class, see Chapter 17, *Drawing with the 2D API.*)

As in C++, a method or variable of an object is accessed in a hierarchical way by appending a dot (`.`) and its name to the object that holds it. We invoked the `drawString()` method of the `Graphics` object (referenced by our g variable) in this way:

```
g.drawString("Hello, Java!", 125, 95);
```

You may need to get used to the idea that our application is drawn by a method that is called by an outside agent at arbitrary times. How can we do anything useful with this? How do we control what gets done and when? These answers will be forthcoming. For now, just think about how you would structure applications that draw themselves on command.

HelloJava2: The Sequel

Let's make our application a little more interactive, shall we? The following improvement, `HelloJava2`, allows us to drag the message around with the mouse.

`HelloJava2` is a new application—another subclass of the `JComponent` class. In that sense, it's a sibling of `HelloJava1`. Having just seen inheritance at work, you might wonder why we aren't creating a subclass of `HelloJava1` and exploiting inheritance to build upon our previous example and extend its functionality. Well, in this case, that would not necessarily be an advantage, and for clarity we simply start over.*

---

* You are left to consider whether such subclassing would even make sense. Should `HelloJava2` really be a kind of `HelloJava`? Are we looking for refinement or just code reuse?

Here is `HelloJava2`:

```java
//file: HelloJava2.java
import java.awt.*;
import java.awt.event.*;
import javax.swing.*;

public class HelloJava2
    extends JComponent implements MouseMotionListener {

  // Coordinates for the message
  int messageX = 125, messageY = 95;
  String theMessage;

  public HelloJava2(String message) {
    theMessage = message;
    addMouseMotionListener(this);
  }

  public void paintComponent(Graphics g) {
    g.drawString(theMessage, messageX, messageY);
  }

  public void mouseDragged(MouseEvent e) {
    // Save the mouse coordinates and paint the message.
    messageX = e.getX();
    messageY = e.getY();
    repaint();
  }

  public void mouseMoved(MouseEvent e) {}

  public static void main(String[] args) {
    JFrame f = new JFrame("HelloJava2");
    // Make the application exit when the window is closed.
    f.addWindowListener(new WindowAdapter() {
      public void windowClosing(WindowEvent we) { System.exit(0); }
    });
    f.setSize(300, 300);
    f.getContentPane().add(new HelloJava2("Hello, Java!"));
    f.setVisible(true);
  }
}
```

Two slashes in a row indicates that the rest of the line is a comment. We've added a few comments to `HelloJava2` to help you keep track of everything.

Place the text of this example in a file called *HelloJava2.java* and compile it as before. You should get a new class file, *HelloJava2.class*, as a result.

To run the new example, use the following command line:

```
% java HelloJava2
```

Feel free to substitute your own salacious comment for the "Hello, Java!" message, and enjoy many hours of fun, dragging the text around with your mouse.

The import Statement

So, what have we added? First you may notice that a few lines are now hovering above our class:

```
import java.awt.*;
import java.awt.event.*;
import javax.swing.*;

public class HelloJava2
...
```

The import statement lists external classes to use in this file and tells the compiler where to look for them. In our first example, we designated the JComponent class as the superclass of HelloJava1. JComponent was not defined by us, and the compiler therefore had to look elsewhere for it. In that case, we referred to JComponent by its fully qualified name, which is javax.swing.JComponent. The JComponent class and all the other classes in the javax.swing package are stored in a standard location, known to the compiler.

In this example, the statement import javax.swing.* enables us to refer to *all* the classes in the javax.swing package by their simple names. For example, we don't have to use fully qualified names to refer to the JComponent and JFrame classes. Our current example uses only the Graphics class from the java.awt package. So we could have used import java.awt.Graphics instead of using the wildcard * to import all of the AWT package's classes. However, we are anticipating using several more classes from this package in the upcoming examples.

We also import all the classes from the package java.awt.event; these classes provide the Event objects that we use to communicate with the user. By listening for events, we find out when the user moved the mouse, clicked a button, and so on. Notice that importing java.awt.* doesn't automatically import the event package. The asterisk imports only the classes in a particular package, not other packages. Packages don't contain other packages, even if the hierarchical naming scheme would seem to imply such a thing.

The import statement may seem a bit like the C or C++ preprocessor #include statement, which injects header files into programs at the appropriate places. This is not true; there are no header files in Java. The import statement does not copy any code into a source file. It's just a convenience. Think of it as "introducing" one or more external classes to the compiler; after they've been introduced, you can call them by their simple names, instead of by their fully-qualified names.

Instance Variables

We have added some variables to our example:

```
int messageX = 125, messageY = 95;
String theMessage;
```

`messageX` and `messageY` are integers that hold the current coordinates of our movable message. They are initialized to default values, which should place the message somewhere near the center of the window. Java integers are always 32-bit signed numbers. There is no fretting about what architecture your code is running on; numeric types in Java are precisely defined. The variable `theMessage` is of type `String` and can hold instances of the `String` class.

You should note that these three variables are declared inside the braces of the class definition, but not inside any particular method in that class. These variables are called *instance variables* or *member variables* because they belong to the entire class, and copies of them appear in each separate instance of the class. Instance variables are always visible (usable) in any of the methods inside their class. Depending on their modifiers, they may also be accessible from outside the class.

Unless otherwise initialized, instance variables are set to a default value of 0 (zero), `false`, or `null`. Numeric types are set to zero, boolean variables are set to `false`, and class type variables always have their value set to `null`, which means "no value." Attempting to use an object with a `null` value results in a runtime error.

Instance variables differ from method arguments and other variables that are declared inside of a single method. The latter are called *local variables*. They are effectively private variables that can be seen only by code inside the method. Java doesn't initialize local variables, so you must assign values yourself. If you try to use a local variable that has not yet been assigned a value, your code will generate a compile-time error. Local variables live only as long as the method is executing and then disappear (which is fine, since nothing outside of the method can see them anyway). Each time the method is invoked, its local variables are recreated and must be assigned values.

We have made some changes to our previously stodgy `paintComponent()` method. All of the arguments in the call to `drawString()` are now variables.

Constructors

The `HelloJava2` class includes a special kind of a method called a *constructor*. A constructor is called to set up a new instance of a class. When a new object is created, Java allocates storage for it, sets instance variables to their default values, and then calls the constructor method for the class to do whatever application-level setup is required.

A *constructor method* is a method with the same name as its class. For example, the constructor for the HelloJava2 class is called HelloJava2(). Constructors don't have a return type; by definition, they return an object of that class. But like other methods, constructors can take arguments. Their sole mission in life is to configure and initialize newly born class instances, possibly using information passed to them in parameters.

An object is created by using the new operator with the constructor for the class and any necessary arguments. The resulting object instance is returned as a value. In our example, a new HelloJava2 is created in the main() method, in this line:

```
f.getContentPane().add(new HelloJava2("Hello, Java!"));
```

This line actually does three things. The following lines are equivalent, and a little easier to understand:

```
HelloJava2 newobj = new HelloJava2("Hello, Java!");
Container content = f.getContentPane();
content.add(newobj);
```

The first line is the important one, where a new HelloJava2 object is created. The HelloJava2 constructor takes a String as an argument and, as it turns out, uses it to set the message that is displayed in the window. A class could also provide methods that allow us to configure an object manually after it's created or to change its configuration at a later time. Many classes do both; the constructor simply takes its arguments and passes them to the appropriate methods or variables. The HelloJava2 class, for example, could have a public method, setMessage(), that allowed us to set the message at any time. Constructors with parameters are therefore a convenience that allows a sort of shorthand to set up a new object.

HelloJava2's constructor does two things: it sets the text of the theMessage instance variable, and it tells the system "Hey, I'm interested in anything that happens involving the mouse":

```
public HelloJava2(String message) {
    theMessage = message;
    addMouseMotionListener(this);
}
```

So what, you may ask, is the type of the argument to the HelloJava2 constructor, back in the main() method? It, too, is a String. With a little magic from the Java compiler, quoted strings in Java source code are turned into String objects. A bit of funny business is going on here, but it's simply for convenience. (See Chapter 9, *Basic Utility Classes*, for a complete discussion of the String class.)

We can use a special read-only variable, called this, to explicitly refer to our object. A method can use this to refer to the instance of the object that holds it. The following two statements are therefore equivalent ways to assign a value to an instance variable:

```
theMessage = message;
```

or:

```
this.theMessage = message;
```

We'll always use the shorter, implicit, form to refer to instance variables. But we'll need the this variable when we have to pass a reference to our object to a method in another class. We often do this so that methods in other classes can invoke our public methods (a *callback*, explained later in this chapter) or use our public variables.

The other method that we call in HelloJava2's constructor is addMouse-MotionListener(). This method is part of the event mechanism, which .we discuss next.

Events

The last two methods of HelloJava2 let us get information from the mouse. Each time the user performs an action, such as pressing a key on the keyboard, moving the mouse, or perhaps banging his or her head against a touch-sensitive screen, Java generates an *event*. An event represents an action that has occurred; it contains information about the action, such as its time and location. Most events are associated with a particular graphical user interface (GUI) component in an application. A keystroke, for instance, could correspond to a character being typed into a particular text entry field. Pressing a mouse button could activate a particular button on the screen. Even just moving the mouse within a certain area of the screen could be intended to trigger effects such as highlighting or changing the cursor's shape.

The way events work was one of the major changes between Java 1.0 and Java 1.1. We're going to talk about the Java 1.1 (and later) events only; they're a big improvement, and there's no sense in learning yesterday's news. In Java 1.1 and later, there are many different event classes including MouseEvent, KeyEvent, and ActionEvent. For the most part, the meaning of these events is fairly intuitive. A MouseEvent occurs when the user does something with the mouse, a KeyEvent occurs when the user types a key, and so on. ActionEvent is a little special; we'll see it at work later in this chapter in our third version of HelloJava. For now, we'll focus on dealing with a MouseEvent.

The various GUI components in Java generate events. For example, if you click the mouse inside a component, the component generates a mouse event. (We can view events as a general-purpose way to communicate between Java objects; but for the moment, let's limit ourselves to the simplest case.) In Java 1.1 and later, any object can ask to receive the events generated by another component. We will call the object that wants to receive events a "listener." For example, to declare that a listener wants to receive a component's mouse-motion events, you invoke that component's addMouseMotionListener() method, specifying the listener object as an argument. That's what our example is doing in its constructor. In this case, the component is calling its own addMouseMotionListener() method, with the argument this, meaning "I want to receive my own mouse-motion events."

That's how we register to receive events. But how do we actually get them? That's what the two remaining methods in our class are for. The mouseDragged() method is called automatically to receive the event generated whenever the user drags the mouse—that is, moves the mouse with any button pressed. The mouseMoved() method is called whenever the user moves the mouse over the area without pressing a button. Our mouseMoved() method is boring: it doesn't do anything. We're ignoring simple mouse motions.

mouseDragged() has a bit more meat to it. It is called repeatedly to give us updates on the position of the mouse. Here it is:

```
public void mouseDragged(MouseEvent e) {
    messageX = e.getX();
    messageY = e.getY();
    repaint();
}
```

The first argument to mouseDragged() is a MouseEvent object, e, that contains all the information we need to know about this event. We ask the MouseEvent to tell us the x and y coordinates of the mouse's current position by calling its getX() and getY() methods. These are saved in the messageX and messageY instance variables. Now, having changed the coordinates for the message, we would like HelloJava2 to redraw itself. We do this by calling repaint(), which asks the system to redraw the screen at a later time. We can't call paintComponent() directly because we don't have a graphics context to pass to it.

There's one other place where we've added an event handler: the main() method. There, we created an event handler that shuts down the application (by calling System.exit()) when the user closes our main window. The syntax might look a little weird; we've used something tricky called an *inner class* to get the job done. Inner classes are discussed in Chapter 6. They're very useful for event handlers.

The real beauty of the event model is that you have to handle only the kinds of events you want. If you don't care about keyboard events, you just don't register a listener for them; the user can type all he or she wants, and you won't be bothered. Java 1.1 and Java 2 don't go around asking potential recipients whether they might be interested in some event, as happened in Java 1.0. If there are no listeners for a particular kind of event, Java won't even generate it. The result is that event handling is quite efficient.

We've danced around one question that may be bothering you by now: how does the system know to call `mouseDragged()` and `mouseMoved()`? And why do we have to supply a `mouseMoved()` method that doesn't do anything? The answer to these questions has to do with interfaces. We'll discuss interfaces after clearing up some unfinished business with `repaint()`.

The repaint( ) Method

We can use the `repaint()` method of the `JComponent` class to request our component be redrawn. `repaint()` causes the Java windowing system to schedule a call to our `paintComponent()` method at the next possible time; Java supplies the necessary `Graphics` object, as shown in Figure 2-4.

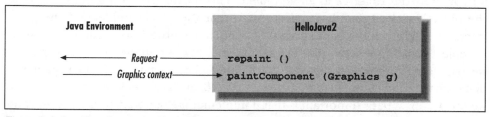

Figure 2-4. Invoking the repaint( ) method

This mode of operation isn't just an inconvenience brought about by not having the right graphics context handy at the moment. The foremost advantage to this mode of operation is that the repainting is handled by someone else, while we are free to go about our business. The Java system has a separate, dedicated thread of execution that handles all `repaint()` requests. It can schedule and consolidate `repaint()` requests as necessary, which helps to prevent the windowing system from being overwhelmed during painting-intensive situations like scrolling. Another advantage is that all of the painting functionality can be kept in our `paintComponent()` method; we aren't tempted to spread it throughout the application.

Interfaces

Now it's time to face up to the question we avoided earlier: how does the system know to call `mouseDragged()` when a mouse event occurs? Is it simply a matter of knowing that `mouseDragged()` is some magic name that our event handling method must have? Not quite; the answer to the question touches on the discussion of interfaces, which are one of the most important features of the Java language.

The first sign of an interface comes on the line of code that introduces the `HelloJava2` class: we say that the class implements the `MouseMotionListener` interface. Essentially, an interface is a list of methods that the class must have; this particular interface requires our class to have methods called `mouseDragged()` and `mouseMoved()`. The interface doesn't say what these methods have to do—and indeed, `mouseMoved()` doesn't do anything. It does say that the methods must take a `MouseEvent` as an argument and return `void` (i.e., no return value).

Another way of looking at an interface is as a contract between you, the code developer, and the compiler. By saying that your class implements the `Mouse-MotionListener` interface, you're saying that these methods will be available for other parts of the system to call. If you don't provide them, a compilation error will occur.

But that's not the only way interfaces impact this program. An interface also acts like a class. For example, a method could return a `MouseMotionListener` or take a `MouseMotionListener` as an argument. This means that you don't care about the object's class; the only requirement is that the object implement the given interface. `addMouseMotionListener()` is such a method: its argument must be an object that implements the `MouseMotionListener` interface. The argument we pass is `this`, the `HelloJava2` object itself. The fact that it's an instance of `JComponent` is irrelevant—it could be a `Cookie`, an `Aardvark`, or any other class we dream up. What's important is that it implements `MouseMotionListener`, and thus declares that it will have the two named methods. That's why we need a `mouseMoved()` method, even though the one we supplied doesn't do anything: the `MouseMotionListener` interface says we have to have one.

In other languages, you'd handle this problem by passing a function pointer; for example, in C, the argument to `addMouseMotionListener()` might be a pointer to the function you want to have called when an event occurs. This technique is called a *callback*. For a variety of reasons, the Java language has eliminated function pointers. Instead, we use interfaces to make contracts between classes and the compiler. (Some new features of the language make it easier to do something similar to a callback, but that's beyond the scope of this discussion.)

The Java distribution comes with many interfaces that define what classes have to do in various situations. This idea of a contract between the compiler and a class is very important. There are many situations like the one we just saw, where you don't care what class something is, you just care that it has some capability, like listening for mouse events. Interfaces give you a way of acting on objects based on their capabilities, without knowing or caring about their actual type.

Furthermore, interfaces provide an important escape clause to the Java rule that any new class can extend only a single class ("single inheritance"). They provide most of the advantages of multiple inheritance (a feature of languages like C++) without the confusion. A class in Java can extend only one class but can implement as many interfaces as it wants; our next example will implement two interfaces, and the final example in this chapter will implement three. In many ways, interfaces are almost like classes, but not quite. They can be used as data types, they can even extend other interfaces (but not classes), and can be inherited by classes (if class A implements interface B, subclasses of A also implement B). The crucial difference is that classes don't actually inherit methods from interfaces; the interfaces merely specify the methods the class must have.

HelloJava3: The Button Strikes!

Well, now that we have those concepts under control, we can move on to some fun stuff. HelloJava3 brings us a new graphical interface component: the JButton.* We add a JButton component to our application that changes the color of our text each time the button is pressed. The draggable-message capability is still there, too. Our new example is:

```
//file: HelloJava3.java
import java.awt.*;
import java.awt.event.*;
import javax.swing.*;

public class HelloJava3
    extends JComponent
    implements MouseMotionListener, ActionListener {

    // Coordinates for the message
    int messageX = 125, messageY = 95;
    String theMessage;

    JButton theButton;

    // Current index into someColors
    int colorIndex;
```

---

* Why isn't it just called a Button? Button is the name that was used in Java's original GUI toolkit, the Abstract Windowing Toolkit (AWT). AWT had some significant shortcomings, so it was extended and essentially replaced by Swing in Java 2. Since AWT already took the reasonable names such as Button and MenuBar, Swing user interface components have names that are prefixed with "J", like JButton and JMenuBar.

```java
static Color[] someColors = { Color.black, Color.red,
    Color.green, Color.blue, Color.magenta };

public HelloJava3(String message) {
  theMessage = message;
  theButton = new JButton("Change Color");
  setLayout(new FlowLayout());
  add(theButton);
  theButton.addActionListener(this);
  addMouseMotionListener(this);
}

public void paintComponent(Graphics g) {
  g.drawString(theMessage, messageX, messageY);
}

public void mouseDragged(MouseEvent e) {
  // Save the mouse coordinates and paint the message.
  messageX = e.getX();
  messageY = e.getY();
  repaint();
}

public void mouseMoved(MouseEvent e) {}

public void actionPerformed(ActionEvent e) {
  // Did somebody push our button?
  if (e.getSource() == theButton)
    changeColor();
}

synchronized private void changeColor() {
  // Change the index to the next color.
  if (++colorIndex == someColors.length)
    colorIndex = 0;
  setForeground(currentColor()); // Use the new color.
  repaint(); // Paint again so we can see the change.
}

synchronized private Color currentColor() {
  return someColors[colorIndex];
}

public static void main(String[] args) {
  JFrame f = new JFrame("HelloJava3");
  // Make the application exit when the window is closed.
  f.addWindowListener(new WindowAdapter() {
    public void windowClosing(WindowEvent we) { System.exit(0); }
  });
```

```
        f.setSize(300, 300);
        f.getContentPane().add(new HelloJava3("Hello, Java!"));
        f.setVisible(true);
    }
}
```

Create `HelloJava3` in the same way as the other applications. Run the example, and you should see the display shown in Figure 2-5. Drag the text. Each time you press the button the color should change. Call your friends! They should be duly impressed.

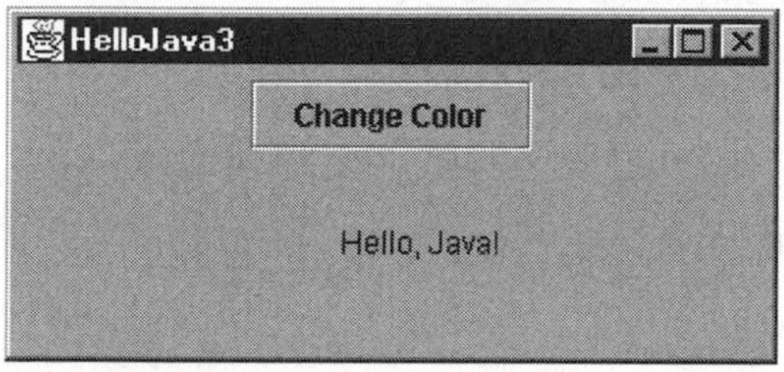

Figure 2-5. The HelloJava3 application

So what have we added this time? Well, for starters we have a new variable:

```
    JButton theButton;
```

The `theButton` variable is of type `JButton` and is going to hold an instance of the `javax.swing.JButton` class. The `JButton` class, as you might expect, represents a graphical button, like other buttons in your windowing system.

Three additional lines in the constructor create the button and display it:

```
    theButton = new JButton("Change Color");
    setLayout(new FlowLayout());
    add(theButton);
```

In the first line, the `new` keyword creates an instance of the `JButton` class. Recall that the variable we have declared is just an empty reference and doesn't yet point to a real object—in this case, an instance of the `JButton` class. This is a fundamental and important concept. The `new` operator provides the general mechanism for instantiating objects. It's the feature of the Java language that creates a new instance of a specified class. It arranges for Java to allocate storage for the object and then calls the constructor method of the object's class to initialize it.

Method Overloading

`JButton` has more than one constructor. A class can have multiple constructors, each taking different parameters and presumably using them to do different kinds of setup. When there are multiple constructors for a class, Java chooses the correct one based on the types of arguments that are passed to it. We call the JButton constructor and pass it a String argument, so Java locates the constructor method of the JButton class that takes a single String argument and uses it to set up the object. This is called *method overloading*. All methods in Java, not just constructors, can be overloaded; this is one aspect of the object-oriented programming principle of *polymorphism.*

Overloaded constructors generally provide a convenient way to initialize a new object. The JButton constructor we've used sets the text of the button as it is created:

```
theButton = new JButton("Change Color");
```

This is shorthand for creating the button and setting its label, like this:

```
theButton = new JButton();
theButton.setText("Change Color");
```

Garbage Collection

We've told you how to create a new object with the new operator, but we haven't said anything about how to get rid of an object when you are done with it. If you are a C programmer, you're probably wondering why not. The reason is that you don't have to do anything to get rid of objects when you are done with them.

The Java runtime system uses a *garbage collection* mechanism to deal with objects no longer in use. The garbage collector sweeps up objects not referenced by any variables and removes them from memory. Garbage collection is one of the most important features of Java. It frees you from the error-prone task of having to worry about details of memory allocation and deallocation.

Components

We have used the terms "component" and "container" somewhat loosely to describe graphical elements of Java applications. But these terms are the names of actual classes in the java.awt package.

Component is a base class from which all of Java's GUI components are derived. It contains variables that represent the location, shape, general appearance, and status of the object, as well as methods for basic painting and event handling. javax. swing.JComponent extends the fundamental Component class for the Swing toolkit. The paintComponent() method we have been using in our example is inherited from the JComponent class. HelloJava3 is a kind of JComponent and inherits all of its public members, just as other (perhaps simpler) types of GUI components do.

The JButton class is also derived from JComponent and therefore shares this functionality. This means that the developer of the JButton class had methods like paintComponent() available with which to implement the behavior of the JButton object, just as we did when creating our example. What's exciting is that we are perfectly free to further subclass components like JButton and override their behavior to create our own special types of user-interface components. JButton and HelloJava3 are, in this respect, equivalent types of things.

Containers

The Container class is an extended type of Component that maintains a list of child components and helps to group them. The Container causes its children to be displayed and arranges them on the screen according to a particular layout strategy. A Container also commonly arranges to receive events related to its child components. This strategy gives us a great deal of flexibility in managing interface components. We implement the strategy here by having JButton's container, HelloJava3, deal with the button's events. (Alternatively, we could create a smart button that handles its own clicks, by subclassing the JButton class and overriding certain methods to deal with the action of being pressed.)

Remember that a Container is a Component, too. It can be placed alongside other Component objects in other Containers, in a hierarchical fashion, as shown in Figure 2-6. Our HelloJava3 class is a kind of Container and can therefore hold and manage other Java components and containers like buttons, sliders, text fields, and panels.

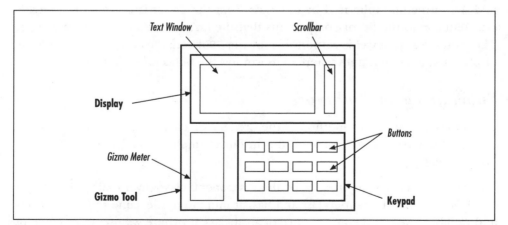

Figure 2-6. Layout of Java containers and components

In Figure 2-6, the italicized items are Components, and the bold items are Containers. The keypad is implemented as a container object that manages a number of keys. The keypad itself is contained in the GizmoTool container object.

Since JComponent descends from Container, it can be both a component and a container. In fact, we've already used it in this capacity in the HelloJava3 example. It does its own drawing and handles events, just like any component. But it also contains a button, just like any container.

Layout

Having created a JButton object, we need to place it in the container (HelloJava3), but where? An object called a LayoutManager determines the location within the HelloJava3 container at which to display the JButton. A LayoutManager object embodies a particular scheme for arranging components on the screen and adjusting their sizes. You'll learn more about layout managers in Chapter 16, *Layout Managers*. There are several standard layout managers to choose from, and we can, of course, create new ones. In our case, we specify one of the standard managers, a FlowLayout. The net result is that the button is centered at the top of the HelloJava3 container:

```
setLayout(new FlowLayout());
```

To add the button to the layout, we invoke the add() method that HelloJava3 inherits from Container, passing the JButton object as a parameter:

```
add(theButton);
```

add() is a method inherited by our class from the Container class. It appends our JButton to the list of components that the HelloJava3 container manages. Thereafter, HelloJava3 is responsible for the JButton: it causes the button to be displayed and it determines where in its window the button should be placed.

Subclassing and Subtypes

If you look up the add() method of the Container class, you'll see that it takes a Component object as an argument. But in our example we've given it a JButton object. What's going on?

JButton is a subclass, indirectly, of the Component class (eventually). Because a subclass is a kind of its superclass and has, at minimum, the same public methods and variables, we can use an instance of a subclass anywhere we use an instance of its superclass. This is a very important concept, and it's a second aspect of the object-oriented principle of polymorphism. JButton is a kind of Component, so any method that expects a Component as an argument will accept a JButton.

More Events and Interfaces

Now that we have a JButton, we need some way to communicate with it: that is, to get the events it generates. We could just listen for mouse clicks within the button and act accordingly. But that would require customization, via subclassing of the JButton; we would be giving up the advantages of using a prebuilt component. Instead, we have the HelloJava3 container object listen for button clicks. A JButton generates a special kind of event called an ActionEvent when someone clicks on it with the mouse. To receive these events, we have added another method to the HelloJava3 class:

```
public void actionPerformed(ActionEvent e) {
  if (e.getSource() == theButton)
    changeColor();
}
```

If you understood the previous example, you shouldn't be surprised to see that HelloJava3 now declares that it implements the ActionListener interface, in addition to MouseMotionListener. ActionListener requires us to implement an actionPerformed() method, which is called whenever an ActionEvent occurs. You also shouldn't be surprised to see that we added a line to the HelloJava3 constructor, registering itself (this) as a listener for the button's action events:

```
theButton.addActionListener(this);
```

The actionPerformed() method takes care of any action events that arise. First, it checks to make sure that the event's source (the component generating the event) is what we think it should be: theButton, the only button we've put in the application. This may seem superfluous; after all, what else could possibly generate an action event? In this application, nothing. But it's a good idea to check, because another application may have several buttons, and you may need to figure out which one has been clicked. Or you may add a second button to this application later, and you don't want it to break something. To check this, we call the getSource() method of the ActionEvent object, e. Then we use the == operator to make sure that the event source matches theButton.

NOTE   In Java, == is a test for identity, not equality; it is true if the event source and theButton are the same object. The distinction between equality and identity is important. We would consider two String objects to be equal if they have the same characters in the same sequence. However, they might not be the same object. In Chapter 7, we'll look at the equals() method, which tests for equality. Once we establish that the event e comes from the right button, we call our changeColor() method, and we're finished.

You may be wondering why we don't have to change `mouseDragged()` now that we have a `JButton` in our application. The rationale is that the coordinates of the event are all that matter for this method. We are not particularly concerned if the event happens to fall within an area of the screen occupied by another component. This means that you can drag the text right through the `JButton` and even lose it behind the `JButton` if you aren't careful: try it and see!

Color Commentary

To support `HelloJava3`'s colorful side, we have added a couple of new variables and two helpful methods. We create and initialize an array of `Color` objects representing the colors through which we cycle when the button is pressed. We also declare an integer variable that serves as an index for this array, specifying the current color:

```
int colorIndex;
static Color[] someColors = { Color.black, Color.red,
    Color.green, Color.blue, Color.magenta };
```

A number of things are going on here. First let's look at the `Color` objects we are putting into the array. Instances of the `java.awt.Color` class represent colors; they are used by all classes in the `java.awt` package that deal with color graphics. Notice that we are referencing variables such as `Color.black` and `Color.red`. These look like normal examples of an object's instance variables; however, `Color` is not an object, it's a class. What is the meaning of this?

Static Members

A class can contain variables and methods that are shared among all instances of the class. These shared members are called *static variables* and *static methods*. The most common use of static variables in a class is to hold predefined constants or unchanging objects, which all of the instances can use.

There are two advantages to this approach. The more obvious advantage is that static members take up space only in the class; the members are not replicated in each instance. The second advantage is that static members can be accessed even if no instances of the class exist. In this example, we use the static variable `Color.red`, without having to create an instance of the `Color` class.

An instance of the `Color` class represents a visible color. For convenience, the `Color` class contains some static, predefined objects with friendly names like `green`, `red`, and (our favorite) `magenta`. The variable `green`, for example, is a static member in the `Color` class. The data type of the variable `green` is `Color`; it is initialized like this:

```
public final static Color green = new Color(0, 255, 0);
```

The green variable and the other static members of Color are not changeable (after they've been initialized), so they are effectively constants and can be optimized as such by the compiler. Constant (or final) static members are the closest thing to a #define construct that you'll find in Java. The alternative to using these predefined colors is to create a color manually by specifying its red, green, and blue (RGB) components using a Color class constructor.

Arrays

Next, we turn our attention to the array. We have declared a variable called someColors, which is an array of Color objects. In Java, arrays are first-class objects. This means that an array is, itself, a type of object that knows how to hold an indexed list of some other type of object. An array is indexed by integers; when you index an array, the resulting value is an object reference—that is, a reference to the object that is located in the array's specified slot. Our code uses the colorIndex variable to index someColors. It's also possible to have an array of simple primitive types, such as floats, rather than objects.

When we declare an array, we can initialize it by using the familiar C-like curly brace construct. Specifying a comma-separated list of elements inside of curly braces is a convenience that instructs the compiler to create an instance of the array with those elements and assign it to our variable. Alternatively, we could have just declared our someColors variable and, later, allocated an array object for it and assigned individual elements to that array's slots. See Chapter 5 for a complete discussion of arrays.

Using Color Methods

So, we now have an array of Color objects and a variable with which to index the array. Two private methods do the actual work for us. The private modifier on these methods specifies that they can be called only by other methods in the same instance of the class. They cannot be accessed outside of the object that contains them. We declare members to be private to hide the detailed inner workings of a class from the outside world. This is called *encapsulation* and is another tenet of object-oriented design, as well as good programming practice. Private methods are also often created as helper functions for use solely in the class implementation.

The first method, currentColor(), is simply a convenience routine that returns the Color object representing the current text color. It returns the Color object in the someColors array at the index specified by our colorIndex variable:

```
synchronized private Color currentColor() {
  return someColors[colorIndex];
}
```

We could just as readily have used the expression someColors[colorIndex] everywhere we use currentColor(); however, creating methods to wrap common tasks is another way of shielding ourselves from the details of our class. In an alternative implementation, we might have shuffled off details of all color-related code into a separate class. We could have created a class that takes an array of colors in its constructor and then provided two methods: one to ask for the current color and one to cycle to the next color (just some food for thought).

The second method, changeColor(), is responsible for incrementing the colorIndex variable to point to the next Color in the array. changeColor() is called from our actionPerformed() method whenever the button is pressed:

```
synchronized private void changeColor() {
  if (++colorIndex == someColors.length)
    colorIndex = 0;
  setForeground(currentColor());
  repaint();
}
```

We increment colorIndex and compare it to the length of the someColors array. All array objects have a variable called length that specifies the number of elements in the array. If we have reached the end of the array, we "wrap around to the beginning" by resetting the index to zero. After changing the currently selected color, we do two things. First, we call the component's setForeground() method, which changes the color used to draw text in the application. Then we call repaint() to cause the component to be redrawn with the new color for the draggable message.

What is the synchronized keyword that appears in front of our currentColor() and changeColor() methods? Synchronization has to do with threads, which we'll examine in the next section. For now, all you need know is that the synchronized keyword indicates these two methods can never be running at the same time. They must always run one after the other.

The reason is that in changeColor() we increment colorIndex before testing its value. That means that for some brief period of time while Java is running through our code, colorIndex can have a value that is past the end of our array. If our currentColor() method happened to run at that same moment, we would see a runtime "array out of bounds" error. There are, of course, ways in which we could fudge around the problem in this case, but this simple example is representative of more general synchronization issues we need to address. In the next section, you'll see that Java makes dealing with these problems easy through language-level synchronization support.

HelloJava4: Netscape's Revenge

We have explored quite a few features of Java with the first three versions of the HelloJava application. But until now, our application has been rather passive; it has waited patiently for events to come its way and responded to the whims of the user. Now our application is going to take some initiative—HelloJava4 will blink! Here is the code for our latest version:

```java
//file: HelloJava4.java
import java.awt.*;
import java.awt.event.*;
import javax.swing.*;

public class HelloJava4
    extends JComponent
    implements MouseMotionListener, ActionListener, Runnable {

  // Coordinates for the message
  int messageX = 125, messageY = 95;
  String theMessage;

  JButton theButton;

  int colorIndex; // Current index into someColors.
  static Color[] someColors = { Color.black, Color.red,
      Color.green, Color.blue, Color.magenta };

  boolean blinkState;

  public HelloJava4(String message) {
    theMessage = message;
    theButton = new JButton("Change Color");
    setLayout(new FlowLayout());
    add(theButton);
    theButton.addActionListener(this);
    addMouseMotionListener(this);
    Thread t = new Thread(this);
    t.start();
  }

  public void paintComponent(Graphics g) {
    g.setColor(blinkState ? getBackground() : currentColor());
    g.drawString(theMessage, messageX, messageY);
  }

  public void mouseDragged(MouseEvent e) {
    messageX = e.getX();
    messageY = e.getY();
```

```
      repaint();
  }

  public void mouseMoved(MouseEvent e) {}

  public void actionPerformed(ActionEvent e) {
    // Did somebody push our button?
    if (e.getSource() == theButton)
      changeColor();
  }

  synchronized private void changeColor() {
    // Change the index to the next color.
    if (++colorIndex == someColors.length)
      colorIndex = 0;
    setForeground(currentColor()); // Use the new color.
    repaint(); // Paint again so we can see the change.
  }

  synchronized private Color currentColor() {
    return someColors[colorIndex];
  }

  public void run() {
    try {
      while(true) {
        blinkState = !blinkState; // Toggle blinkState.
        repaint(); // Show the change.
        Thread.sleep(500);
      }
    }
    catch (InterruptedException ie) {}
  }

  public static void main(String[] args) {
    JFrame f = new JFrame("HelloJava4");
    // Make the application exit when the window is closed.
    f.addWindowListener(new WindowAdapter() {
      public void windowClosing(WindowEvent we) { System.exit(0); }
    });
    f.setSize(300, 300);
    f.getContentPane().add(new HelloJava4("Hello, Java!"));
    f.setVisible(true);
  }
}
```

Compile and run this version of HelloJava just like the others. You'll see that the text does in fact blink. Our apologies if you don't like blinking text—we're not overly fond of it either—but it does make for a simple, instructive example.

Threads

All the changes we've made in HelloJava4 have to do with setting up a separate thread of execution to make the text blink. Java is a *multithreaded* language, which means there can be many threads running at the same time. A *thread* is a separate flow of control within a program. Conceptually, threads are similar to processes, except that unlike processes, multiple threads share the same address space, which means that they can share variables and methods (but also have their own local variables). Threads are also quite lightweight in comparison to processes, so it's conceivable for a single application to be running hundreds of threads concurrently.

Multithreading provides a way for an application to handle many different tasks at the same time. It's easy to imagine multiple things going on at the same time in an application like a web browser. The user could be listening to an audio clip while scrolling an image; at the same time, the browser can be downloading an image. Multithreading is especially useful in GUI-based applications, as it improves the interactive performance of these applications.

Unfortunately for us, programming with multiple threads can be quite a headache. The difficulty lies in making sure routines are implemented so they can be run by multiple concurrent threads. If a routine changes the value of a state variable, for example, then only one thread should be executing the routine at a time. Later in this section, we'll examine briefly the issue of coordinating multiple threads' access to shared data. In other languages, synchronization of threads can be extremely complex and error-prone. You'll see that Java gives you a few simple tools that help you deal with many of these problems. Java threads can be started, stopped, suspended, and prioritized. Threads are preemptive, so a higher priority thread can interrupt a lower priority thread when vying for processor time. See Chapter 8, *Threads*, for a complete discussion of threads.

The Java runtime system creates and manages a number of threads. (Exactly how varies with the implementation.) We've already mentioned the repaint thread, which manages repaint() requests and event processing for GUI components that belong to the java.awt and javax.swing packages. Our example applications have done most of their work in one thread. Methods like mouseDragged() and actionPerformed() are invoked by the windowing thread and run on its time. Similarly, our constructor runs as part of the main application thread. This means we are somewhat limited in the amount of processing we do within these methods. If we were, for instance, to go into an endless loop in our constructor, our application would never appear, as it would never finish initializing. If we want an application to perform any extensive processing, such as animation, a lengthy calculation, or communication, we should create separate threads for these tasks.

The Thread Class

As you might have guessed, threads are created and controlled as Thread objects. An instance of the Thread class corresponds to a single thread. It contains methods to start, control, and stop the thread's execution. Our basic plan is to create a Thread object to handle our blinking code. We call the Thread's start() method to begin execution. Once the thread starts, it continues to run until we call the Thread's interrupt() method to terminate it.

So how do we tell the thread which method to run? Well, the Thread object is rather picky; it always expects to execute a method called run() to perform the action of the thread. The run() method can, however, with a little persuasion, be located in any class we desire.

We specify the location of the run() method in one of two ways. First, the Thread class itself has a method called run(). One way to execute some Java code in a separate thread is to subclass Thread and override its run() method to do our bidding. Invoking the start() method of the subclass object causes its run() method to execute in a separate thread.

It's not always desirable or possible to create a subclass of Thread to contain our run() method. The Thread class has a constructor that takes an object reference as its argument. If we create a Thread object using this constructor and call its start() method, the Thread executes the run() method of the argument object, rather than its own. In order to accomplish this, Java needs a guarantee that the object we are passing it does indeed contain a compatible run() method. We already know how to make such a guarantee: we use an interface. Java provides an interface named Runnable that must be implemented by any class that wants to become a Thread.

The Runnable Interface

We've used the second technique in the HelloJava4 example. To create a thread, a HelloJava4 object passes itself (this) to the Thread constructor. This means that HelloJava4 itself must implement the Runnable interface, by implementing the run() method. This method is called automatically when the runtime system needs to start the thread.

We indicate that the class implements the interface in our class declaration:

```
public class HelloJava4
    extends JComponent
    implements MouseMotionListener, ActionListener, Runnable {...}
```

At compile time, the Java compiler checks to make sure we abide by this statement. We have carried through by adding an appropriate run() method to

HelloJava4. It takes no arguments and returns no value. Our run() method accomplishes blinking by changing the color of our text a couple of times a second. It's a very short routine, but we're going to delay looking at it until we tie up some loose ends in dealing with the Thread itself.

Starting the Thread

We want the blinking to begin when the application starts. So we'll start the thread in the initialization code in HelloJava4's constructor. It takes only two lines:

```
Thread t = new Thread(this);
t.start();
```

First, the constructor creates a new instance of Thread, passing it the object that contains the run() method to the constructor. Since HelloJava4 itself contains our run() method, we pass the special variable this to the constructor. this always refers to our object. After creating the new Thread, we call its start() method to begin execution. This, in turn, invokes HelloJava4's run() method in a separate thread.

Running Code in the Thread

Our run() method does its job by setting the value of the variable blinkState. We have added blinkState, a boolean value, to represent whether we are currently blinking on or off:

```
boolean blinkState;
```

A setColor() call has been added to our paintComponent() method to handle blinking. When blinkState is true, the call to setColor() draws the text in the background color, making it disappear:

```
g.setColor(blinkState ? getBackground() : currentColor());
```

Here we are being somewhat terse, using the C-like ternary operator to return one of two alternative color values based on the value of blinkState.

Finally, we come to the run() method itself:

```
public void run() {
  try {
    while(true) {
      blinkState = !blinkState;
      repaint();
      Thread.sleep(500);
    }
  }
  catch (InterruptedException ie) {}
}
```

Basically, run() is an infinite while loop. This means the method will run continuously until the thread is terminated by a call to the controlling Thread object's interrupt() method.

The body of the loop does three things on each pass:

- Flips the value of blinkState to its opposite value using the not operator, "!"
- Calls repaint() to redraw the text
- Sleeps for 500 milliseconds (half a second)

sleep() is a static method of the Thread class. The method can be invoked from anywhere and has the effect of putting the current thread to sleep for the specified number of milliseconds. The effect here is to give us approximately two blinks per second. The try/catch construct, described in the next section, traps any errors in the call to the sleep() method of the Thread class.

Exceptions

The try/catch statement in Java is used to handle special conditions called *exceptions*. An exception is a message that is sent, normally in response to an error, during the execution of a statement or a method. When an exceptional condition arises, an object is created that contains information about the particular problem or condition. Exceptions act somewhat like events. Java stops execution at the place where the exception occurred, and the exception object is said to be *thrown* by that section of code. Like an event, an exception must be delivered somewhere and handled. The section of code that receives the exception object is said to *catch* the exception. An exception causes the execution of the instigating section of code to stop abruptly and transfers control to the code that receives the exception object.

The try/catch construct allows you to catch exceptions for a section of code. If an exception is caused by any statement inside of a try clause, Java attempts to deliver the exception to the appropriate catch clause. A catch clause looks like a method declaration with one argument and no return type. If Java finds a catch clause with an argument type that matches the type of the exception, that catch clause is invoked. A try clause can have multiple catch clauses with different argument types; Java chooses the appropriate one in a way that is analogous to the selection of overloaded methods. You can catch multiple types of exceptions from a block of code. Depending on the type of exception thrown, the appropriate catch clause will be executed.

If there is no try/catch clause surrounding the code, or a matching catch clause is not found, the exception is thrown up the call stack to the calling method. If the exception is not caught there, it's thrown up another level, and so on until the exception is handled. This provides a very flexible error-handling mechanism, so that exceptions in deeply nested calls can bubble up to the surface of the call stack for handling. As a programmer, you need to know what exceptions a particular statement can generate, so methods in Java are required to declare the exceptions they can throw. If a method doesn't handle an exception itself, it must specify that it can throw that exception, so that its calling method knows that it may have to handle it. See Chapter 4, *The Java Language*, for a complete discussion of exceptions and the `try`/`catch` clause.

So, why do we need a `try`/`catch` clause in the `run()` method? What kind of exception can `Thread`'s `sleep()` method throw and why do we care about it, when we don't seem to check for exceptions anywhere else? Under some circumstances, `Thread`'s `sleep()` method can throw an `InterruptedException`, indicating that it was interrupted by another thread. Since the `run()` method specified in the `Runnable` interface doesn't declare it can throw an `InterruptedException`, we must catch it ourselves, or the compiler will complain. The `try`/`catch` statement in our example has an empty `catch` clause, which means that it handles the exception by ignoring it. In this case, our thread's functionality is so simple it doesn't matter if it's interrupted. All of the other methods we have used either handle their own exceptions or throw only general-purpose exceptions that are assumed to be possible everywhere and don't need to be explicitly declared.

A Word About Synchronization

At any given time, there can be a number of threads running in the Java runtime system. Unless we explicitly coordinate them, these threads will be executing methods without any regard for what the other threads are doing. Problems can arise when these methods share the same data. If one method is changing the value of some variables at the same time that another method is reading these variables, it's possible that the reading thread might catch things in the middle and get some variables with old values and some with new. Depending on the application, this situation could cause a critical error.

In our HelloJava examples, both our `paintComponent()` and `mouseDragged()` methods access the `messageX` and `messageY` variables. Without knowing the implementation of our particular Java environment, we have to assume that these methods could conceivably be called by different threads and run concurrently. `paintComponent()` could be called while `mouseDragged()` is in the midst of updating `messageX` and `messageY`. At that point, the data is in an inconsistent state and if `paintComponent()` gets lucky, it could get the new x value with the old y value. Fortunately, in this case, we probably would not even notice if this were to happen in our application. We did, however, see another case, in our `changeColor()` and `currentColor()` methods, where there is the potential for a more serious "out of bounds" error.

The `synchronized` modifier tells Java to acquire a *lock* for the class that contains the method before executing that method. Only one method can have the lock on a class at any given time, which means that only one synchronized method in that class can be running at a time. This allows a method to alter data and leave it in a consistent state before a concurrently running method is allowed to access it. When the method is done, it releases the lock on the class.

Unlike synchronization in other languages, the `synchronized` keyword in Java provides locking at the language level. This means there is no way that you can forget to unlock a class. Even if the method throws an exception or the thread is terminated, Java will release the lock. This feature makes programming with threads in Java much easier than in other languages. See Chapter 8 for more details on coordinating threads and shared data.

Whew! Now it's time to say goodbye to HelloJava. We hope that you have developed a feel for the major features of the Java language, and that this will help you as you go on to explore the details of programming with Java.

Tools of the Trade

You have many options for Java development environments, from the traditional text-editor-and-command-line environment to IDEs like WebGain's Visual Café, Inprise's JBuilder, Tek-Tools' KAWA, or Sun's Forte for Java. The examples in this book were developed using the Solaris and Windows versions of the Java Software Development Kit (SDK), so we will describe those tools here. When we refer to the compiler or interpreter, we'll be referring to the command-line versions of these tools, so the book is decidedly biased toward those of you who are working in a Unix or DOS-like environment with a shell and filesystem. However, the basic features we'll be describing for Sun's Java interpreter and compiler should be applicable to other Java environments as well.

In this chapter, we'll describe the tools you'll need to compile and run Java applications. The last part of the chapter discusses how to pack Java class files into Java archives (JAR files). Chapter 20, *Applets*, describes the ability to "sign" classes within a JAR file, and to give greater privileges to classes with a signature that you trust.

The Java Interpreter

A Java interpreter is software that implements the Java virtual machine and runs Java applications. It can be a standalone application like the SDK's `java` program, or part of a larger application like the Netscape Navigator web browser. It's likely that the interpreter itself is written in a native, compiled language for your particular platform. Other tools, like Java compilers and development environments, can be written in Java (and should be, we'd argue, in order to maximize the portability of the Java development environment). Sun's Forte for Java is one example of a pure-Java IDE.

The Java interpreter performs all of the activities of the Java runtime system. It loads Java class files and interprets the compiled byte-code. It verifies compiled classes that are loaded from untrusted sources. In an implementation that supports dynamic, or just-in-time, compilation, the interpreter also serves as a specialized compiler that turns Java byte-code into native machine instructions.

Throughout the rest of this book, we'll be building both standalone Java programs and applets. Both are kinds of Java applications run by a Java interpreter. The difference is that a standalone Java application has all of its parts; it's a complete program that runs independently. An applet is more like an embeddable program module. The Java interpreter can't run an applet directly, because it is used as part of a larger application. To run an applet, you can use a web browser like Sun's HotJava or Netscape Navigator, or the `appletviewer` tool that comes with the SDK. Both HotJava and `appletviewer` are standalone Java applications run directly by the Java interpreter; these programs implement the additional structure needed to run Java applets.

Sun's Java interpreter is called `java`. In a standalone Java application, one class includes a `main()` method, which contains the statements to be executed upon startup. To run the application, execute the interpreter, specifying that class as an argument. You can also specify options to the interpreter, as well as arguments to be passed to the application:

```
% java [interpreter options] class_name [program arguments]
```

The class should be specified as a fully qualified class name, including the package name, if any. Note, however, that you don't include the *.class* file extension. Here are a few examples:

```
% java animals.birds.BigBird
% java test
```

The interpreter searches for the class in the *class path*, a list of directories where packages of classes are stored. We'll discuss the class path in detail in the next section. The class path is typically specified by an environment variable, which you can override with the command-line option `-classpath`.

After loading the class specified on the command line, the interpreter executes the class's `main()` method. From there, the application can start additional threads, reference other classes, and create its user interface or other structures, as shown in Figure 3-1.

The `main()` method must have the right *method signature*. A method signature is a collection of information about the method, like a C prototype or a forward function declaration in other languages. It includes the method's name, type, and visibility, as well as its arguments and return type. The `main()` method must be a

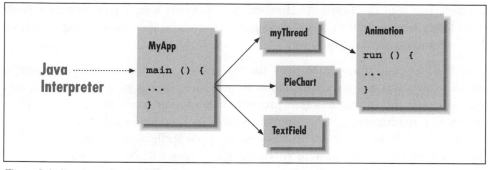

Figure 3-1. Starting a Java application

`public`, `static` method that takes an array of `String` objects as its argument and does not return any value (`void`):

```
public static void main ( String [] myArgs )
```

Because `main()` is a `public` and `static` method, it can be accessed directly from another class using the name of the class that contains it. We'll discuss the implications of visibility modifiers such as `public` and the meaning of `static` in Chapters 4 through 6.

The `main()` method's single argument, the array of `String` objects, holds the command-line arguments passed to the application. As in C, the name that we give the parameter doesn't matter; only the type is important. Unlike C, the content of `myArgs` is a true array. There's no need for an argument count parameter, because `myArgs` knows how many arguments it contains and can happily provide that information:

```
int argc = myArgs.length;
```

Java also differs from C in another respect here: `myArgs[0]` is the first command-line argument, not the name of the application. If you're accustomed to parsing C command-line arguments, you'll need to be careful not to trip over this difference.

The Java interpreter continues to run until the `main()` method of the initial class file has returned, and until any threads that it started are complete. Special threads designated as "daemon" threads are silently killed when the rest of the application has completed.

Policy Files

Java 2 provides a simple mechanism for protecting your computer from evil programs like viruses. If you download a program from somewhere on the Internet, how can you prevent it from stealing information on your computer and sending

it back out into the Internet? How can you prevent a malicious program from
disabling your computer or erasing data on your disk? Most computing platforms
have no answer for these questions.

Java 2 offers powerful ways to limit the actions of running code. Before Java 2,
much of the buzz about security had to do with the security of applets. The applet
ran with security restrictions that prevented the applet from doing questionable
things like reading from or writing to the disk or contacting arbitrary computers
on the network. In Java 2, it's just as easy to apply applet-style security to applications. Furthermore, it's easy to fine-tune the access you allow applications. For
example, you can allow an application to access the disk, but only in a specific
directory, or you can allow network access to certain addresses.

Why is this important? Let's suppose that you need a certain application, like a calendar or an address manager. You go to your favorite Internet search engine and
find a promising-looking Java application that does just what you want. You download and run it. But it's entirely possible that what you've downloaded is not what
you wanted. It could be a computer virus that infects your computer. Or it could
simply be a malicious program that erases files from your disk. In this case, it
would have been a really good idea to restrict the application's actions.

The Default Security Manager

You can use an option of the `java` interpreter to install a default security manager. This security manager enforces many of the same rules as for applets. To see
how this works, let's write a little program that does something questionable, making a network connection to some computer on the Internet. (We'll cover the specifics of network programming later, in Chapters 11 and 12.)

```
//file: EvilEmpire.java
import java.net.*;

public class EvilEmpire {
  public static void main(String[] args) throws Exception{
    try {
      Socket s = new Socket("207.46.131.13", 80);
      System.out.println("Connected!");
    }
    catch (SecurityException e) {
      System.out.println("SecurityException: could not connect.");
    }
  }
}
```

If you just run this program with the Java interpreter, it will make the network
connection:

```
C:\> java EvilEmpire
Connected!

C:\>
```

This is kind of scary. Let's install the default security manager, like this:

```
C:\> java -Djava.security.manager EvilEmpire
SecurityException: could not connect.

C:\>
```

That's better, but suppose that the application actually has a legitimate reason to make its network connection. We'd like to leave the default security manager in place, just to be safe, but we'd like to grant this application permission to make a network connection.

The policytool Utility

To permit our EvilEmpire example to make a network connection, we need to create a *policy file* that contains the appropriate permission. A handy utility called policytool, included in SDK 1.2 and later, helps you make policy files. Fire it up from a command line like this:

```
C:\> policytool
```

You may get an error message when policytool starts up about not finding a default policy file. Don't worry about this; just click **OK** to make the message go away.

We want to add a network permission for the EvilEmpire application. The application is identified by its origin, also called a *codebase*. A codebase is described by a URL. In this case, it will be a file: URL that points to the location of the EvilEmpire application on your disk.

If you started up policytool, you should be looking at its main window, shown in Figure 3-2. Click on **Add Policy Entry**. Another window pops up, like the one shown in Figure 3-3 (but with the fields empty).

First, fill in the codebase with the URL of the directory containing EvilEmpire as shown in the figure. Then click on **Add Permission**. Yet another window pops up, shown in Figure 3-4.

Choose **SocketPermission** from the first combo box. Then fill out the second text field on the right side with the network address that EvilEmpire will connect to. Finally, choose **connect** from the third combo box. Click on **OK**; you should see the new permission in the policy entry window, as shown in Figure 3-3.

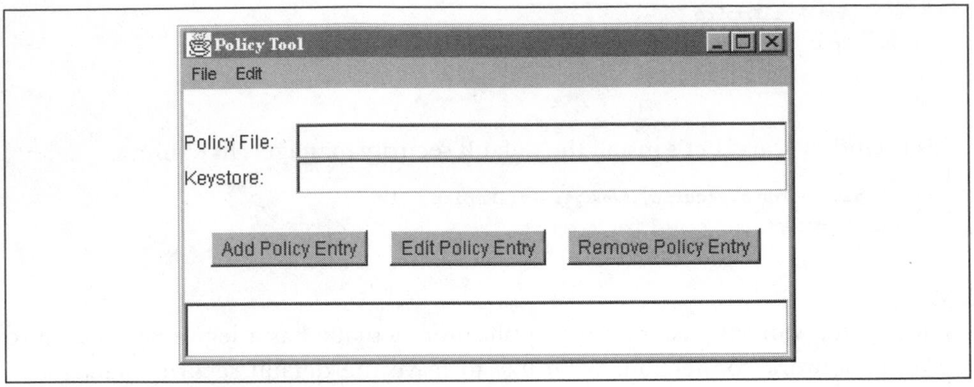

Figure 3-2. The policytool window

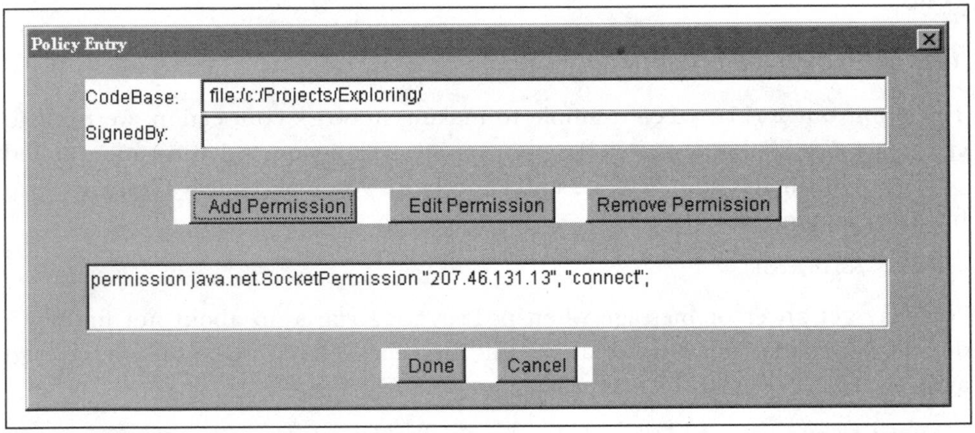

Figure 3-3. Adding a policy entry

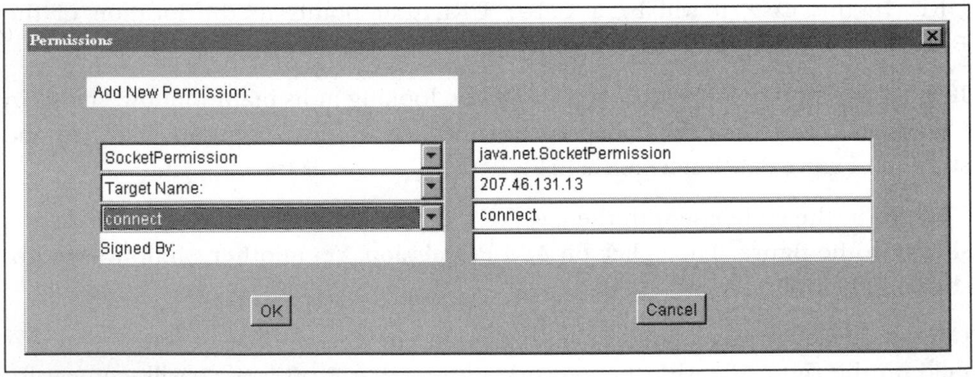

Figure 3-4. Creating a new permission

Click on **Done** to finish creating the policy. Then choose **Save As** from the **File** menu and save the policy file as something memorable, like *EvilEmpire.policy*. You can quit `policytool` now; we're all done with it.

There's nothing magical about the policy file you just created. Take a look at it with a text editor. It has a simple syntax; here's the important part, showing the policy we just created:

```
grant codeBase "file:/c:/Projects/Exploring/" {
  permission java.net.SocketPermission "207.46.131.13", "connect";
};
```

You can eschew `policytool` entirely and just create policy files with a text editor, if you're more comfortable that way.

Using a Policy File with the Default Security Manager

Now that we've gone to the trouble of creating a policy file, let's use it. You can tell the default security manager to use the policy file with another command-line option to the `java` interpreter:

```
C:\> java -Djava.security.manager -Djava.security.policy=EvilEmpire.policy
EvilEmpire
Connected!
```

`EvilEmpire` can now make its socket connection because we have explicitly granted it permission with a policy file. The default security manager still protects us in other ways, however; `EvilEmpire` cannot write or read files on the disk except in the directory it came from; it cannot make connections to any other network addresses except the one we specified. Take a moment and bask in this warm fuzzy feeling.

Later, in Chapter 20, you'll see `policytool` again when we explain signed applets. In this chapter, codebases are identified by URLs, which isn't the most secure option. Through tricky network shenanigans, a clever forger may be able to give you code that appears to be from somewhere it's not. Crytpographically signed code is even more trustworthy; see Chapter 20 for the full details.

The Class Path

The concept of a *path* should be familiar to anyone who has worked on a DOS or Unix platform. It's an environment variable that provides an application with a list of places to look for some resource. The most common example is a path for executable programs. In a Unix shell, the PATH environment variable is a colon-separated list of directories that are searched, in order, when the user types the name of a command. The Java CLASSPATH environment variable, similarly, is a list of locations that can be searched for packages containing Java class files. Both the

Java interpreter and the Java compiler use CLASSPATH when searching for packages and classes on the local host.

A location on the class path can be a directory name or the name of a *class archive file.* Java supports archives of class files in its own Java archive (JAR) format, and in the conventional ZIP format. JAR and ZIP are really the same format, but JAR archives include extra files that describe each archive's contents. JAR files are created with the SDK's jar utility; many tools for creating ZIP archives are publicly available. The archive format enables large groups of classes to be distributed in a single file; the Java interpreter automatically extracts individual class files from an archive, as needed.

The precise means and format for setting the class path vary from system to system. On a Unix system, you set the CLASSPATH environment variable with a colon-separated list of directories and class archive files:

```
CLASSPATH=/home/vicky/Java/classes:/home/josh/oldstuff/foo.zip:.
```

On a Windows system, the CLASSPATH environment variable is set with a semicolon-separated list of directories and class archive files:

```
set CLASSPATH=D:\users\vicky\Java\classes;.
```

The first example above, for Unix, specifies a class path with three locations: a directory in the user's home, a ZIP file in another user's directory, and the current directory, which is always specified with a dot (.). The last component of the class path, the current directory, is useful when tinkering with classes, but as a general rule, it's bad practice to put the current directory in any kind of path.

The Java interpreter and the other command-line tools also know how to find *core* classes, which are the classes included in every Java installation. The classes in the java.lang, java.io, java.net, and javax.swing packages, for example, are all core classes. You don't need to include these classes in your class path; the Java interpreter and the other tools can find them by themselves.

To find other classes, the Java interpreter searches the locations on the class path in order. The search combines the path location and the fully qualified class name. For example, consider a search for the class animals.birds.BigBird. Searching the class path directory */usr/lib/java* means the interpreter looks for an individual class file at */usr/lib/java/animals/birds/BigBird.class.* Searching a ZIP or JAR archive on the class path, say */home/vicky/Java/utils/classutils.jar,* means that the interpreter looks for component file *animals/birds/BigBird.class* in the archive.

For the Java interpreter, java, and the Java compiler, javac, the class path can also be specified with the -classpath option:

```
% javac -classpath /pkg/sdk/lib/classes.zip:/home/pat/java:. Foo.java
```

If you don't specify the CLASSPATH environment variable, it defaults to the current directory (.); this means that the files in your current directory are always available. If you change the class path and don't include the current directory, these files will no longer be accessible.

The Java Compiler

In this section, we'll say a few words about javac, the Java compiler that is supplied as part of Sun's SDK. (If you are happily working in another development environment, you may want to skip ahead to the next section.) The javac compiler is written entirely in Java, so it's available for any platform that supports the Java runtime system. The ability to support its own development environments is an important stage in a language's development. Java makes this bootstrapping automatic by supplying a ready-to-run compiler at the same cost as porting the interpreter.

javac turns Java source code into a compiled class that contains Java virtual machine byte-code. By convention, source files are named with a *.java* extension; the resulting class files have a *.class* extension. Each source code file is a single compilation unit. As you'll see in Chapter 6, *Relationships Among Classes*, classes in a given compilation unit share certain features, such as package and import statements.

javac allows you one public class per file and insists the file have the same name as the class. If the filename and class name don't match, javac issues a compilation error. A single file can contain multiple classes, as long as only one of the classes is public. Avoid packing many classes into a single source file. Including non-public classes in a *.java* file is one easy way to tightly couple such classes to a public class. But you might also consider using inner classes (see Chapter 6).

Now for an example. Place the following source code in file *BigBird.java*:

```
package animals.birds;

public class BigBird extends Bird {
    ...
}
```

Then compile it with:

```
% javac BigBird.java
```

Unlike the Java interpreter, which takes just a class name as its argument, javac needs a filename to process. The previous command produces the class file *BigBird.class* in the same directory as the source file. While it's useful to have the class file in the same directory as the source for testing a simple example, for most real applications you'll need to store the class file in an appropriate place in the class path.

You can use the –d option to javac to specify an alternative directory for storing the class files it generates. The specified directory is used as the root of the class hierarchy, so *.class* files are placed in this directory or in a subdirectory below it, depending on whether the class is contained in a package. (The compiler creates intermediate subdirectories automatically, if necessary.) For example, we can use the following command to create the *BigBird.class* file at */home/vicky/Java/classes/animals/birds/BigBird.class*:

```
% javac -d /home/vicky/Java/classes BigBird.java
```

You can specify multiple *.java* files in a single javac command; the compiler creates a class file for each source file. But you don't need to list source files for other classes that your class references, as long as the other classes have already been compiled. During compilation, Java resolves other class references using the class path. If our class refers to other classes in animals.birds or other packages, the appropriate paths should be listed in the class path at compile time, so that javac can find the appropriate class files.

The Java compiler is more intelligent than your average compiler, replacing some of the functionality of a *make* utility. For example, javac compares the modification times of the source and class files for all referenced classes and recompiles them as necessary. A compiled Java class remembers the source file from which it was compiled, so as long as the source file is in the same directory as the class file, javac can recompile the source if necessary. If, in the previous example, class BigBird references another class, animals.furry.Grover, javac looks for the source file *Grover.java* in an animals.furry package and recompiles it if necessary to bring the *Grover.class* class file up-to-date.

By default, however, javac checks only source files that are referenced directly from other source files. This means that if you have an out-of-date class file that is referenced only by an up-to-date class file, it may not be noticed and recompiled. You can force javac to walk the entire graph of objects using the –depend option. But be warned, this can increase compilation time significantly. And this technique still won't help if you want to keep class libraries or other collections of classes up to date even if they aren't being referenced at all. For that you should consider a *make* utility.

Finally, it's important to note that javac can compile an application even if only the compiled versions of referenced classes are available. You don't need source code for all of your objects. Java class files contain all the data type and method signature information that source files contain, so compiling against binary class files is as type-safe (and exception-safe) as compiling with Java source code.

Java Archive (JAR) Files

Java archive files (JAR files) are Java's suitcases. They are the standard and portable way to pack up all of the parts of your Java application into a compact bundle
for distribution or installation. You can put whatever you want into a JAR file: Java
class files, serialized objects, data files, images, sounds, etc. As we'll see in
Chapter 20, a JAR file can carry one or more digital signatures that attest to the
integrity and authenticity of that data. A signature can be attached to the file as a
whole or to individual items in the file.

The Java runtime system understands JAR files and can load class files directly from
an archive. So you can pack your application's classes in a JAR file and place it in
your CLASSPATH. You can do the equivalent for applets by listing the JAR file in the
ARCHIVE attribute of the HTML <APPLET> tag. Other types of files (data, images,
etc.) contained in your JAR file can be retrieved using the getResource()
method. (described in Chapter 10, *Input/Output Facilities*). Therefore, your code
doesn't have to know whether any resource is a plain file or a member of a JAR
archive. Whether a given class or data file is an item in a JAR file, is an individual
file on the class path, or is located on a remote applet server, you can always refer
to it in a standard way, and let Java's class loader resolve the location.

File Compression

Items stored in JAR files may be compressed with ZLIB* compression. JAR files are
completely compatible with the ZIP archives familiar to Windows users. You could
even use tools like pkzip to create and maintain simple JAR files. But jar, the Java
archive utility, can do a bit more.

Compression makes downloading classes over a network much faster. A quick sur-
vey of the SDK distribution shows that a typical class file shrinks by about 40 percent when it is compressed. Text files such as arbitrary HTML or ASCII containing English words often compress by as much as 75 percent—to one-quarter of
their original size. (On the other hand, image files don't get smaller when compressed; both of the common image formats have compression built in.)

Compression is not the only advantage that a JAR file has for transporting files
over a network. For an application with many components, the amount of time it
takes to transport all of the parts may be less significant than the time involved in
setting up the connections and making the requests for them. This is especially
important for applets loaded via the Web. The typical web browser has to make a
separate HTTP request for each class or data file. An applet comprising 100

---

* See *http://www.cdrom.com/pub/infozip/zlib/* and RFC 1950.

classes, for example, would require at least 100 separate trips to the web server to gather all its parts. Placing all the classes in a single JAR file enables them to be downloaded in a single transaction. Eliminating the overhead of making HTTP requests is likely to be a big savings, since individual class files tend to be small, and a complex applet could easily require many of them.

The jar Utility

The jar utility provided with the SDK is a simple tool for creating and reading JAR files. Its user interface isn't friendly; it mimics the Unix tar (tape archive) command. If you're familiar with tar, you'll recognize the following incantations:

jar -cvf jarFile path [path] [.. .]
>   Create jarFile containing path(s)

jar -tvf jarFile [path] [...]
>   List the contents of jarFile, optionally showing just path(s)

jar -xvf jarFile [path] [...]
>   Extract the contents of jarFile, optionally extracting just path(s)

In these commands, the letters c, t, and x tell jar whether it is creating an archive, listing an archive's contents, or extracting files from an archive. The f means that the next argument will be the name of the JAR file on which to operate. The v tells jar to be more verbose when displaying information about files. In verbose mode you can get information about file sizes, modification times, and compression ratios.

Subsequent items on the command line (i.e., anything aside from the letters telling jar what to do and the file on which jar should operate) are taken as names of archive items. If you're creating an archive, the files and directories you list are placed in it. If you're extracting, only the filenames you list are extracted from the archive. (If you don't list any files, jar extracts everything in the archive.)

For example, let's say we have just completed our new game: "spaceblaster." All the files associated with the game are in three directories. The Java classes themselves are in the *spaceblaster/game* directory; *spaceblaster/images* contains the game's images; and *spaceblaster/docs* contains associated game data. We can pack all of this in an archive with this command:

```
% jar cvf spaceblaster.jar spaceblaster
```

Because we requested verbose output, jar tells us what it is doing:

```
adding:spaceblaster/ (in=0) (out=0) (stored 0%)
adding:spaceblaster/game/ (in=0) (out=0) (stored 0%)
adding:spaceblaster/game/Game.class (in=8035) (out=3936) (deflated 51%)
adding:spaceblaster/game/Planetoid.class (in=6254) (out=3288) (deflated 47%)
```

```
adding:spaceblaster/game/SpaceShip.class (in=2295) (out=1280) (deflated 44%)
adding:spaceblaster/images/ (in=0) (out=0) (stored 0%)
adding:spaceblaster/images/spaceship.gif (in=6174) (out=5936) (deflated 3%)
adding:spaceblaster/images/planetoid.gif (in=23444) (out=23454) (deflated 0%)
adding:spaceblaster/docs/ (in=0) (out=0) (stored 0%)
adding:spaceblaster/docs/help1.html (in=3592) (out=1545) (deflated 56%)
adding:spaceblaster/docs/help2.html (in=3148) (out=1535) (deflated 51%)
```

`jar` creates the file *spaceblaster.jar* and adds the directory *spaceblaster*, in turn adding the directories and files within *spaceblaster* to the archive. In verbose mode, `jar` reports the savings gained by compressing the files in the archive.

We can unpack the archive with this command:

```
% jar xvf spaceblaster.jar
```

Likewise, we can extract an individual file or directory with:

```
% jar xvf spaceblaster.jar filename
```

But you normally don't have to unpack a JAR file to use its contents; Java tools know how to extract files from archives automatically. We can list the contents of our JAR with the command:

```
% jar tvf spaceblaster.jar
```

Here's the output; it lists all the files, their sizes, and creation times:

```
    0 Thu May 15 12:18:54 PDT 1997 META-INF/
 1074 Thu May 15 12:18:54 PDT 1997 META-INF/MANIFEST.MF
    0 Thu May 15 12:09:24 PDT 1997 spaceblaster/
    0 Thu May 15 11:59:32 PDT 1997 spaceblaster/game/
 8035 Thu May 15 12:14:08 PDT 1997 spaceblaster/game/Game.class
 6254 Thu May 15 12:15:18 PDT 1997 spaceblaster/game/Planetoid.class
 2295 Thu May 15 12:15:26 PDT 1997 spaceblaster/game/SpaceShip.class
    0 Thu May 15 12:17:00 PDT 1997 spaceblaster/images/
 6174 Thu May 15 12:16:54 PDT 1997 spaceblaster/images/spaceship.gif
23444 Thu May 15 12:16:58 PDT 1997 spaceblaster/images/planetoid.gif
    0 Thu May 15 12:10:02 PDT 1997 spaceblaster/docs/
 3592 Thu May 15 12:10:16 PDT 1997 spaceblaster/docs/help1.html
 3148 Thu May 15 12:10:02 PDT 1997 spaceblaster/docs/help2.html
```

JAR manifests

Note that `jar` adds a directory called *META-INF* to our archive. It contains one file: *MANIFEST.MF*. The *META-INF* directory holds files describing the contents of the JAR file. The *MANIFEST.MF* file that `jar` adds is an automatically generated packing list naming the files in the archive along with cryptographic checksums for each.

The manifest is a text file containing a set of lines in the form *keyword: value*. The format of the manifest file changed between SDK 1.1 and SDK 1.2. In SDK 1.2 and later, the manifest file is very simple, containing no information on the items in the archive:

```
Manifest-Version: 1.0
Created-By: 1.2.1 (Sun Microsystems Inc.)
```

Basically the file just describes its version number. In SDK 1.1, the manifest contains entries describing each item in the archive. In our case, the beginning of our manifest file looks like this (in SDK 1.1 only):

```
Manifest-Version: 1.0

Name: spaceblaster/game/Game.class
Digest-Algorithms: SHA MD5
SHA-Digest: D5Vi4UV+O+XprdFYaUt0bCv2GDo=
MD5-Digest: 9/W62mC4th6G/x8tTnP2Ng==

Name: spaceblaster/game/Planetoid.class
Digest-Algorithms: SHA MD5
SHA-Digest: SuSUd6pYAASO5JiIGlBrWYzLGVk=
MD5-Digest: KN/4cLDxAxDk/INKHi2emA==

...
```

The first line is the same version number as before. Following it are groups of lines describing each item. The first line tells you the item's name; in this case, the lines describing the files *Game.class* and *Planetoid.class*. The remaining lines in each section describe various attributes of the item. In this case, the `Digest-Algorithms` line specifies that the manifest provides message digests (similar to checksums) in two forms: SHA and MD5.[*] This is followed by the actual message digest for the item, computed using these two algorithms.

As we'll discuss in the next section, the *META-INF* directory and manifest file can also hold digital signature information for items in the archive. Since the message digest information is really necessary only for signed JAR files, it is omitted when you create an archive in SDK 1.2 and later.

You can add your own information to the manifest descriptions by specifying a supplementary manifest file when you create the archive. This is a good place to store other simple kinds of attribute information about the files in the archive, perhaps version or authorship information.

---

[*] SHA and MD5 stand for Secure Hashing Algorithm and Message Digest 5. That's all you really need to know about them; an explanation of these algorithms is beyond the scope of this book.

For example, we can create a file with the following *keyword: value* lines:

```
Name: spaceblaster/images/planetoid.gif
RevisionNumber: 42.7
Artist-Temperment: moody
```

To add this information to the manifest in our archive, place it in a file called *myManifest.mf* and give the following `jar` command:

```
% jar -cvmf myManifest.mf spaceblaster.jar spaceblaster
```

We've added an additional option to the command, `m`, which specifies that `jar` should read additional manifest information from the file given on the command line. How does `jar` know which file is which? Because `m` is before `f`, it expects to find the manifest information before the name of the JAR file it will create. If you think that's awkward, you're right; get the names in the wrong order, and `jar` will do the wrong thing. Be careful.

Aside from information for your own use, there are special values (in SDK 1.2) you can put in the manifest file that are useful. One of these, `Main-Class`, allows you to specify a class that contains a `main()` method:

```
Main-Class: Game
```

If you incorporate this specification in your JAR file manifest (using the `m` option described earlier), you can actually run the JAR from the command line:

```
% java -jar spaceblaster.jar
```

The interpreter looks for the `Main-Class` value in the manifest. Then it loads the named class as the application's initial class.

What can we do with the revision and temperament information we've so cleverly included in the JAR file? Unfortunately, nothing, except for unpacking the archive and reading the manifest. However, if you were writing your own JAR utility or some kind of resource loader, you could include code to look at the manifest, check for your private keywords, and act accordingly—perhaps darkening the display if the artist's temperament is `moody`.

Another important keyword is `Java-Bean`. The value of this keyword should be `true` if the item is a Java Bean; this information is used by the BeanBox and other utilities that work with Beans (see Chapter 19, *Java Beans*).

4

The Java Language

In this chapter, we'll introduce the framework of the Java language and some of its fundamental facilities. We're not going to try to provide a full language reference here. Instead, we'll lay out the basic structures of Java with special attention to how it differs from other languages. For example, we'll take a close look at arrays in Java, because they are significantly different from those in some other languages. We won't, on the other hand, spend much time explaining basic language constructs like loops and control structures. Nor will we talk much about Java's object-oriented side here, as that's covered in detail in Chapters 5 through 7.

As always, we'll try to provide meaningful examples to illustrate how to use Java in everyday programming tasks.

Text Encoding

Java is a language for the Internet. Since the people of the Net speak and write in many different human languages, Java must be able to handle a large number of languages as well. One of the ways in which Java supports international access is through Unicode character encoding. Unicode uses a 16-bit character encoding; it's a worldwide standard that supports the scripts (character sets) of most languages.[*]

Java source code can be written using the Unicode character encoding and stored either in its full 16-bit form or with ASCII-encoded Unicode character values. This makes Java a friendly language for non-English-speaking programmers who can use their native alphabet for class, method, and variable names in Java code.

---

[*] For more information about Unicode, see *http://www.unicode.org*. Ironically, one of the scripts listed as "obsolete and archaic" and not currently supported by the Unicode standard is Javanese—a historical language of the people of the Island of Java.

The Java char type and String objects also support Unicode. But if you're concerned about having to labor with two-byte characters, you can relax. The String API makes the character encoding transparent to you. Unicode is also ASCII-friendly; the first 256 characters are defined to be identical to the first 256 characters in the ISO8859-1 (Latin-1) encoding; if you stick with these values, there's really no distinction between the two.

Most platforms can't display all currently defined Unicode characters. As a result, Java programs can be written with special Unicode escape sequences. A Unicode character can be represented with this escape sequence:

    \u*xxxx*

xxxx is a sequence of one to four hexadecimal digits. The escape sequence indicates an ASCII-encoded Unicode character. This is also the form Java uses to output a Unicode character in an environment that doesn't otherwise support them.

Java stores and manipulates characters and strings internally as Unicode values. Java also comes with classes to read and write Unicode-formatted character streams.

Comments

Java supports both C-style block comments delimited by /* and */ and C++- style line comments indicated by //:

```
/*  This is a
        multiline
           comment.    */

// This is a single-line comment
// and so // is this
```

As in C, block comments can't be nested. Single-line comments are delimited by the end of a line; extra // indicators inside a single line have no effect. Line comments are useful for short comments within methods; they don't conflict with wrapping block comment indicators around large chunks of code during development.

Javadoc Comments

By convention, a block comment beginning with /** indicates a special *doc comment*. A doc comment is designed to be extracted by automated documentation generators, such as the DSK's javadoc program. A doc comment is terminated by the next */, just as with a regular block comment. Leading spacing up to a * on each line is ignored; lines beginning with @ are interpreted as special tags for the documentation generator.

Here's an example:

```
/**
 * I think this class is possibly the most amazing thing you will
 * ever see. Let me tell you about my own personal vision and
 * motivation in creating it.
 * <p>
 * It all began when I was a small child, growing up on the
 * streets of Idaho. Potatoes were the rage, and life was good...
 *
 * @see PotatoPeeler
 * @see PotatoMasher
 * @author John 'Spuds' Smith
 * @version 1.00, 19 Dec 1996
 */
```

`javadoc` creates HTML format documentation of classes by reading the source code and the embedded comments. The author and version information is presented in the output, and the `@see` tags make hypertext links to the appropriate class documentation. The compiler also looks at the doc comments; in particular, it is interested in the `@deprecated` tag, which means that the method has been declared obsolete and should be avoided in new programs. The compiler generates a warning message whenever it sees the usage of a deprecated feature in your code.

Doc comments can appear above class, method, and variable definitions, but some tags may not be applicable to all of these. For example, a variable declaration can contain only a `@see` tag. Table 4-1 summarizes the tags used in doc comments.

Table 4-1. Doc Comment Tags

Tag	Description	Applies to
@see	Associated class name	Class, method, or variable
@author	Author name	Class
@version	Version string	Class
@param	Parameter name and description	Method
@return	Description of return value	Method
@exception	Exception name and description	Method
@deprecated	Declares an item to be obsolete	Class, method, or variable

Types

The type system of a programming language describes how its data elements (variables and constants) are associated with actual storage. In a statically typed language, like C or C++, the type of a data element is a simple, unchanging attribute that often corresponds directly to some underlying hardware phenomenon, like a register value or a pointer indirection. In a more dynamic language like Smalltalk or Lisp, variables can be assigned arbitrary elements and can effectively change their type throughout their lifetime. A considerable amount of overhead goes into validating what happens in these languages at runtime. Scripting languages like Perl and Tcl achieve ease of use by providing drastically simplified type systems in which only certain data elements can be stored in variables, and values are unified into a common representation, such as strings.

Java combines the best features of both statically and dynamically typed languages. As in a statically typed language, every variable and programming element in Java has a type that is known at compile time, so the runtime system doesn't normally have to check the type validity of assignments while the code is executing. Unlike C or C++, though, Java also maintains runtime information about objects and uses this to allow truly safe runtime polymorphism and casting (using an object as a type other than its declared type).

Java data types fall into two categories. *Primitive types* represent simple values that have built-in functionality in the language; they are fixed elements, such as literal constants and numbers. *Reference types* (or class types) include objects and arrays; they are called reference types because they are passed "by reference," as we'll explain shortly.

Primitive Types

Numbers, characters, and boolean values are fundamental elements in Java. Unlike some other (perhaps more pure) object-oriented languages, they are not objects. For those situations where it's desirable to treat a primitive value as an object, Java provides "wrapper" classes (see Chapter 9, *Basic Utility Classes*). One major advantage of treating primitive values as such is that the Java compiler can more readily optimize their usage.

Another important portability feature of Java is that primitive types are precisely defined. For example, you never have to worry about the size of an `int` on a particular platform; it's always a 32-bit, signed, two's complement number. Table 4-2 summarizes Java's primitive types.

Table 4-2. Java Primitive Data Types

Type	Definition
Boolean	`true` or `false`
Char	16-bit Unicode character
Byte	8-bit signed two's complement integer
Short	16-bit signed two's complement integer
Int	32-bit signed two's complement integer

Table 4-2. Java Primitive Data Types (continued)

Type	Definition
Long	64-bit signed two's complement integer
Float	32-bit IEEE 754 floating-point value
Double	64-bit IEEE 754 floating-point value

If you think the primitive types look like an idealization of C scalar types on a 32-bit machine, you're absolutely right. That's how they're supposed to look. The 16-bit characters were forced by Unicode, and ad hoc pointers were deleted for other reasons. But overall, the syntax and semantics of Java primitive types are meant to fit a C programmer's mental habits.

Floating-point precision

Floating-point operations in Java are standardized to follow the IEEE 754 international specification, which means that the result of floating-point calculations will generally be the same on different Java platforms. More recent versions of Java have been enhanced to allow for extended precision on platforms that support it. This can introduce extremely small-valued and arcane differences in the results of high-precision operations. Most applications would never notice this, but if you want to ensure that your application will produce exactly the same results on different platforms, use the special keyword `strictfp` as a class modifier on the class containing the floating-point manipulation.

Variable declaration and initialization

Variables are declared inside of methods or classes in C style. For example:

```
int foo;
double d1, d2;
boolean isFun;
```

Variables can optionally be initialized with an appropriate expression when they are declared:

```
int foo = 42;
double d1 = 3.14, d2 = 2 * 3.14;
boolean isFun = true;
```

Variables that are declared as instance variables in a class are set to default values if they are not initialized. (In this case, they act much like `static` variables in C or C++.) Numeric types default to the appropriate flavor of zero, characters are set to the null character (\0), and boolean variables have the value `false`. Local variables declared in methods, on the other hand, must be explicitly initialized before they can be used.

Integer literals

Integer literals can be specified in octal (base 8), decimal (base 10), or hexadecimal (base 16). A decimal integer is specified by a sequence of digits beginning with one of the characters 1–9:

```
int i = 1230;
```

Octal numbers are distinguished from decimal numbers by a leading zero:

```
int i = 01230;              // i = 664 decimal
```

As in C, a hexadecimal number is denoted by the leading characters 0x or 0X (zero "x"), followed by digits and the characters a–f or A–F, which represent the decimal values 10–15, respectively:

```
int i = 0xFFFF;             // i = 65535 decimal
```

Integer literals are of type int unless they are suffixed with an L, denoting that they are to be produced as a long value:

```
long l = 13L;
long l = 13;        // equivalent: 13 is converted from type int
```

(The lowercase character l ("el") is also acceptable, but should be avoided because it often looks like the numeral 1.)

When a numeric type is used in an assignment or an expression involving a type with a larger range, it can be promoted to the larger type. For example, in the second line of the previous example, the number 13 has the default type of int, but it's promoted to type long for assignment to the long variable. Certain other numeric and comparison operations also cause this kind of arithmetic promotion. A numeric value can never be assigned to a type with a smaller range without an explicit (C-style) cast, however:

```
int i = 13;
byte b = i;             // Compile-time error, explicit cast needed
byte b = (byte) i;      // OK
```

Conversions from floating-point to integer types always require an explicit cast because of the potential loss of precision.

Floating-point literals

Floating-point values can be specified in decimal or scientific notation. Floating-point literals are of type double unless they are suffixed with an f or F denoting that they are to be produced as a float value:

```
double d = 8.31;
double e = 3.00e+8;
float f = 8.31F;
float g = 3.00e+8F;
```

Character literals

A literal character value can be specified either as a single-quoted character or as an escaped ASCII or Unicode sequence:

```
char a = 'a';
char newline = '\n';
char smiley = '\u263a';
```

Reference Types

In C, you can make a new, complex data type by creating a `struct`. In Java (and other object-oriented languages), you instead create a `class` that defines a new type in the language. For instance, if we create a new class called `Foo` in Java, we are also implicitly creating a new type called `Foo`. The type of an item governs how it's used and where it's assigned. An item of type `Foo` can, in general, be assigned to a variable of type `Foo` or passed as an argument to a method that accepts a `Foo` value.

In an object-oriented language like Java, a type is not necessarily just a simple attribute. Reference types are related in the same way as the classes they represent. Classes exist in a hierarchy, where a subclass is a specialized kind of its parent class. The corresponding types have the same relationship, where the type of the child class is considered a subtype of the parent class. Because child classes always extend their parents and have, at a minimum, the same functionality, an object of the child's type can be used in place of an object of the parent's type. For example, if I create a new class, `Bar`, that extends `Foo`, there is a new type `Bar` that is considered a subtype of `Foo`. Objects of type `Bar` can then be used anywhere an object of type `Foo` could be used; an object of type `Bar` is said to be assignable to a variable of type `Foo`. This is called *subtype polymorphism* and is one of the primary features of an object-oriented language. We'll look more closely at classes and objects in Chapter 5, *Objects in Java*.

Primitive types in Java are used and passed "by value." In other words, when a primitive value is assigned or passed as an argument to a method, it's simply copied. Reference types, on the other hand, are always accessed "by reference." A *reference* is simply a handle or a name for an object. What a variable of a reference type holds is a reference to an object of its type (or of a subtype, as described earlier). A reference is like a pointer in C or C++, except that its type is strictly enforced and the reference value itself is a primitive entity that can't be examined directly. A reference value can't be created or changed other than through assignment to an appropriate object. When references are assigned or passed to methods, they are copied by value. You can think of a reference as a pointer type that is automatically dereferenced whenever it's mentioned.

Let's run through an example. We specify a variable of type Foo, called myFoo, and assign it an appropriate object:*

```
Foo myFoo = new Foo();
Foo anotherFoo = myFoo;
```

myFoo is a reference-type variable that holds a reference to the newly constructed Foo object. (For now, don't worry about the details of creating an object; we'll cover that in Chapter 5.) We designate a second Foo type variable, anotherFoo, and assign it to the same object. There are now two identical references: myFoo and anotherFoo. If we change things in the state of the Foo object itself, we will see the same effect by looking at it with either reference.

We can pass an object to a method by specifying a reference-type variable (in this case, either myFoo or anotherFoo) as the argument:

```
myMethod( myFoo );
```

An important, but sometimes confusing, distinction to make at this point is that the reference itself is passed by value. That is, the argument passed to the method (a local variable from the method's point of view) is actually a third copy of the reference. The method can alter the state of the Foo object itself through that reference, but it can't change the caller's notion of the reference to myFoo. That is, the method can't change the caller's myFoo to point to a different Foo object; it can change only its own. For those occasions when we want a method to have the side effect of changing a reference passed in to it, we have to wrap that reference in another object, to provide a layer of indirection.

Reference types always point to objects, and objects are always defined by classes. However, two special kinds of reference types specify the type of object they point to in a slightly different way. Arrays in Java have a special place in the type system. They are a special kind of object automatically created to hold a series of some other type of object, known as the *base type*. Declaring an array-type reference implicitly creates the new class type, as you'll see in the next section.

Interfaces are a bit sneakier. An interface defines a set of methods and a corresponding type. Any object that implements all methods of the interface can be treated as an object of that type. Variables and method arguments can be declared to be of interface types, just like class types, and any object that implements the interface can be assigned to them. This allows Java to cross the lines of the class hierarchy in a type-safe way.

---

* The comparable code in C++ would be:
```
Foo& myFoo      = *(new Foo());
Foo& anotherFoo = myFoo;
```

A Word About Strings

Strings in Java are objects; they are therefore a reference type. String objects do, however, have some special help from the Java compiler that makes them look more like primitive types. Literal string values in Java source code are turned into String objects by the compiler. They can be used directly, passed as arguments to methods, or assigned to String type variables:

```
System.out.println( "Hello World..." );
String s = "I am the walrus...";
String t = "John said: \"I am the walrus...\"";
```

The + symbol in Java is overloaded to provide string concatenation as well as numeric addition. Along with its sister +=, this is the only overloaded operator in Java:

```
String quote = "Four score and " + "seven years ago,";
String more = quote + " our" + " fathers" + " brought...";
```

Java builds a single String object from the concatenated strings and provides it as the result of the expression. We will discuss the String class in Chapter 9.

Statements and Expressions

Although the method declaration syntax of Java is quite different from that of C++, Java statement and expression syntax is like that of C. Again, the intention was to make the low-level details of Java easily accessible to C programmers, so that they can concentrate on learning the parts of the language that are really different. Java *statements* appear inside of methods and classes; they describe all activities of a Java program. Variable declarations and assignments, such as those in the previous section, are statements, as are the basic language structures like conditionals and loops. *Expressions* describe values; an expression is evaluated to produce a result, to be used as part of another expression or in a statement. Method calls, object allocations, and, of course, mathematical expressions are examples of expressions. Technically, since variable assignments can be used as values for further assignments or operations (in somewhat questionable programming style), they can be considered to be both statements and expressions.

One of the tenets of Java is to keep things simple and consistent. To that end, when there are no other constraints, evaluations and initializations in Java always occur in the order in which they appear in the code—from left to right. We'll see this rule used in the evaluation of assignment expressions, method calls, and array indexes, to name a few cases. In some other languages, the order of evaluation is more complicated or even implementation-dependent. Java removes this element of danger by precisely and simply defining how the code is evaluated. This doesn't, however, mean you should start writing obscure and convoluted statements. Relying on the order of evaluation of expressions is a bad programming habit, even when it works. It produces code that is hard to read and harder to modify. Real programmers, however, are not made of stone, and you may catch us doing this once or twice when we can't resist the urge to write terse code.

Statements

As in C or C++, statements and expressions in Java appear within a *code block*. A code block is syntactically just a series of statements surrounded by an open curly brace ({) and a close curly brace (}). The statements in a code block can contain variable declarations:

```
{
    int size = 5;
    setName("Max");
    ...
}
```

Methods, which look like C functions, are in a sense code blocks that take parameters and can be called by name:

```
setUpDog( String name ) {
    int size = 5;
    setName( name );
    ...
}
```

Variable declarations are limited in scope to their enclosing code block. That is, they can't be seen outside of the nearest set of braces:

```
{
    int i = 5;
}

i = 6;          // Compile-time error, no such variable i
```

In this way, code blocks can be used to arbitrarily group other statements and variables. The most common use of code blocks, however, is to define a group of statements for use in a conditional or iterative statement.

Since a code block is itself collectively treated as a statement, we define a conditional like an `if/else` clause as follows:

```
if ( condition )
    statement;
[ else
    statement; ]
```

Thus, the if clause has the familiar (to C/C++ programmers) functionality of taking two different forms:

```
if ( condition )
    statement;
```

or:

```
if ( condition )  {
    [ statement; ]
    [ statement; ]
    [ ... ]
}
```

Here the *condition* is a boolean expression. You can't use an integer expression or a reference type, as in C. In other words, while i==0 is legitimate, i is not (unless i itself is boolean).

In the second form, the statement is a code block, and all of its enclosed statements are executed if the conditional succeeds. Any variables declared within that block are visible only to the statements within the successful branch of the condition. Like the if/else conditional, most of the remaining Java statements are concerned with controlling the flow of execution. They act for the most part like their namesakes in C or C++.

The do and while iterative statements have the familiar functionality; their conditional test is also a boolean expression:

```
while ( condition )
    statement;

do
    statement;
while ( condition );
```

The for statement also looks like it does in C:

```
for ( initialization; condition; incrementor )
    statement;
```

The variable initialization expression can declare a new variable; this variable is limited to the scope of the for statement:

```
for (int i = 0; i < 100; i++ ) {
    System.out.println( i )
    int j = i;
    ...
}
```

Java does not support the C comma operator, which groups multiple expressions into a single expression. However, you can use multiple comma-separated expressions in the initialization and increment sections of the `for` loop. For example:

```
for (int i = 0, j = 10; i < j; i++, j-- ) {
    ...
}
```

The Java `switch` statement takes an integer type (or an argument that can be automatically promoted to an integer type) and selects among a number of alternative `case` branches:

```
switch ( int expression ) {
    case int expression :
        statement;
    [ case int expression
        statement;
    ...
    default :
        statement;  ]
}
```

No two of the `case` expressions can evaluate to the same value. As in C, an optional `default` case can be specified to catch unmatched conditions. Normally, the special statement `break` is used to terminate a branch of the `switch`:

```
switch ( retVal ) {
    case myClass.GOOD :
        // something good
        break;
    case myClass.BAD :
        // something bad
        break;
    default :
        // neither one
        break;
}
```

The Java `break` statement and its friend `continue` perform unconditional jumps out of a loop or conditional statement. They differ from the corresponding statements in C by taking an optional label as an argument. Enclosing statements, like code blocks and iterators, can be labeled with identifier statements:

```
one:
    while ( condition ) {
        ...
        two:
            while ( condition ) {
                ...
                // break or continue point
            }
```

```
            // after two
    }
    // after one
```

In this example, a break or continue without argument at the indicated position would have the normal, C-style effect. A break would cause processing to resume at the point labeled "after two"; a continue would immediately cause the two loop to return to its condition test.

The statement break two at the indicated point would have the same effect as an ordinary break, but break one would break both levels and resume at the point labeled "after one." Similarly, continue two would serve as a normal continue, but continue one would return to the test of the one loop. Multilevel break and continue statements remove the remaining justification for the evil goto statement in C/C++.

There are a few Java statements we aren't going to discuss right now. The try, catch, and finally statements are used in exception handling, as we'll discuss later in this chapter. The synchronized statement in Java is used to coordinate access to statements among multiple threads of execution; see Chapter 8, *Threads*, for a discussion of thread synchronization.

Unreachable statements

On a final note, we should mention that the Java compiler flags "unreachable" statements as compile-time errors. An unreachable statement is one that the compiler determines won't be called at all. Of course there may be many methods that are actually never called in your code, but the compiler will only detect those that it can "prove" will never be called simply by checking at compile time. For example, a method with an unconditional return statement in the middle of it will cause a compile-time error. So will a method with something like this:

```
if (1 < 2)
    return;
// unreachable statements
```

Expressions

An expression produces a result, or value, when it is evaluated. The value of an expression can be a numeric type, as in an arithmetic expression; a reference type, as in an object allocation; or the special type void, which is the declared type of a method that doesn't return a value. In the last case, the expression is evaluated only for its side effects (i.e., the work it does aside from producing a value). The type of an expression is known at compile time. The value produced at runtime is either of this type or, in the case of a reference type, a compatible (assignable) subtype.

Operators

Java supports almost all standard C operators. These operators also have the same precedence in Java as they do in C, as shown in Table 4-3.

Table 4-3. Java Operators

Precedence	Operator	Operand Type	Description
1	++, –	Arithmetic	Increment and decrement
1	+, -	Arithmetic	Unary plus and minus
1	~	Integral	Bitwise complement
1	!	Boolean	Logical complement
1	(*type*)	Any	Cast
2	*, /, %	Arithmetic	Multiplication, division, remainder
3	+, -	Arithmetic	Addition and subtraction
3	+	String	String concatenation
4	<<	Integral	Left shift
4	>>	Integral	Right shift with sign extension
4	>>>	Integral	Right shift with no extension
5	<, <=, >, >=	Arithmetic	Numeric comparison
5	instanceof	Object	Type comparison
6	==, !=	Primitive	Equality and inequality of value
6	==, !=	Object	Equality and inequality of reference
7	&	Integral	Bitwise AND
7	&	Boolean	Boolean AND
8	^	Integral	Bitwise XOR
8	^	Boolean	Boolean XOR
9	|	Integral	Bitwise OR
9	|	Boolean	Boolean OR
10	&&	Boolean	Conditional AND
11	||	Boolean	Conditional OR
12	?:	NA	Conditional ternary operator
13	=	Any	Assignment
13	*=, /=, %=, +=, -=, <<=, >> =, >>>=, &=, ^=, |=	Any	Assignment with operation

There are a few operators missing from the standard C collection. For example, Java doesn't support the comma operator for combining expressions, although the `for` statement allows you to use it in the initialization and increment sections. Java

doesn't allow direct pointer manipulation, so it doesn't support the reference (&),
dereference (*), and sizeof operators that are familiar to C/C++ programmers.

Java also adds some new operators. As we've seen, the + operator can be used with
String values to perform string concatenation. Because all integral types in Java
are signed values, the >> operator performs a right-arithmetic-shift operation with
sign extension. The >>> operator treats the operand as an unsigned number and
performs a right-arithmetic-shift with no sign extension. The new operator, as in
C++, is used to create objects; we will discuss it in detail shortly.

Assignment

While variable initialization (i.e., declaration and assignment together) is considered a statement, with no resulting value, variable assignment alone is also an
expression:

```
int i, j;            // statement
i = 5;               // both expression and statement
```

Normally, we rely on assignment for its side effects alone, but, as in C, an assignment can be used as a value in another part of an expression:

```
j = ( i = 5 );
```

Again, relying on order of evaluation extensively (in this case, using compound
assignments in complex expressions) can make code very obscure and hard to
read. Do so at your own peril.

The null value

The expression null can be assigned to any reference type. It has the meaning of
"no reference." A null reference can't be used to reference anything and attempting to do so generates a NullPointerException at runtime.

Variable access

The dot (.) operator has multiple meanings. It can retrieve the value of an
instance variable (of some object) or a static variable (of some class). It can also
specify a method to be invoked on an object or class. Using the dot (.) to access a
variable in an object is an expression that results in the value of the variable
accessed. This can be either a numeric type or a reference type:

```
int i;
String s;
i = myObject.length;
s = myObject.name;
```

A reference-type expression can be used in further evaluations, by selecting variables or calling methods within it:

```
int len = myObject.name.length();
int initialLen = myObject.name.substring(5, 10).length();
```

Here we have found the length of our name variable by invoking the length() method of the String object. In the second case, we took an intermediate step and asked for a substring of the name string. The substring method of the String class also returns a String reference, for which we ask the length.

Method invocation

A method invocation is essentially a function call: an expression that results in a value. The value's type is the return type of the method. Thus far, we have seen methods invoked by name:

```
System.out.println( "Hello World..." );
int myLength = myString.length();
```

Selecting which method to invoke is more complicated than it appears, because Java allows method overloading and overriding; the details are discussed in Chapter 5.

Like the result of any expression, the result of a method invocation can be used in further evaluations, as we saw earlier. You can allocate intermediate variables to make it absolutely clear what your code is doing, or you can opt for brevity where appropriate; it's all a matter of coding style. The following are equivalent:

```
int initialLen = myObject.name.substring(5, 10).length();
```

and:

```
String temp1 = myObject.name;
String temp2 = temp1.substring(5, 10);
int initialLen = temp2.length();
```

Object creation

Objects in Java are allocated with the new operator:

```
Object o = new Object();
```

The argument to new is the *constructor* for the class. The constructor is a method which always has the same name as the class. The constructor specifies any required parameters to create an instance of the object. The value of the new expression is a reference of the type of the created object. Objects always have one or more constructors.

We'll look at object creation in detail in Chapter 5. For now, just note that object creation is a type of expression, and that the resulting object reference can be used in general expressions. In fact, because the binding of new is "tighter" than that of dot (.), you can easily create a new object and invoke a method in it, without assigning the object to a reference type variable:

```
int hours = new Date().getHours();
```

The Date class is a utility class that represents the current time. Here we create a new instance of Date with the new operator and call its getHours() method to retrieve the current hour as an integer value. The Date object reference lives long enough to service the method call and is then cut loose and garbage-collected at some point in the future.

Calling methods in object references in this way is, again, a matter of style. It would certainly be clearer to allocate an intermediate variable of type Date to hold the new object and then call its getHours() method. However, combining operations like this is common.

The instanceof operator

The instanceof operator can be used to determine the type of an object at runtime. It is used to compare an object against a particular type. instanceof returns a boolean value that indicates whether an object is an instance of a specified class or a subclass of that class:

```
Boolean b;
String str = "foo";
b = ( str instanceof String );    // true
b = ( str instanceof Object );    // also true
b = ( str instanceof Date );      // false, not a Date or subclass
```

instanceof also correctly reports if the object is of the type of an array or a specified interface:

```
if ( foo instanceof byte[] )
    ...
```

It is also important to note that the value null is not considered an instance of any object. So the following test will return false, no matter what the declared type of the variable:

```
String s = null;
if ( s instanceof String )
    // won't happen
```

Exceptions

Java's roots are in embedded systems—software that runs inside specialized devices like hand-held computers, cellular phones, and fancy toasters. In those kinds of applications, it's especially important that software errors be handled robustly. Most users would agree that it's unacceptable for their phone to simply crash or for their toast (and perhaps their house) to burn because their software failed. Given that we can't eliminate the possibility of software errors, it's a step in the right direction to recognize and deal with anticipated application-level errors in a methodical way.

Dealing with errors in a language like C is entirely the responsibility of the programmer. There is no help from the language itself in identifying error types, and there are no tools for dealing with them easily. In C, a routine generally indicates a failure by returning an "unreasonable" value (e.g., the idiomatic -1 or null). As the programmer, you must know what constitutes a bad result, and what it means. It's often awkward to work around the limitations of passing error values in the normal path of data flow.* An even worse problem is that certain types of errors can legitimately occur almost anywhere, and it's prohibitive and unreasonable to explicitly test for them at every point in the software.

Java offers an elegant solution to these problems with exception handling. (Java exception handling is similar to, but not quite the same as, exception handling in C++.) An *exception* indicates an unusual condition or an error condition. Program control becomes unconditionally transferred or "thrown" to a specially designated section of code where it's caught and handled. In this way, error handling is somewhat orthogonal to the normal flow of the program. We don't have to have special return values for all our methods; errors are handled by a separate mechanism. Control can be passed long distance from a deeply nested routine and handled in a single location when that is desirable, or an error can be handled immediately at its source. There are still some methods that return -1 as a special value, but these are generally limited to situations where we are expecting a special value.†

A Java method is required to specify the exceptions it can throw (i.e., the ones that it doesn't catch itself); this means that the compiler can make sure we handle them. In this way, the information about what errors a method can produce is promoted to the same level of importance as its argument and return types. You may still decide to punt and ignore obvious errors, but in Java you must do so explicitly.

---

* The somewhat obscure setjmp() and longjmp() statements in C can save a point in the execution of code and later return to it unconditionally from a deeply buried location. In a limited sense, this is the functionality of exceptions in Java.

† For example, the getHeight() method of the Image class returns -1 if the height isn't known yet. No error has occurred; the height will be available in the future. In this situation, throwing an exception would be inappropriate.

Exceptions and Error Classes

Exceptions are represented by instances of the class `java.lang.Exception` and its subclasses. Subclasses of `Exception` can hold specialized information (and possibly behavior) for different kinds of exceptional conditions. However, more often they are simply "logical" subclasses that serve only to identify a new exception type. Figure 4-1 shows the subclasses of `Exception` in the `java.lang` package. It should give you a feel for how exceptions are organized. Most other packages define their own exception types, which usually are subclasses of `Exception` itself, or of its subclass `RuntimeException`.

Another important exception class is `IOException`, in the package `java.io`. The `IOException` class has many subclasses for typical I/O problems (like `FileNotFoundException`) and networking problems (like `SocketException`). Network exceptions belong to the `java.net` package. Another important descendant of `IOException` is `RemoteException`, which belongs to the `java.rmi` package. It is used when problems arise during remote method invocation (RMI). Throughout this book we'll mention the exceptions you need to be aware of as we run into them.

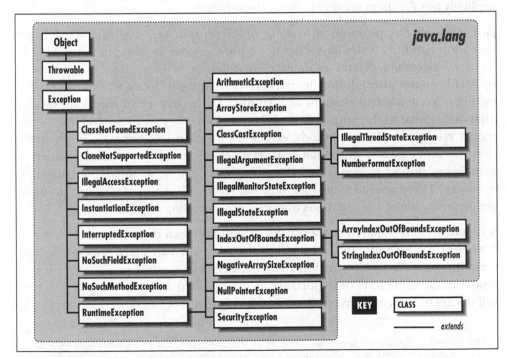

Figure 4-1. The java.lang.Exception subclasses

An `Exception` object is created by the code at the point where the error condition arises. It can hold whatever information is necessary to describe the exceptional condition, optionally including a full stack trace for debugging. The `Exception` object is passed as an argument to the handling block of code, along with the flow of control. This is where the terms "throw" and "catch" come from: the `Exception` object is thrown from one point in the code and caught by the other, where execution resumes.

The Java API also defines the `java.lang.Error` class for unrecoverable errors. The subclasses of `Error` in the `java.lang` package are shown in Figure 4-2. Although a few other packages define their own subclasses of `Error`, subclasses of `Error` are much less common (and less important) than subclasses of `Exception`. You needn't worry about these errors (i.e., you do not have to catch them); they normally indicate fatal linkage problems or virtual machine errors. An error of this kind usually causes the Java interpreter to display a message and exit.

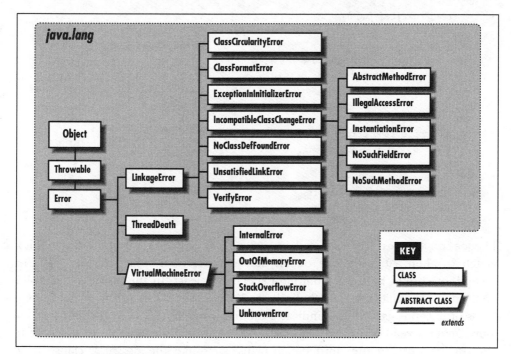

Figure 4-2. The java.lang.Error subclasses

Exception Handling

The `try/catch` guarding statements wrap a block of code and catch designated types of exceptions that occur within it:

```
try {
    readFromFile("foo");
```

```
    ...
    }
catch ( Exception e ) {
    // Handle error
    System.out.println( "Exception while reading file: " + e );
    ...
    }
```

In this example, exceptions that occur within the body of the `try` portion of the statement are directed to the `catch` clause for possible handling. The `catch` clause acts like a method; it specifies an argument of the type of exception it wants to handle and, if it's invoked, it receives the `Exception` object as an argument. Here we receive the object in the variable e and print it along with a message.

A `try` statement can have multiple `catch` clauses that specify different types (subclasses) of `Exception`:

```
try {
    readFromFile("foo");
    ...
}
catch ( FileNotFoundException e ) {
    // Handle file not found
    ...
}
catch ( IOException e ) {
    // Handle read error
    ...
}
catch ( Exception e ) {
    // Handle all other errors
    ...
}
```

The `catch` clauses are evaluated in order, and the first possible (assignable) match is taken. At most, one `catch` clause is executed, which means that the exceptions should be listed from most specific to least. In the previous example, we'll anticipate that the hypothetical `readFromFile()` can throw two different kinds of exceptions: one that indicates the file is not found; the other indicates a more general read error. Any subclass of `Exception` is assignable to the parent type `Exception`, so the third `catch` clause acts like the `default` clause in a `switch` statement and handles any remaining possibilities.

One beauty of the `try`/`catch` scheme is that any statement in the `try` block can assume that all previous statements in the block succeeded. A problem won't arise suddenly because a programmer forgot to check the return value from some method. If an earlier statement fails, execution jumps immediately to the `catch` clause; later statements are never executed.

Bubbling Up

What if we hadn't caught the exception? Where would it have gone? Well, if there is no enclosing `try/catch` statement, the exception pops to the top of the method in which it appeared and is, in turn, thrown from that method up to its caller. If that point in the calling method is within a `try` clause, control passes to the corresponding `catch` clause. Otherwise the exception continues propagating up the call stack. In this way, the exception bubbles up until it's caught, or until it pops out of the top of the program, terminating it with a runtime error message. There's a bit more to it than that because, in this case, the compiler would have reminded us to deal with it, but we'll get back to that in a moment.

Let's look at another example. In Figure 4-3, the method `getContent()` invokes the method `openConnection()` from within a `try/catch` statement. In turn, `openConnection()` invokes the method `sendRequest()`, which calls the method `write()` to send some data.

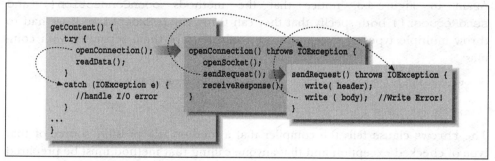

Figure 4-3. Exception propagation

In this figure, the second call to `write()` throws an `IOException`. Since `sendRequest()` doesn't contain a `try/catch` statement to handle the exception, it's thrown again, from the point where it was called in the method `openConnection()`. Since `openConnection()` doesn't catch the exception either, it's thrown once more. Finally it's caught by the `try` statement in `getContent()` and handled by its `catch` clause.

Since an exception can bubble up quite a distance before it is caught and handled, we may need a way to determine exactly where it was thrown. All exceptions can dump a *stack trace* that lists their method of origin and all of the nested method calls that it took to arrive there, using the `printStackTrace()` method.

```
try {
    // complex task
} catch ( Exception e ) {
    // dump information about exactly where the exception occurred
```

```
        e.printStackTrace( System.err );
        ...

    }
```

Checked and Unchecked Exceptions

We explained earlier how Java forces us to be explicit about our error handling. But it's not realistic to require that every conceivable type of error be handled in every situation. So Java exceptions are divided into two categories: *checked exceptions* and *unchecked exceptions*. Most application-level exceptions are checked, which means that any method that throws one, either by generating it itself (as we'll discuss later) or by ignoring one that occurs within it, must declare that it can throw that type of exception in a special throws clause in its method declaration. We haven't yet talked in detail about declaring methods; we'll cover that in Chapter 5. For now all you need know is that methods have to declare the checked exceptions they can throw or allow to be thrown.

Again in Figure 4-3, notice that the methods openConnection() and sendRequest() both specify that they can throw an IOException. If we had to throw multiple types of exceptions, we could declare them separated with commas:

```
    void readFile( String s ) throws IOException, InterruptedException {
        ...
    }
```

The throws clause tells the compiler that a method is a possible source of that type of checked exception and that anyone calling that method must be prepared to deal with it. The caller may use a try/catch block to catch it, or it may declare that it can throw the exception itself.

In contrast, exceptions that are subclasses of either the class java.lang.RuntimeException or the class java.lang.Error are unchecked. See Figure 4-1 for the subclasses of RuntimeException. (Subclasses of Error are generally reserved for serious class linkage or runtime system problems.) It's not a compile-time error to ignore the possibility of these exceptions; methods don't have to declare they can throw them. In all other respects, unchecked exceptions behave the same as other exceptions. We are free to catch them if we wish; we simply aren't required to.

Checked exceptions include application-level problems like missing files and unavailable hosts. As good programmers (and upstanding citizens), we should design software to recover gracefully from these kinds of conditions. Unchecked exceptions include problems such as "out of memory" and "array index out of bounds." While these may indicate application-level programming errors, they can occur almost anywhere and usually aren't easy to recover from. Fortunately, because there are unchecked exceptions, you don't have to wrap every one of your array-index operations in a `try`/`catch` statement.

In sum, checked exceptions are problems that a reasonable application should try to handle gracefully; unchecked exceptions (runtime exceptions or errors) are problems from which we would not expect our software to recover.

Throwing Exceptions

We can throw our own exceptions: either instances of `Exception` or one of its existing subclasses, or our own specialized exception classes. All we have to do is create an instance of the `Exception` and throw it with the `throw` statement:

```
throw new Exception();
```

Execution stops and is transferred to the nearest enclosing `try`/`catch` statement. (There is little point in keeping a reference to the `Exception` object we've created here.) An alternative constructor lets us specify a string with an error message:

```
throw new Exception("Something really bad happened");
```

You can retrieve this string by using the Exception object's `getMessage()` method. Often, though, you can just refer to the object itself; in the first example in the earlier section, "Exception Handling," an exception's string value is automatically provided to the `println()` method.

By convention, all types of `Exception` have a `String` constructor like this. The earlier `String` message is somewhat facetious and vague. Normally you won't be throwing a plain old `Exception`, but a more specific subclass. For example:

```
public void checkRead( String s ) {
    if ( new File(s).isAbsolute() || (s.indexOf("..") != -1) )
        throw new SecurityException(
            "Access to file : "+ s +" denied.");
}
```

In this code, we partially implement a method to check for an illegal path. If we find one, we throw a `SecurityException`, with some information about the transgression.

Of course, we could include whatever other information is useful in our own specialized subclasses of `Exception`. Often, though, just having a new type of exception is good enough, because it's sufficient to help direct the flow of control. For example, if we are building a parser, we might want to make our own kind of exception to indicate a particular kind of failure:

```
class ParseException extends Exception {
    ParseException() {
```

```
        super();
    }
    ParseException( String desc ) {
        super( desc );
    }
}
```

See Chapter 5 for a full description of classes and class constructors. The body of our `Exception` class here simply allows a `ParseException` to be created in the conventional ways that we have created exceptions previously (either generically, or with a simple string description). Now that we have our new exception type, we can guard like this:

```
// Somewhere in our code
...
try {
    parseStream( input );
} catch ( ParseException pe ) {
    // Bad input...
} catch ( IOException ioe ) {
    // Low-level communications problem
}
```

As you can see, although our new exception doesn't currently hold any specialized information about the problem (it certainly could), it does let us distinguish a parse error from an arbitrary I/O error in the same chunk of code.

Re-throwing exceptions

Sometimes you'll want to take some action based on an exception and then turn around and throw a new exception in its place. For example, suppose that we want to handle an `IOException` by freeing up some resources before allowing the failure to pass on to the rest of the application. You can do this in the obvious way, by simply catching the exception and then throwing it again or throwing a new one.

Try Creep

The `try` statement imposes a condition on the statements that it guards. It says that if an exception occurs within it, the remaining statements will be abandoned. This has consequences for local variable initialization. If the compiler can't determine whether a local variable assignment we placed inside a `try`/`catch` block will happen, it won't let us use the variable:

```
void myMethod() {
    int foo;

    try {
        foo = getResults();
    }
```

```
catch ( Exception e ) {
    ...
}

int bar = foo;  // Compile-time error -- foo may not have been initialized
```

In this example, we can't use `foo` in the indicated place because there's a chance it was never assigned a value. One obvious option is to move the assignment inside the `try` statement:

```
try {
    foo = getResults();

    int bar = foo;  // Okay because we get here only
                    // if previous assignment succeeds
}
catch ( Exception e ) {
    ...
}
```

Sometimes this works just fine. However, now we have the same problem if we want to use `bar` later in `myMethod()`. If we're not careful, we might end up pulling everything into the `try` statement. The situation changes if we transfer control out of the method in the `catch` clause:

```
try {
    foo = getResults();
}
catch ( Exception e ) {
    ...
    return;
}

int bar = foo;  // Okay because we get here only
                // if previous assignment succeeds
```

Your code will dictate its own needs; you should just be aware of the options.

The finally Clause

What if we have some cleanup to do before we exit our method from one of the `catch` clauses? To avoid duplicating the code in each `catch` branch and to make the cleanup more explicit, use the `finally` clause. A `finally` clause can be added after a `try` and any associated `catch` clauses. Any statements in the body of the `finally` clause are guaranteed to be executed, no matter why control leaves the `try` body:

```
try {
    // Do something here
```

```
    }
    catch ( FileNotFoundException e ) {
        ...
    }
    catch ( IOException e ) {
        ...
    }
    catch ( Exception e ) {
        ...
    }
    finally {
        // Clean up here
    }
```

In this example, the statements at the cleanup point will be executed eventually, no matter how control leaves the `try`. If control transfers to one of the `catch` clauses, the statements in `finally` are executed after the `catch` completes. If none of the `catch` clauses handles the exception, the `finally` statements are executed before the exception propagates to the next level.

If the statements in the `try` execute cleanly, or if we perform a `return`, `break`, or `continue`, the statements in the `finally` clause are executed. To perform cleanup operations, we can even use `try` and `finally` without any `catch` clauses:

```
    try {
        // Do something here
        return;
    }
    finally {
        System.out.println("Whoo-hoo!");
    }
```

Exceptions that occur in a `catch` or `finally` clause are handled normally; the search for an enclosing `try`/`catch` begins outside the offending `try` statement.

Performance Issues

We mentioned at the beginning of this section that there are methods in the core Java APIs that will still return "out of bounds" values like −1 or `null`, instead of throwing `Exceptions`. Why is this? Well, for some it is simply a matter of convenience; where a special value is easily discernible, we may not want to have to wrap those methods in `try`/`catch` blocks.

But there is also a performance issue. Because of the way the Java virtual machine is implemented, guarding against an exception being thrown (using a `try`) is free. It doesn't add any overhead to the execution of your code. However, throwing an exception is not free. When an exception is thrown, Java has to locate the appropriate `try`/`catch` block and perform other time-consuming activities at runtime.

The result is that you should throw exceptions only in truly "exceptional" circumstances and try to avoid using them for expected conditions, especially when performance is an issue. For example, if you have a loop, it may be better to perform a small test on each pass and avoid throwing the exception, rather than throwing it frequently. On the other hand, if the exception is thrown only one in a gazillion times, you may want to eliminate the overhead of the test code and not worry about the cost of throwing that exception.

Arrays

An *array* is a special type of object that can hold an ordered collection of elements. The type of the elements of the array is called the *base type* of the array; the number of elements it holds is a fixed attribute called its *length*. Java supports arrays of all primitive and reference types.

The basic syntax of arrays looks much like that of C or C++. We create an array of a specified length and access the elements with the index operator, [ ]. Unlike other languages, however, arrays in Java are true, first-class objects. An array is an instance of a special Java array class and has a corresponding type in the type system. This means that to use an array, as with any other object, we first declare a variable of the appropriate type and then use the new operator to create an instance of it.

Array objects differ from other objects in Java in three respects:

- Java implicitly creates a special array class for us whenever we declare an array-type variable. It's not strictly necessary to know about this process in order to use arrays, but it helps in understanding their structure and their relationship to other objects in Java.

- Java lets us use the special [ ] operator to access array elements, so that arrays look as we expect. We could implement our own classes that act like arrays, but because Java doesn't have user-defined operator overloading, we would have to settle for having methods like get ( ) and put ( ) instead of using the special [ ] notation.

- Java provides a corresponding special form of the new operator that lets us construct an instance of an array and specify its length with the [ ] notation.

Array Types

An array-type variable is denoted by a base type followed by the empty brackets, [ ]. Alternatively, Java accepts a C-style declaration, with the brackets placed after the array name.

The following are equivalent:

```
int [] arrayOfInts;
int arrayOfInts [];
```

In each case, `arrayOfInts` is declared as an array of integers. The size of the array is not yet an issue, because we are declaring only the array-type variable. We have not yet created an actual instance of the array class, with its associated storage. It's not even possible to specify the length of an array when creating an array-type variable.

An array of objects can be created in the same way:

```
String [] someStrings;
Button someButtons [];
```

Array Creation and Initialization

The new operator is used to create an instance of an array. After the new operator, we specify the base type of the array and its length, with a bracketed integer expression:

```
arrayOfInts = new int [42];
someStrings = new String [ number + 2 ];
```

We can, of course, combine the steps of declaring and allocating the array:

```
double [] someNumbers = new double [20];
Component widgets [] = new Component [12];
```

As in C, array indices start with zero. Thus, the first element of `someNumbers[]` is 0 and the last element is 19. After creation, the array elements are initialized to the default values for their type. For numeric types, this means the elements are initially zero:

```
int [] grades = new int [30];
grades[0] = 99;
grades[1] = 72;
// grades[2] == 0
```

The elements of an array of objects are references to the objects, not actual instances of the objects. The default value of each element is therefore `null`, until we assign instances of appropriate objects:

```
String names [] = new String [4];
names [0] = new String();
names [1] = "Boofa";
names [2] = someObject.toString();
// names[3] == null
```

This is an important distinction that can cause confusion. In many other languages, the act of creating an array is the same as allocating storage for its elements. In Java, a newly allocated array of objects actually contains only reference variables, each with the value null.* That's not to say that there is no memory associated with an empty array—there is memory needed to hold those references (the empty "slots" in the array). Figure 4-4 illustrates the names array of the previous example.

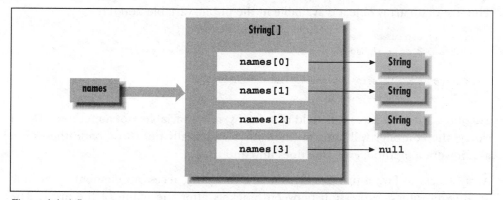

Figure 4-4. A Java array

names is a variable of type String[] (i.e., a string array). This particular String[] object contains four String type variables. We have assigned String objects to the first three array elements. The fourth has the default value null.

Java supports the C-style curly braces {} construct for creating an array and initializing its elements:

```
int [] primes = { 1, 2, 3, 5, 7, 7+4 };    // primes[2] == 3
```

An array object of the proper type and length is implicitly created and the values of the comma-separated list of expressions are assigned to its elements.

We can use the {} syntax with an array of objects. In this case, each of the expressions must evaluate to an object that can be assigned to a variable of the base type of the array, or the value null. Here are some examples:

```
String [] verbs = { "run", "jump", someWord.toString() };
Button [] controls = { stopButton, new Button("Forwards"),
    new Button("Backwards") };
// All types are subtypes of Object
Object [] objects = { stopButton, "A word", null };
```

---

* The analog in C or C++ would be an array of pointers to objects. However, pointers in C or C++ are themselves two- or four-byte values. Allocating an array of pointers is, in actuality, allocating the storage for some number of those pointer objects. An array of references is conceptually similar, although references are not themselves objects. We can't manipulate references or parts of references other than by assignment, and their storage requirements (or lack thereof) are not part of the high-level Java language specification.

The following are equivalent:

```
Button [] threeButtons = new Button [3];
Button [] threeButtons = { null, null, null };
```

Using Arrays

The size of an array object is available in the public variable `length`:

```
char [] alphabet = new char [26];
int alphaLen = alphabet.length;              // alphaLen == 26

String [] musketeers = { "one", "two", "three" };
int num = musketeers.length;                 // num == 3
```

`length` is the only accessible field of an array; it is a variable, not a method. (Don't worry, the compiler will tell you when you accidentally put those parentheses on, as if it were a method; everyone does now and then.)

Array access in Java is just like array access in C; you access an element by putting an integer-valued expression between brackets after the name of the array. The following example creates an array of `Button` objects called `keyPad` and then fills the array with `Button` objects:

```
Button [] keyPad = new Button [ 10 ];
for ( int i=0; i < keyPad.length; i++ )
    keyPad[ i ] = new Button( Integer.toString( i ) );
```

Attempting to access an element that is outside the range of the array generates an `ArrayIndexOutOfBoundsException`. This is a type of `RuntimeException`, so you can either catch and handle it yourself, or ignore it, as we've already discussed:

```
String [] states = new String [50];

try {
    states[0] = "California";
    states[1] = "Oregon";
    ...
    states[50] = "McDonald's Land";  // Error: array out of bounds
}
catch ( ArrayIndexOutOfBoundsException err ) {
    System.out.println( "Handled error: " + err.getMessage() );
}
```

It's a common task to copy a range of elements from one array into another. Java supplies the `arraycopy()` method for this purpose; it's a utility method of the `System` class:

```
System.arraycopy(source,sourceStart,destination,destStart,length);
```

The following example doubles the size of the names array from an earlier example:

```
String [] tmpVar = new String [ 2 * names.length ];
System.arraycopy( names, 0, tmpVar, 0, names.length );
names = tmpVar;
```

A new array, twice the size of names, is allocated and assigned to a temporary variable tmpVar. arraycopy() is used to copy the elements of names to the new array. Finally, the new array is assigned to names. If there are no remaining references to the old array object after names has been copied, it will be garbage-collected on the next pass.

Anonymous Arrays

You often want to create "throw-away" arrays: arrays that are only used in one place and never referenced anywhere else. Such arrays don't need to have a name, because you never need to refer to them again in that context. For example, you may want to create a collection of objects to pass as an argument to some method. It's easy enough to create a normal, named array—but if you don't actually work with the array (if you use the array only as a holder for some collection), you shouldn't have to. Java makes it easy to create "anonymous" (i.e., unnamed) arrays.

Let's say you need to call a method named setPets(), which takes an array of Animal objects as arguments. Cat and Dog are subclasses of Animal. Here's how to call setPets() using an anonymous array:

```
Dog pokey = new Dog ("gray");
Cat squiggles = new Cat ("black");
Cat jasmine = new Cat ("orange");
setPets ( new Animal [] { pokey, squiggles, jasmine });
```

The syntax looks just like the initialization of an array in a variable declaration. We implicitly define the size of the array and fill in its elements using the curly brace notation. However, since this is not a variable declaration, we have to explicitly use the new operator to create the array object.

You can use anonymous arrays to simulate variable-length argument lists (called VARARGS in C), a feature of many programming languages that Java doesn't provide. The advantage of anonymous arrays over variable-length argument lists is that the former allow stricter type checking; the compiler always knows exactly what arguments are expected, and therefore it can verify that method calls are correct.

Multidimensional Arrays

Java supports multidimensional arrays in the form of arrays of array type objects. You create a multidimensional array with C-like syntax, using multiple bracket pairs, one for each dimension. You also use this syntax to access elements at various positions within the array. Here's an example of a multidimensional array that represents a chess board:

```
ChessPiece [][] chessBoard;
chessBoard = new ChessPiece [8][8];
chessBoard[0][0] = new ChessPiece( "Rook" );
chessBoard[1][0] = new ChessPiece( "Pawn" );
...
```

Here `chessBoard` is declared as a variable of type `ChessPiece[][]` (i.e., an array of `ChessPiece` arrays). This declaration implicitly creates the type `ChessPiece[]` as well. The example illustrates the special form of the new operator used to create a multidimensional array. It creates an array of `ChessPiece[]` objects and then, in turn, creates each array of `ChessPiece` objects. We then index `chessBoard` to specify values for particular `ChessPiece` elements. (We'll neglect the color of the pieces here.)

Of course, you can create arrays with more than two dimensions. Here's a slightly impractical example:

```
Color [][][] rgbCube = new Color [256][256][256];
rgbCube[0][0][0] = Color.black;
rgbCube[255][255][0] = Color.yellow;
...
```

As in C, we can specify the initial index of a multidimensional array to get an array-type object with fewer dimensions. In our example, the variable `chessBoard` is of type `ChessPiece[][]`. The expression `chessBoard[0]` is valid and refers to the first element of `chessBoard`, which is of type `ChessPiece[]`. For example, we can create a row for our chess board:

```
ChessPiece [] startRow = {
    new ChessPiece("Rook"), new ChessPiece("Knight"),
    new ChessPiece("Bishop"), new ChessPiece("King"),
    new ChessPiece("Queen"), new ChessPiece("Bishop"),
    new ChessPiece("Knight"), new ChessPiece("Rook")
};

chessBoard[0] = startRow;
```

We don't necessarily have to specify the dimension sizes of a multidimensional array with a single new operation. The syntax of the new operator lets us leave the sizes of some dimensions unspecified. The size of at least the first dimension (the most significant dimension of the array) has to be specified, but the sizes of any number of the less significant array dimensions may be left undefined. We can assign appropriate array-type values later.

We can create a checkerboard of boolean values (which is not quite sufficient for a real game of checkers) using this technique:

```
boolean [][] checkerBoard;
checkerBoard = new boolean [8][];
```

Here, `checkerBoard` is declared and created, but its elements, the eight `boolean[]` objects of the next level, are left empty. Thus, for example, `checker-Board[0]` is `null` until we explicitly create an array and assign it, as follows:

```
checkerBoard[0] = new boolean [8];
checkerBoard[1] = new boolean [8];
...
checkerBoard[7] = new boolean [8];
```

The code of the previous two examples is equivalent to:

```
boolean [][] checkerBoard = new boolean [8][8];
```

One reason we might want to leave dimensions of an array unspecified is so that we can store arrays given to us by another method.

Note that since the length of the array is not part of its type, the arrays in the checkerboard do not necessarily have to be of the same length. That is, multi-dimensional arrays do not have to be rectangular. Here's a defective (but perfectly legal, to Java) checkerboard:

```
checkerBoard[2] = new boolean [3];
checkerBoard[3] = new boolean [10];
```

And here's how you could create and initialize a triangular array:

```
int [][] triangle = new int [5][];
for (int i = 0; i < triangle.length; i++) {
    triangle[i] = new int [i + 1];
    for (int j = 0; j < i + 1; j++)
        triangle[i][j] = i + j;
}
```

Inside Arrays

We said earlier that arrays are instances of special array classes in the Java language. If arrays have classes, where do they fit into the class hierarchy and how are they related? These are good questions; however, we need to talk more about the object-oriented aspects of Java before answering them. That's the subject of the next chapter. For now, take it on faith that arrays fit into the class hierarchy.

5

In this chapter:
- *Classes*
- *Methods*
- *Object Creation*
- *Object Destruction*

Objects in Java

In this chapter, we'll get to the heart of Java and explore the object-oriented aspects of the language. Object-oriented design is the art of decomposing an application into some number of objects—self-contained application components that work together. The goal is to break the problem down into a number of smaller problems that are simpler and easier to understand. Ideally, the components can be implemented as straightforward objects in the Java language. And if things are truly ideal, the components correspond to well-known objects that already exist, so they don't have to be created at all.

An object design methodology is a system or a set of rules created to help you identify objects in your application domain and pick the real ones from the noise. In other words, such a methodology helps you factor your application into a good set of reusable objects. The problem is that though it wants to be a science, good object-oriented design is still pretty much an art form. While you can learn from the various off-the-shelf design methodologies, none of them will help you in all situations. The truth is that there is no substitute for experience.

We won't try to push you into a particular methodology here; there are shelves full of books to do that.* Instead, we'll provide a few hints to get you started. Here are some general design guidelines, which should be taken with a liberal amount of salt and common sense:

- Think of an object in terms of its interface, not its implementation. It's perfectly fine for an object's internals to be unfathomably complex, as long as its "public face" is easy to understand.

---

* Once you have some experience with basic object-oriented concepts, you might want to take a look at *Design Patterns: Elements of Reusable Object-Oriented Software,* by Gamma, Helm, Johnson, Vlissides (Addison-Wesley). This book catalogs useful object-oriented designs that have been refined over the years by experience. Many appear in the design of the Java APIs.

- Hide and abstract as much of your implementation as possible. Avoid public variables in your objects, with the possible exception of constants. Instead define *accessor* methods to set and return values (even if they are simple types). Later, when you need to, you'll be able to modify and extend the behavior of your objects without breaking other classes that rely on them.

- Specialize objects only when you have to. When you use an object in its existing form, as a piece of a new object, you are *composing* objects. When you change or refine the behavior of an object, you are using *inheritance*. You should try to reuse objects by composition rather than inheritance whenever possible, because when you compose objects you are taking full advantage of existing tools. Inheritance involves breaking down the barrier of an object and should be done only when there's a real advantage. Ask yourself if you really need to inherit the whole public interface of an object (do you want to be a "kind" of that object), or if you can just delegate certain jobs to the object and use it by composition.

- Minimize relationships between objects and try to organize related objects in packages. To enhance your code's reusability, write it as if there *is* a tomorrow. Determine what one object needs to know about another to get its job done and try to minimize the coupling between them.

Classes

Classes are the building blocks of a Java application. A *class* can contain methods, variables, initialization code, and, as we'll discuss later on, even other classes. It serves as a blueprint for making class *instances*, which are runtime objects that implement the class structure. You declare a class with the `class` keyword. Methods and variables of the class appear inside the braces of the class declaration:

```
class Pendulum {
    float mass;
    float length = 1.0;
    int cycles;

    float position ( float time ) {
        ...
    }
    ...
}
```

The `Pendulum` class contains three variables: `mass`, `length`, and `cycles`. It also defines a method called `position()`, which takes a `float` value as an argument and returns a `float` value. Variables and method declarations can appear in any order, but variable initializers can't use forward references to uninitialized variables. Once we've defined the `Pendulum` class, we can create a `Pendulum` object (an instance of that class) as follows:

```
Pendulum p;
p = new Pendulum();
```

Recall that our declaration of the variable p does not create a `Pendulum` object; it simply creates a variable that refers to an object of type `Pendulum`. We still have to create the object, using the `new` keyword. Now that we've created a `Pendulum` object, we can access its variables and methods, as we've already seen many times:

```
p.mass = 5.0;
float pos = p.position( 1.0 );
```

Two kinds of variables can be defined in a class: *instance variables* and *static variables*. Every object has its own set of instance variables; the values of these variables in one object can differ from the values in another object. If you don't initialize an instance variable when you declare it, it's given a default value appropriate for its type.

Figure 5-1 shows a hypothetical `TextBook` application, which uses two instances of `Pendulum` through the reference-type variables `bigPendulum` and `small-Pendulum`. Each of these `Pendulum` objects has its own copy of `mass`, `length`, and `cycles`. As with variables, methods defined in a class may be *instance methods* or *static methods*. An instance method is associated with an instance of the class, but each instance doesn't really have its own copy of the method. Instead, there's just one copy of the method, which operates on the values of the instance variables of a particular object. As you'll see in Chapter 6, *Relationships Among Classes*, we talk about subclassing; there's more to learn about how methods see variables.

Accessing Fields and Methods

Inside a class, we can access instance variables and call instance methods of the class directly by name. Here's an example that expands upon our `Pendulum`:

```
class Pendulum {
    ...
    void resetEverything() {
        mass = 1.0;
        length = 1.0;
        cycles = 0;
        ...
        float startingPosition = position( 0.0 );
    }
    ...
}
```

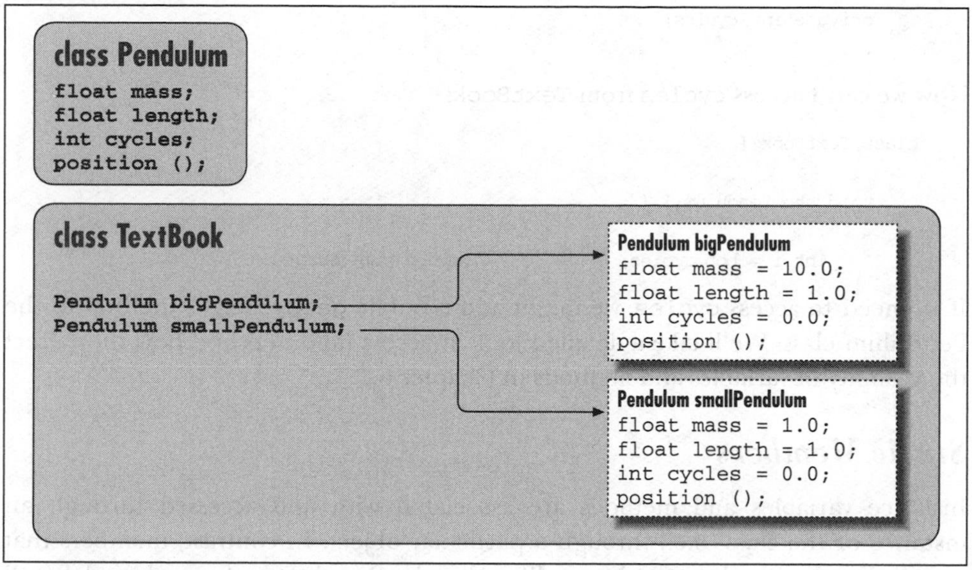

Figure 5-1. Instances of the Pendulum class

Other classes access members of an object through a reference, using the C-style dot notation:

```
class TextBook {
    ...
    void showPendulum() {
        Pendulum bob = new Pendulum();
        ...
        int i = bob.cycles;
        bob.resetEverything();
        bob.mass = 1.01;
        ...
    }
    ...
}
```

Here we have created a second class, TextBook, that uses a Pendulum object. It creates an instance in showPendulum() and then invokes methods and accesses variables of the object through the reference bob. Several factors affect whether class members can be accessed from outside the class. You can use the visibility modifiers public, private, and protected to control access; classes can also be placed into packages, which affects their scope. The private modifier, for example, designates a variable or method for use only by other members of the class itself. In the previous example, we could change the declaration of our variable cycles to private:

```
class Pendulum {
    ...
```

```
        private int cycles;
        ...
```

Now we can't access `cycles` from TextBook:

```
    class TextBook {
        ...
        void showPendulum() {
            ...
            int i = bob.cycles;            // Compile time error
```

If we need to access `cycles`, we might add a public `getCycles()` method to the Pendulum class. We'll take a detailed look at access modifiers and how they affect the visibility of variables and methods in Chapter 6.

Static Members

Instance variables and methods are associated with and accessed through an instance of the class—i.e., through a particular object. In contrast, members that are declared with the `static` modifier live in the class and are shared by all instances of the class. Variables declared with the `static` modifier are called *static variables* or *class variables*; similarly, these kinds of methods are called *static methods* or *class methods*. We can add a static variable to our Pendulum example:

```
    class Pendulum {
        ...
        static float gravAccel = 9.80;
        ...
```

We have declared the new `float` variable `gravAccel` as `static`. That means if we change its value in any instance of a `Pendulum`, the value changes for all `Pendulum` objects, as shown in Figure 5-2.

Static members can be accessed like instance members. Inside our `Pendulum` class, we can refer to `gravAccel` by name, like an instance variable:

```
    class Pendulum {
        ...
        float getWeight () {
            return mass * gravAccel;
        }
        ...
    }
```

However, since static members exist in the class itself, independent of any instance, we can also access them directly through the class. We don't need a `Pendulum` object to set the variable `gravAccel`; instead we can use the class name in place of a reference-type variable:

```
    Pendulum.gravAccel = 8.76;
```

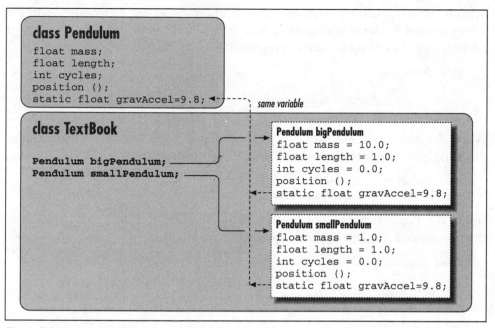

Figure 5-2. Static variables shared by all instances of a class

This changes the value of `gravAccel` for any current or future instances. Why would we want to change the value of `gravAccel`? Well, perhaps we want to explore how pendulums would work on different planets. Static variables are also very useful for other kinds of data shared among classes at runtime. For instance, you can create methods to register your objects so that they can communicate, or you can count references to them. We can use static variables to define constant values. In this case, we use the `static` modifier along with the `final` modifier. So, if we cared only about pendulums under the influence of the Earth's gravitational pull, we could change `Pendulum` as follows:

```
class Pendulum {
    ...
    static final float EARTH_G = 9.80;
    ...
```

We have followed a common convention and named our constant with capital letters; C programmers should recognize the capitalization convention, which resembles the C convention for #define statements. Now the value of EARTH_G is a constant; it can be accessed by any instance of `Pendulum` (or anywhere, for that matter), but its value can't be changed at runtime.

It's important to use the combination of `static` and `final` only for things that are really constant. That's because the compiler is allowed to "inline" such values within classes that reference them. This is probably okay for constants like π, but it may not be ideal for other variables. Static members are useful as flags and identifiers, which can be accessed from anywhere. They are especially useful for values needed in the construction of an instance itself. In our example, we might declare a number of static values to represent various kinds of Pendulum objects:

```
class Pendulum {
    ...
    static int SIMPLE = 0, ONE_SPRING = 1, TWO_SPRING = 2;
    ...
```

We might then use these flags in a method that sets the type of a Pendulum or, more likely, in a special constructor, as we'll discuss shortly:

```
Pendulum pendy = new Pendulum();
pendy.setType( Pendulum.ONE_SPRING );
```

Inside the Pendulum class, we can use static members directly by name, as well; there's no need for the Pendulum. prefix:

```
class Pendulum {
    ...
    void resetEverything() {
        setType ( SIMPLE );
        ...
    }
    ...
}
```

Methods

Methods appear inside class bodies. They contain local variable declarations and other Java statements that are executed by a calling thread when the method is invoked. Method declarations in Java look like ANSI C-style function declarations with two restrictions: a method in Java always specifies a return type (there's no default). The returned value can be a primitive type, a reference type, or the type void, which indicates no returned value. A method always has a fixed number of arguments. The combination of method overloading and true arrays lessens the need for a variable number of arguments. These techniques are type-safe and easier to use than C's variable-argument list mechanism.

Here's a simple example:

```
class Bird {
    int xPos, yPos;

    double fly ( int x, int y ) {
        double distance = Math.sqrt( x*x + y*y );
        flap( distance );
        xPos = x;
        yPos = y;
```

```
        return distance;
    }
    ...
}
```

In this example, the class `Bird` defines a method, `fly()`, that takes as arguments two integers: `x` and `y`. It returns a `double` type value as a result.

Local Variables

The `fly()` method declares a local variable called `distance`, which it uses to compute the distance flown. A local variable is temporary; it exists only within the scope of its method. Local variables are allocated and initialized when a method is invoked; they are normally destroyed when the method returns. They can't be referenced from outside the method itself. If the method is executing concurrently in different threads, each thread has its own copies of the method's local variables. A method's arguments also serve as local variables within the scope of the method.

An object created within a method and assigned to a local variable may or may not persist after the method has returned. As with all objects in Java, it depends on whether any references to the object remain. If an object is created, assigned to a local variable, and never used anywhere else, that object will no longer be referenced when the local variable is destroyed, so garbage collection will remove the object. If, however, we assign the object to an instance variable, pass it as an argument to another method, or pass it back as a return value, it may be saved by another variable holding its reference. We'll discuss object creation and garbage collection in more detail shortly.

Shadowing

If a local variable and an instance variable have the same name, the local variable *shadows* or hides the name of the instance variable within the scope of the method. In the following example, the local variables `xPos` and `yPos` hide the instance variables of the same name:

```
class Bird {
    int xPos, yPos;
    int xNest, yNest;
    ...
    double flyToNest() {
        int xPos = xNest;
        int yPos = yNest:
        return ( fly( xPos, yPos ) );
    }
    ...
}
```

When we set the values of the local variables in `flyToNest()`, it has no effect on the values of the instance variables.

The "this" reference

You can use the special reference `this` any time you need to refer explicitly to the current object. At times you don't need to use `this`, because the reference to the current object is implicit; this is the case with using instance variables and methods inside a class. But we can use `this` to refer explicitly to instance variables in the object, even if they are shadowed. The following example shows how we can use `this` to allow argument names that shadow instance variable names. This is a fairly common technique, as it saves your having to make up alternative names. Here's how we could implement our `fly()` method with shadowed variables:

```java
class Bird {
    int xPos, yPos;

    double fly ( int xPos, int yPos ) {
        double distance = Math.sqrt( xPos*xPos + yPos*yPos );
        flap( distance );
        this.xPos = xPos;
        this.yPos = yPos;
        return distance;
    }
    ...
}
```

In this example, the expression `this.xPos` refers to the instance variable `xPos` and assigns it the value of the local variable `xPos`, which would otherwise hide its name. The only reason we need to use `this` in the previous example is because we've used argument names that hide our instance variables, and we want to refer to the instance variables.

Static Methods

Static methods (class methods), like static variables, belong to the class and not to an individual instance of the class. What does this mean? Well, foremost, a static method lives outside of any particular class instance. It can be invoked by name, through the class name, without any objects around. Because it is not bound to a particular object instance, a static method can directly access only other static members of the class. It can't directly see any instance variables or call any instance methods, because to do so we'd have to ask, "on which instance?" Static methods can be called from instances, just like instance methods, but the important thing is that they can also be used independently.

Our `fly()` method uses a static method: `Math.sqrt()`, which is defined by the `java.lang.Math` class; we'll explore this class in detail in Chapter 9, *Basic Utility*

Classes. For now, the important thing to note is that Math is the name of a class and not an instance of a Math object. (It so happens that you can't even make an instance of the Math class.) Because static methods can be invoked wherever the class name is available, class methods are closer to normal C-style functions. Static methods are particularly useful for utility methods that perform work that is useful either independently of instances or in creating instances. For example, in our Bird class we can enumerate all types of birds that can be created:

```
class Bird {
    ...
    static String [] getBirdTypes( ) {
        String [] types;
        // Create list...
        return types;
    }
    ...
}
```

Here we've defined a static method getBirdTypes(), which returns an array of strings containing bird names. We can use getBirdTypes() from within an instance of Bird, just like an instance method. However, we can also call it from other classes, using the Bird class name as a reference:

```
String [] names = Bird.getBirdTypes();
```

Perhaps a special version of the Bird class constructor accepts the name of a bird type. We could use this list to decide what kind of bird to create.

Initializing Local Variables

In the flyToNest() example, we made a point of initializing the local variables xPos and yPos. Unlike instance variables, local variables must be initialized before they can be used. It's a compile-time error to try to access a local variable without first assigning it a value:

```
void myMethod() {
    int foo = 42;
    int bar;

    // bar += 1;  Would cause compile-time error, bar uninitialized

    bar = 99;
    bar += 1;      // OK here
}
```

Notice that this doesn't imply local variables have to be initialized when declared, just that the first time they are referenced must be in an assignment. More subtle possibilities arise when making assignments inside of conditionals:

```
void myMethod {
    int foo;
```

```
    if ( someCondition ) {
      foo = 42;
      ...
    }
    foo += 1;    // Compile-time error, foo may not be initialized
}
```

In this example, foo is initialized only if someCondition is true. The compiler doesn't let you make this wager, so it flags the use of foo as an error. We could correct this situation in several ways. We could initialize the variable to a default value in advance or move the usage inside of the conditional. We could also make sure the path of execution doesn't reach the uninitialized variable through some other means, depending on what makes sense for our particular application. For example, we could return from the method abruptly:

```
int foo;
...
if ( someCondition ) {
    foo = 42;
    ...
} else
    return;

foo += 1;
```

In this case, there's no chance of reaching foo in an uninitialized state, so the compiler allows the use of foo after the conditional.

Why is Java so picky about local variables? One of the most common (and insidious) sources of error in C or C++ is forgetting to initialize local variables, so Java tries to help us out. If it didn't, Java would suffer the same potential irregularities as C or C++.[*]

Argument Passing and References

Let's consider what happens when you pass arguments to a method. All primitive data types (e.g., int, char, float) are passed by value. Now you're probably used to the idea that reference types (i.e., any kind of object, including arrays and strings) are used through references. An important distinction is that the references themselves (the pointers to these objects) are actually primitive types and are passed by value too.

---

[*] As with malloc'ed storage in C or C++, Java objects and their instance variables are allocated on a heap, which allows them default values once, when they are created. Local variables, however, are allocated on the Java virtual machine stack. As with the stack in C and C++, failing to initialize these could mean successive method calls could receive garbage values, and program execution might be inconsistent or implementation-dependent.

Consider the following piece of code:

```
...
int i = 0;
SomeKindOfObject obj = new SomeKindOfObject();
myMethod( i, obj );
...
void myMethod(int j, SomeKindOfObject o) {
...
}
```

The first chunk of code calls myMethod(), passing it two arguments. The first argument, i, is passed by value; when the method is called, the value of i is copied into the method's parameter, j. If myMethod() changes the value of i, it's changing only its copy of the local variable.

In the same way, a copy of the reference to obj is placed into the reference variable o of myMethod(). Both references refer to the same object, so any changes made through either reference affect the actual (single) object instance. If we change the value of, say, o.size, the change is visible either as o.size (inside myMethod()) or as obj.size (in the calling method). However, if myMethod() changes the reference o itself—to point to another object—it's affecting only its copy. It doesn't affect the variable obj, which still refers to the original object. In this sense, passing the reference is like passing a pointer in C and unlike passing by reference in C++.

What if myMethod() needs to modify the calling method's notion of the obj reference as well (i.e., make obj point to a different object)? The easy way to do that is to wrap obj inside some kind of object. One example would be to wrap the object up as the lone element in an array:

```
SomeKindOfObject [] wrapper = new SomeKindOfObject [] { obj };
```

All parties could then refer to the object as wrapper[0] and would have the ability to change the reference. This is not aesthetically pleasing, but it does illustrate that what is needed is the level of indirection.

Another possibility is to use this to pass a reference to the calling object. In that case, the calling object serves as the wrapper for the reference. Let's look at a piece of code that could be from an implementation of a linked list:

```
class Element {
    public Element nextElement;

    void addToList( List list ) {
        list.addToList( this );
    }
}
```

```
class List {
    void addToList( Element element ) {
        ...
        element.nextElement = getNextElement();
    }
}
```

Every element in a linked list contains a pointer to the next element in the list. In this code, the `Element` class represents one element; it includes a method for adding itself to the list. The `List` class itself contains a method for adding an arbitrary `Element` to the list. The method `addToList()` calls `addToList()` with the argument `this` (which is, of course, an `Element`). `addToList()` can use the `this` reference to modify the `Element`'s `nextElement` instance variable. The same technique can be used in conjunction with interfaces to implement callbacks for arbitrary method invocations.

Method Overloading

Method overloading is the ability to define multiple methods with the same name in a class; when the method is invoked, the compiler picks the correct one based on the arguments passed to the method. This implies that overloaded methods must have different numbers or types of arguments. (In Chapter 6, we'll look at *method overriding*, which occurs when we declare methods with identical signatures in different classes.)

Method overloading (also called *ad-hoc polymorphism*) is a powerful and useful feature. The idea is to create methods that act in the same way on different types of arguments. This creates the illusion that a single method can operate on any of the types. The `print()` method in the standard `PrintStream` class is a good example of method overloading in action. As you've probably deduced by now, you can print a string representation of just about anything using this expression:

```
System.out.print( argument )
```

The variable `out` is a reference to an object (a `PrintStream`) that defines nine different versions of the `print()` method. The versions take arguments of the following types: `Object`, `String`, `char[]`, `char`, `int`, `long`, `float`, `double`, and `boolean`.

```
class PrintStream {
    void print( Object arg ) { ... }
    void print( String arg ) { ... }
    void print( char [] arg ) { ... }
    ...
}
```

You can invoke the `print()` method with any of these types as an argument, and it's printed in an appropriate way. In a language without method overloading, this would require something more cumbersome, such as a uniquely named method for printing each type of object. Then it would be your responsibility to remember what method to use for each data type. In the previous example, `print()` has been overloaded to support two reference types: `Object` and `String`.

What if we try to call `print()` with some other reference type? Say, perhaps, a `Date` object? When there's not an exact type match, the compiler searches for an acceptable, assignable match. Since `Date`, like all classes, is a subclass of `Object`, a `Date` object can be assigned to a variable of type `Object`. It's therefore an acceptable match, and the `Object` method is selected.

What if there's more than one possible match? Say, for example, we tried to print a subclass of `String` called `MyString`. (The `String` class is `final`, so it can't be subclassed, but allow me this brief transgression for purposes of explanation.) `MyString` is assignable to either `String` or to `Object`. Here the compiler makes a determination as to which match is "better" and selects that method. In this case, it's the `String` method.

The intuitive explanation is that the `String` class is closer to `MyString` in the inheritance hierarchy. It is a more specific match. A more rigorous way of specifying it would be to say that a given method is more specific than another method if the argument types of the first method are all assignable to the argument types of the second method. In this case, the `String` method is more specific to a subclass of `String` than the `Object` method because type `String` is assignable to type `Object`. The reverse is not true.

If you're paying close attention, you may have noticed we said that the compiler resolves overloaded methods. Method overloading is not something that happens at runtime; this is an important distinction. It means that the selected method is chosen once, when the code is compiled. Once the overloaded method is selected, the choice is fixed until the code is recompiled, even if the class containing the called method is later revised and an even more specific overloaded method is added. This is in contrast to overridden (virtual) methods, which are located at runtime and can be found even if they didn't exist when the calling class was compiled. We'll talk about method overriding later in the chapter.

One last note about overloading. In earlier chapters, we've pointed out that Java doesn't support programmer-defined overloaded operators, and that + is the only system-defined overloaded operator. If you've been wondering what an overloaded operator is, I can finally clear up that mystery. In a language like C++, you can customize operators such as + and * to work with objects that you create. For example, you could create a class `Complex` that implements complex numbers,

and then overload methods corresponding to + and * to add and multiply
Complex objects. Some people argue that operator overloading makes for elegant
and readable programs, while others say it's just "syntactic sugar" that makes for
obfuscated code. The Java designers clearly espoused the latter opinion when they
chose not to support programmer-defined overloaded operators.

Object Creation

Objects in Java are allocated from a system heap space, much like malloc'ed storage in C or C++. Unlike in C or C++, however, we needn't manage that memory
ourselves. Java takes care of memory allocation and deallocation for you. Java
explicitly allocates storage for an object when you create it with the new operator.
More importantly, objects are removed by garbage collection when they're no
longer referenced.

Constructors

Objects are allocated by specifying the new operator with an *object constructor*. A
constructor is a special method with the same name as its class and no return type.
It's called when a new class instance is created, which gives the class an opportunity to set up the object for use. Constructors, like other methods, can accept arguments and can be overloaded (they are not, however, inherited like other
methods; we'll discuss inheritance in Chapter 6).

```
class Date {
    long time;

    Date() {
        time = currentTime();
    }

    Date( String date ) {
        time = parseDate( date );
    }
    ...
}
```

In this example, the class Date has two constructors. The first takes no arguments;
it's known as the *default constructor*. Default constructors play a special role: if we
don't define any constructors for a class, an empty default constructor is supplied
for us. The default constructor is what gets called whenever you create an object
by calling its constructor with no arguments. Here we have implemented the
default constructor so that it sets the instance variable time by calling a hypothetical method, currentTime(), which resembles the functionality of the real java.
util.Date class. The second constructor takes a String argument. Presumably,

this `String` contains a string representation of the time that can be parsed to set the `time` variable. Given the constructors in the previous example, we create a `Date` object in the following ways:

```
Date now = new Date();
Date christmas = new Date("Dec 25, 1999");
```

In each case, Java chooses the appropriate constructor at compile time based on the rules for overloaded method selection.

If we later remove all references to an allocated object, it'll be garbage-collected, as we'll discuss shortly:

```
christmas = null;        // fair game for the garbage collector
```

Setting this reference to `null` means it's no longer pointing to the "Dec 25, 1999" object. (So would setting `christmas` to any other value.) Unless that object is referenced by another variable, it's now inaccessible and can be garbage-collected.

A few more notes: constructors can't be `abstract`, `synchronized`, or `final`. Constructors can, however, be declared with the visibility modifiers `public`, `private`, or `protected`, to control their accessibility. We'll talk in detail about visibility modifiers later in the chapter.

Working with Overloaded Constructors

A constructor can refer to another constructor in the same class or the immediate superclass using special forms of the `this` and `super` references. We'll discuss the first case here, and return to that of the superclass constructor after we have talked more about subclassing and inheritance. A constructor can invoke another, overloaded constructor in its class using the reference `this()` with appropriate arguments to select the desired constructor. If a constructor calls another constructor, it must do so as its first statement:

```
class Car {
    String model;
    int doors;

    Car( String m, int d ) {
        model = m;
        doors = d;
        // other, complicated setup
        ...
    }

    Car( String m ) {
        this( m, 4 );
    }
    ...
}
```

In this example, the class Car has two constructors. The first, more explicit one, accepts arguments specifying the car's model and its number of doors. The second constructor takes just the model as an argument and, in turn, calls the first constructor with a default value of four doors. The advantage of this approach is that you can have a single constructor do all the complicated setup work; other auxiliary constructors simply feed the appropriate arguments to that constructor.

The call to this() must appear as the first statement in our second constructor. The syntax is restricted in this way because there's a need to identify a clear chain of command in the calling of constructors. At one end of the chain, Java invokes the constructor of the superclass (if we don't do it explicitly) to ensure that inherited members are initialized properly before we proceed.

There's also a point in the chain, just after the constructor of the superclass is invoked, where the initializers of the current class's instance variables are evaluated. Before that point, we can't even reference the instance variables of our class. We'll explain this situation again in complete detail after we have talked about inheritance.

For now, all you need to know is that you can invoke a second constructor only as the first statement of another constructor. For example, the following code is illegal and causes a compile-time error:

```
Car( String m ) {
    int doors = determineDoors();
    this( m, doors );   // Error: constructor call
                        // must be first statement
}
```

The simple model name constructor can't do any additional setup before calling the more explicit constructor. It can't even refer to an instance member for a constant value:

```
class Car {
    ...
    final int default_doors = 4;
    ...

    Car( String m ) {
        this( m, default_doors ); // Error: referencing
                                  // uninitialized variable
    }
    ...
}
```

The instance variable defaultDoors is not initialized until a later point in the chain of constructor calls, so the compiler doesn't let us access it yet. Fortunately, we can solve this particular problem by using a static variable instead of an instance variable:

```
class Car {
    ...
    static final int DEFAULT_DOORS = 4;
    ...

    Car( String m ) {
        this( m, DEFAULT_DOORS );  // Okay now
    }
    ...

}
```

The static members of a class are initialized when the class is first loaded, so it's safe to access them in a constructor.

Static and Nonstatic Code Blocks

It's possible to declare a code block (some statements within curly braces) directly within the scope of a class. This code block doesn't belong to any method; instead, it's executed once, at the time the object is constructed, or, in the case of a code block marked static, at the time the class is loaded.

Nonstatic code blocks can be thought of as extensions of instance variable initialization. They're called at the time the instance variable's initializers are evaluated (after superclass construction), in the order that they appear in the Java source:

```
class MyClass {
    Properties myProps = new Properties();
    // set up myProps
    {
        myProps.put("foo", "bar");
        myProps.put("boo", "gee");
    }
    int a = 5;
    ...
```

You can use static code blocks to initialize static class members. So the static members of a class can have complex initialization just like objects:

```
class ColorWheel {
    static Hashtable colors = new Hashtable();

    // set up colors
    static {
        colors.put("Red", Color.red );
        colors.put("Green", Color.green );
        colors.put("Blue", Color.blue );
        ...
    }
    ...
}
```

The class `ColorWheel` provides a variable `colors` that maps the names of colors to `Color` objects in a `Hashtable`. The first time the class `ColorWheel` is referenced and loaded, the static components of `ColorWheel` are evaluated, in the order they appear in the source. In this case, the static code block simply adds elements to the `colors Hashtable`.

Object Destruction

Now that we've seen how to create objects, it's time to talk about their destruction. If you're accustomed to programming in C or C++, you've probably spent time hunting down memory leaks in your code. Java takes care of object destruction for you; you don't have to worry about memory leaks, and you can concentrate on more important programming tasks.

Garbage Collection

Java uses a technique known as *garbage collection* to remove objects that are no longer needed. The garbage collector is Java's grim reaper. It lingers, usually in a low-priority thread, stalking objects and awaiting their demise. It finds them, watches them, and periodically counts references to them to see when their time has come. When all references to an object are gone, so it's no longer accessible, the garbage-collection mechanism reclaims it and returns the space to the available pool of resources.

There are many different algorithms for garbage collection; the Java virtual machine architecture doesn't specify a particular scheme. It's worth noting, though, that current implementations of Java use a conservative mark-and-sweep system. Under this scheme, Java first walks through the tree of all accessible object references and marks them as alive. Then Java scans the heap looking for identifiable objects that aren't so marked. Java finds objects on the heap because they are stored in a characteristic way and have a particular signature of bits in their handles unlikely to be reproduced naturally. This kind of algorithm doesn't suffer from the problem of cyclic references, where detached objects can mutually reference each other and appear alive.

By default, the Java virtual machine is configured to run the garbage collector in a low-priority thread, so that the garbage collector runs periodically to collect stray objects. With the SDK's `java` interpreter, you can turn off garbage collection by using the `-noasyncgc` command-line option. If you do this, the garbage collector will be run only if it's requested explicitly or if the Java virtual machine runs out of memory. In newer runtime implementations like HotSpot, garbage collections effectively runs continuously in a very efficient way and should never cause a significant delay in execution.

You can prompt the garbage collector to make a sweep explicitly by invoking the `System.gc()` method. An extremely time-sensitive Java application might use this to its advantage by deactivating asynchronous garbage collection and scheduling its own cleanup periods. But this is probably not a good idea. This issue is necessarily implementation-dependent, because on different platforms, garbage collection may be implemented in different ways. On some systems it may even be running in hardware.

Finalization

Before an object is removed by garbage collection, its `finalize()` method is invoked to give it a last opportunity to clean up its act and free other kinds of resources it may be holding. While the garbage collector can reclaim memory resources, it may not take care of things like closing files and terminating network connections gracefully or efficiently. That's what the `finalize()` method is for. An object's `finalize()` method is called once and only once before the object is garbage-collected. However, there's no guarantee when that will happen. Garbage collection may never run on a system that is not short of memory. It is also interesting to note that finalization and collection occur in two distinct phases of the garbage-collection process. First items are finalized; then they are collected. It is therefore possible that finalization could (intentionally or unintentionally) create a lingering reference to the object in question, postponing its garbage collection. The object could, of course, be subject to collection later, if the reference goes away, but its `finalize()` method would not be called again.

The `finalize()` methods of superclasses are not invoked automatically for you. If you need to invoke the finalization routine of your parent classes, you should invoke the `finalize()` method of your superclass, using `super.finalize()`. We discuss inheritance and overridden methods in Chapter 6.

6

Relationships Among Classes

So far, we know how to create a Java class and to create objects, which are instances of a class. But an object by itself isn't very interesting—no more interesting than, say, a table knife. You can marvel at a table knife's perfection, but you can't really do anything with it until you have some other pieces of cutlery and food to use the cutlery on. The same is true of objects and classes in Java: they're interesting by themselves, but what's really important comes from relationships that you establish among them.

That's what we'll cover in this chapter. In particular, we'll be looking at several kinds of relationships:

Inheritance relationships
> How a class inherits methods and variables from its parent class

Interfaces
> How to declare that a class supports certain behavior and define a type to refer to that behavior

Packaging
> How to organize objects into logical groups

Inner classes
> A generalization of classes that lets you nest a class definition inside of another class definition

Subclassing and Inheritance

Classes in Java exist in a class hierarchy. A class in Java can be declared as a *subclass* of another class using the `extends` keyword. A subclass *inherits* variables and methods from its *superclass* and uses them as if they were declared within the subclass itself:

```
class Animal {
    float weight;
    ...
    void eat() {
        ...
    }
    ...
}

class Mammal extends Animal {
    int heartRate;
    // inherits weight
    ...
    void breathe() {
        ...
    }
    // inherits eat()
}
```

In this example, an object of type Mammal has both the instance variable weight and the method eat(). They are inherited from Animal.

A class can extend only one other class. To use the proper terminology, Java allows *single inheritance* of class implementation. Later in this chapter we'll talk about interfaces, which take the place of *multiple inheritance* as it's primarily used in C++.

A subclass can be further subclassed. Normally, subclassing specializes or refines a class by adding variables and methods:

```
class Cat extends Mammal {
    boolean longHair;
    // inherits weight and heartRate
    ...
    void purr() {
        ...
    }
    // inherits eat() and breathe()
}
```

The Cat class is a type of Mammal that is ultimately a type of Animal. Cat objects inherit all the characteristics of Mammal objects and, in turn, Animal objects. Cat also provides additional behavior in the form of the purr() method and the longHair variable. We can denote the class relationship in a diagram, as shown in Figure 6-1.

A subclass inherits all members of its superclass not designated as private. As we'll discuss shortly, other levels of visibility affect what inherited members of the class can be seen from outside of the class and its subclasses, but at a minimum, a subclass always has the same set of visible members as its parent. For this reason, the type of a subclass can be considered a subtype of its parent, and instances of

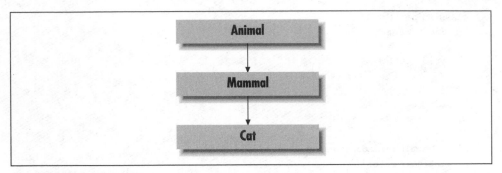

Figure 6-1. A class hierarchy

the subtype can be used anywhere instances of the supertype are allowed. Consider the following example:

```
Cat simon = new Cat();
Animal creature = simon;
```

The `Cat` `simon` in this example can be assigned to the `Animal` type variable `creature` because `Cat` is a subtype of `Animal`.

Shadowed Variables

In the section on methods in Chapter 5, *Objects in Java*, we saw that a local variable of the same name as an instance variable *shadows* (hides) the instance variable. Similarly, an instance variable in a subclass can shadow an instance variable of the same name in its parent class, as shown in Figure 6-2.

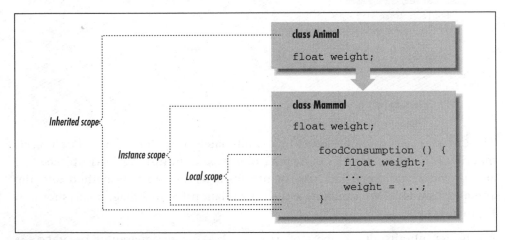

Figure 6-2. The scope of shadowed variables

In Figure 6-2, the variable `weight` is declared in three places: as a local variable in the method `foodConsumption()` of the class `Mammal`, as an instance variable of the class `Mammal`, and as an instance variable of the class `Animal`. The actual variable selected depends on the scope in which we are working.

In the previous example, all variables were of the same type. About the only reason for declaring a variable with the same type in a subclass is to provide an alternate initializer.

A more important use of shadowed variables involves changing their types. We could, for example, shadow an `int` variable with a `double` variable in a subclass that needs decimal values instead of integer values. We do this without changing the existing code because, as its name suggests, when we shadow variables, we don't replace them but instead mask them. Both variables still exist; methods of the superclass see the original variable, and methods of the subclass see the new version. The determination of what variables the various methods see occurs at compile time.

Here's a simple example:

```
class IntegerCalculator {
    int sum;
    ...
}

class DecimalCalculator extends IntegerCalculator {
    double sum;
    ...
}
```

In this example, we shadow the instance variable `sum` to change its type from `int` to `double`.* Methods defined in the class `IntegerCalculator` see the integer variable `sum`, while methods defined in `DecimalCalculator` see the floating-point variable `sum`. However, both variables actually exist for a given instance of `DecimalCalculator`, and they can have independent values. In fact, any methods that `DecimalCalculator` inherits from `IntegerCalculator` actually see the integer variable `sum`.

Since both variables exist in `DecimalCalculator`, we need to reference the variable inherited from `IntegerCalculator`. We do that using the `super` reference:

```
int s = super.sum;
```

Inside of `DecimalCalculator`, the `super` keyword used in this manner refers to the `sum` variable defined in the superclass. We'll explain the use of `super` more fully in a bit.

---

* Note that a better way to design our calculators would be to have an abstract `Calculator` class with two subclasses: `IntegerCalculator` and `DecimalCalculator`.

Another important point about shadowed variables has to do with how they work when we refer to an object by way of a less derived type. For example, we can refer to a `DecimalCalculator` object as an `IntegerCalculator`. If we do so and then access the variable `sum`, we get the integer variable, not the decimal one:

```
DecimalCalculator dc = new DecimalCalculator();
IntegerCalculator ic = dc;

int s = ic.sum;         // accesses IntegerCalculator sum
```

After this detailed explanation, you may still be wondering what shadowed variables are good for. Well, to be honest, the usefulness of shadowed variables is limited, but it's important to understand the concepts before we talk about doing the same thing with methods. We'll see a different and more dynamic type of behavior with method shadowing, or more correctly, *method overriding*.

Overriding Methods

In Chapter 5, we saw we could declare *overloaded methods* (i.e., methods with the same name but a different number or type of arguments) within a class. Overloaded method selection works in the way we described on all methods available to a class, including inherited ones. This means that a subclass can define some overloaded methods that augment the overloaded methods provided by a superclass.

But a subclass does more than that; it can define a method that has exactly the *same* method signature (arguments and return type) as a method in its superclass. In that case, the method in the subclass *overrides* the method in the superclass and effectively replaces its implementation, as shown in Figure 6-3. Overriding methods to change the behavior of objects is called *sub-type polymorphism*. It's the kind that most people think of when they talk about the power of object-oriented languages.

In Figure 6-3, `Mammal` overrides the `reproduce()` method of `Animal`, perhaps to specialize the method for the peculiar behavior of mammals' giving live birth.* The `Cat` object's sleeping behavior is overridden to be different from that of a general `Animal`, perhaps to accommodate cat naps. The `Cat` class also adds the more unique behaviors of purring and hunting mice.

From what you've seen so far, overridden methods probably look like they shadow methods in superclasses, just as variables do. But overridden methods are actually more powerful than that. An overridden method in Java acts like a `virtual` method in C++. When there are multiple implementations of a method in the inheritance hierarchy of an object, the one in the "most derived" class (the lowest

---

* We'll ignore the platypus, which is an obscure nonovoviviparous mammal.

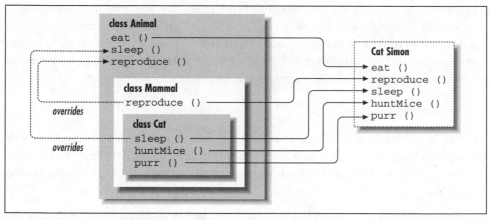

Figure 6-3. Method overriding

one in the hierarchy) always overrides the others, even if we refer to the object by way of a less derived type. For example, if we have a Cat instance assigned to a variable of the more general type Animal and we call its sleep() method, we get the sleep() method implemented in the Cat class, not the one in Animal:

```
Cat simon = new Cat();
Animal creature = simon;
    ...
creature.sleep();        // accesses Cat sleep();
```

In other respects, the variable creature looks like an Animal. For example, access to a shadowed variable would find the implementation in the Animal class, not the Cat class. However, because methods are virtual, the appropriate method in the Cat class can be located, even though we are dealing with an Animal object. This means we can deal with specialized objects as if they were more general types of objects and still take advantage of their specialized implementations of behavior.

A common programming error in Java is to miss and accidentally overload a method when trying to override it. Any difference in the number or type of arguments produces two overloaded methods instead of a single, overridden method. Make it a habit to look twice when overriding methods.

Overridden methods and dynamic binding

In a previous section, we mentioned that overloaded methods are selected by the compiler at compile time. Overridden methods, on the other hand, are selected dynamically at runtime. Even if we create an instance of a subclass, our code has never seen before (perhaps a new object type loaded from the network), any overriding methods that it contains will be located and invoked at runtime to replace those that existed when we last compiled our code.

In contrast, if we load a new class that implements an additional, more specific overloaded method, our code will continue to use the implementation it discovered at compile time. Another effect of this is that casting (i.e., explicitly telling the compiler to treat an object as one of its assignable types) affects the selection of overloaded methods, but not overridden methods.

Static method binding

static methods do not belong to any object instance; they are accessed directly through a class name, so they are not dynamically selected at runtime like instance methods. That is why static methods are called "static"—they are always bound at compile time.

A static method in a superclass can be shadowed by another static method in a subclass, as long as the original method was not declared final. However, you can't override a static method with a nonstatic method. In other words, you can't change a static method in a superclass into an instance method in a subclass.

Dynamic method selection and performance

When Java has to search dynamically for overridden methods in subclasses, there's a small performance penalty. In languages like C++, the default is for methods to act like shadowed variables, so you have to declare explicitly the methods you want to be dynamic (or, as C++ terms them, virtual).

In Java, instance methods are, by default, dynamic. But you can use the final modifier to declare that an instance method can't be overridden, so it won't be subject to dynamic binding and its performance won't suffer. We have seen final used with variables to effectively make them constants. When applied to a method, final means that its implementation is constant; no overriding allowed. final can also be applied to an entire class, which means the class can't be subclassed.

Newer runtime systems like Sun's HotSpot should, however, eliminate the need for this kind of specificity. A profiling runtime should be able to determine which methods are not being overridden and "optimistically inline" them.

Compiler optimizations

When javac, the Java compiler, is run with the –O switch, it performs certain optimizations. It can inline final methods to improve performance (while slightly increasing the size of the resulting class file). private methods, which are effectively final, can also be inlined, and final classes may also benefit from more powerful optimizations.

Another kind of optimization allows you to include debugging code in your Java source without penalty. Java doesn't have a preprocessor to explicitly control what source is included, but you can get some of the same effects by making a block of code conditional on a constant (i.e., `static` and `final`) variable. The Java compiler is smart enough to remove this code when it determines that it won't be called. For example:

```
static final boolean DEBUG = false;
...
final void debug (String message) {
    if (DEBUG) {
        System.err.println(message);
        // do other stuff
        ...
    }
}
```

If we compile this code using the –O switch, the compiler can recognize that the condition on the DEBUG variable is always false, and the body of the `debug()` method will be optimized away. But that's not all—since `debug()` itself is also `final`, it can be inlined, and an empty inlined method generates no code at all. So when we compile with DEBUG set to `false`, calls to the `debug()` method generate no residual code at all.

NOTE   The –O compiler switch is something that may eventually go away in favor of smarter runtime systems, like Sun's HotSpot, which can inline arbitrary chunks of code dynamically. In some recent versions of Java, the –O switch is documented not to work at all! We document it here mainly for completeness.

Method selection revisited

By now you should have a good, intuitive idea as to how methods are selected from the pool of potentially overloaded and overridden method names of a class. If, however, you are dying for a dry definition, we'll provide one now. If you are satisfied with your understanding, you may wish to skip this little exercise in logic.

In a previous section, we offered an inductive rule for overloaded method resolution. It said that a method is considered more specific than another if its arguments are assignable to the arguments of the second method. We can now expand this rule to include the resolution of overridden methods by adding the following condition: to be more specific than another method, the type of the class containing the method must also be assignable to the type of the class holding the second method.

What does that mean? Well, the only classes whose types are assignable are classes in the same inheritance hierarchy. So, what we're talking about now is the set of all methods of the same name in a class or any of its parent or child classes. Since subclass types are assignable to superclass types, but not vice versa, the resolution is pushed, in the way that we expect, down the chain, toward the subclasses. This effectively adds a second dimension to the search, in which resolution is pushed down the inheritance tree towards more refined classes and, simultaneously, toward the most specific overloaded method within a given class.

Exceptions and overridden methods

When we talked about exception handling in Chapter 4, *The Java Language*, we didn't mention an important restriction that applies when you override a method. When you override a method, the new method (the overriding method) must adhere to the throws clause of the method it overrides. In other words, if an overridden method declares that it can throw an exception, the overriding method must also specify that it can throw the same kind of exception, or a subtype of that exception. By allowing the exception to be a subtype of the one specified by the parent, the overriding method can refine the type of exception thrown, to go along with its new behavior. For example:

```
class MeatInedibleException extends InedibleException {
    ...
}

class Animal {
    void eat( Food f ) throws InedibleException {
        ...
    }
}
class Herbivore extends Animal {
    void eat( Food f ) throws InedibleException {
        if ( f instanceof Meat )
            throw new MeatInedibleException();
        ...
    }
}
```

In this code, Animal specifies that it can throw an InedibleException from its eat() method. Herbivore is a subclass of Animal, so its eat() method must also be able to throw an InedibleException. However, Herbivore's eat() method actually throws a more specific exception: MeatInedibleException. It can do this because MeatInedibleException is a subtype of InedibleException (remember that exceptions are classes, too). Our calling code's catch clause can therefore be more specific:

```
Animal creature = ...
try {
    creature.eat( food );
} catch ( MeatInedibleException ) {
    // creature can't eat this food because it's meat
} catch ( InedibleException ) {
    // creature can't eat this food
}
```

However, if we don't care why the food is inedible, we're free to catch
`InedibleException` alone, because a `MeatInedibleException` is also an
`InedibleException`.

NOTE   The `eat()` method in the `Herbivore` class could have declared that
it throws a `MeatInedibleException`, not a plain old `Inedible-`
`Exception`. But it should do so only if eating meat is the only cause
of herbivore indigestion.

Special References: this and super

The special references `this` and `super` allow you to refer to the members of the
current object instance or to members of the superclass, respectively. We have
seen `this` used elsewhere to pass a reference to the current object and to refer to
shadowed instance variables. The reference `super` does the same for the parents
of a class. You can use it to refer to members of a superclass that have been shadowed or overridden. A common arrangement is for an overridding method in a
subclass to do some preliminary work and then defer to the overridden method of
the superclass to finish the job:

```
class Animal {
    void eat( Food f ) throws InedibleException {
        // consume food
    }
}

class Herbivore extends Animal {
    void eat( Food f ) throws MeatInedibleException {
        // check if edible
        ...
        super.eat( f );
    }
}
```

In this example, our `Herbivore` class overrides the `Animal` `eat()` method to first
do some checking on the food object. After doing its job, it uses `super.eat()` to
call the (otherwise overridden) implementation of `eat()` in its superclass.

super prompts a search for the method or variable to begin in the scope of the
immediate superclass rather than the current class. The inherited method or variable found may reside in the immediate superclass, or in a more distant one. The
usage of the super reference when applied to overridden methods of a superclass
is special; it tells the method resolution system to stop the dynamic method search
at the superclass, instead of at the most derived class (as it otherwise does). Without super, there would be no way to access overridden methods.

Casting

As in C++, a *cast* explicitly tells the compiler to change the apparent type of an
object reference. Unlike in C++, casts in Java are checked both at compile time
and at runtime to make sure they are legal. Attempting to cast an object to an
incompatible type at runtime results in a ClassCastException. Only casts
between objects in the same inheritance hierarchy (and as we'll see later, to appropriate interfaces) are legal in Java and pass the scrutiny of the compiler and the
runtime system.

Casts in Java affect only the treatment of references; they never change the form of
the actual object. This is an important rule to keep in mind. You never change the
object pointed to by a reference by casting it; you change only the compiler's (or
runtime system's) notion of it.

A cast can be used to *narrow* the type of a reference—to make it more specific.
Often, we'll do this when we have to retrieve an object from a more general type
of collection or when it has been previously used as a less derived type. (The prototypical example is using an object in a Vector or Hashtable, as you'll see in
Chapter 9, *Basic Utility Classes*.) Continuing with our Cat example:

```
Animal creature = ...
Cat simon = ...

creature = simon;        // OK
// simon = creature;      // Compile time error, incompatible type
simon = (Cat)creature;    // OK
```

We can't reassign the reference in creature to the variable simon even though
we know it holds an instance of a Cat (Simon). We have to perform the indicated
cast. This is also called *downcasting* the reference.

Note that an implicit cast was performed when we went the other way to *widen* the
reference simon to type Animal during the first assignment. In this case, an
explicit cast would have been legal, but superfluous.

If casting seems complicated, here's a simple way to think about it. Basically, you
can't lie about what an object is. If you have a Cat object, you can cast it to a less

derived type (i.e., a type above it in the class hierarchy) such as `Animal` or even `Object`, since all Java classes are a subclass of `Object`. If you have an `Object` you know is a `Cat`, you can downcast the `Object` to be an `Animal` or a `Cat`. However, if you aren't sure if the `Object` is a `Cat` or a `Dog` at runtime, you should check it with `instanceof` before you perform the cast. If you get the cast wrong, the runtime system throws a `ClassCastException`.

As we mentioned earlier, casting can affect the selection of compile-time items such as variables and overloaded methods, but not the selection of overridden methods. Figure 6-4 shows the difference. As shown in the top half of the diagram, casting the reference `simon` to type `Animal` (widening it) affects the selection of the shadowed variable `weight` within it. However, as the lower half of the diagram indicates, the cast doesn't affect the selection of the overridden method `sleep()`.

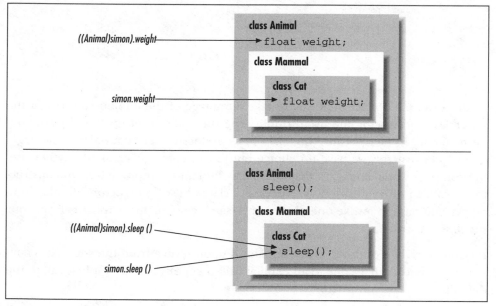

Figure 6-4. Casting and selection of methods and variables

Using Superclass Constructors

When we talked earlier about constructors, we discussed how the special statement `this()` invokes an overloaded constructor upon entry to another constructor. Similarly, the statement `super()` explicitly invokes the constructor of a superclass. Of course, we also talked about how Java makes a chain of constructor calls that includes the superclass's constructor, so why use `super()` explicitly? When Java makes an implicit call to the superclass constructor, it calls the default constructor. So, if we want to invoke a superclass constructor that takes arguments, we have to do so explicitly using super().

If we are going to call a superclass constructor with super(), it must be the first statement of our constructor, just as this() must be the first call we make in an overloaded constructor. Here's a simple example:

```
class Person {
    Person ( String name ) {
        // setup based on name
        ...
    }
    ...
}

class Doctor extends Person {
    Doctor ( String name, String specialty ) {
        super( name );
        // setup based on specialty
        ...
    }
    ...
}
```

In this example, we use super() to take advantage of the implementation of the superclass constructor and avoid duplicating the code to set up the object based on its name. In fact, because the class Person doesn't define a default (no arguments) constructor, we have no choice but to call super() explicitly. Otherwise, the compiler would complain that it couldn't find an appropriate default constructor to call. In other words, if you subclass a class whose constructors all take arguments, you have to invoke one of the superclass's constructors explicitly from your subclass constructor.

Instance variables of the class are initialized upon return from the superclass constructor, whether that's due to an explicit call to super() or an implicit call to the default superclass constructor.

Full Disclosure: Constructors and Initialization

We can now give the full story of how constructors are chained together and when instance variable initialization occurs. The rule has three parts and is applied repeatedly for each successive constructor invoked.

- If the first statement of a constructor is an ordinary statement—i.e., not a call to this() or super()—Java inserts an implicit call to super() to invoke the default constructor of the superclass. Upon returning from that call, Java initializes the instance variables of the current class and proceeds to execute the statements of the current constructor.

- If the first statement of a constructor is a call to a superclass constructor via `super()`, Java invokes the selected superclass constructor. Upon its return, Java initializes the current class's instance variables and proceeds with the statements of the current constructor.

- If the first statement of a constructor is a call to an overloaded constructor via `this()`, Java invokes the selected constructor and upon its return simply proceeds with the statements of the current constructor. The call to the superclass's constructor has happened within the overloaded constructor, either explicitly or implicitly, so the initialization of instance variables has already occurred.

Abstract Methods and Classes

A method in Java can be declared with the `abstract` modifier to indicate that it's just a prototype. An abstract method has no body; it's simply a signature declaration followed by a semicolon. You can't directly use a class that contains an abstract method; you must instead create a subclass that implements the abstract method's body.

```
abstract void vaporMethod( String name );
```

In Java, a class that contains one or more abstract methods must be explicitly declared as an abstract class, also using the `abstract` modifier:

```
abstract class vaporClass {
    ...
    abstract void vaporMethod( String name );
    ...
}
```

An abstract class can contain other, nonabstract methods and ordinary variable declarations; however, it can't be instantiated. To be used, it must be subclassed and its abstract methods must be overridden with methods that implement a body. Not all abstract methods have to be implemented in a single subclass, but a subclass that doesn't override all its superclass's abstract methods with actual, concrete implementations must also be declared `abstract`.

Abstract classes provide a framework for classes that are to be "filled in" by the implementor. The `java.io.InputStream` class, for example, has a single abstract method called `read()`. Various subclasses of `InputStream` implement `read()` in their own ways to read from their own sources. The rest of the `InputStream` class, however, provides extended functionality built on the simple `read()` method. A subclass of `InputStream` inherits these nonabstract methods that provide functionality based on the simple `read()` method that the subclass implements.

Interfaces

Java expands on the abstract method concept with its interfaces scheme. It's often desirable to specify the prototypes for a set of methods and provide no implementation. In Java, this is called an *interface*. An interface defines a set of methods that a class must implement (i.e., some or all of the class's behavior). A class in Java can declare that it *implements* an interface and then go about implementing the required methods. A class that implements an interface doesn't have to inherit from any particular part of the inheritance hierarchy or use a particular implementation.

Interfaces are kind of like Boy Scout or Girl Scout merit badges. A scout who has learned to build a birdhouse can walk around wearing a little sleeve patch with a picture of one. This says to the world, "I know how to build a birdhouse." Similarly, an *interface* is a list of methods that define some set of behavior for an object. Any class that implements each of the methods listed in the interface can declare that it implements the interface and wear, as its merit badge, an extra type—the interface's type.

Interface types act like class types. You can declare variables to be of an interface type, you can declare arguments of methods to accept interface types, and you can even specify that the return type of a method is an interface type. In each of these cases, what is meant is that any object that implements the interface (i.e., wears the right merit badge) can fill that spot. In this sense, interfaces are orthogonal to the class hierarchy. They cut across the boundaries of what kind of object an item *is* and deal with it only in terms of what it can *do*. A class can implement as many interfaces as it desires. In this way, interfaces in Java replace the need for C++'s multiple inheritance (and all of its messy side effects).

An interface looks like a purely `abstract` class (i.e., a class with only `abstract` methods). You define an interface with the `interface` keyword and list its methods with no bodies, just prototypes:

```
interface Driveable {
    boolean startEngine();
    void stopEngine();
    float accelerate( float acc );
    boolean turn( Direction dir );
}
```

The previous example defines an interface called `Driveable` with four methods. It's acceptable, but not necessary, to declare the methods in an interface with the `abstract` modifier; we haven't done that here. More importantly, the methods of an interface are always considered public, and you can optionally declare them as so. Why public? Well, the user of the interface wouldn't necessarily be able to see them otherwise.

Interfaces define capabilities, so it's common to name interfaces after their capabilities. `Driveable`, `Runnable`, and `Updateable` are good interface names. Any class that implements all the methods can then declare it implements the interface by using a special `implements` clause in its class definition. For example:

```
class Automobile implements Driveable {
    ...
    public boolean startEngine() {
        if ( notTooCold )
            engineRunning = true;
        ...
    }

    public void stopEngine() {
        engineRunning = false;
    }

    public float accelerate( float acc ) {
        ...
    }

    public boolean turn( Direction dir ) {
        ...
    }
    ...
}
```

Here, the class `Automobile` implements the methods of the `Driveable` interface and declares itself `Driveable` using an `implements` clause.

As shown in Figure 6-5, another class, such as `Lawnmower`, can also implement the `Driveable` interface. The figure illustrates the `Driveable` interface being implemented by two different classes. While it's possible that both `Automobile` and `Lawnmower` could derive from some primitive kind of vehicle, they don't have to in this scenario. This is a significant advantage of interfaces over standard multiple inheritance, as implemented in C++.

After declaring the interface, we have a new type, `Driveable`. We can declare variables of type `Driveable` and assign them any instance of a `Driveable` object:

```
Automobile auto = new Automobile();
Lawnmower mower = new Lawnmower();
Driveable vehicle;

vehicle = auto;
vehicle.startEngine();
vehicle.stopEngine();

vehicle = mower;
```

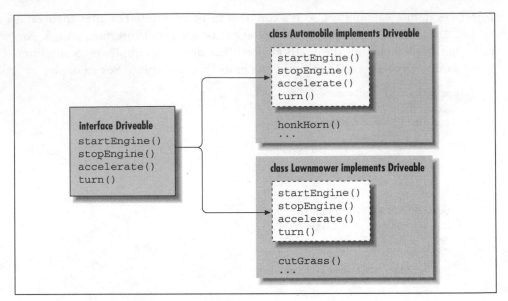

Figure 6-5. Implementing the Driveable interface

```
vehicle.startEngine();
vehicle.stopEngine();
```

Both `Automobile` and `Lawnmower` implement `Driveable`, so they can be considered of that type.

Interfaces as Callbacks

Interfaces can be used to implement callbacks in Java. An object can, in effect, pass one of its methods to another object. The callback occurs when the other object subsequently invokes the method. In C or C++, this is prime territory for function pointers; Java uses interfaces instead.

Consider two classes: a `TickerTape` class that displays data and a `TextSource` class that provides an information feed. We'd like our `TextSource` to send any new text data. We could have `TextSource` store a reference to a `TickerTape` object, but then we could never use our `TextSource` to send data to any other kind of object. Instead, we'd have to proliferate subclasses of `TextSource` that dealt with different types. A more elegant solution is to have `TextSource` store a reference to an interface type, `TextUpdateable`:

```
interface TextUpdateable {
    void doTextUpdate( String text );
}

class TickerTape implements TextUpdateable {
    public void doTextUpdate( String text ) {
```

```
            System.out.println("TICKER:\n" + text + "\n");
        }
    }

    class TextSource {
        TextUpdateable receiver;

        TextSource( TextUpdateable r ) {
            receiver = r;
        }

        public void sendText( String s ) {
            receiver.doTextUpdate( s );
        }
    }
```

The only thing the TextSource really cares about is finding the right method to invoke in order to output some text. Using an interface establishes a "well-known" name, doTextUpdate, for that method.

When the TextSource is constructed, a reference to the TickerTape (which implements the interface) is stored in an instance variable. This "registers" the TickerTape as the TextSource's "output device." Whenever it needs to output data, the TextSource calls the output device's doTextUpdate() method.

Interface Variables

Although interfaces mostly allow us to specify behavior without implementation, there's one exception. An interface can contain constants (static final variables), which appear in any class that implements the interface. This feature enables predefined parameters for use with the methods:

```
    interface Scaleable {
        static final int BIG = 0, MEDIUM = 1, SMALL = 2;
        void setScale( int size );
    }
```

The Scaleable interface defines three integers: BIG, MEDIUM, and SMALL. All variables defined in interfaces are implicitly final and static; we don't have to use the modifiers, but for clarity, we recommend you do. A class that implements Scaleable sees these variables:

```
    class Box implements Scaleable {

        void setScale( int size ) {
            switch( size ) {
                case BIG:
                    ...
                case MEDIUM:
```

```
            ...
        case SMALL:
            ...
      }
    }
    ...
  }
```

Empty interfaces

Sometimes, interfaces are created just to hold constants; anyone who implements the interfaces can see the constant names, as if they were included by a C/C++ *include* file. This is a somewhat degenerate, but acceptable, use of interfaces.

Sometimes completely empty interfaces serve as a marker that a class has a special property. The `java.io.Serializeable` interface is a good example. Classes that implement `Serializable` don't add any methods or variables. Their additional type simply identifies them to Java as classes that want to be able to be serialized.

Subinterfaces

An interface can extend another interface, just as a class can extend another class. Such an interface is called a *subinterface*. For example:

```
interface DynamicallyScaleable extends Scaleable {
    void changeScale( int size );
}
```

The interface `DynamicallyScaleable` extends our previous `Scaleable` interface and adds an additional method. A class that implements `Dynamically-Scaleable` must implement all the methods of both interfaces.

Note here that we are using the term "extends" and not "implements" to subclass the interface. Interfaces can't implement anything! But an interface is allowed to extend as many interfaces as it wants. If you want to extend two or more interfaces, list them after the `extends` keyword, separated by commas:

```
interface DynamicallyScaleable extends Scaleable, SomethingElseable {
    ...
}
```

Keep in mind that although Java supports multiple inheritance of interfaces, each class can extend only a single parent class.

Packages and Compilation Units

A *package* is a name for a group of related classes and interfaces. In Chapter 3, *Tools of the Trade*, we discussed how Java uses package names to locate classes during compilation and at runtime. In this sense, packages are somewhat like libraries; they organize and manage sets of classes. Packages provide more than just source-code-level organization though. They also create an additional level of scope for their classes and the variables and methods within them. We'll talk about the visibility of classes later in this section. In the next section, we'll discuss the effect that packages have on access to variables and methods among classes.

Compilation Units

The source code for a Java class is organized into *compilation units*. A simple compilation unit contains a single class definition and is named for that class. The definition of a class named `MyClass`, for instance, would appear in a file named *MyClass.java*. For most of us, a compilation unit is just a file with a *.java* extension, but in an integrated development environment, it could be an arbitrary entity. For brevity here, we'll refer to a compilation unit simply as a file.

The division of classes into their own compilation units is important because the Java compiler assumes much of the responsibility of a *make* utility. The compiler relies on the names of source files to find and compile dependent classes. It's possible (and common) to put more than one class definition into a single file, but there are some restrictions we'll discuss shortly.

A class is declared to belong to a particular package with the `package` statement. The `package` statement must appear as the first statement in a compilation unit. There can be only one `package` statement, and it applies to the entire file:

```
package mytools.text;

class TextComponent {
    ...
}
```

In this example, the class `TextComponent` is placed in the package `mytools.text`.

Package Names

Package names are constructed in a hierarchical way, using a dot-separated naming convention. Package-name components construct a unique path for the compiler and runtime systems to locate files; however, they don't affect the contents directly in any other way. There is no such thing as a subpackage; the package namespace is really flat, not hierarchical. Packages under a particular part of a package hierarchy are related only by informal association. For example, if we create another package called `mytools.text.poetry` (presumably for text classes specialized in some way to work with poetry), those classes won't be part of the `mytools.text` package; they won't have the access privileges of package members. In this sense, the package-naming convention can be misleading.

Class Visibility

By default, a class is accessible only to other classes within its package. This means that the class `TextComponent` is available only to other classes in the `mytools.text` package. To be visible elsewhere, a class must be declared as `public`:

```
package mytools.text;

public class TextEditor {
    ...
}
```

The class `TextEditor` can now be referenced anywhere. There can be only a single `public` class defined in a compilation unit; the file must be named for that class.

By hiding unimportant or extraneous classes, a package builds a subsystem that has a well-defined interface to the rest of the world. Public classes provide a facade for the operation of the system. The details of its inner workings can remain hidden, as shown in Figure 6-6. In this sense, packages hide classes in the way classes hide private members.

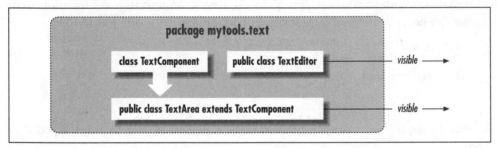

Figure 6-6. Packages and class visibility

Figure 6-6 shows part of the hypothetical `mytools.text` package. The classes `TextArea` and `TextEditor` are declared `public`, so they can be used elsewhere in an application. The class `TextComponent` is part of the implementation of `TextArea` and is not accessible from outside of the package.

Importing Classes

Classes within a package can refer to each other by their simple names. However, to locate a class in another package, we have to supply a qualifier. Continuing with the previous example, an application refers directly to our editor class by its fully qualified name of `mytools.text.TextEditor`. But we'd quickly grow tired of typing such long class names, so Java gives us the `import` statement. One or more `import` statements can appear at the top of a compilation unit, beneath the `package` statement. The `import` statements list the fully qualified names of classes to be used within the file.

Like a `package` statement, an `import` statement applies to the entire compilation unit. Here's how you might use an `import` statement:

```
package somewhere.else;
import mytools.text.TextEditor;

class MyClass {
    TextEditor editBoy;
    ...
}
```

As shown in this example, once a class is imported, it can be referenced by its simple name throughout the code.

It is also possible to import all of the classes in a package using the * wildcard notation:

```
import mytools.text.*;
```

Now we can refer to all `public` classes in the `mytools.text` package by their simple names.

Obviously, there can be a problem with importing classes that have conflicting names. If two different packages contain classes that use the same name, you just have to fall back to using fully qualified names to refer to those classes. Other than the potential for naming conflicts, there's no penalty for importing classes. Java doesn't carry extra baggage into the compiled class files. In other words, Java class files don't contain other class definitions—they only reference them.

The Unnamed Package

A class that is defined in a compilation unit that doesn't specify a package falls into the large, amorphous, unnamed package. Classes in this nameless package can refer to each other by their simple names. Their path at compile time and runtime is considered to be the current directory, so package-less classes are useful for experimentation and testing, and for brevity in examples in books about Java.

Visibility of Variables and Methods

One of the most important aspects of object-oriented design is data hiding, or *encapsulation*. By treating an object in some respects as a "black box" and ignoring the details of its implementation, we can write stronger, simpler code with components that can be easily reused.

Basic Access Modifiers

By default, the variables and methods of a class are accessible to members of the class itself and to other classes in the same package. To borrow from C++ terminology, classes in the same package are *friendly*. We'll call this the default level of visibility. As you'll see as we go on, the default visibility lies in the middle of the range of restrictiveness that can be specified.

The modifiers `public` and `private`, on the other hand, define the extremes. As we mentioned earlier, methods and variables declared as `private` are accessible only within their class. At the other end of the spectrum, members declared as `public` are accessible from any class in any package, provided the class itself can be seen. (The class that contains the methods must be `public` to be seen outside of its package, as we discussed previously.) The `public` members of a class should define its most general functionality—what the black box is supposed to do.

Figure 6-7 illustrates the four simplest levels of visibility, continuing the example from the previous section. Public members in `TextArea` are accessible from anywhere. Private members are not visible from outside the class. The default visibility allows access by other classes in the package.

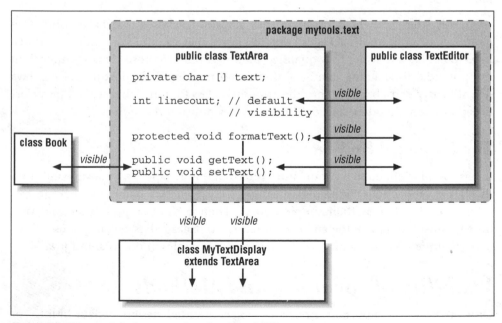

Figure 6-7. Private, default, protected, and public visibility

The `protected` modifier allows special access permissions for subclasses. Contrary to how it might sound, `protected` is slightly less restrictive than the default level of accessibility. In addition to the default access afforded classes in the same package, `protected` members are visible to subclasses of the class, even if they are defined in a different package. If you are a C++ programmer and so are used to more restrictive meanings, this may rub you the wrong way. *

Table 6-1 summarizes the levels of visibility available in Java; it runs generally from most restrictive to least. Methods and variables are always visible within a class, so the table doesn't address those.

Table 6-1. Visibility Modifiers

Modifier	Visibility
private	None
none (default)	Classes in the package
protected	Classes in package and subclasses inside or outside the package
public	All classes

Subclasses and Visibility

Subclasses add two important (but unrelated) complications to the topic of visibility. First, when you override methods in a subclass, the overriding method must be at least as visible as the overridden method. While it is possible to take a `private` method and override it with a `public` method in a subclass, the reverse is not possible; you can't override a `public` method with a `private` method. This restriction makes sense if you realize that subtypes have to be usable as instances of their supertype (e.g., a `Mammal` is a subclass of `Animal` and therefore must be usable as an `Animal`). If we could override a method with a less visible method, we would have a problem: our `Mammal` might not be able to do all the things an `Animal` can. However, we can reduce the visibility of a variable. In this case, the variable acts like any other shadowed variable; the two variables are distinct and can have separate visibilities in different classes.

The next complication is a bit harder to follow: the `protected` variables of a class are visible to its subclasses, but only through objects of the subclass's type or its subtypes. In other words, a subclass can see a `protected` variable of its superclass as an inherited variable, but it can't access that same variable in a separate instance of the superclass itself. This can be confusing, because we often forget

---

* Early on, the Java language allowed for certain combinations of modifiers, one of which was `privateprotected`. The meaning of private protected was to limit visibility strictly to subclasses (and remove package access). This was later deemed confusing and overly complex. It is no longer supported.

that visibility modifiers don't restrict access between instances of the same class in the same way that they restrict access between instances of different classes. Two instances of the same type of object can normally access all of each other's members, including private ones. Said another way: two instances of Cat can access all of each other's variables and methods (including private ones), but a Cat can't access a protected member in an instance of Animal unless the compiler can prove that the Animal is a Cat. If you found this hard to follow, don't worry too much. You shouldn't run into these issues very often.

Interfaces and Visibility

Interfaces behave like classes within packages. An interface can be declared public to make it visible outside of its package. Under the default visibility, an interface is visible only inside of its package. There can be only one public interface declared in a compilation unit.

Arrays and the Class Hierarchy

At the end of Chapter 4, we mentioned that arrays have a place in the Java class hierarchy, but we didn't give you any details. Now that we've discussed the object-oriented aspects of Java, we can give you the whole story.

Array classes live in a parallel Java class hierarchy under the Object class. If a class is a direct subclass of Object, then an array class for that base type also exists as a direct subclass of Object. Arrays of more derived classes are subclasses of the corresponding array classes. For example, consider the following class types:

```
class Animal { ... }
class Bird extends Animal { ... }
class Penguin extends Bird { ... }
```

Figure 6-8 illustrates the class hierarchy for arrays of these classes. Arrays of the same dimension are related to one another in the same manner as their base type classes. In our example, Bird is a subclass of Animal, which means that the Bird[] type is a subtype of Animal[]. In the same way a Bird object can be used in place of an Animal object, a Bird[] array can be assigned to a variable of type Animal[]:

```
Animal [][] animals;
Bird [][] birds = new Bird [10][10];
birds[0][0] = new Bird();

// make animals and birds reference the same array object
animals = birds;
Observe( animals[0][0] );                // processes Bird object
```

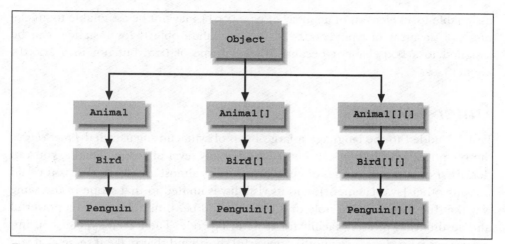

Figure 6-8. Arrays in the Java class hierarchy

Because arrays are part of the class hierarchy, we can use instanceof to check the type of an array:

```
if ( birds instanceof Animal[][] )      // true
```

An array is a subtype of Object and can therefore be assigned to Object type variables:

```
Object something;
something = animals;
```

Since Java knows the actual type of all objects, you can also cast back if appropriate:

```
animals = (Animal [][])something;
```

Under unusual circumstances, Java may not be able to check the types of objects you place into arrays at compile time. In those cases, it's possible to receive an ArrayStoreException if you try to assign the wrong type of object to an array element. Consider the following:

```
class Dog { ... }
class Poodle extends Dog { ... }
class Chihuahua extends Dog { ... }

Dog [] dogs;
Poodle [] poodles = new Poodle [10];

dogs = poodles;
dogs[3] = new Chihuahua();  // runtime error, ArrayStoreException
```

Both Poodle and Chihuahua are subclasses of Dog, so an array of Poodle objects can therefore be assigned to an array of Dog objects. The problem is that an object assignable to an element of an array of type `Dog[]` may not be assignable to an element of an array of type `Poodle[]`. A `Chihuahua` object, for instance, can be assigned to a `Dog` element because it's a subtype of `Dog`, but not to a `Poodle` element.*

Inner Classes

Java 1.1 added to the language a large heap of syntactic sugar called *inner classes*. Simply put, classes in Java can be declared at any level of scope. That is, you can declare a class within any set of curly braces (i.e., almost anywhere that you could put any other Java statement), and its visibility is limited to that scope in the same way that the name of a variable or method would be. Inner classes are a powerful and aesthetically pleasing facility for structuring code. Their even sweeter cousins, *anonymous inner classes*, are another powerful shorthand that make it seem as if you can create classes dynamically within Java's statically typed environment.

However, if you delve into the inner workings of Java, inner classes are not quite as aesthetically pleasing or dynamic. We said that they are syntactic sugar; this means that they let you leverage the compiler by writing a few lines of code that trigger a lot of behind-the-scenes work somewhere between the compiler's front end and the byte-code. Inner classes rely on code generation; they are a feature of the Java language, but not of the Java virtual machine. As a programmer you may never need be aware of this; you can simply rely on inner classes like any other language construct. However, you should know a little about how inner classes work, to better understand the results and a few potential side effects.

To this point, all of our classes have been *top-level* classes. We have declared them, freestanding, at the package level. Inner classes are essentially nested classes, like this:

```
Class Animal {
    Class Brain {
        ...
    }
}
```

Here the class `Brain` is an inner class: it is a class declared inside the scope of class `Animal`. Although the details of what that means require a fair bit of explanation,

---

* In some sense, this could be considered a hole in the Java type system. It doesn't occur elsewhere in Java—only with arrays. This is because array objects exhibit *covariance* in overriding their assignment and extraction methods. Covariance allows array subclasses to override methods with arguments or return values that are subtypes of the overridden methods, where the methods would normally be overloaded or prohibited. This allows array subclasses to operate on their base types with type safety, but also means that subclasses have different capabilities than their parents, leading to the problem shown earlier.

we'll start by saying that the Java language tries to make the meaning, as much as possible, the same as for the other Java entities (methods and variables) living at that level of scope. For example, let's add a method to the Animal class:

```
Class Animal {
    Class Brain {
        ...
    }
    void performBehavior() { ... }
}
```

Both the inner class Brain and the method performBehavior() are within the scope of Animal. Therefore, anywhere within Animal we can refer to Brain and performBehavior() directly, by name. Within Animal we can call the constructor for Brain (new Brain()) to get a Brain object, or invoke performBehavior() to carry out that method's function. But neither Brain nor performBehavior() are accessible outside of the class Animal without some additional qualification.

Within the body of the Brain class and the body of the performBehavior() method, we have direct access to all of the other methods and variables of the Animal class. So, just as the performBehavior() method could work with the Brain class and create instances of Brain, code within the Brain class can invoke the performBehavior() method of Animal as well as work with any other methods and variables declared in Animal.

That last bit has important consequences. From within Brain we can invoke the method performBehavior(); that is, from within an instance of Brain we can invoke the performBehavior() method of an instance of Animal. Well, which instance of Animal? If we have several Animal objects around (say, a few Cats and Dogs), we need to know whose performBehavior() method we are calling. What does it mean for a class definition to be "inside" another class definition? The answer is that a Brain object always lives within a single instance of Animal: the one that it was told about when it was created. We'll call the object that contains any instance of Brain its *enclosing instance*.

A Brain object cannot live outside of an enclosing instance of an Animal object. Anywhere you see an instance of Brain, it will be tethered to an instance of Animal. Although it is possible to construct a Brain object from elsewhere (i.e., another class), Brain always requires an enclosing instance of Animal to "hold" it. We'll also say now that if Brain is to be referred to from outside of Animal, it acts something like an Animal.Brain class. And just as with the performBehavior() method, modifiers can be applied to restrict its visibility. There is even an interpretation of the static modifier, which we'll talk about a bit later. However, the details are somewhat boring and not immediately useful. For more information, consult a full language reference, such as *Java Language Reference, Second Edition*, by

Mark Grand (O'Reilly & Associates). Before we get too far afield, let's turn to a more compelling example.

A particularly important use of inner classes is to make *adapter classes*. An adapter class is a "helper" class that ties one class to another in a very specific way. Using adapter classes, you can write your classes more naturally, without having to anticipate every conceivable user's needs in advance. Instead, you provide adapter classes that marry your class to a particular interface. As an example, let's say that we have an `EmployeeList` object:

```
public class EmployeeList {
    private Employee [] employees = ... ;
    ...
}
```

`EmployeeList` holds information about a set of employees. Let's say that we would like to have `EmployeeList` provide its elements via an iterator. An iterator is a simple interface to a list of objects. The `java.util.Iterator` interface has several methods:

```
public interface Iterator {
    boolean hasMore ();
    Object next();
    void remove();
}
```

It lets us step through its elements, asking for the next one and testing to see if more remain. The iterator is a good candidate for an adapter class because it is an interface that our `EmployeeList` can't readily implement itself. Why can't the list implement the iterator directly? Because an iterator is a "one-way," disposable view of our data. It isn't intended to be reset and used again. It may also be necessary for there to be multiple iterators walking through the list at different points. We must therefore keep the iterator implementation separate from the `Employee-List` itself. This is crying out for a simple class to provide the iterator capability. But what should that class look like?

Well, before we knew about inner classes, our only recourse would have been to make a new "top-level" class. We would probably feel obliged to call it `EmployeeListIterator`:

```
class EmployeeListIterator implements Iterator {
    // lots of knowledge about EmployeeList
    ...
}
```

Here we have a comment representing the machinery that the `EmployeeList-Iterator` requires. Think for just a second about what you'd have to do to implement that machinery. The resulting class would be completely coupled to the

EmployeeList and unusable in other situations. Worse, to function it must have access to the inner workings of EmployeeList. We would have to allow EmployeeListIterator access to the private array in EmployeeList, exposing this data more widely than it should be. This is less than ideal.

This sounds like a job for inner classes. We already said that Employee-ListIterator was useless without an EmployeeList; this sounds a lot like the "lives inside" relationship we described earlier. Furthermore, an inner class lets us avoid the encapsulation problem, because it can access all the members of its enclosing instance. Therefore, if we use an inner class to implement the iterator, the array employees can remain private, invisible outside the EmployeeList. So let's just shove that helper class inside the scope of our EmployeeList:

```
public class EmployeeList {
    private Employee [] employees = ... ;
    ...

    class Iterator implements java.util.Iterator {
        int element = 0;

        boolean hasMore() {
            return  element < employees.length ;
        }

        Object next() {
            if ( hasMoreElements() )
                return employees[ element++ ];
            else
                throw new NoSuchElementException();
        }

        void remove() {
            throw new UnsupportedOperationException();
        }
    }
}
```

Now EmployeeList can provide an accessor method like the following to let other classes work with the list:

```
Iterator getIterator() {
    return new Iterator();
}
```

One effect of the move is that we are free to be a little more familiar in the naming of our iterator class. Since it is no longer a top-level class, we can give it a name that is appropriate only within the EmployeeList. In this case, we've named it Iterator to emphasize what it does—but we don't need a name like EmployeeIterator that shows the relationship to the EmployeeList class because that's implicit. We've also filled in the guts of the Iterator class. As you can see, now that it is inside the scope of EmployeeList, Iterator has direct access to its private members, so it can directly access the employees array. This greatly simplifies the code and maintains compile-time safety.

Before we move on, we should note that inner classes can have constructors, even though we didn't need one in this example. They are in all respects real classes.

Inner Classes Within Methods

Inner classes may also be declared within the body of a method. Returning to the Animal class, we could put Brain inside the performBehavior() method if we decided that the class was useful only inside of that method:

```
Class Animal {
    void performBehavior() {
        Class Brain {
            ...
        }
    }
}
```

In this situation, the rules governing what Brain can see are the same as in our earlier example. The body of Brain can see anything in the scope of performBehavior() and above it (in the body of Animal). This includes local variables of performBehavior() and its arguments. But there are a few limitations and additional restrictions, as described in the following sections.

Limitations on inner classes

performBehavior() is a method, and methods have limited lifetimes. When they exit, their local variables normally disappear into the stacky abyss. But an instance of Brain (like any object) lives on as long as it is referenced. So Java must make sure that any local variables used by instances of Brain created within an invocation of performBehavior() also live on. Furthermore, all of the instances of Brain that we make within a single invocation of performBehavior() must see the same local variables. To accomplish this, the compiler must be allowed to make copies of local variables. Thus, their values cannot change once an inner class has seen them. This means that any of the method's local variables that are referenced by the inner class must be declared final. The final modifier means that they are constant once assigned. This is a little confusing and easy to forget, but the compiler will graciously remind you.

Static inner classes

We mentioned earlier that the inner class Brain of the class Animal could in some ways be considered an Animal.Brain class. That is, it is possible to work with a `Brain` from outside the `Animal` class, using just such a qualified name: `Animal.Brain`. But given that our `Animal.Brain` class always requires an instance of an `Animal` as its enclosing instance, some explicit setup is needed.*

But there is another situation in which we might use inner classes by name. An inner class that lives within the body of a top-level class (not within a method or another inner class) can be declared `static`. For example:

```
class Animal  {
    static class MigrationPattern {
        ...
    }
    ...
}
```

A static inner class such as this acts just like a new top-level class called `Animal.MigrationPattern`. We can use it just like any other class, without regard to any enclosing instances. Although this seems strange, it is not inconsistent, since a static member never has an object instance associated with it. The requirement that the inner class be defined directly inside a top-level class ensures that an enclosing instance won't be needed. If we have permission, we can create an instance of the class using the qualified name:

```
Animal.MigrationPattern stlToSanFrancisco =
    new Animal.MigrationPattern();
```

As you see, the effect is that `Animal` acts something like a mini-package, holding the `MigrationPattern` class. Here we have used the fully qualified name, but we could also import it like any other class:

```
Import Animal.MigrationPattern;
```

This enables us to refer to it simply as `MigrationPattern`. We can use all of the standard visibility modifiers on inner classes, so a static inner class could be private, protected, default, or publicly visible.

Another example: the Java 2D API uses static inner classes to implement specialized shape classes. For example, the `java.awt.geom.Rectangle2D` class has two inner classes, `Float` and `Double`, that implement two different precisions. These are actually trivial subclasses; it would have been sad to have to multiply the number of top-level classes by three to accommodate them.

Anonymous inner classes

Now we get to the best part. As a general rule, the more deeply encapsulated and limited in scope our classes are, the more freedom we have in naming them. We

---

* Specifically, we would have to follow a design pattern and pass a reference to the enclosing instance of `Animal` into the `Animal.Brain` constructor. See a Java language reference for more information. We don't expect you to run into this situation very often.

saw this in our previous iterator example. This is not just a purely aesthetic issue. Naming is an important part of writing readable and maintainable code. We generally want to give things the most concise and meaningful names possible. A corollary to this is that we prefer to avoid doling out names for purely ephemeral objects that are going to be used only once.

Anonymous inner classes are an extension of the syntax of the new operation. When you create an anonymous inner class, you combine the class's declaration with the allocation of an instance of that class. After the new operator, you specify either the name of a class or an interface, followed by a class body. The class body becomes an inner class, which either extends the specified class or, in the case of an interface, is expected to implement the specified interface. A single instance of the class is created and returned as the value.

For example, we could do away with the declaration of the Iterator class in the EmployeeList example by using an anonymous inner class in the getIterator() method:

```
Iterator getIterator() {
    return new Iterator() {
        int element = 0;
        boolean hasMore() {
            return  element < employees.length ;
        }
        Object next() {
            if ( hasMoreElements() )
                return employees[ element++ ];
            else
                throw new NoSuchElementException();
        }
        void remove() {
            throw new UnsupportedOperationException();
        }
    };
}
```

Here we have simply moved the guts of Iterator into the body of an anonymous inner class. The call to new implies a class that implements the Iterator interface and returns an instance of the class as its result. Note the extent of the curly braces and the semicolon at the end. The getIteratgor() method contains a single return statement.

But the previous code certainly does not improve readability. Inner classes are best used when you want to implement a few lines of code, when the verbiage and conspicuousness of declaring a separate class detracts from the task at hand.

Here's a better example. Suppose that we want to start a new thread to execute the performBehavior() method of our Animal:

```
new Thread() {
    public void run() {  performBehavior();  }
}.start();
```

Here we have gone over to the terse side. We've allocated and started a new
Thread, using an anonymous inner class that extends the Thread class and
invokes our performBehavior() method in its run() method. The effect is similar to using a method pointer in some other language. However, the inner class
allows the compiler to check type consistency, which would be more difficult (or
impossible) with a true method pointer. At the same time, our anonymous adapter
class with its three lines of code is much more efficient and readable than creating
a new, top-level adapter class named AnimalBehaviorThreadAdapter.

While we're getting a bit ahead of the story, anonymous adapter classes are a perfect fit for event handling (which we'll cover fully in Chapter 13, *Swing*). Skipping
a lot of explanation, let's say you want the method handleClicks() to be called
whenever the user clicks the mouse. You would write code like this:

```
addMouseListener(new MouseInputAdapter() {
    public void mouseClicked(MouseEvent e) { handleClicks(e); }
});
```

In this case, the anonymous class extends the MouseInputAdapter class by overriding its mouseClicked() method to call our method. A lot is going on in a very
small space, but the result is clean, readable code. You get to assign method names
that are meaningful to you, while allowing Java to do its job of type checking.

Scoping of the "this" reference

Sometimes an inner class may want to get a handle on its "parent" enclosing
instance. It might want to pass a reference to its parent, or to refer to one of the
parent's variables or methods that has been hidden by one of its own. For
example:

```
class Animal {
    int size;
    class Brain {
        int size;
    }
}
```

Here, as far as Brain is concerned, the variable size in Animal is hidden by its
own version.

Normally an object refers to itself using the special this reference (implicitly or
explicitly). But what is the meaning of this for an object with one or more enclosing instances? The answer is that an inner class has multiple this references. You
can specify which this you want by prepending the name of the class. So, for

instance (no pun intended), we can get a reference to our `Animal` from within `Brain` like so:

```
class Brain {
    Animal ourAnimal = Animal.this;
    ...
}
```

Similarly, we could refer to the `size` variable in `Animal`:

```
class Brain {
    int animalSize = Animal.this.size;
    ...
}
```

How do inner classes really work?

Finally, we'll get our hands dirty and take a look at what's really going on when we use an inner class. We've said that the compiler is doing all of the things that we had hoped to forget about. Let's see what's actually happening. Try compiling this trivial example:

```
class Animal {
    class Brain {
    }
}
```

What you'll find is that the compiler generates two *.class* files: *Animal.class* and *Animal$Brain.class.*

The second file is the class file for our inner class. Yes, as we feared, inner classes are really just compiler magic. The compiler has created the inner class for us as a normal, top-level class and named it by combining the class names with a dollar sign. The dollar sign is a valid character in class names, but is intended for use only by automated tools. (Please don't start naming your classes with dollar signs.) Had our class been more deeply nested, the intervening inner-class names would have been attached in the same way to generate a unique top-level name.

Now take a look at it with the SDK's `javap` utility (don't quote the argument on a Windows system):

```
% javap 'Animal$Brain'
class Animal$Brain extends java.lang.Object {
    Animal$Brain(Animal);
}
```

You'll see that the compiler has given our inner class a constructor that takes a reference to an `Animal` as an argument. This is how the real inner class gets the handle on its enclosing instance.

The worst thing about these additional class files is that you need to know they are there. Utilities like `jar` don't automatically find them; when you're invoking a utility like `jar`, you need to specify these files explicitly or use a wildcard that finds them.

Security implications

Given what we just saw—that the inner class really does exist as an automatically generated top-level class—how does it get access to private variables? The answer, unfortunately, is that the compiler is forced to break the encapsulation of your object and insert accessor methods so that the inner class can reach them. The accessor methods will be given package-level access, so your object is still safe within its package walls, but it is conceivable that this difference could be meaningful if people were allowed to create new classes within your package.

The visibility modifiers on inner classes also have some problems. Current implementations of the virtual machine do not implement the notion of a `private` or `protected` class within a package, so giving your inner class anything other than `public` or default visibility is only a compile-time guarantee. It is difficult to conceive of how these security issues could be abused, but it is interesting to note that Java is straining a bit to stay within its original design.

7

Working with Objects and Classes

In the previous two chapters, we came to know Java objects and then their inter-relationships. We have now climbed the scaffolding of the Java class hierarchy and reached the top. In this chapter, we'll talk about the `Object` class itself, which is the "grandmother" of all classes in Java. We'll also describe the even more fundamental `Class` class (the class named "Class") that represents Java classes in the Java virtual machine. We'll discuss what you can do with these objects in their own right. Finally, this will lead us to a more general topic: the reflection interface, which lets a Java program inspect and interact with (possibly unknown) objects on the fly.

The Object Class

`java.lang.Object` is the ancestor of all objects; it's the primordial class from which all other classes are ultimately derived. Methods defined in `Object` are therefore very important because they appear in every instance of any class, throughout all of Java. At last count, there were nine `public` methods in `Object`. Five of these are versions of `wait()` and `notify()` that are used to synchronize threads on object instances, as we'll discuss in Chapter 8, *Threads*. The remaining four methods are used for basic comparison, conversion, and administration.

Every object has a `toString()` method that is called implicitly when it's to be represented as a text value. `PrintStream` objects use `toString()` to print data, as discussed in Chapter 10, *Input/Output Facilities*. `toString()` is also used when an object is referenced in a string concatenation. Here are some examples:

```
MyObj myObject = new MyObj();
Answer theAnswer = new Answer();

System.out.println( myObject );
String s = "The answer is: " + theAnswer ;
```

To be friendly, a new kind of object should override `toString()` and implement its own version that provides appropriate printing functionality. Two other methods, `equals()` and `hashCode()`, may also require specialization when you create a new class.

Equality and Equivalence

`equals()` determines whether two objects are equivalent. Precisely what that means for a particular class is something that you'll have to decide for yourself. Two `String` objects, for example, are considered equivalent if they hold precisely the same characters in the same sequence:

```
String userName = "Joe";
...
if ( userName.equals( suspectName ) )
    arrest( userName );
```

Using `equals()` is *not* the same as:

```
if ( userName == suspectName )        // Wrong!
```

This code tests whether the two reference variables, `userName` and `suspectName`, refer to the same object; which is sufficient but not necessary for them to be equivalent objects.

A class should override the `equals()` method if it needs to implement its own notion of equality. If you have no need to compare objects of a particular class, you don't need to override `equals()`.

Watch out for accidentally overloading `equals()` when you mean to override it. With overloading, the method signatures differ; with overriding, they must be the same. The `equals()` method signature specifies an `Object` argument and a boolean return value. You'll probably want to check only objects of the same type for equivalence. But in order to override (not overload) `equals()`, the method must specify its argument to be an `Object`.

Here's an example of correctly overriding an `equals()` method in class `Shoes` with an `equals()` method in subclass `Sneakers`. Using its own method, a `Sneakers` object can compare itself with any other object.

```
class Sneakers extends Shoes {
    public boolean equals( Object arg ) {
        if ( (arg != null) && (arg instanceof Sneakers) ) {
            // compare arg with this object to check equivalence
            // If comparison is okay...
            return true;
        }
```

```
        return false;
    }
    ...
}
```

If we specified `public boolean equals(Sneakers arg)` ... in the `Sneakers` class, we'd overload the `equals()` method instead of overriding it. If the other object happens to be assigned to a non-`Sneakers` variable, the method signature won't match. The result: superclass `Shoes`'s implementation of `equals()` will be called, possibly causing an error.

Hashcodes

The `hashCode()` method returns an integer that is a *hashcode* for the object. A hashcode is like a signature or checksum for an object; it's a random-looking identifying number that is usually generated from the contents of the object. The hashcode should always be different for instances of the class that contain different data, but should normally be the same for instances that compare "equal" with the `equals()` method. Hashcodes are used in the process of storing objects in a `Hashtable`, or a similar kind of collection. The hashcode helps the `Hashtable` optimize its storage of objects by serving as an identifier for distributing them into storage evenly, and locating them quickly later.

The default implementation of `hashCode()` in `Object` assigns each object instance a unique number. If you don't override this method when you create a subclass, each instance of your class will have a unique hashcode. This is sufficient for some objects. However, if your classes have a notion of equivalent objects (if you have overriden `equals()`) and you want equal objects to serve as equivalent keys in a `Hashtable`, then you should override `hashCode()` so that your equivalent objects generate the same hashcode value.

Cloning Objects

Objects can use the `clone()` method of the `Object` class to make copies of themselves. A copied object will be a new object instance, separate from the original. It may or may not contain exactly the same state (the same instance variable values) as the original—that's controlled by the object being copied. Just as important, the decision as to whether the object allows itself to be cloned at all is up to the object.

The Java `Object` class provides the mechanism to make a simple copy of an object including all of its state—a bitwise copy. But by default this capability is turned off. (We'll hit upon why in a moment.) To make itself cloneable, an object must implement the `java.lang.Cloneable` interface. This is a flag interface indicating to Java that the object wants to cooperate in being cloned (the interface does not actually contain any methods). If the object isn't cloneable, the `clone()` method throws a `CloneNotSupportedException`.

clone() is a protected method, so by default it can be called only by an object on itself, an object in the same package, or another object of the same type or a subtype. If we want to make an object cloneable by everyone, we have to override its clone() method and make it public.

Here is a simple, cloneable class—Sheep:

```
import java.util.Hashtable;

public class Sheep implements Cloneable {
    Hashtable flock = new Hashtable();

    public Object clone() {
        try {
            return super.clone();
        } catch (CloneNotSupportedException e ) {
            throw new Error("This should never happen!");
        }
    }
}
```

Sheep has one instance variable, a Hashtable called flock (which the sheep uses to keep track of its fellow sheep). Our class implements the Cloneable interface, indicating that it is okay to copy Sheep and it has overridden the clone() method to make it public. Our clone() simply returns the object created by the superclass's clone() method—a copy of our Sheep. Unfortunately, the compiler is not smart enough to figure out that the object we're cloning will never throw the CloneNotSupportedException, so we have to guard against it anyway. Our sheep is now cloneable. We can make copies like so:

```
Sheep one = new Sheep();
Sheep anotherOne = (Sheep)one.clone();
```

The cast is necessary here because the return type of clone() is Object.*

We now have two sheep instead of one. The equals() method would tell us that the sheep are equivalent, but == tells us that they aren't equal—that is, they are two distinct objects. Java has made a "shallow" copy of our Sheep. What's so shallow about it? Java has simply copied the bits of our variables. That means that the flock instance variable in each of our Sheep still holds the same information—that is, both sheep have a reference to the same Hashtable. The situation looks like that shown in Figure 7-1.

---

* You might think that we could override the clone() method in our objects to refine the return type of the clone() method. However this is currently not possible in Java. You can't override methods and change their return types. Technically this would be called *covariant return typing*. It's something that may find its way into the language eventually.

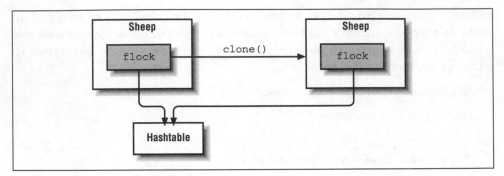

Figure 7-1. Shallow copy of an object

This may or may not be what you intended. If we instead want our Sheep to have separate copies of all of its variables (or something in between), we can take control ourselves. In the following example, DeepSheep, we implement a "deep" copy, duplicating our own flock variable:

```
public class DeepSheep implements Cloneable {
    Hashtable flock = new Hashtable();

    public Object clone() {
        try {
            DeepSheep copy = (DeepSheep)super.clone();
            copy.flock = (Hashtable)flock.clone();
            return copy;
        } catch (CloneNotSupportedException e ) {
            throw new Error("This should never happen!");
        }
    }
}
```

Our clone() method now clones the Hashtable as well. Now, when a DeepSheep is cloned, the situation looks more like that shown in Figure 7-2.

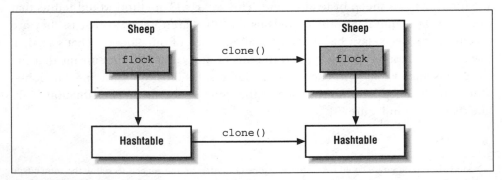

Figure 7-2. Deep copy of an object

Each `DeepSheep` now has its own hashtable. You can see now why objects are not cloneable by default. It would make no sense to assume that all objects can be sensibly duplicated with a shallow copy. Likewise, it makes no sense to assume that a deep copy is necessary, or even correct. In this case, we probably don't need a deep copy; the flock contains the same members no matter which sheep you're looking at, so there's no need to copy the `Hashtable`. But the decision depends on the object itself and its requirements.

The Class Class

The last method of `Object` we need to discuss is `getClass()`. This method returns a reference to the `Class` object that produced the `Object` instance.

A good measure of the complexity of an object-oriented language is the degree of abstraction of its class structures. We know that every object in Java is an instance of a class, but what exactly is a class? In C++, objects are formulated by and instantiated from classes, but classes are really just artifacts of the compiler. Thus, you see classes only mentioned in C++ source code, not at runtime. By comparison, classes in Smalltalk are real, runtime entities in the language that are themselves described by "metaclasses" and "metaclass classes." Java strikes a happy medium between these two languages with what is effectively a two-tiered system that uses `Class` objects.

Classes in Java source code are represented at runtime by instances of the `java.lang.Class` class. There's a `Class` object for every class you use; this `Class` object is responsible for producing instances for its class. You don't have to worry about any of this unless you are interested in loading new kinds of classes dynamically at runtime. The `Class` object is also the basis for "reflecting" on a class to find out its methods and other properties; we'll discuss this feature in the next section.

We get the `Class` associated with a particular object with the `getClass()` method:

```
String myString = "Foo!"
Class c = myString.getClass();
```

We can also get the `Class` reference for a particular class statically, using the special `.class` notation:

```
Class c = String.class;
```

The `.class` reference looks like a static field that exists in every class. However, it is really resolved by the compiler.

One thing we can do with the `Class` object is ask for the name of the object's class:

```
String s = "Boofa!";
Class mycls= s.getClass();
System.out.println( mycls.getName() );    // "java.lang.String"
```

Another thing that we can do with a `Class` is to ask it to produce a new instance of its type of object. Continuing with the previous example:

```
try {
    String s2 = (String)strClass.newInstance();
}
catch ( InstantiationException e ) { ... }
catch ( IllegalAccessException e ) { ... }
```

`newInstance()` has a return type of `Object`, so we have to cast it to a reference of the appropriate type. (`newInstance()` has to be able to return any kind of constructed object.) A couple of problems can occur here. An `Instantiation-Exception` indicates we're trying to instantiate an `abstract` class or an interface. `IllegalAccessException` is a more general exception that indicates we can't access a constructor for the object. Note that `newInstance()` can create only an instance of a class that has an accessible default constructor. It doesn't allow us to pass any arguments to a constructor. (But see "Accessing Constructors" later in this chapter.)

All this becomes more meaningful when we add the capability to look up a class by name. `forName()` is a `static` method of `Class` that returns a `Class` object given its name as a `String`:

```
try {
    Class sneakersClass = Class.forName("Sneakers");
}
catch ( ClassNotFoundException e ) { ... }
```

A `ClassNotFoundException` is thrown if the class can't be located.

Combining these tools, we have the power to load new kinds of classes dynamically. When combined with the power of interfaces, we can use new data types by name in our applications:

```
interface Typewriter {
    void typeLine( String s );
    ...
}

class Printer implements Typewriter {
    ...
}

class MyApplication {
    ...
    String outputDeviceName = "Printer";

    try {
        Class newClass = Class.forName( outputDeviceName );
```

```
        Typewriter device = (Typewriter)newClass.newInstance();
        ...
        device.typeLine("Hello...");
    }
    catch ( Exception e ) { ... }
}
```

Here we have an application loading a class implementation (`Printer` which implements the `Typewriter` interface) knowing only its name. Imagine the name was entered by the user or looked up from a configuration file.

Reflection

In this section, we'll take a look at the Java reflection API, supported by the classes in the `java.lang.reflect` package. As its name suggests, reflection is the ability for a class or object to examine itself. Reflection lets Java code look at an object (more precisely, the class of the object) and determine its structure. Within the limits imposed by the security manager, you can find out what constructors, methods, and fields a class has, as well as their attributes. You can even change the value of fields, dynamically invoke methods, and construct new objects, much as if Java had primitive pointers to variables and methods. And you can do all of this on objects that your code has never even seen before.

We don't have room here to fully cover the reflection API. As you might expect, the `reflect` package is complex and rich in details. But reflection has been designed so that you can do a lot with relatively little effort; 20 percent of the effort will give you 80 percent of the fun.

The reflection API is used by JavaBeans to determine the capabilities of objects at runtime. It's also used at a lower level by object serialization to tear apart and build objects for transport over streams or into persistent storage. Obviously, the power to pick apart objects and see their internals must be zealously guarded by the security manager. Your code is not allowed to do anything with the reflection API that it couldn't do with static (ordinary, compiled) Java code. In short, reflection is a powerful tool, but it isn't a loophole. An object can't use it to find out about data fields that it wouldn't normally be able to access (for example, another object's private fields), and you can't use it to modify any data inappropriately.

The three primary features of a class are its fields (variables), methods, and constructors. For purposes of describing or accessing an object, these three features are represented by separate classes in the reflection API: `java.lang.reflect.Field`, `java.lang.reflect.Method`, and `java.lang.reflect.Constructor`. We can create these objects using the `Class` object

The Class class provides two pairs of methods for getting at each type of feature. One pair allows access to a class's public features (including those inherited from its superclasses), while the other pair allows access to any public or nonpublic item declared within the class (but not features that are inherited), subject to security considerations. Some examples:

- getFields() returns an array of Field objects representing all of a class's public variables, including those it inherits.

- getDeclaredFields() returns an array representing all the variables declared in the class, regardless of their access modifiers (not including variables the security manager won't let you see), but not including inherited variables.

- For constructors, the distinction between "all constructors" and "declared constructors" is meaningful, so getConstructors() and getDeclared-Constructors() differ only in that the former returns public constructors, while the latter returns all the class's constructors.

Each pair of methods includes a method for listing all of the items at once (for example, getFields()) and a method for looking up a particular item by name and—for methods and constructors—by signature (for example, getField(), which takes the field name as an argument).

The following listing shows the methods in the Class class:

Field [] **getFields**();
    Get all public variables, including inherited ones.

Field **getField**(String *name*);
    Get the specified public variable, which may be inherited.

Field [] **getDeclaredFields**();
    Get all public and nonpublic variables declared in this class (not including those inherited from superclasses).

Field **getDeclaredField**(String *name*);
    Get the specified variable, public or nonpublic, declared in this class (inherited variables not considered).

Method [] **getMethods**();
    Get all public methods, including inherited ones.

Method **getMethod**(String *name*, Class [] *argumentTypes*);
    Get the specified public method whose arguments match the types listed in argumentTypes. The method may be inherited.

Method [] **getDeclaredMethods**();
    Get all public and nonpublic methods declared in this class (not including those inherited from superclasses).

Method **getDeclaredMethod**(String *name*, Class [] *argumentTypes*);
Get the specified method, public or nonpublic, whose arguments match the types listed in argumentTypes, and which is declared in this class (inherited methods not considered).

Constructor [] **getConstructors**();
Get all public constructors of this class.

Constructor **getConstructor**(Class [] *argumentTypes*);
Get the specified public constructor of this class whose arguments match the types listed in argumentTypes.

Constructor [] **getDeclaredConstructors**();
Get all public and nonpublic constructors of this class.

Constructor **getDeclaredConstructor**(Class [] *argumentTypes*);
Get the specified constructor, public or nonpublic, whose arguments match the types listed in argumentTypes.

As a quick example, we'll show how easy it is to list all of the public methods of the java.util.Calendar class:

```
Method [] methods = Calendar.class.getMethods();
for (int i=0; i < methods.length; i++)
    System.out.println( methods[i] );
```

Here we have used the .class notation to get a reference to the Class of Calendar. Remember the discussion of the Class class—the reflection methods don't belong to a particular instance of Calendar itself; they belong to the java.lang.Class object that describes the Calendar class. If we wanted to start from an instance of Calendar (or, say, an unknown object), we could have used the getClass() method of the object instead:

```
Method [] methods = myUnknownObject.getClass().getMethods();
```

Security

Access to the reflection API is governed by a security manager. A fully trusted application has access to all of the previously discussed functionality—it can gain access to members of classes at the level of restriction normally granted code within its scope. There is currently no "special" access granted by the reflection API. It is possible that in the future, the full power of the reflection API will be available to completely trusted code; currently, user code can see only what it could have seen at compile time. Untrusted code (for example, an unsigned applet) has the normal level of access to classes loaded from its own origin (classes sharing its class loader), but can rely only on the ability to access the public members of public classes that originate elsewhere.

Accessing Fields

The class `java.lang.reflect.Field` is used to represent static variables and instance variables. `Field` has a full set of accessor methods for all of the base types (for example, `getInt()` and `setInt()`, `getBoolean()` and `setBoolean()`) and `get()` and `set()` methods for accessing members that are object references. For example, consider this class:

```
class BankAccount {
    public int balance;
}
```

With the reflection API, we can read and modify the value of the public integer field `balance`:

```
BankAccount myBankAccount = ...;
...
try {
    Field balanceField = BankAccount.class.getField("balance");
    // read it
    int mybalance = balanceField.getInt( myBankAccount );
    // change it
    balanceField.setInt( myBankAccount, 42 );
} catch ( NoSuchFieldException e ) {
    ... // there is no "balance" field in this class
} catch ( IllegalAccessException e2) {
    ... // we don't have permission to access the field
}
```

In this example, we are assuming that we already know the structure of a `BankAccount` object. However the real power of reflection is in examining objects that we've never seen before.

The various methods of `Field` take a reference to the particular object instance that we want to access. In the code shown earlier, the `getField()` method returns a `Field` object that represents the `balance` of the `BankAccount` class; this object doesn't refer to any specific `BankAccount`. Therefore, to read or modify any specific `BankAccount`, we call `getInt()` and `setInt()` with a reference to `myBankAccount`, which is the particular account we want to work with. An exception occurs if we try to access to a field that doesn't exist, or if we don't have the proper permission to read or write to the field. If we make `balance` a `private` field, we can still look up the `Field` object that describes it, but we won't be able to read or write its value.

Therefore, we aren't doing anything that we couldn't have done with static code at compile time; as long as `balance` is a `public` member of a class that we can access, we can write code to read and modify its value. What's important is that we're accessing `balance` at runtime, and could use this technique to examine the `balance` field in a class that was dynamically loaded.

Accessing Methods

The class `java.lang.reflect.Method` represents a static or instance method. Subject to the normal security rules, a `Method` object's `invoke()` method can be used to call the underlying object's method with specified arguments. Yes, Java has something like a method pointer!

As an example, we'll write a Java application called `Invoke` that takes as command-line arguments the name of a Java class and the name of a method to invoke. For simplicity, we'll assume that the method is static and takes no arguments:

```
//file: Invoke.java
import java.lang.reflect.*;

class Invoke {
    public static void main( String [] args ) {
    try {
        Class c = Class.forName( args[0] );
        Method m = c.getMethod( args[1], new Class [] { } );
        Object ret =  m.invoke( null, null );
        System.out.println(
            "Invoked static method: " + args[1]
            + " of class: " + args[0]
            + " with no args\nResults: " + ret );
        } catch ( ClassNotFoundException e ) {
        // Class.forName() can't find the class
        } catch ( NoSuchMethodException e2 ) {
        // that method doesn't exist
        } catch ( IllegalAccessException e3 ) {
        // we don't have permission to invoke that method
        } catch ( InvocationTargetException e4 ) {
        // an exception occurred while invoking that method
        System.out.println(
            "Method threw an: " + e4.getTargetException() );
    }
  }
}
```

We can run `invoke` to fetch the value of the system clock:

```
% java Invoke java.lang.System currentTimeMillis
Invoked static method: currentTimeMillis of class:
java.lang.System with no args
Results: 861129235818
```

Our first task is to look up the specified `Class` by name. To do so, we call the `forName()` method with the name of the desired class (the first command-line argument). We then ask for the specified method by its name. `getMethod()` has two arguments: the first is the method name (the second command-line argument), and the second is an array of `Class` objects that specifies the method's signature. (Remember that any method may be overloaded; you must specify the signature to make it clear which version you want.) Since our simple program calls only methods with no arguments, we create an anonymous empty array of `Class` objects. Had we wanted to invoke a method that takes arguments, we would have passed an array of the classes of their respective types, in the proper order. For primitive types we would have used the necessary wrappers. The classes of primitive types are represented by the static `TYPE` fields of their respective wrappers; for example, use `Integer.TYPE` for the class of an `int`.

Once we have the `Method` object, we call its `invoke()` method. This calls our target method and returns the result as an `Object`. To do anything nontrivial with this object, you have to cast it to something more specific. Presumably, since you're calling the method, you know what kind of object to expect. If the returned value is a primitive type like `int` or `boolean`, it will be wrapped in the standard wrapper class for its type. (Wrappers for primitive types are discussed in Chapter 9, *Basic Utility Classes*.) If the method returns `void`, `invoke()` returns a `Void` object. This is the wrapper class that represents `void` return values.

The first argument to `invoke()` is the object on which we would like to invoke the method. If the method is static, there is no object, so we set the first argument to `null`. That's the case in our example. The second argument is an array of objects to be passed as arguments to the method. The types of these should match the types specified in the call to `getMethod()`. Because we're calling a method with no arguments, we can pass `null` for the second argument to `invoke()`. As with the return value, you must use wrapper classes for primitive argument types.

The exceptions shown in the previous code occur if we can't find or don't have permission to access the method. Additionally, an `InvocationTargetException` occurs if the method being invoked throws some kind of exception itself. You can find out what it threw by calling the `getTargetException()` method of `InvocationTargetException`.

Accessing Constructors

The `java.lang.reflect.Constructor` class represents an object constructor that accepts arguments. You can use it, subject to the security manager, to create a new instance of an object. (Recall that you can create instances of a class with `Class.newInstance()`, but you cannot specify arguments with that method.)

Here we'll create an instance of `java.util.Date`, passing a string argument to the constructor:

```
try {
    Constructor c =
        Date.class.getConstructor(new Class [] { String.class } );
```

```
        Object o = c.newInstance( new Object [] { "Jan 1, 2000" } );
        Date d = (Date)o;
        System.out.println(d);
    } catch ( NoSuchMethodException e ) {
        // getConstructor() couldn't find the constructor we described
    } catch ( InstantiationException e2 ) {
        // the class is abstract
    } catch ( IllegalAccessException e3 ) {
        // we don't have permission to create an instance
    } catch ( InvocationTargetException e4 ) {
        // the construct threw an exception
    }
```

The story is much the same as with a method invocation; after all, a constructor is really no more than a method with some strange properties. We look up the appropriate constructor for our Date class—the one that takes a single String as its argument—by passing getConstructor() an array containing the String class as its only element. (If the constructor required more arguments, we would put additional objects in the array, representing the class of each argument.) We can then invoke newInstance(), passing it a corresponding array of argument objects. Again, to pass primitive types, we would wrap them in their wrapper types first. Finally, we cast the resulting object to a Date and print it.

The exceptions from the previous example apply here, too, along with Illegal-ArgumentException and InstantiationException. The latter is thrown if the class is abstract, and so can't be instantiated.

What About Arrays?

The reflection API allows you to create and inspect arrays of base types using the java.lang.reflect.Array class. The process is very much the same as with the other classes, so we won't cover it here. For more information, look in your favorite Java language reference.

Dynamic Interface Adapters

Ideally, Java reflection would allow us to do everything at runtime that we can do at compile time (without forcing us to generate and compile source into byte-code). But prior to SDK 1.3, there was an important piece missing from the puzzle. Although we could dynamically load and create instances of objects at runtime using the Class.forName(), there was no way to create new types or implementations of objects—for which no class files pre-exist—on the fly.

In SDK 1.3, the java.lang.reflect.Proxy class takes a step towards solving this problem, by allowing the creation of adapter objects that implement arbitrary interfaces. The Proxy class is a factory that can generate an adapter class implementing any interface you want. When methods are invoked on the adapter class, they are delegated to a designated `InvocationHandler` object. You can use this to create implementations of any kind of interface at runtime and handle the method calls anywhere you want. This is particularly important for tools that work with JavaBeans, which must dynamically register event listeners. (We'll mention this again in Chapter 19, *Java Beans.*)

In the following snippet, we take an interface name and construct a proxy implementing the interface. It will output a message whenever any of the interface's methods is invoked.

```
import java.lang.reflect.*;

InvocationHandler handler =
  new InvocationHandler() {
    public Object
    invoke( Object proxy, Method method, Object[] args ) {
        System.out.println( "Method: "+ method.getName() +"()"
                          +" of interface: "+ interfaceName
                          + " invoked on proxy." );
        return null;
    }
  };

Class clas = Class.forName( interfaceName );

Object interfaceProxy =
    Proxy.newProxyInstance( clas.getClassLoader(),
                          new Class[] { clas }, handler );
```

The resulting object, `interfaceProxy`, can be cast to the type of the interface we specified in `interfaceName`. It will call our handler whenever any of its methods is called.

First we make an implementation of `InvocationHandler`. This is an object with an `invoke()` method that takes as its argument the `Method` being called and an array of objects representing the arguments to the method call. Then we fetch the class of the interface that we're going to implement using `Class.forName()`. Finally we ask the proxy to create an adapter for us, specifying the types of interfaces (you can specify more than one) that we want implemented and the handler to use. `invoke()` is expected to return an object of the correct type for the method call. If it returns the wrong type, a special runtime exception is thrown. Any primitive types in the arguments or in the return value should be wrapped in the appropriate wrapper class. (The runtime system unwraps the return value, if necessary.)

What Is Reflection Good for?

In Chapter 19, we'll learn how reflection is used to dynamically discover capabilities and features of Java Bean objects. But these are somewhat behind-the-scenes applications. What can reflection do for us in everyday situations?

Well, we could use reflection to go about acting as if Java had dynamic method invocation and other useful capabilities; in Chapter 19, we'll also develop a dynamic adapter class using reflection. But as a general coding practice, dynamic method invocation is a bad idea. One of the primary features of Java is its strong typing and safety. You abandon much of that when you take a dip in the reflecting pool.

More appropriately, you can use reflection in situations where you need to work with objects that you can't know about in advance. Reflection puts Java on a higher plane of programming languages, opening up possibilities for new kinds of applications. As we hinted earlier, one of the most important uses for reflection will be in integrating Java with scripting languages. With reflection, one could write a source code interpreter in Java that could access the full Java APIs, create objects, invoke methods, modify variables and do all of the other things that a Java program can do at compile time, while it is running. In fact someone has done this— one of the authors of this book!

The BeanShell application

Pat here . . . I can't resist inserting a plug here for BeanShell—my free, open source, light-weight Java scripting language. BeanShell is just what I alluded to in the previous section—a Java application that uses the reflection API to execute Java statements and expressions dynamically. You can use BeanShell interactively to quickly try out some of the examples in this book (although you can't create classes per se). BeanShell exercises the Java reflection API to its fullest and serves as a demonstration of how dynamic the Java runtime environment really is.

You can find a copy of BeanShell on the CD-ROM that accompanies this book, on the book's web page, *http://www.oreilly.com/catalog/learnjava*, or at *http://www. beanshell.org*. See Appendix B, *BeanShell: Simple Java Scripting*, for more information on getting started. I hope you find it both interesting and useful!

8

Threads

Threads have been around for some time, but few programmers have actually worked with them. There is even some debate over whether the average programmer *can* use threads effectively. In Java, working with threads can be easy and productive (at least for the most common cases). In fact, threads provide the only reasonable way to handle certain kinds of tasks. So it's important that you become familiar with threads early in your exploration of Java.

Threads are integral to the way Java works. For example, an applet's `paint()` method isn't called by the applet itself, but rather by another thread within the Java runtime system. At any given time, there may be many such background threads, performing activities in parallel with your application. In fact, it's easy to get half a dozen or more threads running in an applet without even trying, simply by requesting images, updating the screen, playing audio, and so on. But these things happen behind the scenes; you don't normally have to worry about them. In this chapter, we'll talk about writing applications that create and use their own threads explicitly.

Introducing Threads

Conceptually, a *thread* is a flow of control within a program. A thread is similar to the more familiar notion of a process, except that multiple threads within the same application share much of the same state—in particular, they run in the same address space. It's not unlike a golf course, which many golfers use at the same time. Sharing the same address space means that threads share instance variables but not local variables, just like players share the golf course but not personal things like clubs and balls.

188

Multiple threads in an application have the same problems as the golfers—in a word, *synchronization*. Just as you can't have two sets of players blindly playing the same green at the same time, you can't have several threads trying to access the same variables without some kind of coordination. Someone is bound to get hurt. A thread can reserve the right to use an object until it's finished with its task, just as a golf party gets exclusive rights to the green until it's done. And a thread that is more important can raise its priority, asserting its right to play through.

The devil is in the details, of course, and those details have historically made threads difficult to use. Java makes creating, controlling, and coordinating threads much simpler. When creating a new thread is the best way to accomplish some task, it should be as easy as adding a new component to your application.

It is common to stumble over threads when you first look at them, because creating a thread exercises many of your new Java skills all at once. You can avoid confusion by remembering there are always two players involved in running a thread: a Java language object that represents the thread itself and an arbitrary target object that contains the method that the thread is to execute. Later, you will see that it is possible to play some sleight of hand and combine these two roles, but that special case just changes the packaging, not the relationship.

The Thread Class and the Runnable Interface

A new thread is born when we create an instance of the `java.lang.Thread` class. The `Thread` object represents a real thread in the Java interpreter and serves as a handle for controlling and synchronizing its execution. With it, we can start the thread, stop the thread, or suspend it temporarily. The constructor for the `Thread` class accepts information about where the thread should begin its execution. Conceptually, we would like to simply tell it what method to run, but since there are no pointers to methods in Java, we can't specify one directly. Instead, we have to take a short detour and use the `java.lang.Runnable` interface to create an object that contains a "runnable" method. Runnable defines a single, general-purpose method:

```
public interface Runnable {
    abstract public void run();
}
```

Every thread begins its life by executing the `run()` method in the `Runnable` object (the "target object") that was passed to the thread. The `run()` method can contain any code, but it must be public, take no arguments, have no return value, and throw no exceptions.

Any class that contains an appropriate `run()` method can declare that it implements the `Runnable` interface. An instance of this class is then a runnable object

that can serve as the target of a new Thread. If you don't want to put the run()
method directly in your object (and very often you don't), you can always make an
adapter class that serves as the Runnable for you. The adapter's run() method
can call any method it wants to after the thread is started.

Creating and starting threads

A newly born Thread remains idle until we give it a figurative slap on the bottom
by calling its start() method. The thread then wakes up and proceeds to execute the run() method of its target object. start() can be called only once in
the lifetime of a Thread. Once a thread starts, it continues running until the target object's run() method returns. The start() method has a sort of evil twin
method called stop(), which kills the thread permanently. However, this method
is deprecated and should no longer be used. We'll explain why and give some
examples of a better way to stop your threads later in this chapter. We will also
look at some other methods you can use to control a thread's progress while it is
running.

Now let's look at an example. The following class, Animation, implements a run()
method to drive its drawing loop:

```
class Animation implements Runnable {
    ...
    public void run() {
        while ( true ) {
            // draw Frames
            ...
        }
    }
}
```

To use it, we create a Thread object, passing it an instance of Animation as its target object, and invoke its start() method. We can perform these steps explicitly:

```
Animation happy = new Animation("Mr. Happy");
Thread myThread = new Thread( happy );
myThread.start();
```

Here we have created an instance of our Animation class and passed it as the
argument to the constructor for myThread. When we call the start() method,
myThread begins to execute Animation's run() method. Let the show begin!

This situation is not terribly object-oriented. More often, we want an object to handle its own threads, as shown in Figure 8-1, which depicts a Runnable object that
creates and starts its own Thread. We'll show our Animation class performing
these actions in its constructor, although in practice it might be better to place
them in a more explicit controller method (e.g., startAnimation()):

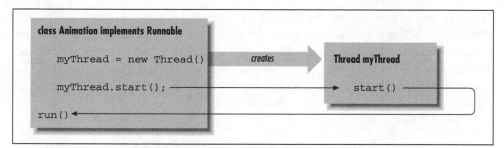

Figure 8-1. Interaction between Animation and its thread

```
class Animation implements Runnable {
    Thread myThread;
    Animation (String name) {
        myThread = new Thread( this );
        myThread.start();
    }
    ...
}
```

In this case, the argument we pass to the Thread constructor is this, the current object (which is a Runnable). We keep the Thread reference in the instance variable myThread, in case we want to interrupt the show or exercise some other kind of control later.

The Runnable interface lets us make an arbitrary object the target of a thread, as we did earlier. This is the most important general usage of the Thread class. In most situations in which you need to use threads, you'll create a class (possibly a simple adapter class) that implements the Runnable interface.

A natural-born thread

We'd be remiss not to show you the other technique for creating a thread. Another design option is to make our target class a subclass of a type that is already runnable. As it turns out, the Thread class itself conveniently implements the Runnable interface; it has its own run() method, which we can override directly to do our bidding:

```
class Animation extends Thread {
    ...
    public void run() {
        while (true ) {
            // draw Frames
            ...
        }
    }
}
```

The skeleton of our `Animation` class looks much the same as before, except that our class is now a subclass of `Thread`. To go along with this scheme, the default constructor of the `Thread` class makes itself the default target. That is, by default, the `Thread` executes its own `run()` method when we call the `start()` method, as shown in Figure 8-2. So now our subclass can just override the `run()` method in the `Thread` class. (`Thread` itself defines an empty `run()` method.)

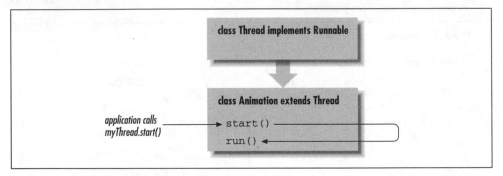

Figure 8-2. Animation as a subclass of Thread

Now we create an instance of `Animation` and call its `start()` method (which it also inherited from `Thread`):

```
Animation bouncy = new Animation("Bouncy");
bouncy.start();
```

Alternatively, we can have the `Animation` object start its thread when it is created, as before:

```
class Animation extends Thread {
    ...
    Animation (String name) {
        start();
    }
    ...
}
```

Here our `Animation` object just calls its own `start()` method when an instance is created. (Again, it's probably better form to start and stop our objects explicitly after they're created, rather than starting threads as a hidden side effect of object creation.)

Subclassing `Thread` seems like a convenient way to bundle a `Thread` and its target `run()` method. However, this approach often isn't the best design. If you subclass `Thread` to implement a thread, you are saying you need a new type of object that is a kind of `Thread`. While there is something unnaturally satisfying about taking an object that's primarily concerned with performing a task and making it a `Thread`, the actual situations where you'll want to create a subclass of `Thread` should not be very common. In most cases, it will be more natural to let the requirements of your program dictate the class structure. If you find you're subclassing Thread left and right, you may want to examine whether you are falling into the design trap of making objects that are simply glorified functions.

Using an adapter

Finally, as we have suggested, we can build an adapter class to give us more control over how to structure the code. It is particularly convenient to create an anonymous inner class that implements Runnable and invokes an arbitrary method in our object. This almost gives the feel of starting a thread and specifying an arbitrary method to run, as if we had method pointers. For example, suppose that our Animation class provides a method called startAnimating(), which performs setup (loads the images, etc.) and then starts a thread to perform the animation. We'll say that the actual guts of the animation loop are in a private method called drawFrames(). We could use an adapter to run drawFrames() for us:

```
class Animation {

    public void startAnimating() {
        // do setup, load images, etc.
        ...

        // start a drawing thread
        myThread = new Thread ( new Runnable() {
            public void run() { drawFrames(); }
        } );
        myThread.start();
    }

    private void drawFrames() {
        // do animation ...
    }
}
```

In this code, the anonymous inner class implementing Runnable is generated for us by the compiler. We create a Thread with this anonymous object as its target and have its run() method call our drawFrames() method. We have avoided implementing a generic run() method in our application code, but at the expense of generating an extra class.

Note that we could be a bit more terse in the previous example by simply having our anonymous inner class extend Thread rather than implement Runnable:

```
myThread = new Thread() {
    public void run() { drawFrames(); }
};
myThread.start();
```

Controlling Threads

We have seen the start() method used to bring a newly created Thread to life. Several other instance methods let us explicitly control a Thread's execution:

- The sleep() method causes the current thread to wait for a designated period of time, without consuming much (if any) CPU time.

- The interrupt() method wakes up a thread that is sleeping or is otherwise blocked on a long I/O operation.*

- The methods wait() and join() coordinate the execution of two or more threads. We'll discuss them in detail when we talk about thread synchronization later in this chapter.

Deprecated methods

We should also mention that there are three deprecated thread control methods: stop(), suspend(), and resume(). The stop() method complements start(); it destroys the thread. start(), and the deprecated stop() method can be called only once in the life cycle of a Thread. By contrast, the deprecated suspend() and resume() methods were used to arbitrarily pause and then restart the execution of a Thread.

Although these deprecated methods still exist in the latest version of Java, they shouldn't be used in new code development. The problem with both stop() and suspend() is that they seize control of a thread's execution in an uncoordinated and harsh way. This make programming difficult—it's not always easy for an application to anticipate and properly recover from being interrupted at an arbitrary point in its execution. Moreover, when a thread is seized using one of these methods, the Java runtime system must release all of its internal locks used for thread synchronization. This can cause unexpected behavior and, in the case of suspend(), can lead to deadlock situations.

A better way to affect the execution of a thread—which requires just a bit more work on your part—is by creating some simple logic in your thread's code using monitor variables (flags), possibly in conjunction with the interrupt() method, which allows you to wake up a sleeping thread. In other words, you should cause your thread to stop or resume what it is doing by asking it to nicely, rather than by pulling the rug out from under it unexpectedly. The thread examples in this book will use this technique in one way or another.

---

* interrupt() does not work in versions of Java prior to 1.1.

The sleep( ) method

We often need to tell a thread to sit idle, or "sleep," for a fixed period of time. While a thread is asleep, or otherwise blocked on input of some kind, it shouldn't consume CPU time or compete with other threads for processing. For this, we can either call the thread's `sleep()` instance method or use the static convenience method `Thread.sleep()`. Either way, the call causes the currently executing thread to delay for a specified number of milliseconds:

```
try {
    // static convenience method
    Thread.sleep( 1000 );
    // instance method
    sleep( 500 );
}
catch ( InterruptedException e ) {
    // someone woke us up prematurely
}
```

In either case, `sleep()` throws an `InterruptedException` if it is interrupted by another Thread via its `interrupt()` method. As you see in the previous code, the thread can catch this exception and take the opportunity to perform some action—such as checking a variable to determine whether or not it should exit—or perhaps just perform some housekeeping and then go back to sleep.

The join( ) method

Finally, if you need to coordinate your activities with another thread by waiting for the other thread to complete its task, you can use the `join()` method. Calling a thread's `join()` method causes the caller to block until the target thread dies. Alternatively, you can poll the thread by calling `join()` with a number of milliseconds to wait. This is a very coarse form of thread synchronization. Later in this chapter, we'll look at a much more general and powerful mechanism for coordinating the activities of threads: `wait()` and `notify()`.

A Thread's Life

A thread continues to execute until one of the following things happens:

- It explicitly returns from its target `run()` method.

- It encounters an uncaught runtime exception.

- The evil and nasty deprecated `stop()` method is called.

So what happens if none of these things occurs and the `run()` method for a thread never terminates? The answer is that the thread can live on, even after what is ostensibly the part of the application that created it has finished. This means we have to be aware of how our threads eventually terminate, or an application can end up leaving orphaned threads that unnecessarily consume resources.

In many cases, we really want to create background threads that do simple, periodic tasks in an application. The `setDaemon()` method can be used to mark a Thread as a daemon thread that should be killed and discarded when no other application threads remain. Normally, the Java interpreter continues to run until all threads have completed. But when daemon threads are the only threads still alive, the interpreter will exit.

Here's a devilish example using daemon threads:

```
class Devil extends Thread {
    Devil() {
        setDaemon( true );
        start();
    }

    public void run() {
        // perform evil tasks
    }
}
```

In this example, the `Devil` thread sets its daemon status when it is created. If any `Devil` threads remain when our application is otherwise complete, the runtime system kills them for us. We don't have to worry about cleaning them up.

Daemon threads are primarily useful in standalone Java applications and in the implementation of the Java runtime system itself, but not in applets. Since an applet runs inside of another Java application, any daemon threads it creates could continue to live until the controlling application exits—probably not the desired effect. A browser or any other application can use `ThreadGroups` to contain all of the threads created by subsystems of an application and then clean them up if necessary.

Threads in Applets

Applets are embeddable Java applications that are expected to be able to start and stop themselves on command. Applets may be asked to start and stop themselves any number of times. A Java-enabled web browser normally starts an applet when the applet is displayed and stops it when the user moves to another page or (in theory) when the user scrolls the applet out of view. To conform to the semantics of the API, we would like an applet to cease its nonessential activity when it is stopped and resume it when started again. (If you're not familiar with applets, you may want to take a look at Chapter 20, *Applets*, at this point.)

In this section, we will build `UpdateApplet`, a simple base class for an applet that maintains a thread to automatically update its display at regular intervals. Although we're building an applet here, the general technique is important for all threaded applications.

`UpdateApplet` handles the basic starting and stopping behavior for us:

```
//file: UpdateApplet.java
public class UpdateApplet extends java.applet.Applet
    implements Runnable {

    private Thread updateThread;
    int updateInterval = 1000;

    public void run() {
        while ( updateThread != null ) {
            try {
                Thread.sleep( updateInterval );
            }
            catch (InterruptedException e ) {
                return;
            }
            repaint();
        }
    }

    public void start() {
        if ( updateThread == null ) {
            updateThread = new Thread(this);
            updateThread.start();
        }
    }

    public void stop() {
        if ( updateThread != null ) {
            Thread runner = updateThread;
            updateThread = null;  // flag to quit
            runner.interrupt();   // wake up if asleep
        }
    }
}
```

`UpdateApplet` is a `Runnable` object that alternately sleeps and calls its `repaint()` method. (There's nothing to paint, though, so running this applet is kind of boring. Later in this section, we'll subclass it to implement a digital clock.) It has two other public methods: `start()` and `stop()`. These are methods of the `Applet` class we are overriding; don't confuse them with the similarly named methods of the `Thread` class. These `start()` and `stop()` methods are called by the Java runtime system, to tell the applet when it should and should not be running.

UpdateApplet illustrates an environmentally friendly way to deal with threads in a simple applet. UpdateApplet effectively kills its thread each time the applet is stopped and recreates it if the applet is restarted. When UpdateApplet's start() method is called, we first check to make sure there is no currently executing updateThread. We then create one to begin our execution. When our applet is subsequently asked to stop, we set a flag indicating that it should stop and then make sure it is awake by invoking its interrupt() method. In our stop() method, we set updateThread to null, which serves three purposes: it allows the garbage collector to clean up the dead Thread object; it indicates to Update-Applet's start() method that the thread is gone, so that another one can be started when necessary; and we use it as the flag to indicate to the running thread that it is time to quit. If you feel that we have overburdened this variable, you might consider using a separate boolean variable for the flag condition.

One thing about Applets: in truth, an Applet's start() and stop() methods are guaranteed to be called in sequence. As a result, we shouldn't have to check for the existence of updateThread in start(). (It should always be null.) However, it's good programming practice to perform the test. If we didn't, and for some reason stop() were to fail at its job, we might inadvertently start a lot of threads.

With UpdateApplet doing all of the work for us, we can now create the world's simplest clock applet with just a few lines of code. Figure 8-3 shows our Clock. (This might be a good one to run on your Java wristwatch.)

```
//file: Clock.java
public class Clock extends UpdateApplet {
    public void paint( java.awt.Graphics g ) {
        g.drawString( new java.util.Date().toString(), 10, 25 );
    }
}
```

```
Sat Apr 22 09:37:51 MDT 2000
```

Figure 8-3. The Clock applet

The java.util.Date().toString() method creates a string that contains the current time.

Our Clock applet provides a good example of a simple thread; we don't mind throwing it away and subsequently rebuilding it if the user should happen to wander on and off of our web page a few times. But what if the task that our thread handles isn't so simple? What if, for instance, we have to open a socket and establish a connection with another system? One solution is to use Thread's suspend() and resume() methods, as we'll show you in a moment.

Now if you're concerned about being so cavalier in creating and discarding Thread objects, you might rightly ask if we couldn't simply do a little more logic and save our thread. Perhaps we could teach the start() method to have the existing thread begin again., rather than having to create a new thread. It should be apparent how to go about this using the wait() and notify() methods after you read the next section on thread synchronization.

However, an issue with applets is that we have no control over how a user navigates web pages. For example, say a user scrolls our applet out of view, and we pause our thread. Now we have no way of ensuring that the user will bring the applet back into view before moving on to another page. And actually, the same situation would occur if the user simply moves on to another page and never comes back. That's not a problem in this simple example, but there may be cases in which we need to do some application cleanup before we die. For this situation the Applet API gives us the destroy() method. destroy() is called by the Java runtime system when the applet is going to be removed (often from a cache). It provides a place at which we can free up any resources the applet is holding.

Synchronization

Every thread has a life of its own. Normally, a thread goes about its business without any regard for what other threads in the application are doing. Threads may be time-sliced, which means they can run in arbitrary spurts and bursts as directed by the operating system. On a multiprocessor system, it is even possible for many different threads to be running simultaneously on different CPUs. This section is about coordinating the activities of two or more threads, so they can work together and not collide in their use of the same address space.

Java provides a few simple structures for synchronizing the activities of threads. They are all based on the concept of monitors, a widely used synchronization scheme developed by C.A.R. Hoare. You don't have to know the details about how monitors work to be able to use them, but it may help you to have a picture in mind.

A monitor is essentially a lock. The lock is attached to a resource that many threads may need to access, but that should be accessed by only one thread at a time. It's not unlike a restroom with a door that locks. If the resource is not being used, the thread can acquire the lock and access the resource. By the same token, if the restroom is unlocked, you can enter and lock the door. When the thread is done, it relinquishes the lock, just as you unlock the door and leave it open for the next person. However, if another thread already has the lock for the resource, all other threads have to wait until the current thread finishes and releases the lock. This is just like when the restroom is locked when you arrive: you have to wait until the current occupant is done and unlocks the door.

Fortunately, Java makes the process of synchronizing access to resources quite easy. The language handles setting up and acquiring locks; all you have to do is specify which resources require locks.

Serializing Access to Methods

The most common need for synchronization among threads in Java is to serialize their access to some resource (an object)—in other words, to make sure that only one thread at a time can manipulate an object or variable.* In Java, every object has a lock associated with it. To be more specific, every class and every instance of a class has its own lock. The synchronized keyword marks places where a thread must acquire the lock before proceeding.

For example, say we implemented a SpeechSynthesizer class that contains a say() method. We don't want multiple threads calling say() at the same time or we wouldn't be able to understand anything being said. So we mark the say() method as synchronized, which means that a thread has to acquire the lock on the SpeechSynthesizer object before it can speak:

```
class SpeechSynthesizer {
    synchronized void say( String words ) {
        // speak
    }
}
```

Because say() is an instance method, a thread has to acquire the lock on the particular SpeechSynthesizer instance it is using before it can invoke the say() method. When say() has completed, it gives up the lock, which allows the next waiting thread to acquire the lock and run the method. Note that it doesn't matter whether the thread is owned by the SpeechSynthesizer itself or some other object; every thread has to acquire the same lock, that of the SpeechSynthesizer instance. If say() were a class (static) method instead of an instance method, we could still mark it as synchronized. But in this case as there is no instance object involved, the lock would be on the class object itself.

Often, you want to synchronize multiple methods of the same class, so that only one of the methods modifies or examines parts of the class at a time. All static syn-

---

* Don't confuse the term "serialize" in this context with Java object serialization, which is a mechanism for making objects persistent. But the underlying meaning (to place one thing after another) does apply to both. In the case of object serialization, it is the object's data which is laid out, byte for byte, in a certain order.

chronized methods in a class use the same class object lock. By the same token, all instance methods in a class use the same instance object lock. In this way, Java can guarantee that only one of a set of synchronized methods is running at a time. For example, a `SpreadSheet` class might contain a number of instance variables that represent cell values, as well as some methods that manipulate the cells in a row:

```
class SpreadSheet {

    int cellA1, cellA2, cellA3;

    synchronized int sumRow() {
        return cellA1 + cellA2 + cellA3;
    }

    synchronized void setRow( int a1, int a2, int a3 ) {
        cellA1 = a1;
        cellA2 = a2;
        cellA3 = a3;
    }
    ...
}
```

In this example, both methods `setRow()` and `sumRow()` access the cell values. You can see that problems might arise if one thread were changing the values of the variables in `setRow()` at the same moment another thread were reading the values in `sumRow()`. To prevent this, we have marked both methods as `synchronized`. When threads are synchronized, only one will be run at a time. If a thread is in the middle of executing `setRow()` when another thread calls `sumRow()`, the second thread waits until the first one is done executing `setRow()` before it gets to run `sumRow()`. This synchronization allows us to preserve the consistency of the `SpreadSheet`. And the best part is that all of this locking and waiting is handled by Java; it's transparent to the programmer.

In addition to synchronizing entire methods, the `synchronized` keyword can be used in a special construct to guard arbitrary blocks of code. In this form it also takes an explicit argument that specifies the object for which it is to acquire a lock:

```
synchronized ( myObject ) {
    // Functionality that needs to be synced
}
```

This code block can appear in any method. When it is reached, the thread has to acquire the lock on `myObject` before proceeding. In this way, we can synchronize methods (or parts of methods) in different classes in the same way as methods in the same class.

A synchronized instance method is, therefore, equivalent to a method with its statements synchronized on the current object. Thus:

```
synchronized void myMethod () {
    ...
}
```

is equivalent to:

```
void myMethod () {
    synchronized ( this ) {
        ...
    }
}
```

Accessing instance variables

In the SpreadSheet example, we guarded access to a set of instance variables with a synchronized method, which we did mainly so that we wouldn't change one of the variables while someone was reading the rest of them. We wanted to keep them coordinated. But what about individual variable types? Do they need to be synchronized? Normally the answer is no. Almost all operations on primitives and object reference types in Java happen "atomically": they are handled by the virtual machine in one step, with no opportunity for two threads to collide. You can't be in the middle of changing a reference and be only "part way" done when another thread looks at the reference.

But watch out—we did say "almost." If you read the Java virtual machine specification carefully, you will see that the double and long primitive types are not guaranteed to be handled atomically. Both of these types represent 64-bit values. The problem has to do with how the Java Virtual Machine's stack handles them. It is possible that this specification will be beefed up in the future. But for now, if you have any fears, synchronize access to your double and long instance variables through accessor methods.

The wait() and notify() Methods

With the synchronized keyword, we can serialize the execution of complete methods and blocks of code. The wait() and notify() methods of the Object class extend this capability. Every object in Java is a subclass of Object, so every object inherits these methods. By using wait() and notify(), a thread can effectively give up its hold on a lock at an arbitrary point and then wait for another thread to give it back before continuing.* All of the coordinated activity still

---

* In actuality, they don't really pass the lock around; the lock becomes available and, as we'll describe, a thread that is scheduled to run acquires it.

happens inside of synchronized blocks, and still only one thread is executing at a given time.

By executing `wait()` from a synchronized block, a thread gives up its hold on the lock and goes to sleep. A thread might do this if it needs to wait for something to happen in another part of the application, as we'll see shortly. Later, when the necessary event happens, the thread that is running it calls `notify()` from a block synchronized on the same object. Now the first thread wakes up and begins trying to acquire the lock again.

When the first thread manages to reacquire the lock, it continues from the point it left off. However, the thread that waited may not get the lock immediately (or perhaps ever). It depends on when the second thread eventually releases the lock and which thread manages to snag it next. Note also that the first thread won't wake up from the `wait()` unless another thread calls `notify()`. There is an overloaded version of `wait()`, however, that allows us to specify a timeout period. If another thread doesn't call `notify()` in the specified period, the waiting thread automatically wakes up.

Let's look at a simple scenario to see what's going on. In the following example, we'll assume there are three threads—one waiting to execute each of the three synchronized methods of the `MyThing` class. We'll call them the *waiter, notifier,* and *related* threads. Here's a code fragment to illustrate:

```
class MyThing {
    synchronized void waiterMethod() {
        // do some stuff
        wait();        // now wait for notifier to do something
        // continue where we left off
    }

    synchronized void notifierMethod() {
        // do some stuff
        notify();    // notify waiter that we've done it
        // do more things
    }

    synchronized void relatedMethod() {
        // do some related stuff
    }
    ...
}
```

Let's assume *waiter* gets through the gate first and begins executing `waiter-Method()`. The two other threads are initially blocked, trying to acquire the lock for the `MyThing` object. When waiter executes the `wait()` method, it relinquishes its hold on the lock and goes to sleep. Now there are now two viable threads waiting for the lock. Which thread gets it depends on several factors, including chance and the priorities of the threads. (We'll discuss thread scheduling in the next section.)

Let's say that *notifier* is the next thread to acquire the lock, so it begins to run `notifierMethod()`. *waiter* continues to sleep and *related* languishes, waiting for its turn. When *notifier* executes the call to `notify()`, the runtime system prods the *waiter* thread, effectively telling it something has changed. *waiter* then wakes up and rejoins *related* in vying for the `MyThing` lock. Note that it doesn't receive the lock automatically; it just changes from saying "leave me alone" to "I want the lock."

At this point, *notifier* still owns the lock and continues to hold it until the synchronized `notifierMethod()` returns—or perhaps executes a `wait()` itself. At that point, the other two methods get to fight over the lock. *waiter* would like to continue executing `waiterMethod()` from the point it left off, while *related*, which has been patient, would like to get started. We'll let you choose your own ending for the story.

For each call to `notify()`, the runtime system wakes up just one method that is asleep in a `wait()` call. If there are multiple threads waiting, Java picks a thread on an arbitrary basis, which may be implementation-dependent. The `Object` class also provides a `notifyAll()` call to wake up all waiting threads. In most cases, you'll probably want to use `notifyAll()` rather than `notify()`. Keep in mind that `notify()` really means "Hey, something related to this object has changed. The condition you are waiting for may have changed, so check it again." In general, there is no reason to assume only one thread at a time is interested in the change or able to act upon it. Different threads might look upon whatever has changed in different ways.

Often, our *waiter* thread is waiting for a particular condition to change and we will want to sit in a loop like the following:

```
while ( condition != true )
    wait();
```

Other synchronized threads call `notify()` or `notifyAll()` when they have modified the environment so that *waiter* can check the condition again. Using "wait conditions" like this is the civilized alternative to polling and sleeping, as you'll see in the following section.

Passing Messages

Now we'll illustrate a classic interaction between two threads: a `Producer` and a `Consumer`. A producer thread creates messages and places them into a queue, while a consumer reads them out and displays them. To be realistic, we'll give the queue a maximum depth. And to make things really interesting, we'll have our

consumer thread be lazy and run much more slowly than the producer. This
means that Producer occasionally has to stop and wait for Consumer to catch up.
Here are the Producer and Consumer classes:

```
//file: Consumer.java
import java.util.Vector;

class Producer extends Thread {
    static final int MAXQUEUE = 5;
    private Vector messages = new Vector();

    public void run() {
        try {
            while ( true ) {
                putMessage();
                sleep( 1000 );
            }
        }
        catch( InterruptedException e ) { }
    }

    private synchronized void putMessage()
      throws InterruptedException {

        while ( messages.size() == MAXQUEUE )
            wait();
        messages.addElement( new java.util.Date().toString() );
        notify();
    }

    // called by Consumer
    public synchronized String getMessage()
      throws InterruptedException {
        notify();
        while ( messages.size() == 0 )
            wait();
        String message = (String)messages.firstElement();
        messages.removeElement( message );
        return message;
    }
} // end of class Producer

public class Consumer extends Thread {
    Producer producer;

    Consumer(Producer p) {
        producer = p;
    }
```

```
        public void run() {
            try {
                while ( true ) {
                    String message = producer.getMessage();
                    System.out.println("Got message: " + message);
                    sleep( 2000 );
                }
            }
            catch( InterruptedException e ) { }
        }

        public static void main(String args[]) {
            Producer producer = new Producer();

            producer.start();
            new Consumer( producer ).start();
        }
    }
```

For convenience, we have included a main() method in the Consumer class that
runs the complete example. It creates a Consumer that is tied to a Producer and
starts the two classes. You can run the example as follows:

```
% java Consumer
```

The output is the timestamp messages created by the Producer:

```
Got message: Sun Dec 19 03:35:55 CST 1999
Got message: Sun Dec 19 03:35:56 CST 1999
Got message: Sun Dec 19 03:35:57 CST 1999
...
```

The timestamps initially show a spacing of one second, although they appear every
two seconds. Our Producer runs faster than our Consumer. Producer would like
to generate a new message every second, while Consumer gets around to reading
and displaying a message only every two seconds. Can you see how long it will take
the message queue to fill up? What will happen when it does?

Let's look at the code. We are using a few new tools here. Producer and
Consumer are subclasses of Thread. It would have been a better design decision to
have Producer and Consumer implement the Runnable interface, but we took
the slightly easier path and subclassed Thread. You should find it fairly simple to
use the other technique; you might try it as an exercise.

The Producer and Consumer classes pass messages through an instance of a
java.util.Vector object. We haven't discussed the Vector class yet. Think of
this one as a queue: we add and remove elements in first-in, first-out order.

The important activity is in the synchronized methods: putMessage() and
getMessage(). Although one of the methods is used by the Producer thread and

the other by the `Consumer` thread, they both live in the `Producer` class so that we can coordinate them simply by declaring them `synchronized`. Here they both implicitly use the `Producer` object's lock. If the queue is empty, the `Consumer` blocks in a call in the `Producer`, waiting for another message.

Another design option would implement the `getMessage()` method in the `Consumer` class and use a `synchronized` code block to synchronize explicitly on the `Producer` object. In either case, synchronizing on the `Producer` enables us to have multiple `Consumer` objects that feed on the same `Producer`. We'll do that later in this section.

`putMessage()`'s job is to add a new message to the queue. It can't do this if the queue is already full, so it first checks the number of elements in `messages`. If there is room, it stuffs in another timestamp message. If the queue is at its limit, however, `putMessage()` has to wait until there's space. In this situation, `putMessage()` executes a `wait()` and relies on the consumer to call `notify()` to wake it up after a message has been read. Here we have `putMessage()` testing the condition in a loop. In this simple example, the test probably isn't necessary; we could assume that when `putMessage()` wakes up, there is a free spot. However, this test is another example of good programming practice. Before it finishes, `putMessage()` calls `notify()` itself to prod any `Consumer` that might be waiting on an empty queue.

`getMessage()` retrieves a message for the `Consumer`. It enters a loop like that of `putMessage()`, waiting for the queue to have at least one element before proceeding. If the queue is empty, it executes a `wait()` and expects the `Producer` to call `notify()` when more items are available. Notice that `getMessage()` makes its own unconditional call to `notify()`. This is a somewhat lazy way of keeping the `Producer` on its toes, so that the queue should generally be full. Alternatively, `getMessage()` might test to see if the queue had fallen below a low-water mark before waking up the producer.

Now let's add another consumer to the scenario, just to make things really interesting. Most of the necessary changes are in the `Consumer` class; here's the code for the modified class, now called `NamedConsumer`:

```
//file: NamedConsumer.java
public class NamedConsumer extends Thread {
    Producer producer;
    String name;

    NamedConsumer(String name, Producer producer) {
        this.producer = producer;
        this.name = name;
    }
```

```
    public void run() {
        try {
            while ( true ) {
                String message = producer.getMessage();
                System.out.println(name + " got message: " + message);
                sleep( 2000 );
            }
        }
        catch( InterruptedException e ) { }
    }

    public static void main(String args[]) {
        Producer producer = new Producer();
        producer.start();

        // start two this time
        new NamedConsumer( "One", producer ).start();
        new NamedConsumer( "Two", producer ).start();
    }
}
```

The NamedConsumer constructor takes a string name, to identify each consumer. The run() method uses this name in the call to println() to identify which consumer received the message.

The only required modification to the Producer code is to change the notify() calls to notifyAll() calls in putMessage() and getMessage(). (We could have used notifyAll() in the first place.) Now, instead of the consumer and producer playing tag with the queue, we can have many players waiting on the condition of the queue to change. We might have a number of consumers waiting for a message, or we might have the producer waiting for a consumer to take a message. Whenever the condition of the queue changes, we prod all of the waiting methods to reevaluate the situation by calling notifyAll().

Here is some sample output when there are two NamedConsumers running, as in the main() method shown previously:

```
One got message: Sat Mar 20 20:00:01 CST 1999
Two got message: Sat Mar 20 20:00:02 CST 1999
One got message: Sat Mar 20 20:00:03 CST 1999
Two got message: Sat Mar 20 20:00:04 CST 1999
One got message: Sat Mar 20 20:00:05 CST 1999
Two got message: Sat Mar 20 20:00:06 CST 1999
One got message: Sat Mar 20 20:00:07 CST 1999
Two got message: Sat Mar 20 20:00:08 CST 1999
...
```

We see nice, orderly alternation between the two consumers, as a result of the calls to sleep() in the various methods. Interesting things would happen, however, if we were to remove all of the calls to `sleep()` and let things run at full speed. The threads would compete and their behavior would depend on whether the system is using time-slicing. On a time-sliced system, there should be a fairly random distribution between the two consumers, while on a nontime-sliced system, a single consumer could monopolize the messages. And since you're probably wondering about time-slicing, let's talk about thread priority and scheduling.

Scheduling and Priority

Java makes few guarantees about how it schedules threads. Almost all of Java's thread scheduling is left up to the Java implementation and, to some degree, the application. Although it might have made sense (and would certainly have made many developers happier) if Java's developers had specified a scheduling algorithm, a single scheduling algorithm isn't necessarily suitable for all of the roles that Java can play. Instead, Sun decided to put the burden on you to write robust code that works whatever the scheduling algorithm, and let the implementation tune the algorithm for whatever is best.

Therefore, the priority rules that we'll describe next are carefully worded in the Java language specification to be a general guideline for thread scheduling. You should be able to rely on this behavior overall (statistically), but it is not a good idea to write code that relies on very specific features of the scheduler to work properly. You should instead use the control and synchronization tools that we have described in this chapter to coordinate your threads.[*]

Every thread has a priority value. If at any time a thread of a higher priority than the current thread becomes runnable, it preempts the lower-priority thread and begins executing. By default, threads at the same priority are scheduled round-robin, which means once a thread starts to run, it continues until it does one of the following:

- Sleeps, by calling `Thread.sleep()` or `wait()`

- Waits for a lock, in order to run a `synchronized` method

- Blocks on I/O, for example, in a `read()` or `accept()` call

- Explicitly yields control, by calling `yield()`

- Terminates, by completing its target method or with a `stop()` call (deprecated)

This situation looks something like Figure 8-4.

---

[*] *Java Threads*, by Scott Oaks and Henry Wong (O'Reilly & Associates), includes a detailed discussion of synchronization, scheduling, and other thread-related issues.

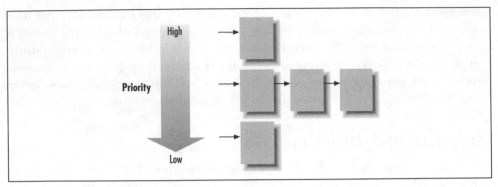

Figure 8-4. Priority preemptive, round-robin scheduling

Time-Slicing

In addition to prioritization, many systems implement time-slicing of threads.* In a time-sliced system, thread processing is chopped up, so that each thread runs for a short period of time before the context is switched to the next thread, as shown in Figure 8-5.

Higher-priority threads still preempt lower-priority threads in this scheme. The addition of time-slicing mixes up the processing among threads of the same priority; on a multiprocessor machine, threads may even be run simultaneously. This can introduce a difference in behavior for applications that don't use threads and synchronization properly.

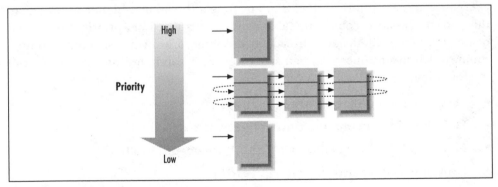

Figure 8-5. Priority preemptive, time-sliced scheduling

Since Java doesn't guarantee time-slicing, you shouldn't write code that relies on this type of scheduling; any software you write needs to function under the default

---

* As of Java Release 1.0, Sun's Java Interpreter for Windows uses time-slicing, as does the Netscape Navigator Java environment. Sun's Java 1.0 for the Solaris Unix platforms doesn't.

round-robin scheduling. If you're wondering what your particular flavor of Java does, try the following experiment:

```java
//file: Thready.java
public class Thready {
    public static void main( String args [] ) {
        new MyThread("Foo").start();
        new MyThread("Bar").start();
    }
} // end of class Thready

class MyThread extends Thread {
    String message;

    MyThread ( String message ) {
        this.message = message;
    }

    public void run() {
        while ( true )
            System.out.println( message );
    }
}
```

The Thready class starts up two MyThread objects. Thready is a thread that goes into a hard loop (very bad form) and prints its message. Since we don't specify a priority for either thread, they both inherit the priority of their creator, so they have the same priority. When you run this example, you will see how your Java implementation does its scheduling. Under a round-robin scheme, only "Foo" should be printed; "Bar" never appears. In a time-slicing implementation, you should occasionally see the "Foo" and "Bar" messages alternate.

Priorities

Now let's change the priority of the second thread:

```java
class Thready {
    public static void main( String args [] ) {
        new MyThread("Foo").start();
        Thread bar = new MyThread("Bar");
        bar.setPriority( Thread.NORM_PRIORITY + 1 );
        bar.start();
    }
}
```

As you might expect, this changes how our example behaves. Now you may see a few "Foo" messages, but "Bar" should quickly take over and not relinquish control, regardless of the scheduling policy.

Here we have used the setPriority() method of the Thread class to adjust our thread's priority. The Thread class defines three standard priority values (they're integers): MIN_PRIORITY, NORM_PRIORITY, and MAX_PRIORITY.

If you need to change the priority of a thread, you should use one of these values, possibly with a small increment or decrement. Avoid using values near MAX_PRIORITY; if you elevate many threads to this priority level, priority will quickly become meaningless. A slight increase in priority should be enough for most needs. For example, specifying NORM_PRIORITY + 1 in our example is enough to beat out our other thread.

We should also note that in an applet environment you may not have access to maximum priority because you're limited by the maximum priority of the thread group in which you were created (see "Thread Groups" later in this chapter).

User-Controlled Time-Slicing

There is a rough technique that you can use to get the effect similar to time-slicing in a Java application, even if the Java runtime system does not support it directly. The idea is simply to create a high (maximum) priority thread that does nothing but repeatedly sleep for a short interval and then wake up. Since the higher-priority thread will (in general) interrupt any lower-priority threads when it becomes runnable, you will effectively chop up the execution time of your lower-priority threads, which should then execute in the standard round-robin fashion. We call this technique rough because of the weakness of the specification for Java threads with respect to their pre-emptiveness. If you use this technique, you should consider it only a potential optimization.

Yielding

Whenever a thread sleeps, waits, or blocks on I/O, it gives up its time slot, and another thread is scheduled. So as long as you don't write methods that use hard loops, all threads should get their due. However, a Thread can also signal that it is willing to give up its time voluntarily at any point with the yield() call. We can change our previous example to include a yield() on each iteration:

```
class MyThread extends Thread {
    ...

    public void run() {
        while ( true ) {
            System.out.println( message );
            yield();
        }
    }
}
```

Now you should see "Foo" and "Bar" messages strictly alternating. If you have threads that perform very intensive calculations or otherwise eat a lot of CPU time, you might want to find an appropriate place for them to yield control occasionally. Alternatively, you might want to drop the priority of your compute-intensive thread, so that more important processing can proceed around it.

Unfortunately the Java language specification is very weak with respect to yield(). It is another one of these things that you should consider an optimization rather than a guarantee. In the worst case, the runtime system may simply ignore calls to yield().

Native Threads

We mentioned the possibility that different threads could run on different processors. This would be an ideal Java implementation. Unfortunately, most implementations don't even allow multiple threads to run in parallel with other processes running on the same machine. The most common implementations of threads today effectively simulate threading for an individual process like the Java interpreter. One feature that you might want to look for in choosing a Java implementation is called *native threads*. This means that the Java runtime system is able to use the real (native) threading mechanism of the host environment, which should perform better and, ideally, can allow multiprocessor operation.

Thread Groups

The ThreadGroup class allows us to deal with threads "wholesale": we can use it to arrange threads in groups and deal with the groups as a whole. A ThreadGroup can contain other ThreadGroups, in addition to individual threads, so our arrangements can be hierarchical. Thread groups are particularly useful when we want to start a task that might create many threads of its own. By assigning the task a thread group, we can later identify and control all of the task's threads. ThreadGroups are also the subject of restrictions that can be imposed by the Java Security Manager. So we can restrict a thread's behavior according to its thread group. For example, we can forbid threads in a particular group from interacting with threads in other groups. This is one way that web browsers can prevent threads started by Java applets from stopping important system threads.

When we create a Thread, it normally becomes part of the ThreadGroup that the currently running thread belongs to. To create a new ThreadGroup of our own, we can call the constructor:

```
ThreadGroup myTaskGroup = new ThreadGroup("My Task Group");
```

The `ThreadGroup` constructor takes a name, which a debugger can use to help you identify the group. (You can also assign names to the threads themselves.) Once we have a group, we can put threads in the group by supplying the `ThreadGroup` object as an argument to the `Thread` constructor:

```
Thread myTask = new Thread( myTaskGroup, taskPerformer );
```

Here, `myTaskGroup` is the thread group, and `taskPerformer` is the target object (the `Runnable` object that performs the task). Any additional threads that `myTask` creates will also belong to the `myTaskGroup` thread group.

Working with the ThreadGroup Class

Creating thread groups isn't interesting unless you do things to them. The `ThreadGroup` class exists so that you can control threads in batches. It has methods that parallel the basic `Thread` control methods—even the deprecated `stop()`, `suspend()`, and `resume()`. These methods in the `ThreadGroup` operate on all of the threads they contain. You can also mark a `ThreadGroup` as a "daemon"; a daemon thread group is automatically removed when all of its children are gone. If a thread group isn't a daemon, you have to call `destroy()` to remove it when it is empty.

We can set the maximum priority for any thread in a `ThreadGroup` by calling `setMaximumPriority()`. Thereafter, no threads can be created with a priority higher than the maximum; threads that change their priority can't set their new priority higher than the maximum.

Finally, you can get a list of all of the threads in a group. The method `activeCount()` tells you how many threads are in the group; the method `enumerate()` gives you a list of them. The argument to `enumerate()` is an array of `Thread`s, which `enumerate()` fills in with the group's threads. (Use `activeCount()` to make an array of the right size.) Both `activeCount()` and `enumerate()` operate recursively on all thread groups that the group contains.

It is also the responsibility of the `ThreadGroup` to handle uncaught runtime exceptions thrown by the `run()` methods of its threads. You can override the `uncaughtException()` method of `ThreadGroup` when making your own `ThreadGroup`s to control this behavior.

9

Basic Utility Classes

If you've been reading this book sequentially, you've read all about the core Java language constructs, including the object-oriented aspects of the language and the use of threads. Now it's time to shift gears and talk about the Java Application Programming Interface (API), the collection of classes that comes with every Java implementation. The Java API encompasses all the public methods and variables in the classes that make up the core Java packages. Table 9-1 lists the most important packages in the API and shows which chapters in this book discuss each of the packages.

Table 9-1. Packages of the Java API

Package	Contents	Chapter
`java.lang`	Basic language classes	4, 5, 6, 7, 8, 9
`java.lang.reflect`	Reflection	7
`java.io`	Input and output	10
`java.util`	Utilities and collections classes	9, 10, 11
`java.text`	International text classes	9
`java.net`	Sockets and URLs	11, 12
`java.applet`	The applet API	20
`javax.swing`, `java.awt`	Swing and 2D graphics	13, 14, 15, 16, 17
`javax.swing.event`, `java.awt.event`	Event classes	13, 14, 15
`java.awt.image`	2D image-processing classes	18
`java.beans`	JavaBeans API	19
`java.rmi`	RMI classes	11

As you can see in Table 9-1, we've already examined some of the classes in `java.lang` in earlier chapters on the core language constructs. Starting with this chapter, we'll throw open the Java toolbox and begin examining the rest of the classes in the API.

We'll begin our exploration with some of the fundamental language classes in `java.lang`, including strings and math utilities. Figure 9-1 shows the class hierarchy of the `java.lang` package.

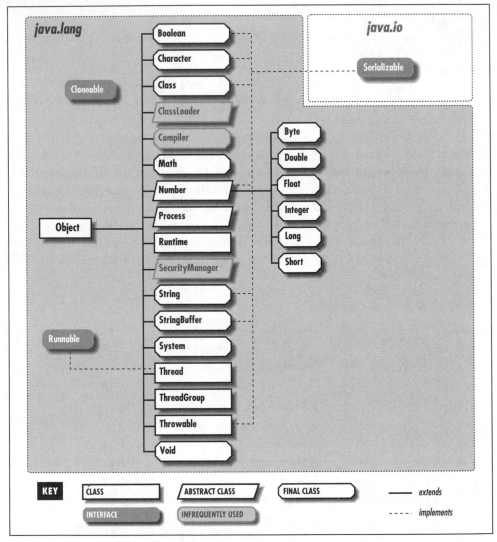

Figure 9-1. The java.lang package

We'll cover some of the classes in `java.util`, such as classes that support date and time values, random numbers, vectors, and hashtables. Figure 9-2 shows the class hierarchy of the `java.util` package.

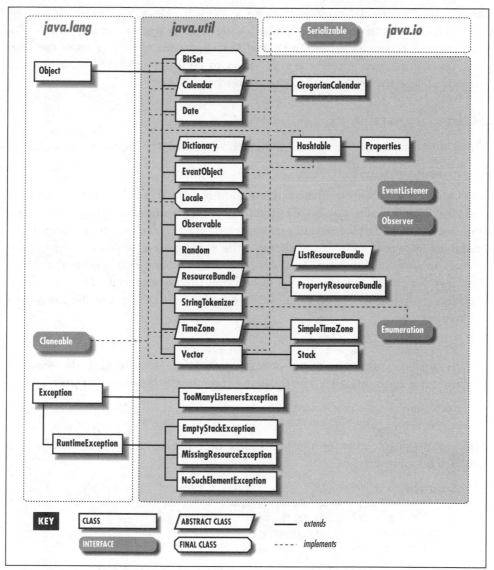

Figure 9-2. The java.util package

Strings

In this section, we take a closer look at the Java `String` class (or more specifically, `java.lang.String`). Because strings are used so extensively throughout Java (or any programming language, for that matter), the Java `String` class has quite a bit of functionality. We'll test-drive most of the important features, but before you go off and write a complex parser or regular expression library, you should refer to a Java class reference manual for additional details. For example, see *Java Fundamental Classes Reference*, by Mark Grand and Jonathan Knudsen (O'Reilly & Associates).

Strings are immutable; once you create a `String` object, you can't change its value. Operations that would otherwise change the characters or the length of a string instead return a new `String` object that copies the needed parts of the original. (Java implementations make an effort to consolidate identical strings and string literals in the same class into a shared-string pool.)

String Constructors

To create a string, assign a double-quoted constant to a `String` variable:

```
String quote = "To be or not to be";
```

Java automatically converts the string literal into a `String` object. If you're a C or C++ programmer, you may be wondering if `quote` is null-terminated. This question doesn't make any sense with Java strings. The `String` class actually uses a Java character array internally. It's `private` to the `String` class, so you can't get at the characters and change them. As always, arrays in Java are real objects that know their own length, so `String` objects in Java don't require special terminators (not even internally). If you need to know the length of a `String`, use the `length()` method:

```
int length = quote.length();
```

Strings can take advantage of the only overloaded operator in Java, the + operator, for string concatenation. The following code produces equivalent strings:

```
String name = "John " + "Smith";
String name = "John ".concat("Smith");
```

Literal strings can't span lines in Java source files, but we can concatenate lines to produce the same effect:

```
String poem =
    "'Twas brillig, and the slithy toves\n" +
    "    Did gyre and gimble in the wabe:\n" +
    "All mimsy were the borogoves,\n" +
    "    And the mome raths outgrabe.\n";
```

Embedding lengthy text in source code should now be a thing of the past, given that we can retrieve a `String` from anywhere on the planet via a URL. In Chapter 12, *Programming for the Web*, we'll see how to do things like this:

```
String poem = (String) new URL(
    "http://myserver/~dodgson/jabberwocky.txt").getContent();
```

In addition to making strings from literal expressions, we can construct a `String` from an array of characters:

```
char [] data = { 'L', 'e', 'm', 'm', 'i', 'n', 'g' };
String lemming = new String( data );
```

or from an array of bytes:

```
byte [] data = { 97, 98, 99 };
String abc = new String(data, "8859_5");
```

The second argument to the `String` constructor for byte arrays is the name of an encoding scheme. It's used to convert the given bytes to the string's Unicode characters. Unless you know something about Unicode, you can use the form of the constructor that accepts a byte array only; the default encoding scheme will be used.*

Strings from Things

We can get the string representation of most things with the static `String. valueOf()` method. Various overloaded versions of this method give us string values for all of the primitive types:

```
String one = String.valueOf( 1 );
String two = String.valueOf( 2.384f );
String notTrue = String.valueOf( false );
```

All objects in Java have a `toString()` method, inherited from the `Object` class. For class-type references, `String.valueOf()` invokes the object's `toString()` method to get its string representation. If the reference is `null`, the result is the literal string "null":

```
String date = String.valueOf( new Date() );
System.out.println( date );        // "Sun Dec 19 05:45:34 CST 1999"

date = null;
System.out.println( date );        // "null"
```

Things from Strings

Producing primitives like numbers from `String` objects is not a function of the `String` class. For that we need the primitive wrapper classes; they are described in the "Math Utilities" section later in this chapter. The wrapper classes provide `valueOf()` methods that produce an object from a `String`, as well as corresponding methods to retrieve the value in various primitive forms. Two examples are:

```
int i = Integer.valueOf("123").intValue();
double d = Double.valueOf("123.0").doubleValue();
```

In this code, the `Integer.valueOf()` call yields an Integer object that represents the value 123. An `Integer` object can provide its primitive value in the form of an int with the `intValue()` method.

---

* In Windows, the default encoding is CP1252; in Solaris, it's ISO8859_1.

Although these techniques may work for simple cases, they will not work internationally. Let's pretend for a moment that we are programming Java in the rolling hills of Tuscany. We would follow the local customs for representing numbers and write code like the following:

```
double d = Double.valueOf("1.234,56").doubleValue();   // oops!
```

Unfortunately, this code throws a NumberFormatException. The java.text package, which we'll discuss later, contains the tools we need to generate and parse strings for different countries and languages.

The charAt() method of the String class lets us get at the characters of a String in an array-like fashion:

```
String s = "Newton";
for ( int i = 0; i < s.length(); i++ )
    System.out.println( s.charAt( i ) );
```

This code prints the characters of the string one at a time. Alternately, we can get the characters all at once with toCharArray(). Here's a way to save typing a bunch of single quotes:

```
char [] abcs = "abcdefghijklmnopqrstuvwxyz".toCharArray();
```

Comparisons

Just as in C, you can't compare strings for equality with == because as in C, strings are accessed by reference. Even the expression "foo" == "foo" will return false, unless your Java compiler happens to coalesce multiple instances of the same string literal to a single string-pool item. String comparisons with <, >, <=, and >= don't work at all, because Java can't convert references to integers.

Use the equals() method to compare strings:

```
String one = "Foo";
char [] c = { 'F', 'o', 'o' };
String two = new String ( c );

if ( one.equals( two ) )                // true
```

An alternative version, equalsIgnoreCase(), can be used to check the equivalence of strings in a case-insensitive way:

```
String one = "FOO";
String two = "foo";

if ( one.equalsIgnoreCase( two ) )      // true
```

The compareTo() method compares the lexical value of the String against another String. It returns an integer that is less than, equal to, or greater than zero, just like the C routine string():

```
String abc = "abc";
String def = "def";
String num = "123";

if ( abc.compareTo( def ) < 0 )          // true
if ( abc.compareTo( abc ) == 0 )         // true
if ( abc.compareTo( num ) > 0 )          // true
```

On some systems, the behavior of lexical comparison is complex, and obscure alternative character sets exist. Java avoids this problem by comparing characters strictly by their position in the Unicode specification.

The Collator class

In Java 1.1 and later, the java.text package provides a sophisticated set of classes for comparing strings, even in different languages. German, for example, has vowels with umlauts over them and a beta-like character that represents a double "s". How should we sort these? Although the rules for sorting these characters are precisely defined, you can't assume that the lexical comparison we used earlier works correctly for languages other than English. Fortunately, the Collator class takes care of these complex sorting problems.

In the following example, we use a Collator designed to compare German strings. (We'll talk about Locales in a later section.) You can obtain a default Collator by calling the Collator.getInstance() method, with no arguments. Once you have an appropriate Collator instance, you can use its compare() method, which returns values just like String's compareTo() method. The following code creates two strings for the German translations of "fun" and "later," using Unicode constants for these two special characters. It then compares them, using a Collator for the German locale; the result is that "fun" (Spaß) sorts before "later" (später).

```
String fun = "Spa\u00df";
String later = "sp\u00e4ter";
Collator german = Collator.getInstance(Locale.GERMAN);
if (german.compare(fun, later) < 0) // true
```

Using collators is essential if you're working with languages other than English. In Spanish, for example, *ll* and *ch* are treated as separate characters and alphabetized separately. A collator handles cases like these automatically.

Searching

The `String` class provides several methods for finding substrings within a string. The `startsWith()` and `endsWith()` methods compare an argument `String` with the beginning and end of the `String`, respectively:

```
String url = "http://foo.bar.com/";
if ( url.startsWith("http:") )           // true
```

Overloaded versions of `indexOf()` search for the first occurrence of a character or substring:

```
String abcs = "abcdefghijklmnopqrstuvwxyz";
int i = abcs.indexOf( 'p' );             // 15
int i = abcs.indexOf( "def" );           // 3
```

Correspondingly, overloaded versions of `lastIndexOf()` search for the last occurrence of a character or substring.

Editing

A number of methods operate on the `String` and return a new `String` as a result. While this is useful, you should be aware that creating lots of strings in this manner can affect performance. If you need to modify a string often, you should use the `StringBuffer` class, as we'll discuss shortly.

`trim()` is a useful method that removes leading and trailing whitespace (i.e., carriage return, newline, and tab) from the `String`:

```
String str = "   abc   ";
str = str.trim();                        // "abc"
```

In this example, we have thrown away the original `String` (with excess whitespace), so it will be garbage-collected.

The `toUpperCase()` and `toLowerCase()` methods return a new `String` of the appropriate case:

```
String down = "FOO".toLowerCase();       // "foo"
String up   = down.toUpperCase();        // "FOO"
```

`substring()` returns a specified range of characters. The starting index is inclusive; the ending is exclusive:

```
String abcs = "abcdefghijklmnopqrstuvwxyz";
String cde = abcs.substring(2, 5);       // "cde"
```

String Method Summary

Many people complain when they discover that the Java String class is final (i.e., it can't be subclassed). There is a lot of functionality in String, and it would be nice to be able to modify its behavior directly. Unfortunately, there is also a serious need to optimize and rely on the performance of String objects. The Java compiler can optimize final classes by inlining methods when appropriate. The implementation of final classes can also be trusted by classes that work closely together, allowing for special cooperative optimizations. If you want to make a new string class that uses basic String functionality, use a String object in your class and provide methods that delegate method calls to the appropriate String methods.

Table 9-2 summarizes the methods provided by the String class.

Table 9-2. String Methods

Method	Functionality
charAt()	Gets at a particular character in the string
compareTo()	Compares the string with another string
concat()	Concatenates the string with another string
copyValueOf()	Returns a string equivalent to the specified character array
endsWith()	Checks whether the string ends with a specified suffix
equals()	Compares the string with another string
equalsIgnore-Case()	Compares the string with another string, ignoring case
getBytes()	Copies characters from the string into a byte array
getChars()	Copies characters from the string into a character array
hashCode()	Returns a hashcode for the string
indexOf()	Searches for the first occurrence of a character or substring in the string
intern()	Fetches a unique instance of the string from a global shared string pool
lastIndexOf()	Searches for the last occurrence of a character or substring in a string
length()	Returns the length of the string
regionMatches()	Checks whether a region of the string matches the specified region of another string
replace()	Replaces all occurrences of a character in the string with another character
startsWith()	Checks whether the string starts with a specified prefix
substring()	Returns a substring from the string
toCharArray()	Returns the array of characters from the string
toLowerCase()	Converts the string to lowercase

Table 9-2. String Methods (continued)

Method	Functionality
toString()	Returns the string value of an object
toUpperCase()	Converts the string to uppercase
trim()	Removes leading and trailing white space from the string
valueOf()	Returns a string representation of a value

The java.lang.StringBuffer Class

The `java.lang.StringBuffer` class is a growable buffer for characters. It's an efficient alternative to code like the following:

```
String ball = "Hello";
ball = ball + " there.";
ball = ball + " How are you?";
```

This example repeatedly produces new `String` objects. This means that the character array must be copied over and over, which can adversely affect performance. A more economical alternative is to use a `StringBuffer` object and its `append()` method:

```
StringBuffer ball = new StringBuffer("Hello");
ball.append(" there.");
ball.append(" How are you?");
```

The `StringBuffer` class provides a number of overloaded `append()` methods for appending various types of data to the buffer.

We can get a `String` from the `StringBuffer` with its `toString()` method:

```
String message = ball.toString();
```

You can also retrieve part of a `StringBuffer`, as a `String`, using one of the `substring()` methods.

`StringBuffer` also provides a number of overloaded `insert()` methods for inserting various types of data at a particular location in the string buffer. Furthermore, you can remove a single character or a range of characters with the `deleteCharAt()` and `delete()` methods. Finally, you can replace part of the `StringBuffer` with the contents of a `String` using the `replace()` method.

The `String` and `StringBuffer` classes cooperate, so that even in this last operation, no copy has to be made. The string data is shared between the objects, unless and until we try to change it in the `StringBuffer`.

So, when should you use a `StringBuffer` instead of a `String`? If you need to keep adding characters to a string, use a `StringBuffer`; it's designed to efficiently handle such modifications. You'll still have to convert the `StringBuffer` to a `String` when you need to use any of the methods in the `String` class. But you can print a `StringBuffer` directly using `System.out.println()`, because `println()` calls the `toString()` for you.

Another thing you should know about `StringBuffer` methods is that they are thread-safe, just like all public methods in the Java API. This means that only one thread at a time can change the state of a `StringBuffer` instance. Any time you modify a `StringBuffer`, you don't have to worry about another thread coming along and messing up the string while you are modifying it.

You might be interested to know that the compiler uses a `StringBuffer` to implement `String` concatenation. Consider the following expression:

```
String foo = "To " + "be " + "or";
```

This is equivalent to:

```
String foo = new
    StringBuffer().append("To ").append("be ").append("or").toString();
```

This kind of chaining of expressions is one of the things operator overloading hides in other languages.

The java.util.StringTokenizer Class

A common programming task involves parsing a string of text into words or "tokens" that are separated by some set of delimiter characters. The `java.util.StringTokenizer` class is a utility that does just this. The following example reads words from the string `text`:

```
String text = "Now is the time for all good men (and women)...";
StringTokenizer st = new StringTokenizer( text );

while ( st.hasMoreTokens() )  {
    String word = st.nextToken();
    ...
}
```

First, we create a new `StringTokenizer` from the `String`. We invoke the `hasMoreTokens()` and `nextToken()` methods to loop over the words of the text. By default, we use whitespace (i.e., carriage return, newline, and tab) as delimiters.

The `StringTokenizer` implements the `java.util.Enumeration` interface, which means that `StringTokenizer` also implements two more general methods for accessing elements: `hasMoreElements()` and `nextElement()`. These methods are defined by the `Enumeration` interface; they provide a standard way of returning a sequence of values. The advantage of `nextToken()` is that it returns a `String`, while `nextElement()` returns an `Object`. (We'll see an example in the

"Properties" section later in this chapter.) The Enumeration interface is implemented by many items that return sequences or collections of objects. Those of
you who have used the C strtok() function should appreciate how useful this
object-oriented equivalent is.

You can also specify your own set of delimiter characters in the StringTokenizer
constructor, using another String argument to the constructor. Any combination of the specified characters is treated as the equivalent of whitespace for
tokenizing:

```
text = "http://foo.bar.com/";
tok = new StringTokenizer( text, "/:" );

if ( tok.countTokens() < 2 )          // bad URL

String protocol = tok.nextToken();    // "http"
String host = tok.nextToken();        // "foo.bar.com"
```

This example parses a URL specification to get at the protocol and host components. The characters / and : are used as separators. The countTokens()
method provides a fast way to see how many tokens will be returned by
nextToken(), without actually creating the String objects.

An overloaded form of nextToken() accepts a string that defines a new delimiter
set for that and subsequent reads. The StringTokenizer constructor accepts a
flag that specifies that separator characters are to be returned individually as
tokens themselves. By default, the token separators are not returned.

Math Utilities

Java supports integer and floating-point arithmetic directly. Higher-level math
operations are supported through the java.lang.Math class. Java provides wrapper classes for all primitive data types, so you can treat them as objects if necessary. Java also provides the java.util.Random class for generating random
numbers.

Java handles errors in integer arithmetic by throwing an ArithmeticException:

```
int zero = 0;

try {
    int i = 72 / zero;
}
catch ( ArithmeticException e ) {
    // division by zero
}
```

To generate the error in this example, we created the intermediate variable `zero`. The compiler is somewhat crafty and would have caught us if we had blatantly tried to perform a division by a literal zero.

Floating-point arithmetic expressions, on the other hand, don't throw exceptions. Instead, they take on the special out-of-range values shown in Table 9-3.

Table 9-3. Special Floating-Point Values

Value	Mathematical Representation
POSITIVE_INFINITY	1.0/0.0
NEGATIVE_INFINITY	−1.0/0.0
NaN	0.0/0.0

The following example generates an infinite result:

```
double zero = 0.0;
double d = 1.0/zero;

if ( d == Double.POSITIVE_INFINITY )
    System.out.println( "Division by zero" );
```

The special value `NaN` indicates the result is "not a number." The value `NaN` has the special distinction of not being equal to itself (`NaN != NaN` evaluates to `true`). Use `Float.isNaN()` or `Double.isNaN()` to test for `NaN`.

The java.lang.Math Class

The `java.lang.Math` class provides Java's math library. All its methods are static and used directly; you don't have to (and you can't) instantiate a `Math` object. We use this kind of degenerate class when we really want methods to approximate standard C-like functions. While this tactic defies the principles of object-oriented design, it makes sense in this case, as it provides a means of grouping some related utility functions in a single class. Table 9-4 summarizes the methods in `java.lang.Math`.

Table 9-4. Methods in java.lang.Math

Method	Argument Type(s)	Functionality
Math.abs(a)	int, long, float, double	Absolute value
Math.acos(a)	double	Arc cosine
Math.asin(a)	double	Arc sine
Math.atan(a)	double	Arc tangent
Math.atan2(a,b)	double	Angle part of rectangular-to-polar coordinate transform

Table 9-4. Methods in java.lang.Math (continued)

Method	Argument Type(s)	Functionality
`Math.ceil(a)`	`double`	Smallest whole number greater than or equal to a
`Math.cos(a)`	`double`	Cosine
`Math.exp(a)`	`double`	`Math.E` to the power a
`Math.floor(a)`	`double`	Largest whole number less than or equal to a
`Math.log(a)`	`double`	Natural logarithm of a
`Math.max(a, b)`	`int, long, float, double`	Maximum
`Math.min(a, b)`	`int, long, float, double`	Minimum
`Math.pow(a, b)`	`double`	a to the power b
`Math.random()`	None	Random-number generator
`Math.rint(a)`	`double`	Converts double value to integral value in double format
`Math.round(a)`	`float, double`	Rounds to whole number
`Math.sin(a)`	`double`	Sine
`Math.sqrt(a)`	`double`	Square root
`Math.tan(a)`	`double`	Tangent

`log()`, `pow()`, and `sqrt()` can throw an `ArithmeticException`. `abs()`, `max()`, and `min()` are overloaded for all the scalar values, `int`, `long`, `float`, or `double`, and return the corresponding type. Versions of `Math.round()` accept either `float` or `double` and return `int` or `long`, respectively. The rest of the methods operate on and return `double` values:

```
double irrational = Math.sqrt( 2.0 );
int bigger = Math.max( 3, 4 );
long one = Math.round( 1.125798 );
```

For convenience, `Math` also contains the static final double values `E` and `PI`:

```
double circumference = diameter * Math.PI;
```

The java.math Class

If a `long` or a `double` just isn't big enough for you, the `java.math` package provides two classes, `BigInteger` and `BigDecimal`, that support arbitrary-precision numbers. These are full-featured classes with a bevy of methods for performing arbitrary-precision math. In the following example, we use `BigDecimal` to add two numbers:

```
try {
    BigDecimal twentyone = new BigDecimal("21");
```

```
        BigDecimal seven = new BigDecimal("7");
        BigDecimal sum = twentyone.add(seven);

        int answer= sum.intValue();              // 28
    }
    catch (NumberFormatException nfe) { }
    catch (ArithmeticException ae) { }
```

If you implement cryptographic algorithms for fun, `BigInteger` is crucial. But other than that, you're not likely to need these classes.

Wrappers for Primitive Types

In languages like Smalltalk, numbers and other simple types are objects, which makes for an elegant language design, but has trade-offs in efficiency and complexity. By contrast, there is a schism in the Java world between class types (i.e., objects) and primitive types (i.e., numbers, characters, and boolean values). Java accepts this trade-off simply for efficiency reasons. When you're crunching numbers, you want your computations to be lightweight; having to use objects for primitive types would seriously affect performance. For the times you want to treat values as objects, Java supplies a wrapper class for each of the primitive types, as shown in Table 9-5.

Table 9-5. Primitive Type Wrappers

Primitive	Wrapper
void	java.lang.Void
boolean	java.lang.Boolean
char	java.lang.Character
byte	java.lang.Byte
short	java.lang.Short
int	java.lang.Integer
long	java.lang.Long
float	java.lang.Float
double	java.lang.Double

An instance of a wrapper class encapsulates a single value of its corresponding type. It's an immutable object that serves as a container to hold the value and let us retrieve it later. You can construct a wrapper object from a primitive value or from a `String` representation of the value. The following statements are equivalent:

```
Float pi = new Float( 3.14 );
Float pi = new Float( "3.14" );
```

Wrapper classes throw a `NumberFormatException` when there is an error in parsing a string:

```
try {
    Double bogus = new Double( "huh?" );
}
catch ( NumberFormatException e ) {      // bad number
}
```

You should arrange to catch this exception if you want to deal with it. Otherwise, since it's a subclass of `RuntimeException`, it will propagate up the call stack and cause a runtime error if not caught.

Sometimes you'll use the wrapper classes simply to parse the `String` representation of a number:

```
String sheep = getParameter("sheep");
int n = new Integer( sheep ).intValue();
```

Here we are retrieving the value of the `sheep` parameter. This value is returned as a `String`, so we need to convert it to a numeric value before we can use it. Every wrapper class provides methods to get primitive values out of the wrapper; we are using `intValue()` to retrieve an `int` out of `Integer`. Since parsing a `String` representation of a number is such a common thing to do, the `Integer` and `Long` classes also provide the static methods `Integer.parseInt()` and `Long.parseLong()` that read a `String` and return the appropriate type. So the second line in the previous example is equivalent to:

```
int n = Integer.parseInt( sheep );
```

Likewise, the `Float` and `Double` classes provide the static methods `Float.parseFloat()` and `Double.parseDouble()`, for parsing strings into floating-point primitives.

All wrappers provide access to their values in various forms. You can retrieve scalar values with the methods `doubleValue()`, `floatValue()`, `longValue()`, and `intValue()`:

```
Double size = new Double ( 32.76 );

double d = size.doubleValue();       // 32.76
float f = size.floatValue();         // 32.76
long l = size.longValue();           // 32
int i = size.intValue();             // 32
```

This code is equivalent to casting the primitive double value to the various types.

You also need a wraper when you want to use a primitive value in a situation that requires an object. As you'll see shortly, a `Vector` is an extensible array of

Objects. We can use wrappers to hold numbers in a `Vector`, along with other objects:

```
Vector myNumbers = new Vector();
Integer thirtyThree = new Integer( 33 );
myNumbers.addElement( thirtyThree );
```

Here we have created an `Integer` wrapper object so that we can insert the number into the `Vector`, using `addElement()`. Later, when we are extracting elements from the `Vector`, we can recover the `int` value as follows:

```
Integer theNumber = (Integer)myNumbers.firstElement();
int n = theNumber.intValue();            // 33
```

Random Numbers

You can use the `java.util.Random` class to generate random values. It's a pseudo-random number generator that can be initialized with a 48-bit seed.* The default constructor uses the current time as a seed, but if you want a repeatable sequence, specify your own seed with:

```
long seed = mySeed;
Random rnums = new Random( seed );
```

This code creates a random-number generator. Once you have a generator, you can ask for random values of various types using the methods listed in Table 9-6.

Table 9-6. Random Number Methods

Method	Range
nextBoolean()	true or false
nextInt()	–2147483648 to 2147483647
nextInt(int n)	0 to (n – 1) inclusive
nextLong()	–9223372036854775808 to 9223372036854775807
nextFloat()	–1.0 to 1.0
nextDouble()	–1.0 to 1.0

By default, the values are uniformly distributed. You can use the `nextGaussian()` method to create a Gaussian (bell curve) distribution of `double` values, with a mean of 0.0 and a standard deviation of 1.0.

The `static` method `Math.random()` retrieves a random `double` value. This method initializes a `private` random-number generator in the `Math` class, using the default `Random` constructor. So every call to `Math.random()` corresponds to a call to `nextDouble()` on that random-number generator.

---

* The generator uses a linear congruential formula. See *The Art of Computer Programming*, Volume 2, "Semi-numerical Algorithms," by Donald Knuth (Addison-Wesley).

Dates

Working with dates and times without the proper tools can be a chore.* In SDK 1.1 and later, you get three classes that do all the hard work for you. The `java.util.Date` class encapsulates a point in time. The `java.util.GregorianCalendar` class, which descends from the abstract `java.util.Calendar`, translates between a point in time and calendar fields like month, day, and year. Finally, the `java.text.DateFormat` class knows how to generate and parse string representations of dates and times.†

The separation of the `Date` class and the `GregorianCalendar` class is analogous to having a class representing temperature and a class that translates that temperature to Celsius units. Conceivably, we could define other subclasses of `Calendar`, say `JulianCalendar` or `LunarCalendar`.

The default `GregorianCalendar` constructor creates an object that represents the current time, as determined by the system clock:

```
GregorianCalendar now = new GregorianCalendar();
```

Other constructors accept values to specify the point in time. In the first statement in the following code, we construct an object representing August 9, 1996; the second statement specifies both a date and a time, yielding an object that represents 9:01 a.m., April 8, 1997.

```
GregorianCalendar daphne =
    new GregorianCalendar(1996, Calendar.AUGUST, 9);
GregorianCalendar sometime =
    new GregorianCalendar(1997, Calendar.APRIL, 8, 9, 1); // 9:01 AM
```

We can also create a `GregorianCalendar` by setting specific fields using the `set()` method. The `Calendar` class contains a torrent of constants representing both calendar fields and field values. The first argument to the `set()` method is a field constant; the second argument is the new value for the field.

```
GregorianCalendar kristen = new GregorianCalendar();
kristen.set(Calendar.YEAR, 1972);
kristen.set(Calendar.MONTH, Calendar.MAY);
kristen.set(Calendar.DATE, 20);
```

---

* For a wealth of information about time and world time-keeping conventions, see *http://tycho.usno.navy.mil*, the U.S. Navy Directorate of Time. For a fascinating history of the Gregorian and Julian calendars, try *http://www.magnet.ch/serendipity/hermetic/cal_stud/cal_art.htm*.

† In Java 1.0.2, the `Date` class performed all three functions. In Java 1.1 and later, most of its methods have been deprecated, so that the only purpose of the `Date` class is to represent a point in time.

A `GregorianCalendar` is created in the default time zone. Setting the time zone of the calendar is as easy as obtaining the desired `TimeZone` and giving it to the `GregorianCalendar`:

```
GregorianCalendar smokey = new GregorianCalendar();
smokey.setTimeZone(TimeZone.getTimeZone("MST"));
```

To represent a `GregorianCalendar`'s date as a string, first create a `Date` object:

```
Date mydate = smokey.getTime();
```

To create a string representing a point in time, create a `DateFormat` object and apply its `format()` method to a `Date` object. Although `DateFormat` itself is abstract, it has several static ("factory") methods that return useful `DateFormat` subclass instances. To get a default `DateFormat`, simply call `getInstance()`:

```
DateFormat plain = DateFormat.getInstance();
String now = plain.format(new Date());          // 4/12/00 6:06 AM
```

You can generate a date string or a time string, or both, using the `get-DateInstance()`, `getTimeInstance()`, and `getDateTimeInstance()` factory methods. The argument to these methods describes what level of detail you'd like to see. `DateFormat` defines four constants representing detail levels: they are SHORT, MEDIUM, LONG, and FULL. There is also a DEFAULT, which is the same as MEDIUM. The following code creates three `DateFormat` instances: one to format a date, one to format a time, and one to format a date and time together. Note that `getDateTimeInstance()` requires two arguments: the first specifies how to format the date, the second how to format the time:

```
// 12-Apr-00
DateFormat df  = DateFormat.getDateInstance(DateFormat.DEFAULT);

// 9:18:27 AM
DateFormat tf  = DateFormat.getTimeInstance(DateFormat.DEFAULT);

// Wednesday, April 12, 2000 9:18:27 o'clock AM EDT
DateFormat dtf =
   DateFormat.getDateTimeInstance(DateFormat.FULL, DateFormat.FULL);
```

We're showing only how to create the `DateFormat` objects here; to actually generate a `String` from a date, you'll need to call the `format()` method of these objects.

Formatting dates and times for other countries is just as easy. Overloaded factory methods accept a `Locale` argument:

```
// 12 avr. 00
DateFormat df =
   DateFormat.getDateInstance(DateFormat.DEFAULT, Locale.FRANCE);
```

```
// 9:27:49
DateFormat tf =
  DateFormat.getTimeInstance(DateFormat.DEFAULT, Locale.GERMANY);

// mercoledi 12 aprile 2000 9.27.49 GMT-04:00
DateFormat dtf =
    DateFormat.getDateTimeInstance(
        DateFormat.FULL, DateFormat.FULL, Locale. ITALY);
```

To parse a string representing a date, we use the parse() method of the
DateFormat class. The result is a Date object. The parsing algorithms are finicky,
so it's safest to parse dates and times that are in the same format that is produced
by the DateFormat. The parse() method throws a ParseException if it doesn't
understand the string you give it. All of the following calls to parse() succeed
except the last; we don't supply a time zone, but the format for the time is LONG.
Other exceptions are occasionally thrown from the parse() method. To cover all
the bases, catch NullPointerExceptions and StringIndexOutOfBounds-
Exceptions, also.

```
try {
  Date d;
  DateFormat df;

  df = DateFormat.getDateTimeInstance(
          DateFormat.FULL, DateFormat.FULL);
  d = df.parse("Wednesday, April 12, 2000 2:22:22 o'clock PM EDT");

  df = DateFormat.getDateTimeInstance(
          DateFormat.MEDIUM, DateFormat.MEDIUM);
  d = df.parse("12-Apr-00 2:22:22 PM");

  df = DateFormat.getDateTimeInstance(
          DateFormat.LONG, DateFormat.LONG);
  d = df.parse("April 12, 2000 2:22:22 PM EDT");

  // throws a ParseException; detail level mismatch
  d = df.parse("12-Apr-00 2:22:22 PM");
}
catch (Exception e) { ... }
```

Timers

The Java 2 SDK 1.3 includes two handy classes for timed code execution. If you
write a clock application, for example, you want to update the display every second or so. Or you might want to play an alarm sound at some predetermined time.
You could accomplish these tasks with multiple threads and calls to Thread.
sleep(). But it's simpler to use the java.util.Timer and java.util.Timer-
Task classes.

Instances of `Timer` watch the clock and execute `TimerTasks` at appropriate times. You could, for example, schedule a task to run at a specific time like this:

```
import java.util.*;

public class Y2K {
  public static void main(String[] args) {
    Timer timer = new Timer();

    TimerTask task = new TimerTask() {
      public void run() {
        System.out.println("Boom!");
      }
    };

    Calendar c = new GregorianCalendar(2000, Calendar.JANUARY, 1);
    timer.schedule(task, c.getTime());
  }
}
```

`TimerTask` implements the `Runnable` interface. To create a task, you can simply subclass `TimerTask` and supply a `run()` method. Here we've created a simple anonymous subclass of `TimerTask`, which prints a message to `System.out`. Using the `schedule()` method of `Timer`, we've asked that the task be run on January 1, 2000. (Oops—too late! But you get the idea.)

There are some other varieties of `schedule()`; you can run tasks once or at recurring intervals. There are two kinds of recurring tasks—*fixed delay* and *fixed rate.* Fixed delay means that a fixed amount of time elapses between the end of the task's execution and the beginning of the next execution. Fixed rate means that the task should begin execution at fixed time intervals.

You could, for example, update a clock display every second with code like this:

```
Timer timer = new Timer();

TimerTask task = new TimerTask() {
    public void run() {
        repaint(); // update the clock display
    }
};

timer.schedule(task, 0, 1000);
```

`Timer` can't really make any guarantees about exactly when things are executed; you'd need a real-time operating system for that kind of precision. However, `Timer` can give you reasonable assurance that tasks will be executed at particular times, provided the tasks are not overly complex; with a slow-running task, the end of one execution might spill into the start time for the next execution.

Collections

Collections are a fundamental idea in programming. Applications frequently need to keep track of many related things, like a group of employees or a set of images. To support the concept of *many* at a fundamental level, of course, Java includes the concept of arrays. Since a one-dimensional array has a fixed length, arrays are awkward for sets of things that grow and shrink over the lifetime of an application. Ever since SDK 1.0, the Java platform has had two handy classes for keeping track of sets. The `java.util.Vector` class represents a dynamic list of objects, and the `java.util.Hashtable` class is a set of key/value pairs. The Java 2 platform introduces a more comprehensive approach to collections called the Collections Framework. The `Vector` and `Hashtable` classes still exist, but they are now a part of the framework.

If you work with dictionaries or associative arrays in other languages, you should understand how useful these classes are. If you are someone who has worked in C or another static language, you should find collections to be truly magical. They are part of what makes Java powerful and dynamic. Being able to work with lists of objects and make associations between them is an abstraction from the details of the types. It lets you think about the problems at a higher level and saves you from having to reproduce common structures every time you need them.

The Collections Framework is based around a handful of interfaces in the `java.util` package. These interfaces are divided into two hierarchies. The first hierarchy descends from the `Collection` interface. This interface (and its descendants) represents a box that holds other objects. The second hierarchy is based on the `Map` interface, which represents a group of key/value pairs.

The Collection Interface

The mother of all collections is an interface appropriately named `Collection`. It serves as a box that holds other objects, its *elements*. It doesn't specify whether duplicate objects are allowed or whether the objects will be ordered in some way. These kinds of details are left to child interfaces. Nevertheless, the `Collection` interface does define some basic operations:

public boolean **add**(Object o)
>   This method adds the supplied object to this collection. If the operation succeeds, this method returns `true`. If the object already exists in this collection and the collection does not permit duplicates, `false` is returned. Furthermore, some collections are read-only. These collections will throw an `UnsupportedOperationException` if this method is called.

```
public boolean remove(Object o)
```
This method removes the supplied object from this collection. Like the add()
method, this method returns true if the object is removed from the collection. If the object doesn't exist in this collection, false is returned. Read-only
collections throw an UnsupportedOperationException if this method is
called.

```
public boolean contains(Object o)
```
This method returns true if the collection contains the specified object.

```
public int size()
```
Use this method to find the number of elements in this collection.

```
public boolean isEmpty()
```
This method returns true if there are no elements in this collection.

```
public Iterator iterator()
```
Use this method to examine all the elements in this collection. This method
returns an Iterator, which is an object that you can use to step through the
collection's elements. We'll talk more about iterators in the next section.

As a special convenience, the elements of a collection can be placed into an array
using the following methods:

```
public Object[] toArray()
public Object[] toArray(Object[] a)
```

These methods return an array that contains all the elements in this collection.
The second version of this method returns an array of the same type as the array a.

Remember, these methods are common to every Collection implementation.
Any class that implements Collection or one of its child interfaces will have
these methods.

A Collection is a dynamic array; it can grow to accommodate new items. For
example, a List is a kind of Collection that implements a dynamic array. You
can insert and remove elements at arbitrary positions within a List. Collections
work directly with the type Object, so we can use Collections with instances of
any class.* We can even put different kinds of Objects in a Collection together;
the Collection doesn't know the difference.

As you might guess, this is where things get tricky. To do anything useful with an
Object after we take it back out of a Collection, we have to cast it back (narrow
it) to its original type. This can be done safely in Java because the cast is checked

---

* In C++, where classes don't derive from a single Object class that supplies a base type and common
  methods, the elements of a collection would usually be derived from some common collectable class.
  This forces the use of multiple inheritance and brings its associated problems.

at runtime. Java throws a `ClassCastException` if we try to cast an object to the wrong type. However, this need for casting means that your code must remember types or methodically test them with `instanceof`. That is the price we pay for having a completely dynamic collection class that operates on all types.

You might wonder if you can implement `Collection` to produce a class that works on just one type of element in a type-safe way. Unfortunately, the answer is no. We could implement `Collection`'s methods to make a `Collection` that rejects the wrong type of element at runtime, but this does not provide any new compile time, static type safety. In C++, templates provide a safe mechanism for parameterizing types by restricting the types of objects used at compile time. For a glimpse at Java language work in this area, see *http://www.math.luc.edu/pizza/gj*.

Iterators

What does the `java.util.Iterator` interface do? An `Iterator` is an object that lets you step through another object's data.*

public Object next()
> This method returns the next element of the associated Collection.

public boolean hasNext()
> This method returns `true` if you have not yet stepped through all of the `Collection`'s elements. In other words, it returns `true` if you can call `next()` to get the next element.

The following example shows how you could use an `Iterator` to print out every element of a collection:

```
public void printElements(Collection c, PrintStream out) {
    Iterator iterator = c.iterator();

    while (iterator.hasNext())
        out.println(iterator.next());
}
```

Finally, `Iterator` offers the ability to remove an element from a collection:

public void remove()
> This method removes the last object returned from `next()` from the associated `Collection`. Not all iterators implement `remove()`. It doesn't make sense to be able to remove an element from a read-only collection, for example. If element removal is not allowed, an `UnsupportedOperationException` is thrown from this method. If you call `remove()` before first calling `next()`,

---

* If you're familiar with earlier versions of Java, it will help you to know that `Iterator` is the successor to `Enumeration`, kind of an `Enumeration` on steroids.

or if you call `remove()` twice in a row, you'll get an `IllegalState-Exception`.

Collection Flavors

The `Collection` interface has two child interfaces: `Set` represents a collection in which duplicate elements are not allowed, and `List` is a collection whose elements have a specific order.

`Set` has no methods besides the ones it inherits from `Collection`. It does, however, enforce the rule that duplicate elements are not allowed. If you try to add an element that already exists in a `Set`, the `add()` method will return false.

`SortedSet` adds only a few methods to `Set`. As you call `add()` and `remove()`, the set maintains its order. You can retrieve subsets (which are also sorted) using the `subSet()`, `headSet()`, and `tailSet()` methods. The `first()`, `last()`, and `comparator()` methods provide access to the first element, the last element, and the object used to compare elements (more on this later).

The last child interface of `Collection` is `List`. The `List` interface adds the ability to manipulate elements at specific positions in the list:

public void **add**(int *index*, Object *element*)
> This method adds the given object at the supplied list position. If the position is less than zero or greater than the list length, an `IndexOutOf-BoundsException` will be thrown. The element that was previously at the supplied position and all elements after it will be moved up by one index position.

public void **remove**(int *index*)
> This method removes the element at the supplied position. All subsequent elements will move down by one index position.

public void **get**(int *index*)
> This method returns the element at the given position.

public void **set**(int *index*, Object *element*)
> This method changes the element at the given position to be the supplied object.

The Map Interface

The Collections Framework also includes the concept of a `Map`, which is a collection of key/value pairs. Another way of looking at a map is that it is a dictionary, similar to an associative array. Maps store and retrieve elements with key values; they are very useful for things like caches and minimalist databases. When you store a value in a map, you associate a key object with that value. When you need to look up the value, the map retrieves it using the key.

The `java.util.Map` interface specifies a map that, like `Collection`, operates on the type `Object`. A `Map` stores an element of type `Object` and associates it with a key, also of type `Object`. In this way, we can index arbitrary types of elements using arbitrary types as keys. As with `Collection`, casting is generally required to narrow objects back to their original type after pulling them out of a map.

The basic operations are straightforward:

public Object **put**(Object *key*, Object *value*)
> This method adds the specified key/value pair to the map. If the map already contains a value for the specified key, the old value is replaced.

public Object **get**(Object *key*)
> This method retrieves the value corresponding to key from the map.

public Object **remove**(Object *key*)
> This method removes the value corresponding to key from the map.

public int **size**()
> Use this method to find the number of key/value pairs in this map.

You can retrieve all the keys or values in the map:

public Set **keySet**()
> This method returns a `Set` that contains all of the keys in this map.

public Collection **values**()
> Use this method to retrieve all of the values in this map. The returned `Collection` can contain duplicate elements.

`Map` has one child interface, `SortedMap`. `SortedMap` maintains its key/value pairs in sorted order according to the key values. It provides `subMap()`, `headMap()`, and `tailMap()` methods for retrieving sorted map subsets. Like `SortedSet`, it also provides a `comparator()` method that returns an object that determines how the map keys are sorted. We'll talk more about this later.

Implementations

Up until this point, we've talked only about interfaces. But you can't instantiate interfaces. The Collections Framework includes useful implementations of the collections interfaces. These implementations are listed in Table 9-7, according to the interface they implement.

Table 9-7. Collections Framework Implementation Classes

Interface	Implementation
Set	HashSet
SortedSet	TreeSet

Table 9-7. Collections Framework Implementation Classes (continued)

Interface	Implementation
List	ArrayList, LinkedList, Vector
Map	HashMap, Hashtable
SortedMap	TreeMap

ArrayList offers good performance if you add to the end of the list frequently, while LinkedList offers better performance for frequent insertions and deletions. Vector has been around since SDK 1.0; it's now retrofitted to implement the List methods. Vector offers the advantage (and overhead) of synchronized methods, which is essential for multithreaded access. The old Hashtable has been updated so that it now implements the Map interface. It also has the advantage and overhead of synchronized operations. As you'll see, there are other, more general ways to get synchronized collections.

Hashcodes and key values

If you've used a hashtable before, you've probably guessed that there's more going on behind the scenes with maps than we've let on. An element in a hashtable is not associated with a key strictly by the key object's identity, but rather by the key's contents. This allows keys that are equivalent to access the same object. By "equivalent," we mean those objects that compare true with equals(). So, if you store an object in a Hashtable using one object as a key, you can use any other object that equals() tells you is equivalent to retrieve the stored object.

It's easy to see why equivalence is important if you remember our discussion of strings. You may create two String objects that have the same text in them but that come from different sources in Java. In this case, the == operator will tell you that the objects are different, but the equals() method of the String class will tell you that they are equivalent. Because they are equivalent, if we store an object in a Hashtable using one of the String objects as a key, we can retrieve it using the other.

Since Hashtables have a notion of equivalent keys, what does the hashcode do? The hashcode is like a fingerprint of the object's data content. The Hashtable uses the hashcode to store the objects so that they can be retrieved efficiently. The hashcode is nothing more than a number (an integer) that is a function of the data. The number always turns out the same for identical data, but the hashing function is intentionally designed to generate as random a number as possible for different combinations of data. That is, a very small change in the data should produce a big difference in the number. It is unlikely that two similar data sets will produce the same hashcode.

A `Hashtable` really just keeps a number of lists of objects, but it puts objects into the lists based on their hashcode. So when it wants to find the object again, it can look at the hashcode and know immediately how to get to the appropriate list. The `Hashtable` still might end up with a number of objects to examine, but the list should be short. For each object it finds, it does the following comparison to see if the key matches:

```
if ((keyHashcode == storedKeyHashcode) && key.equals(storedKey))
    return object;
```

There is no prescribed way to generate hashcodes. The only requirement is that they be somewhat randomly distributed and reproducible (based on the data). This means that two objects that are not the same could end up with the same hashcode by accident. This is unlikely (there are 2^{32} possible integer values); moreover, it doesn't cause a problem, because the `Hashtable` ultimately checks the actual keys, as well as the hashcodes, to see if they are equal. Therefore, even if two objects have the same hashcode, they can still co-exist in the hashtable.

Hashcodes are computed by an object's `hashCode()` method, which is inherited from the `Object` class if it isn't overridden. The default `hashCode()` method simply assigns each object instance a unique number to be used as a hashcode. If a class does not override this method, each instance of the class will have a unique hashcode. This goes along well with the default implementation of `equals()` in `Object`, which only compares objects for identity using `==`.

You must override `equals()` in any classes for which equivalence of different objects is meaningful. Likewise, if you want equivalent objects to serve as equivalent keys, you need to override the `hashCode()` method, as well, to return identical hashcode values. To do this, you need to create some suitably complex and arbitrary function of the contents of your object. The only criterion for the function is that it should be almost certain to return different values for objects with different data, but the same value for objects with identical data.

Slam Dunking with Collections

The `java.util.Collections` class is full of handy static methods that operate on `Sets` and `Maps`. (It's not the same as the `java.util.Collection` interface, which we've already talked about.) Since all the static methods in `Collections` operate on interfaces, they will work regardless of the actual implementation classes you're using. This is pretty powerful stuff.

The `Collections` class includes these methods:

```
public static Collection synchronizedCollection(Collection c)
public static Set synchronizedSet(Set s)
public static List synchronizedList(List list)
```

```
public static Map synchronizedMap(Map m)
public static SortedSet synchronizedSortedSet(SortedSet s)
public static SortedMap synchronizedSortedMap(SortedMap m)
```

These methods create synchronized, thread-safe versions of the supplied collection. This is useful if you're planning to access the collection from more than one thread. We'll talk a more about this later in this chapter.

Furthermore, you can use the Collections class to create read-only versions of any collection:

```
public static Collection unmodifiableCollection(Collection c)
public static Set unmodifiableSet(Set s)
public static List unmodifiableList(List list)
public static Map unmodifiableMap(Map m)
public static SortedSet unmodifiableSortedSet(SortedSet s)
public static SortedMap unmodifiableSortedMap(SortedMap m)
```

Sorting for Free

Collections includes other methods for performing common operations like sorting. Sorting comes in two varieties:

public static void **sort**(List *list*)
>   This method sorts the given list. You can use this method only on lists whose elements implement the java.lang.Comparable interface. Luckily, many classes already implement this interface, including String, Date, BigInteger, and the wrapper classes for the primitive types (Integer, Double, etc.).

public static void **sort**(List *list,* Comparator *c*)
>   Use this method to sort a list whose elements don't implement the Comparable interface. The supplied java.util.Comparator does the work of comparing elements. You might, for example, write an ImaginaryNumber class and want to sort a list of them. You would then create a Comparator implementation that knew how to compare two imaginary numbers.

Collections gives you some other interesting capabilities, too. If you're interested in finding out more, check out the min(), max(), binarySearch(), and reverse() methods.

A Thrilling Example

Collections is a bread-and-butter topic, which means it's hard to make exciting examples about it. The example in this section reads a text file, parses all its words,

counts the number of occurrences, sorts them, and writes the results to another
file. It will give you a good feel for how to use collections in your own programs.

```java
//file: WordSort.java
import java.io.*;
import java.util.*;

public class WordSort {
  public static void main(String[] args) throws IOException {
    // get the command-line arguments
    if (args.length < 2) {
      System.out.println("Usage: WordSort inputfile outputfile");
      return;
    }
    String inputfile = args[0];
    String outputfile = args[1];


/* Create the word map. Each key is a word and each value is an
 * Integer that represents the number of times the word occurs
 * in the input file.
 */

    Map map = new TreeMap();

    // read every line of the input file
    BufferedReader in =
        new BufferedReader(new FileReader(inputfile));
    String line;

    while ((line = in.readLine()) != null) {
      // examine each word on the line
      StringTokenizer st = new StringTokenizer(line);
      while (st.hasMoreTokens()) {
        String word = st.nextToken();
        Object o = map.get(word);
        // if there's no entry for this word, add one
        if (o == null) map.put(word, new Integer(1));
        // otherwise, increment the count for this word
        else {
          Integer count = (Integer)o;
          map.put(word, new Integer(count.intValue() + 1));
        }
      }
    }
    in.close();

    // get the map's keys and sort them
    List keys = new ArrayList(map.keySet());
```

```
        Collections.sort(keys);

        // write the results to the output file
        PrintWriter out = new PrintWriter(new FileWriter(outputfile));
        Iterator iterator = keys.iterator();
        while (iterator.hasNext()) {
          Object key = iterator.next();
          out.println(key + " : " + map.get(key));
        }
        out.close();
      }
    }
```

Suppose, for example, that you have an input file named *Ian Moore.txt*:

```
Well it was my love that kept you going
Kept you strong enough to fall
And it was my heart you were breaking
When he hurt your pride

So how does it feel
How does it feel
How does it feel
How does it feel
```

You could run the example on this file using the following command line:

```
java WordSort "Ian Moore.txt" count.txt
```

The output file, *count.txt*, looks like this:

```
And : 1
How : 3
Kept : 1
So : 1
Well : 1
When : 1
breaking : 1
does : 4
enough : 1
fall : 1
feel : 4
going : 1
he : 1
heart : 1
how : 1
hurt : 1
it : 6
kept : 1
love : 1
my : 2
```

```
pride : 1
strong : 1
that : 1
to : 1
was : 2
were : 1
you : 3
your : 1
```

The results are case-sensitive: "How" is recorded separately from "how". You could modify this behavior by converting words to all lowercase after retrieving them from the `StringTokenizer`:

```
String word = st.nextToken().toLowerCase();
```

Thread Safety and Iterators

If a collection will be accessed by more than one thread (see Chapter 8, *Threads*), things get a little tricky. Operations on the collection should be fast, but on the other hand, you need to make sure that different threads don't step on each other's toes with respect to the collection.

The `Collections` class provides methods that will create a thread-safe version of any `Collection`. There are methods for each subtype of `Collection`. The following example shows how to create a thread-safe `List`:

```
List list = new ArrayList();
List syncList = Collections.synchronizedList(list);
```

Although synchronized collections are thread-safe, the `Iterators` returned from them are not. This is an important point. If you obtain an `Iterator` from a collection, you should do your own synchronization to ensure that the collection does not change as you're iterating through its elements. You can do this with the `synchronized` keyword:

```
synchronized(syncList) {
    Iterator iterator = syncList.iterator();
    // do stuff with the iterator here
}
```

WeakHashMap: An Interesting Variation

`WeakHashMap` is an especially interesting collection. In some respects, it looks and behaves like a `HashMap`. What's interesting is that the key values in `WeakHashMap` are allowed to be harvested by the garbage collector.

`WeakHashMap` makes use of weak references. As you'll recall, objects in Java are garbage-collected when there are no longer any references to them. A *weak reference* is a special kind of reference that doesn't prevent the garbage collector from cleaning up the referenced object. Weak references and their siblings, *soft references* and *phantom references*, are implemented in the `java.lang.ref` package. We won't go into detail here; just the concept of a weak reference is important.

Why is `WeakHashMap` useful? It means you don't have to remove key/value pairs from a `Map` when you're finished with them. Normally if you removed all references to a key object in the rest of your application, the `Map` would still contain a reference and keep the object "alive." `WeakHashMap` changes this; once you remove references to a key object in the rest of the application, the `WeakHashMap` lets go of it too.

Properties

The `java.util.Properties` class is a specialized hashtable for strings. Java uses the `Properties` object to replace the environment variables used in other programming environments. You can use a `Properties` object (or "table") to hold arbitrary configuration information for an application in an easily accessible format. The `Properties` object can also load and store information using streams (see Chapter 10, *Input/Output Facilities*, for information on streams).

Any string values can be stored as key/value pairs in a `Properties` table. However, the convention is to use a dot-separated naming hierarchy to group property names into logical structures, as is done with X Window System resources on Unix systems.* The `java.lang.System` class provides system-environment information in this way, through a system `Properties` table we'll describe shortly.

Create an empty `Properties` table and add `String` key/value pairs just as with any `Hashtable`:

```
Properties props = new Properties();
props.put("myApp.xsize", "52");
props.put("myApp.ysize", "79");
```

Thereafter, you can retrieve values with the `getProperty()` method:

```
String xsize = props.getProperty( "myApp.xsize" );
```

If the named property doesn't exist, `getProperty()` returns `null`. You can get an `Enumeration` of the property names with the `propertyNames()` method:

```
for ( Enumeration e = props.propertyNames(); e.hasMoreElements; ) {
    String name = e.nextElement();
    ...
}
```

---

* Unfortunately, this is just a naming convention right now, so you can't access logical groups of properties as you can with X resources.

Default Values

When you create a `Properties` table, you can specify a second table for default property values:

```
Properties defaults;
...
Properties props = new Properties( defaults );
```

Now when you call `getProperty()`, the method searches the default table if it doesn't find the named property in the current table. An alternative version of `getProperty()` also accepts a default value; this value instead of `null` is returned, if the property is not found in the current list or in the default list:

```
String xsize = props.getProperty( "myApp.xsize", "50" );
```

Loading and Storing

You can save a `Properties` table to an `OutputStream` using the `save()` method. The property information is output in flat ASCII format. Continuing with the previous example, output the property information to `System.out` as follows:

```
props.save( System.out, "Application Parameters" );
```

`System.out` is a standard output stream similar to C's `stdout`. We could also save the information to a file by using a `FileOutputStream` as the first argument to `save()`. The second argument to `save()` is a `String` that is used as a header for the data. The previous code outputs something like the following to `System.out`:

```
#Application Parameters
#Mon Feb 12 09:24:23 CST 1999
myApp.ysize=79
myApp.xsize=52
```

The `load()` method reads the previously saved contents of a `Properties` object from an `InputStream`:

```
FileInputStream fin;
...
Properties props = new Properties()
props.load( fin );
```

The `list()` method is useful for debugging. It prints the contents to an `OutputStream` in a format that is more human-readable but not retrievable by `load()`. It truncates long lines with an ellipsis (. . .).

System Properties

The `java.lang.System` class provides access to basic system environment information through the static `System.getProperty()` method. This method returns a `Properties` table that contains system properties. System properties take the place of environment variables in some programming environments. Table 9-8 summarizes system properties that are guaranteed to be defined in any Java environment.

Table 9-8. System Properties

System Property	Meaning
`java.vendor`	Vendor-specific string
`java.vendor.url`	URL of vendor
`java.version`	Java version
`java.home`	Java installation directory
`java.class.version`	Java class version
`java.class.path`	The class path
`os.name`	Operating system name
`os.arch`	Operating system architecture
`os.version`	Operating system version
`file.separator`	File separator (such as / or \)
`path.separator`	Path separator (such as : or ;)
`line.separator`	Line separator (such as \n or \r\n)
`user.name`	User account name
`user.home`	User's home directory
`user.dir`	Current working directory

Applets are, by current web browser conventions, prevented from reading the following properties: `java.home`, `java.class.path`, `user.name`, `user.home`, and `user.dir`. As you'll see later, these restrictions are implemented by a `SecurityManager` object.

Your application can set system properties with the static method `System.setProperty()`. You can also set system properties when you run the Java interpreter, using the –D option:

```
%java -Dfoo=bar -Dcat=Boojum MyApp
```

Since it is common to use system properties to provide parameters such as numbers and colors, Java provides some convenience routines for retrieving property values and parsing them into their appropriate types. The classes `Boolean`, `Integer`, `Long`, and `Color` each come with a "get" method that looks up and parses a system property. For example, `Integer.getInteger("foo")` looks for a system property called `foo` and then returns it as an `Integer`. `Color.getColor("foo")` parses the property as an RGB value and returns a `Color` object.

Observers and Observables

The java.util.Observer interface and java.util.Observable class are relatively small utilities, but they provide a peek at a fundamental design pattern. The concept of observers and observables is part of the MVC (Model View Controller) framework. It is an abstraction that lets a number of client objects (the *observers*) be notified whenever a certain object or resource (the *observable*) changes in some way. We will see this pattern used extensively in Java's event mechanism.

The basic idea behind observers and observables is that the Observable object has a method that an Observer calls to register its interest. When a change happens, the Observable sends a notification by calling a method in each of the Observers. The observers implement the Observer interface, which specifies that notification causes an Observer object's update() method to be called.

In the following example, we create a MessageBoard object that holds a String message. MessageBoard extends Observable, from which it inherits the mechanism for registering observers (addObserver()) and notifying observers (notifyObservers()). To observe the MessageBoard, we have Student objects that implement the Observer interface so that they can be notified when the message changes:

```
//file: MessageBoard.java
import java.util.*;

public class MessageBoard extends Observable {
    private String message;

    public String getMessage() {
        return message;
    }
    public void changeMessage( String message ) {
        this.message = message;
        setChanged();
        notifyObservers( message );
    }
    public static void main( String [] args ) {
        MessageBoard board = new MessageBoard();
        Student bob = new Student();
        Student joe = new Student();
        board.addObserver( bob );
        board.addObserver( joe );
        board.changeMessage("More Homework!");
    }
} // end of class MessageBoard

class Student implements Observer {
    public void update(Observable o, Object arg) {
```

```
           System.out.println( "Message board changed: " + arg );
     }
  }
```

Our `MessageBoard` object extends `Observable`, which provides a method called `addObserver()`. Each of our `Student` objects registers itself using this method and receives updates via its `update()` method. When a new message string is set, using the `MessageBoard`'s `changeMessage()` method, the `Observable` calls the `setChanged()` and `notifyObservers()` methods to notify the observers. `notifyObservers()` can take as an argument an `Object` to pass along as an indication of the change. This object, in this case the `String` containing the new message, is passed to the observer's `update()` method, as its second argument. The first argument to `update()` is the `Observable` object itself.

The `main()` method of `MessageBoard` creates a `MessageBoard` and registers two `Student` objects with it. Then it changes the message. When you run the code, you should see each `Student` object print the message as it is notified.

You can imagine how you could implement the observer/observable relationship yourself using a `Vector` to hold the list of observers. In Chapter 13, *Swing*, and beyond, we'll see that the `Swing` event model extends this design patttern to use strongly typed notification objects and observers; these are *events* and *event listeners*.

The Security Manager

A Java application's access to system resources, such as the display, the filesystem, threads, external processes, and the network, can be controlled at a single point with a security manager. The class that implements this functionality in the Java API is the `java.lang.SecurityManager` class.

As you saw in Chapter 3, *Tools of the Trade*, the Java 2 platform provides a default security manager that you can use with the Java interpreter. For many applications, this default security manager is sufficient; for some types of applications, such as those that do custom class loading, you may need to write your own security manager.

An instance of the `SecurityManager` class can be installed once, and only once, in the life of the Java runtime environment. Thereafter, every access to a fundamental system resource is filtered through specific methods of the `SecurityManager` object by the core Java packages. By installing a specialized `SecurityManager`, we can implement arbitrarily complex (or simple) security policies for allowing access to individual resources.

When the Java runtime system starts executing, it's in a wide-open state until a `SecurityManager` is installed. The "null" security manager grants all requests, so the Java runtime system can perform any activity with the same level of access as other programs running under the user's authority. If the application that is running needs to ensure a secure environment, it can install a `SecurityManager` with the static `System.setSecurityManager()` method. For example, a Java-enabled web browser such as Netscape Navigator installs a `SecurityManager` before it runs any Java applets.

`java.lang.SecurityManager` must be subclassed to be used. This class does not actually contain any abstract methods; it's `abstract` as an indication that its default implementation is not very useful. By default, each security method in `SecurityManager` is implemented to provide the strictest level of security. In other words, the default `SecurityManager` simply rejects all requests.

The following example, `MyApp`, installs a trivial subclass of `SecurityManager` as one of its first activities:

```
class FascistSecurityManager extends SecurityManager { }

public class MyApp {
    public static void main( String [] args ) {
        System.setSecurityManager( new FascistSecurityManager() );
        // no access to files, network, windows, etc.
        ...
    }
}
```

In this scenario, `MyApp` does little aside from reading from `System.in` and writing to `System.out`. Any attempt to read or write files, access the network, or even open a window results in a `SecurityException` being thrown.

After this draconian `SecurityManager` is installed, it's impossible to change the `SecurityManager` in any way. The security of this feature is not dependent on the `SecurityManager` itself; it's built into the Java runtime system. You can't replace or modify the `SecurityManager` under any circumstances. The upshot of this is that you have to install one that handles all your needs up front.

To do something more useful, we can override the methods that are consulted for access to various kinds of resources. Table 9-9 lists some of the more important access methods. You should not normally have to call these methods yourself, although you could. They are called by the core Java classes before granting particular types of access.

Table 9-9. SecurityManager Methods

Method	Can I . . .
checkAccess(Thread g)	Access this thread?
checkExit(int status)	Execute a `System.exit()`?

Table 9-9. SecurityManager Methods (continued)

Method	Can I . . .
checkExec(String cmd)	exec() this process?
checkRead(String file)	Read a file?
checkWrite(String file)	Write a file?
checkDelete(String file)	Delete a file?
checkConnect(String host, int port)	Connect a socket to a host?
checkListen(int port)	Create a server socket?
checkAccept(String host, int port)	Accept this connection?
checkPropertyAccess(String key)	Access this system property?
checkTopLevelWindow(Object window)	Create this new top-level window?

Most of these methods simply return to grant access. If access is not granted, they throw a SecurityException. checkTopLevelWindow() is different; it returns a boolean value: true indicates the access is granted; false indicates the access is granted, but with the restriction that the new window should provide a warning border that serves to identify it as an untrusted window.

Let's implement a silly SecurityManager that allows only files whose names begin with *foo* to be read:

```
class FooFileSecurityManager extends SecurityManager {

    public void checkRead( String s ) {
        if ( s.startsWith("foo") ) {
            return true;
        } else {
            throw new SecurityException("Access to non-foo file: "
                + s + " not allowed." );
        }
    }
}
```

Once the FooFileSecurityManager is installed, any attempt to read a badly named file from any class will fail and cause a SecurityException to be thrown. All other security methods are inherited from SecurityManager, so they are left at their default restrictiveness.

As we've shown, security managers can make their decisions about what to allow and disallow based on any kind of criterion. One very powerful facility that the SecurityManager class provides is the classDepth() method. classDepth() takes as an argument the name of a Java class; it returns an integer indicating the depth of that class if it is present on the Java stack. The depth indicates the number of nested method invocations that occurred between the call to classDepth() and the last method invocation from the given class. This can be used to determine what class required the security check.

For example, if a class shows a depth of 1, the security check must have been caused by a method in that class—there are no method calls intervening between the last call to that class and the call requiring the check. You could allow or refuse an operation based on the knowledge that it came from a specific class.

All restrictions placed on applets by an applet-viewer application are enforced through a `SecurityManager`, including whether to allow untrusted code loaded from over the network to be executed. The `AppletSecurityManager` is responsible for applying the various rules for untrusted applets and allowing user configured access to trusted (signed) applets.

Internationalization

In order to deliver on the promise "write once, run anywhere," the engineers at Java designed the famous Java Virtual Machine. True, your program will run anywhere there is a JVM, but what about users in other countries? Will they have to know English to use your application? Java 1.1 answers that question with a resounding "no," backed up by various classes that are designed to make it easy for you to write a "global" application. In this section, we'll talk about the concepts of internationalization and the classes that support them.

The java.util.Locale Class

Internationalization programming revolves around the `Locale` class. The class itself is very simple; it encapsulates a country code, a language code, and a rarely used variant code. Commonly used languages and countries are defined as constants in the `Locale` class. (It's ironic that these names are all in English.) You can retrieve the codes or readable names, as follows:

```
Locale l = Locale.ITALIAN;
System.out.println(l.getCountry());            // IT
System.out.println(l.getDisplayCountry());     // Italy
System.out.println(l.getLanguage());           // it
System.out.println(l.getDisplayLanguage());    // Italian
```

The country codes comply with ISO639. A complete list of country codes is at *http://www.ics.uci.edu/pub/ietf/http/related/iso639.txt*. The language codes comply with ISO3166. A complete list of language codes is at *http://www.chemie.fu-berlin.de/diverse/doc/ISO_3166.html*. There is no official set of variant codes; they are designated as vendor-specific or platform-specific.

Various classes throughout the Java API use a `Locale` to decide how to represent themselves. We have already seen how the `DateFormat` class uses `Locale`s to determine how to format and parse strings.

Resource Bundles

If you're writing an internationalized program, you want all the text that is displayed by your application to be in the correct language. Given what you have just learned about Locale, you could print out different messages by testing the Locale. This gets cumbersome quickly, however, because the messages for all Locales are embedded in your source code. ResourceBundle and its subclasses offer a cleaner, more flexible solution.

A ResourceBundle is a collection of objects that your application can access by name, much like a Hashtable with String keys. The same ResourceBundle may be defined for many different Locales. To get a particular ResourceBundle, call the factory method ResourceBundle.getBundle(), which accepts the name of a ResourceBundle and a Locale. The following example gets the Resource-Bundle named "Message" for two Locales; from each bundle, it retrieves the message whose key is "HelloMessage" and prints the message.

```
//file: Hello.java
import java.util.*;

public class Hello {
  public static void main(String[] args) {
    ResourceBundle bun;
    bun = ResourceBundle.getBundle("Message", Locale.ITALY);
    System.out.println(bun.getString("HelloMessage"));
    bun = ResourceBundle.getBundle("Message", Locale.US);
    System.out.println(bun.getString("HelloMessage"));
  }
}
```

The getBundle() method throws the runtime exception MissingResource-Exception if an appropriate ResourceBundle cannot be located.

Locales are defined in three ways. They can be standalone classes, in which case they will be either subclasses of ListResourceBundle or direct subclasses of ResourceBundle. They can also be defined by a property file, in which case they will be represented at runtime by a PropertyResourceBundle object. Resource-Bundle.getBundle() returns either a matching class or an instance of PropertyResourceBundle corresponding to a matching property file. The algorithm used by getBundle() is based on appending the country and language codes of the requested Locale to the name of the resource. Specifically, it searches for resources in this order:

```
name_language_country_variant
name_language_country
name_language
name
```

```
name_default-language_default-country_default-variant
name_default-language_default-country
name_default-language
```

In this example, when we try to get the ResourceBundle named Message, specific to Locale.ITALY, it searches for the following names (no variant codes are in the Locales we are using):

```
Message_it_IT
Message_it
Message
Message_en_US
Message_en
```

Let's define the Message_it_IT ResourceBundle now, using a subclass of ListResourceBundle:

```
import java.util.*;

public class Message_it_IT extends ListResourceBundle {
  public Object[][] getContents() {
    return contents;
  }

  static final Object[][] contents = {
    {"HelloMessage", "Buon giorno, world!"},
    {"OtherMessage", "Ciao."},
  };
}
```

ListResourceBundle makes it easy to define a ResourceBundle class; all we have to do is override the getContents() method. This method simply returns a two-dimensional array containing the names and values of its resources. In this example, contents[1][0] is the second key (OtherMessage), and contents [1][1] is the corresponding message (Ciao.).

Now let's define a ResourceBundle for Locale.US. This time, we'll make a property file. Save the following data in a file called Message_en_US.properties:

```
HelloMessage=Hello, world!
OtherMessage=Bye.
```

So what happens if somebody runs your program in Locale.FRANCE, and no ResourceBundle is defined for that Locale? To avoid a runtime Missing-ResourceException, it's a good idea to define a default ResourceBundle. So in our example, you could change the name of the property file to Message. properties. That way, if a language- or country-specific ResourceBundle cannot be found, your application can still run.

The java.text Class

The `java.text` package includes, among other things, a set of classes designed for generating and parsing string representations of objects. We have already seen one of these classes, `DateFormat`. In this section we'll talk about the other format classes: `NumberFormat`, `ChoiceFormat`, and `MessageFormat`.

The `NumberFormat` class can be used to format and parse currency, percents, or plain old numbers. Like `DateFormat`, `NumberFormat` is an abstract class. However, it has several useful factory methods. For example, to generate currency strings, use `getCurrencyInstance()`:

```
double salary = 1234.56;
String here =        // $1,234.56
    NumberFormat.getCurrencyInstance().format(salary);
String italy =       // L 1.234,56
    NumberFormat.getCurrencyInstance(Locale.ITALY).format(salary);
```

The first statement generates an American salary, with a dollar sign, a comma to separate thousands, and a period as a decimal point. The second statement presents the same string in Italian, with a lire sign, a period to separate thousands, and a comma as a decimal point. Remember that `NumberFormat` worries about format only; it doesn't attempt to do currency conversion. (Among other things, that would require access to a dynamically updated table and exchange rates—a good opportunity for a Java Bean but too much to ask of a simple formatter.)

Likewise, `getPercentInstance()` returns a formatter you can use for generating and parsing percents. If you do not specify a `Locale` when calling a `getInstance()` method, the default `Locale` is used:

```
int progress = 44;
NumberFormat pf = NumberFormat.getPercentInstance();
System.out.println(pf.format(progress));       // "44%"
try {
    System.out.println(pf.parse("77.2%"));     // "0.772"
}
catch (ParseException e) {}
```

And if you just want to generate and parse plain old numbers, use a `Number-Format` returned by `getInstance()` or its equivalent, `getNumberInstance()`:

```
NumberFormat guiseppe = NumberFormat.getInstance(Locale.ITALY);

// defaults to Locale.US
NumberFormat joe = NumberFormat.getInstance();

try {
  double theValue = guiseppe.parse("34.663,252").doubleValue();
  System.out.println(joe.format(theValue));  // "34,663.252"
```

```
    }
    catch (ParseException e) {}
```

We use guiseppe to parse a number in Italian format (periods separate thousands, comma is the decimal point). The return type of parse() is Number, so we use the doubleValue() method to retrieve the value of the Number as a double. Then we use joe to format the number correctly for the default (U.S.) locale.

Here's a list of the factory methods for text formatters in the java.text package:

```
DateFormat.getDateInstance()
DateFormat.getDateInstance(int style)
DateFormat.getDateInstance(int style, Locale aLocale)
DateFormat.getDateTimeInstance()
DateFormat.getDateTimeInstance(int dateStyle, int timeStyle)
DateFormat.getDateTimeInstance(int dateStyle, int timeStyle, Locale aLocale)
DateFormat.getInstance()
DateFormat.getTimeInstance()
DateFormat.getTimeInstance(int style)
DateFormat.getTimeInstance(int style, Locale aLocale)
NumberFormat.getCurrencyInstance()
NumberFormat.getCurrencyInstance(Locale inLocale)
NumberFormat.getInstance()
NumberFormat.getInstance(Locale inLocale)
NumberFormat.getNumberInstance()
NumberFormat.getNumberInstance(Locale inLocale)
NumberFormat.getPercentInstance()
NumberFormat.getPercentInstance(Locale inLocale)
```

Thus far we've seen how to format dates and numbers as text. Now we'll take a look at a class, ChoiceFormat, that maps numerical ranges to text. ChoiceFormat is constructed by specifying the numerical ranges and the strings that correspond to them. One constructor accepts an array of doubles and an array of Strings, where each string corresponds to the range running from the matching number up through (but not including) the next number:

```
double[] limits = {0, 20, 40};
String[] labels = {"young", "less young", "old"};
ChoiceFormat cf = new ChoiceFormat(limits, labels);
System.out.println(cf.format(12)); // young
System.out.println(cf.format(26)); // less young
```

You can specify both the limits and the labels using a special string in an alternative ChoiceFormat constructor:

```
ChoiceFormat cf = new ChoiceFormat("0#young|20#less young|40#old");
System.out.println(cf.format(40)); // old
System.out.println(cf.format(50)); // old
```

The limit and value pairs are separated by vertical bar (|) characters; the number sign (#) separates each limit from its corresponding value.

To complete our discussion of the formatting classes, we'll take a look at another class, `MessageFormat`, that helps you construct human-readable messages. To construct a `MessageFormat`, pass it a pattern string. A pattern string is a lot like the string you feed to `printf()` in C, although the syntax is different. Arguments are delineated by curly brackets and may include information about how they should be formatted. Each argument consists of a number, an optional type, and an optional style. These are summarized in Table 9-10.

Table 9-10. MessageFormat Arguments

Type	Styles
choice	*pattern*
date	short, medium, long, full, *pattern*
number	integer, percent, currency, *pattern*
time	short, medium, long, full, *pattern*

Let's use an example to clarify all of this:

```
MessageFormat mf = new MessageFormat("You have {0} messages.");
Object[] arguments = {"no"};
System.out.println(mf.format(arguments)); // "You have no messages."
```

We start by constructing a `MessageFormat` object; the argument to the constructor is the pattern on which messages will be based. The special incantation `{0}` means "in this position, substitute element 0 from the array passed as an argument to the `format()` method." Thus, we construct a `MessageFormat` object. When we generate a message, by calling `format()`, we pass in values to replace the placeholders (`{0}`, `{1}`, . . .) in the template. In this case, we pass the array `arguments[]` to `mf.format`; this substitutes `arguments[0]`, yielding the result `You have no messages`.

Let's try this example again, except we'll show how to format a number and a date instead of a string argument:

```
MessageFormat mf = new MessageFormat(
    "You have {0, number, integer} messages on {1, date, long}.");
Object[] arguments = {new Integer(93), new Date()};

// "You have 93 messages on April 10, 1999."
System.out.println(mf.format(arguments));
```

In this example, we need to fill in two spaces in the template, and therefore we need two elements in the `arguments[]` array. Element 0 must be a number and is formatted as an integer. Element 1 must be a `Date` and will be printed in the long format. When we call `format()`, the `arguments[]` array supplies these two values.

This is still sloppy. What if there is only one message? To make this grammatically correct, we can embed a ChoiceFormat-style pattern string in our Message-Format pattern string:

```
MessageFormat mf = new MessageFormat(
    "You have {0, number, integer} message{0, choice, 0#s|1#|2#s}.");
Object[] arguments = {new Integer(1)};


// "You have 1 message."
System.out.println(mf.format(arguments));
```

In this case, we use element 0 of arguments[] twice: once to supply the number of messages, and once to provide input to the ChoiceFormat pattern. The pattern says to add an s if argument 0 has the value zero or is two or more.

Finally, a few words on how to be clever. If you want to write international programs, you can use resource bundles to supply the strings for your Message-Format objects. This way, you can automatically format messages that are in the appropriate language with dates and other language-dependent fields handled appropriately.

In this context, it's helpful to realize that messages don't need to read elements from the array in order. In English, you would say "Disk C has 123 files"; in some other language, you might say "123 files are on Disk C." You could implement both messages with the same set of arguments:

```
MessageFormat m1 = new MessageFormat(
    "Disk {0} has {1, number, integer} files.");
MessageFormat m2 = new MessageFormat(
    "{1, number, integer} files are on disk {0}.");
Object[] arguments = {"C", new Integer(123)};
```

In real life, the code could be even more compact; you'd only use a single MessageFormat object, initialized with a string taken from a resource bundle.

10

Input/Output Facilities

In this chapter, we'll continue our exploration of the Java API by looking at many of the classes in the `java.io` package. Figure 10-1 shows the class hierarchy of the `java.io` package.

We'll start by looking at the stream classes in `java.io`; these classes are all sub-classes of the basic `InputStream`, `OutputStream`, `Reader`, and `Writer` classes. Then we'll examine the `File` class and discuss how you can interact with the file-system using classes in `java.io`. Finally, we'll take a quick look at the data compression classes provided in `java.util.zip`.

Streams

All fundamental I/O in Java is based on *streams*. A stream represents a flow of data, or a channel of communication with (at least conceptually) a *writer* at one end and a *reader* at the other. When you are working with terminal input and output, read-ing or writing files, or communicating through sockets in Java, you are using a stream of one type or another. So that you can see the forest without being dis-tracted by the trees, we'll start by summarizing the classes involved with the differ-ent types of streams:

`InputStream/OutputStream`

    Abstract classes that define the basic functionality for reading or writing an unstructured sequence of bytes. All other byte streams in Java are built on top of the basic `InputStream` and `OutputStream`.

`Reader/Writer`

    Abstract classes that define the basic functionality for reading or writing a sequence of character data, with support for Unicode. All other character streams in Java are built on top of `Reader` and `Writer`.

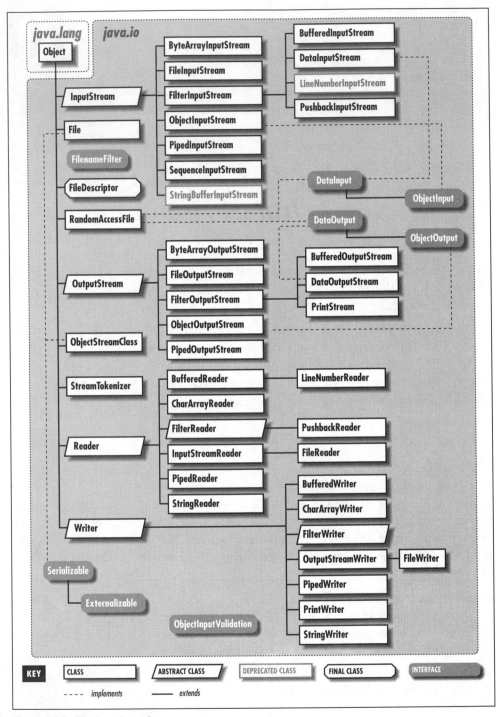

Figure 10-1. The java.io package

InputStreamReader/OutputStreamWriter

"Bridge" classes that convert bytes to characters and vice versa. Remember: in Unicode, a character is not a byte!

DataInputStream/DataOutputStream

Specialized stream filters that add the ability to read and write simple data types, such as numeric primitives and String objects, in a universal format.

ObjectInputStream/ObjectOutputStream

Specialized stream filters that are capable of writing serialized Java objects and reconstructing them.

BufferedInputStream/BufferedOutputStream/BufferedReader/
BufferedWriter

Specialized stream filters that add buffering for additional efficiency.

PrintWriter

A specialized character stream that makes it simple to print text.

PipedInputStream/PipedOutputStream/PipedReader/PipedWriter

"Double-ended" streams that normally occur in pairs. Data written into a PipedOutputStream or PipedWriter is read from its corresponding PipedInputStream or PipedReader.

FileInputStream/FileOutputStream/FileReader/FileWriter

Implementations of InputStream, OutputStream, Reader, and Writer that read from and write to files on the local filesystem.

Streams in Java are one-way streets. The java.io input and output classes represent the ends of a simple stream, as shown in Figure 10-2. For bidirectional conversations, we use one of each type of stream.

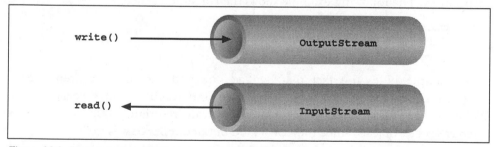

Figure 10-2. Basic input and output stream functionality

InputStream and OutputStream are abstract classes that define the lowest-level interface for all byte streams. They contain methods for reading or writing an unstructured flow of byte-level data. Because these classes are abstract, you can't create a generic input or output stream. Java implements subclasses of these for activities like reading from and writing to files and communicating with sockets.

Because all byte streams inherit the structure of InputStream or OutputStream, the various kinds of byte streams can be used interchangeably. A method specifying an InputStream as an argument can, of course, accept any subclass of InputStream. Specialized types of streams can also be layered to provide features, such as buffering, filtering, or handling larger data types.

In Java 1.1, new classes based around Reader and Writer were added to the java.io package. Reader and Writer are very much like InputStream and OutputStream, except that they deal with characters instead of bytes. As true character streams, these classes correctly handle Unicode characters, which was not always the case with the byte streams. However, some sort of bridge is needed between these character streams and the byte streams of physical devices like disks and networks. InputStreamReader and OutputStreamWriter are special classes that use an *encoding scheme* to translate between character and byte streams.

We'll discuss all of the interesting stream types in this section, with the exception of FileInputStream, FileOutputStream, FileReader, and FileWriter. We'll postpone the discussion of file streams until the next section, where we'll cover issues involved with accessing the filesystem in Java.

Terminal I/O

The prototypical example of an InputStream object is the "standard input" of a Java application. Like stdin in C or cin in C++, this object reads data from the program's environment, which is usually a terminal window or a command pipe. The java.lang.System class, a general repository for system-related resources, provides a reference to standard input in the static variable in. System also provides objects for standard output and standard error in the out and err variables, respectively. The following example shows the correspondence:

```
InputStream stdin = System.in;
OutputStream stdout = System.out;
OutputStream stderr = System.err;
```

This example hides the fact that System.out and System.err aren't really OutputStream objects, but more specialized and useful PrintStream objects. We'll explain these later, but for now we can reference out and err as OutputStream objects, since they are a kind of OutputStream as well.

We can read a single byte at a time from standard input with the InputStream's read() method. If you look closely at the API, you'll see that the read() method of the base InputStream class is an abstract method. What lies behind System.in is a particular implementation of InputStream—the subclass provides a real implementation of the read() method.

```
try {
    int val = System.in.read();
```

```
        ...
    }
    catch ( IOException e ) {
        ...
    }
```

As is the convention in C, `read()` provides a byte of information, but its return type is `int`. A return value of −1 indicates a normal end of stream has been reached; you'll need to test for this condition when using the simple `read()` method. If an error occurs during the read, an `IOException` is thrown. All basic input and output stream commands can throw an `IOException`, so you should arrange to catch and handle them appropriately.

To retrieve the value as a byte, perform a cast:

```
    byte b = (byte) val;
```

Be sure to check for the end-of-stream condition before you perform the cast.

An overloaded form of `read()` fills a byte array with as much data as possible up to the capacity of the array, and returns the number of bytes read:

```
    byte [] bity = new byte [1024];
    int got = System.in.read( bity );
```

We can also check the number of bytes available for reading on an `InputStream` with the `available()` method. Using that information, we could create an array of exactly the right size:

```
    int waiting = System.in.available();
    if ( waiting > 0 ) {
        byte [] data = new byte [ waiting ];
        System.in.read( data );
        ...
    }
```

However, the reliability of this technique depends on the ability of the underlying stream implementation to detect how much data is arriving.

`InputStream` provides the `skip()` method as a way of jumping over a number of bytes. Depending on the implementation of the stream, skipping bytes may be more efficient than reading them. The `close()` method shuts down the stream and frees up any associated system resources. It's a good idea to close a stream when you are done using it.

Character Streams

Some `InputStream` and `OutputStream` subclasses of early versions of Java included methods for reading and writing strings, but most of them operated by assuming that a 16-bit Unicode character was equivalent to an 8-bit byte in the stream. This works only for Latin-1 (ISO 8859-1) characters, so the character stream classes `Reader` and `Writer` were introduced in Java 1.1. Two special classes, `InputStreamReader` and `OutputStreamWriter`, bridge the gap between the world of character streams and the world of byte streams. These are character streams that are wrapped around an underlying byte stream. An encoding scheme is used to convert between bytes and characters. An encoding scheme name can be specified in the constructor of `InputStreamReader` or `OutputStreamWriter`. Or the default constructor can be used, which uses the system's default encoding scheme. For example, let's parse a human-readable string from the standard input into an integer. We'll assume that the bytes coming from `System.in` use the system's default encoding scheme:

```
try {
    InputStreamReader converter = new InputStreamReader(System.in);
    BufferedReader in = new BufferedReader(converter);

    String text = in.readLine();
    int i = NumberFormat.getInstance().parse(text).intValue();
}
catch ( IOException e ) { }
catch ( ParseException pe ) { }
```

First, we wrap an `InputStreamReader` around `System.in`. This object converts the incoming bytes of `System.in` to characters using the default encoding scheme. Then, we wrap a `BufferedReader` around the `InputStreamReader`. `BufferedReader` gives us the `readLine()` method, which we can use to convert a full line of text into a `String`. The string is then parsed into an integer using the techniques described in Chapter 9, *Basic Utility Classes*.

We could have programmed the previous example using only byte streams, and it would have worked for users in the United States, at least. So why go to the extra trouble of using character streams? Character streams were introduced in Java 1.1 to correctly support Unicode strings. Unicode was designed to support almost all of the written languages of the world. If you want to write a program that works in any part of the world, in any language, you definitely want to use streams that don't mangle Unicode.

So how do you decide when you need a byte stream (`InputStream` or `Output-Stream`) and when you need a character stream? If you want to read or write character strings, use some variety of `Reader` or `Writer`. Otherwise, a byte stream should suffice. Let's say, for example, that you want to read strings from a file that was written by an earlier Java application. In this case, you could simply create a `FileReader`, which will convert the bytes in the file to characters using the system's default encoding scheme. If you have a file in a specific encoding scheme, you can create an `InputStreamReader` with the specified encoding scheme wrapped around a `FileInputStream` and read characters from it.

Another example comes from the Internet. Web servers serve files as byte streams. If you want to read Unicode strings with a particular encoding scheme from a file on the network, you'll need an appropriate InputStreamReader wrapped around the InputStream of the web server's socket.

Stream Wrappers

What if we want to do more than read and write a sequence of bytes or characters? We can use a "filter" stream, which is a type of InputStream, OutputStream, Reader, or Writer that wraps another stream and adds new features. A filter stream takes the target stream as an argument in its constructor and delegates calls to it after doing some additional processing of its own. For example, you could construct a BufferedInputStream to wrap the system standard input:

```
InputStream bufferedIn = new BufferedInputStream( System.in );
```

The BufferedInputStream is a type of filter stream that reads ahead and buffers a certain amount of data. (We'll talk more about it later in this chapter.) The BufferedInputSream wraps an additional layer of functionality around the underlying stream. Figure 10-3 shows this arrangment for a DataInputStream.

As you can see from the previous code snippet, the BufferedInputStream filter is a type of InputStream. Because filter streams are themselves subclasses of the basic stream types, they can be used as arguments to the construction of other filter streams. This allows filter streams to be layered on top of on another to provide different combinations of features. For example, we could first wrap our System.in with a BufferedInputStream and then wrap the Buffered-InputSream with a DataInputStream for reading special data types.

There are four superclasses corresponding to the four types of filter streams: FilterInputStream, FilterOutputStream, FilterReader, and Filter-Writer. The first two are for filtering byte streams, and the last two are for filtering character streams. These superclasses provide the basic machinery for a "no op" filter (a filter that doesn't do anything) by delegating all of their method calls to their underlying stream. Real filter streams subclass these and override various methods to add their additional processing. We'll make a filter stream a little later in this chapter.

Data streams

DataInputStream and DataOutputStream are filter streams that let you read or write strings and primitive data types that comprise more than a single byte. DataInputStream and DataOutputStream implement the DataInput and DataOutput interfaces, respectively. These interfaces define the methods required for streams that read and write strings and Java primitive numeric and boolean types in a machine-independent manner.

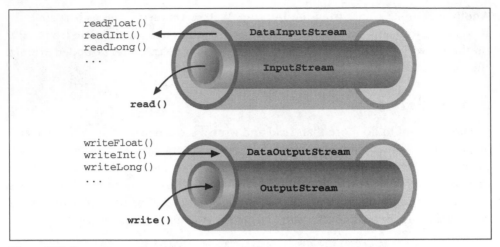

Figure 10-3. Layered streams

You can construct a `DataInputStream` from an `InputStream` and then use a method like `readDouble()` to read a primitive data type:

```
DataInputStream dis = new DataInputStream( System.in );
double d = dis.readDouble();
```

This example wraps the standard input stream in a `DataInputStream` and uses it to read a double value. `readDouble()` reads bytes from the stream and constructs a `double` from them. The `DataInputStream` methods expect the bytes of numeric data types to be in *network byte order*, a standard that specifies that the high order bytes are sent first.

The `DataOutputStream` class provides write methods that correspond to the read methods in `DataInputStream`. For example, `writeInt()` writes an integer in binary format to the underlying output stream.

The `readUTF()` and `writeUTF()` methods of `DataInputStream` and `DataOutputStream` read and write a Java `String` of Unicode characters using the UTF-8 "transformation format." UTF-8 is an ASCII-compatible encoding of Unicode characters commonly used for the transmission and storage of Unicode text. This differs from the `Reader` and `Writer` streams, which can use arbitrary encodings and may not preserve all of the Unicode characters.

We can use a `DataInputStream` with any kind of input stream, whether it be from a file, a socket, or standard input. The same applies to using a `DataOutputStream`, or, for that matter, any other specialized streams in `java.io`.

Buffered streams

The `BufferedInputStream`, `BufferedOutputStream`, `BufferedReader`, and `BufferedWriter` classes add a data buffer of a specified size to the stream path. A buffer can increase efficiency by reducing the number of physical read or write operations that correspond to read() or write() method calls. You create a buffered stream with an appropriate input or output stream and a buffer size. (You can also wrap another stream around a buffered stream, so that it benefits from the buffering.) Here's a simple buffered input stream:

```
BufferedInputStream bis =
    new BufferedInputStream(myInputStream, 4096);
...
bis.read();
```

In this example, we specify a buffer size of 4096 bytes. If we leave off the size of the buffer in the constructor, a reasonably sized one is chosen for us. On our first call to read(), bis tries to fill the entire 4096-byte buffer with data. Thereafter, calls to read() retrieve data from the buffer, which is refilled as necessary.

A BufferedOutputStream works in a similar way. Calls to write() store the data in a buffer; data is actually written only when the buffer fills up. You can also use the flush() method to wring out the contents of a BufferedOutputStream at any time. The flush() method is actually a method of the OutputStream class itself. It's important because it allows you to be sure that all data in any underlying streams and filter streams has been sent (before, for example, you wait for a response).

Some input streams like BufferedInputStream support the ability to mark a location in the data and later reset the stream to that position. The mark() method sets the return point in the stream. It takes an integer value that specifies the number of bytes that can be read before the stream gives up and forgets about the mark. The reset() method returns the stream to the marked point; any data read after the call to mark() is read again.

This functionality is especially useful when you are reading the stream in a parser. You may occasionally fail to parse a structure and so must try something else. In this situation, you can have your parser generate an error (a homemade ParseException) and then reset the stream to the point before it began parsing the structure:

```
BufferedInputStream input;
...
try {
    input.mark( MAX_DATA_STRUCTURE_SIZE );
    return( parseDataStructure( input ) );
}
catch ( ParseException e ) {
    input.reset();
    ...
}
```

The `BufferedReader` and `BufferedWriter` classes work just like their byte-based counterparts, but operate on characters instead of bytes.

Print streams

Another useful wrapper stream is `java.io.PrintWriter`. This class provides a suite of overloaded `print()` methods that turn their arguments into strings and push them out the stream. A complementary set of `println()` methods adds a newline to the end of the strings. `PrintWriter` is an unusual character stream because it can wrap either an `OutputStream` or another `Writer`.

`PrintWriter` is the more capable big brother of the `PrintStream` byte stream. The `System.out` and `System.err` streams are `PrintStream` objects; you have already seen such streams strewn throughout this book:

```
System.out.print("Hello world...\n");
System.out.println("Hello world...");
System.out.println( "The answer is: " + 17 );
System.out.println( 3.14 );
```

`PrintWriter` and `PrintStream` have a strange, overlapping history. Early versions of Java did not have the `Reader` and `Writer` classes and streams like `PrintStream`, which must of necessity convert bytes to characters simply made assumptions about the character encoding. As of Java 1.1, the `PrintStream` class was enhanced to translate characters to bytes using the system's default encoding scheme. For all new development, however, use a `PrintWriter` instead of a `PrintStream`. Because a `PrintWriter` can wrap an `OutputStream`, the two classes are more or less interchangeable.

When you create a `PrintWriter` object, you can pass an additional boolean value to the constructor. If this value is `true`, the `PrintWriter` automatically performs a `flush()` on the underlying `OutputStream` or `Writer` each time it sends a newline:

```
boolean autoFlush = true;
PrintWriter p = new PrintWriter( myOutputStream, autoFlush );
```

When this technique is used with a buffered output stream, it corresponds to the behavior of terminals that send data line by line.

Unlike methods in other stream classes, the methods of `PrintWriter` and `PrintStream` do not throw `IOExceptions`. This makes life a lot easier for printing text, which is a very common operation. Instead, if we are interested, we can check for errors with the `checkError()` method:

```
System.out.println( reallyLongString );
if ( System.out.checkError() )                  // uh oh
```

Pipes

Normally, our applications are directly involved with one side of a given stream at a time. `PipedInputStream` and `PipedOutputStream` (or `PipedReader` and `PipedWriter`), however, let us create two sides of a stream and connect them together, as shown in Figure 10-4. This can be used to provide a stream of communication between threads, for example, or as a "loop-back" for testing.

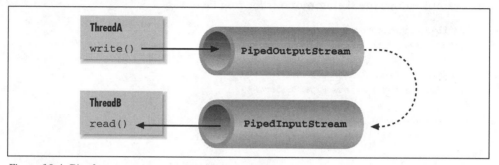

Figure 10-4. Piped streams

To create a byte stream pipe, we use both a `PipedInputStream` and a `PipedOutputStream`. We can simply choose a side and then construct the other side using the first as an argument:

```
PipedInputStream pin = new PipedInputStream();
PipedOutputStream pout = new PipedOutputStream( pin );
```

Alternatively:

```
PipedOutputStream pout = new PipedOutputStream( );
PipedInputStream pin = new PipedInputStream( pout );
```

In each of these examples, the effect is to produce an input stream, `pin`, and an output stream, `pout`, that are connected. Data written to `pout` can then be read by `pin`. It is also possible to create the `PipedInputStream` and the `PipedOutputStream` separately, and then connect them with the `connect()` method.

We can do exactly the same thing in the character-based world, using `PipedReader` and `PipedWriter` in place of `PipedInputStream` and `PipedOutputStream`.

Once the two ends of the pipe are connected, use the two streams as you would other input and output streams. You can use `read()` to read data from the `PipedInputStream` (or `PipedReader`) and `write()` to write data to the `PipedOutputStream` (or `PipedWriter`). If the internal buffer of the pipe fills up, the writer blocks and waits until space is available. Conversely, if the pipe is empty, the reader blocks and waits until some data is available.

One advantage to using piped streams is that they provide stream functionality in
our code, without compelling us to build new, specialized streams. For example,
we can use pipes to create a simple logging facility for our application. We can
send messages to the logging facility through an ordinary PrintWriter, and then
it can do whatever processing or buffering is required before sending the messages off to their ultimate location. Because we are dealing with string messages,
we use the character-based PipedReader and PipedWriter classes. The following example shows the skeleton of our logging facility:

```java
//file: LoggerDaemon.java
import java.io.*;

class LoggerDaemon extends Thread {
    PipedReader in = new PipedReader();

    LoggerDaemon() {
        start();
    }

    public void run() {
        BufferedReader bin = new BufferedReader( in );
        String s;

        try {
            while ( (s = bin.readLine()) != null ) {
                // process line of data
                // ...
            }
        }
        catch (IOException e ) { }
    }

    PrintWriter getWriter() throws IOException {
        return new PrintWriter( new PipedWriter( in ) );
    }
}

class myApplication {
    public static void main ( String [] args ) throws IOException {
        PrintWriter out = new LoggerDaemon().getWriter();

        out.println("Application starting...");
        // ...
        out.println("Warning: does not compute!");
        // ...
    }
}
```

LoggerDaemon reads strings from its end of the pipe, the PipedReader named in. LoggerDaemon also provides a method, getWriter(), that returns a PipedWriter that is connected to its input stream. To begin sending messages, we create a new LoggerDaemon and fetch the output stream.

In order to read strings with the readLine() method, LoggerDaemon wraps a BufferedReader around its PipedReader. For convenience, it also presents its output pipe as a PrintWriter, rather than a simple Writer.

One advantage of implementing LoggerDaemon with pipes is that we can log messages as easily as we write text to a terminal or any other stream. In other words, we can use all our normal tools and techniques. Another advantage is that the processing happens in another thread, so we can go about our business while the processing takes place.

There is nothing stopping us from connecting more than two piped streams. For example, we could chain multiple pipes together to perform a series of filtering operations. Note that in this example, there is nothing to prevent messages printed to the pipe from different threads being mixed together. To do that we might have to create a number of pipes, one for each thread, in the getWriter() method.

Strings to Streams and Back

StringReader is another useful stream class; it essentially wraps stream functionality around a String. Here's how to use a StringReader:

```
String data = "There once was a man from Nantucket...";
StringReader sr = new StringReader( data );

char T = (char)sr.read();
char h = (char)sr.read();
char e = (char)sr.read();
```

Note that you will still have to catch IOExceptions thrown by some of the StringReader's methods.

The StringReader class is useful when you want to read data in a String as if it were coming from a stream, such as a file, pipe, or socket. For example, suppose you create a parser that expects to read tokens from a stream. But you want to provide a method that also parses a big string. You can easily add one using StringReader.

Turning things around, the StringWriter class lets us write to a character buffer through an output stream. The internal buffer grows as necessary to accommodate the data. When we are done we can fetch the contents of the buffer as a

`String`. In the following example, we create a `StringWriter` and wrap it in a `PrintWriter` for convenience:

```
StringWriter buffer = new StringWriter();
PrintWriter out = new PrintWriter( buffer );

out.println("A moose once bit my sister.");
out.println("No, really!");

String results = buffer.toString();
```

First we print a few lines to the output stream, to give it some data, then retrieve the results as a string with the `toString()` method. Alternately, we could get the results as a `StringBuffer` object using the `getBuffer()` method.

The `StringWriter` class is useful if you want to capture the output of something that normally sends output to a stream, such as a file or the console. A `PrintWriter` wrapped around a `StringWriter` is a viable alternative to using a `StringBuffer` to construct large strings piece by piece.

The rot13InputStream Class

Before we leave streams, let's try our hand at making one of our own. I mentioned earlier that specialized stream wrappers are built on top of the `Filter-InputStream` and `FilterOutputStream` classes. It's quite easy to create our own subclass of `FilterInputStream` that can be wrapped around other streams to add new functionality.

The following example, `rot13InputStream`, performs a *rot13* (rotate by 13 letters) operation on the bytes that it reads. *rot13* is a trivial obfuscation algorithm that shifts alphanumeric letters to make them not quite human-readable; it's cute because it's symmetric. That is, to "un-rot13" some text, simply *rot13* it again. We'll use the `rot13InputStream` class again in the `crypt` protocol handler example in Appendix A, *Content and Protocol Handlers*, so we've put the class in the `learningjava.io` package to facilitate reuse. Here's our `rot13InputStream` class:

```
//file: rot13InputStream.java
package learningjava.io;
import java.io.*;

public class rot13InputStream extends FilterInputStream {

    public rot13InputStream ( InputStream i ) {
        super( i );
    }
```

```
        public int read() throws IOException {
            return rot13( in.read() );
        }

        private int rot13 ( int c ) {
            if ( (c >= 'A') && (c <= 'Z') )
                c=(((c-'A')+13)%26)+'A';
            if ( (c >= 'a') && (c <= 'z') )
                c=(((c-'a')+13)%26)+'a';
            return c;
        }

    }
```

The `FilterInputStream` needs to be initialized with an `InputStream`; this is the stream to be filtered. We provide an appropriate constructor for the `rot13-InputStream` class and invoke the parent constructor with a call to `super()`. `FilterInputStream` contains a protected instance variable, `in`, where it stores a reference to the specified InputStream, making it available to the rest of our class.

The primary feature of a `FilterInputStream` is that it delegates its input tasks to the underlying `InputStream`. So, for instance, a call to `FilterInputStream`'s `read()` simply turns around and calls the `read()` method of the underlying `InputStream`, to fetch a byte.

Filtering amounts to doing extra work (such as encryption) on the data as it passes through. In our example, the `read()` method to fetches a byte from the underlying `InputStream`, in, and then performs the *rot13* shift on the byte before returning it. Note that the `rot13()` method shifts alphabetic characters, while simply passing all other values, including the end-of-stream value (-1). Our subclass is now a *rot13* filter.

`run()` is the only `InputStream` method that `FilterInputStream` overrides. All other normal functionality of an `InputStream`, like `skip()` and `available()`, is unmodified, so calls to these methods are answered by the underlying `InputStream`.

Strictly speaking, `rot13InputStream` works only on an ASCII byte stream, since the underlying algorithm is based on the Roman alphabet. A more generalized character-scrambling algorithm would have to be based on `FilterReader` to handle 16-bit Unicode classescorrectly. (Anyone want to try rot32768?)

Files

Unless otherwise restricted, a Java application can read and write to the host file-system with the same level of access as the user who runs the Java interpreter. Java applets and other kinds of untrusted applications can, of course, be restricted by the security policy and cut off from these services. We'll discuss applet access at the end of this section. First, let's take a look at the tools for basic file access.

Working with files in Java is still somewhat problematic. The host filesystem lies outside of Java's virtual environment, in the real world, and can therefore still suffer from architecture and implementation differences. Java tries to mask some of these differences by providing information to help an application tailor itself to the local environment; we'll mention these areas as they occur.

The java.io.File Class

The `java.io.File` class encapsulates access to information about a file or directory entry in the filesystem. It can be used to get attribute information about a file, list the entries in a directory, and perform basic filesystem operations like removing a file or making a directory. While the `File` object handles these tasks, it doesn't provide direct access for reading and writing file data; there are specialized streams for that purpose.

File constructors

You can create an instance of `File` from a `String` pathname:

```
File fooFile = new File( "/tmp/foo.txt" );
File barDir = new File( "/tmp/bar" );
```

You can also create a file with a relative path:

```
File f = new File( "foo" );
```

In this case, Java works relative to the current directory of the Java interpreter. You can determine the current directory by checking the `user.dir` property in the `System Properties` list:

```
System.getProperty("user.dir"));
```

An overloaded version of the `File` constructor lets you specify the directory path and filename as separate `String` objects:

```
File fooFile = new File( "/tmp", "foo.txt" );
```

With yet another variation, you can specify the directory with a `File` object and the filename with a `String`:

```
File tmpDir = new File( "/tmp" );
File fooFile = new File ( tmpDir, "foo.txt" );
```

None of the `File` constructors throw any exceptions. This means the object is created whether or not the file or directory actually exists; it isn't an error to create a `File` object for a nonexistent file. You can use the object's `exists()` instance method to find out whether the file or directory exists. The `File` object simply exists as a handle for getting information about what is (potentially at least) a file or directory.

Path localization

One of the reasons that working with files in Java is problematic is that pathnames are expected to follow the conventions of the local filesystem. Java's designers intend to provide an abstraction that deals with most system-dependent filename features, such as the file separator, path separator, device specifier, and root directory. Unfortunately, not all these features are implemented in the current version.

On some systems, Java can compensate for differences such as the direction of the file separator slashes in a pathname. For example, in the current implementation on Windows platforms, Java accepts paths with either forward slashes or backslashes. However, under Solaris, Java accepts only paths with forward slashes.

Your best bet is to make sure you follow the filename conventions of the host filesystem. If your application is just opening and saving files at the user's request, you should be able to handle that functionality with the Swing JFileDialog class. This class encapsulates a graphical file–selection dialog box. The methods of the JFileDialog take care of system-dependent filename features for you.

If your application needs to deal with files on its own behalf, however, things get a little more complicated. The File class contains a few static variables to make this task possible. File.separator defines a String that specifies the file separator on the local host (e.g., / on Unix and Macintosh systems and \ on Windows systems); File.separatorChar provides the same information as a char. File.pathSeparator defines a String that separates items in a path (e.g., : on Unix systems and ; on Macintosh and Windows systems); File.pathSeparatorChar provides the information as a char.

You can use this system-dependent information in several ways. Probably the simplest way to localize pathnames is to pick a convention you use internally, for instance the forward slash, and do a String replace to substitute for the localized separator character:

```
// we'll use forward slash as our standard
String path = "mail/1999/june/merle";
path = path.replace('/', File.separatorChar);
File mailbox = new File( path );
```

Alternately, you could work with the components of a pathname and build the local pathname when you need it:

```
String [] path = { "mail", "1999", "june", "merle" };

StringBuffer sb = new StringBuffer(path[0]);
```

```
    for (int i=1; i< path.length; i++)
        sb.append( File.separator + path[i] );
    File mailbox = new File( sb.toString() );
```

One thing to remember is that Java interprets the backslash character (\) as an escape character when used in a `String`. To get a backslash in a `String`, you have to use \\.

Another issue to grapple with is that some operating systems use special identifiers for the "roots" of filesystems. For example, Windows uses `C:\`. Should you need it, the `File` class provides the static method `listRoots()`, which returns an array of `File` objects corresponding to the filesystem root directories.

File operations

Once we have a `File` object, we can use it to ask for information about the file or directory and to perform standard operations on it. A number of methods let us ask certain questions about the `File`. For example, `isFile()` returns `true` if the `File` represents a file, while `isDirectory()` returns `true` if it's a directory. `isAbsolute()` indicates if the `File` has an absolute or relative path specification.

Components of the `File` pathname are available through the following methods: `getName()`, `getPath()`, `getAbsolutePath()`, and `getParent()`. `getName()` returns a `String` for the filename without any directory information; `getPath()` returns the directory information without the filename. If the `File` has an absolute path specification, `getAbsolutePath()` returns that path. Otherwise it returns the relative path appended to the current working directory. `getParent()` returns the parent directory of the `File`.

Interestingly, the string returned by `getPath()` or `getAbsolutePath()` may not follow the same case-conventions as the underlying filesystem. You can retrieve the filesystem's own or "canonical" version of the file's path using the method `getCanonicalPath()`. In Windows, for example, you can create a `File` object whose `getAbsolutePath()` is `C:\Autoexec.bat`, but whose `getCanonical-Path()` is `C:\AUTOEXEC.BAT`. This is useful for comparing filenames that may have been supplied with different case conventions.

You can get or set the modification time of a file or directory with `lastModified()` and `setLastModified()` methods. The value is a `long` that is the number of milliseconds since the *epoch* (Jan 1, 1970, 00:00:00 GMT). We can also get the size of the file in bytes with `length()`.

Here's a fragment of code that prints some information about a file:

```
    File fooFile = new File( "/tmp/boofa" );

    String type = fooFile.isFile() ? "File " : "Directory ";
```

```
String name = fooFile.getName();
long len = fooFile.length();
System.out.println(type + name + ", " + len + " bytes " );
```

If the `File` object corresponds to a directory, we can list the files in the directory with the `list()` method or the `listFiles()` method:

```
String [] fileNames = fooFile.list();
File [] files = fooFile.listFiles();
```

`list()` returns an array of `String` objects that contains filenames. `listFiles()` returns an array of `File` objects. Note that in neither case are the files guaranteed to be in any kind of order (alphabetical, for example).

If the `File` refers to a nonexistent directory, we can create the directory with `mkdir()` or `mkdirs()`. `mkdir()` creates a single directory; `mkdirs()` also creates all of the intervening directories in a `File` specification. Use `renameTo()` to rename a file or directory and `delete()` to delete a file or directory.

Note that using the `File` object itself isn't generally the way to create a file; that's normally done implicitly with a `FileOutputStream` or `FileWriter`, as we'll discuss in a moment. The exception is the `createNewFile()` method, which can be used to attempt to create a new zero-length file at the location pointed to by the `File` object. The useful thing about this method is that the operation is guaranteed to be "atomic" with respect to all other file creation. `createNewFile()` returns a boolean value which tells you whether the file was created.

You can use this to implement file locking from Java. This is useful in combination with `deleteOnExit()`, which flags the file to be automatically removed when the Java Virtual Machine exits. Another file creation method related to the `File` class itself is the static method `createTempFile()`, which creates a file in a specified location using an automatically generated unique name. This, too, is useful in combination with `deleteOnExit()`.

The `toURL()` method converts a file path to a `file:` URL object. We'll talk about URLs in Chapter 12, *Programming for the Web*. They are an abstraction that allows you to point to any kind of object anywhere on the Net. Converting a `File` reference to a URL may be useful for consistency with more general routines that deal with URLs.

Table 10-1 summarizes the methods provided by the `File` class.

Table 10-1. File Methods

Method	Return Type	Description
canRead()	boolean	Is the file (or directory) readable?
canWrite()	boolean	Is the file (or directory) writable?

Table 10-1. File Methods (continued)

Method	Return Type	Description
createNewFile()	boolean	Creates a new file
createTempFile (String *pfx*, String *sfx*)	static File	Creates a new file, with the specified prefix and suffix, in the default temp-file directory
delete()	boolean	Deletes the file (or directory)
deleteOnExit()	void	When it exits, Java runtime system will delete the file
exists()	boolean	Does the file (or directory) exist?
getAbsolutePath()	String	Returns the absolute path of the file (or directory)
getCanonicalPath()	String	Returns the absolute, case-correct path of the file (or directory)
getName()	String	Returns the name of the file (or directory)
getParent()	String	Returns the name of the parent directory of the file (or directory)
getPath()	String	Returns the path of the file (or directory)
isAbsolute()	boolean	Is the filename (or directory name) absolute?
isDirectory()	boolean	Is the item a directory?
isFile()	boolean	Is the item a file?
lastModified()	long	Returns the last modification time of the file (or directory)
length()	long	Returns the length of the file
list()	String []	Returns a list of files in the directory
listfiles()	File[]	Returns the contents of the directory as an array of File objects
mkdir()	boolean	Creates the directory
mkdirs()	boolean	Creates all directories in the path
renameTo(File *dest*)	boolean	Renames the file (or directory)
setLastModified()	boolean	Sets the last-modified time of the file (or directory)
setReadOnly()	boolean	Sets the file to read-only status
toURL()	java.net. URL	Generates a URL object for the Thefile (or directory)

File Streams

Java provides two specialized streams for reading and writing files in the file-system: `FileInputStream` and `FileOutputStream`. These streams provide the basic `InputStream` and `OutputStream` functionality applied to reading and writing the contents of files. They can be combined with the filter streams described earlier to work with files in the same way we do other stream communications.

Because `FileInputStream` is a subclass of `InputStream`, it inherits all standard `InputStream` functionality for reading the contents of a file. `FileInputStream` provides only a low-level interface to reading data, however, so you'll typically wrap it with another stream, such as a `DataInputStream`.

You can create a `FileInputStream` from a `String` pathname or a `File` object:

```
FileInputStream foois = new FileInputStream( fooFile );
FileInputStream passwdis = new FileInputStream( "/etc/passwd" );
```

When you create a `FileInputStream`, the Java runtime system attempts to open the specified file. Thus, the `FileInputStream` constructors can throw a `FileNotFoundException` if the specified file doesn't exist, or an `IOException` if some other I/O error occurs. Be sure to catch and handle these exceptions in your code. When the stream is first created, its `available()` method and the `File` object's `length()` method should return the same value. Be sure to call the `close()` method when you are done with the file.

To read characters from a file, you can wrap an `InputStreamReader` around a `FileInputStream`. If you want to use the default character-encoding scheme, you can use the `FileReader` class instead, which is provided as a convenience. `FileReader` works just like `FileInputStream`, except that it reads characters instead of bytes and wraps a `Reader` instead of an `InputStream`.

The following class, `ListIt`, is a small utility that sends the contents of a file or directory to standard output:

```java
//file: ListIt.java
import java.io.*;

class ListIt {
    public static void main ( String args[] ) throws Exception {
        File file =  new File( args[0] );

        if ( !file.exists() || !file.canRead() ) {
            System.out.println( "Can't read " + file );
            return;
        }

        if ( file.isDirectory() ) {
            String [] files = file.list();
            for (int i=0; i< files.length; i++)
                System.out.println( files[i] );
        }
        else
            try {
                FileReader fr = new FileReader ( file );
                BufferedReader in = new BufferedReader( fr );
                String line;
                while ((line = in.readLine()) != null)
```

```
            System.out.println(line);
        }
        catch ( FileNotFoundException e ) {
            System.out.println( "File Disappeared" );
        }
    }
}
```

ListIt constructs a File object from its first command-line argument and tests the File to see whether it exists and is readable. If the File is a directory, ListIt outputs the names of the files in the directory. Otherwise, ListIt reads and outputs the file.

FileOutputStream is a subclass of OutputStream, so it inherits all the standard OutputStream functionality for writing to a file. Just like FileInputStream though, FileOutputStream provides only a low-level interface to writing data. You'll typically wrap another stream, like a DataOutputStream or a PrintWriter, around the FileOutputStream to provide higher-level functionality.

You can create a FileOutputStream from a String pathname or a File object. Unlike FileInputStream, however, the FileOutputStream constructors don't throw a FileNotFoundException. If the specified file doesn't exist, the FileOutputStream creates the file. The FileOutputStream constructors can throw an IOException if some other I/O error occurs, so you still need to handle this exception.

If the specified file does exist, the FileOutputStream opens it for writing. When you subsequently call the write() method, the new data overwrites the current contents of the file. If you need to append data to an existing file, you should use a different constructor that accepts an append flag:

```
FileInputStream foois = new FileOutputStream( fooFile, true);
FileInputStream psis = new FileOutputStream("/etc/passwd", true);
```

Another way to append data to files is with a RandomAccessFile, as we'll discuss shortly.

To write characters (instead of bytes) to a file, you can wrap an Output-StreamWriter around a FileOutputStream. If you want to use the default character-encoding scheme, you can use instead the FileWriter class, which is provided as a convenience. FileWriter works just like FileOutputStream, except that it writes characters instead of bytes and wraps a Writer instead of an OutputStream.

The following example reads a line of data from standard input and writes it to the file */tmp/foo.txt*:

```
String s = new BufferedReader(
    new InputStreamReader( System.in ) ).readLine();
```

```
File out = new File( "/tmp/foo.txt" );
FileWriter fw = new FileWriter ( out );
PrintWriter pw = new PrintWriter( fw )
pw.println( s );
fw.close();
```

Notice how we have wrapped a `PrintWriter` around the `FileWriter` to facilitate writing the data. Also, to be a good filesystem citizen, we've called the `close()` method when we're done with the `FileWriter`.

The java.io.RandomAccessFile Class

The `java.io.RandomAccessFile` class provides the ability to read and write data from or to any specified location in a file. `RandomAccessFile` implements both the `DataInput` and `DataOutput` interfaces, so you can use it to read and write strings and primitive types. In other words, `RandomAccessFile` defines the same methods for reading and writing data as `DataInputStream` and `DataOutputStream`. However, because the class provides random, rather than sequential, access to file data, it's not a subclass of either `InputStream` or `OutputStream`.

You can create a `RandomAccessFile` from a `String` pathname or a `File` object. The constructor also takes a second `String` argument that specifies the mode of the file. Use `"r"` for a read-only file or `"rw"` for a read-write file. Here's how we would start to create a simple database to keep track of user information:

```
try {
    RandomAccessFile users =
        new RandomAccessFile( "Users", "rw" );
    ...
}
catch (IOException e) { ... }
```

When you create a `RandomAccessFile` in read-only mode, Java tries to open the specified file. If the file doesn't exist, `RandomAccessFile` throws an `IOException`. If, however, you are creating a `RandomAccessFile` in read-write mode, the object creates the file if it doesn't exist. The constructor can still throw an `IOException` if some other I/O error occurs, so you still need to handle this exception.

After you have created a `RandomAccessFile`, call any of the normal reading and writing methods, just as you would with a `DataInputStream` or `DataOutputStream`. If you try to write to a read-only file, the write method throws an `IOException`.

What makes a `RandomAccessFile` special is the `seek()` method. This method takes a `long` value and uses it to set the location for reading and writing in the file.

You can use the getFilePointer() method to get the current location. If you need to append data to the end of the file, use length() to determine that location, then seek() to it. You can write or seek beyond the end of a file, but you can't read beyond the end of a file. The read() method throws an EOFException if you try to do this.

Here's an example of writing some data to our user database:

```
users.seek( userNum * RECORDSIZE );
users.writeUTF( userName );
users.writeInt( userID );
```

One caveat to notice with this example is that we need to be sure that the String length for userName, along with any data that comes after it, fits within the specified record size.

Applets and Files

For security reasons, untrusted applets and applications are not permitted to read from and write to arbitrary places in the filesystem. The ability of untrusted code to read and write files, as with any kind of system resource, is under the control of the system security policy, through a SecurityManager object. A Security-Manager is installed by the application that is running the untrusted code, such as *appletviewer* or a Java-enabled web browser. All filesystem access must first pass the scrutiny of the SecurityManager.

For example, Sun's HotJava web browser allows even untrusted applets to have access to specific files designated by the user in an access-control list. Netscape Navigator, on the other hand, currently doesn't allow untrusted applets any access to the filesystem. In both cases, trusted applets can be given arbitrary access to the filesystem, just like a standalone Java application.

It isn't unusual to want an applet to maintain some kind of state information on the system on which it's running. But for a Java applet that is restricted from access to the local filesystem, the only option is to store data over the network on its server. Applets have at their disposal powerful general means for communicating data over networks. The only limitation is that, by convention, an applet's network communication is restricted to the server that launched it. This limits the options for where the data will reside.

Currently, the only way for a Java program to send data to a server is through a network socket or tools like RMI, which run over sockets. In Chapter 11, *Network Programming with Sockets and RMI*, we'll take a detailed look at building networked applications with sockets. With the tools described in that chapter, it's possible to build powerful client/server applications. Sun also has a Java extension called

WebNFS, which allows applets and applications to work with files on an NFS server in much the same way as the ordinary File API.

Loading Application Resources

We often have data files and other objects that we want our programs to use. Java provides many ways to access these resources. In a standalone application, we can simply open files and read the bytes. In both standalone applications and applets, we can construct URLs to well-known locations. The problem with these methods is that we have to know where our application lives in order to find our data. This is not always as easy as it seems. What is needed is a universal way to access resources associated with our application and our application's individual classes. The `Class` class's `getResource()` method provides just this.

What does `getResource()` do for us? To construct a URL to a file, we normally have to figure out a home directory for our code and construct a path relative to that. In an applet, we could use `getCodeBase()` or `getDocumentBase()` to find the base URL, and use that base to create the URL for the resource we want. But these methods don't help a standalone application—and there's no reason that a standalone application and an applet shouldn't be able to share classes anyway. To solve this problem, the `getResource()` method provides a standard way to get objects relative to a given class file or to the system classpath. `getResource()` returns a special URL that uses the class's class loader. This means that no matter where the class came from—a web server, the local filesystem, or even a JAR file—we can simply ask for an object, get a URL for the object, and use the URL to access the object.

`getResource()` takes as an argument a slash-separated pathname for the resource and returns a URL. There are two kinds of paths: absolute and relative. An absolute path begins with a slash. For example: */foo/bar/blah.txt*. In this case, the search for the object begins at the top of the class path. If there is a directory *foo/bar* in the class path, `getResource()` searches that directory for the *blah.txt* file. A relative URL does not begin with a slash. In this case, the search begins at the location of the class file, whether it is local, on a remote server, or in a JAR file (either local or remote). So if we were calling `getResource()` on a class loader that loaded a class in the `foo.bar` package, we could refer to the file as *blah.txt*. In this case, the class itself would be loaded from the directory *foo/bar* somewhere on the class path, and we'd expect to find the file in the same directory.

For example, here's an application that looks up some resources:

```
//file: FindResources.java
package mypackage;
import java.net.URL;
import java.io.IOException;
```

```
public class FindResources {
  public static void main( String [] args ) throws IOException {
    // absolute from the classpath
    URL url = FindResources.class.getResource("/mypackage/foo.txt");
    // relative to the class location
    url = FindResources.class.getResource("foo.txt");
    // another relative document
    url = FindResources.class.getResource("docs/bar.txt");
  }
}
```

The FindResources class belongs to the mypackage package, so its class file will live in a *mypackage* directory somewhere on the class path. FindResources locates the document *foo.txt* using an absolute and then a relative URL. At the end, FindResources uses a relative path to reach a document in the *mypackage/docs* directory. In each case we refer to the FindResources's Class object using the static .class notation. Alternatively, if we had an instance of the object, we could use its getClass() method to reach the Class object.

For an applet, the search is similar but occurs on the host from which the applet was loaded. getResource() first checks any JAR files loaded with the applet, and then searches the normal remote applet class path, constructed relative to the applet's codebase URL.

getResource() returns a URL for whatever type of object you reference. This could be a text file or properties file that you want to read as a stream, or it might be an image or sound file or some other object. If you want the data as a stream, the Class class also provides a getResourceAsStream() method. In the case of an image, you'd probably hand the URL over to the getImage() method of the Applet class or one of the components of the Swing package for loading.

Serialization

Using a DataOutputStream, you could write an application that saves the data content of an arbitrary object as simple types. However Java provides an even more powerful mechanism called *object serialization* that does almost all of the work for you. In its simplest form, object serialization is an automatic way to save and load the state of an object. However, object serialization has depths that we cannot plumb within the scope of this book, including complete control over the serialization process and interesting conundrums like class versioning.

Basically, an object of any class that implements the Serializable interface can be saved and restored from a stream. Special stream subclasses, Object-InputStream and ObjectOutputStream, are used to serialize primitive types and objects. Subclasses of Serializable classes are also serializable. The default serialization mechanism saves the value of an object's nonstatic and nontransient (see the following explanation) member variables.

One of the most important (and tricky) things about serialization is that when an object is serialized, any object references it contains are also serialized. Serialization can capture entire "graphs" of interconnected objects and put them back together on the receiving end (we'll demonstrate this in an upcoming example). The implication is that any object we serialize must contain only references to other `Serializable` objects. We can take control by marking nonserializable members as `transient` or overriding the default serialization mechanisms. The `transient` modifier can be applied to any instance variable to indicate that its contents are not useful outside of the current context and should never be saved.

In the following example, we create a `Hashtable` and write it to a disk file called *h.ser*. The `Hashtable` object is serializable because it implements the `Serializable` interface.

```
//file: Save.java
import java.io.*;
import java.util.*;

public class Save {
  public static void main(String[] args) {
    Hashtable h = new Hashtable();
    h.put("string", "Gabriel Garcia Marquez");
    h.put("int", new Integer(26));
    h.put("double", new Double(Math.PI));

    try {
      FileOutputStream fileOut = new FileOutputStream("h.ser");
      ObjectOutputStream out = new ObjectOutputStream(fileOut);
      out.writeObject(h);
    }
    catch (Exception e) {
      System.out.println(e);
    }
  }
}
```

First we construct a `Hashtable` with a few elements in it. Then, in the three lines of code inside the `try` block, we write the `Hashtable` to a file called *h.ser*, using the `writeObject()` method of `ObjectOutputStream`. The `ObjectOutput-Stream` class is a lot like the `DataOutputStream` class, except that it includes the powerful `writeObject()` method.

The `Hashtable` we created has internal references to the items it contains. Thus, these components are automatically serialized along with the `Hashtable`. We'll see this in the next example when we deserialize the `Hashtable`.

```
//file: Load.java
import java.io.*;
import java.util.*;

public class Load {
  public static void main(String[] args) {
    try {
      FileInputStream fileIn = new FileInputStream("h.ser");
      ObjectInputStream in = new ObjectInputStream(fileIn);
      Hashtable h = (Hashtable)in.readObject();
      System.out.println(h.toString());
    }
    catch (Exception e) {
      System.out.println(e);
    }
  }
}
```

In this example, we read the Hashtable from the *h.ser* file, using the readObject() method of ObjectInputStream. The ObjectInputStream class is a lot like DataInputStream, except that it includes the readObject() method. The return type of readObject() is Object, so we need to cast it to a Hashtable. Finally, we print out the contents of the Hashtable using its toString() method.

We'll show more examples of serialization at work in Chapter 19, *Java Beans*, when we discuss JavaBeans. There we'll see that it is even possible to serialize graphical GUI components in mid-use and bring them back to life later.

Data Compression

The java.util.zip package contains classes you can use for data compression. In this section, we'll talk about how to use these classes. We'll also present two useful example programs that build on what you have just learned about streams and files.

The classes in the java.util.zip package support two widespread compression formats: GZIP and ZIP. Both of these are based on the ZLIB compression algorithm, which is discussed in RFC 1950, RFC 1951, and RFC 1952. These documents are available at *http://www.faqs.org/rfcs*. But you don't need to read them unless you want to implement your own compression algorithm or otherwise extend the functionality of the java.util.zip package.

Compressing Data

The java.util.zip class provides two FilterOutputStream subclasses to write compressed data to a stream. To write compressed data in the GZIP format, simply wrap a `GZIPOutputStream` around an underlying stream and write to it. The following is a complete example that shows how to compress a file using the GZIP format:

```java
//file: GZip.java
import java.io.*;
import java.util.zip.*;

public class GZip {
  public static int sChunk = 8192;

  public static void main(String[] args) {
    if (args.length != 1) {
      System.out.println("Usage: GZip source");
      return;
    }
    // create output stream
    String zipname = args[0] + ".gz";
    GZIPOutputStream zipout;
    try {
      FileOutputStream out = new FileOutputStream(zipname);
      zipout = new GZIPOutputStream(out);
    }
    catch (IOException e) {
      System.out.println("Couldn't create " + zipname + ".");
      return;
    }
    byte[] buffer = new byte[sChunk];
    // compress the file
    try {
      FileInputStream in = new FileInputStream(args[0]);
      int length;
      while ((length = in.read(buffer, 0, sChunk)) != -1)
        zipout.write(buffer, 0, length);
      in.close();
    }
    catch (IOException e) {
      System.out.println("Couldn't compress " + args[0] + ".");
    }
    try { zipout.close(); }
    catch (IOException e) {}
  }
}
```

First we check to make sure we have a command-line argument representing a filename. Then we construct a `GZIPOutputStream` wrapped around a `FileOutputStream` representing the given filename, with the *.gz* suffix appended. With this in place, we open the source file. We read chunks of data from it and write them into the `GZIPOutputStream`. Finally, we clean up by closing our open streams.

Writing data to a ZIP file is a little more involved but still quite manageable. While a GZIP file contains only one compressed file, a ZIP file is actually a collection of files, some (or all) of which may be compressed. Each item in the ZIP file is represented by a `ZipEntry` object. When writing to a `ZipOutputStream`, you'll need to call `putNextEntry()` before writing the data for each item. The following example shows how to create a `ZipOutputStream`. You'll notice it's just like creating a `GZIPOutputStream`:

```
ZipOutputStream zipout;
try {
  FileOutputStream out = new FileOutputStream("archive.zip");
  zipout = new ZipOutputStream(out);
}
catch (IOException e) {}
```

Let's say we have two files we want to write into this archive. Before we begin writing, we need to call `putNextEntry()`. We'll create a simple entry with just a name. There are other fields in `ZipEntry` that you can set, but most of the time you won't need to bother with them.

```
try {
  ZipEntry entry = new ZipEntry("First");
  zipout.putNextEntry(entry);
}
catch (IOException e) {}
```

At this point, you can write the contents of the first file into the archive. When you're ready to write the second file into the archive, simply call `putNextEntry()` again:

```
try {
  ZipEntry entry = new ZipEntry("Second");
  zipout.putNextEntry(entry);
}
catch (IOException e) {}
```

Decompressing Data

To decompress data, you can use one of the two `FilterInputStream` subclasses provided in `java.util.zip`. To decompress data in the GZIP format, simply wrap a `GZIPInputStream` around an underlying `FileInputStream` and read from it. The following is a complete example that shows how to decompress a GZIP file:

```
//file: GUnzip.java
import java.io.*;
import java.util.zip.*;
```

```
public class GUnzip {
  public static int sChunk = 8192;
  public static void main(String[] args) {
    if (args.length != 1) {
      System.out.println("Usage: GUnzip source");
      return;
    }
    // create input stream
    String zipname, source;
    if (args[0].endsWith(".gz")) {
      zipname = args[0];
      source = args[0].substring(0, args[0].length() - 3);
    }
    else {
      zipname = args[0] + ".gz";
      source = args[0];
    }
    GZIPInputStream zipin;
    try {
      FileInputStream in = new FileInputStream(zipname);
      zipin = new GZIPInputStream(in);
    }
    catch (IOException e) {
      System.out.println("Couldn't open " + zipname + ".");
      return;
    }
    byte[] buffer = new byte[sChunk];
    // decompress the file
    try {
      FileOutputStream out = new FileOutputStream(source);
      int length;
      while ((length = zipin.read(buffer, 0, sChunk)) != -1)
        out.write(buffer, 0, length);
      out.close();
    }
    catch (IOException e) {
      System.out.println("Couldn't decompress " + args[0] + ".");
    }
    try { zipin.close(); }
    catch (IOException e) {}
  }
}
```

First we check to make sure we have a command-line argument representing a file-name. If the argument ends with *.gz*, we figure out what the filename for the uncompressed file should be. Otherwise, we use the given argument and assume the compressed file has the *.gz* suffix. Then we construct a GZIPInputStream wrapped around a FileInputStream, representing the compressed file. With this

in place, we open the target file. We read chunks of data from the GZIP-
InputStream and write them into the target file. Finally, we clean up by closing
our open streams.

Again, the ZIP archive presents a little more complexity than the GZIP file. When
reading from a ZipInputStream, you should call getNextEntry() before reading each item. When getNextEntry() returns null, there are no more items to
read. The following example shows how to create a ZipInputStream. You'll
notice it's just like creating a GZIPInputStream:

```
ZipInputStream zipin;
try {
  FileInputStream in = new FileInputStream("archive.zip");
  zipin = new ZipInputStream(in);
}
catch (IOException e) {}
```

Suppose we want to read two files from this archive. Before we begin reading, we
need to call getNextEntry(). At the least, the entry will give us a name of the
item we are reading from the archive:

```
try {
  ZipEntry first = zipin.getNextEntry();
}
catch (IOException e) {}
```

At this point, you can read the contents of the first item in the archive. When you
come to the end of the item, the read() method will return −1. Now you can call
getNextEntry() again to read the second item from the archive:

```
try {
  ZipEntry second = zipin.getNextEntry();
}
catch (IOException e) {}
```

If you call getNextEntry() and it returns null, there are no more items, and
you have reached the end of the archive.

11

In this chapter:
- *Sockets*
- *Datagram Sockets*
- *Simple Serialized Object Protocols*
- *Remote Method Invocation (RMI)*

Network Programming with Sockets and RMI

The network is the soul of Java. Most of what is new and exciting about Java centers around the potential for new kinds of dynamic, networked applications. In this chapter, we'll start our discussion of the `java.net` package, which contains the fundamental classes for communications and working with networked resources. We'll also talk about the `java.rmi` package, which provides Java's powerful, high-level, Remote Method Invocation facilities.

The classes of `java.net` fall into two categories: the sockets API and tools for working with Uniform Resource Locators (URLs). Figure 11-1 shows the `java.net` package.

Java's sockets API provides access to the standard network protocols used for communications between hosts on the Internet. Sockets are the mechanism underlying all other kinds of portable networked communications. Sockets are a low-level tool—you can use sockets for any kind of communications between client and server server or peer applications on the Net, but you have to implement your own application-level protocols for handling and interpreting the data. Higher-level networking tools, like remote method invocation and other distributed object systems, are implemented on top of sockets.

Java remote method invocation (RMI) is a powerful tool that leverages Java object serialization, allowing you to transparently work with objects on remote machines as if they were local. With RMI it is easy to write distributed applications in which clients and servers work with each other's data as full-fledged Java objects, rather than streams or packets of data.

In this chapter, we'll provide some simple and practical examples of Java network programming at both levels, using sockets and RMI. In the next chapter, we'll look at the other half of the `java.net` package, which works with URLs, content

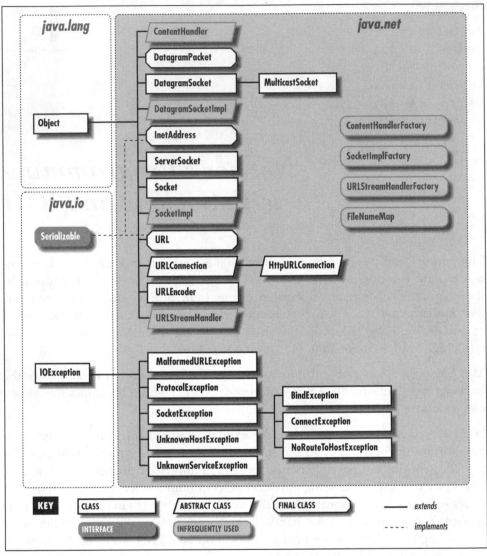

Figure 11-1. The java.net package

handlers, and protocol handlers; we'll also cover servlets, which allow you to write application components for web servers.

Sockets

Sockets are a low-level programming interface for networked communications. They send streams of data between applications that may or may not be on the same host. Sockets originated in BSD Unix and are, in other languages, hairy and complicated things with lots of small parts that can break off and choke little children. The reason for this is that most socket APIs can be used with almost any kind of underlying network protocol. Since the protocols that transport data across the network can have radically different features, the socket interface can be quite complex.*

Java supports a simplified object-oriented interface to sockets that makes network communications considerably easier. If you have done network programming using sockets in C or another structured language, you should be pleasantly surprised at how simple things can be when objects encapsulate the gory details. If this is the first time you've come across sockets, you'll find that talking to another application over the network can be as simple as reading a file or getting user input from a terminal. Most forms of I/O in Java, including most network I/O, use the stream classes described in Chapter 10, *Input/Output Facilities*. Streams provide a unified I/O interface; reading or writing across the Internet is similar to reading or writing a file on the local system.

Java provides different kinds of sockets to support three different distinct classes of underlying protocols. In this first section, we'll look at Java's basic `Socket` class, which uses a *connection-oriented* protocol. A connection-oriented protocol gives you the equivalent of a telephone conversation; after establishing a connection, two applications can send data back and forth—the connection stays in place even when no one is talking. The protocol ensures that no data is lost and that whatever you send always arrives in order that you sent it. In the next section, we'll look at the `DatagramSocket` class, which uses a *connectionless protocol*. A connectionless protocol is more like the postal service. Applications can send short messages to each other, but no end-to-end connection is set up in advance and no attempt is made to keep the messages in order. It is not even guaranteed that the messages will arrive at all. A `MulticastSocket` is a variation of a `DatagramSocket` that can be used to send data to multiple recipients (multicasting). Working with mutlicast sockets is very much like working with datagram sockets. However, multicasting is not widely supported across the Internet at this time, so we will not cover it here.

Again, in theory, just about any protocol family can be used underneath the socket layer: Novell's IPX, Apple's AppleTalk, even the old ChaosNet protocols. But in practice, there's only one protocol family people care about on the Internet, and only one protocol family Java supports: the Internet Protocol, IP. The `Socket` class speaks TCP, and the `DatagramSocket` class speaks UDP, both standard Internet protocols. These protocols are generally available on any system that is connected to the Internet.

---

* For a discussion of sockets in general, see *Unix Network Programming*, by Richard Stevens (Prentice-Hall). For a complete discussion of network programming in Java, see *Java Network Programming*, by Elliotte Rusty Harold (O'Reilly & Associates).

Clients and Servers

When writing network applications, it's common to talk about clients and servers. The distinction is increasingly vague, but the side that initiates the conversation is usually considered the *client*. The side that accepts the request to talk is usually the *server*. In the case where there are two peer applications using sockets to talk, the distinction is less important, but for simplicity we'll use this definition.

For our purposes, the most important difference between a client and a server is that a client can create a socket to initiate a conversation with a server application at any time, while a server must prepare to listen for incoming conversations in advance. The `java.net.Socket` class represents one side of an individual socket connection on both the client and server. In addition, the server uses the `java. net.ServerSocket` class to listen for connections from clients. An application (or thread) acting as a server creates a `ServerSocket` object and waits, blocked in a call to its `accept()` method, until a connection arrives. When it does, the `accept()` method creates a `Socket` object the server uses to communicate with the client. A server may carry on conversations with multiple clients at once; in this case there will still be only a single `ServerSocket` but the server will have multiple `Socket` objects—one associated with each client, as shown in Figure 11-2.

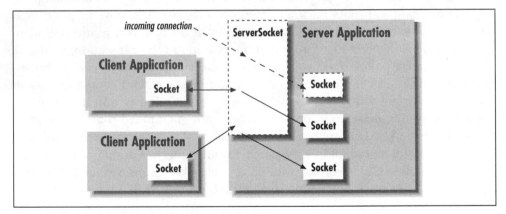

Figure 11-2. Clients and servers, Sockets and ServerSockets

A client needs two pieces of information to locate and connect to another server on the Internet: a *hostname* (used to find the host's network address) and a *port number*. The port number is an identifier that differentiates between multiple clients or servers on the same host. A server application listens on a prearranged port while waiting for connections. Clients select the port number assigned to the service they want to access. If you think of the host computers as hotels and the applications as guests, then the ports are like the guests' room numbers. For one person to call another, he or she must know the other party's hotel name and room number.

Clients

A client application opens a connection to a server by constructing a `Socket` that specifies the hostname and port number of the desired server:

```
try {
    Socket sock = new Socket("wupost.wustl.edu", 25);
}
catch ( UnknownHostException e ) {
    System.out.println("Can't find host.");
}
catch ( IOException e ) {
    System.out.println("Error connecting to host.");
}
```

This code fragment attempts to connect a `Socket` to port 25 (the SMTP mail service) of the host *wupost.wustl.edu*. The client handles the possibility that the hostname can't be resolved (`UnknownHostException`) and that it might not be able to connect to it (`IOException`). As an alternative to using a hostname, you can provide a string version of the host's IP address:

```
Socket sock = new Socket("22.66.89.167", 25);
```

Once a connection is made, input and output streams can be retrieved with the `Socket getInputStream()` and `getOutputStream()` methods. The following (rather arbitrary) code sends and receives some data with the streams:

```
try {
    Socket server = new Socket("foo.bar.com", 1234);
    InputStream in = server.getInputStream();
    OutputStream out = server.getOutputStream();

    // write a byte
    out.write(42);

    // write a newline or carriage return delimited string
    PrintWriter pout = new PrintWriter( out, true );
    pout.println("Hello!");

    // read a byte
    byte back = (byte)in.read();

    // read a newline or carriage return delimited string
    BufferedReader bin =
      new BufferedReader( new InputStreamReader( in ) );
    String response = bin.readLine();

    // send a serialized Java object
    ObjectOutputStream oout = new ObjectOutputStream( out );
    oout.writeObject( new java.util.Date() );
```

```
    oout.flush();

    server.close();
}
catch (IOException e ) { ... }
```

In this exchange, the client first creates a Socket for communicating with the server. The Socket constructor specifies the server's hostname (*foo.bar.com*) and a prearranged port number (1234). Once the connection is established, the client writes a single byte to the server using the OutputStream's write() method. It then wraps a PrintWriter around the OutputStream in order to send a string of text more easily. Next, it performs the complementary operations: reading a byte from the server using InputStream's read() and then creating a Buffered-Reader from which to get a full string of text. Finally, we do something really funky and send a serialized Java object to the server, using an Object-OutputStream. (We'll talk in depth about sending serialized objects later in this chapter.) The client then terminates the connection with the close() method. All these operations have the potential to generate IOExceptions; the catch clause is where our application would deal with these.

Servers

After a connection is established, a server application uses the same kind of Socket object for its side of the communications. However, to accept a connection from a client, it must first create a ServerSocket, bound to the correct port. Let's re-create the previous conversation from the server's point of view:

```
// meanwhile, on foo.bar.com...
try {
    ServerSocket listener = new ServerSocket( 1234 );

    while ( !finished ) {
        Socket client = listener.accept();  // wait for connection

        InputStream in = client.getInputStream();
        OutputStream out = client.getOutputStream();

        // read a byte
        byte someByte = (byte)in.read();

        // read a newline or carriage-return-delimited string
        BufferedReader bin =
          new BufferedReader( new InputStreamReader( in ) );
        String someString = bin.readLine();

        // write a byte
        out.write(43);
```

```
        // say goodbye
        PrintWriter pout = new PrintWriter( out, true );
        pout.println("Goodbye!");

        // read a serialized Java object
        ObjectInputStream oin = new ObjectInputStream( in );
        Date date = (Date)oin.readObject();

        client.close();
    }

    listener.close();
}
catch (IOException e ) { ... }
catch (ClassNotFoundException e2 ) { ... }
```

First, our server creates a `ServerSocket` attached to port 1234. On some systems, there are rules about what ports an application can use. Port numbers below 1024 are usually reserved for system processes and standard, well-known services, so we pick a port number outside of this range. The `ServerSocket` need be created only once; thereafter we can accept as many connections as arrive.

Next we enter a loop, waiting for the `accept()` method of the `ServerSocket` to return an active `Socket` connection from a client. When a connection has been established, we perform the server side of our dialog, then close the connection and return to the top of the loop to wait for another connection. Finally, when the server application wants to stop listening for connections altogether, it calls the `close()` method of the `ServerSocket`.

This server is single-threaded; it handles one connection at a time, not calling `accept()` to listen for a new connection until it's finished with the current connection. A more realistic server would have a loop that accepts connections concurrently and passes them off to their own threads for processing. (Our tiny web server example later in this chapter will do just this.)

Sockets and security

The previous examples presuppose that the client has permission to connect to the server, and that the server is allowed to listen on the specified socket. This is not always the case. Specifically, applets and other untrusted applications run under the auspices of a `SecurityManager` that can impose arbitrary restrictions on what hosts they may or may not talk to, and whether or not they can listen for connections.

The security policy imposed on applets by the SDK `appletviewer` and the current version of Netscape allows untrusted applets to open socket connections only to the host that served them. That is, they can talk back only to the server from which their class files were retrieved. Untrusted applets are not allowed to open server sockets themselves. Now, this doesn't mean that an untrusted applet can't cooperate with its server to communicate with anyone, anywhere. The applet's server could run a proxy that lets the applet communicate indirectly with anyone it likes. What this security policy prevents is malicious applets roaming around inside corporate firewalls, making connections to trusted services. It places the burden of security on the originating server, and not the client machine. Restricting access to the originating server limits the usefulness of "trojan" applications that do annoying things from the client side. (You probably won't let your proxy mail-bomb people, because you'll be blamed.)

While fully trusted code and applications that are run without any security manager can perform any kind of activities, the default security policy that comes with SDK 1.2 and later dissallows most network access. So if you are going to run your application under the default security manager (using the `–Djava.security.manager` option on the command line or by manually installing the security manager within your application) you will have to modify the policy file to grant the appropriate permissions to your code. (See the section "Policy Files" in Chapter 3, *Tools of the Trade.*)

The following policy file fragment sets the socket permissions to allow connections to or from any host, on any nonprivileged port:

```
grant {
  permission java.net.SocketPermission
    "*:1024-", "listen,accept,connect";
};
```

When starting the Java interpreter, you can install the security manager and use this file (call it *mysecurity.policy*):

```
java –Djava.security.manager
    –Djava.security.policy=mysecurity.policy MyApplication
```

The DateAtHost Client

Many networked workstations run a time service that dispenses their local clock time on a well-known port. This was a precursor of NTP, the more general Network Time Protocol. In the next example, `DateAtHost`, we'll make a specialized subclass of `java.util.Date` that fetches the time from a remote host instead of initializing itself from the local clock. (See Chapter 9, *Basic Utility Classes*, for a complete discussion of the `Date` class.)

`DateAtHost` connects to the time service (port 37) and reads four bytes representing the time on the remote host. These four bytes are interpreted as an integer representing the number of seconds since the beginning of the 20th century. DateAtHost converts this to Java's variant of the absolute time (milliseconds since January 1, 1970, a date that should be familiar to Unix users). The conversion first creates a `long` value, which is the unsigned equivalent of the integer `time`. It subtracts an offset to make the time relative to the epoch (January 1, 1970) rather than the century, and multiplies by 1000 to convert to milliseconds. It then uses the converted time to initialize itself:

```java
//file: DateAtHost.java
import java.net.Socket;
import java.io.*;

public class DateAtHost extends java.util.Date {
    static int timePort = 37;
    // seconds from start of 20th century to Jan 1, 1970 00:00 GMT
    static final long offset = 2208988800L;

    public DateAtHost( String host ) throws IOException {
        this( host, timePort );
    }

    public DateAtHost( String host, int port ) throws IOException {
        Socket server = new Socket( host, port );
        DataInputStream din =
          new DataInputStream( server.getInputStream() );
        int time = din.readInt();
        server.close();

        setTime( (((1L << 32) + time) - offset) * 1000 );
    }
}
```

That's all there is to it. It's not very long, even with a few frills. We have supplied two possible constructors for DateAtHost. Normally we'd expect to use the first, which simply takes the name of the remote host as an argument. The second constructor specifies the hostname and the port number of the remote time service. (If the time service were running on a nonstandard port, we would use the second constructor to specify the alternate port number.) This second constructor does the work of making the connection and setting the time. The first constructor simply invokes the second (using the `this()` construct) with the default port as an argument. Supplying simplified constructors that invoke their siblings with default arguments is a common and useful technique; that is the only reason we've shown it here.

The second constructor opens a socket to the specified port on the remote host. It creates a DataInputStream to wrap the input stream and then reads a four-byte integer using the readInt() method. It's no coincidence that the bytes are in the right order. Java's `DataInputStream` and `DataOutputStream` classes work with the bytes of integer types in *network byte order* (most significant to least significant). The time protocol (and other standard network protocols that deal with binary data) also uses the network byte order, so we don't need to call any conversion routines. Explicit data conversions would probably be necessary if we were using a nonstandard protocol, especially when talking to a non-Java client or server. In that case we'd have to read byte by byte and do some rearranging to get our four-byte value. After reading the data, we're finished with the socket, so we close it, terminating the connection to the server. Finally, the constructor initializes the rest of the object by calling `Date`'s `setTime()` method with the calculated time value.

The `DateAtHost` class can work with a time retrieved from a remote host almost as easily as `Date` is used with the time on the local host. The only additional overhead is that we have to deal with the possible `IOException` that can be thrown by the `DateAtHost` constructor:

```
try {
    Date d = new DateAtHost( "sura.net" );
    System.out.println( "The time over there is: " + d );
}
catch ( IOException e ) { ... }
```

This example fetches the time at the host *sura.net* and prints its value.

The TinyHttpd Server

Have you ever wanted your very own web server? Well, you're in luck. In this section, we're going to build `TinyHttpd`, a minimal but functional HTTP daemon. `TinyHttpd` listens on a specified port and services simple HTTP "get file" requests. They look something like this:

```
GET /path/filename [ optional stuff ]
```

Your web browser sends one or more of these requests for each document it retrieves from a web server. Upon reading a request, our server will attempt to open the specified file and send its contents. If that document contains references to images or other items to be displayed inline, the browser continues with additional `GET` requests. For best performance `TinyHttpd` services each request in its own thread. Therefore, `TinyHttpd` can service several requests concurrently.

Over and above the limitations imposed by its simplicity, `TinyHttpd` suffers from the limitations imposed by the fickleness of filesystem access in Java. It's important to remember that file pathnames are still somewhat architecture-dependent—as is the concept of a filesystem to begin with. This example should work, as is, on Unix and DOS-like systems, but may require some customizations to account for differences on other platforms. It's possible to write slightly more elaborate code that uses the environmental information provided by Java to tailor itself to the local system. (Chapter 10 gives some hints about how.)

WARNING   Unless run with the security manager, the next example will serve files from your host without protection. Don't try this at work.

Now, without further ado, here's `TinyHttpd`:

```java
//file: TinyHttpd.java
import java.net.*;
import java.io.*;
import java.util.*;

public class TinyHttpd {
  public static void main( String argv[] ) throws IOException {
    ServerSocket ss =
        new ServerSocket( Integer.parseInt(argv[0]) );
    while ( true )
      new TinyHttpdConnection( ss.accept() ).start();
  }
} // end of class TinyHttpd

class TinyHttpdConnection extends Thread {
  Socket client;
  TinyHttpdConnection ( Socket client ) throws SocketException {
    this.client = client;
    setPriority( NORM_PRIORITY - 1 );
  }

  public void run() {
    try {
      BufferedReader in = new BufferedReader(
        new InputStreamReader(client.getInputStream(), "8859_1" ));
      OutputStream out = client.getOutputStream();
      PrintWriter pout = new PrintWriter(
        new OutputStreamWriter(out, "8859_1"), true );
      String request = in.readLine();
      System.out.println( "Request: "+request );

      StringTokenizer st = new StringTokenizer( request );
      if ( (st.countTokens() >= 2)
            && st.nextToken().equals("GET") ) {
        if ( (request = st.nextToken()).startsWith("/") )
          request = request.substring( 1 );
        if ( request.endsWith("/") || request.equals("") )
          request = request + "index.html";
        try {
          FileInputStream fis = new FileInputStream ( request );
```

```
            byte [] data = new byte [ fis.available() ];
            fis.read( data );
            out.write( data );
            out.flush();
          } catch ( FileNotFoundException e ) {
            pout.println( "404 Object Not Found" ); }
        } else
          pout.println( "400 Bad Request" );
        client.close();
      } catch ( IOException e ) {
        System.out.println( "I/O error " + e ); }
    }
  }
```

Compile TinyHttpd and place it in your class path, as described in Chapter 3. Go to a directory with some interesting documents and start the daemon, specifying an unused port number as an argument. For example:

% java TinyHttpd 1234

You should now be able to use your web browser to retrieve files from your host. You'll have to specify the port number you chose in the URL. For example, if your hostname is *foo.bar.com*, and you started the server as shown, you could reference a file as in:

```
http://foo.bar.com:1234/welcome.html
```

TinyHttpd looks for files relative to its current directory, so the pathnames you provide should be relative to that location. Retrieved some files? (Did you notice that when you retrieved an HTML file your web browser automatically generated more requests for items like images that were contained within it?) Let's take a closer look.

The TinyHttpd application has two classes. The public TinyHttpd class contains the main() method of our standalone application. It begins by creating a ServerSocket, attached to the specified port. It then loops, waiting for client connections and creating instances of the second class, a TinyHttpdConnection thread, to service each request. The while loop waits for the ServerSocket accept() method to return a new Socket for each client connection. The Socket is passed as an argument to construct the TinyHttpdConnection thread that handles it.

TinyHttpdConnection is a subclass of Thread. It lives long enough to process one client connection and then dies. TinyHttpdConnection's constructor does two things. After saving the Socket argument for its caller, it adjusts its priority. By lowering its priority to NORM_PRIORITY-1 (just below the default priority), we ensure that the threads servicing established connections won't block TinyHttpd's main thread from accepting new requests. (On a time-slicing system, this is less important.) After our object is constructed, its `start()` method is invoked to bring the `run()` method to life.

The body of `TinyHttpdConnection`'s `run()` method is where all the magic happens. First, we fetch an `OutputStream` for talking back to our client. The second line reads the `GET` request from the `InputStream` into the variable `req`. This request is a single newline-terminated `String` that looks like the `GET` request we described earlier. For this we use a `BufferedInputStream` wrapped around an `InputStreamReader`. (We'll say more about the `InputStreamReader` in a moment.)

We then parse the contents of `req` to extract a filename. The next few lines are a brief exercise in string manipulation. We create a `StringTokenizer` and make sure there are at least two tokens. Using `nextToken()`, we take the first token and make sure it's the word `GET`. (If both conditions aren't met, we have an error.) Then we take the next token (which should be a filename), assign it to `req`, and check whether it begins with a forward slash. If so, we use `substring()` to strip the first character, giving us a filename relative to the current directory. If it doesn't begin with a forward slash, the filename is already relative to the current directory. Finally, we check to see if the requested filename looks like a directory name (i.e., ends in a slash) or is empty. In these cases, we append the familiar default filename *index.html* as a convenience.

Once we have the filename, we try to open the specified file and load its contents into a large byte array. If all goes well, we write the data out to the client on the `OutputStream`. If we can't parse the request or the file doesn't exist, we wrap our `OutputStream` with a `PrintStream` to make it easier to send a textual message. Then we return an appropriate HTTP error message. Finally, we close the socket and return from `run()`, removing our `Thread`.

Do French web servers speak French?

In `TinyHttpd`, we explicitly created the `InputStreamReader` for our `Buffered-Read` and the `OutputStreamWriter` for our `PrintWriter`. We do this so that we can specify the character encoding to use when converting to and from the byte representation of the HTTP protocol messages. (Note that we're not talking about the body of the file we will be sending—that is simply a stream of raw bytes to us; rather we're talking here about the `GET` and response messages.) If we didn't specify, we'd get the default character encoding for the local system. For many purposes that may be correct, but in this case we are speaking of a well-defined international protocol, and we should be specific. The RFC for HTTP specifies that web clients and servers should use the ISO8859-1 character encoding. We specify this encoding explicitly when we construct the `InputStreamReader` and `Output-StreamWriter`. Now as it turns out, ISO8859-1 is just plain ASCII and conversion to and from Unicode should always leave ASCII values unchanged, so again we would probably not be in any trouble if we we did not specify an encoding. But it's important to think about these things at least once—and now you have.

Taming the daemon

An important problem with TinyHttpd is that there are no restrictions on the files it will serve. With a little trickery, the daemon will happily send any file in your file-system to the client. It would be nice if we could enforce the restriction that TinyHttpd serve only files that are in the current working directory or a subdirectory, as it normally does. An easy way to do this is to activate the Java Security Manager. Normally, a security manager is used to prevent Java code downloaded over the Net from doing anything suspicious. However, the security manager will serve nicely to restrict file access in our application as well.

You can use a policy like the simple one that we provided in the section "Sockets and security" earlier in this chapter; it allows the server to accept connections on a specified range of sockets. As a happy bonus, the default file access security policy does just what we want: allows an application access to files in its current working directory and subdirectories. So simply installing the security manager will provide exactly the kind of file protection that we wanted in this case. (It would be easy to add additional permissions if you wish to extend the server's range to other well-defined areas.)

With the security manager in place, the daemon will not be able to access anything that isn't within the current directory or a subdirectory. If it tries to, the security manager throws an exception and prevents access to the file. In that case, we should have TinyHttpd catch the SecurityException and return a proper message to the web browser. Add the following catch clause after the File-NotFoundException's catch clause:

```
    ...
    } catch ( Security Exception e ) {
        pout.println("403 Forbidden");
    }
```

Room for improvement

TinyHttpd still has quite a bit of room for improvement. First, it consumes a lot of memory by allocating a huge array to read the entire contents of the file all at once. A more realistic implementation would use a buffer and send large amounts of data in several passes. Reading and sending the data iteratively would also allow us to handle the contingency where the first read does not return all of the data. In practice, this will not happen when reading from files, but the possibility is left open by the API and a responsible application should handle it. Finally,

`TinyHttpd` is of course not fully compliant with the HTTP 1.0 protocol, but only implements a rudimentary portion of the `GET` command. A modern web server would expect and send additional "meta" information about the requested file in HTTP header text. As an additional convenience, it wouldn't be hard to add a few lines of code to read directories and generate linked HTML listings as most web servers do. Have fun with this example and you can learn quite a bit!

Socket Options

The Java sockets API is a simplified interface to the general socket mechanisms. In a C environment, where all of the gory details of the network are visible to you, a lot of complex and sometimes esoteric options can be set on sockets to govern the behavior of the underlying protocols. Java gives us access to a few of the important ones. We'll refer to them by their C language names so that you can recognize them in other networking books.

SO_TIMEOUT

The `SO_TIMEOUT` option sets a timer on all I/O methods of a socket that block so that you don't have to wait forever if they don't return. This works for operations such as `accept()` on server sockets and `read()` or `write()` on all sockets. If the timer expires before the operation would complete, an `InterruptedIO-Exception` is thrown. You can catch the exception and continue to use the socket normally if it is appropriate, or you can take the opportunity to bail out of the operation. Servers should use this sort of technique for their "shutdown" logic:

```
serverSocket.setSoTimeout( 2000 ); // 2 seconds

while ( !shutdown ) {
    try {
        Socket client = serverSocket.accept();
        handleClient( client );
    } catch ( InterruptedIOException e ) {
        // ignore the exception
    }

    // exit
}
```

You set the timer by calling the `setSoTimeout()` method of the `Socket` class with the timeout period, in milliseconds, as an `int` argument. This works for regular `Sockets` and `ServerSockets` (TCP) and `DatagramSockets` (UDP), which we'll discuss in the next section.

To find out the current timeout value, call `getSoTimeout()`.

TCP_NODELAY

This option turns off a feature of TCP called Nagle's algorithm, which tries to prevent certain interactive applications from flooding the network with very tiny packets. Turn this off if you have a fast network and you want all packets sent as soon as possible. The `Socket setTcpNoDelay()` method takes a boolean argument specifying whether the delay is on or off.

To find out whether the `TCP_NODELAY` option is enabled, call `getTcpNoDelay()`, which returns a `boolean`.

SO_LINGER

This option controls what happens to any unsent data when you perform a `close()` on an active socket connection. Normally the system tries to deliver any network buffered data and close the connection gracefully. The `setSoLinger()` method of the `Socket` class takes two arguments: a boolean that enables or disables the option, and an `int` that sets the "linger" value, in seconds. If you set the linger value to 0, any unsent data is discarded, and the TCP connection is aborted (terminated with a reset).

To find out the current linger value, call `getSoLinger()`.

TCP_KEEPALIVE

This option can be enabled with the `setKeepAlive()` method. It triggers a feature of TCP that polls the other side every two hours if there is no other activity. Normally, when there is no data flowing on a TCP connection, no packets are sent at all. This can make it difficult to tell the difference between the other side simply being quiet and having disappeared. If one side of the connection closes it properly, this will be detected. But if the other side simply disappears, we will not know unless and until we try to talk to them. For this reason, servers often use this feature to detect lost client connections (where they might otherwise only respond to requests, rather than initiate them). `Keepalive` is not part of the TCP specification; it's an add-on that's not guaranteed to be implemented everywhere. If you have the option, the best way to be sure of detecting lost clients is to implement the polling as part of your own protocol.

"Half Close"

In TCP, it is technically possible to close one direction of a stream but not the other. In other words, you can shut down sending but not receiving, or vice versa. A few protocols use this to indicate the end of a client request by closing the client side of the stream, allowing the end of stream to be detected by the server. You can shut down either half of a socket connection with `shutdownOutput()` or `shutdownInput()`.

Proxies and Firewalls

Many networks are behind *firewalls*, which prevent applications from opening direct socket connections to the outside network. Instead, they provide a service called SOCKS (named for sockets) that serves as a *proxy server* for socket connections, giving the administrators more control over what connections are allowed.

Java has built-in support for SOCKS. All you have to do is set some system properties in your application (in an applet, this should be already taken care of for you, since you wouldn't have authority to set those properties). Here's a list of the properties that configure Java to use a proxy server:

`http.proxySet`
> A boolean (`true` or `false`) indicating whether to use the proxy

`http.proxyHost`
> The proxy server name

`http.proxyPort`
> The proxy port number

You can set these properties on the command line using the Java interpreter's `-D` option or by calling the `System.setProperty()` method. The following command runs `MyProgram` using the proxy server at *foo.bar.com* on port 1234:

```
% java -Dhttp.proxySet=true -Dhttp.proxyServer=foo.bar.com
    -Dhttp.proxyPort=1234 MyProgram
```

In SDK 1.0.2, the names didn't have the `http.` prefix. SDK 1.1 and later checks for the new names and then the old names. If the firewall does not allow any outside socket connections, your applet or application may still be able to communicate with the outside world by using HTTP to send and receive data. See Chapter 12, *Programming for the Web*, for an example of how to perform an HTTP POST.

Datagram Sockets

`TinyHttpd` used a `Socket` to create a connection to the client using the TCP protocol. In that example, TCP itself took care of data integrity; we didn't have to worry about data arriving out of order or incorrect. Now we'll take a walk on the wild side. We'll build an applet that uses a `java.net.DatagramSocket`, which uses the UDP protocol. A datagram is sort of like a letter sent via the postal service: it's a discrete chunk of data transmitted in one packet. Unlike the previous example, where we could get a convenient `OutputStream` from our `Socket` and write the data as if writing to a file, with a `DatagramSocket` we have to work one datagram at a time. (Of course, the TCP protocol was taking our `OutputStream` and slicing the data into packets, but we didn't have to worry about those details.)

UDP doesn't guarantee that the data will get through. If the data packets do get through, they may not arrive in the order in which we sent them; it's even possible for duplicate datagrams to arrive (under rare circumstances). Using UDP is something like cutting the pages out of the encyclopedia, putting them into separate envelopes, and mailing them to your friend. If your friend wants to read the encyclopedia, it's his or her job to put the pages in order. If some pages got lost in the mail, your friend has to send you a letter asking for replacements.

Obviously, you wouldn't use UDP to send a huge amount of data without error correction. But it's significantly more efficient than TCP, particularly if you don't care about the order in which messages arrive, or whether 100% of their arrival is guaranteed. For example, in a simple periodic database lookup, the client can send a query; the server's response itself constitutes an acknowledgment. If the response doesn't arrive within a certain time, the client can send another query. It shouldn't be hard for the client to match responses to its original queries. Some important applications that use UDP are the Domain Name System (DNS) and Sun's Network Filesystem (NFS).

The HeartBeat Applet

In this section, we'll build a simple applet, HeartBeat, that sends a datagram to its server each time it's started and stopped. We'll also build a simple standalone server application, Pulse, that receives these datagrams and prints them. By tracking the output, you could have a crude measure of who is currently looking at your web page at any given time. This is an ideal application for UDP: we don't want the overhead of a TCP socket, and if datagrams get lost, it's no big deal.

First, the HeartBeat applet:

```
//file: HeartBeat.java
import java.net.*;
import java.io.*;

public class HeartBeat extends java.applet.Applet {
    String myHost;
    int myPort;

    public void init() {
        myHost = getCodeBase().getHost();
        myPort = Integer.parseInt( getParameter("myPort") );
    }

    private void sendMessage( String message ) {
        try {
            byte [] data = message.getBytes();
            InetAddress addr = InetAddress.getByName( myHost );
            DatagramPacket pack =
```

```
                    new DatagramPacket(data, data.length, addr, myPort );
                DatagramSocket ds = new DatagramSocket();
                ds.send( pack );
                ds.close();
            } catch ( IOException e ) {
                System.out.println( e );  // Error creating socket
            }
        }

    public void start() {
        sendMessage("Arrived");
    }
    public void stop() {
        sendMessage("Departed");
    }

    }
```

Compile the applet and include it in an HTML document with an <APPLET> tag:

```
<APPLET height=10 width=10 code=HeartBeat>
    <PARAM name="myPort" value="1234">
</APPLET>
```

Make sure to place the `HeartBeat.class` file in the same directory as the HTML document. If you're not familiar with embedding applets in HTML documents, consult Chapter 20, *Applets.*

The `myPort` parameter should specify the port number on which our server application listens for data.

Next, the server-side application, `Pulse`:

```
//file: Pulse.java
import java.net.*;
import java.io.*;

public class Pulse {
    public static void main( String [] argv ) throws IOException {
        DatagramSocket s =
          new DatagramSocket( Integer.parseInt(argv[0]) );

        while ( true ) {
            DatagramPacket packet =
              new DatagramPacket(new byte [1024], 1024);
            s.receive( packet );
            String message = new String( packet.getData() );
            System.out.println( "Heartbeat from: "
              + packet.getAddress().getHostName()
              + " - " + message );
        }
    }
}
```

Compile `Pulse` and run it on your web server, specifying a port number as an argument:

```
% java Pulse 1234
```

The port number should be the same as the one you used in the `myPort` parameter of the `<APPLET>` tag for `HeartBeat`.

Now, pull up the web page in your browser. You won't see anything interesting there (a better application might do something visual as well), but you should get a blip from the `Pulse` application. Leave the page and return to it a few times. Each time the applet is started or stopped, it sends a message and `Pulse` reports it

```
Heartbeat from: foo.bar.com - Arrived
Heartbeat from: foo.bar.com - Departed
Heartbeat from: foo.bar.com - Arrived
Heartbeat from: foo.bar.com - Departed
...
```

Cool, eh? Just remember the datagrams are not guaranteed to arrive (although it's highly unlikely you'll ever see them fail on a normal network), and it's possible that you could miss an arrival or a departure. Now let's look at the code.

The HeartBeat applet code

`HeartBeat` overrides the `init()`, `start()`, and `stop()` methods of the `Applet` class, and implements one private method of its own, `sendMessage()`, that sends a datagram. `HeartBeat` begins its life in `init()`, where it determines the destination for its messages. It uses the `Applet getCodeBase()` and `getHost()` methods to find the name of its originating host and fetches the correct port number from the `myPort` parameter of the `<APPLET>` tag. After `init()` has finished, the `start()` and `stop()` methods are called whenever the applet is started or stopped. These methods merely call `sendMessage()` with the appropriate message.

`sendMessage()` is responsible for sending a `String` message to the server as a datagram. It takes the text as an argument, constructs a datagram packet containing the message, and then sends the datagram. All of the datagram information is packed into a `java.net.DatagramPacket` object, including the destination and port number. The `DatagramPacket` is like an addressed envelope, stuffed with our bytes. After the `DatagramPacket` is created, `sendMessage()` simply has to open a `DatagramSocket` and send it.

The first five lines of `sendMessage()` build the `DatagramPacket`:

```
try {
    byte [] data = message.getBytes();
    InetAddress addr = InetAddress.getByName( myHost );
```

```
DatagramPacket pack =
    new DatagramPacket(data, data.length, addr, myPort );
```

First, the contents of message are placed into an array of bytes called data. Next a java.net.InetAddress object is created from the name myHost. An Inet-Address holds the network address information for a host in a special format. We get an InetAddress object for our host by using the static getByName() method of the InetAddress class. (We can't construct an InetAddress object directly.) Finally, we call the DatagramPacket constructor with four arguments: the byte array containing our data, the length of the data, the destination address object, and the port number.

The remaining lines construct a default client DatagramSocket and call its send() method to transmit the DatagramPacket. After sending the datagram, we close the socket:

```
DatagramSocket ds = new DatagramSocket();
ds.send( pack );
ds.close();
```

Two operations throw a type of IOException: the InetAddress.getByName() lookup and the DatagramSocket send(). InetAddress.getByName() can throw an UnknownHostException, which is a type of IOException that indicates that the hostname can't be resolved. If send() throws an IOException, it implies a serious client-side problem in talking to the network. We need to catch these exceptions; our catch block simply prints a message telling us that something went wrong. If we get one of these exceptions, we can assume the datagram never arrived. However, we can't assume the inverse: even if we don't get an exception, we still don't know that the host is actually accessible or that the data actually arrived. With a DatagramSocket, we never find out from the API.

The Pulse server code

The Pulse server corresponds to the HeartBeat applet. First, it creates a DatagramSocket to listen on our prearranged port. This time, we specify a port number in the constructor; we get the port number from the command line as a string (argv[0]) and convert it to an integer with Integer.parseInt(). Note the difference between this call to the constructor and the call in HeartBeat. In the server, we need to listen for incoming datagrams on a prearranged port, so we need to specify the port when creating the DatagramSocket. The client just sends datagrams, so we don't have to specify the port in advance; we build the port number into the DatagramPacket itself.

Second, Pulse creates an empty DatagramPacket of a fixed size to receive an incoming datagram. This alternative constructor for DatagramPacket takes a byte array and a length as arguments. As much data as possible is stored in the byte array when it's received. (A practical limit on the size of a UDP datagram that can be sent over the Internet is 8K, although they can be larger for local network use.) Finally, `Pulse` calls the `DatagramSocket`'s `receive()` method to wait for a packet to arrive. When a packet arrives, its contents are printed.

As you can see, working with `DatagramSocket` is slightly more tedious than working with `Sockets`. With datagrams, it's harder to spackle over the messiness of the socket interface. The Java API rather slavishly follows the Unix interface, and that doesn't help. It's easy to imagine conveniences that would make all of this simpler; perhaps we'll have them in a future release.

Simple Serialized Object Protocols

Earlier in this chapter, we showed a hypothetical conversation in which a client and server exchanged some primitive data and a serialized Java object. Passing an object between two programs may not have seemed like a big deal at the time, but in the context of Java as a portable byte-code language, it has profound implications. In this section, we'll show how a protocol can be built using serialized Java objects.

Before we move on, it's worth considering network protocols. Most programmers would consider working with sockets to be "low-level" and unfriendly. Even though Java makes sockets much much easier to use than many other languages, sockets still provide only an unstructured flow of bytes between their endpoints. If you want to do serious communications using sockets, the first thing you have to do is come up with a protocol that defines the data you'll be sending and receiving. The most complex part of that protocol usually involves how to marshal (package) your data for transfer over the Net and unpack it on the other side.

As we've seen, Java's `DataInputStream` and `DataOuputStream` classes solve this problem for simple data types. We can read and write numbers, `Strings`, and Java primitives in a recognizable format that can be understood on any other Java platform. But to do real work, we need to be able to put simple types together into larger structures. Java object serialization solves this problem elegantly, by allowing us to send our data just as we use it, as the state of Java objects. Serialization can even pack up entire graphs of interconnected objects and put them back together at a later time, possibly in another Java VM.

A Simple Object-Based Server

In the following example, a client will send a serialized object to the server, and the server will respond in kind. The client object represents a request and the server object represents a response. The conversation ends when the client closes the connection. It's hard to imagine a simpler protocol. All the hairy details are taken care of by object serialization, so we can keep them out of our design.

To start we'll define a class, Request, to serve as a base class for the various kinds of requests we make to the server. Using a common base class is a convenient way to identify the object as a type of request. In a real application, we might also use it to hold basic information like client names and passwords, timestamps, serial numbers, etc. In our example, Request can be an empty class that exists so others can extend it:

```
//file: Request.java
public class Request implements java.io.Serializable {}
```

Request implements Serializable, so all of its subclasses will be serializable by default. Next we'll create some specific kinds of Requests. The first, Date-Request, is also a trivial class. We'll use it to ask the server to send us a java.util.Date object as a response:

```
//file: DateRequest.java
public class DateRequest extends Request {}
```

Next, we'll create a generic WorkRequest object. The client sends a WorkRequest to get the server to perform some computation for it. The server calls the WorkRequest object's execute() method and returns the resulting object as a response:

```
//file: WorkRequest.java
public abstract class WorkRequest extends Request {
    public abstract Object execute();
}
```

For our application, we'll subclass WorkRequest to create MyCalculation, which adds code that performs a specific calculation; in this case, we will just square a number:

```
//file: MyCalculation.java
public class MyCalculation extends WorkRequest {
    int n;

    public MyCalculation( int n ) {
        this.n = n;
    }
    public Object execute() {
        return new Integer( n * n );
    }
}
```

As far as data content is concerned, MyCalculation really doesn't do much; it only transports an integer value for us. But keep in mind that a request object could hold lots of data, including references to many other objects in complex structures like arrays or linked lists. An interesting part here is that MyCalculation also contains behavior—the execute() operation. In our discussion of RMI below, we'll see how Java's ability to dynamically download byte-code for serialized objects makes both the data content and behavior portable over the network.

Now that we have our protocol, we need the server. The following `Server` class looks a lot like the `TinyHttpd` server that we developed earlier in this chapter:

```java
//file: Server.java
import java.net.*;
import java.io.*;

public class Server {
  public static void main( String argv[] ) throws IOException {
    ServerSocket ss = new ServerSocket( Integer.parseInt(argv[0]) );
    while ( true )
      new ServerConnection( ss.accept() ).start();
  }
} // end of class Server

class ServerConnection extends Thread {
  Socket client;
  ServerConnection ( Socket client ) throws SocketException {
    this.client = client;
    setPriority( NORM_PRIORITY - 1 );
  }

  public void run() {
    try {
      ObjectInputStream in =
        new ObjectInputStream( client.getInputStream() );
      ObjectOutputStream out =
        new ObjectOutputStream( client.getOutputStream() );
      while ( true ) {
        out.writeObject( processRequest( in.readObject() ) );
        out.flush();
      }
    } catch ( EOFException e3 ) { // Normal EOF
      try {
        client.close();
      } catch ( IOException e ) { }
    } catch ( IOException e ) {
      System.out.println( "I/O error " + e ); // I/O error
    } catch ( ClassNotFoundException e2 ) {
      System.out.println( e2 ); // unknown type of request object
    }
  }

  private Object processRequest( Object request ) {
    if ( request instanceof DateRequest )
```

```
            return new java.util.Date();
         else if ( request instanceof WorkRequest )
           return ((WorkRequest)request).execute();
         else
           return null;
    }
  }
```

The `Server` services each request in a separate thread. For each connection, the `run()` method creates an `ObjectInputStream` and an `ObjectOutputStream`, which the server uses to receive the request and send the response. The `processRequest()` method decides what the request means and comes up with the response. To figure out what kind of request we have, we use the `instanceof` operator to look at the object's type.

Finally, we get to our `Client`, which is even simpler:

```
//file: Client.java
import java.net.*;
import java.io.*;

public class Client {
  public static void main( String argv[] ) {
    try {
      Socket server =
        new Socket( argv[0], Integer.parseInt(argv[1]) );
      ObjectOutputStream out =
        new ObjectOutputStream( server.getOutputStream() );
      ObjectInputStream in =
        new ObjectInputStream( server.getInputStream() );

      out.writeObject( new DateRequest() );
      out.flush();
      System.out.println( in.readObject() );

      out.writeObject( new MyCalculation( 2 ) );
      out.flush();
      System.out.println( in.readObject() );

      server.close();
    } catch ( IOException e ) {
      System.out.println( "I/O error " + e ); // I/O error
    } catch ( ClassNotFoundException e2 ) {
      System.out.println( e2 ); // unknown type of response object
    }
  }
}
```

Just like the server, `Client` creates the pair of object streams. It sends a `DateRequest` and prints the response; it then sends a `MyCalculation` object and prints the response. Finally, it closes the connection. On both the client and the server, we call the flush() method after each call to writeObject(). This method forces the system to send any buffered data; it's important because it ensures that the other side sees the entire request before we wait for a response. When the client closes the connection, our server catches the EOFException that is thrown and ends the session. Alternatively, our client could write a special object, perhaps null, to end the session; the server could watch for this item in its main loop.

The order in which we construct the object streams is important. We create the output streams first because the constructor of an ObjectInputStream tries to read a header from the stream to make sure that the InputStream really is an object stream. If we tried to create both of our input streams first, we would deadlock waiting for the other side to write the headers.

Finally, we can run the example. Run the Server, giving it a port number as an argument:

```
% java Server 1234
```

Then run the Client, telling it the server's hostname and port number:

```
% java Client flatland 1234
```

The result should look like this:

```
Sun Jul 11 14:25:25 PDT 1999
4
```

All right, the result isn't that impressive, but it's easy to imagine more substantial applications. Imagine that you needed to perform some complex computation on many large data sets. Using serialized objects makes maintenance of the data objects natural and sending them over the wire trivial. There is no need to deal with byte-level protocols at all.

Limitations

There is one catch in this scenario: both the client and server need access to the necessary classes. That is, all of the Request classes—including MyCalculation, which is really the property of the Client—have to be in the class path on both the client and the server machines. As we hinted earlier, in the next section we'll see that it's possible to send the Java bytecode along with serialized objects to allow completely new kinds of objects to be transported over the network dynamically. We could create this solution on our own, adding to the earlier example using a network class loader to load the classes for us. But we don't have to: Java's RMI facility automates that for us. The ability to send both serialized data and class definitions over the network makes Java a powerful tool for developing advanced distributed applications.

Remote Method Invocation (RMI)

The most fundamental means of inter-object communication in Java is method invocation. Mechanisms like the Java event model are built on simple method invocations between objects in the same virtual machine. Therefore, when we want to communicate between virtual machines on different hosts, it's natural to want a mechanism with similar capabilities and semantics. Java's Remote Method Invocation mechanism does just that. It lets us get a reference to an object on a remote host and use it as if it were in our own virtual machine. RMI lets us invoke methods on remote objects, passing real Java objects as arguments and getting real Java objects as returned values.

Remote invocation is nothing new. For many years C programmers have used remote procedure calls (RPC) to execute a C function on a remote host and return the results. The primary difference between RPC and RMI is that RPC, being an offshoot of the C language, is primarily concerned with data structures. It's relatively easy to pack up data and ship it around, but for Java, that's not enough. In Java we don't just work with data structures; we work with objects, which contain both data and methods for operating on the data. Not only do we have to be able to ship the state of an object (the data) over the wire, but also the recipient has to be able to interact with the object (use its methods) after receiving it.

It should be no surprise that RMI uses object serialization, which allows us to send graphs of objects (objects and all of the connected objects that they reference). When necessary, RMI can also use dynamic class loading and the security manager to transport Java classes safely. Thus, the real breakthrough of RMI is that it's possible to ship both data and behavior (code) around the Net.

Remote and Non-Remote Objects

Before an object can be used with RMI, it must be serializable. But that's not sufficient. Remote objects in RMI are real distributed objects. As the name suggests, a remote object can be an object on a different machine; it can also be an object on the local host. The term *remote* means that the object is used through a special kind of object reference that can be passed over the network. Like normal Java objects, remote objects are passed by reference. Regardless of where the reference is used, the method invocation occurs at the original object, which still lives on its original host. If a remote host returns a reference to one of its objects to you, you can call the object's methods; the actual method invocations will happen on the remote host, where the object resides.

Nonremote objects are simpler. They are just normal serializable objects. (You can pass these over the network as we did in the "Simple Object Based Server" section earlier.) The catch is that when you pass a nonremote object over the network it is simply copied. So references to the object on one host are not the same as those on the remote host. Nonremote objects are passed by copy (as opposed to by reference). This may be acceptable for many kinds of data-oriented objects in your application, especially those that are not being modified.

Stubs and skeletons

No, we're not talking about a gruesome horror movie. Stubs and skeletons are used in the implementation of remote objects. When you invoke a method on a remote object (which could be on a different host), you are actually calling some local code that serves as a proxy for that object. This is the *stub*. (It is called a *stub* because it is something like a truncated placeholder for the object.) The *skeleton* is another proxy that lives with the real object on its original host. It receives remote method invocations from the stub and passes them to the object.

After you create stubs and skeletons you never have to work with them directly; they are hidden from you (in the closet, so to speak). Stubs and skeletons for your remote objects are created by running the rmic (RMI compiler) utility. After compiling your Java source files normally, you run rmic on the remote object classes as a second pass. It's easy; we'll show you how in the following examples.

Remote interfaces

Remote objects are objects that implement a special *remote interface* that specifies which of the object's methods can be invoked remotely. The remote interface must extend the java.rmi.Remote interface. Your remote object will implement its remote interface; as will the stub object that is automatically generated for it. In the rest of your code, you should then refer to the remote object as an instance of the remote interface—not as an instance of its actual class. Because both the real object and stub implement the remote interface, they are equivalent as far as we are concerned (for method invocation); locally, we never have to worry about whether we have a reference to a stub or to an actual object. This "type equivalence" means that we can use normal language features, like casting with remote objects. Of course public fields (variables) of the remote object are not accessible through an interface, so you must make accessor methods if you want to manipulate the remote object's fields.

All methods in the remote interface must declare that they can throw the exception java.rmi.RemoteException. This exception (actually, one of many subclasses to RemoteException) is thrown when any kind of networking error happens: for example, the server could crash, the network could fail, or you could be requesting an object that for some reason isn't available.

Here's a simple example of the remote interface that defines the behavior of RemoteObject; we'll give it two methods that can be invoked remotely, both of which return some kind of Widget object:

```
import java.rmi.*;


public interface RemoteObject extends Remote {
    public Widget doSomething() throws RemoteException;
    public Widget doSomethingElse() throws RemoteException;
}
```

The UnicastRemoteObject class

The actual implementation of a remote object (not the interface we discussed previously) will usually extend java.rmi.server.UnicastRemoteObject. This is the RMI equivalent to the familiar Object class. When a subclass of Unicast-RemoteObject is constructed, the RMI runtime system automatically "exports" it to start listening for network connections from remote interfaces (stubs) for the object. Like java.lang.Object, this superclass also provides implementations of equals(), hashcode(), and toString() that make sense for a remote object.

Here's a remote object class that implements the RemoteObject interface; we haven't supplied implementations for the two methods or the constructor:

```
public class MyRemoteObject implements RemoteObject
        extends java.rmi.UnicastRemoteObject
{
    public RemoteObjectImpl() throws RemoteException {...}
    public Widget doSomething() throws RemoteException {...}
    public Widget doSomethingElse() throws RemoteException {...}
    // other non-public methods
    ...
}
```

This class can have as many additional methods as it needs; presumably, most of them will be private, but that isn't strictly necessary. We have to supply a constructor explicitly, even if the constructor does nothing, because the constructor (like any method) can throw a RemoteException; we therefore can't use the default constructor.

What if we can't or don't want to make our remote object implementation a subclass of UnicastRemoteObject? Suppose, for example, that it has to be a subclass of BankAccount or some other special base type for our system. Well, we can simply export the object ourselves using the static method exportObject() of UnicastRemoteObject. The exportObject() method takes as an argument a Remote interface and accomplishes what the UnicastRemoteObject constructor normally does for us. It returns as a value the remote object's stub. However, you will normally not do anything with this directly. In the next section, we'll discuss how to get stubs to your client through the RMI registry.

Normally, exported objects listen on individual ephemeral (randomly assigned) port numbers by default. (This is implementation-dependent.) You can control the port number allocation explicitly by exporting your objects using another form of `UnicastRemoteObject.exportObject()`, which takes both a `Remote` interface and a port number as arguments.

Finally, the name `UnicastRemoteObject` suggests the question, "what other kinds of remote objects are there?" Right now, none. It's possible that Sun will develop remote objects using other protocols or multicast techniques in the future. They would take their place alongside `UnicastRemoteObject`.

The RMI registry

The registry is the RMI phone book. You use the registry to look up a reference to a registered remote object on another host. We've already described how remote references can be passed back and forth by remote method calls. But the registry is needed to bootstrap the process: the client needs some way of looking up some initial object.

The registry is implemented by a class called `Naming` and an application called `rmiregistry`. This application must be running on the local host before you start a Java program that uses the registry. You can then create instances of remote objects and bind them to particular names in the registry. (Remote objects that bind themselves to the registry sometimes provide a `main()` method for this purpose.) A registry name can be anything you choose; it takes the form of a slash-separated path. When a client object wants to find your object, it constructs a special URL with the `rmi:` protocol, the hostname, and the object name. On the client, the RMI `Naming` class then talks to the registry and returns the remote object reference.

Which objects need to register themselves with the registry? Well, initially any object that the client has no other way of finding. But a call to a remote method can return another remote object without using the registry. Likewise, a call to a remote method can have another remote object as its argument, without requiring the registry. So you could design your system such that only one object registers itself, and then serves as a factory for any other remote objects you need. In other words, it wouldn't be hard to build a simple object request "bouncer" (we won't say "broker") that returns references to all of the remote objects that your application uses. Depending on how you structure your application, this may happen naturally anyway.

Why avoid using the registry for everything? The current RMI registry is not very sophisticated, and lookups tend to be slow. It is not intended to be a general-purpose directory service (like JNDI, the Java API for accessing directory/name services), but simply to bootstrap RMI communications. It wouldn't be surprising if Sun releases a much improved registry in the future, but that's not the one we have now. Besides, the factory design pattern is extremely flexible and useful.

An RMI Example

The first thing we'll implement using RMI is a duplication of the simple serialized object protocol from the previous section. We'll make a remote RMI object called MyServer on which we can invoke methods to get a Date object or execute a WorkRequest object. First, we'll define our Remote interface:

```java
//file: RmtServer.java
import java.rmi.*;
import java.util.*;

public interface RmtServer extends Remote {
    Date getDate() throws RemoteException;
    Object execute( WorkRequest work ) throws RemoteException;
}
```

The RmtServer interface extends the java.rmi.Remote interface, which identifies objects that implement it as remote objects. We supply two methods that take the place of our old protocol: getDate() and execute().

Next, we'll implement this interface in a class called MyServer that defines the bodies of these methods. (Note that a more common convention for naming the implementation of remote interfaces is to postfix the class name with "Impl". Using that convention MyServer would instead be named something like ServerImpl.)

```java
//file: MyServer.java
import java.rmi.*;
import java.util.*;

public class MyServer
    extends java.rmi.server.UnicastRemoteObject
    implements RmtServer {

    public MyServer() throws RemoteException { }

    // implement the RmtServer interface
    public Date getDate() throws RemoteException {
        return new Date();
    }

    public Object execute( WorkRequest work )
      throws RemoteException {
```

```
        return work.execute();
    }

    public static void main(String args[]) {
        try {
            RmtServer server = new MyServer();
            Naming.rebind("NiftyServer", server);
        } catch (java.io.IOException e) {
            // problem registering server
        }
    }
}
```

`MyServer` extends `java.rmi.UnicastRemoteObject`, so when we create an instance of `MyServer`, it will automatically be exported and start listening to the network. We start by providing a constructor, which must throw `RemoteException`, accommodating errors that might occur in exporting an instance. (We can't use the automatically generated default constructor, because it won't throw the exception.) Next, `MyServer` implements the methods of the remote `RmtServer` interface. These methods are straightforward.

The last method in this class is `main()`. This method lets the object set itself up as a server. `main()` creates an instance of the `MyServer` object and then calls the static method `Naming.rebind()` to register the object with the registry. The arguments to `rebind()` are the name of the remote object in the registry (`NiftyServer`), which clients will use to look up the object, and a reference to the server object itself. We could have called `bind()` instead, but `rebind()` is less prone to problems: if there's already a `NiftyServer` registered, `rebind()` replaces it.

We wouldn't need the `main()` method or this `Naming` business if we weren't expecting clients to use the registry to find the server. That is, we could omit `main()` and still use this object as a remote object. We would be limited to passing the object in method invocations or returning it from method invocations—but that could be part of a factory design, as we discussed before.

Now we need our client:

```
//file: MyClient.java
import java.rmi.*;
import java.util.*;

public class MyClient {

    public static void main(String [] args)
      throws RemoteException {
        new MyClient( args[0] );
    }
```

```
        public MyClient(String host) {
            try {
                RmtServer server = (RmtServer)
                    Naming.lookup("rmi://"+host+"/NiftyServer");
                System.out.println( server.getDate() );
                System.out.println(
                    server.execute( new MyCalculation(2) ) );
            } catch (java.io.IOException e) {
                // I/O Error or bad URL
            } catch (NotBoundException e) {
                // NiftyServer isn't registered
            }
        }
    }
}
```

When we run `MyClient`, we pass it the hostname of the server on which the registry is running. The `main()` method creates an instance of the `MyClient` object, passing the hostname from the command line as an argument to the constructor.

The constructor for `MyClient` uses the hostname to construct a URL for the object. The URL will look something like this: *rmi://hostname/NiftyServer*. (Remember, `NiftyServer` is the name under which we registered our `RmtServer`.) We pass the URL to the static `Naming.lookup()` method. If all goes well, we get back a reference to a `RmtServer` (the remote interface). The registry has no idea what kind of object it will return; `lookup()` therefore returns an `Object`, which we must cast to `RmtServer`.

Compile all of the code. Then run `rmic`, the RMI compiler, to make the stub and skeleton files for `MyServer`:

```
% rmic MyServer
```

Let's run the code. For the first pass, we'll assume that you have all of the class files, including the stubs and skeletons generated by `rmic`, available in the class path on both the client and server machines. (You can run this example on a single host to test it if you want.) Make sure your class path is correct and then start the registry; then start the server:

```
% rmiregistry &     (on Windows: start rmiregistry)
% java MyServer
```

In each case, make sure the registry application has the class path including your server classes so that it can load the stub class. (Be warned, we're going to tell you to do the opposite later as part of setting up the dynamic class loading!)

Finally, on the client machine, run `MyClient`, passing the hostname of the server:

```
% java MyClient myhost
```

The client should print the date and the number 4, which the server graciously calculated. Hooray! With just a few lines of code you have created a powerful client/server application.

Dynamic class loading

Before running the example, we told you to distribute all the class files to both the client and server machines. However, RMI was designed to ship classes, in addition to data, around the network; you shouldn't have to distribute all the classes in advance. Let's go a step further, and have RMI load classes for us, as needed. This involves several steps.

First, we need to tell RMI where to find any other classes it needs. We can use the system property `java.rmi.server.codebase` to specify a URL on a web server (or FTP server) when we run our client or server. This URL specifies the location of a JAR file or a base directory in which RMI will begin its search for classes. When RMI sends a serialized object (i.e., an object's data) to some client, it also sends this URL. If the recipient needs the class file in addition to the data, it fetches the file at the specified URL. In addition to stub classes, other classes referenced by remote objects in the application can be loaded dynamically. Therefore, we don't have to distribute many class files to the client; we can let the client download them as necessary. In Figure 11-3, we see an example as `MyClient` is going to the registry to get a reference to the `RmtServer` object. Then `MyClient` dynamically downloads the stub class for `RmtMyServer` from a web server running on the server object's host.

We can now split our class files between the server and client machines. For example, we could withhold the `MyCalculation` class from the server, since it really belongs to the client. Instead, we can make the `MyCalculation` class available via a web server on some machine (probably our client's) and specify the URL when we run `MyClient`:

```
java -Djava.rmi.server.codebase="http://myserver/foo/" ...
```

In this case, we would expect that `MyCalculation` would be accessible at the URL *http://myserver/foo/MyCalculation.class/*. (Note that the trailing slash in the URL is important: it says that the location is a base directory that contains the class files.)

Next we have to set up security. Since we will be loading class files over the network and executing their methods, we must have a security manager in place to restrict the kinds of things those classes may do, at least in the case where they are not coming from a trusted code source. RMI will not load any classes dynamically unless a security manager is installed. One easy way to meet this condition is to install the `RMISecurityManager` as the system security manager for your application. It is an example security manager that works with the default system policy

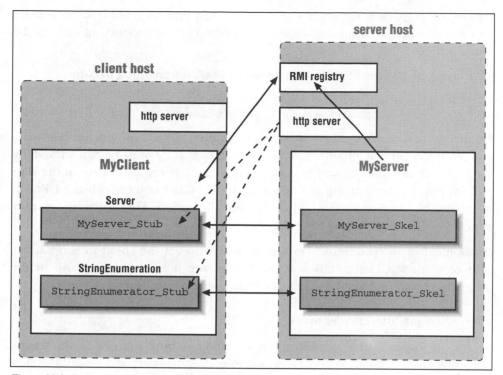

Figure 11-3. RMI applications and dynamic class loading

and imposes some basic restrictions on what downloaded classes can do. To install the `RMISecurityManager`, simply add the following line to the beginning of the `main()` method of both the client and server applications (yes, we'll be sending code both ways in the next section):

```
main() {
    System.setSecurityManager( new RMISecurityManager() );
    ...
```

The `RMISecurityManager` will work with the system security policy file to enforce restrictions. So you'll have to provide a policy file that allows the client and server to do basic operations like make network connections. Unfortunately allowing all of the operations needed to load classes dynamically would require us listing a lot of permission information and we don't want to get into that here. So we're going to resort to suggesting that for this example you simply grant the code all permissions. Here is an example policy file—call it *mysecurity.policy*:

```
grant {
    permission java.security.AllPermission ;
};
```

(It's exceedingly lame to install a security manager and then tell it to enforce no real security, but we're more interested in looking at the networking code at the moment.)

So, to run our MyServer application we would now do something like this:

```
java -Djava.rmi.server.codebase='http://myserver/foo/'
     -Djava.security.policy=mysecurity.policy MyServer
```

Finally, there is one last magic incantation required to enable dynamic class loading. As of the current implementation, the `rmiregistry` must be run *without* the classes which are to be loaded being in its class path. If the classes are in the class path of `rmiregistry`, it will not annotate the serialized objects with the URLs of their class files and no classes will be dynamically loaded. This limitation is really annoying; all we can say is to heed the warning for now.

If you meet these conditions, you should be able to get the client to run starting with only the `MyClient` class and the `RmtServer` remote interface. All of the other classes will be loaded dynamically from a remote location.

Passing remote object references

So far, we haven't done anything that we couldn't have done with the simple object protocol. We only used one remote object, `MyServer`, and we got its reference from the RMI registry. Now we'll extend our example to pass some remote references between the client and server (these will be prime candidates for dynamic class loading). We'll add two methods to our remote `RmtServer` interface:

```
public interface RmtServer extends Remote {
    ...
    StringIterator getList() throws RemoteException;
    void asyncExecute( WorkRequest work, WorkListener listener )
        throws RemoteException;
}
```

`getList()` retrieves a new kind of object from the server: a `StringIterator`. The `StringIterator` is a simple list of strings, with some methods for accessing the strings in order. We will make it a remote object, so that implementations of `StringIterator` stay on the server.

Next we'll spice up our work request feature by adding an `asyncExecute()` method. `asyncExecute()` lets us hand off a `WorkRequest` object as before, but it does the calulation on its own time. The return type for `asyncExecute()` is void, because it doesn't actually return a value; we get the result later. Along with the request, our client passes a reference to a `WorkListener` object that is to be notified when the `WorkRequest` is done. We'll have our client implement `WorkListener` itself.

Because this is to be a remote object, our interface must extend Remote, and its methods must throw RemoteExceptions:

```
//file: StringIterator.java
import java.rmi.*;

public interface StringIterator extends Remote {
    public boolean hasNext() throws RemoteException;
    public String next() throws RemoteException;
}
```

Next, we provide a simple implementation of StringIterator, called MyStringIterator:

```
//file: MyStringIterator.java
import java.rmi.*;

public class MyStringIterator
  extends java.rmi.server.UnicastRemoteObject
  implements StringIterator {

    String [] list;
    int index = 0;

    public MyStringIterator( String [] list )
      throws RemoteException {
        this.list = list;
    }
    public boolean hasNext() throws RemoteException {
        return index < list.length;
    }
    public String next() throws RemoteException {
        return list[index++];
    }
}
```

MyStringIterator extends UnicastRemoteObject. Its methods are simple: it can give you the next string in the list, and it can tell you whether there are any strings that you haven't seen yet.

Next, we'll define the WorkListener remote interface. This is the interface that defines how an object should listen for a completed WorkRequest. It has one method, workCompleted(), which the server that is executing a WorkRequest calls when the job is done:

```
//file: WorkListener.java
import java.rmi.*;

public interface WorkListener extends Remote {
    public void workCompleted(WorkRequest request, Object result )
```

```
            throws RemoteException;
    }
```

Next, let's add the new features to MyServer. We need to add implementations of the getList() and asyncExecute() methods, which we just added to the RmtServer interface:

```
public class MyServer extends java.rmi.server.UnicastRemoteObject
                        implements RmtServer {
    ...
    public StringIterator getList() throws RemoteException {
      return new MyStringIterator(
          new String [] { "Foo", "Bar", "Gee" } );
    }

    public void asyncExecute(
        WorkRequest request , WorkListener listener )
        throws java.rmi.RemoteException {

        // should really do this in another thread
        Object result = request.execute();
        listener.workCompleted( request, result );
    }
}
```

getList() just returns a StringIterator with some stuff in it. asyncExecute() calls a WorkRequest's execute() method and notifies the listener when it's done. (Our implementation of asyncExecute() is a little cheesy. If we were forming a more complex calculation we would want to start a thread to do the calculation, and return immediately from asyncExecute(), so the client won't block. The thread would call workCompleted() at a later time, when the computation was done. In this simple example, it would probably take longer to start the thread than to perform the calculation.)

We have to modify MyClient to implement the remote WorkListener interface. This turns MyClient into a remote object, so we must make it a Unicast-RemoteObject. We also add the workCompleted() method that the Work-Listener interface requires:

```
public class MyClient
    extends java.rmi.server.UnicastRemoteObject
    implements WorkListener {
      ...
    public void workCompleted( WorkRequest request, Object result)
      throws RemoteException {
        System.out.println("Async work result = " + result);
      }
}
```

Finally, we want `MyClient` to exercise the new features. Add these lines after the calls to `getDate()` and `execute()`:

```
// MyClient constructor
   ...
StringIterator se = server.getList();
while ( se.hasNext() )
    System.out.println( se.next() );


server.asyncExecute( new MyCalculation(100), this );
```

We use `getList()` to get the iterator from the server, then loop, printing the strings. We also call `asyncExecute()` to perform another calculation; this time, we square the number 100. The second argument to `asyncExecute()` is the `WorkListener` to notify when the data is ready; we pass a reference to ourself (`this`).

Now all we have to do is compile everything and run `rmic` to make the stubs for all our remote objects:

```
rmic MyClient MyServer MyStringIterator
```

Restart the RMI registry and `MyServer` on your server, and run the client somewhere. You should get the following:

```
Fri Jul 11 23:57:19 PDT 1999
4
Foo
Bar
Gee
Async work result = 10000
```

If you are experimenting with dynamic class loading, you should be able to have the client download all of the server's auxiliary classes (the stubs and the `StringIterator`) from a web server. And, conversely, you should be able to have the `MyServer` download the `Client` stub and `WorkRequest` related classes when it needs them.

We hope that this introduction has given you a feel for the tremendous power that RMI offers through object serialization and dynamic class loading. Java is one of the first programming languages to offer this kind of powerful framework for distributed applications.

RMI Object Activation

One of the newest features of RMI is the ability to create remote objects that are persistent. They can save their state and be reactivated when a request from a client arrives. This is an important feature for large systems with remote objects that must remain accessible across long periods of time. RMI activation effectively allows a remote object to be stored away—in a database, for example—and automatically be reincarnated when it is needed. RMI activation is not particularly easy to use and would not have benefited us in any of our simple examples; we won't delve into it here. Much of the functionality of activatable objects can be achieved by using factories of shorter-lived objects that know how to retrieve some state from a database (or other location). The primary users of RMI activation may be systems like Enterprise JavaBeans, which need a generalized mechanism to save remotely accessible objects and revive them at later times.

RMI and CORBA

Java supports an important alternative to RMI, called CORBA (Common Object Request Broker Architecture). We won't say much about CORBA here, but you should know that it exists. CORBA is a distributed object standard developed by the Object Management Group (OMG), of which Sun Microsystems is one of the founding members. Its major advantage is that it works across languages: a Java program can use CORBA to talk to objects written in other languages, like C or C++. This is may be a considerable advantage if you want to build a Java front end for an older program that you can't afford to re-implement. CORBA also provides other services similar to those in the Java Enterprise APIs. CORBA's major disadvantages are that it's complex, inelegant, and somewhat arcane.

Sun and OMG have been making efforts to bridge RMI and CORBA. There is an implementation of RMI that can use IIOP (the Internet Inter-Object Protocol) to allow some RMI-to-CORBA interoperability. However, CORBA currently does not have many of the semantics necessary to support true RMI style distributed objects. So this solution is somewhat limited at this time.

In this chapter:
- *Uniform Resource Locators (URLs)*
- *The URL Class*
- *Web Browsers and Handlers*
- *Talking to CGI Programs and Servlets*
- *Implementing Servlets*

12

Programming for the Web

When we think about the World Wide Web, we normally think of applications—web browsers, web servers—and the many kinds of content that those applications move around the network. But it's important to note that standards and protocols, not the applications themselves, have enabled the Web's growth. Ever since the first days of the Internet, there have been ways to move files from here to there, and document formats that were just as good as HTML, but there was not a unifying model for how to identify, retrieve, and display information; nor was there a universal way for applications to interact with that data over the network. As we all know, HTML came to provide a common data basis for documents. In this chapter, we're going to talk about how to use HTTP, the protocol that governs communications between web clients and servers, and URLs, which provide a standard for naming and addressing objects on the Web.

In this chapter, we're also going to talk about web programming: making the Web intelligent, making it do what you want. This involves writing code for both clients and servers. Java provides a powerful API for dealing with URLs, which will be the first focus of our discussion. Then we'll discuss how to write web clients that can interact with the standard CGI interface, using the GET and POST methods. Finally, we'll take a look at servlets, simple Java programs that run on web servers and provide an effective way to build intelligence into your web pages. Servlets have been one of the most important and popular developments in Java over the past couple of years.

Uniform Resource Locators (URLs)

A URL points to an object on the Internet. It's (usually) a text string that identifies an item, tells you where to find it, and specifies a method for communicating with it or retrieving it from its source. A URL can refer to any kind of information source. It might point to static data, such as a file on a local filesystem, a web server, or an FTP archive; or it can point to a more dynamic object such as a news article on a news spool or a record in a database. URLs can even refer to less tangible resources such as telnet sessions and mailing addresses.

The Java URL classes provide an API for accessing well-defined networked resources, like documents and applications on servers. The classes use an extensible set of prefabricated protocol and content handlers to perform the necessary communication and data conversion for accessing URL resources. With URLs, an application can fetch a complete file or database record from a server on the network with just a few lines of code. Applications like web browsers, which deal with networked content, use the URL class to simplify the task of network programming. They also take advantage of the dynamic nature of Java, which allows handlers for new types of URLs to be added on the fly. As new types of servers and new formats for content evolve, additional URL handlers can be supplied to retrieve and interpret the data without modifying the original application.

A URL is usually presented as a string of text, like an address.* Since there are many different ways to locate an item on the Net, and different mediums and transports require different kinds of information, there are different formats for different kinds of URLs. The most common form has three components: a network host or server, the name of the item and its location on that host, and a protocol by which the host should communicate:

> *protocol://hostname/location/item-name*

protocol (also called the "scheme") is an identifier such as http, ftp, or gopher; *hostname* is an Internet hostname; and the *location* and *item* components form a path that identifies the object on that host. Variants of this form allow extra information to be packed into the URL, specifying things like port numbers for the communications protocol and fragment identifiers that reference parts inside the object.

We sometimes speak of a URL that is relative to another URL, called a *base URL*. In that case we are using the base URL as a starting point and supplying additional information. For example, the base URL might point to a directory on a web server; a relative URL might name a particular file in that directory.

---

* The term URL was coined by the Uniform Resource Identifier (URI) working group of the IETF to distinguish URLs from the more general notion of Uniform Resource Names or URNs. URLs are really just static addresses, whereas URNs would be more persistent and abstract identifiers used to resolve the location of an object anywhere on the Net. URLs are defined in RFC 1738 and RFC 1808.

The URL Class

A URL is represented by an instance of the java.net.URL class. A URL object manages all the component information within a URL string and provides methods for retrieving the object it identifies. We can construct a URL object from a URL specification string or from its component parts:

```
try {
    URL aDoc =
        new URL( "http://foo.bar.com/documents/homepage.html" );
    URL sameDoc =
        new URL("http","foo.bar.com","documents/homepage.html");
}
catch ( MalformedURLException e ) { }
```

These two URL objects point to the same network resource, the *homepage.html* document on the server *foo.bar.com*. Whether the resource actually exists and is available isn't known until we try to access it. At this point, the URL object just contains data about the object's location and how to access it. No connection to the server has been made. We can examine the URL's components with the getProtocol(), getHost(), and getFile() methods. We can also compare it to another URL with the sameFile() method (which has an unfortunate name for something which may not point to a file). sameFile() determines whether two URLs point to the same resource. It can be fooled, but sameFile() does more than compare the URLs for equality; it takes into account the possibility that one server may have several names, and other factors.

When a URL is created, its specification is parsed to identify just the protocol component. If the protocol doesn't make sense, or if Java can't find a protocol handler for it, the URL constructor throws a MalformedURLException. A *protocol handler* is a Java class that implements the communications protocol for accessing the URL resource. For example, given an http URL, Java prepares to use the HTTP protocol handler to retrieve documents from the specified server.

Stream Data

The lowest level way to get data back from URL is to ask for an InputStream from the URL by calling openStream(). Currently, if you're writing an applet or working in an otherwise untrusted environment this is about your only choice. Getting the data as a stream may be useful if you want to receive continuous updates from a dynamic information source. The drawback is that you have to parse the contents of the object yourself. Not all types of URLs support the openStream() method because not all types of URLs refer to concrete data; you'll get an UnknownServiceException if the URL doesn't.

The following code prints the contents of an HTML file:

```
try {
    URL url = new URL("http://server/index.html");

    BufferedReader bin = new BufferedReader (
        new InputStreamReader( url.openStream() ));

    String line;
    while ( (line = bin.readLine()) != null )
        System.out.println( line );
} catch (Exception e) { }
```

We ask for an `InputStream` with `openStream()` and wrap it in a `Buffered-Reader` to read the lines of text. Because we specify the `http` protocol in the URL, we require the services of an HTTP protocol handler. As we'll discuss later, that raises some questions about what kinds of handlers we have available. This example partially works around those issues because no content handler is involved; we read the data and interpret the content ourselves (by simply printing it).

Applets have additional restrictions. To be sure that you can access the specified URL and the correct protocol handler, construct URLs relative to the base URL that identifies the applet's *codebase*—the location of the applet code. For example:

```
new URL( getCodeBase(), "foo/bar.gif" );
```

This should guarantee that the needed protocol is available and accessible to the applet. However if you are just trying to get data files or media associated with an applet, there is a more general way; see the discussion of `getResource()` in Chapter 10, *Input/Output Facilities*.

Getting the Content as an Object

`openStream()` operates at a lower level than the more general content-handling mechanism implemented by the URL class. We showed it first because, until some things are settled, you'll be limited as to when you can use URLs in their more powerful role. When a proper content handler is installed, you can retrieve the item the URL addresses as a Java object, by calling the URL's `getContent()` method. Currently, this only works if you supply one with your application or install one in the local classpath. (The HotJava web browser also provides a mechanism for adding new handlers.) In this mode of operation `getContent()` initiates a connection to the host, fetches the data for you, determines the MIME (Multipurpose Internet Mail Extensions) type of the contents, and invokes a content handler to turn the bytes into a Java object. MIME is a standard that was developed to facilitate multimedia email, but it has become widely used as a general way to specify how to treat data; Java uses MIME to help it pick the right content handler.

For example, given the URL *http://foo.bar.com/index.html,* a call to getContent()
would use the HTTP protocol handler to retrieve data and an HTML content handler to turn the data into an appropriate document object. A URL that points to a
plain-text file might use a text-content handler that returns a String object. Similarly, a GIF file might be turned into an ImageProducer object using a GIF content handler. If we accessed the GIF file using an "ftp" URL, Java would use the
same content handler but would use the FTP protocol handler to receive the data.

getContent() returns the output of the content handler, but leaves us wondering what kind of object we got. Since the content handler has to be able to return
anything, the return type of getContent() is Object. In a moment, we'll
describe how we could ask the protocol handler about the object's MIME type,
which it discovered. Based on this, and whatever other knowledge we have about
the kind of object we are expecting, we can cast the Object to its appropriate,
more specific type. For example, if we expect a String, we'll cast the result of
getContent() to a String:

```
try {
    String content = (String)myURL.getContent();
} catch ( ClassCastException e ) { ... }
```

If we're wrong about the type, we'll get a ClassCastException. As an alternative, we could check the type of the returned object using the instanceof operator, like this:

```
if ( content instanceof String ) {
    String s = (String)content;
    ...
```

Various kinds of errors can occur when trying to retrieve the data. For example,
getContent() can throw an IOException if there is a communications error.
Other kinds of errors can occur at the application level: some knowledge of how
the application-specific content and protocol handlers deal with errors is necessary.

One problem that could arise is that a content handler for the data's MIME type
wouldn't be available. In this case, getContent() just invokes an "unknown type"
handler and returns the data as a raw InputStream. A sophisticated application
might specialize this behavior to try to decide what to do with the data on its own.

In some situations, we may also need knowledge of the protocol handler. For
example, consider a URL that refers to a nonexistent file on an HTTP server. When
requested, the server probably returns a valid HTML document that contains the
familiar "404 Not Found" message. In a naive implementation, an HTML content
handler might be invoked to interpret this message and return it as it would any
other HTML document. To check the validity of protocol-specific operations like
this, we may need to talk to the protocol handler.

The openStream() and getContent() methods both implicitly create the connection to the remote URL object. When the connection is set up, the protocol handler is consulted to create a URLConnection object. The URLConnection manages the protocol-specific communications. We can get a URLConnection for our URL with the openConnection() method. One of the things we can do with the URLConnection is ask for the object's content type. For example:

```
URLConnection connection = myURL.openConnection();
String mimeType = connection.getContentType();
...
Object contents = myURL.getContents();
```

We can also get protocol-specific information. Different protocols provide different types of URLConnection objects. The HttpURLConnection object, for instance, can interpret the "404 Not Found" message and tell us about the problem. (We'll examine URLConnections in detail in Appendix A, *Content and Protocol Handlers.*)

Web Browsers and Handlers

The content- and protocol-handler mechanisms we've introduced can be used by any application that accesses data via URLs. This mechanism is extremely flexible; to handle a URL, you need only the appropriate protocol and content handlers. One obvious application is for Java-based web browsers that can handle new and specialized kinds of URLs.

Furthermore, Java's ability to load new classes over the Net means that, in theory, the handlers don't even need to be owned by the browser. Content and protocol handlers could be downloaded over the Net from the same site that supplies the data, and used by the browser. If you wanted to supply some completely new data type, using a completely new protocol, you could make your data file plus a content handler and a protocol handler available on your web server; anyone using a Web browser supporting Java could automatically get the appropriate handlers whenever they access your data. In short, Java could allow you to build dynamically extensible web applications. Instead of gigantic do-everything software, you could build a lightweight scaffold that dynamically incorporates extensions as needed.

Figure 12-1 shows the conceptual operation of a downloadable content handler in a web browser; Figure 12-2 does the same for a protocol handler.

Unfortunately, a few nasty flies are stuck in this ointment. The schemes depicted in these figures have been part of the Java scene since it was an alpha product, but they are still hypothetical. There is no API for dynamically downloading new content and protocol handlers. In fact, there is no API for determining what content and protocol handlers exist on a given platform. Although content and protocol

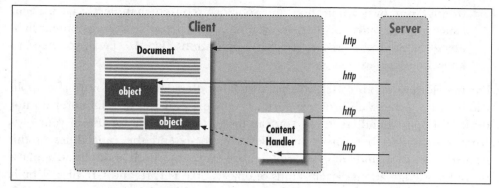

Figure 12-1. A content handler at work

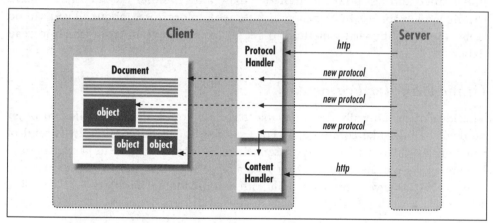

Figure 12-2. A protocol handler at work

handlers are part of the Java API and an intrinsic part of the mechanism for working with URLs, specific content and protocol handlers aren't defined. The standard Java classes don't, for example, include content handlers for HTML, GIF, MPEG, or other common data types. Sun's SDK and all of the other Java environments do come with these kinds of handlers, but these are installed on an application-level basis.

There are two real issues here:

- There isn't a standard that says that certain types of handlers have to be provided in each environment along with the core Java API. Instead we have to rely on the application to decide what kinds of data types it needs. This makes sense but is frustrating when it should be reasonable to expect certain basic types to be covered in all environments.

- There isn't any standard that tells you what kind of object the content handler should return. Maybe GIF data should be returned as an `ImageProducer` object, but at the moment, that's an application-level decision. If you're writing your own application and your own content handlers, that isn't an issue: you can make any decision you want. But if you're writing content handlers that are to be used by arbitrary applications (like HotJava), you need to know what they expect.

For the HotJava web browser, you can install handlers locally (as for all Java applications), but other web browsers such as Netscape and Internet Explorer do not directly support handlers at all. You can install them locally for use in your own (intranet) applets but you cannot use them to extend the capabilities of the browser. Netscape and Internet Explorer are currently classic monolithic applications: knowledge about certain kinds of objects, like HTML and GIF files, is built in. These browsers can be extended via a plug-in mechanism, which is a much less fine grained and less powerful approach than Java's handler mechanism. If you're writing applets for use in Netscape or Internet Explorer now, about all you can do is use the openStream() method to get a raw input stream from which to read data.

Other Handler Frameworks

The idea of dynamically downloadable handlers could also be applied to other kinds of handler-like components. For example, the XML community is fond of referring to XML as a way to apply semantics to documents and to Java as a portable way to supply the behavior that goes along with those semantics. It's possible that an XML viewer could be built with downloadable handlers for displaying XML tags.

The JavaBeans APIs also touch upon this subject with the Java Activation Framework. The JAF provides a way to detect the type of a stream of data and "encapsulate access to it" in a Java Bean. If this sounds suspiciously like the content handler's job, it is. Unfortunately, it looks like these APIs will not be merged in the future.

Writing Content and Protocol Handlers

If you're adventurous and want to start leveraging content and protocol handlers in your own applications, you can find all the information you'll need in Appendix A, which covers writing content and protocol handlers.

Talking to CGI Programs and Servlets

CGI stands for Common Gateway Interface; it is an API for writing applications (often scripts) that can be run by a web server to service a particular range of URLs. Servlets are an implementation very similar to CGI using a component-ized framework in Java. CGI programs and servlets can perform dynamic activities like automatically generating web documents. More important, they can accept data sent from the browser; they are most frequently used to process forms.

The name/value pairs of HTML form fields are encoded by the client web browser in a special format and sent to the application using one of two methods. The first method, using the HTTP command GET, encodes the user's input into the URL and requests the corresponding document. The server recognizes that the first part of the URL refers to a program and invokes it, passing along the information encoded in the URL as a parameter. The second method uses the HTTP command POST to ask the server to accept the encoded data and pass it to the CGI program as a stream.

In Java, we can create a URL that refers to a CGI program and send it data using either the GET or POST methods. Why would we want to talk to a CGI? Well, CGI remains a widely used technique for building web applications. Other techniques such as opening sockets or talking via RMI are coming on strong, but CGI has been in widespread use for several years. Another important reason for using CGI is that many firewalls block socket connections entirely. But all firewalls that allow web access have to let us use GET and POST to talk to CGIs. So CGI programs can be used as a last resort communications mechanism between applets and servers.

In this section, we'll talk about writing the client side of these applications. Later in this chapter we'll talk about writing servlets for the server side of the application. We'll present the two data sending techniques GET and POST lightly here and in more detail when we revisit them in the "Implementing Servlets" section.

Using the GET Method

Using the GET method of encoding data in a URL is pretty easy. All we have to do is create a URL pointing to a server program and use a simple convention to tack on the encoded name/value pairs that make up our data. For example, the following code snippet opens a URL to a CGI program called *login.cgi* on the server *myhost* and passes it two name/value pairs. It then prints whatever text the CGI sends back:

```
URL url = new URL(
    // this string should be URL-encoded as well
    "http://myhost/cgi-bin/login.cgi?Name=Pat&Password=foobar");

BufferedReader bin = new BufferedReader (
  new InputStreamReader( url.openStream() ));

String line;
while ( (line = bin.readLine()) != null )
    System.out.println( line );
```

To form the new URL, we start with the URL of *login.cgi*; we add a question mark (?), which marks the beginning of the form data, followed by the first name/value pair. We can add as many pairs as we want, separated by ampersand (&) characters. The rest of our code simply opens the stream and reads back the response from the server. Remember that creating a URL doesn't actually open the connection. In this case, the URL connection was made implicitly when we called openStream(). Although we are assuming here that our CGI sends back text, it could send anything. (In theory of course we could use the getContentType() method of the URL to check the MIME type of any returned data, and try to retrieve the data as an object using getContent() as well).

It's important to point out that we have skipped a step here. This example works because our name/value pairs happen to be simple text. If any "non-printable" or special characters (including ? or &) are in the pairs, they have to be encoded first. The java.net.URLEncoder class provides a utility for encoding the data. We'll show how to use it in the next example.

Another important thing to note is that although this example sends a password field, you should never do so using this simplistic approach. All of the data we're sending goes in clear text across the network (it is not encrypted). And in this case the password field would appear anywhere the URL is printed as well (e.g., server logs). We'll talk about secure web communications later in this chapter.

Using the POST Method

Next we'll create a small application that acts like an HTML form. It gathers data from two text fields—name and password—and posts the data to a specified URL using the HTTP POST method. If you look ahead to Chapter 15, which covers the Swing GUI text components, you will see that that writing an application that displays actual HTML text and can post using forms just like a web browser is simple. So why would we want to do things the hard way?

There are many reasons that an application (or applet) might want to communicate with a CGI or servlet. For example, compatability with another web-based application might be important, or you might need to gain access to a server through a firewall where direct socket connections (and hence normal RMI) are not available. HTTP has become the lingua franca of the Net and despite its limitations (or more likely because of its simplicity) it has rapidly become one of the most widely supported protocols in the world. All of the other reasons that one would write a client GUI application (as opposed to a pure web/HTML-based application) also present themselves: a client-side GUI can do sophisticated presentation and field validation while, with the technique presented here, still use web-enabled services over the network.

Here's the code:

```
//file: Post.java
import java.net.*;
import java.io.*;
import java.awt.*;
import java.awt.event.*;
import javax.swing.*;

public class Post extends JPanel implements ActionListener {
  JTextField nameField, passwordField;
  String postURL;

  GridBagConstraints constraints = new GridBagConstraints();
  void addGB( Component component, int x, int y ) {
    constraints.gridx = x;  constraints.gridy = y;
    add ( component, constraints );
  }

  public Post( String postURL ) {
    this.postURL = postURL;
    JButton postButton = new JButton("Post");
    postButton.addActionListener( this );
    setLayout( new GridBagLayout() );
    addGB( new JLabel("Name:"), 0,0 );
    addGB( nameField = new JTextField(20), 1,0 );
    addGB( new JLabel("Password:"), 0,1 );
    addGB( passwordField = new JPasswordField(20),1,1 );
    constraints.gridwidth = 2;
    addGB( postButton, 0,2 );
  }

  public void actionPerformed(ActionEvent e) {
    postData();
  }

  protected void postData() {
    StringBuffer sb = new StringBuffer();
    sb.append( URLEncoder.encode("Name") + "=" );
    sb.append( URLEncoder.encode(nameField.getText()) );
    sb.append( "&" + URLEncoder.encode("Password") + "=" );
    sb.append( URLEncoder.encode(passwordField.getText()) );
    String formData = sb.toString();

    try {
      URL url = new URL( postURL );
      HttpURLConnection urlcon =
          (HttpURLConnection) url.openConnection();
      urlcon.setRequestMethod("POST");
      urlcon.setRequestProperty("Content-type",
```

```
        "application/x-www-form-urlencoded");
    urlcon.setDoOutput(true);
    urlcon.setDoInput(true);
    PrintWriter pout = new PrintWriter( new OutputStreamWriter(
        urlcon.getOutputStream(), "8859_1"), true );
    pout.print( formData );
    pout.flush();

    // read results...
    if ( urlcon.getResponseCode() != HttpURLConnection.HTTP_OK )
      System.out.println("Posted ok!");
    else {
      System.out.println("Bad post...");
      return;
    }
    //InputStream in = urlcon.getInputStream();
    // ...

  } catch (MalformedURLException e) {
    System.out.println(e);       // bad postURL
  } catch (IOException e2) {
    System.out.println(e2);      // I/O error
  }
}

public static void main( String [] args ) {
  JFrame frame = new JFrame("SimplePost");
  frame.getContentPane().add( new Post( args[0] ), "Center" );
  frame.pack();
  frame.setVisible(true);
}
}
```

When you run this application, you must specify the URL of the server program on the command line. For example:

```
% java Post http://www.myserver.example/cgi-bin/login.cgi
```

The beginning of the application creates the form; there's nothing here that won't be obvious after you've read the chapters on Swing. All the magic happens in the protected postData() method. First we create a StringBuffer and load it with name/value pairs, separated by ampersands. (We don't need the initial question mark when we're using the POST method, because we're not appending to a URL string.) Each pair is first encoded using the static URLEncoder.encode() method. We ran the name fields through the encoder as well as the value fields, even though we know that they contain no special characters.

Next we set up the connection to the CGI program. In our previous example, we didn't have to do anything special to send the data, because the request was made by the web browser for us. Here, we have to carry some of the weight of talking to the remote web server. Fortunately, the HttpURLConnection object does most of the work for us; we just have to tell it that we want to do a POST to the URL and the type of data we are sending. We ask for the URLConnection object using the URL's openConnection() method. We know that we are using the HTTP protocol, so we should be able to cast it safely to an HttpURLConnection type, which has the support we need.

Next we use setRequestMethod() to tell the connection we want to do a POST operation. We also use setRequestProperty() to set the "Content-Type" field of our HTTP request to the appropriate type—in this case, the proper MIME type for encoded form data. (This helps the server sort out what we're sending.) Finally, we use the setDoOutput() and setDoInput() methods to tell the connection that we want to both send and receive stream data. The URL connection infers from this combination that we are going to do a POST operation. Next we get an output stream from the connection with getOutputStream() and create a PrintWriter so we can easily write our encoded data.

After we post the data, our application calls getResponseCode() to see whether the HTTP response code from the server indicates that the POST was successful. Other response codes (defined as constants in HttpURLConnection) indicate various failures. At the end, we indicate where we could have read back the text of the response. For this application, we'll assume that simply knowing the post was successful was sufficient.

Although form-encoded data (as indicated by the MIME type we specified for the Content-Type field) is the most common, other types of communications are possible. We could have used the input and output streams to exchange arbitrary data types with the CGI program (provided that the CGI program was capable of listening for a connection from us). One great feature of servlets, which we'll discuss momentarily, is that they can easily exchange arbitrary data with the client.

If you are writing a server application that needs to decode form data, you can use the java.net.URLDecoder to undo the operation of the URLEncoder.

SSL and Secure Web Communications

The previous examples sent a field called Password to the server. However, standard HTTP doesn't provide encryption to hide our data. Fortunately, adding security for GET and POST operations is easy. Where available you simply have to use a secure form of the HTTP protocol—HTTPS.

HTTPS is a version of the standard HTTP protocol run over SSL (Secure Socket Layer) sockets, which use public-key encryption techniques to encrypt the data sent. Most web browsers currently come with built-in support for HTTPS (or raw

SSL sockets). Therefore, if your web server supports HTTPS, you can use a browser to send and receive secure data simply by specifying the https protocol in your URLs. This is not something your code has to deal with directly. Applets written using the Java plug-in have access to the HTTPS protocol handler. For other applications you will have to make sure that your environments have supplied an HTTPS (SSL) protocol handler, or set up the data connection yourself using other secure means.

Implementing Servlets

Now we're going to take a leap from the client side over to the server side, to write Java applications for web servers. The Java servlet API is a framework for writing *servlets*, which are application components for a web server or other type of server; just as *applets* are application components for a web browser.

The servlet APIs live in the javax.servlet package, which is a standard Java API extension, not part of the core Java APIs. In this book we haven't talked about many standard extension packages, but this is one is particularly important. (It should probably be a core API.) You'll want to grab the latest Java Servlet Development Kit (JSDK) from *http://java.sun.com/products/servlet*.

The servlet APIs are useless without a server on which to run them, so you'll also want to find an implementation of the servlet environment for your favorite web server: Netscape, Apache, or whatever. We won't try to anticipate which environment you have in this book, so the details about how to install your servlets and invoke them will be up to you. But it should be pretty easy.

Why Servlets?

Why would we want to use Java on the server side, as opposed to a scripting language, such as Perl? The simplest answer to that question is: for the same reasons that you would use Java anywhere else. Servlets simply let you write in Java and derive all of the benefits of Java and the virtual machine environment on the server side. (You also have the limitations of Java.) Historically, servlets had speed advantages over CGI programs written in scripting languages or even in C/C++. That is because servlets execute in a multithreaded way within one instance of a virtual machine. Older CGI applications required the server to start a separate process, "pipe" data to it, and then receive the response as a stream as well. Speed is still a factor, but a more important reason for using Java is that Java makes writing large applications much more manageable. Java isn't as easy to use as a scripting language, but it's much easier to come back to your program next year and add a new feature, and it's a lot better at scaling to large applications.

Writing server code with servlets allows you to access all of the standard Java APIs within the virtual machine while your servlets are handling requests. This means that your Java server code can access "live" database connections, or communicate with other network services that have already been established. This kind of behavior has been hacked into other CGI environments, but it has always been there in Java in a robust and natural way.

The Servlet Life Cycle

The Servlet API is very simple, almost exactly paralleling the Applet API. There are three life-cycle methods, init(), service(), and destroy(), along with a couple of methods for getting configuration parameters and servlet info. Before a servlet is used for the first time, it is initialized by the server through its init() method. Thereafter the servlet spends its time handling service() requests and doing its job until (presumably) the server is shut down and the servlet's destroy() method is called, giving it an opportunity to clean up.

The service() method of a servlet accepts two parameters: a servlet "request" object and a servlet "response" object. These provide tools for reading the client request and generating output; we'll talk about them in detail in the examples.

By default, servlets are expected to handle multithreaded requests; that is, the servlet's service methods may be invoked by many threads at the same time. This means that you cannot store client-related data in instance variables of your servlet object. (Of course, you can store general data related to the servlet's operation, as long as it does not change on a per-request basis.) Per-client state information can be stored in a client "session" object, which persists across client requests. We'll talk about that in detail later.

If for some reason you have developed a servlet that cannot support multithreaded access, you can tell the runtime system this by implementing the flag interface SingleThreadModel. It has no methods, serving only to indicate that the servlet should be invoked in a single-threaded manner.

HTTP (Web) Servlets

There are actually two packages of interest in the Servlet API. The first is the javax.servlet package, which contains the most general servlet APIs. The second important package is javax.servlet.http, which contains APIs specific to servlets that handle HTTP requests for web servers. In the rest of this section, we are going to discuss servlets pretty much as if all servlets were HTTP-related. Although you can write servlets for other protocols, that's not what we're currently interested in.

The primary tool provided by the `javax.servlet.http` package is the `HttpServlet` base class. This is an abstract servlet that provides some basic implementation related to handling an HTTP request. In particular, it overrides the generic servlet `service()` request and breaks it out into several HTTP-related methods for you, including: `doGet()`, `doPost()`, `doPut()`, and `doDelete()`. The default `service()` method examines the request to determine what kind it is and dispatches it to one of these methods, so you can override one or more of them to implement the corresponding web server behavior.

`doGet()` and `doPost()` correspond to the standard HTTP `GET` and `POST` operations. `GET` is the standard request for the object at a specified URL: e. g., a file or document. `POST` is the method by which a client sends data to the server. HTML forms are the most common example of users of `POST`.

To round these out, `HttpServlet` provides the `doPut()` and `doDelete()` methods. These methods correspond to a poorly supported part of the HTTP protocol, meant to provide a way to upload and remove files. `doPut()` is supposed to be like POST but with different semantics; `doDelete()` would be its opposite.

`HttpServlet` also implements three other HTTP related methods for you: `doHead()`, `doTrace()`, and `doOptions()`. You don't normally need to override these methods. `doHead()` implements the HTTP `HEAD` request, which asks for the headers of a `GET` request without the body. (`HttpServlet` implements this by performing the `GET` and then sending only the headers). `doTrace()` and `doOptions()` implement other features of HTTP that allow for debugging and for simple client/server capabilities negotiation. Again, you generally shouldn't need to override these.

Along with `HttpServlet`, `javax.servlet.http` also includes subclasses of the `ServletRequest` and `ServletResponse` objects, namely: `HttpServletRequest` and `HttpServletResponse`. These provide (respectively) the input and output streams needed to read and write client data. They also provide the APIs for getting or setting HTTP header information and, as we'll see, client session information. Rather than document these dryly, we'll just show them in the context of some examples. As usual, we'll start with the simplest example possible.

The HelloClient Servlet

Here's our "Hello World" of servlet land, `HelloClient`:

```
//file: HelloClient.java
import java.io.*;
import javax.servlet.ServletException;
import javax.servlet.http.*;

public class HelloClient extends HttpServlet {
```

```
public void doGet(HttpServletRequest request,
                  HttpServletResponse response)
    throws ServletException, IOException {

    // must come first
    response.setContentType("text/html");
    PrintWriter out = response.getWriter();

    out.println(
        "<html><head><title>Hello Client</title></head><body>"
        + "<h1> Hello Client </h1>"
        + "</body></html>" );
    out.close();
}
}
```

`HelloClient` extends the base `HttpServlet` class and overrides the `doGet()` method to handle simple requests. In this case, we want to respond to any GET request by sending back a one-line HTML document that says "Hello Client". We get the output writer from our `HttpServletResponse` parameter using the `getWriter()` method and print the message to it. Then we close the stream to indicate that we are done generating output.

Content Types

Before fetching the output stream and writing to it, however, it's very important that we specify what kind of output we are sending by calling the `response` parameter's `setContentType()` method.

In this case, we set the content type to `text/html`, which is the proper MIME type for an HTML document. But in general, it's possible for a servlet to generate any kind of data, including sound, video, or some other kind of text. If we were writing a generic `FileServlet` that serves files like a regular web server, we might inspect the filename extension and determine the MIME type from that, or from direct inspection of the data.

The content type is used in the `Content-Type:` header of the server's HTTP response, which tells the client what to expect even before it starts reading the result. This is how your web browser is able to prompt you with the "Save File" dialog when you click on a zip archive or executable program. When the content type string is used in its full form to specify the character encoding (for example, `text/html; charset=ISO-8859-1`) that information is also used by the servlet engine to set the character encoding of the `PrintWriter` output stream. So you should call the `setContentType()` method before fetching the writer with the `getWriter()` method.

Servlet Parameters

Our first example shows how to accept a basic request. You can imagine how we might do arbitrary processing, database queries, etc., to generate an interesting response. Of course, to do anything really useful we are going to have to get some information from the user. Fortunately, the servlet engine handles this for us, interpreting both GET- and POST-encoded form information from the client and providing it to us through the simple getParameter() method of the servlet request.

GET, POST, and the "extra path"

There are essentially two ways to pass information from your web browser to a servlet or CGI program. The most general is to "post" it, which means that your client encodes the information and sends it as a stream to the program, which decodes it. Posting can be used to upload large amounts of form data or other data, including files. The other way is to somehow encode the information in the URL of your client's request. The primary way to do this is to use GET-style encoding of parameters in the URL string. In this case the web browser will append the parameters to the end of the URL string in an encoded way and the server will decode them and pass them to the application.

As we described earlier in this chapter, GET-style encoding says that you take the parameters and append them to the URL in a name/value fashion, with the first parameter preceded by a question mark (?) and the rest separated by ampersands (&). The entire string is expected to be *URL-encoded*: any special characters (like spaces, ?, and & in the string) are specially encoded.

A less sophisticated form of encoding data in the URL is called *extra path*. This simply means that when the server has located your servlet or CGI program as the target of a URL, it takes any remaining path components of the URL string and simply hands it over as an extra part of the URL. For example, consider these URLs:

```
http://www.myserver.example/servlets/MyServlet
http://www.myserver.example/servlets/MyServlet/foo/bar
```

Suppose the server maps the first URL to the servlet called MyServlet. When subsequently given the second URL, the server would still invoke MyServlet, but would consider /foo/bar to be "extra path" that could be retrieved through the servlet request getExtraPath() method.

Both GET and POST encoding can be used with HTML forms on the client, simply by specifying get or post in the action attribute of the form tag. The browser handles the encoding; on the server side, the servlet engine will handle the decoding.

Which one to use?

To users, the primary difference between GET and POST is that they can see the GET information in the encoded URL shown in their web browser. This can be useful because the user can cut and paste that URL (the result of a search for example) and mail it to a friend or bookmark it for future reference. POST information is never visible to the user and ceases to exist after it's sent to the server. This behavior goes along with the protocol's perspective that GET and POST are intended to have different semantics. By definition, the result of a GET operation is not supposed to have any side effects. That is, it's not supposed to cause the server to perform any consequential operations (such as making an e-commerce purchase). In theory, that's the job of POST. That's why your web browser warns you about "re-posting form data" if you hit reload on a page that was the result of a form posting.

The extra path method is not useful for form data, but would be useful if you wanted to make a servlet that retrieves files or handles a range of URLs not driven by forms.

The ShowParameters Servlet

Our first example didn't do anything interesting. This example prints the values of any parameters that were received. We'll start by handling GET requests and then make some trivial modifications to handle POST as well. Here's the code:

```java
//file: ShowParameters.java
import java.io.*;
import javax.servlet.ServletException;
import javax.servlet.http.*;
import java.util.Enumeration;

public class ShowParameters extends HttpServlet {

    public void doGet(HttpServletRequest request,
                      HttpServletResponse response)
      throws ServletException, IOException {
        showRequestParameters( request, response );
    }

    void showRequestParameters(HttpServletRequest request,
                      HttpServletResponse response)
      throws IOException {
        response.setContentType("text/html");
        PrintWriter out = response.getWriter();

        out.println(
          "<html><head><title>Show Parameters</title></head><body>"
```

```
              + "<h1>Parameters</h1><ul>");

         for ( Enumeration e=request.getParameterNames();
                 e.hasMoreElements(); ) {
             String name = (String)e.nextElement();
             String value = request.getParameter( name );
             if (! value.equals("") )
                 out.println("<li>"+ name +" = "+ value );
         }

         out.close();
     }
 }
```

There's not much new here. As in the first example, we override the doGet()
method. Here, we delegate the request to a helper method that we've created,
called showRequestParameters(). All this method does is enumerate the parameters using the request object's getParameterNames() method and print the
names and values. (To make it pretty, we've listed them in an HTML list by
prepending each with an <li> tag.)

As it stands, our servlet would respond to any URL that contains a GET request.
Let's round it out by adding our own form to the output and also accommodating
POST method requests. To accept posts, we simply override the doPost() method.
The implementation of doPost() could simply call our showRequest-
Parameters() method as well, but we can make it simpler still. The API lets us
treat GET and POST requests interchangeably, because the servlet engine handles
the decoding of request parameters. So we simply delegate the doPost() opera-
tion to doGet().

Add the following method to the example:

```
    public void doPost( HttpServletRequest request,
                        HttpServletResponse response)
      throws ServletException, IOException {
        doGet( request, response );
    }
```

Now let's add an HTML form to the output. The form lets the user fill in some
parameters and submit them to the servlet. Add this line to the
showRequestParameters() method before the call to out.close():

```
    out.println(
      "</ul><p><form method=\"POST\" action=\""
      + request.getRequestURI() + "\">"
      + "Field 1 <input name=\"Field 1\" size=20><br>"
      + "Field 2 <input name=\"Field 2\" size=20><br>"
      + "<br><input type=\"submit\" value=\"Submit\"></form>"
    );
```

The form's `action` attribute is the URL of our servlet, so that it will get the data. We use the `getRequestURI()` method to ask for the location of our servlet. For the `method` attribute we've specified a `POST` operation; but you can try changing the operation to `GET` to see both styles.

So far, we haven't done anything that you couldn't do easily with your average CGI script. Next, we'll show some more interesting stuff: how to manage a user session.

User Session Management

One of the nicest features of the servlet API is that it provides a simple mechanism for managing a user session. By a session, we mean that the servlet can maintain information over multiple pages and through multiple transactions as navigated by the user. Providing continuity through a series of web pages is important in many kinds of applications, like providing a login process or tracking purchases in a shopping cart. In a sense, session data takes the place of instance data in your servlet object. It lets you store data between invocations of your service methods.

Session tracking is supported by the servlet engine; you don't have to worry about the details of how it's accomplished. It's done in one of two ways: using client-side *cookies*, or *URL rewriting*. Client-side cookies are a standard HTTP mechanism for getting the client web browser to cooperate in storing some state information for you. A cookie is basically just a name/value attribute that is issued by the server, stored on the client, and returned by the client whenever it is accessing a certain group of URLs on a specified server. First, we'll talk about cookies that live only for the duration of a typical user session (although it is possible to use cookies to store state across multiple user visits).

URL rewriting appends the session tracking information to the URL, using `GET`-style encoding or extra path information. The term "rewriting" applies because the server rewrites the URL before it is seen by the client and absorbs the extra information before it is passed back to the servlet.

To the servlet programmer, the state information is made available through an `HttpSession` object, which acts like a hashtable for storing whatever objects you would like to carry through the session. The objects stay on the server side; a special identifier is sent to the client through a cookie or URL rewriting. On the way back, the identifier is mapped to a session and the session is associated with the servlet again.

The ShowSession servlet

Here's a simple servlet that shows how to store some string information in a session.

```java
//file: ShowSession.java
import java.io.*;
import javax.servlet.ServletException;
import javax.servlet.http.*;
import java.util.Enumeration;

public class ShowSession extends HttpServlet {

    public void doPost( HttpServletRequest request,
                          HttpServletResponse response)
      throws ServletException, IOException {
        doGet( request, response );
    }

    public void doGet(HttpServletRequest request,
                        HttpServletResponse response)
      throws ServletException, IOException {
        response.setContentType("text/html");
        PrintWriter out = response.getWriter();

        out.println(
          "<html><head><title>Show Session</title></head><body>");
        HttpSession session = request.getSession();

        out.println("<h1>In this session:</h1><ul>");
        String [] names = session.getValueNames();
        for (int i=0; i< names.length; i++)
            out.println(
              "<li>"+names[i]+" = "+session.getValue( names[i] ));

        // add new name-value to session
        String name = request.getParameter("Name");
        if ( name != null ) {
            String value = request.getParameter("Value");
            session.putValue( name, value );
        }

        out.println(
          "</ul><p><hr><h1>Add String</h1>"
          + "<form method=\"POST\" action=\""
          + request.getRequestURI() +"\">"
          + "Name: <input name=\"Name\" size=20><br>"
          + "Value: <input name=\"Value\" size=20><br>"
          + "<br><input type=\"submit\" value=\"Submit\"></form>"
        );

        out.close();
    }
}
```

When you invoke the servlet, you are presented with a form that prompts you to enter a name and a value. The value string is stored in a session object under the name provided. Each time the servlet is called, it outputs the list of all data items associated with the session. You will see the session grow as each item is added (in this case, until you restart your web browser or the server).

The basic mechanics are much like our `ShowParameters` servlet. Our `doGet()` method generates the form, which refers back to our servlet via a POST method. We override `doPost()` to delegate back to our `doGet()` method, allowing it to handle everything. Once in `doGet()`, we attempt to fetch the user session object from the `request` parameter using `getSession()`. The `HttpSession` object supplied by the request functions like a hashtable. There is a `putValue()` method, which takes a string name and an `Object` argument and a corresponding `getValue()` method. In our example, we use the `getValueNames()` method to enumerate the values currently stored in the session and print them.

By default, `getSession()` creates a session if one does not yet exist. If you want to test for a session or explicitly control when one is created, you can call the overloaded version `getSession(false)`, which does not automatically create a new session. This method returns `null` if there is no session yet.

The ShoppingCart servlet

Next, we'll build on the previous example to make a servlet that could be used as part of an online store. `ShoppingCart` lets users choose items and add them to their basket until check-out time:

```
//file: ShoppingCart.java
import java.io.*;
import javax.servlet.ServletException;
import javax.servlet.http.*;
import java.util.Enumeration;

public class ShoppingCart extends HttpServlet {
    // from your database
    String [] items = new String [] {
        "Chocolate Covered Crickets", "Raspberry Roaches",
        "Buttery Butterflies", "Chicken Flavored Chicklets(tm)" };

    public void doPost( HttpServletRequest request,
                        HttpServletResponse response)
        throws IOException, ServletException {
        doGet( request, response );
    }

    public void doGet( HttpServletRequest request,
                       HttpServletResponse response)
```

```java
            throws ServletException, IOException {
        response.setContentType("text/html");
        PrintWriter out = response.getWriter();

        // get or create the session information
        HttpSession session = request.getSession();
        int [] purchases = (int [])session.getValue("purchases");
        if ( purchases == null ) {
            purchases = new int [ items.length ];
            session.putValue( "purchases", purchases );
        }

        out.println( "<html><head><title>Shopping Cart</title>"
                    + "</title></head><body><p>" );
        if ( request.getParameter("checkout") != null )
            out.println("<h1>Thanks for ordering!</h1>");
        else {
            if ( request.getParameter("add") != null ) {
                addPurchases( request, purchases );
                out.println(
                    "<h1>Purchase added.  Please continue</h1>");
            } else {
                if ( request.getParameter("clear") != null )
                    for (int i=0; i<purchases.length; i++)
                        purchases[i] = 0;
                out.println("<h1>Please Select Your Items!</h1>");
            }
            doForm( out, purchases, request.getRequestURI() );
        }
        showPurchases( out, purchases );
        out.close();
    }


void addPurchases( HttpServletRequest request,
                    int [] purchases ) {
    for (int i=0; i<items.length; i++) {
        String added = (String)request.getParameter( items[i] );
        if ( !added.equals("") )
            purchases[i] += Integer.parseInt( added );
    }
}

void doForm( PrintWriter out, int [] purchases,
            String requestURI) {
    out.println( "<form method=POST action="+ requestURI +">" );

    for(int i=0; i< items.length; i++)
        out.println( "Quantity <input name=\"" + items[i]
            + "\" value=0 size=3> of: " + items[i] + "<br>");
```

```
        out.println(
          "<p><input type=submit name=add value=\"Add To Cart\">"
        + "<input type=submit name=checkout value=\"Check Out\">"
        + "<input type=submit name=clear value=\"Clear Cart\">"
        + "</form>" );
    }

  void showPurchases( PrintWriter out, int [] purchases )
      throws IOException {

    out.println("<hr><h2>Your Shopping Basket</h2>");
    for (int i=0; i<items.length; i++)
      if ( purchases[i] != 0 )
        out.println( purchases[i] +"  "+ items[i] +"<br>" );
  }
}
```

First we should point out that ShoppingCart has some instance data: a String array that holds a list of products. We're making the assumption that the product selection is the same for all customers. If it's not, we'd have to generate the product list on the fly or put it in the session for the user.

Next, we see the same basic pattern as in our previous servlets, with doPost() delegating to doGet() and doGet() generating the body of the output and a form for gathering new data. Here we've broken down the work using a few helper methods: doForm(), addPurchases() and showPurchases(). Our shopping cart form has three submit buttons: one for adding items to the cart, one for check-out, and one for clearing the cart. In each case we show the user what his or her purchases are. Depending on the button chosen in the form, we either add new purchases, clear the list, or simply show the results as a check out window.

The form is generated by our doForm() method, using the list of items for sale. As in the other examples, we supply our servlet's address as the target of the form. Next, we have placed an integer array called purchases into the user session. Each element in purchases holds a count of the number of each item the user wants to buy. We create the array after retrieving the session simply by asking the session for it. If this is a new session and the array hasn't been created, getValue() gives us a null array that we can then populate. Since we generate our form using the names from the items array, it's easy for addPurchases() to check for each name using getParameter(), and increment the purchases array for the number of items requested.* Finally, showPurchases() simply loops over the purchases array and prints the name and quantity for each item that the user has purchased.

---

* We also test for the value being equal to the null string, because some web browsers send empty strings for all field values.

Cookies

In our previous examples, a session lived only until you shut down your web browser or the server. You can do more long-lived kinds of user tracking or identification by managing cookies explicitly. You can send a cookie to the client by creating a `javax.servlet.http.Cookie` object and adding it to the servlet response using the `addCookie()` method. Later you can retrieve the cookie information from the servlet request and use it to look up persistent information in a database. The following servlet sends a "Learning Java" cookie to your web browser and displays it when you return to the page:

```java
//file: CookieCutter.java
import java.io.*;
import java.text.*;
import java.util.*;
import javax.servlet.*;
import javax.servlet.http.*;

public class CookieCutter extends HttpServlet {

    public void doGet(HttpServletRequest request,
                        HttpServletResponse response)
      throws IOException, ServletException {
        response.setContentType("text/html");
        PrintWriter out = response.getWriter();

        if ( request.getParameter("setcookie") != null ) {
            Cookie cookie = new Cookie("Learningjava", "Cookies!");
            cookie.setMaxAge(3600);
            response.addCookie(cookie);
            out.println("<html><body><h1>Cookie Set...</h1>");
        } else {
            out.println("<html><body>");
            Cookie[] cookies = request.getCookies();
            if ( cookies.length == 0 )
                out.println("<h1>No cookies found...</h1>");
            else
                for (int i = 0; i < cookies.length; i++)
                    out.print("<h1>Name: "+ cookies[i].getName()
                            + "<br>"
                            + "Value: " + cookies[i].getValue()
                            + "</h1>" );
            out.println("<p><a href=\""+ request.getRequestURI()
                +"?setcookie=true\">"
                +"Reset the Learning Java cookie.</a>");
        }
        out.println("</body></html>");
```

```
        out.close();
    }
}
```

This example simply enumerates the cookies supplied by the request object using the getCookies() method, and prints their names and values. We provide a GET-style link that points back to our servlet with a parameter setcookie, indicating that we should set the cookie. In that case, we create a Cookie object using the specified name and value and add it to the response with the addCookie() method. We set the maximum age of the cookie to 3600 seconds, so it will remain in a web browser for one hour before being discarded. You can specify an arbitrary time period here, or a negative time period to indicate that the cookie should not be stored persistently on the client.

Two other methods of Cookie are of interest: setDomain() and setPath(). These allow you to specify the domain name and path component that limits the servers to which the client will send the cookie. (If you're writing some kind of purchase applet for L.L. Bean, you don't want clients sending your cookies over to Eddie Bauer.) The default domain is the domain of the server sending the cookie. (You may not be able to specify other domains for security reasons.) The path parameter defaults to the base URL of the servlet, but you can specify a wider (or narrower) range of URLs on the server by setting this parameter manually.

13

In this chapter:
- *Components*
- *Containers*
- *Events*
- *Event Summary*
- *Multithreading in Swing*

Swing

Swing is Java's user interface toolkit. It was developed during the life of SDK 1.1 and now is part of the core APIs in Java 2 (née JDK 1.2). Swing provides classes representing interface items like windows, buttons, combo boxes, trees, grids, and menus—everything you need to build a user interface for your Java application. The `javax.swing` package (and its numerous subpackages) contain the Swing user interface classes.*

Swing is part of a larger collection of software called the Java Foundation Classes (JFC). JFC includes the following APIs:

- The Abstract Window Toolkit (AWT), the original user interface toolkit

- Swing, the new user interface toolkit

- Accessibility, which provides tools for integrating nonstandard input and output devices into your user interfaces

- The 2D API, a comprehensive set of classes for high-quality drawing

- Drag and Drop, an API that supports the drag-and-drop metaphor

JFC is the largest and most complicated part of the standard Java platform, so it shouldn't be any surprise that we'll take several chapters to discuss it. In fact, we won't even get to talk about all of it, just the most important parts—Swing and the 2D API. Here's the lay of the land:

- This chapter covers the basic concepts you need to understand how to build user interfaces with Swing.

---

* Don't be fooled by the `javax` prefix, which usually denotes a standard extension API. Swing is part of the core APIs in Java 2; every Java 2 implementation includes Swing.

- Chapter 14, *Using Swing Components*, discusses the basic components from which user interfaces are built: lists, text fields, checkboxes, and so on.

- Chapter 15, *More Swing Components*, dives further into the Swing toolkit, describing text components, trees, tables, and other neat stuff.

- Chapter 16, *Layout Managers* discusses layout managers, which are responsible for arranging components within a window.

- Chapter 17, *Drawing with the 2D API* discusses the fundamentals of drawing, including simple image displays.

- Chapter 18, *Working with Images and Other Media*, covers the image generation and processing tools that are in the `java.awt.image` package. We'll throw in audio and video for good measure.

We can't cover the full functionality of Swing in this book; if you want the whole story, see *Java Swing*, by Robert Eckstein, Marc Loy, and Dave Wood (O'Reilly & Associates). Instead, we'll cover the basic tools you are most likely to use and show some examples of what can be done with some of the more advanced features. Figure 13-1 shows the user interface component classes of the `javax.swing` package.

To understand Swing, it helps to understand its predecessor, the Abstract Window Toolkit (AWT). As its name suggests, AWT is an abstraction. Its classes and functionality are the same for all Java implementations, so Java applications built with AWT should work in the same way on all platforms. You could choose to write your code under Windows, and then run it on an X Window System or a Macintosh. To achieve platform independence, AWT uses interchangeable *toolkits* that interact with the host windowing system to display user interface components. This shields your application from the details of the environment it's running in. Let's say you ask AWT to create a button. When your application or applet runs, a toolkit appropriate to the host environment renders the button appropriately: on Windows, you can get a button that looks like other Windows buttons; on a Macintosh, you can get a Mac button; and so on.

AWT had some serious shortcomings. The worst was that the use of platform-specific toolkits meant that AWT applications might be subtly incompatible on different platforms. Furthermore, AWT was lacking advanced user interface components, like trees and grids.

Swing takes a fundamentally different approach. Instead of using native toolkits to supply interface items like buttons and combo boxes, components in Swing are implemented in Java itself. This means that, whatever platform you're using, a Swing button (for example) looks the same. It also makes Swing much less prone to platform-specific bugs, which were a problem for AWT.

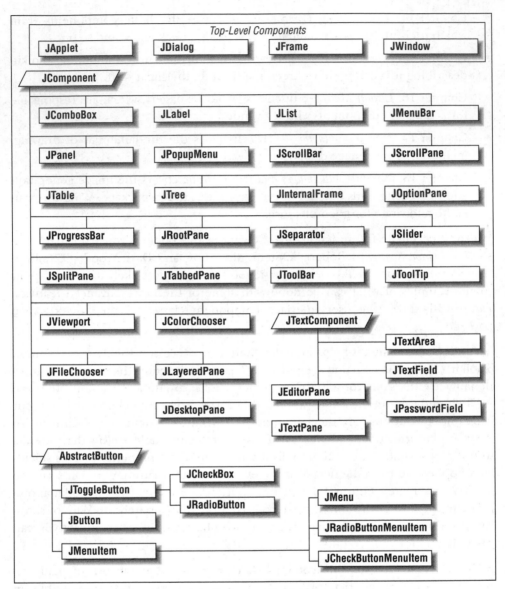

Figure 13-1. User interface components in the javax.swing package

If you already know AWT, you'll be able to transfer a lot of your knowledge into the Swing world. However, there's a lot more material in Swing than in AWT, so be prepared to learn. If you've never programmed with AWT, this chapter and the next two provide a gentle introduction to building user interfaces with Swing.

Working with user interface components in Swing is meant to be easy. When building a user interface for your application, you'll be working with prefabricated components. It's easy to assemble a collection of user interface components (buttons, text areas, etc.) and arrange them inside containers to build complex layouts. You can also use simple components as building blocks for making entirely new kinds of interface gadgets that are completely portable and reusable.

Swing uses *layout managers* to arrange *components* inside *containers* and control their sizing and positioning. Layout managers define a strategy for arranging components instead of specifying absolute positions. For example, you can define a user interface with a collection of buttons and text areas and be reasonably confident that it will always display correctly, even if the user resizes the application window. It doesn't matter what platform or user interface look-and-feel you're using; the layout manager should still position them sensibly with respect to each other.

The next two chapters contain examples using most of the components in the javax.swing package. But before we dive into those examples, we need to spend a bit of time talking about the concepts Swing uses for creating and handling user interfaces. This material should get you up to speed on GUI concepts and on how they are used in Java.

Components

A *component* is the fundamental user interface object in Java. Everything you see on the display in a Java application is a component. This includes things like windows, drawing canvases, buttons, checkboxes, scrollbars, lists, menus, and text fields. To be used, a component usually must be placed in a *container*. Container objects group components, arrange them for display using a layout manager, and associate them with a particular display device. All Swing components are derived from the abstract javax.swing.JComponent class, as you saw in Figure 13-1. For example, the JButton class is a subclass of AbstractButton, which is itself a subclass of the JComponent class.

JComponent is the root of the Swing component hierarchy, but it descends from the AWT Container class. Intuitively, we can say that Swing is a very large extension to AWT. Container's superclass is Component, the root of all AWT components, and Component's superclass is, finally, Object. Because JComponent inherits from Container, it has the the capabilities of both a component and a container.

AWT and Swing, then, have parallel hierarchies. The root of AWT's hierarchy is Component, while Swing's components are based on JComponent. You'll find similar classes in both hierarchies, like Button and JButton. But Swing is much more than simply a replacement for AWT—it contains sophisticated components, like trees and grids, as well as a real implementation of the Model View Controller (MVC) paradigm, which we'll discuss later.

For the sake of simplicity, we can split the functionality of the JComponent class into two categories: appearance and behavior. The JComponent class contains methods and variables that control an object's general appearance. This includes basic attributes such as its visibility, its current size and location, and certain common graphical defaults, like font and color. The JComponent class also contains methods implemented by specific subclasses to produce the graphical displays.

When a component is first displayed, it's associated with a particular display device. The JComponent class encapsulates access to its display area on that device. This includes methods for accessing graphics and for working with off-screen drawing buffers for the display.

By a "component's behavior," we mean the way it responds to user-driven events. When the user performs an action (like pressing the mouse button) within a component's display area, a Swing thread delivers an event object that describes "what happened." The event is delivered to objects that have registered themselves as "listeners" for that type of event from that component. For example, when the user clicks on a button, the button delivers an ActionEvent object. To receive those events, an object registers with the button as an ActionListener.

Events are delivered by invoking designated event-handler methods within the receiving object (the "listener"). A listener object prepares itself to receive events by implementing methods (e.g., actionPerformed()) for the types of events in which it interested. Specific types of events cover different categories of component user interaction. For example, MouseEvents describe activities of the mouse within a component's area, KeyEvents describe key presses, and higher-level events (such as ActionEvents) indicate that a user interface component has done its job.

We will describe events thoroughly in this chapter, because they are so fundamental to the way in which user interfaces function in Java But they aren't limited to building user interfaces; they are an important interobject communications mechanism, which may be used by completely nongraphical parts of an application, as well. They are particularly important in the context of JavaBeans, which uses events as an extremely general notification mechanism.

Swing's event architecture enables containers to take on certain responsibilities for the components that they hold. Instead of every component listening for and handling events for its own bit of the user interface, a container may register itself or another object to receive the events for its child components and "glue" those events to the correct application logic.

One responsibility a container always has is laying out the components it contains. A component informs its container when it does something that might affect other components in the container, such as changing its size or visibility. The container then tells its layout manager that it is time to rearrange the child components.

As you've seen, Swing components are also containers. Containers can manage and arrange JComponent objects without knowing what they are and what they are doing. Components can be swapped and replaced with new versions easily and combined into composite user interface objects that can be treated as individual components. This lends itself well to building larger, reusable user interface items.

Peers

Swing components are *peerless* or *lightweight.* To understand these terms, you'll have to understand the peer system that AWT used. The cold truth is that getting data out to a display medium and receiving events from input devices involve crossing the line from Java to the real world. The real world is a nasty place full of architecture dependence, local peculiarities, and strange physical devices like mice, trackballs, and '69 Buicks.

At some level, our components will have to talk to objects that contain native methods to interact with the host operating environment. To keep this interaction as clean and well-defined as possible, AWT used a set of *peer* interfaces. The peer interface made it possible for a pure Java-language graphic component to use a corresponding real component—the peer object—in the native environment. You didn't generally deal directly with peer interfaces or the objects behind them; peer handling was encapsulated within the Component class.

AWT relied heavily on peers. For example, if you created a window and added eight buttons to it, AWT would create nine peers for you—one for the window and one for each of the buttons. As an application programmer, you wouldn't ever have to worry about the peers, but they would always be lurking under the surface, doing the real work of interacting with your operating system's windowing toolkit.

In Swing, by contrast, most components are peerless, or lightweight. This means that Swing components don't have any direct interaction with the underlying windowing system. They draw themselves in their parent container and respond to user events, all without the aid of a peer. All of the components in Swing are written in pure Java, with no native code involved. In Swing, only top-level windows interact with the windowing system. These Swing containers descend from AWT counterparts, and thus still have peers. In Swing, if you create a window and add eight buttons to it, only one peer is created—for the window. Having far fewer interactions with the underlying windowing system than AWT, Swing is more reliable.

Another consquence of using lightweight components is that it is easy to change the appearance of components. Since each component draws itself, instead of relying on a peer, it can decide at runtime how to draw itself. Accordingly, Swing supports different *look-and-feel* schemes, which can be changed at runtime. (A look-and-feel is the collected appearance of components in an application.) Look-and-feels based on Windows and Solaris are available, as well as an entirely original one called Metal, which is the default scheme.

Why the Move from AWT to Swing?

Java's developers initially decided to implement the standard AWT components with a "mostly native" toolkit. As we described earlier, that means that most of the important functionality of these classes is delegated to peer objects, which live in the native operating system. Using native peers allows Java to take on the look-and-feel of the local operating environment. Macintosh users see Mac applications, PC users see Windows' windows, and Unix users can have their Motif motif; warm fuzzy feelings abound. Java's chameleon-like ability to blend into the native environment was considered by many to be an integral part of platform independence. However, there are a few important downsides to this arrangement.

First, using native peer implementations makes it much more difficult (if not impossible) to subclass these components to specialize or modify their behavior. Most of their behavior comes from the native peer, and therefore can't be overridden or extended easily. As it turns out, this is not a terrible problem because of the ease with which we can make our own components in Java. It is also true that a sophisticated new component, like an HTML viewer, would benefit little in deriving from a more primitive text-viewing component like TextArea.

Next, as we mentioned before, porting the native code makes it much more difficult to bring Java to a new platform. For the user, this can only mean one thing—bugs. Basically, there were too many places where AWT was interacting with the underlying windowing system—one peer per component. There were too many places where something might go wrong, or peers might behave in subtly different ways on different platforms.

Finally, we come to a somewhat counterintuitive problem with the use of native peers. In most current implementations of Java, the native peers are quite "heavy" and consume a lot of resources. You might expect that relying on native code would be much more efficient than creating the components in Java. However, it can take a long time to instantiate a large number of GUI elements when each requires the creation of a native peer from the toolkit. And in some cases you may find that once the native peers are created, they don't perform as well as the pure Java equivalents that you can create yourself.

An extreme example would be a spreadsheet that uses an AWT TextField for each cell. Creating hundreds of TextFieldPeer objects would be something between slow and impossible. While simply saying "don't do that" might be a valid answer, this prompts the question: how do you create large applications with complex GUIs? The answer, of course, is Swing. Swing's peerless architecture means that it's possible to build large, complicated user interfaces and have them work efficiently.

The Model/View/Controller Framework

Before continuing our discussion of GUI concepts, we want to make a brief aside and talk about the Model/View/Controller (MVC) framework. MVC is a method of building reusable components that logically separates the structure, presentation, and behavior of a component into separate pieces. MVC is primarily concerned with building user interface components, but the basic ideas can be applied to many design issues; its principles can be seen throughout Java.

The fundamental idea behind MVC is the separation of the data model for an item from its presentation. For example, we can draw different representations (e.g., bar graphs, pie charts) of the data in a spreadsheet. The data is the *model*; the particular representation is the *view*. A single model can have many views that present the data differently. A user interface component's *controller* defines and governs its behavior. Typically, this includes changes to the model, which, in turn, cause the view(s) to change, also. For a checkbox component, the data model could be a single boolean variable, indicating whether it's checked or not. The behavior for handling mouse-press events would alter the model, and the view would examine that data when it draws the on-screen representation.

The way in which Swing objects communicate, by passing events from sources to listeners, is part of this MVC concept of separation. Event listeners are "observers" (controllers) and event sources are "observables" (models). When an observable changes or performs a function, it notifies all of its observers of the activity.

Swing components explicitly support MVC. Each component is actually composed of two pieces. One piece, called the UI-delegate, is responsible for the "view" and "controller" roles. It takes care of drawing the component and responding to user events. The second piece is the data model itself. This separation makes it possible for multiple Swing components to share a single data model. For example, a read-only text box and a drop-down list box could use the same list of strings as a data model.*

---

* In Chapter 9, *Basic Utility Classes*, we described the Observer class and Observable interface of the java.util package. Swing doesn't use these classes directly, but it does use exactly the same design pattern for handling event sources and listeners.

Painting

In an event-driven environment like Swing, components can be asked to draw themselves at any time. In a more procedural programming environment, you might expect a component to be involved in drawing only when first created or when it changes its appearance. In Java, components act in a way that is closely tied to the underlying behavior of the display environment. For example, when you obscure a component with another window and then re-expose it, a Swing thread asks the component to redraw itself.

Swing asks a component to draw itself by calling its paint() method. paint() may be called at any time, but in practice, it's called when the object is first made visible, whenever it changes its appearance, and whenever some tragedy in the display system messes up its area. Because paint() can't make any assumptions about why it was called, it must redraw the component's entire display. The system may limit the drawing if only part of the component needs to be redrawn, but you don't have to worry about this.

A component never calls its paint() method directly. Instead, when a component requires redrawing, it schedules a call to paint() by invoking repaint(). The repaint() method asks Swing to schedule the component for repainting. At some point in the future, a call to paint() occurs. Swing is allowed to manage these requests in whatever way is most efficient. If there are too many requests to handle, or if there are multiple requests for the same component, the thread can reschedule a number of repaint requests into a single call to paint(). This means that you can't predict exactly when paint() will be called in response to a repaint(); all you can expect is that it happens at least once, after you request it.

Calling repaint() is normally an implicit request to be updated as soon as possible. Another form of repaint() allows you to specify a time period within which you would like an update, giving the system more flexibility in scheduling the request. The system will try to repaint the component within the time you specify. An application can use this method to govern its refresh rate. For example, the rate at which you render frames for an animation might vary, depending on other factors (like the complexity of the image). You could impose an effective maximum frame rate by calling repaint() with a time (the inverse of the frame rate) as an argument. If you then happen to make more than one repaint request within that time period, Swing is not obliged to physically repaint for each one. It can simply condense them to carry out a single update within the time you have specified.

Swing components can act as containers, holding other components. Because every Swing component does its own drawing, Swing components are responsible for telling contained components to draw themselves. Fortunately, this is all taken care of for you by a component's default paint() method. If you override this method, however, you have to make sure to call the superclass's implementation like this:

```
public void paint(Graphics g) {
    super.paint(g);
    ...
}
```

There's another, cleaner way around this problem. All Swing components have a method called paintComponent(). While paint() is responsible for drawing the component as well as its contained components, paintComponent()'s sole responsibility is drawing the component itself. If you override paintComponent() instead of paint(), you won't have to worry about drawing contained components.

Both paint() and paintComponent() take a single argument: a Graphics object. The Graphics object represents the component's graphics context. It corresponds to the area of the screen on which the component can draw and provides the methods for performing primitive drawing and image manipulation. (We'll look at the Graphics class in detail in Chapter 17.)

All components paint and update themselves using this mechanism. Because all Swing components are peerless, it's easy to draw on any of them. (With an AWT component, the presence of the native peer component can make such drawing operations difficult.) In practice, it won't make sense very often to draw on the prebuilt components, like buttons and list boxes. When creating your own components, you'll probably just subclass JComponent directly.

Enabling and Disabling Components

Standard Swing components can be turned on and off by calling the setEnabled() method. When a component like a JButton or JTextField is disabled, it becomes "ghosted" or "greyed-out" and doesn't respond to user input.

For example, let's see how to create a component that can be used only once. This requires getting ahead of the story; we won't explain some aspects of this example until later. Earlier, we said that a JButton generates an ActionEvent when it is pressed. This event is delivered to the listeners' actionPerformed() method. The following code disables whatever component generated the event:

```
public boolean void actionPerformed(ActionEvent e ) {
    ...
    ((JComponent)e.getSource()).setEnabled(false);
}
```

This code calls getSource() to find out which component generated the event. We cast the result to JComponent because we don't necessarily know what kind of component we're dealing with; it might not be a button, because other kinds of components can generate action events. Once we know which component generated the event, we disable it.

You can also disable an entire container. Disabling a `JPanel`, for instance, disables all the components it contains. This is one of the things that used to be unpredictable in AWT, because of the peers involved. In Swing, it just works.

Focus, Please

In order to receive keyboard events, a component has to have keyboard *focus*. The component with the focus is simply the currently selected input component. It receives all keyboard event information until the focus changes. A component can ask for focus with the `JComponent`'s `requestFocus()` method. Text components like `JTextField` and `JTextArea` do this automatically whenever you click the mouse in their area. A component can find out when it gains or loses focus through the `FocusListener` interface (see Table 13-1 and Table 13-2 later in this chapter). If you want to create your own text-oriented component, you could implement this behavior yourself. For instance, you might request focus when the mouse is clicked in your component's area. After receiving focus, you could change the cursor or do something else to highlight the component.

Many user interfaces are designed so that the focus automatically jumps to the "next available" component when the user presses the Tab key. This behavior is particularly common in forms; users often expect to be able to tab to the next text entry field. Swing handles automatic focus traversal for you. You can get control over the behavior through the `transferFocus()`, `setNextFocusable-Component()`, and `setFocusTraversable()` methods of `JComponent`. The method `transferFocus()` passes the focus to the next appropriate component. If you want to change the traversal order, you can call `setNextFocusable-Component()` to tell each component which component should be next. The `setFocus-Traversable()` accepts a `boolean` value that determines whether the component should be considered eligible for receiving focus. You can use this method to determine whether your components can be tabbed to.

Other Component Methods

The `JComponent` class is very large; it has to provide the base-level functionality for all of the various kinds of Java GUI objects. It inherits a lot of functionality from its parent `Container` and `Component` classes. We don't have room to document every method of the `JComponent` class here, but we'll flesh out our discussion by covering some more of the important ones:

Container **getParent**()
    Return the container that holds this component.

String **getName**()
void **setName**(String *name*)

> Get or assign the String name of this component. Naming a component is useful for debugging. The name is returned by toString().

void **setVisible**(boolean *visible*)

> Make the component visible or invisible, within its container. If you change the component's visibility, the container's layout manager automatically lays out its visible components.

Color **getForeground**()
void **setForeground**(Color *c*)
Color **getBackground**()
void **setBackground**(Color *c*)

> Get and set the foreground and background colors for this component. The foreground color of any component is the default color used for drawing. For example, it is the color used for text in a text field; it is also the default drawing color for the Graphics object passed to the component's paint() and paintComponent() methods. The background color is used to fill the component's area when it is cleared by the default implementation of update().

Dimension **getSize**()
void **setSize**(int *width,* int *height*)

> Get and set the current size of the component. Note that a layout manager may change the size of a component even after you've set its size yourself. To change the size a component "wants" to be, use setPreferredSize(). There are other methods in JComponent to set its location, but normally this is the job of a layout manager.

Dimension **getPreferredSize**()
void **setPreferredSize**(Dimension *preferredSize*)

> Use these methods to examine or set the preferred size of a component. Layout managers attempt to set components to their preferred sizes. If you change a component's preferred size, remember to call revalidate() on the component to get it laid out again.

Cursor **getCursor**()
void **setCursor**(Cursor *cursor*)

> Get or set the type of cursor (mouse pointer) used when the mouse is over this component's area. For example:

```
JComponent myComponent = ...;
Cursor crossHairs =
    Cursor.getPredefinedCursor( Cursor.CROSSHAIR_CURSOR );
    myComponent.setCursor( crossHairs );
```

Containers

A container is a kind of component that holds and manages other components. JComponent objects can be containers, because the JComponent class descends from the Container class.

Three of the most useful container types are JFrame, JPanel, and JApplet. A JFrame is a top-level window on your display. JFrame is derived from JWindow, which is pretty much the same but lacks a border. A JPanel is a generic container element used to group components inside of JFrames and other JPanels. The JApplet class is a kind of container that provides the foundation for applets that run inside web browsers. Like every other JComponent, a JApplet has the ability to contain other user interface components. You can also use the JComponent class directly, like a JPanel, to hold components inside of another container. With the exception of JFrame and JWindow, all the components and containers in Swing are lightweight.

A container maintains the list of "child" components that it manages, and has methods for dealing with those components. Note that this child relationship refers to a visual hierarchy, not a subclass/superclass hierarchy. By themselves, most components aren't very useful until they are added to a container and displayed. The add() method of the Container class adds a component to the container. Thereafter, this component can be displayed in the container's display area and positioned by its layout manager. You can remove a component from a container with the remove() method.

Layout Managers

A *layout manager* is an object that controls the placement and sizing of components within the display area of a container. A layout manager is like a window manager in a display system; it controls where the components go and how big they are. Every container has a default layout manager, but you can install a new one by calling the container's setLayout() method.

Swing comes with a few layout managers that implement common layout schemes. The default layout manager for a JPanel is a FlowLayout, which tries to place objects at their preferred size from left to right and top to bottom in the container. The default for a JFrame is a BorderLayout, which places a limited number of objects at named locations within the window, such as NORTH, SOUTH, and CENTER. Another layout manager, GridLayout, arranges components in a rectangular grid. The most general (and difficult to use) layout manager is GridBagLayout, which lets you do the kinds of things you can do with HTML tables. (We'll get into the details of all of these layout managers in Chapter 16.)

When you add a component to a container, you'll often use the version of add() that takes a single Component as an argument. However, if you're using a layout manager that uses "constraints," like BorderLayout or GridBagLayout, you must specify additional information about where to put the new component. For that you can use the version that takes a constraint object. For example, here's how to place a component at the top edge of a container that uses a BorderLayout manager:

```
myContainer.add(myComponent, BorderLayout.NORTH);
```

In this case, the constraint object is the static member variable NORTH. GridBag-Layout uses a much more complex constraint object to specify positioning.

Insets

Insets specify a container's margins; the space specified by the container's insets won't be used by a layout manager. Insets are described by an Insets object, which has four public int fields: top, bottom, left, and right. You normally don't need to worry about the insets; the container will set them automatically, taking into account extras like the menu bar that may appear at the top of a frame. To find out the insets, call the component's getInsets() method, which returns an Insets object.

Z-Ordering (Stacking Components)

With the standard layout managers, components are not allowed to overlap. However, if you use custom-built layout managers or absolute positioning, components within a container may overlap. If they do, the order in which components were added to a container matters. When components overlap they are "stacked" in the order in which they were added: the first component added to the container is on top; the last is on the bottom. To give you more control over stacking, two additional forms of the add() method take an additional integer argument that lets you specify the component's exact position in the container's stacking order.

The revalidate() and doLayout() Methods

A layout manager arranges the components in a container only when asked to. Several things can mess up a container after it's initially laid out:

- Changing its size
- Resizing or moving one of its child components
- Adding, showing, removing, or hiding a child component

Any of these actions cause the container or its components to be marked *invalid*. This means it needs to have its child components readjusted by its layout manager. In most cases, Swing will re-layout container automatically. There are a few cases where you may need to tell Swing to fix things. One example is when you change the preferred size of a component. To fix up the layout, call the `revalidate()` method. `revalidate()` marks a component (or container) invalid and calls `Container`'s `doLayout()` method, which asks the layout manager to do its job. In addition, `revalidate()` also notes that the `Container` has been fixed (i.e., it's valid again) and looks at each child component of the container, recursively validating any containers or components that are also messed up.

So if you have a small `JPanel`—say a keypad holding some buttons—and you change the preferred size of the `JPanel` by calling its `setPreferredSize()` method, you should also call `revalidate()` on the panel or its container. The layout manager of the panel's container may then reposition or resize the keypad. It also automatically calls `revalidate()` for the keypad itself, so that it can rearrange its buttons to fit inside its new area.

All components, not just containers, maintain a notion of when they are valid or invalid. If the size, location, or internal layout of a component changes, its `revalidate()` will automatically be called.

Child containers are validated only if they are invalid. That means that if you have an invalid component nested inside a valid component and you validate a container above both, the invalid component may never be reached. To help avoid this situation, the `invalidate()` method that marks a container as dirty automatically marks parent containers as well, all the way up the container hierarchy.

Managing Components

There are a few additional tools of the `Container` class that we should mention:

Component[] **getComponents**()
:   Returns the container's components in an array.

void **list**(PrintWriter *out*, int *indent*)
:   Generates a list of the components in this container and writes them to the specified `PrintWriter`.

Component **getComponentAt**(int *x*, int *y*)
:   Tells you what component is at the specified coordinates in the container's coordinate system.

Listening for Components

You can use the `ContainerListener` interface to automate the setting up of a container's new components. A container that implements this interface can receive an event whenever it gains or loses a component. This facility makes it easy for a container to micro-manage its components.

Windows and Frames

Windows and frames are the top-level containers for Java components. A JWindow is simply a plain, graphical screen that displays in your windowing system. Windows have no frills; they are mainly suitable for making "splash" screens and dialogs. JFrame, on the other hand, is a subclass of JWindow that has a border and can hold a menu bar. You can drag a frame around on the screen and resize it, using the ordinary controls for your windowing environment. Figure 13-2 shows a JFrame on the left and a JWindow on the right.

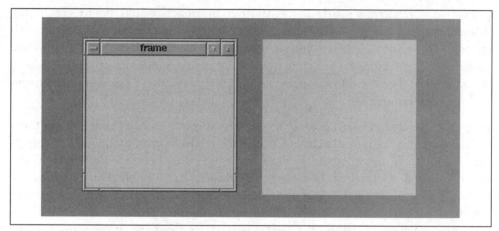

Figure 13-2. A frame and a window

All other Swing components and containers must be held, at some level, inside of a JWindow or JFrame. Applets are a kind of Container. Even applets must be housed in a frame or window, though normally you don't see an applet's parent frame because it is part of (or simply is) the browser or *appletviewer* displaying the applet.

JFrames and JWindows are the only components that can be displayed without being added or attached to another Container. After creating a JFrame or JWindow, you can call the setVisible() method to display it. The following short application creates a JFrame and a JWindow and displays them side by side, just like in Figure 13-2.

```
//file: TopLevelWindows.java
import javax.swing.*;

public class TopLevelWindows {
```

```
   public static void main(String[] args) {
     JFrame f = new JFrame("The Frame");
     f.setSize(300, 300);
     f.setLocation(100, 100);

     JWindow w = new JWindow();
     w.setSize(300, 300);
     w.setLocation(500, 100);

     f.setVisible(true);
     w.setVisible(true);
   }
 }
```

The JFrame constructor can take a String argument that supplies a title, displayed in the JFrame's title bar. (Another approach would be to create the JFrame with no title and call setTitle() to supply the title later.) The JFrame's size and location on your desktop is determined by the calls to setSize() and setLocation(). After creating the JFrame, we create a JWindow in almost exactly the same way. The JWindow doesn't have a title bar, so there are no arguments to the JWindow constructor.

Once the JFrame and JWindow are set up, we call setVisible(true) to get them on the screen. The setVisible() method returns immediately, without blocking. Fortunately, our application does not exit, even though we've reached the end of the main() method, because the windows are still visible. You can close the JFrame by clicking on the close button in the title bar. JFrame's default behavior is to hide itself when you click on the box by calling setVisible(false). You can alter this behavior by calling the setDefaultCloseOperation() method, or by adding an event listener, which we'll cover later.

There's no way to close the JWindow inside our application. You will have to hit Ctrl-C or whatever keystroke kills a process on your machine to stop execution of the TopLevelWindows application.

Other Methods for Controlling Frames

The setLocation() method of the Component class can be used on a JFrame or JWindow to set its position on the screen. The x and y coordinates are relative to the screen's origin (the top left corner).

You can use the toFront() and toBack() methods to place a JFrame or JWindow in front of, or behind, other windows. By default, a user is allowed to resize a JFrame, but you can prevent resizing by calling setResizable(false) before showing the JFrame.

On most systems, frames can be "iconified"; that is, they can be represented by a little icon image. You can get and set a frame's icon image by calling getIconImage() and setIconImage(). As you can with all components, you set the cursor by calling the setCursor() method.

Using Content Panes

Windows and frames don't behave exactly like regular containers. With other containers, you can add child components with the add() method. JFrame and JWindow have some extra stuff in them (mostly to support Swing's peerless components), so you can't just add() components directly. Instead, you need to add the components to the associated *content pane*. The content pane is just a Container that covers the visible area of the JFrame or JWindow. Whenever you create a new JFrame or JWindow, a content pane is automatically created for you. You can retrieve it with getContentPane(). Here's another example that creates a JFrame and adds some components to its content pane:

```
//file: MangoMango1.java
import java.awt.*;
import javax.swing.*;

public class MangoMango1 {
  public static void main(String[] args) {
    JFrame f = new JFrame("The Frame");
    f.setLocation(100, 100);

    Container content = f.getContentPane();
    content.setLayout(new FlowLayout());
    content.add(new JLabel("Mango"));
    content.add(new JButton("Mango"));

    f.pack();
    f.setVisible(true);
  }
}
```

The call to JFrame's pack() method tells the frame window to resize itself so it exactly fits its components. Instead of having to determine the size of the JFrame, we just tell it to be "just big enough." If you do ever want to set the absolute size of the JFrame yourself, call setSize() instead.

If you create your own Container, you can make it the content pane of a JFrame or JWindow by passing it to setContentPane(). Using this strategy, you could rewrite the previous example as follows:

```
//file: MangoMango2.java
import java.awt.*;
```

```java
import javax.swing.*;

public class MangoMango2 {
  public static void main(String[] args) {
    JFrame f = new JFrame("The Frame");
    f.setLocation(100, 100);

    Container content = new JPanel();
    content.add(new JLabel("Mango"));
    content.add(new JButton("Mango"));
    f.setContentPane(content);

    f.pack();
    f.setVisible(true);
  }
}
```

We'll cover labels and buttons in Chapter 14 and layouts in Chapter 16. The important thing to remember is that you can't add components directly to a JFrame or JWindow. Instead, add them to the automatically created content pane, or create an entirely new content pane.

Events

We've spent a lot of time discussing the different kinds of objects in Swing—components, containers, and special containers like frames and windows. Now it's time to discuss interobject communication in detail.

Swing objects communicate by sending events. The way we talk about "firing" events and "handling" them makes it sound as if they are part of some special Java language feature. But they aren't. An event is simply an ordinary Java object that is delivered to its receiver by invoking an ordinary Java method. Everything else, however interesting, is purely convention. The entire Java event mechanism is really just a set of conventions for the kinds of descriptive objects that should be delivered; these conventions prescribe when, how, and to whom events should be delivered.

Events are sent from a single source object to one or more *listeners* (or *receivers*). A listener implements prescribed event-handling methods that enable it to receive a type of event. It then registers itself with a source of that kind of event. Sometimes an *adapter* object may be interposed between the event source and the listener, but in any case, registration of a listener is always established before any events are delivered.

An event object is an instance of a subclass of `java.util.EventObject`; it holds information about something that's happened to its source. The `EventObject` class itself serves mainly to identify event objects; the only information it contains is a reference to the event source (the object that sent the event). Components do not normally send or receive `EventObjects` as such; they work with subclasses that provide more specific information. `AWTEvent` is a subclass of `EventObject` that is used within AWT; further subclasses of `AWTEvent` provide information about specific event types. Swing has events of its own that descend directly from `EventObject`. For the most part, you'll just be working with specific event subclasses, which are used in the same ways in AWT and Swing.

`ActionEvents` correspond to a decisive "action" that a user has taken with the component—like pressing a button or pressing Enter. An `ActionEvent` thus carries the name of an action to be performed (the *action command*) by the program. `MouseEvents` are generated when a user operates the mouse within a component's area. They describe the state of the mouse, and therefore carry information like the x and y coordinates and the state of your mouse buttons at the time the `MouseEvent` was created.

`ActionEvent` operates at a higher semantic level than `MouseEvent`: an `ActionEvent` lets us know that a component has performed its job, while a `MouseEvent` simply confers a lot of information about the mouse at a given time. You could figure out that somebody clicked on a `JButton` by examining mouse events, but it is simpler to work with action events. The precise meaning of an event, however, can depend on the context in which it is received.

Event Receivers and Listener Interfaces

An event is delivered by passing it as an argument to the receiving object's event-handler method. `ActionEvents`, for example, are always delivered to a method called `actionPerformed()` in the receiver:

```
public void actionPerformed( ActionEvent e ) {
    ...
}
```

For each type of event, there is a corresponding listener interface that prescribes the method(s) it must provide to receive those events. In this case, any object that receives `ActionEvents` must implement the `ActionListener` interface:

```
public interface ActionListener extends java.util.EventListener {
    public void actionPerformed( ActionEvent e );
}
```

All listener interfaces are subinterfaces of `java.util.EventListener`, which is an empty interface. It exists only to help the compiler identify listener interfaces.

Listener interfaces are required for a number of reasons. First, they help to identify objects that are capable of receiving a given type of event. This way we can give the event-handler methods friendly, descriptive names and still make it easy for documentation, tools, and humans to recognize them in a class. Next, listener interfaces are useful because several methods can be specified for an event receiver. For example, the FocusListener interface contains two methods:

```
abstract void focusGained( FocusEvent e );
abstract void focusLost( FocusEvent e );
```

Athough these methods both take a FocusEvent as an argument, they correspond to different reasons for firing the event; in this case, whether the FocusEvent means that focus was received or lost. You could figure out what happened by inspecting the event; all AWTEvents contain a constant specifying the event's subtype. By requiring two methods, the FocusListener interface saves you the effort: if focusGained() is called, you know the event type was FOCUS_GAINED.

Similarly, the MouseListener interface defines five methods for receiving mouse events (and MouseMotionListener defines two more), each of which gives you some additional information about why the event occurred. In general, the listener interfaces group sets of related event-handler methods; the method called in any given situation provides a context for the information in the event object.

There can be more than one listener interface for dealing with a particular kind of event. For example, the MouseListener interface describes methods for receiving MouseEvents when the mouse enters or exits an area or a mouse button is pressed or released. MouseMotionListener is an entirely separate interface that describes methods to get mouse events when the mouse is moved (no buttons pressed) or dragged (buttons pressed). By separating mouse events into these two categories, Java lets you be a little more selective about the circumstances under which you want to receive MouseEvents. You can register as a listener for mouse events without receiving mouse motion events; since mouse motion events are extremely common, you don't want to handle them if you don't need to.

Two simple patterns govern the naming of Swing event listener interfaces and handler methods:

- Event-handler methods are public methods that return type void and take a single event object (a subclass of java.util.EventObject) as an argument.*

- Listener interfaces are subclasses of java.util.EventListener that are named with the suffix "Listener"—for example, MouseListener and Action-Listener.

---

* This rule is not complete. JavaBeans allows event-handler methods to take additional arguments when absolutely necessary and also to throw checked exceptions.

These may seem pretty obvious, but they are important because they are our first hint of a *design pattern* governing how to build components that work with events.

Event Sources

The previous section described the machinery that an event receiver uses to listen for events. In this section, we'll describe how a receiver tells an event source to send it events, as they occur.

To receive events, an eligible listener must register itself with an event source. It does this by calling an "add listener" method in the event source and passing a reference to itself. (Thus, this scheme implements a *callback* facility.) For example, the Swing JButton class is a source of ActionEvents. Here's how a TheReceiver object might register to receive these events:

```
// source of ActionEvents
JButton theButton = new JButton("Belly");

// receiver of ActionEvents
class TheReceiver implements ActionListener {

    setupReceiver() {
        ...
        theButton.addActionListener( this );
    }

    public void actionPerformed( ActionEvent e ) {
        // Belly Button pushed...
    }
```

The receiver makes a call to addActionListener() to become eligible to receive ActionEvents from the button when they occur. It passes the reference this to register itself as an ActionListener.

To manage its listeners, an ActionEvent source (like the JButton) always implements two methods:

```
// ActionEvent source
public void addActionListener(ActionListener listener) {
    ...
}
public void removeActionListener(ActionListener listener) {
    ...
}
```

The removeActionListener() method removes the listener from the list so that it will not receive future events of that kind. Swing components supply implementations of both methods; normally, you won't need to implement them yourself.

Now, you may be expecting an EventSource interface listing these two methods, but there isn't one. There are no event source interfaces in the current conventions. If you are analyzing a class and trying to determine what events it generates, you have to look for the add and remove methods. For example, the presence of the addActionListener() and removeActionListener() methods define the object as a source of ActionEvents. If you happen to be a human being, you can simply look at the documentation; but if the documentation isn't available, or if you're writing a program that needs to analyze a class (a process called "reflection"), you can look for this *design pattern*:

> A source of FooEvent events for the FooListener interface must implement a pair of add/remove methods:
>
> **addFooListener**(FooListener *listener*)
> **removeFooListener**(FooListener *listener*)

If an event source can support only one event listener (unicast delivery), the add listener method can throw the checked exception java.util.TooMany-ListenersException.

So what do all the naming patterns up to this point accomplish? Well, for one thing, they make it possible for automated tools and integrated development environments to divine what are sources of particular events. Tools that work with Java Beans will use the Java reflection and introspection APIs to search for these kinds of design patterns and identify the events that can be fired by a component.

It also means that event hookups are strongly typed, just like the rest of Java. So it's not easy to accidentally hook up the wrong kind of components; for example, you can't register to receive ItemEvents from a JButton, because a button doesn't have an addItemListener() method. Java knows at compile time what types of events can be delivered to whom.

Event Delivery

Swing and AWT events are multicast; every event is associated with a single source but can be delivered to any number of receivers. When an event is fired, it is delivered individually to each listener on the list (Figure 13-3).

There are no guarantees about the order in which events will be delivered. Neither are there any guarantees about what happens if you register yourself more than once with an event source; you may or may not get the event more than once. Similarly, you should assume that every listener receives the same event data. Events are immutable; they can't be changed by their listeners.

To be complete, we could say that event delivery is synchronous with respect to the event source, but that follows from the fact that the event delivery is really just the

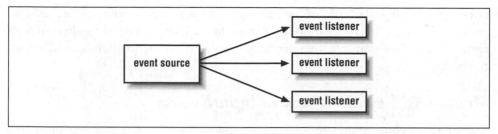

Figure 13-3. Event delivery

invocation of a normal Java method. The source of the event calls the handler method of each listener. However, listeners shouldn't assume that all of the events will be sent in the same thread. An event source could decide to send out events to all of the listeners in parallel, each in its own thread.

Event Types

All of the events used by Swing GUI components are subclasses of `java.util.EventObject`. You can use or subclass any of the `EventObject` types for use in your own components. We'll describe the important event types here.

The events and listeners that are used by Swing fall into two packages: `java.awt.event` and `javax.swing.event`. As we've discussed, the structure of components has changed significantly between AWT and Swing. The event mechanism, however, is fundamentally the same, so the events and listeners in `java.awt.event` are still used by the new Swing components. In addition, Swing has added its own event types and listeners in the `javax.swing.event` package.

`java.awt.event.ComponentEvent` is the base class for events that can be fired by any component. This includes events that provide notification when a component changes its dimensions or visibility, as well as the other event types for mouse operation and key presses. `ContainerEvent`s are fired by containers when components are added or removed.

The java.awt.event.InputEvent Class

`MouseEvent`s, which track the state of the mouse, and `KeyEvent`s, which are fired when the user uses the keyboard, are kinds of `java.awt.event.InputEvent`. When the user presses a key or moves the mouse within a component's area, the events are generated with that component as the source.

Input events and some other GUI events are placed on a special event queue that is managed by Swing. This gives Swing control over how the events are delivered. First, under some circumstances, a sequence of the same type of event may be compressed into a single event. This is done to make some event types more efficient—in particular, mouse events and some special internal events used to control repainting. Perhaps more important to us, input events are delivered with extra information that lets listeners decide if the component itself should act on the event.

Mouse and Key Modifiers on InputEvents

InputEvents come with a set of flags for special modifiers. These let you detect whether the Shift or Alt key was held down during a mouse button or key press, and detect which mouse button was pressed. The following are the flag values contained in java.awt.event.InputEvent:

SHIFT_MASK
CTRL_MASK
META_MASK
ALT_MASK
BUTTON1_MASK
BUTTON2_MASK
BUTTON3_MASK

To check for one or more flags, evaluate the boolean AND of the complete set of modifiers and the flag or flags you're interested in. The complete set of modifiers involved in the event is returned by the InputEvent's getModifiers() method:

```
public void mousePressed (MouseEvent e) {
    int mods = e.getModifiers();
    if ((mods & InputEvent.SHIFT_MASK) != 0) {
        // shifted Mouse Button press
    }
}
```

The three BUTTON flags can be used to detect which mouse button was pressed on a two- or three-button mouse. If you use these, you run the risk that your program won't work on platforms without multibutton mice. Currently, BUTTON2_MASK is equivalent to ALT_MASK, and BUTTON3_MASK is equivalent to META_MASK. This means that pushing the second mouse button is equivalent to pressing the first (or only) button with the Alt key depressed, and the third button is equivalent to the first with the Meta key depressed. However, if you really want to guarantee portability, you should limit yourself to a single button, possibly in combination with keyboard modifiers, rather than relying on the button masks.

Event Summary

Table 13-1 and Table 13-2 summarize the commonly used Swing events, which Swing components fire them, and the methods of the listener interfaces that receive them. The events and listeners are divided between the java.awt.event and javax.swing.event packages.

In Swing, a component's model and view are distinct. Strictly speaking, components don't fire events; models do. When you press a JButton, for example, it's actually the button's data model that fires an ActionEvent, not the button itself. But JButton has a convenience method for registering ActionListeners; this methods passes its argument through to register the listener with the button model. In many cases (as with JButtons), you don't have to deal with the data model separately from the view, so we can speak loosely of the component itself firing the events.

Table 13-1. Swing Component and Container Events

Event	Fired by	Listener Interface	Handler Method
java.awt.event. ComponentEvent	All components	Component- Listener	component- Resized()
			componentMoved()
			componentShown()
			componentHidden()
java.awt.event. FocusEvent	All components	FocusListener	focusGained()
			focusLost()
java.awt.event. KeyEvent	All components	KeyListener	keyTyped()
			keyPressed()
			keyReleased()
java.awt.event. MouseEvent	All components	MouseListener	mouseClicked()
			mousePressed()
			mouseReleased()
			mouseEntered()
			mouseExited()
		MouseMotion- Listener	mouseDragged()
			mouseMoved()
java.awt.event. ContainerEvent	All containers	Container- Listener	componentAdded()
			component- Removed()

Table 13-2. Component-Specific Swing Events

Event	Fired by	Listener Interface	Handler Method
java.awt.event. ActionEvent	JButton	ActionListener	action-Performed()
	JCheckBoxMenu-Item		
	JComboBox		
	JFileChooser		
	JList		
	JRadioButton-MenuItem		
	JTextField		
	JToggleButton		
java.awt.event. AdjustmentEvent	JScrollBar	Adjustment-Listener	adjustmentValue-Changed()
javax.swing. event.Caret-Event	JTextComponent	CaretListener	caretUpdate()
javax.swing. event.Hyper-linkEvent	JEditorPane, JTextPane	Hyperlink-Listener	hyperlink-Update()
java.awt.event. InternalFrame-Event	JInternalFrame	InternalFrame-Listener	internalFrame-Activated()
			internalFrame-Closed()
			internalFrame-Closing()
			internalFrame-Deactivated()
			internalFrame-Deiconified()
			internalFrame-Iconified()
			internalFrame-Opened()
java.awt.event. ItemEvent	JCheckBoxMenu-Item	ItemListener	itemState-Changed()
	JComboBox		
	JRadioButton-MenuItem		
	JToggleButton		

Table 13-2. Component-Specific Swing Events (continued)

Event	Fired by	Listener Interface	Handler Method
`javax.swing.event.ListData-Event`	`ListModel`	`ListData-Listener`	`contents-Changed()`
			`intervalAdded()`
			`interval-Removed()`
`javax.swing.event.List-SelectionEvent`	`JList` `ListSelection-Model`	`ListSelection-Listener`	`valueChanged()`
`javax.swing.event.MenuEvent`	`JMenu`	`MenuListener`	`menuCanceled()`
			`menu-Deselected()`
			`menuSelected()`
`javax.swing.event.Popup-MenuEvent`	`JPopupMenu`	`PopupMenu-Listener`	`popupMenu-Canceled()`
			`popupMenuWill-BecomeInvisible()`
			`popupMenuWill-BecomeVisible()`
`javax.swing.event.MenuKey-Event`	`JMenuItem`	`MenuKeyListener`	`menuKeyPressed()`
			`menuKeyReleased()`
			`menuKeyTyped()`
`javax.swing.event.MenuDrag-MouseEvent`	`JMenuItem`	`MenuDragMouse-Listener`	`menuDragMouse-Dragged()`
			`menuDragMouse-Entered()`
			`menuDragMouse-Exited()`
			`menuDragMouse-Released()`
`javax.swing.event.Table-ColumnModel-Event`	`TableColumn-Model`[a]	`TableColumn-ModelListener`	`columnAdded()`
			`columnMargin-Changed()`

Table 13-2. Component-Specific Swing Events (continued)

Event	Fired by	Listener Interface	Handler Method
			`columnMoved()`
			`columnRemoved()`
			`columnSelection-Changed()`
`javax.swing.event.Table-ModelEvent`	`TableModel`	`TableModel-Listener`	`tableChanged()`
`javax.swing.event.Tree-ExpansionEvent`	`JTree`	`TreeExpansion-Listener`	`treeCollapsed()`
			`treeExpanded()`
`javax.swing.event.Tree-ModelEvent`	`TreeModel`	`TreeModel-Listener`	`treeNodes-Changed()`
			`treeNodes-Inserted()`
			`treeNodes-Removed()`
			`treeStructure-Changed()`
`javax.swing.event.Tree-SelectionEvent`	`JTree`	`TreeSelection-Listener`	`valueChanged()`
	`TreeSelection-Model`		
`javax.swing.event.Undoable-EditEvent`	`javax.swing.text.Document`	`UndoableEdit-Listener`	`undoableEdit-Happened()`
`java.awt.event.WindowEvent`	`JDialog`	`WindowListener`	`windowOpened()`
	`JFrame`		`windowClosing()`
	`JWindow`		`windowClosed()`
			`window-Iconified()`
			`window-Deiconified()`
			`window-Activated()`
			`window-Deactivated()`

^a The `TableColumnModel` class breaks with convention in the names of the methods that add listeners. They are `addColumnModelListener()` and `removeColumnModelListener()`.

Adapter Classes

It's not usually ideal to have your application components implement a listener interface and receive events directly. Sometimes it's not even possible. Being an event receiver forces you to modify or subclass your objects to implement the appropriate event listener interfaces and add the code necessary to handle the events. Since we are talking about Swing events here, a more subtle issue is that you are, of necessity, building GUI logic into parts of your application that shouldn't have to know anything about the GUI. Let's look at an example.

In Figure 13-4, we have drawn the plans for our Vegomatic food processor. Here, we have made our `Vegomatic` object implement the `ActionListener` interface, so that it can receive events directly from the three `JButton` components: `Chop`, `Puree`, and `Frappe`. The problem is that our `Vegomatic` object now has to know more than how to mangle food. It also has to be aware that it will be driven by three controls—specifically, buttons that send action commands—and be aware of which methods in itself it should invoke for those commands. Our boxes labeling the GUI and application code overlap in an unwholesome way. If the marketing people should later want to add or remove buttons or perhaps just change the names, we have to be careful. We may have to modify the logic in our `Vegomatic` object. All is not well.

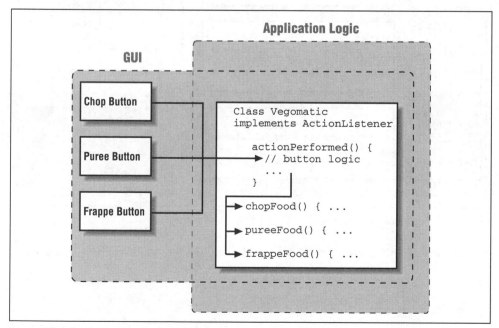

Figure 13-4. Implementing the ActionListener interface directly

An alternative is to place an adapter class between our event source and receiver. An *adapter* is a simple object whose sole purpose is to map an incoming event to an outgoing method.

Figure 13-5 shows a better design that uses three adapter classes, one for each button. The implementation of the first adapter might look like:

```
class VegomaticAdapter1 implements ActionListener {
    Vegomatic vegomatic;
    VegomaticAdapter1 ( Vegotmatic vegomatic ) {
        this.vegomatic = vegomatic;
    }
    public void actionPerformed( ActionEvent e ) {
        vegomatic.chopFood();
    }
}
```

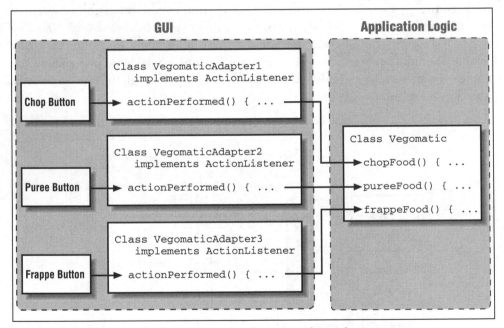

Figure 13-5. Implementing the ActionListener interface using adapter classes

So somewhere in the code where we build our GUI, we could register our listener like this:

```
Vegomatic theVegomatic = ...;
Button chopButton = ...;

// make the hookup
chopButton.addActionListener( new VegomaticAdapter1(theVegomatic) );
```

Instead of registering itself (`this`) as the Button's listener, the adapter registers the `Vegomatic` object (`theVegomatic`). In this way, the adapter acts as an intermediary, hooking up an event source (the button) with an event receiver (the virtual chopper).

We have completely separated the messiness of our GUI from the application code. However, we have added three new classes to our application, none of which does very much. Is that good? That depends on your vantage point.

Under different circumstances, our buttons may have been able to share a common adapter class that was simply instantiated with different parameters. Various trade-offs can be made between size, efficiency, and elegance of code. Adapter classes will often be generated automatically by development tools. The way we have named our adapter classes `VegomaticAdapter1`, `VegomaticAdapter2`, and `VegomaticAdapter3` hints at this. More often, when hand-coding, you'll use an inner class. At the other extreme, we can forsake Java's strong typing and use the reflection API to create a completely dynamic hookup between an event source It'sand its listener.

Dummy Adapters

Many listener interfaces contain more than one event-handler method. Unfortunately, this means that to register yourself as interested in any one of those events, you must implement the whole listener interface. And to accomplish this you might find yourself typing in dummy "stubbed-out" methods, simply to complete the interface. There is really nothing wrong with this, but it is a bit tedious. To save you some trouble, AWT and Swing provide some helper classes that implement these dummy methods for you. For each of the most common listener interfaces containing more than one method, there is an adapter class containing the stubbed methods. You can use the adapter class as a base class for your own adapters. So when you need a class to patch together your event source and listener, you can simply subclass the adapter and override only the methods you want.

For example, the `MouseAdapter` class implements the `MouseListener` interface and provides the following implementation:

```
public void mouseClicked(MouseEvent e) {};
public void mousePressed(MouseEvent e) {};
public void mouseReleased(MouseEvent e) {};
public void mouseEntered(MouseEvent e) {};
public void mouseExited(MouseEvent e) {};
```

This isn't a tremendous time saver; it's simply a bit of sugar. The primary advantage comes into play when we use the `MouseAdapter` as the base for our own adapter in an anonymous inner class. For example, suppose we want to catch a

`mousePressed()` event in some component and blow up a building. We can use
the following to make the hookup:

```
someComponent.addMouseListener( new MouseAdapter() {
    public void MousePressed(MouseEvent e) {
        building.blowUp();
    }
} );
```

We've taken artistic liberties with the formatting, but it's very readable. Moreover,
we've avoided creating stub methods for the four unused event-handler methods.
Writing adapters is common enough that it's nice to avoid typing those extra few
lines and perhaps stave off the onset of carpal tunnel syndrome for a few more
hours. Remember that any time you use an inner class, the compiler is generating
a class for you, so the messiness you've saved in your source still exists in the output classes.

Old-Style and New-Style Event Processing

Although Java is still a youngster, it has a bit of a legacy. Versions of Java before 1.1
used a different style of event delivery. Back in the old days (a couple of years
ago), event types were limited, and an event was delivered only to the `Component`
that generated it or one of its parent containers. The old style component event-
handler methods (now deprecated) returned a `boolean` value declaring whether
or not they had handled the event:

```
boolean handleEvent( Event e ) {
    ...
}
```

If the method returns `false`, the event is automatically redelivered to the component's container to give it a chance. If the container does not handle it, it is passed
on to its parent container, and so on. In this way, events were propagated up the
containment hierarchy until they were either consumed or passed over to the component peer, just as current `InputEvents` are ultimately interpreted using the
peer if no registered event listeners have consumed them.

Note that this older style of event processing applies only to AWT components.
The newer Swing components handle only events with the new model.

Although this style of event delivery was convenient for some simple applications,
it is not very flexible. Events could be handled only by components, which meant
that you always had to subclass a `Component` or `Container` type to handle events.
This was a degenerate use of inheritance (i.e., bad design) that led to the creation
of lots of unnecessary classes.

We could, alternatively, receive the events for many embedded components in a single parent container, but that would often lead to very convoluted logic in the container's event-handling methods. It is also very costly to run every single AWT event through a gauntlet of (often empty) tests as it traverses its way up the tree of containers. This is why Swing now provides the more dynamic and general event source/listener model that we have described in this chapter. The old-style events and event-handler methods are, however, still with us.

Java is not allowed to simply change and break an established API. Instead, older ways of doing things are simply deprecated in favor of the new ones. This means that code using the old-style event handler methods will still work; you may see old-style code around for a long time. The problem with relying on old-style event delivery, however, is that the old and new ways of doing things cannot be mixed.

By default, Java is obligated to perform the old behavior—offering events to the component and each of its parent containers. However, Java turns off the old-style delivery whenever it thinks that we have elected to use the new style. Java determines whether a Component should receive old-style or new-style events based on whether any event listeners are registered, or whether new style events have been explicitly enabled. When an event listener is registered with a Component, new-style events are implicitly turned on (a flag is set). Additionally, a mask is set telling the component the types of events it should process. The mask allows components to be more selective about which events they process.

processEvent( )

When new-style events are enabled, all events are first routed to the dispatch-Event() method of the Component class. The dispatchEvent() method examines the component's event mask and decides whether the event should be processed or ignored. Events that have been enabled are sent to the processEvent() method, which looks at the event's type and delegates it to a helper processing method named for its type. The helper processing method finally dispatches the event to the set of registered listeners for its type.

This process closely parallels the way in which old-style events are processed and the way in which events are first directed to a single handleEvent() method that dispatches them to more specific handler methods in the Component class. The differences are that new-style events are not delivered unless someone is listening for them, and the listener registration mechanism means that we don't have to subclass the component in order to override its event-handler methods and insert our own code.

Enabling new-style events explicitly

Still, if you are subclassing a Component or you really want to process all events in a single method, you should be aware that it is possible to emulate the old-style event handling and override your component's event-processing methods. Call the Component's enableEvents() method with the appropriate mask value to turn on processing for the given type of event. You can then override the corresponding method and insert your code. The mask values, listed in Table 13-3, are found in the java.awt.AWTEvent class.

Table 13-3. AWTEvent Masks

java.awt.AWTEvent mask	Method
COMPONENT_EVENT_MASK	ProcessComponentEvent()
FOCUS_EVENT_MASK	processFocusEvent()
KEY_EVENT_MASK	processKeyEvent()
MOUSE_EVENT_MASK	processMouseEvent()
MOUSE_MOTION_EVENT_MASK	ProcessMouseMotionEvent()

For example:

```
public void init() {
    ...
    enableEvent( AWTEvent.KEY_EVENT_MASK ):
}

public void processKeyEvent(KeyEvent e) {
    if ( e.getID() == KeyEvent.KEY_TYPED ) {
        // do work
    }
    super.processKeyEvent(e);
}
```

If you do this, it is very important that you remember to make a call to super. process...Event() in order to allow normal event delegation to continue. Of course, by emulating old-style event handling, we're giving up the virtues of the new style; this code is a lot less flexible than the code we could write with the new event model. As we've seen, the user interface is hopelessly tangled with the actual work your program does. A compromise solution would be to have your subclass declare that it implements the appropriate listener interface and register itself, as we have done in the simpler examples in this book:

```
class MyApplet implements KeyListener ...
    public void init() {
        addKeyListener( this ):
        ...
    }
```

```
public void keyTyped(KeyEvent e) {
    // do work
}
```

Multithreading in Swing

Multithreading programs need to be careful about updating Swing components. The issue arises because Swing has its own event-dispatching thread. If your application is changing components in a different thread, bad things might happen: misshapen components or race conditions.

The fundamental rule is simple: if you need to update a Swing component from your own thread, do it using invokeAndWait() or invokeLater(). These are static methods in the javax.swing.SwingUtilities class.

public static void **invokeLater**(Runnable *doRun*)

Use this method to ask Swing to execute the run() method of the specified Runnable.

public static void **invokeAndWait**(Runnable *doRun*)

throws InterruptedException, InvocationTargetException

This method is just like invokeLater(), except that it waits until the run() method has completed before returning.

A simple example is a download progress indicator. If your application downloads a lot of data from the network, it should show a progress meter that indicates how much data has been downloaded and how much remains. You shouldn't update this meter directly from the download thread; instead, you should package updates in a Runnable and use invokeLater() or invokeAndWait().

14

Using Swing Components

In the previous chapter, we discussed a number of concepts, including how Java's user interface facility is put together and how the larger pieces work. You should understand what components and containers are, how you use them to create a display, what events are, how components use them to communicate with the rest of your application, and what layout managers are.

Now that we're through with the general concepts and background, we'll get to the fun stuff: how to do things with Swing. We will cover most of the components that the Swing package supplies, how to use these components in applets and applications, and how to build your own components. We will have lots of code and lots of pretty examples to look at.

There's more material than fits in a single chapter. In this chapter, we'll cover all the basic user interface components. In the next chapter, we'll cover some of the more involved topics: text components, trees, tables, and creating your own components.

Buttons and Labels

We'll start with the simplest components: buttons and labels. Frankly, there isn't much to say about them. If you've seen one button, you've seen them all; and you've already seen buttons in the applications in Chapter 2, *A First Application* (`HelloJava3` and `HelloJava4`). A button generates an `ActionEvent` when the user presses it. To receive these events, your program registers an `Action-Listener`, which must implement the `actionPerformed()` method. The argument passed to `actionPerformed()` is the event itself.

There's one more thing worth saying about buttons, which applies to any component that generates an action event. Java lets us specify an "action command" string for buttons (and other components, like menu items, that can generate action events). The action command is less interesting than it sounds. It is just a `String` that serves to identify the component that sent the event. By default, the action command of a `JButton` is the same as its label; it is included in action events, so you can use it to figure out which button an event came from.

To get the action command from an action event, call the event's `getAction-Command()` method. The following code checks whether the user pressed the **Yes** button:

```
public void actionPerformed(ActionEvent e){
    if (e.getActionCommand().equals("Yes") {
        //the user pressed "Yes"; do something
        ...
    }
}
```

You can change the action command by calling the button's `setActionCommand()` method. The following code changes button `myButton`'s action command to "confirm":

```
myButton.setActionCommand("confirm");
```

It's a good idea to get used to setting action commands explicitly; this helps to prevent your code from breaking when you or some other developer "internationalizes" it, or otherwise changes the button's label. If you rely on the button's label, your code will stop working as soon as that label changes; a French user might see the label `Oui` rather than `Yes`. By setting the action command, you eliminate one source of bugs; for example, the button `myButton` in the previous example will always generate the action command `confirm`, regardless of what its label says.

Swing buttons can have an image in addition to a label. The `JButton` class includes constructors that accept an `Icon` object, which knows how to draw itself. You can create buttons with captions, images, or both. A handy class called `ImageIcon` takes care of loading an image for you and can be used to easily add an image to a button. The following example shows how this works:

```
//file: PictureButton.java
import java.awt.*;
import java.awt.event.*;
import javax.swing.*;

public class PictureButton extends JFrame {

  public PictureButton() {
    super("PictureButton v1.0");
```

```
    setSize(200, 200);
    setLocation(200, 200);

    Icon icon = new ImageIcon("rhino.gif");
    JButton button = new JButton(icon);
    button.addActionListener(new ActionListener() {
      public void actionPerformed(ActionEvent ae) {
        System.out.println("Urp!");
      }
    });

    Container content = getContentPane();
    content.setLayout(new FlowLayout());
    content.add(button);
  }

  public static void main(String[] args) {
    JFrame f = new PictureButton();
    f.addWindowListener(new WindowAdapter() {
      public void windowClosing(WindowEvent we) { System.exit(0); }
    });
    f.setVisible(true);
  }
}
```

The example creates an **ImageIcon** from the *rhino.gif* file. Then a **JButton** is created from the **ImageIcon**. The whole thing is displayed in a **JFrame**. This example also shows the idiom of using an anonymous inner class as an
ActionListener.

There's even less to be said about **JLabel** components. They're just text strings or
images housed in a component. There aren't any special events associated with
labels; about all you can do is specify the text's alignment, which controls the position of the text within the label's display area. As with buttons, **JLabels** can be created with **Icons** if you want to create a picture label. The following code creates
some labels with different options:

```
// default alignment (CENTER)
JLabel label1 = new JLabel("Lions");

// left aligned
JLabel label2 = new JLabel("Tigers", SwingConstants.LEFT);

//label with no text, default alignment
JLabel label3 = new JLabel();

// create image icon
Icon icon = new ImageIcon("rhino.gif");
```

```
// create image label
JLabel label4 = new JLabel(icon);

// assigning text to label3
label3.setText("and Bears");

// set alignment
label3.setHorizontalAlignment(SwingConstants.RIGHT);
```

The alignment constants are defined in the `SwingConstants` interface.

Now we've built several labels, using a variety of constructors and several of the class's methods. To display the labels, just add them to a container by calling the container's `add()` method.

The other characteristics you might like to set on labels, such as changing their font or color, are accomplished using the methods of the `Component` class, `JLabel`'s distant ancestor. For example, you can call `setFont()` and `setColor()` on a label, as with any other component.

Given that labels are so simple, why do we need them at all? Why not just draw a text string directly on the container object? Remember that a `JLabel` is a `JComponent`. That's important; it means that labels have the normal complement of methods for setting fonts and colors that we mentioned earlier, as well as the ability to be managed sensibly by a layout manager. Therefore, they're much more flexible than a text string drawn at an absolute location within a container.

Speaking of layouts—if you use the `setText()` method to change the text of your label, the label's preferred size may change. But the label's container will automatically lay out its components when this happens, so you don't have to worry about it.

Swing can interpret HTML-formatted text in `JLabel` and `JButton` labels. The following example shows how to create a button with HTML-formatted text:

```
JButton button = new JButton(
  "<html>"
  + "S<font size=-1>MALL<font size=+0> "
  + "C<font size=-1>APITALS");
```

Checkboxes and Radio Buttons

A checkbox is a labeled toggle switch. Each time the user clicks it, its state toggles between checked and unchecked. Swing implements the checkbox as a special kind of button. Radio buttons are similar to checkboxes, but they are usually arranged in groups. Click on one radio button in the group, and the others automatically turn off. They are named for the preset buttons on old car radios.

Checkboxes and radio buttons are represented by instances of JCheckBox and JRadioButton, respectively. Radio buttons can be tethered together using an instance of another class called ButtonGroup. By now you're probably well into the swing of things (no pun intended) and could easily master these classes on your own. We'll use an example to illustrate a different way of dealing with the state of components and to show off a few more things about containers.

A JCheckBox sends ItemEvents when it's pushed. Since a checkbox is a kind of button, it also fires ActionEvents when it becomes checked. For something like a checkbox, we might want to be lazy and check on the state of the buttons only at some later time, such as when the user commits an action. It's like filling out a form; you can change your choices until you submit the form.

The following application, DriveThrough, lets us check off selections on a fast food menu, as shown in Figure 14-1. DriveThrough prints the results when we press the **Place Order** button. Therefore, we can ignore all the events generated by our checkboxes and radio buttons and listen only for the action events generated by the regular button.

```
//file: DriveThrough.java
import java.awt.*;
import java.awt.event.*;

import javax.swing.*;

public class DriveThrough {
  public static void main(String[] args) {
    JFrame f = new JFrame("Lister v1.0");
    f.setSize(300, 150);
    f.setLocation(200, 200);
    f.addWindowListener(new WindowAdapter() {
      public void windowClosing(WindowEvent we) { System.exit(0); }
    });

    JPanel entreePanel = new JPanel();
    final ButtonGroup entreeGroup = new ButtonGroup();
    JRadioButton radioButton;
    entreePanel.add(radioButton = new JRadioButton("Beef"));
    radioButton.setActionCommand("Beef");
    entreeGroup.add(radioButton);
    entreePanel.add(radioButton = new JRadioButton("Chicken"));
    radioButton.setActionCommand("Chicken");
    entreeGroup.add(radioButton);
    entreePanel.add(radioButton = new JRadioButton("Veggie", true));
    radioButton.setActionCommand("Veggie");
    entreeGroup.add(radioButton);

    final JPanel condimentsPanel = new JPanel();
```

```
        condimentsPanel.add(new JCheckBox("Ketchup"));
        condimentsPanel.add(new JCheckBox("Mustard"));
        condimentsPanel.add(new JCheckBox("Pickles"));

        JPanel orderPanel = new JPanel();
        JButton orderButton = new JButton("Place Order");
        orderPanel.add(orderButton);

        Container content = f.getContentPane();
        content.setLayout(new GridLayout(3, 1));
        content.add(entreePanel);
        content.add(condimentsPanel);
        content.add(orderPanel);

        orderButton.addActionListener(new ActionListener() {
          public void actionPerformed(ActionEvent ae) {
            String entree =
              entreeGroup.getSelection().getActionCommand();
            System.out.println(entree + " sandwich");
            Component[] components = condimentsPanel.getComponents();
            for (int i = 0; i < components.length; i++) {
              JCheckBox cb = (JCheckBox)components[i];
              if (cb.isSelected())
                System.out.println("With " + cb.getText());
            }
          }
        });

        f.setVisible(true);
      }
    }
```

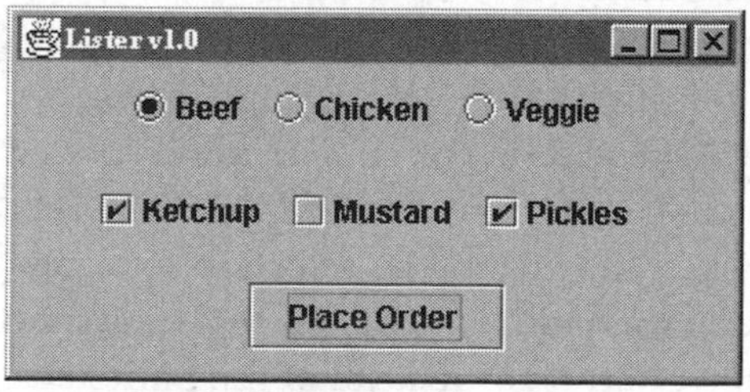

Figure 14-1. The DriveThrough application

DriveThrough lays out three panels. The radio buttons in the entreePanel are tied together through a ButtonGroup object. We add() the buttons to a ButtonGroup to make them mutually exclusive. The ButtonGroup object is an odd animal. One expects it to be a container or a component, but it isn't; it's simply a helper object that allows only one RadioButton to be selected at a time.

In this example, the button group forces you to choose a beef, chicken, or veggie entree, but not more than one. The condiment choices, which are `JCheckBoxes`, aren't in a button group, so you can request any combination of ketchup, mustard, and pickles on your sandwich.

When the **Place Order** button is pushed, we receive an `ActionEvent` in the `actionPerformed()` method of our inner `ActionListener`. At this point, we gather the information in the radio buttons and checkboxes and print it. `actionPerformed()` simply reads the state of the various buttons. We could have saved references to the buttons in a number of ways; this example demonstrates two. First, we find out which entree was selected. To do so, we call the `ButtonGroup`'s `getSelection()` method. This returns a `ButtonModel`, upon which we immediately call `getActionCommand()`. This returns the action command as we set it when we created the radio buttons. The action commands for the buttons are the entrée names, which is exactly what we need.

To find out which condiments were selected, we use a more complicated procedure. The problem is that condiments aren't mutually exclusive, so we don't have the convenience of a `ButtonGroup`. Instead, we ask the condiments `JPanel` for a list of its components. The `getComponents()` method returns an array of references to the container's child components. We'll use this to loop over the components and print the results. We cast each element of the array back to `JCheckBox` and call its `isSelected()` method to see if the checkbox is on or off. If we were dealing with different types of components in the array, we could determine each component's type with the `instanceof` operator.

Lists and Combo Boxes

`JLists` and `JComboBoxes` are a step up on the evolutionary chain from `JButtons` and `JLabels`. Lists let the user choose from a group of alternatives. They can be configured to force the user to choose a single selection or to allow multiple choices. Usually, only a small group of choices are displayed at a time; a scrollbar lets the user move to the choices that aren't visible. The user can select an item by clicking on it. He or she can expand the selection to a range of items by holding down Shift and clicking on another item. To make discontinuous selections, the user can hold down the Control key instead of the Shift key.

A combo box is a cross-breed between a text field and a list. It displays a single line of text (possibly with an image) and a downward pointing arrow at one side. If you click on the arrow, the combo box opens up and displays a list of choices. You can select a single choice by clicking on it. After a selection is made, the combo box closes up; the list disappears and the new selection is shown in the text field.

Like every other component in Swing, lists and combo boxes have data models that are distinct from visual components. The list also has a *selection model* that controls how selections may be made on the list data.

Lists and combo boxes are similar because they have similar data models. Each is simply an array of acceptable choices. This similarity is reflected in Swing, of course: the type of a JComboBox's data model is a subclass of the type used for a JList's data model. The next example demonstrates this relationship.

The following example creates a window with a combo box, a list, and a button. The combo box and the list use the same data model. When you press the button, the program writes out the current set of selected items in the list. Figure 14-2 shows the example; the code itself follows.

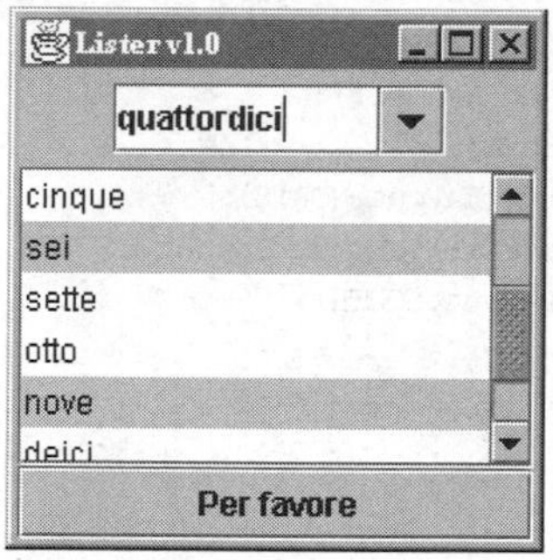

Figure 14-2. A combo box and a list using the same data model

```
/file: Lister.java
import java.awt.*;
import java.awt.event.*;
import javax.swing.*;

public class Lister {
  public static void main(String[] args) {
    JFrame f = new JFrame("Lister v1.0");
    f.setSize(200, 200);
    f.setLocation(200, 200);
    f.addWindowListener(new WindowAdapter() {
      public void windowClosing(WindowEvent we) { System.exit(0); }
    });

    // create a combo box
    String [] items = { "uno", "due", "tre", "quattro", "cinque",
                        "sei", "sette", "otto", "nove", "deici",
                        "undici", "dodici" };
    JComboBox comboBox = new JComboBox(items);
    comboBox.setEditable(true);
```

```
    // create a list with the same data model
    final JList list = new JList(comboBox.getModel());

    // create a button; when it's pressed, print out
    // the selection in the list
    JButton button = new JButton("Per favore");
    button.addActionListener(new ActionListener() {
      public void actionPerformed(ActionEvent ae) {
        Object[] selection = list.getSelectedValues();
        System.out.println("-----");
        for (int i = 0; i < selection.length; i++)
          System.out.println(selection[i]);
      }
    });

    // put the controls the content pane
    Container c = f.getContentPane();
    JPanel comboPanel = new JPanel();
    comboPanel.add(comboBox);
    c.add(comboPanel, BorderLayout.NORTH);
    c.add(new JScrollPane(list), BorderLayout.CENTER);
    c.add(button, BorderLayout.SOUTH);

    f.setVisible(true);
  }
}
```

The combo box is created from an array of strings. This is a convenience—behind the scenes, the JComboBox constructor creates a data model from the strings you supply and sets the JComboBox to use that data model. The list is created using the data model of the combo box. This works because JList expects to use a ListModel for its data model, and the ComboBoxModel used by the JComboBox is a subclass of ListModel.

The button's action event handler simply prints out the selected items in the list, which are retrieved with a call to getSelectedValues(). This method actually returns an object array, not a string array. List and combo box items, like many other things in Swing, are not limited to text. You can use images, or drawings, or some combination of text and images.

You might expect that selecting one item in the combo box would select the same item in the list. In Swing components, selection is controlled by a *selection model.* The combo box and the list have distinct selection models; after all, you can select only one item from the combo box, while it's possible to select multiple items from the list. Thus, while the two components share a data model, they have separate selection models.

We've made the combo box editable. By default, it would not be editable: the user could choose only one of the items in the drop-down list. With an editable combo box, the user can type in a selection, as if it were a text field. Non-editable combo boxes are useful if you just want to offer a limited set of choices; editable combo boxes are handy when you want to accept any input but offer some common choices.

There's a great class tucked away in the last example that deserves some recognition. It's JScrollPane. In Lister, you'll notice we created one when we added the List to the main window.

JScrollPane simply wraps itself around another Component and provides scrollbars as necessary. The scrollbars show up if the contained Component's preferred size (as returned by getPreferredSize()) is greater than the size of the JScrollPane itself. In the previous example, the scrollbars show up whenever the size of the List exceeds the available space.

You can use JScrollPane to wrap any Component, including components with drawings or images or complex user interface panels. We'll discuss JScrollPane in more detail later in this chapter, and we'll use it frequently with the text components in the next chapter.

Borders

Any Swing component can have a decorative border. JComponent includes a method called setBorder(); all you have to do is call setBorder(), passing it an appropriate implementation of the Border interface.

Swing provides many useful Border implementations in the javax.swing. border package. You could create an instance of one of these classes and pass it to a component's setBorder() method, but there's an even simpler technique.

The BorderFactory class can create any kind of border for you using static "factory" methods. Creating and setting a component's border, then, is simple:

```
JLabel labelTwo = new JLabel("I have an etched border.");
labelTwo.setBorder(BorderFactory.createEtchedBorder());
```

Every component has a setBorder() method, from simple labels and buttons right up to the fancy text and table components we'll cover in the next chapter.

BorderFactory is convenient, but it does not offer every option of every border type. For example, if you want to create a raised EtchedBorder instead of the default lowered border, you'll need to use EtchedBorder's constructor rather than a method in BorderFactory, like this:

```
JLabel labelTwo = new JLabel("I have a raised etched border.");
labelTwo.setBorder( new EtchedBorder(EtchedBorder.RAISED) );
```

The `Border` implementation classes are listed and briefly described here:

`BevelBorder`

This border draws raised or lowered beveled edges, giving an illusion of depth.

`SoftBevelBorder`

This border is similar to `BevelBorder`, but thinner.

`EmptyBorder`

Doesn't do any drawing, but does take up space. You can use it to give a component a little breathing room in a crowded user interface.

`EtchedBorder`

A lowered etched border gives the appearance of a rectangle that has been chiseled into a piece of stone. A raised etched border looks like it is standing out from the surface of the screen.

`LineBorder`

Draws a simple rectangle around a component. You can specify the color and width of the line in `LineBorder`'s constructor.

`MatteBorder`

A souped-up version of `LineBorder`. You can create a `MatteBorder` with a certain color and specify the size of the border on the left, top, right, and bottom of the component. `MatteBorder` also allows you to pass in an `Icon` that will be used to draw the border. This could be an image (`ImageIcon`) or any other implementation of the `Icon` interface.

`TitledBorder`

A regular border with a title. `TitledBorder` doesn't actually draw a border; it just draws a title in conjunction with another border object. You can specify the locations of the title, its justification, and its font. This border type is particularly useful for grouping different sets of controls in a complicated interface.

`CompoundBorder`

A border that contains two other borders. This is especially handy if you want to enclose a component in an `EmptyBorder` and then put something decorative around it, like an `EtchedBorder` or a `MatteBorder`.

The following example shows off some different border types. It's only a sampler, though; many more border types are available. Furthermore, the example only encloses labels with borders. You can put a border around any component in Swing. The example is shown in Figure 14-3; the source code follows.

```
//file: Borders.java
import java.awt.*;
import java.awt.event.*;
import javax.swing.*;
```

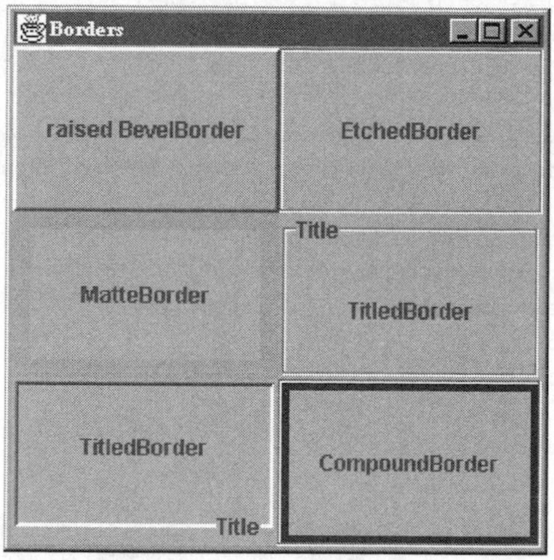

Figure 14-3. A bevy of borders

```java
import javax.swing.border.*;

public class Borders {
  public static void main(String[] args) {
    // create a JFrame to hold everything
    JFrame f = new JFrame("Borders");
    f.addWindowListener(new WindowAdapter() {
      public void windowClosing(WindowEvent we) { System.exit(0); }
    });
    f.setSize(300, 300);
    f.setLocation(200, 200);

    // Create labels with borders.
    int center = SwingConstants.CENTER;
    JLabel labelOne = new JLabel("raised BevelBorder", center);
    labelOne.setBorder(
        BorderFactory.createBevelBorder(BevelBorder.RAISED));
    JLabel labelTwo = new JLabel("EtchedBorder", center);
    labelTwo.setBorder(BorderFactory.createEtchedBorder());
    JLabel labelThree = new JLabel("MatteBorder", center);
    labelThree.setBorder(
        BorderFactory.createMatteBorder(10, 10, 10, 10, Color.pink));
    JLabel labelFour = new JLabel("TitledBorder", center);
    Border etch = BorderFactory.createEtchedBorder();
    labelFour.setBorder(
        BorderFactory.createTitledBorder(etch, "Title"));
    JLabel labelFive = new JLabel("TitledBorder", center);
    Border low = BorderFactory.createLoweredBevelBorder();
    labelFive.setBorder(
        BorderFactory.createTitledBorder(low, "Title",
```

```
            TitledBorder.RIGHT, TitledBorder.BOTTOM));
    JLabel labelSix = new JLabel("CompoundBorder", center);
    Border one = BorderFactory.createEtchedBorder();
    Border two =
        BorderFactory.createMatteBorder(4, 4, 4, 4, Color.blue);
    labelSix.setBorder(BorderFactory.createCompoundBorder(one, two));

    // add components to the content pane
    Container c = f.getContentPane();
    c.setLayout(new GridLayout(3, 2));
    c.add(labelOne);
    c.add(labelTwo);
    c.add(labelThree);
    c.add(labelFour);
    c.add(labelFive);
    c.add(labelSix);

    f.setVisible(true);
  }
}
```

Menus

A JMenu is a standard pull-down menu with a fixed name. Menus can hold other menus as submenu items, enabling you to implement complex menu structures. In Swing, menus are first-class components, just like everything else. You can place them wherever a component would go. Another class, JMenuBar, holds menus in a horizontal bar. Menu bars are real components, too, so you can place them wherever you want in a container: top, bottom, or middle. But in the middle of a container, it usually makes more sense to use a JComboBox rather than some kind of menu.

Menu items may have associated images and shortcut keys; there are even menu items that look like checkboxes and radio buttons. Menu items are really a kind of button. Like buttons, menu items fire action events when they are selected. You can respond to menu items by registering action listeners with them.

There are two ways to use the keyboard with menus. The first is called *mnemonics*. A mnemonic is one character in the menu name. If you hold down the Alt key and type a menu's mnemonic, the menu will drop down, just as if you had clicked on it with the mouse. Menu items may also have mnemonics. Once a menu is dropped down, you can select individual items in the same way.

Menu items may also have *accelerators*. An accelerator is a key combination that selects the menu item, whether or not the menu that contains it is showing. A common example is the accelerator Ctrl-C, which is frequently used as a shortcut for the **Copy** item in the **Edit** menu.

The following example demonstrates several different features of menus. It creates a menu bar with three different menus. The first, **Utensils**, contains several menu items, a submenu, a separator, and a **Quit** item that includes both a mnemonic and an accelerator. The second menu, **Spices**, contains menu items that look and act like checkboxes. Finally, the **Cheese** menu demonstrates how radio button menu items can be used.

This application is shown in Figure 14-4 with one of its menus dropped down. Choosing **Quit** from the menu (or pressing Ctrl-Q) removes the window. Give it a try.

```java
//file: DinnerMenu.java
import java.awt.*;
import java.awt.event.*;
import javax.swing.*;

public class DinnerMenu extends JFrame {

  public DinnerMenu() {
    super("DinnerMenu v1.0");
    setSize(200, 200);
    setLocation(200, 200);

    // create the Utensils menu
    JMenu utensils = new JMenu("Utensils");
    utensils.setMnemonic(KeyEvent.VK_U);
    utensils.add(new JMenuItem("Fork"));
    utensils.add(new JMenuItem("Knife"));
    utensils.add(new JMenuItem("Spoon"));
    JMenu hybrid = new JMenu("Hybrid");
    hybrid.add(new JMenuItem("Spork"));
    hybrid.add(new JMenuItem("Spife"));
    hybrid.add(new JMenuItem("Knork"));
    utensils.add(hybrid);
    utensils.addSeparator();

    // do some fancy stuff with the Quit item
    JMenuItem quitItem = new JMenuItem("Quit");
    quitItem.setMnemonic(KeyEvent.VK_Q);
    quitItem.setAccelerator(
        KeyStroke.getKeyStroke(KeyEvent.VK_Q, Event.CTRL_MASK));
    quitItem.addActionListener(new ActionListener() {
      public void actionPerformed(ActionEvent e) { System.exit(0); }
    });
    utensils.add(quitItem);

    // create the Spices menu
    JMenu spices = new JMenu("Spices");
    spices.setMnemonic(KeyEvent.VK_S);
```

```
        spices.add(new JCheckBoxMenuItem("Thyme"));
        spices.add(new JCheckBoxMenuItem("Rosemary"));
        spices.add(new JCheckBoxMenuItem("Oregano", true));
        spices.add(new JCheckBoxMenuItem("Fennel"));

        // create the Cheese menu
        JMenu cheese = new JMenu("Cheese");
        cheese.setMnemonic(KeyEvent.VK_C);
        ButtonGroup group = new ButtonGroup();
        JRadioButtonMenuItem rbmi;
        rbmi = new JRadioButtonMenuItem("Regular", true);
        group.add(rbmi);
        cheese.add(rbmi);
        rbmi = new JRadioButtonMenuItem("Extra");
        group.add(rbmi);
        cheese.add(rbmi);
        rbmi = new JRadioButtonMenuItem("Blue");
        group.add(rbmi);
        cheese.add(rbmi);

        // create a menu bar and use it in this JFrame
        JMenuBar menuBar = new JMenuBar();
        menuBar.add(utensils);
        menuBar.add(spices);
        menuBar.add(cheese);
        setJMenuBar(menuBar);
    }

    public static void main(String[] args) {
      JFrame f = new DinnerMenu();
      f.addWindowListener(new WindowAdapter() {
        public void windowClosing(WindowEvent we) { System.exit(0); }
      });
      f.setVisible(true);
    }
}
```

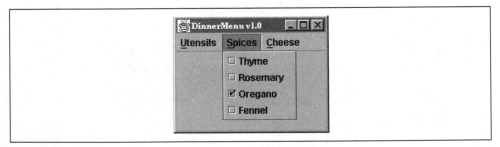

Figure 14-4. The DinnerMenu application

Yes, we know. **Quit** doesn't belong in the **Utensils** menu. If it's driving you crazy, you can go back and add a **File** menu as an exercise when we're through.

Creating menus is pretty simple work. You create a JMenu object, specifying the menu's title.* Then you just add JMenuItems to the JMenu. You can also add JMenus to a JMenu; they show up as submenus. This is shown in the creation of the **Utensils** menu:

```
JMenu utensils = new JMenu("Utensils");
utensils.setMnemonic(KeyEvent.VK_U);
utensils.add(new JMenuItem("Fork"));
utensils.add(new JMenuItem("Knife"));
utensils.add(new JMenuItem("Spoon"));
JMenu hybrid = new JMenu("Hybrid");
hybrid.add(new JMenuItem("Spork"));
hybrid.add(new JMenuItem("Spife"));
hybrid.add(new JMenuItem("Knork"));
utensils.add(hybrid);
```

In the second line, we set the mnemonic for this menu using a constant defined in the KeyEvent class.

You can add those pretty separator lines with a single call:

```
utensils.addSeparator();
```

The **Quit** menu item has some bells and whistles we should explain. First, we create the menu item and set its mnemonic, just as we did before for the **Utensils** menu:

```
JMenuItem quitItem = new JMenuItem("Quit");
quitItem.setMnemonic(KeyEvent.VK_Q);
```

Now we want to create an accelerator for the menu item. We do this with the help of a class called KeyStroke:

```
quitItem.setAccelerator(
    KeyStroke.getKeyStroke(KeyEvent.VK_Q, Event.CTRL_MASK));
```

Finally, to actually do something in response to the menu item, we register an action listener:

```
quitItem.addActionListener(new ActionListener() {
    public void actionPerformed(ActionEvent e) { System.exit(0); }
});
```

Our action listener exits the application when the **Quit** item is selected.

---

* Like the text of JButtons and JLabels, menu labels can contain simple HTML.

Creating the **Spices** menu is just as easy, except that we use `JCheckBoxMenuItems` instead of regular `JMenuItems`. The result is a menu full of items that behave like checkboxes.

The next menu, **Cheese**, is a little more tricky. We want the items to be radio buttons, but we need to place them in a `ButtonGroup` to ensure they are mutually exclusive. Each item, then, is created, added to the button group, and added to the menu itself.

The final step is to place the menus we've just created in a `JMenuBar`. This is simply a component that lays out menus in a horizontal bar. We have two options for adding it to our `JFrame`. Since the `JMenuBar` is a real component, we could add it to the content pane of the `JFrame`. Instead, we use a convenience method called `setJMenuBar()`, which automatically places the `JMenuBar` at the top of the frame's content pane. This saves us the trouble of altering the layout or size of the content pane; it is adjusted to coexist peacefully with the menu bar.

The PopupMenu Class

One of Swing's nifty components is `JPopupMenu`, a menu that automatically appears when you press the appropriate mouse button inside of a component. (On a Windows system, for example, clicking the right mouse button invokes a popup menu.) Which button you press depends on the platform you're using; fortunately, you don't have to care—Swing figures it out for you.

The care and feeding of `JPopupMenu` is basically the same as any other menu. You use a different constructor (`JPopupMenu()`) to create it, but otherwise, you build a menu and add elements to it the same way. The big difference is you don't need to attach it to a `JMenuBar`. Instead, just pop up the menu whenever you need it.

The following example, `PopupColorMenu`, contains three buttons. You can use a `JPopupMenu` to set the color of each button or the frame itself, depending on where you press the mouse. Figure 14-5 shows the example in action; the user is preparing to change the color of the bottom button.

```java
//file: PopUpColorMenu.java
import java.awt.*;
import java.awt.event.*;
import javax.swing.*;

public class PopUpColorMenu extends JFrame
                            implements ActionListener {
  JPopupMenu colorMenu;
  Component selectedComponent;

  public PopUpColorMenu() {
```

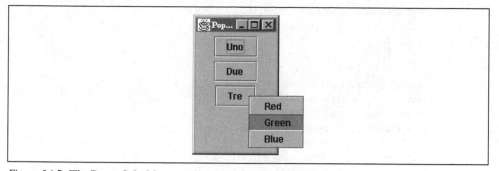

Figure 14-5. The PopupColorMenu application

```
super("PopUpColorMenu v1.0");
setSize(100, 200);
setLocation(200, 200);
addWindowListener(new WindowAdapter() {
  public void windowClosing(WindowEvent e) { System.exit(0); }
});

MouseListener mouseListener = new MouseAdapter() {
  public void mousePressed(MouseEvent e) { checkPopup(e); }
  public void mouseClicked(MouseEvent e) { checkPopup(e); }
  public void mouseReleased(MouseEvent e) { checkPopup(e); }
  private void checkPopup(MouseEvent e) {
    if (e.isPopupTrigger()) {
      selectedComponent = e.getComponent();
      colorMenu.show(e.getComponent(), e.getX(), e.getY());
    }
  }
};

final Container content = getContentPane();
content.setLayout(new FlowLayout());
JButton button = new JButton("Uno");
button.addMouseListener(mouseListener);
content.add(button);
button = new JButton("Due");
button.addMouseListener(mouseListener);
content.add(button);
button = new JButton("Tre");
button.addMouseListener(mouseListener);
content.add(button);

colorMenu = new JPopupMenu("Color");
colorMenu.add(makeMenuItem("Red"));
colorMenu.add(makeMenuItem("Green"));
colorMenu.add(makeMenuItem("Blue"));
```

```
        getContentPane().addMouseListener(mouseListener);

        setVisible(true);
    }

    public void actionPerformed(ActionEvent e) {
        String color = e.getActionCommand();
        if (color.equals("Red"))
            selectedComponent.setBackground(Color.red);
        else if (color.equals("Green"))
            selectedComponent.setBackground(Color.green);
        else if (color.equals("Blue"))
            selectedComponent.setBackground(Color.blue);
    }

    private JMenuItem makeMenuItem(String label) {
        JMenuItem item = new JMenuItem(label);
        item.addActionListener( this );
        return item;
    }

    public static void main(String[] args) {
        new PopUpColorMenu();
    }
}
```

Because the popup menu is triggered by mouse events, we need to register a
MouseListener for any of the components to which it applies. In this example, all
three buttons and the content pane of the frame are eligible for the color popup
menu. Therefore, we add a mouse event listener for all of these components
explicitly. The same instance of an anonymous inner MouseAdapter subclass is
used in each case. In this class, we override the mousePressed(), mouse-
Released(), and mouseClicked() methods to display the popup menu when we
get an appropriate event. How do we know what an "appropriate event" is? Fortunately, we don't need to worry about the specifics of our user's platform; we just
need to call the event's isPopupTrigger() method. If this method returns true,
we know the user has done whatever normally displays a popup menu on his or
her system.

Once we know that the user wants to raise a popup menu, we display the popup
menu by calling its show() method with the mouse event coordinates as arguments.

If we wanted to provide different menus for different types of components or the
background, we'd create different mouse listeners for each different kind of component. The mouse listeners would invoke different kinds of popup menus as
appropriate.

The only thing left is to handle the action events from the popup menu items. We use a helper method called makeMenuItem() to register the PopUpColorMenu window as an action listener for every item we add. The example implements ActionListener and has the required actionPerformed() method. This method reads the action command from the event, which is equal to the selected menu item's label by default. It then sets the background color of the selected component appropriately.

The JScrollPane Class

We used JScrollPane earlier in this chapter without explaining much about it. In this section we'll remedy the situation.

A JScrollPane is a container that can hold one component. Said another way, a JScrollPane *wraps* another component. By default, if the wrapped component is larger than the JScrollPane itself, the JScrollPane supplies scrollbars. JScrollPane handles the events from the scrollbars and displays the appropriate portion of the contained component.

Technically, JScrollPane is a Container, but it's a funny one. It has its own layout manager, which can't be changed. It can accommodate only one component at a time. This seems like a big limitation, but it isn't. If you want to put a lot of stuff in a JScrollPane, just put your components into a JPanel, with whatever layout manager you like, and put that panel into the JScrollPane.

When you create a JScrollPane, you can specify the conditions under which its scrollbars will be displayed. This is called the *scrollbar display policy*; a separate policy is used for the horizontal and vertical scrollbars. The following constants can be used to specify the policy for each of the scrollbars:

HORIZONTAL_SCROLLBAR_AS_NEEDED
> Displays a scrollbar only if the wrapped component doesn't fit.

HORIZONTAL_SCROLLBAR_ALWAYS
> Always shows a scrollbar, regardless of the contained component's size.

HORIZONTAL_SCROLLBAR_NEVER
> Never shows a scrollbar, even if the contained component won't fit. If you use this policy, you should provide some other way to manipulate the JScrollPane.

VERTICAL_SCROLLBAR_AS_NEEDED
> Displays a scrollbar only if the wrapped component doesn't fit.

VERTICAL_SCROLLBAR_ALWAYS
> Always shows a scrollbar, regardless of the contained component's size.

VERTICAL_SCROLLBAR_NEVER

Never shows a scrollbar, even if the contained component won't fit. If you use this policy, you should provide some other way to manipulate the JScroll-Pane.

By default, the policies are HORIZONTAL_SCROLLBAR_AS_NEEDED and VERTICAL_SCROLLBAR_AS_NEEDED.

Here's an example that uses a JScrollPane to display a large image. The application itself is very simple; all we do is place the image in an ImageComponent, wrap a JScrollPane around it, and put the JScrollPane in a JFrame's content pane. Here's the code:

```
//file: ScrollPaneFrame.java
import java.awt.*;
import java.awt.event.*;
import javax.swing.*;

public class ScrollPaneFrame {
  public static void main(String[] args) {
    String filename = "Piazza di Spagna.jpg";
    if (args.length > 0)
      filename = args[0];

    JFrame f = new JFrame("ScrollPaneFrame v1.0");
    f.setSize(300, 300);
    f.setLocation(200, 200);
    f.addWindowListener(new WindowAdapter() {
      public void windowClosing(WindowEvent e) { System.exit(0); }
    });

    Image image = Toolkit.getDefaultToolkit().getImage(filename);
    f.getContentPane().add(
      new JScrollPane(new ImageComponent(image)));
    f.setVisible(true);
  }
}
```

And here's the ImageComponent. It waits for the image to load, using a MediaTracker, and sets its size to the size of the image. It also provides a paint() method to draw the image. This takes a single call to drawImage(). The first argument is the image itself; the next two are the coordinates of the image relative to the ImageComponent; and the last is a reference to the ImageComponent itself (this), which serves as an image observer. (We'll discuss image observers in Chapter 18, *Working with Images and Other Media*; for the time being, take this on faith.)

```
//file: ImageComponent.java
import java.awt.*;
```

```
import javax.swing.*;

public class ImageComponent extends JComponent {
  Image image;
  Dimension size;

  public ImageComponent(Image image) {
    this.image = image;
    MediaTracker mt = new MediaTracker(this);
    mt.addImage(image, 0);
    try {
      mt.waitForAll();
    }
    catch (InterruptedException e) {
      // error ...
    };

    size = new Dimension (image.getWidth(null),
                          image.getHeight(null));
    setSize(size);
  }

  public void paint(Graphics g) {
    g.drawImage(image, 0, 0, this);
  }

  public Dimension getPreferredSize() {
    return size;
  }
}
```

Finally, `ImageComponent` provides a `getPreferredSize()` method, overriding the method it inherits from `Component`. This method simply returns the image's size, which is a `Dimension` object. When you're using `JScrollPane`, it's important for the object you're scrolling to provide a reliable indication of its size. Figure 14-6 shows the `ScrollPaneFrame` with the `ImageComponent`.

The JSplitPane Class

A *split pane* is a special container that holds two components, each in its own sub-pane. A *splitter bar* adjusts the sizes of the two sub-panes. In a document viewer, you could use a split pane to show a table of contents next to a full document.

The following example capitalizes on the `ImageComponent` class from the previous example. It displays two `ImageComponents`, wrapped in `JScrollPanes`, in either side of a `JSplitPane`. You can drag the splitter bar back and forth to adjust the sizes of the two contained components.

Figure 14-6. The ScrollPaneFrame application

```
//file: SplitPaneFrame.java
import java.awt.*;
import java.awt.event.*;
import javax.swing.*;
import javax.swing.border.*;

public class SplitPaneFrame {
  public static void main(String[] args) {
    String fileOne = "Piazza di Spagna.jpg";
    String fileTwo = "L1-Light.jpg";

    if (args.length > 0) fileOne = args[0];
    if (args.length > 1) fileTwo = args[1];

    // create a JFrame to hold everything
    JFrame f = new JFrame("SplitPaneFrame");
    f.addWindowListener(new WindowAdapter() {
      public void windowClosing(WindowEvent we) { System.exit(0); }
    });
    f.setSize(300, 200);
    f.setLocation(200, 200);

    Image leftImage = Toolkit.getDefaultToolkit().getImage(fileOne);
    Component left =
      new JScrollPane(new ImageComponent(leftImage));
    Image rightImage = Toolkit.getDefaultToolkit().getImage(fileTwo);
    Component right =
      new JScrollPane(new ImageComponent(rightImage));
    JSplitPane split =
      new JSplitPane(JSplitPane.HORIZONTAL_SPLIT, left, right);
```

```
            split.setDividerLocation(100);
            f.getContentPane().add(split);

            f.setVisible(true);
        }
    }
```

This example is shown in Figure 14-7.

Figure 14-7. Using a split pane

The JTabbedPane Class

If you've ever dealt with the System control panel in Windows, you already know what a JTabbedPane is. It's a container with labeled tabs. When you click on a tab, a new set of controls is shown in the body of the JTabbedPane. In Swing, JTabbedPane is simply a specialized container.

Each tab has a name. To add a tab to the JTabbedPane, simply call addTab(). You'll need to specify the name of the tab as well as a component that supplies the tab's contents. Typically, it's a container holding other components.

Even though the JTabbedPane only shows one set of components at a time, be aware that all the components on all the pages are in memory at one time. If you have components that hog processor time or memory, try to put them into some "sleep" state when they are not showing.

The following example shows how to create a JTabbedPane. It adds standard Swing components to a first tab, named **Controls**. The second tab is filled with an instance of ImageComponent, which was presented earlier in this chapter.

```
//file: TabbedPaneFrame.java
import java.awt.*;
import java.awt.event.*;
import javax.swing.*;
import javax.swing.border.*;
```

```java
public class TabbedPaneFrame {
  public static void main(String[] args) {
    // create a JFrame to hold everything
    JFrame f = new JFrame("TabbedPaneFrame");
    f.addWindowListener(new WindowAdapter() {
      public void windowClosing(WindowEvent we) { System.exit(0); }
    });
    f.setSize(200, 200);
    f.setLocation(200, 200);

    JTabbedPane tabby = new JTabbedPane();

    // create a controls pane
    JPanel controls = new JPanel();
    controls.add(new JLabel("Service:"));
    JList list = new JList(
        new String[] { "Web server", "FTP server" });
    list.setBorder(BorderFactory.createEtchedBorder());
    controls.add(list);
    controls.add(new JButton("Start"));

    // create an image pane
    String filename = "Piazza di Spagna.jpg";
    Image image = Toolkit.getDefaultToolkit().getImage(filename);
    JComponent picture = new JScrollPane(new ImageComponent(image));

    tabby.addTab("Controls", controls);
    tabby.addTab("Picture", picture);

    f.getContentPane().add(tabby);
    f.setVisible(true);
  }
}
```

The code is not especially fancy, but the result is an impressive-looking user interface. The first tab is a `JPanel` that contains some other components, including a `JList` with an etched border. The second tab simply contains an `Image-Component` wrapped in a `JScrollPane`. The running example is shown in Figure 14-8.

Scrollbars and Sliders

`JScrollPane` is such a handy component that you may not ever need to use scrollbars by themselves. In fact, if you ever do find yourself using a scrollbar by itself, chances are you really want to use another component called a *slider*.

There's not much point in describing the appearance and functionality of scrollbars and sliders. Instead, let's jump right in with an example that includes both

Figure 14-8. Using a tabbed pane

components. Figure 14-9 shows a simple example with both a scrollbar and a slider.

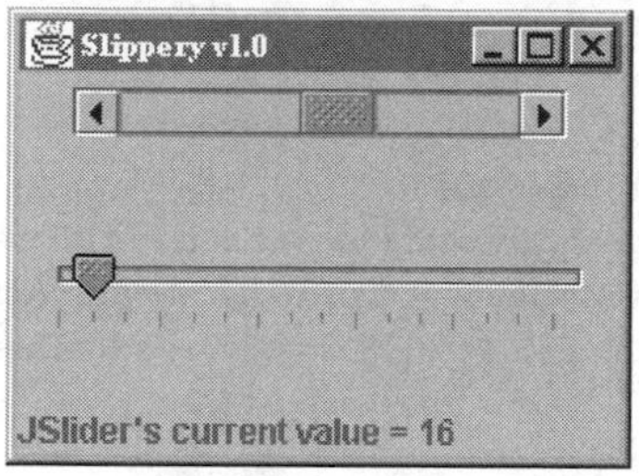

Figure 14-9. Using a scrollbar and a slider

Here is the source code for this example:

```java
//file: Slippery.java
import java.awt.*;
import java.awt.event.*;
import javax.swing.*;
import javax.swing.event.*;

public class Slippery extends JFrame {

  public Slippery() {
    super("Slippery v1.0");
    setSize(220, 160);
    setLocation(200, 200);

    Container content = getContentPane();

    JPanel main = new JPanel(new GridLayout(2, 1));
    JPanel scrollBarPanel = new JPanel();
    final JScrollBar scrollBar =
```

```
        new JScrollBar(JScrollBar.HORIZONTAL, 0, 48, 0, 255);
    int height = scrollBar.getPreferredSize().height;
    scrollBar.setPreferredSize(new Dimension(175, height));
    scrollBarPanel.add(scrollBar);
    main.add(scrollBarPanel);

    JPanel sliderPanel = new JPanel();
    final JSlider slider =
        new JSlider(JSlider.HORIZONTAL, 0, 255, 128);
    slider.setMajorTickSpacing(48);
    slider.setMinorTickSpacing(16);
    slider.setPaintTicks(true);
    sliderPanel.add(slider);
    main.add(sliderPanel);

    content.add(main, BorderLayout.CENTER);

    final JLabel statusLabel =
        new JLabel("Welcome to Slippery v1.0");
    content.add(statusLabel, BorderLayout.SOUTH);

    // wire up the event handlers
    scrollBar.addAdjustmentListener(new AdjustmentListener() {
      public void adjustmentValueChanged(AdjustmentEvent e) {
        statusLabel.setText("JScrollBar's current value = "
                            + scrollBar.getValue());
      }
    });

    slider.addChangeListener(new ChangeListener() {
      public void stateChanged(ChangeEvent e) {
        statusLabel.setText("JSlider's current value = "
                            + slider.getValue());
      }
    });
  }

  public static void main(String[] args) {
    JFrame f = new Slippery();
    f.addWindowListener(new WindowAdapter() {
      public void windowClosing(WindowEvent e) { System.exit(0); }
    });
    f.setVisible(true);
  }
}
```

All we've really done here is added a JScrollBar and a JSlider to our main window. If the user adjusts either of these components, the current value of the component is displayed in a JLabel at the bottom of the window.

The `JScrollBar` and `JSlider` are both created by specifying an orientation, either `HORIZONTAL` or `VERTICAL`. You can also specify the minimum and maximum values for the components, as well as the initial value. The `JScrollBar` supports one additional parameter, the *extent*. The extent simply refers to what range of values is represented by the slider within the scroll bar. For example, in a scrollbar that runs from 0 to 255, an extent of 128 means that the slider will be half the width of the scrollable area of the scrollbar.

`JSlider` supports the idea of tick marks, which are lines drawn at certain values along the slider's length. *Major* tick marks are slightly larger than *minor* tick marks. To draw tick marks, just specify an interval for major and minor tick marks, and then paint the tick marks:

```
slider.setMajorTickSpacing(48);
slider.setMinorTickSpacing(16);
slider.setPaintTicks(true);
```

`JSlider` also supports labeling the ticks with text strings, using the `setLabel-Table()` method.

Responding to events from the two components is straightforward. The `JScroll-Bar` sends out `AdjustmentEvents` every time something happens; the `JSlider` fires off `ChangeEvents` when its value changes. In our simple example, we display the new value of the changed component in the `JLabel` at the bottom of the window.

Dialogs

A dialog is another standard feature of user interfaces. Dialogs are frequently used to present information to the user ("Your fruit salad is ready.") or to ask a question ("Shall I bring the car around?"). Dialogs are used so commonly in GUI applications that Swing includes a handy set of pre-built dialogs. These are accessible from static methods in the `JOptionPane` class. Many variations are possible; `JOptionPane` groups them into four basic types:

message dialog
Displays a message to the user, usually accompanied by an **OK** button.

confirmation dialog
Ask a question and displays answer buttons, usually **Yes**, **No**, and **Cancel**.

input dialog
Asks the user to type in a string.

option dialogs
The most general type—you pass it your own components, which are displayed in the dialog.

A confirmation dialog is shown in Figure 14-10.

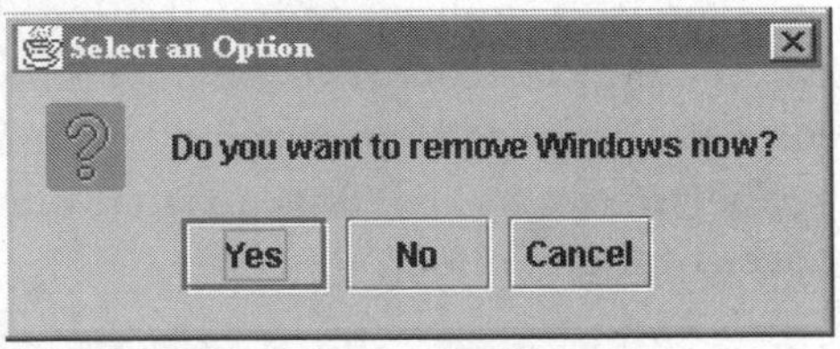

Figure 14-10. Using a confirmation dialog

Let's look at examples of each kind of dialog. The following code produces a message dialog:

```
JOptionPane.showMessageDialog(f, "You have mail.");
```

The first parameter to **showMessageDialog()** is the parent component (in this case f, an existing **JFrame**). The dialog will be centered on the parent component. If you pass **null** for the parent component, the dialog is centered in your screen. The dialogs that **JOptionPane** displays are *modal*, which means they block other input to your application while they are showing.

Here's a slightly fancier message dialog. We've specified a title for the dialog and a message type, which affects the icon that is displayed:

```
JOptionPane.showMessageDialog(f, "You are low on memory.",
        "Apocalyptic message", JOptionPane.WARNING_MESSAGE);
```

Here's how to display the confirmation dialog shown in Figure 14-10:

```
int result = JOptionPane.showConfirmDialog(null,
        "Do you want to remove Windows now?");
```

In this case, we've passed **null** for the parent component. Special values are returned from **showConfirmDialog()** to indicate which button was pressed. There's a full example below that shows how to use this return value.

Sometimes you need to ask the user to type some input. The following code puts up a dialog requesting the user's name:

```
String name = JOptionPane.showInputDialog(null,
        "Please enter your name.");
```

Whatever the user types is returned as a **String**, or **null** if the user presses the **Cancel** button.

The most general type of dialog is the option dialog. You supply an array of objects that you wish to be displayed; **JOptionPane** takes care of formatting them and displaying the dialog. The following example displays a text label, a **JTextField**, and a **JPasswordField**. (Text components are described in the next chapter.)

```
JTextField userField = new JTextField();
JPasswordField passField = new JPasswordField();
String message = "Please enter your user name and password.";
result = JOptionPane.showOptionDialog(f,
    new Object[] { message, userField, passField },
    "Login", JOptionPane.OK_CANCEL_OPTION,
    JOptionPane.QUESTION_MESSAGE,
    null, null, null);
```

We've also specified a dialog title ("Login") in the call to showOptionDialog(). We want **OK** and **Cancel** buttons, so we pass OK_CANCEL_OPTION as the dialog type. The QUESTION_MESSAGE argument indicates we'd like to see the question mark icon. The last three items are optional: an Icon, an array of different choices, and a current selection. Since the icon parameter is null, a default is used. If the array of choices and the current selection parameters were not null, JOptionPane might try to display the choices in a list or combo box.

The following application includes all the examples we've covered:

```
import javax.swing.*;

public class ExerciseOptions {
  public static void main(String[] args) {
    JFrame f = new JFrame("ExerciseOptions v1.0");
    f.setSize(200, 200);
    f.setLocation(200, 200);
    f.setVisible(true);

    JOptionPane.showMessageDialog(f, "You have mail.");
    JOptionPane.showMessageDialog(f, "You are low on memory.",
        "Apocalyptic message", JOptionPane.WARNING_MESSAGE);

    int result = JOptionPane.showConfirmDialog(null,
        "Do you want to remove Windows now?");
    switch (result) {
      case JOptionPane.YES_OPTION:
        System.out.println("Yes"); break;
      case JOptionPane.NO_OPTION:
        System.out.println("No"); break;
      case JOptionPane.CANCEL_OPTION:
        System.out.println("Cancel"); break;
      case JOptionPane.CLOSED_OPTION:
        System.out.println("Closed"); break;
    }

    String name = JOptionPane.showInputDialog(null,
        "Please enter your name.");
    System.out.println(name);
```

```
JTextField userField = new JTextField();
JPasswordField passField = new JPasswordField();
String message = "Please enter your user name and password.";
result = JOptionPane.showOptionDialog(f,
    new Object[] { message, userField, passField },
    "Login", JOptionPane.OK_CANCEL_OPTION,
    JOptionPane.QUESTION_MESSAGE,
    null, null, null);
if (result == JOptionPane.OK_OPTION)
  System.out.println(userField.getText() +
      " " + new String(passField.getPassword()));

System.exit(0);
  }
}
```

File Selection Dialog

A JFileChooser is a standard file-selection box. As with other Swing components, JFileChooser is implemented in pure Java, so it looks and acts the same on different platforms.

Selecting files all day can be pretty boring without a greater purpose, so we'll exercise the JFileChooser in a mini-editor application. Editor provides a text area in which we can load and work with files. (The JFileChooser created by Editor is shown in Figure 14-11.) We'll stop just shy of the capability to save and let you fill in the blanks (with a few caveats):

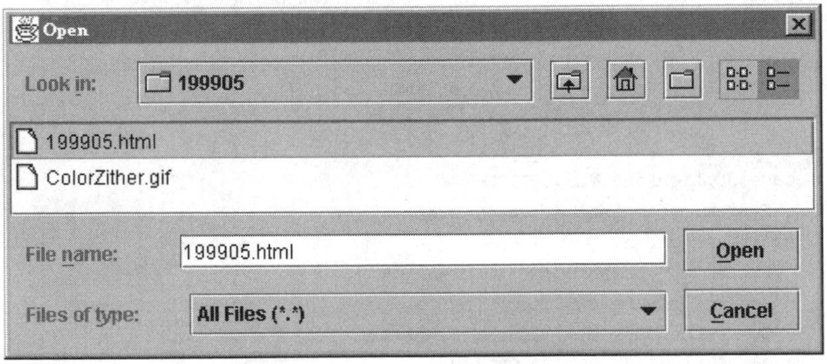

Figure 14-11. Using a JFileChooser

```
import java.awt.*;
import java.awt.event.*;
import java.io.*;

import javax.swing.*;
```

```java
public class Editor
    extends JFrame
    implements ActionListener {
  public static void main(String[] s) { new Editor(); }

  private JEditorPane textPane = new JEditorPane();

  public Editor() {
    super("Editor v1.0");
    addWindowListener(new WindowAdapter() {
      public void windowClosing(WindowEvent e) { System.exit(0); }
    });
    Container content = getContentPane();
    content.add(new JScrollPane(textPane), BorderLayout.CENTER);
    JMenu menu = new JMenu("File");
    menu.add(makeMenuItem("Open"));
    menu.add(makeMenuItem("Save"));
    menu.add(makeMenuItem("Quit"));
    JMenuBar menuBar = new JMenuBar();
    menuBar.add(menu);
    setJMenuBar(menuBar);
    setSize(300, 300);
    setLocation(200, 200);
    setVisible(true);
  }

  public void actionPerformed(ActionEvent e) {
    String command = e.getActionCommand();
    if (command.equals("Quit")) System.exit(0);
    else if (command.equals("Open")) loadFile();
    else if (command.equals("Save")) saveFile();
  }

  private void loadFile () {
    JFileChooser chooser = new JFileChooser();
    int result = chooser.showOpenDialog(this);
    if (result == JFileChooser.CANCEL_OPTION) return;
    try {
      File file = chooser.getSelectedFile();
      java.net.URL url = file.toURL();
      textPane.setPage(url);
    }
    catch (Exception e) {
      textPane.setText("Could not load file: " + e);
    }
  }

  private void saveFile() {
    JFileChooser chooser = new JFileChooser();
```

```
        chooser.showSaveDialog(this);
        // Save file data...
    }

    private JMenuItem makeMenuItem( String name ) {
      JMenuItem m = new JMenuItem( name );
      m.addActionListener( this );
      return m;
    }
  }
```

Editor is a JFrame that lays itself out with a JEditorPane (which will be covered in the next chapter) and a pull-down menu. From the pull-down **File** menu, we can **Open**, **Save**, or **Quit**. The actionPerformed() method catches the events associated with these menu selections and takes the appropriate action.

The interesting parts of Editor are the private methods loadFile() and saveFile().loadFile() creates a new JFileChooser and calls its showOpen-Dialog() method.

A JFileChooser does its work when the showOpenDialog() method is called. This method blocks the caller until the dialog completes its job, at which time the file chooser disappears. After that, we can retrieve the designated file with the getFile() method. In loadFile(), we convert the selected File to a URL and pass it to the JEditorPane, which displays the selected file. As you'll learn in the next chapter, JEditorPane can display HTML and RTF files.

You can fill out the unfinished saveFile() method if you wish, but it would be prudent to add the standard safety precautions. For example, you could use one of the confirmation dialogs we just looked at to prompt the user before overwriting an existing file.

The Color Chooser

Swing is chock full of goodies. JColorChooser is yet another ready-made dialog supplied with Swing; it allows your users to choose colors. The following very brief example shows how easy it is to use JColorChooser:

```java
import java.awt.*;
import java.awt.event.*;

import javax.swing.*;

public class LocalColor {
  public static void main(String[] args) {
    final JFrame f = new JFrame("LocalColor v1.0");
    f.addWindowListener(new WindowAdapter() {
      public void windowClosing(WindowEvent e) { System.exit(0); }
```

```
    });
    f.setSize(200, 200);
    f.setLocation(200, 200);
    final Container content = f.getContentPane();
    content.setLayout(new GridBagLayout());
    JButton button = new JButton("Change color...");
    content.add(button);

    button.addActionListener(new ActionListener() {
      public void actionPerformed(ActionEvent e) {
        Color c = JColorChooser.showDialog(f,
            "Choose a color", content.getBackground());
        if (c != null) content.setBackground(c);
      }
    });

    f.setVisible(true);
  }
}
```

This examples shows a frame window with a single button. When you click on the button, a color chooser pops up. After you select a color, it becomes the background color of the frame window.

Basically all we have to do is call JColorChooser's static method showDialog(). In this example, we've specified a parent component, a dialog title, and an initial color value. But you can get away with just specifying a parent component. Whatever color the user chooses is returned; if the user presses the **Cancel** button, null is returned.

15

More Swing Components

In the previous chapter, we described most of the components that Swing offers for building user interfaces. In this chapter, you'll find out about the rest. These include Swing's text components, trees, and tables. These types of components have considerable depth, but are quite easy to use if you accept their default options. We'll show you the easy way to use these components, and start to describe the more advanced features of each. The chapter ends with a brief description of how to implement your own components in Swing.

Text Components

Swing gives us sophisticated text components, from plain text entry boxes to HTML interpreters. For full coverage of Swing's text capabilities, see *Java Swing*, by Robert Eckstein, Marc Loy, and Dave Wood (O'Reilly & Associates). In that encyclopedic book, six meaty chapters are devoted to text. It's a huge subject; we'll just scratch the surface here.

Let's begin by examining the simpler text components: `JTextArea` is a multiline text editor; `JTextField` is a simple, single-line text editor. Both `JTextField` and `JTextArea` derive from the `JTextComponent` class, which provides the functionality they have in common. This includes methods for setting and retrieving the displayed text, specifying whether the text is "editable" or read-only, manipulating the cursor position within the text, and manipulating text selections.

Observing changes in text components requires an understanding of how the components implement the Model-View-Controller (MVC) architecture. You may recall from the last chapter that Swing components implement a true MVC architecture. It's in the text components that you first get an inkling of a clear separation between the M and VC parts of the MVC architecture. The model for text components is an object called a Document. When you add or remove text from a JTextField or a JTextArea, the corresponding Document is changed. It's the document itself, not the visual components, that generates text events when something changes. To receive notification of JTextArea changes, therefore, you register with the underlying Document, not with the JTextArea component itself:

```
JTextArea textArea = new JTextArea();
Document d = textArea.getDocument();
d.addDocumentListener(someListener);
```

As you'll see in an upcoming example, you can easily have more than one visual text component use the same underlying data model, or Document.

In addition, JTextField components generate an ActionEvent whenever the user presses the Return key within the field. To get these events, implement the ActionListener interface, and call addActionListener() to register.

The next sections contain a couple of simple applications that show you how to work with text areas and fields.

The TextEntryBox Application

Our first example, TextEntryBox, creates a JTextArea and ties it to a JTextField, as you can see in Figure 15-1. When the user hits Return in the JTextField, we receive an ActionEvent and add the line to the JTextArea's display. Try it out. You may have to click your mouse in the JTextField to give it focus before typing in it. If you fill up the display with lines, you can test drive the scrollbar:

```java
//file: TextEntryBox.java
import java.awt.*;
import java.awt.event.*;
import javax.swing.*;

public class TextEntryBox extends JFrame {

  public TextEntryBox() {
    super("TextEntryBox v1.0");
    setSize(200, 300);
    setLocation(200, 200);

    final JTextArea area = new JTextArea();
    area.setFont(new Font("Serif", Font.BOLD, 18));
    area.setText("Howdy!\n");
    final JTextField field = new JTextField();

    Container content = getContentPane();
    content.add(new JScrollPane(area), BorderLayout.CENTER);
```

```
      content.add(field, BorderLayout.SOUTH);
      setVisible(true);
      field.requestFocus();

      field.addActionListener(new ActionListener() {
        public void actionPerformed(ActionEvent ae) {
          area.append(field.getText() + '\n');
          field.setText("");
        }
      });
    }

  public static void main(String[] args) {
    JFrame f = new TextEntryBox();
    f.addWindowListener(new WindowAdapter() {
      public void windowClosing(WindowEvent we) { System.exit(0); }
    });
    f.setVisible(true);
  }
}
```

Figure 15-1. The TextEntryBox application

TextEntryBox is exceedingly simple; we've done a few things to make it more interesting. We give the text area a bigger font using Component's setFont() method; fonts are discussed in Chapter 17, *Drawing with the 2D API*. Finally, we want to be notified whenever the user presses Return in the text field, so we register an anonymous inner class as a listener for action events.

Pressing Return in the JTextField generates an action event, and that's where the fun begins. We handle the event in the actionPerformed() method of our inner ActionListener implementation. Then we use the getText() and setText() methods to manipulate the text the user has typed. These methods can be used for both JTextField and JTextArea, because these components are derived from the JTextComponent class, and therefore have some common functionality.

The event handler, `actionPerformed()`, calls `field.getText()` to read the text that the user typed into our `JTextField`. It then adds this text to the `JTextArea` by calling `area.append()`. Finally, we clear the text field by calling the method `field.setText("")`, preparing it for more input.

Remember, the text components really are distinct from the text data model, the `Document`. When you call `setText()`, `getText()`, or `append()`, these methods are shorthand for operations on an underlying `Document`.

By default, `JTextField` and `JTextArea` are editable; you can type and edit in both text components. They can be changed to output-only areas by calling `setEditable(false)`. Both text components also support *selections*. A selection is a range of text that is highlighted for copying and pasting in your windowing system. You select text by dragging the mouse over it; you can then copy and paste it into other text windows. The current text selection is returned by `getSelected-Text()`.

Notice how `JTextArea` fits neatly inside a `JScrollPane`. The scroll pane gives us the expected scrollbars and scrolling behavior if the text in the `JTextArea` becomes too large for the available space.

Say the Magic Word

Swing includes a class just for typing passwords, called `JPasswordField`. A `JPasswordField` behaves just like a `JTextField` (it's a subclass), except every character that's typed is echoed as a single character, typically an asterisk. Figure 15-2 shows the option dialog example that was presented in Chapter 14, *Using Swing Components*. The example includes a `JTextField` and a `JPassword-Field`.

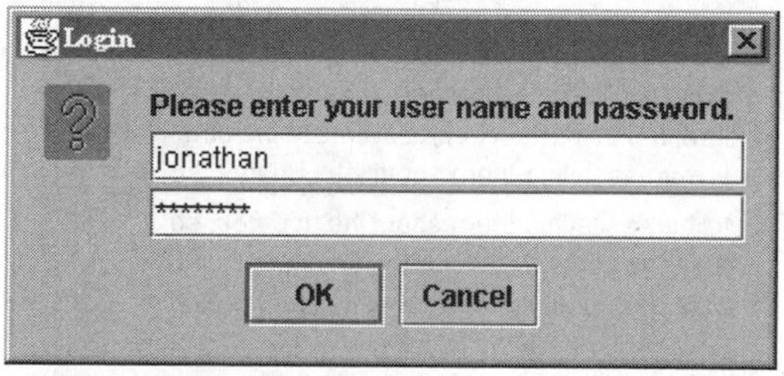

Figure 15-2. Using a JPasswordField in a dialog

The creation and use of `JPasswordField` is basically the same as for `JTextField`. If you find asterisks distasteful, you can tell the `JPasswordField` to use a different character using the `setEchoChar()` method.

Normally, you would use `getText()` to retrieve the text typed into the `JPasswordField`. This method, however, is deprecated; you should use `getPassword()` instead. The `getPassword()` method returns a character array rather than a `String` object. This is done because character arrays are less vulnerable than `Strings` to discovery by memory-snooping password sniffer programs. If you're not that concerned, you can simply create a new `String` from the character array. Note that methods in the Java cryptographic classes accept passwords as character arrays, not strings, so it makes a lot of sense to pass the results of a `getPassword()` call directly to methods in the cryptographic classes, without ever creating a `String`.

Sharing a Data Model

Our next example shows how easy it is to make two or more text components share the same `Document`; Figure 15-3 shows what the application looks like. Anything the user types into any text area is reflected in all of them. All we had to do is make all the text areas use the same data model, like this:

```
JTextArea areaFiftyOne = new JTextArea();
JTextArea areaFiftyTwo = new JTextArea();
areaFiftyTwo.setDocument(areaFiftyOne.getDocument());
JTextArea areaFiftyThree = new JTextArea();
areaFiftyThree.setDocument(areaFiftyOne.getDocument());
```

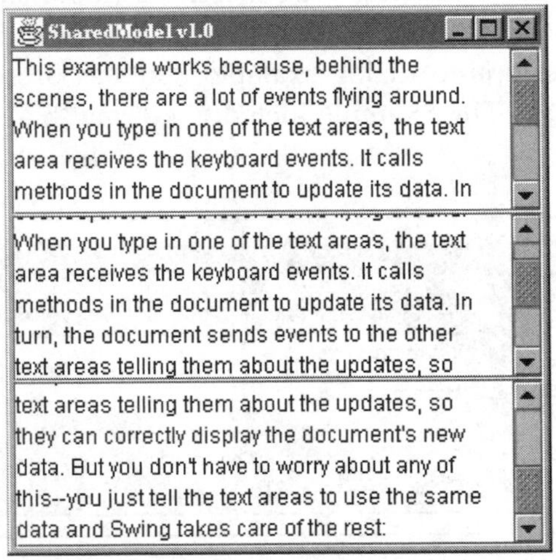

Figure 15-3. Three views of the same data model

We could just as easily make seven text areas sharing the same document, or seventy. While this example may not look very useful, keep in mind that you can scroll different text areas to different places in the same document. That's one of the beauties of putting multiple views on the same data—you get to examine different parts of it. Another useful technique is viewing the same data in different ways. You could, for example, view some tabular numerical data as both a spreadsheet and a pie chart. The MVC architecture that Swing uses means that it's possible to do this in an intelligent way, so that if numbers in a spreadsheet are updated, a pie chart that uses the same data will automatically be updated also.

This example works because behind the scenes, there are a lot of events flying around. When you type in one of the text areas, the text area receives the keyboard events. It calls methods in the document to update its data. In turn, the document sends events to the other text areas telling them about the updates, so they can correctly display the document's new data. But you don't have to worry about any of this—you just tell the text areas to use the same data and Swing takes care of the rest:

```java
//file: SharedModel.java
import java.awt.*;
import java.awt.event.*;
import javax.swing.*;

public class SharedModel extends JFrame {

  public SharedModel() {
    super("SharedModel v1.0");
    setSize(300, 300);
    setLocation(200, 200);

    JTextArea areaFiftyOne = new JTextArea();
    JTextArea areaFiftyTwo = new JTextArea();
    areaFiftyTwo.setDocument(areaFiftyOne.getDocument());
    JTextArea areaFiftyThree = new JTextArea();
    areaFiftyThree.setDocument(areaFiftyOne.getDocument());

    Container content = getContentPane();
    content.setLayout(new GridLayout(3, 1));
    content.add(new JScrollPane(areaFiftyOne));
    content.add(new JScrollPane(areaFiftyTwo));
    content.add(new JScrollPane(areaFiftyThree));
    setVisible(true);
  }

  public static void main(String[] args) {
    JFrame f = new SharedModel();
    f.addWindowListener(new WindowAdapter() {
      public void windowClosing(WindowEvent we) { System.exit(0); }
    });
    f.setVisible(true);
  }
}
```

Setting up the display is simple. We use a `GridLayout` (discussed in the next chapter) and add three text areas to the layout. Then all we have to do is tell the text areas to use the same `Document`.

HTML and RTF for Free

Most user interfaces will use only two subclasses of `JTextComponent`. These are the simple `JTextField` and `JTextArea` classes that we just covered. That's just the tip of the iceberg, however. Swing offers sophisticated text capabilities through two other subclasses of `JTextComponent`: `JEditorPane` and `JTextPane`.

The first of these, `JEditorPane`, can display HTML and RTF documents. It also fires one more type of event, a `HyperlinkEvent`. Subtypes of this event are fired off when the mouse enters, exits, or clicks on a hyperlink. Combined with `JEditorPane`'s HTML display capabilities, it's very easy to build a simple browser. Here's one in fewer than 100 lines:

```java
//file: CanisMinor.java
import java.awt.*;
import java.awt.event.*;
import java.net.*;
import javax.swing.*;
import javax.swing.event.*;

public class CanisMinor extends JFrame {
  protected JEditorPane mEditorPane;
  protected JTextField mURLField;

  public CanisMinor(String urlString) {
    super("CanisMinor v1.0");
    createUI(urlString);
    setVisible(true);
  }

  protected void createUI(String urlString) {
    setSize(500, 600);
    center();
    Container content = getContentPane();
    content.setLayout(new BorderLayout());

    // add the URL control
    JToolBar urlToolBar = new JToolBar();
    mURLField = new JTextField(urlString, 40);
    urlToolBar.add(new JLabel("Location:"));
    urlToolBar.add(mURLField);
    content.add(urlToolBar, BorderLayout.NORTH);

    // add the editor pane
```

```java
    mEditorPane = new JEditorPane();
    mEditorPane.setEditable(false);
    content.add(new JScrollPane(mEditorPane), BorderLayout.CENTER);

    // open the initial URL
    openURL(urlString);

    // go to a new location when enter is pressed in the URL field
    mURLField.addActionListener(new ActionListener() {
      public void actionPerformed(ActionEvent ae) {
        openURL(ae.getActionCommand());
      }
    });

    // add the plumbing to make links work
    mEditorPane.addHyperlinkListener(new LinkActivator());

    // exit the application when the window is closed
    addWindowListener(new WindowAdapter() {
      public void windowClosing(WindowEvent e) { System.exit(0); }
    });
  }

  protected void center() {
    Dimension screen = Toolkit.getDefaultToolkit().getScreenSize();
    Dimension us = getSize();
    int x = (screen.width - us.width) / 2;
    int y = (screen.height - us.height) / 2;
    setLocation(x, y);
  }

  protected void openURL(String urlString) {
    try {
      URL url = new URL(urlString);
      mEditorPane.setPage(url);
      mURLField.setText(url.toExternalForm());
    }
    catch (Exception e) {
      System.out.println("Couldn't open " + urlString + ":" + e);
    }
  }

  class LinkActivator implements HyperlinkListener {
    public void hyperlinkUpdate(HyperlinkEvent he) {
      HyperlinkEvent.EventType type = he.getEventType();
      if (type == HyperlinkEvent.EventType.ENTERED)
        mEditorPane.setCursor(
            Cursor.getPredefinedCursor(Cursor.HAND_CURSOR));
      else if (type == HyperlinkEvent.EventType.EXITED)
```

```
          mEditorPane.setCursor(Cursor.getDefaultCursor());
        else if (type == HyperlinkEvent.EventType.ACTIVATED)
          openURL(he.getURL().toExternalForm());
    }
  }

  public static void main(String[] args) {
    String urlString = "http://www.oreilly.com/catalog/java2d/";
    if (args.length > 0)
      urlString = args[0];
    new CanisMinor(urlString);
  }
}
```

This browser is shown in Figure 15-4.

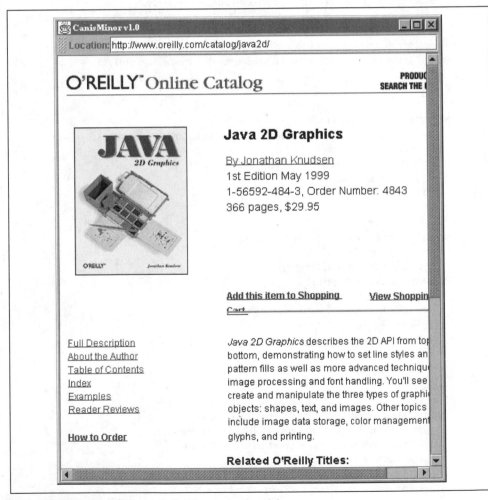

Figure 15-4. The CanisMinor application, a simple web browser

JEditorPane is the center of this little application. Passing a URL to setPage() causes the JEditorPane to load a new page, either from a local file or from somewhere across the Internet. To go to a new page, enter it in the text field at the top of the window and press Return. This fires an ActionEvent which sets the new page location of the JEditorPane. It can display RTF files, too. (RTF is the text or non-binary storage format for Microsoft Word documents.)

Responding to hyperlinks correctly is simply a matter of responding to the HyperlinkEvents thrown by the JEditorPane. This behavior is encapsulated in the LinkActivator inner class. If the mouse enters a hyperlink area, the cursor is changed to a hand. It's changed back when the mouse exits a hyperlink. If the user "activates" the hyperlink by clicking on it, we set the location of the JEditorPane to the location given under the hyperlink. Surf away!

Behind the scenes, something called an EditorKit handles displaying documents for the JEditorPane. Different kinds of EditorKits are used to display different kinds of documents. For HTML, the HTMLEditorKit class (in the javax. swing.text.html package) handles the display. Currently, this class supports HTML 3.2. Subsequent releases of the SDK will contain enhancements to the capabilities of HTMLEditorKit; eventually, it will support HTML 4.0.

There's another component here that we haven't covered before—the JToolBar. This nifty container houses our URL text field. Initially, the JToolBar starts out at the top of the window. But you can pick it up by clicking on the little dotted box near its left edge, then drag it around to different parts of the window. You can place this toolbar at the top, left, right, or bottom of the window, or you can drag it outside the window entirely. It will then inhabit a window of its own. All this behavior comes for free from the JToolBar class. All we had to do was create a JToolBar and add some components to it. The JToolBar is just a container, so we add it to the content pane of our window to give it an initial location.

Managing Text Yourself

Swing offers one last subclass of JTextComponent that can do just about anything you want: JTextPane. The basic text components, JTextField and JTextArea, are limited to a single font in a single style. But JTextPane, a subclass of JEditorPane, can display multiple fonts and multiple styles in the same component. It also includes support for a cursor (caret), highlighting, image embedding, and other advanced features.

We'll just take a peek at JTextPane here by creating a text pane with some styled text. Remember, the text itself is stored in an underlying data model, the Document. To create styled text, we simply associate a set of *text attributes* with different parts of the document's text. Swing includes classes and methods for manipulating sets of attributes, like specifying a bold font or a different color for the text. Attributes themselves are contained in a class called `SimpleAttributeSet`; these attribute sets are manipulated with static methods in the `StyleConstants` class. For example, to create a set of attributes that specifies the color red, you could do this:

```
SimpleAttributeSet redstyle = new SimpleAttributeSet();
StyleConstants.setForeground(redstyle, Color.red);
```

To add some red text to a document, you would just pass the text and the attributes to the document's `insertString()` method, like this:

```
document.insertString(6, "Some red text", redstyle);
```

The first argument to `insertString()` is an offset into the text. An exception is thrown if you pass in an offset that's greater than the current length of the document. If you pass `null` for the attribute set, the text is added in the `JTextPane`'s default font and style.

Our simple example creates several attribute sets and uses them to add plain and styled text to a `JTextPane`, as shown in Figure 15-5.

```java
//file: Styling.java
import java.awt.*;
import java.awt.event.*;
import javax.swing.*;
import javax.swing.text.*;

public class Styling extends JFrame {
  private JTextPane textPane;

  public Styling() {
    super("Styling v1.0");
    setSize(300, 200);
    setLocation(200, 200);

    textPane = new JTextPane();
    textPane.setFont(new Font("Serif", Font.PLAIN, 24));

    // create some handy attribute sets
    SimpleAttributeSet red = new SimpleAttributeSet();
    StyleConstants.setForeground(red, Color.red);
    StyleConstants.setBold(red, true);
    SimpleAttributeSet blue = new SimpleAttributeSet();
    StyleConstants.setForeground(blue, Color.blue);
    SimpleAttributeSet italic = new SimpleAttributeSet();
    StyleConstants.setItalic(italic, true);
    StyleConstants.setForeground(italic, Color.orange);

    // add the text
    append("In a ", null);
```

```
            append("sky", blue);
            append(" full of people\nOnly some want to ", null);
            append("fly", italic);
            append("\nIsn't that ", null);
            append("crazy", red);
            append("?", null);

            Container content = getContentPane();
            content.add(new JScrollPane(textPane), BorderLayout.CENTER);
            setVisible(true);
    }

    protected void append(String s, AttributeSet attributes) {
        Document d = textPane.getDocument();
        try { d.insertString(d.getLength(), s, attributes); }
        catch (BadLocationException ble) {}
    }

    public static void main(String[] args) {
        JFrame f = new Styling();
        f.addWindowListener(new WindowAdapter() {
            public void windowClosing(WindowEvent we) { System.exit(0); }
        });
        f.setVisible(true);
    }
}
```

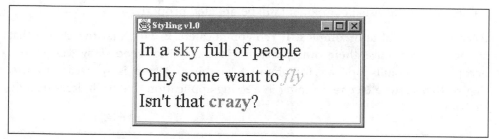

Figure 15-5. Using styled text in a JTextPane

This example creates a JTextPane, which is saved away in a member variable. Three different attribute sets are created, using combinations of text styles and foreground colors. Then, using a helper method called append(), text is added to the JTextPane.

The append() method tacks a text String on the end of the JTextPane's document, using the supplied attributes. Remember that if the attributes are null, the text is displayed with the JTextPane's default font and style.

You can go ahead and add your own text, if you wish. If you place the caret inside one of the differently styled words and type, the new text comes out in the appropriate style. Pretty cool, eh? You'll also notice that JTextPane gives us word-wrapping behavior for free. And since we've wrapped the JTextPane in a JScrollPane, we get scrolling for free, too. Swing allows you to do some really cool stuff without breaking a sweat. Just wait—there's plenty more to come.

This simple example should give you some idea of what JTextPane can do. It's reasonably easy to build a simple word processor with JTextPane, and complex commercial-grade word processors are definitely possible.

If JTextPane still isn't good enough for you, or you need some finer control over character, word, and paragraph layout, you can actually draw text, carets, and highlight shapes yourself. A class in the 2D API called TextLayout simplifies much of this work, but it's outside the scope of this book. For coverage of TextLayout and other advanced text drawing topics, see *Java 2D Graphics* by Jonathan Knudsen (O'Reilly & Associates).

Trees

One of Swing's advanced components is JTree. Trees are good for representing hierarchical information, like the contents of a disk drive or a company's organizational chart. As with all Swing components, the data model is distinct from the visual representation. This means you can do things like update the data model and trust that the visual component will be updated properly.

JTree is powerful and complex. It's so complicated, in fact, that the classes that support JTree have their own package, javax.swing.tree. However, if you accept the defaults options for almost everything, JTree is very easy to use. Figure 15-6 shows a JTree running in a Swing application that we'll describe a little later.

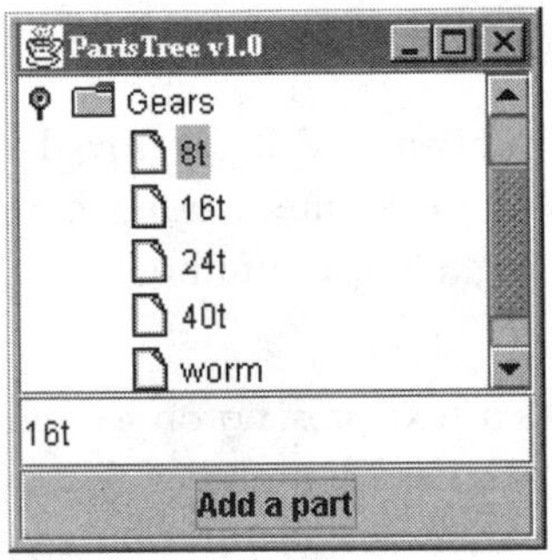

Figure 15-6. The JTree class in action

Nodes and Models

A tree's data model is made up of interconnected nodes. A node has a name, typically, a parent, and some number of children (possibly 0). In Swing, a node is represented by the TreeNode interface. Nodes that can be modified are represented by MutableTreeNode. A concrete implementation of this interface is Default-MutableTreeNode. One node, called the *root* node, usually resides at the top of the hierarchy.

A tree's data model is represented by the TreeModel interface. Swing provides an implementation of this interface called DefaultTreeModel. You can create a DefaultTreeModel by passing a root TreeNode to its constructor.

You could create a TreeModel with just one node like this:

```
TreeNode root = new DefaultMutableTreeNode("Root node");
TreeModel model = new DefaultTreeModel(root);
```

Here's another example with a real hierarchy. The root node contains two nodes, Node 1 and Group. The Group node contains Node 2 and Node 3 as subnodes.

```
MutableTreeNode root = new DefaultMutableTreeNode("Root node");
MutableTreeNode group = new DefaultMutableTreeNode("Group");
root.insert(group, 0);
root.insert(new DefaultMutableTreeNode("Node 1"), 1);
group.insert(new DefaultMutableTreeNode("Node 2"), 0);
group.insert(new DefaultMutableTreeNode("Node 3"), 1);
```

Once you've got your nodes organized, you can create a TreeModel in the same way as before:

```
TreeModel model = new DefaultTreeModel(root);
```

Save a Tree

Once you have a tree model, creating a JTree is simple:

```
JTree tree = new JTree(model);
```

The JTree behaves like a souped-up JList. As Figure 15-6 shows, the JTree automatically shows nodes with no children as a sheet of paper, while nodes that contain other nodes are shown as folders. You can expand and collapse nodes by clicking on the little knobs to the left of the folder icons. You can also expand and collapse nodes by double-clicking on them. You can select nodes; multiple selections are possible using the Shift and Ctrl keys. And, like a JList, you should put a JTree in a JScrollPane if you want it to scroll.

Tree Events

A tree fires off several flavors of events. You can find out when nodes have been expanded and collapsed, when nodes are *about to be* expanded or collapsed (because the user has clicked on them), and when selections occur. Three distinct event listener interfaces handle this information: `TreeExpansionListener`, `TreeWillExpandListener`, and `TreeSelectionListener`.

Tree selections are a tricky business. You can select any combination of nodes by using the Control key and clicking on nodes. Tree selections are described by a `TreePath`, which describes how to get from the root node to the selected nodes.

The following example registers an event listener that prints out the last selected node:

```
tree.addTreeSelectionListener(new TreeSelectionListener() {
  public void valueChanged(TreeSelectionEvent e) {
    TreePath tp = e.getNewLeadSelectionPath();
    System.out.println(tp.getLastPathComponent());
  }
});
```

A Complete Example

This section contains a complete example that showcases the following tree techniques:

- Construction of a tree model, using `DefaultMutableTreeNode`

- Creation and display of a `JTree`

- Listening for tree selection events

- Modifying the tree's data model while the `JTree` is showing

Here's the source code for the example:

```
//file: PartsTree.java
import java.awt.*;
import java.awt.event.*;
import javax.swing.*;
import javax.swing.event.*;
import javax.swing.tree.*;

public class PartsTree {
  public static void main(String[] args) {
    // create a hierarchy of nodes
    MutableTreeNode root = new DefaultMutableTreeNode("Parts");
    MutableTreeNode beams = new DefaultMutableTreeNode("Beams");
    MutableTreeNode gears = new DefaultMutableTreeNode("Gears");
    root.insert(beams, 0);
```

```
root.insert(gears, 1);
beams.insert(new DefaultMutableTreeNode("1x4 black"), 0);
beams.insert(new DefaultMutableTreeNode("1x6 black"), 1);
beams.insert(new DefaultMutableTreeNode("1x8 black"), 2);
beams.insert(new DefaultMutableTreeNode("1x12 black"), 3);
gears.insert(new DefaultMutableTreeNode("8t"), 0);
gears.insert(new DefaultMutableTreeNode("24t"), 1);
gears.insert(new DefaultMutableTreeNode("40t"), 2);
gears.insert(new DefaultMutableTreeNode("worm"), 3);
gears.insert(new DefaultMutableTreeNode("crown"), 4);

// create a JFrame to hold the tree
JFrame f = new JFrame("PartsTree v1.0");
f.addWindowListener(new WindowAdapter() {
  public void windowClosing(WindowEvent e) { System.exit(0); }
});
f.setSize(200, 200);
f.setLocation(200, 200);

// create the JTree
final DefaultTreeModel model = new DefaultTreeModel(root);
final JTree tree = new JTree(model);

// create a text field and button to modify the data model
final JTextField nameField = new JTextField("16t");
final JButton button = new JButton("Add a part");
button.setEnabled(false);
button.addActionListener(new ActionListener() {
  public void actionPerformed(ActionEvent e) {
    TreePath tp = tree.getSelectionPath();
    MutableTreeNode insertNode =
        (MutableTreeNode)tp.getLastPathComponent();
    int insertIndex = 0;
    if (insertNode.getParent() != null) {
      MutableTreeNode parent =
          (MutableTreeNode)insertNode.getParent();
      insertIndex = parent.getIndex(insertNode) + 1;
      insertNode = parent;
    }
    MutableTreeNode node =
        new DefaultMutableTreeNode(nameField.getText());
    model.insertNodeInto(node, insertNode, insertIndex);
  }
});
JPanel addPanel = new JPanel(new GridLayout(2, 1));
addPanel.add(nameField);
addPanel.add(button);

// listen for selections
```

```
        tree.addTreeSelectionListener(new TreeSelectionListener() {
          public void valueChanged(TreeSelectionEvent e) {
            TreePath tp = e.getNewLeadSelectionPath();
            button.setEnabled(tp != null);
          }
        });

        // put it all together
        f.getContentPane().add(new JScrollPane(tree));
        f.getContentPane().add(addPanel, BorderLayout.SOUTH);
        f.setVisible(true);
      }
    }
```

The example begins by creating a node hierarchy. The root node is called Parts. It contains two subnodes, Beams and Gears, as shown:

```
MutableTreeNode root = new DefaultMutableTreeNode("Parts");
MutableTreeNode beams = new DefaultMutableTreeNode("Beams");
MutableTreeNode gears = new DefaultMutableTreeNode("Gears");
root.insert(beams, 0);
root.insert(gears, 1);
```

The Beams and Gears nodes contain a handful of items each.

The **Add a part** button inserts a new item into the tree at the level of the current node, and just after it. You can specify the name of the new node by typing it in the text field above the button. To determine where the node should be added, the current selection is first obtained, in the anonymous inner `ActionListener`:

```
TreePath tp = tree.getSelectionPath();
MutableTreeNode insertNode =
    (MutableTreeNode)tp.getLastPathComponent();
```

The new node should be added to the parent node of the current node, so it ends up being a sibling of the current node. The only hitch here is that if the current node is the root node, it won't have a parent. If a parent does exist, we determine the index of the currently selected node, and then add the new node at the next index:

```
int insertIndex = 0;
if (insertNode.getParent() != null) {
  MutableTreeNode parent =
      (MutableTreeNode)insertNode.getParent();
  insertIndex = parent.getIndex(insertNode) + 1;
  insertNode = parent;
}
MutableTreeNode node =
    new DefaultMutableTreeNode(nameField.getText());
model.insertNodeInto(node, insertNode, insertIndex);
```

You must add the new node to the tree's data model, using `insertNodeInto()`, not to the `MutableTableNode` itself. The model notifies the `JTree` that it needs to update itself.

We have another event handler in this example, one that listens for tree selection events. Basically, we want to enable our **Add a part** button only if a current selection exists:

```
tree.addTreeSelectionListener(new TreeSelectionListener() {
  public void valueChanged(TreeSelectionEvent e) {
    TreePath tp = e.getNewLeadSelectionPath();
    button.setEnabled(tp != null);
  }
});
```

When you first start this application, the button is disabled. As soon as you select something, it is enabled and you can add nodes to the tree with abandon. If you want to see the button disabled again, you can unselect everything by holding the Control key and clicking on the current selection.

Tables

Tables present information in orderly rows and columns. This is useful for presenting financial figures or representing data from a relational database. Like trees, tables in Swing are incredibly powerful. If you go with the default options, however, they're also pretty easy to use.

The `JTable` class represents a visual table component. A `JTable` is based on a `TableModel`, one of a dozen or so supporting interfaces and classes in the `javax.swing.table` package.

A First Stab: Freeloading

`JTable` has one constructor that creates a default table model for you from arrays of data. You just need to supply it with the names of your column headers and a two-dimensional array of `Objects` representing the table's data. The first index selects the table's row; the second index selects the column. The following example shows how easy it is to get going with tables using this constructor:

```
//file: DullShipTable.java
import java.awt.*;
import java.awt.event.*;
import javax.swing.*;
import javax.swing.table.*;

public class DullShipTable {
  public static void main(String[] args) {
```

```
// create some tabular data
String[] headings =
  new String[] {"Number", "Hot?", "Origin",
                "Destination", "Ship Date", "Weight" };
Object[][] data = new Object[][] {
  { "100420", Boolean.FALSE, "Des Moines IA", "Spokane WA",
    "02/06/2000", new Float(450) },
  { "202174", Boolean.TRUE, "Basking Ridge NJ", "Princeton NJ",
    "05/20/2000", new Float(1250) },
  { "450877", Boolean.TRUE, "St. Paul MN", "Austin TX",
    "03/20/2000", new Float(1745) },
  { "101891", Boolean.FALSE, "Boston MA", "Albany NY",
    "04/04/2000", new Float(88) }
};

// create a JFrame to hold the table
JFrame f = new JFrame("DullShipTable v1.0");
f.addWindowListener(new WindowAdapter() {
  public void windowClosing(WindowEvent e) { System.exit(0); }
});
f.setSize(500, 200);
f.setLocation(200, 200);

// create the data model and the JTable
JTable table = new JTable(data, headings);

// put it all together
f.getContentPane().add(new JScrollPane(table));
f.setVisible(true);
  }
}
```

This small application produces the display shown in Figure 15-7.

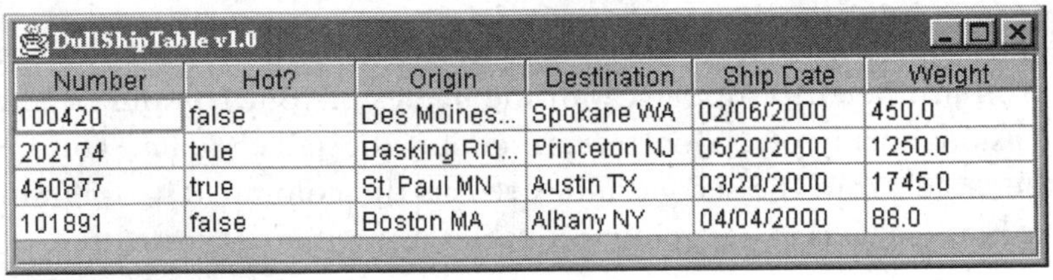

DullShipTable v1.0					
Number	Hot?	Origin	Destination	Ship Date	Weight
100420	false	Des Moines...	Spokane WA	02/06/2000	450.0
202174	true	Basking Rid...	Princeton NJ	05/20/2000	1250.0
450877	true	St. Paul MN	Austin TX	03/20/2000	1745.0
101891	false	Boston MA	Albany NY	04/04/2000	88.0

Figure 15-7. A rudimentary JTable

For a very little typing, we've gotten some pretty impressive stuff. Here are a few things that come for free:

Column headings

The JTable has automatically formatted the column headings differently than the table cells. It's clear that they are not part of the table's data area.

Cell overflow

If a cell's data is too long to fit in the cell, it is automatically truncated and shown with an ellipses (…). This is shown in the "Origin" cell in the first two rows in Figure 15-7.

Row selection

You can click on any cell in the table to select its entire row. This behavior is controllable; you can select single cells, entire rows, entire columns, or some combination of these. To configure the `JTable`'s selection behavior, use the `setCellSelectionEnabled()`, `setColumnSelectionAllowed()`, and `set-RowSelectionAllowed()` methods.

Cell editing

Double-clicking on a cell opens it for editing; you'll get a little cursor in the cell. You can type directly into the cell to change the cell's data.

Column sizing

If you position the mouse cursor between two column headings, you'll get a little left-right arrow cursor. Click and drag to change the size of the column to the left. Depending on how the `JTable` is configured, the other columns may also change size. The resizing behavior is controlled with the `setAutoResizeMode()` method.

Column reordering

If you click and drag on a column heading, you can move *the entire column* to another part of the table.

Play with this for a while; it's fun.

Round Two: Creating a Table Model

`JTable` is a very powerful component. You get a lot of very nice behavior for free. However, the default settings are not quite what we wanted for this simple example. In particular, we intended the table entries to be read-only; they should not be editable. Also, we'd like entries in the "Hot?" column to be checkboxes instead of words. Finally, it would be nice if the "Weight" column were formatted appropriately for numbers rather than for text.

To achieve more flexibility with `JTable`, we'll write our own data model by implementing the `TableModel` interface. Fortunately, Swing makes this easy by supplying a class that does most of the work, `AbstractTableModel`. To create a table model, we'll just subclass `AbstractTableModel` and override whatever behavior we want to change.

At a minimum, all `AbstractTableModel` subclasses have to define the following three methods.

```
public int getRowCount()
public int getColumnCount()
```
These methods return the number of rows and columns in this data model.

```
public Object getValueAt(int row, int column)
```
This method returns the value for the given cell.

When the JTable needs data values, it calls the getValueAt() method in the table model. To get an idea of the total size of the table, JTable calls the getRowCount() and getColumnCount() methods in the table model.

A very simple table model looks like this:

```
public static class ShipTableModel extends AbstractTableModel {
    private Object[][] data = new Object[][] {
        { "100420", Boolean.FALSE, "Des Moines IA", "Spokane WA",
            "02/06/2000", new Float(450) },
        { "202174", Boolean.TRUE, "Basking Ridge NJ", "Princeton NJ",
            "05/20/2000", new Float(1250) },
        { "450877", Boolean.TRUE, "St. Paul MN", "Austin TX",
            "03/20/2000", new Float(1745) },
        { "101891", Boolean.FALSE, "Boston MA", "Albany NY",
            "04/04/2000", new Float(88) }
    };

    public int getRowCount() { return data.length; }
    public int getColumnCount() { return data[0].length; }

    public Object getValueAt(int row, int column) {
        return data[row][column];
    }
}
```

We'd like to use the same column headings we used in the previous example. The table model supplies these through a method called getColumnName(). We could add column headings to our simple table model like this:

```
private String[] headings = new String[] {
    "Number", "Hot?", "Origin", "Destination", "Ship Date", "Weight"
};

public String getColumnName(int column) {
    return headings[column];
}
```

By default, AbstractTableModel makes all its cells non-editable, which is what we wanted. No changes need to be made for this.

The final modification is to have the "Hot?" column and the "Weight" column show up formatted specially. To do this, we give our table model some knowledge about the column types. JTable automatically generates checkbox cells for Boolean column types and specially formatted number cells for Number types. To give the table model some intelligence about its column types, we override the getColumnClass() method. The JTable calls this method to determine the data type of each column. It may then represent the data in a special way. This table model returns the class of the item in the first row of its data:

```
public Class getColumnClass(int column) {
  return data[0][column].getClass();
}
```

That's really all there is to do. The following complete example illustrates how you can use your own table model to create a JTable, using the techniques just described. The running application is shown in Figure 15-8.

```
//file: ShipTable.java
import java.awt.*;
import java.awt.event.*;
import javax.swing.*;
import javax.swing.table.*;

public class ShipTable {
  public static class ShipTableModel extends AbstractTableModel {
    private String[] headings = new String[] {
      "Number", "Hot?", "Origin", "Destination", "Ship Date", "Weight"
    };
    private Object[][] data = new Object[][] {
      { "100420", Boolean.FALSE, "Des Moines IA", "Spokane WA",
          "02/06/2000", new Float(450) },
      { "202174", Boolean.TRUE, "Basking Ridge NJ", "Princeton NJ",
          "05/20/2000", new Float(1250) },
      { "450877", Boolean.TRUE, "St. Paul MN", "Austin TX",
          "03/20/2000", new Float(1745) },
      { "101891", Boolean.FALSE, "Boston MA", "Albany NY",
          "04/04/2000", new Float(88) }
    };

    public int getRowCount() { return data.length; }
    public int getColumnCount() { return data[0].length; }

    public Object getValueAt(int row, int column) {
      return data[row][column];
    }

    public String getColumnName(int column) {
      return headings[column];
    }

    public Class getColumnClass(int column) {
```

```
      return data[0][column].getClass();
    }
}

public static void main(String[] args) {
    // create a JFrame to hold the table
    JFrame f = new JFrame("ShipTable v1.0");
    f.addWindowListener(new WindowAdapter() {
      public void windowClosing(WindowEvent e) { System.exit(0); }
    });
    f.setSize(500, 200);
    f.setLocation(200, 200);

    // create the data model and the JTable
    TableModel model = new ShipTableModel();
    JTable table = new JTable(model);

    table.setAutoResizeMode(JTable.AUTO_RESIZE_OFF);

    // put it all together
    f.getContentPane().add(new JScrollPane(table));
    f.setVisible(true);
  }
}
```

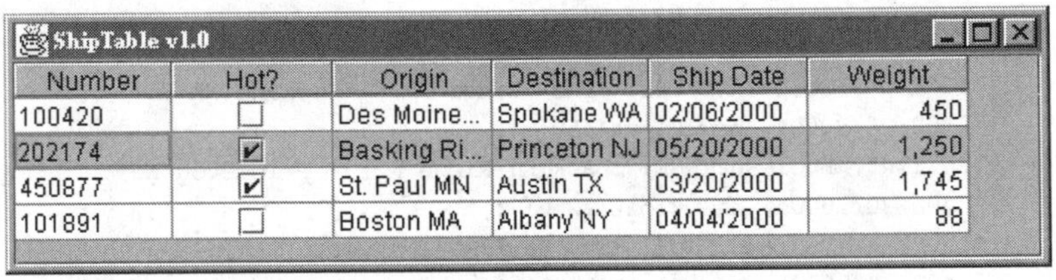

Number	Hot?	Origin	Destination	Ship Date	Weight
100420	☐	Des Moine...	Spokane WA	02/06/2000	450
202174	☑	Basking Ri...	Princeton NJ	05/20/2000	1,250
450877	☑	St. Paul MN	Austin TX	03/20/2000	1,745
101891	☐	Boston MA	Albany NY	04/04/2000	88

Figure 15-8. Customizing a table

Round Three: A Simple Spreadsheet

To illustrate just how powerful and flexible the separation of the data model from the GUI can be, we'll show a more complex model. In the following example, we'll implement a very slim but functional spreadsheet (see Figure 15-9) using almost no customization of the JTable. All of the data processing is in a TableModel called SpreadSheetModel.

Our spreadsheet will do the expected stuff—allowing you to enter numbers or mathematical expression like (A1*B2)+C3 into each cell. All of the cell editing and updating is driven by the standard JTable. We implement the methods necessary to set and retrieve cell data. Of course we don't do any real validation here, so it's easy to break our table. (For example, there is no check for circular dependencies, which may be undesirable.)

As you will see, the bulk of the code in this example is in the inner class used to parse the value of the equations in the cells. If you don't find this part interesting you might want to skip ahead. But if you have never seen an example of this kind of parsing before, we think you will find it to be very cool. Through the magic of recursion and Java's powerful String manipulation, it will take us only about fifty lines of code to implement a parser capable of handling basic arithmetic with arbitrarily nested parentheses.*

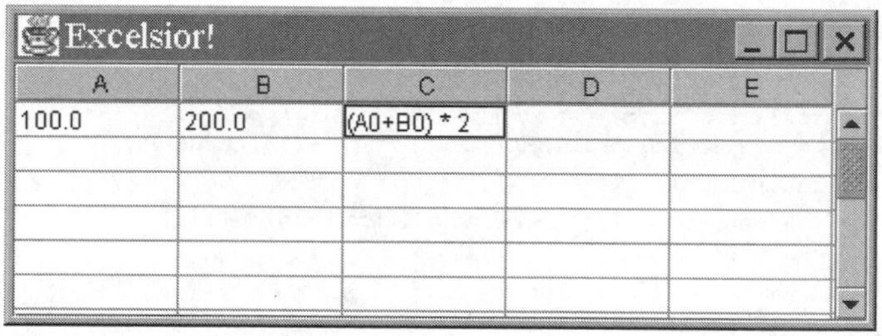

Figure 15-9. A simple spreadsheet

Here is the code:

```
//file: SpreadsheetModel.java
import java.util.StringTokenizer;
import javax.swing.*;
import javax.swing.table.AbstractTableModel;
import java.awt.event.*;

public class SpreadsheetModel extends AbstractTableModel {
  Expression [][] data;

  public SpreadsheetModel( int rows, int cols ) {
    data = new Expression [rows][cols];
  }

  public void setValueAt(Object value, int row, int col) {
    data[row][col] = new Expression( (String)value );
    fireTableDataChanged();
  }

  public Object getValueAt( int row, int col ) {
    if ( data[row][col] != null )
```

---

* You may need to double-click on a cell to edit it.

```
        try { return data[row][col].eval() + ""; }
        catch ( BadExpression e ) { return "Error"; }
      return "";
  }
  public int getRowCount() { return data.length; }
  public int getColumnCount() { return data[0].length; }
  public boolean isCellEditable(int row, int col) { return true; }

  class Expression {
    String text;
    StringTokenizer tokens;
    String token;

    Expression( String text ) { this.text = text.trim(); }

    float eval() throws BadExpression {
      tokens = new StringTokenizer( text, " */+-()", true );
      try { return sum(); }
      catch ( Exception e ) { throw new BadExpression(); }
    }

    private float sum() {
      float value = term();
      while( more() && match("+-") )
        if ( match("+") ) { consume(); value = value + term(); }
        else { consume(); value = value - term(); }
      return value;
    }
    private float term() {
      float value = element();
      while( more() && match( "*/") )
        if ( match("*") ) { consume(); value = value * element(); }
        else { consume(); value = value / element(); }
      return value;
    }
    private float element() {
      float value;
      if ( match( "(") ) { consume(); value = sum(); }
      else {
        String svalue;
        if ( Character.isLetter( token().charAt(0) ) ) {
          int col = findColumn( token().charAt(0) + "" );
          int row = Character.digit( token().charAt(1), 10 );
          svalue = (String)getValueAt( row, col );
        } else
          svalue = token();
        value = Float.valueOf( svalue ).floatValue();;
      }
      consume(); // ")" or value token
```

```
        return value;
      }
      private String token() {
        if ( token == null )
          while ( (token=tokens.nextToken()).equals(" ") );
        return token;
      }
      private void consume() { token = null; }
      private boolean match( String s ) { return s.indexOf( token() )!=-1; }
      private boolean more() { return tokens.hasMoreTokens(); }
    }

    class BadExpression extends Exception { }

    public static void main( String [] args ) {
      JFrame frame = new JFrame("Excelsior!");
      frame.addWindowListener(new WindowAdapter() {
        public void windowClosing(WindowEvent we) { System.exit(0); }
      });
      JTable table = new JTable( new SpreadsheetModel(15, 5) );
      table.setPreferredScrollableViewportSize(
          table.getPreferredSize() );
      table.setCellSelectionEnabled(true);
      frame.getContentPane().add( new JScrollPane( table ) );
      frame.pack(); frame.show();
    }
  }
```

Our model extends `AbstractTableModel` and overrides just a few methods. As you can see, our data is stored in a two-dimensional array of `Expression` objects. The `setValueAt()` method of our model creates `Expression` objects from the strings typed by the user and stores them in the array. The `getValueAt()` method returns a value for a cell by calling the expression's `eval()` method. If the user enters some invalid text in a cell, a `BadExpression` exception is thrown and the word "error" is placed in the cell as a value. The only other methods of `TableModel` that we must override are `getRowCount()`, `getColumnCount()` and `isCellEditable()` to determine the dimensions of the spreadsheet and to allow the user to edit the fields. That's it!

Now on to the good stuff. We'll employ our old friend `StringTokenizer` to read the expression string as separate values and the mathematical symbols +-*/() one by one. These tokens will then be processed by the three parser methods: `sum()`, `term()`, and `element()`. The methods call one another generally in that order (from the top down), but it might be easier to read them in reverse to see what's happening.

At the bottom level, element() reads individual numeric values or cell names, e.g., 5.0 or B2. Above that, the term() method operates on the values supplied by element() and applies any multiplication or division operations. And at the top, sum() operates on the values that are returned by term() and applies addition or subtraction to them. If the element() method encounters parentheses, it makes a call to sum() to handle the nested expression. Eventually the nested sum will return (possibly after further recursion) and the parenthesized expression will have been reduced to a single value, which is returned by element(). The magic of recursion has untangled the nesting for us. The other small piece of magic here is in the ordering of the three parser methods. Having sum() call term() and term() call element() imposes the precedence of operators; i.e., "atomic" values are parsed first (at the bottom), then multiplications happen, and finally addition or subtraction of terms is applied.

The grammar parsing relies on four simple helper methods; token(), consume( ), match(), and more() make the code more manageable. token() calls the string tokenizer to get the next value and match() compares it with a specified value. consume() is used to move to the next token, and more() indicates when the final token has been processed.

Desktops

At this point, you might be thinking that there's nothing more that Swing could possibly do. But it just keeps getting better. If you've ever wished that you could have windows within windows in Java, Swing now makes it possible with JDesktopPane and JInternalFrame. Figure 15-10 shows how this works.

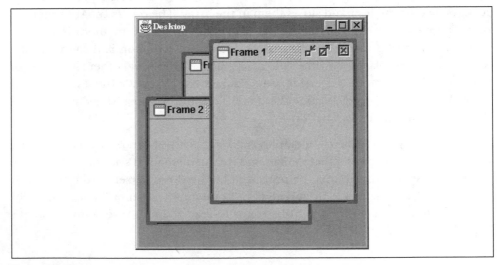

Figure 15-10. Using internal frames on a JDesktopPane

You get a lot of behavior for free from `JInternalFrame`. Internal frames can be moved by clicking and dragging the title bar. They can be resized by clicking and dragging on the window's borders. Internal frames can be iconified, which means reducing them to a small icon representation on the desktop. Internal frames may also be made to fit the entire size of the desktop (maximized). To you, the programmer, the internal frame is just a kind of special container. You can put your application's data inside an internal frame.

The following brief example shows how to create the windows shown in Figure 15-10.

```java
//file: Desktop.java
import java.awt.*;
import java.awt.event.*;
import javax.swing.*;
import javax.swing.border.*;

public class Desktop {
  public static void main(String[] args) {
    // create a JFrame to hold everything
    JFrame f = new JFrame("Desktop");
    f.addWindowListener(new WindowAdapter() {
      public void windowClosing(WindowEvent we) { System.exit(0); }
    });
    f.setSize(300, 300);
    f.setLocation(200, 200);

    JDesktopPane desktop = new JDesktopPane();
    for (int i = 0; i < 5; i++) {
      JInternalFrame internal =
          new JInternalFrame("Frame " + i, true, true, true, true);
      internal.setSize(180, 180);
      internal.setLocation(i * 20, i * 20);
      internal.setVisible(true);
      desktop.add(internal);
    }

    f.setContentPane(desktop);
    f.setVisible(true);
  }
}
```

All we've done here is to create a `JDesktopPane` and add internal frames to it. When each `JInternalFrame` is constructed, we specify a window title. The four `true` values passed in the constructor specify that the new window should be resizable, closable, maximizable, and iconifiable.

`JInternalFrames` fire off their own set of events. However, `InternalFrame-Event` and `InternalFrameListener` are just like `WindowEvent` and `Window-Listener`, with the names changed. If you want to hear about a `JInternalFrame` closing, just register an `InternalFrameListener` and define the `internal-FrameClosing()` method. This is just like defining the `windowClosing()` method for a `JFrame`.

Pluggable Look-and-Feel

We mentioned before that Swing's peerless components can easily change their appearance, like master spies or thespians. Generally, different kinds of components have appearances that are similar in some way. For example, they probably use the same font and the same basic color scheme. The collection of appearances for different components is called a look-and-feel (L&F).

Part of the job of designing a GUI for an operating system is designing the L&F. MacOS, therefore, has its own distinctive L&F, as does Windows. Java 2 offers not one, not two, but three different L&F schemes for Swing components. If you're adept at graphic design, you can write your own L&F schemes and easily convince Swing to use them. This chameleon-like ability to change appearance is called *pluggable look-and-feel*, sometimes abbreviated PLAF.

Seeing is believing. Here's an example that creates a handful of Swing components. Menu items allow you to change the L&F dynamically, as the application is running:

```
//file: QuickChange.java
import java.awt.*;
import java.awt.event.*;
import javax.swing.*;

public class QuickChange extends JFrame {

  public QuickChange() {
    super("QuickChange v1.0");
    createUI();
    setVisible(true);
  }

  protected void createUI() {
    setSize(300, 200);
    setLocation(200, 200);

    // create a simple File menu
    JMenu file = new JMenu("File", true);
    JMenuItem quit = new JMenuItem("Quit");
    file.add(quit);
```

```
      quit.addActionListener(new ActionListener() {
        public void actionPerformed(ActionEvent e) { System.exit(0); }
      });

      // create the Look & Feel menu
      JMenu lnf = new JMenu("Look & Feel", true);
      ButtonGroup buttonGroup = new ButtonGroup();
      final UIManager.LookAndFeelInfo[] info =
          UIManager.getInstalledLookAndFeels();
      for (int i = 0; i < info.length; i++) {
        JRadioButtonMenuItem item = new
            JRadioButtonMenuItem(info[i].getName(), i == 0);
        final String className = info[i].getClassName();
        item.addActionListener(new ActionListener() {
          public void actionPerformed(ActionEvent ae) {
            try { UIManager.setLookAndFeel(className); }
            catch (Exception e) { System.out.println(e); }
            SwingUtilities.updateComponentTreeUI(QuickChange.this);
          }
        });
        buttonGroup.add(item);
        lnf.add(item);
      }

      // add the menu bar
      JMenuBar mb = new JMenuBar();
      mb.add(file);
      mb.add(lnf);
      setJMenuBar(mb);

      // add some components
      JPanel jp = new JPanel();
      jp.add(new JCheckBox("JCheckBox"));
      String[] names =
        new String[] { "Tosca", "Cavaradossi", "Scarpia",
                       "Angelotti", "Spoletta", "Sciarrone",
                       "Carceriere", "Il sagrestano", "Un pastore" };
      jp.add(new JComboBox(names));
      jp.add(new JButton("JButton"));
      jp.add(new JLabel("JLabel"));
      jp.add(new JTextField("JTextField"));
      JPanel main = new JPanel(new GridLayout(1, 2));
      main.add(jp);
      main.add(new JScrollPane(new JList(names)));
      setContentPane(main);
    }

  public static void main(String[] args) {
    JFrame f = new QuickChange();
```

```
      f.addWindowListener(new WindowAdapter() {
        public void windowClosing(WindowEvent e) { System.exit(0); }
      });
      f.setVisible(true);
    }
  }
```

The interesting part of this application is creating a menu of the available L& Fs. First, we ask a class called `UIManager` to tell us all about the available L&Fs on our computer:

```
final UIManager.LookAndFeelInfo[] info =
       UIManager.getInstalledLookAndFeels();
```

Information about L&Fs is returned as instances of `UIManager.LookAnd-FeelInfo`. Despite the long name, there's not much to this class—it just associates a name, like "Metal," and the name of the class that implements the L&F, like *javax.swing.plaf.metal.MetalLookAndFeel*. In the `QuickChange` example, we create a menu item from each L&F name. If the menu item is selected, we tell the `UIManager` to use the selected L&F class. Then, to make sure all the components are redrawn with the new L&F, we call a static method in the `SwingUtilities` class called `updateComponentTreeUI()`.

The regular SDK includes three L&Fs, one that resembles Windows, one that resembles Motif, and an entirely new L&F called Metal. Metal is used by default; you've been staring at it through all the examples in this chapter and the last chapter.

If you're running Swing on MacOS, there's a MacOS L&F you can install and use. It does not, however, run on any other platforms.

Creating Custom Components

In this chapter and the previous chapter, we've worked with many different user interface objects and made a lot of new classes that are sort of like components. Our new classes do one particular thing well; a number of them can be added to applets or other containers just like the standard Swing components; and several of them are lightweight components that use system resources efficiently because they don't rely on a peer. But we haven't created new components; we've just used Swing's impressive repertoire of components as building blocks. In this section, we'll create an entirely new component, a *dial*.

Up until now, our new classes still haven't really been components. If you think about it, all our classes have been fairly self-contained; they know everything about what to do and don't rely on other parts of the program to do much processing. Therefore, they are overly specialized. Our menu example created a `DinnerFrame` class that had a menu of dinner options, but it included all the processing needed to handle the user's selections. If we wanted to process the selections differently, we'd have to modify the class. A true component separates the detection of user choices from the processing of those choices. It lets the user take some action and then calls another part of the program to process the action.

Generating Events

So we need a way for our new classes to communicate with other parts of the program. Since we want our new classes to be components, they should communicate the way components communicate: by generating event objects and sending those events to listeners. So far, we've written a lot of code that listened for events but haven't seen any examples that generated its own custom events.

Generating events sounds like it ought to be difficult, but it isn't. You can either create new kinds of events by subclassing `java.util.EventObject`, or use one of the standard event types. In either case, you need to register listeners for your events and provide a means to deliver events to your listeners. Swing's `JComponent` class provides a protected member variable, `listenerList`, that you can use to keep track of event listeners. It's an instance of `EventListenerList`; basically it acts like the maître d' at a restaurant, keeping track of all event listeners, sorted by type.

Often, you won't event need to worry about creating a custom event type. `JComponent` has methods that support firing off `PropertyChangeEvents` whenever one of the component's properties changes. The example we'll look at next uses this infrastructure to fire `PropertyChangeEvents` whenever a value changes.

A Dial Component

The standard Swing classes don't have a component that's similar to an old fashioned dial—for example, the volume control on your radio. In this section, we implement a `Dial` class. The dial has a value that can be adjusted by clicking and dragging to "twist" the dial. As the value of the dial changes, `DialEvents` are fired off by the component. The dial can be used just like any other Java component. We even have a custom `DialListener` interface that matches the `DialEvent` class. Figure 15-11 shows what the dial looks like; it is followed by the `Dial` code.

```
//file: Dial.java
import java.awt.*;
import java.awt.event.*;
import java.beans.*;
import java.util.*;
import javax.swing.*;
```

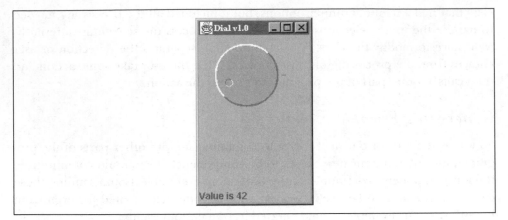

Figure 15-11. The Dial component

```java
public class Dial extends JComponent {
  int minValue, value, maxValue, radius;

  public Dial() { this(0, 100, 0); }

  public Dial(int minValue, int maxValue, int value) {
    this.minValue = minValue;
    this.maxValue = maxValue;
    this.value = value;
    setForeground(Color.lightGray);

    addMouseListener(new MouseAdapter() {
      public void mousePressed(MouseEvent e) { spin(e); }
    });
    addMouseMotionListener(new MouseMotionAdapter() {
      public void mouseDragged(MouseEvent e) { spin(e); }
    });
  }

  protected void spin(MouseEvent e) {
    int y = e.getY();
    int x = e.getX();
    double th = Math.atan((1.0 * y - radius) / (x - radius));
    int value=((int)(th / (2 * Math.PI) * (maxValue - minValue)));
    if (x < radius)
      setValue(value + maxValue / 2);
    else if (y < radius)
      setValue(value + maxValue);
    else
      setValue(value);
  }

  public void paintComponent(Graphics g) {
```

```
      Graphics2D g2 = (Graphics2D)g;
      int tick = 10;
      radius = getSize().width / 2 - tick;
      g2.setPaint(getForeground().darker());
      g2.drawLine(radius * 2 + tick / 2, radius,
          radius * 2 + tick, radius);
      g2.setStroke(new BasicStroke(2));
      draw3DCircle(g2, 0, 0, radius, true);
      int knobRadius = radius / 7;
      double th = value * (2 * Math.PI) / (maxValue - minValue);
      int x = (int)(Math.cos(th) * (radius - knobRadius * 3)),
      y = (int)(Math.sin(th) * (radius - knobRadius * 3));
      g2.setStroke(new BasicStroke(1));
      draw3DCircle(g2, x + radius - knobRadius,
                  y + radius - knobRadius, knobRadius, false );
   }


   private void draw3DCircle( Graphics g, int x, int y,
                              int radius, boolean raised) {
     Color foreground = getForeground();
     Color light = foreground.brighter();
     Color dark = foreground.darker();
     g.setColor(foreground);
     g.fillOval(x, y, radius * 2, radius * 2);
     g.setColor(raised ? light : dark);
     g.drawArc(x, y, radius * 2, radius * 2, 45, 180);
     g.setColor(raised ? dark : light);
     g.drawArc(x, y, radius * 2, radius * 2, 225, 180);
   }


   public Dimension getPreferredSize() {
     return new Dimension(100, 100);
   }


   public void setValue(int value) {
     firePropertyChange( "value", this.value, value );
     this.value = value;
     repaint();
     fireEvent();
   }
   public int getValue()  { return value; }
   public void setMinimum(int minValue)  { this.minValue = minValue; }
   public int getMinimum()  { return minValue; }
   public void setMaximum(int maxValue)  { this.maxValue = maxValue; }
   public int getMaximum()  { return maxValue; }


   public void addDialListener(DialListener listener) {
     listenerList.add( DialListener.class, listener );
   }
```

```java
    public void removeDialListener(DialListener listener) {
      listenerList.remove( DialListener.class, listener );
    }

    void fireEvent() {
      Object[] listeners = listenerList.getListenerList();
      for ( int i = 0; i < listeners.length; i += 2 )
        if ( listeners[i] == DialListener.class )
          ((DialListener)listeners[i + 1]).dialAdjusted(
            new DialEvent(this, value) );
    }

    public static void main(String[] args) {
      JFrame f = new JFrame("Dial v1.0");
      f.addWindowListener( new WindowAdapter() {
        public void windowClosing(WindowEvent e) { System.exit(0); }
      });
      f.setSize(150, 150);

      final JLabel statusLabel = new JLabel("Welcome to Dial v1.0");
      final Dial dial = new Dial();
      JPanel dialPanel = new JPanel();
      dialPanel.add(dial);
      f.getContentPane().add(dialPanel, BorderLayout.CENTER);
      f.getContentPane().add(statusLabel, BorderLayout.SOUTH);

      dial.addDialListener(new DialListener() {
        public void dialAdjusted(DialEvent e) {
          statusLabel.setText("Value is " + e.getValue());
        }
      });
      f.setVisible( true );
    }
  }
```

Here's DialEvent, a simple subclass of java.util.EventObject:

```java
//file: DialEvent.java
import java.awt.*;

public class DialEvent extends java.util.EventObject {
    int value;

    DialEvent( Dial source, int value ) {
        super( source );
        this.value = value;
    }

    public int getValue() {
```

```
                    return value;
            }
        }
```

Finally, here's the code for `DialListener`:

```
//file: DialListener.java
public interface DialListener extends java.util.EventListener {
    void dialAdjusted( DialEvent e );
}
```

Let's start from the top of the `Dial` class. We'll focus on the structure and leave you to figure out the trigonometry on your own.

`Dial`'s `main()` method demonstrates how to use the dial to build a user interface. It creates a `Dial` and adds it to a `JFrame`. Then `main()` registers a dial listener on the dial. Whenever a `DialEvent` is received, the value of the dial is examined and displayed in a `JLabel` at the bottom of the frame window.

The constructor for the Dial class stores the dial's minimum, maximum, and current values; a default constructor provides a minimum of 0, a maximum of 100, and a current value of 0. The constructor sets the foreground color of the dial and registers listeners for mouse events. If the mouse is pressed or dragged, `Dial`'s `spin()` method is called to update the dial's value. `spin()` performs some basic trigonometry to figure out what the new value of the dial should be.

`paintComponent()` and `draw3DCircle()` do a lot of trigonometry to figure out how to display the dial. `draw3DCircle()` is a private helper method that draws a circle that appears either raised or depressed; we use this to make the dial look three-dimensional.

The next group of methods provides ways to retrieve or change the dial's current setting and the minimum and maximum values. The important thing to notice here is the pattern of "getter" and "setter" methods for all of the important values used by the `Dial`. We will talk more about this in Chapter 19, *Java Beans*. Also, notice that the `setValue()` method does two important things: it repaints the component to reflect the new value and fires an event signifying the change.

If you examine `setValue()` closely, you'll notice that `Dial` actually fires off two events when its value changes. The first of these is a `PropertyChangeEvent`, a standard event type in the Java Beans architecture. The second event is our custom `DialEvent` type.

The final group of methods in the `Dial` class provide the plumbing that is necessary for event firing. `addDialListener()` and `removeDialListener()` take care of maintaining the listener list. Using the `listenerList` member variable we inherited from `JComponent` makes this an easy task. The `fireEvent()` method retrieves the registered listeners for this component. It sends a `DialEvent` to any registered `DialListeners`.

Model and View Separation

The `Dial` example is overly simplified. All Swing components, as we've discussed, keep their data model and view separate. In the `Dial` component, we've combined these elements in a single class, which limits its reusability. To have `Dial` implement the MVC paradigm, we would have developed a dial data model and something called a UI-delegate that handled displaying the component and responding to user events. For a full treatment of this subject, see the `JogShuttle` example in *Java Swing*, by Robert Eckstein, Marc Loy, and Dave Wood (O'Reilly & Associates).

16

Layout Managers

A *layout manager* arranges the child components of a container, as shown in Figure 16-1. It positions and sets the size of components within the container's display area according to a particular layout scheme. The layout manager's job is to fit the components into the available area while maintaining the proper spatial relationships among the components. Swing comes with a few standard layout managers that will collectively handle most situations; you can make your own layout managers if you have special requirements.

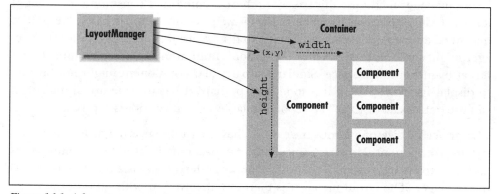

Figure 16-1. A layout manager at work

Every container has a default layout manager; therefore, when you make a new container, it comes with a LayoutManager object of the appropriate type. You can install a new layout manager at any time with the setLayout() method. For example, we can set the layout manager of a container to a BorderLayout:

```
setLayout (new BorderLayout());
```

Notice that we call the `BorderLayout` constructor, but we don't even save a reference to the layout manager. This is typical; once you have installed a layout manager, it does its work behind the scenes, interacting with the container. You rarely call the layout manager's methods directly, so you don't usually need a reference (a notable exception is `CardLayout`). However, you do need to know what the layout manager is going to do with your components as you work with them.

The `LayoutManager` is consulted whenever a container's `doLayout()` method is called to reorganize the contents. It does its job by calling the `setLocation()` and `setBounds()` methods of the individual child components to arrange them in the container's display area. A container is laid out the first time it is displayed, and thereafter whenever the container's `revalidate()` method is called. Containers that are a subclass of the `Window` class (`Frame`, `JFrame`, and `JWindow`) are automatically validated whenever they are packed or resized. Calling `pack()` sets the window's size as small as possible while holding all its components at their preferred sizes.

Every component determines three important pieces of information used by the layout manager in placing and sizing it: a minimum size, a maximum size, and a preferred size. These sizes are reported by the `getMinimumSize()`, `getMaximumSize()`, and `getPreferredSize()` methods of `Component`, respectively. For example, a plain `JButton` object can normally be changed to any size. However, the button's designer can provide a preferred size for a good-looking button. The layout manager might use this size when there are no other constraints, or it might ignore it, depending on its scheme. Now if we give the button a label, the button may need a new minimum size in order to display itself properly. The layout manager might show more respect for the button's minimum size and guarantee that it has at least that much space. Similarly, a particular component might not be able to display itself properly if it is too large (perhaps it has to scale up an image); it can use `getMaximumSize()` to report the largest size it considers acceptable.

The preferred size of a `Container` object has the same meaning as for any other type of component. However, since a `Container` may hold its own components and want to arrange them in its own layout, its preferred size is a function of its layout manager. The layout manager is therefore involved in both sides of the issue. It asks the components in its container for their preferred (or minimum) sizes in order to arrange them. Based on those values, it calculates the preferred size of its own container (which can be communicated to the container's parent).

When a layout manager is called to arrange its components, it is working within a fixed area. It usually begins by looking at its container's dimensions, and the preferred or minimum sizes of the child components. It then doles out screen area and sets the sizes of components according to its scheme. You can override the `getMinimumSize()`, `getMaximumSize()`, and `getPreferredSize()` methods of a component, but you should do this only if you are actually specializing the component, and it has new needs. If you find yourself fighting with a layout manager because it's changing the size of one of your components, you are probably using the wrong kind of layout manager or not composing your user interface properly. Remember that it's possible to use a number of JPanel objects in a given display, each one with its own LayoutManager. Try breaking down the problem: place related components in their own JPanel and then arrange the panels in the container. When that becomes too complicated, you can choose to use a constraint-based layout manager like GridBagLayout, which we'll discuss later in this chapter.

FlowLayout

FlowLayout is a simple layout manager that tries to arrange components with their preferred sizes, from left to right and top to bottom in the container. A FlowLayout can have a specified row justification of LEFT, CENTER, or RIGHT, and a fixed horizontal and vertical padding. By default, a flow layout uses CENTER justification, meaning that all components are centered within the area allotted to them. FlowLayout is the default for JPanels.

The following example adds five buttons to the content pane of a JFrame using the default FlowLayout; the result is shown in Figure 16-2.

```java
//file: Flow.java
import java.awt.*;
import java.awt.event.*;
import javax.swing.*;

public class Flow extends JPanel {

  public Flow() {
    // FlowLayout is default layout manager for a JPanel
    add(new JButton("One"));
    add(new JButton("Two"));
    add(new JButton("Three"));
    add(new JButton("Four"));
    add(new JButton("Five"));
  }

  public static void main(String[] args) {
    JFrame f = new JFrame("Flow");
    f.addWindowListener(new WindowAdapter() {
      public void windowClosing(WindowEvent e) { System.exit(0); }
    });
    f.setSize(400, 75);
    f.setLocation(200, 200);
```

```
        Flow flow = new Flow();
        f.setContentPane(flow);
        f.setVisible(true);
    }
}
```

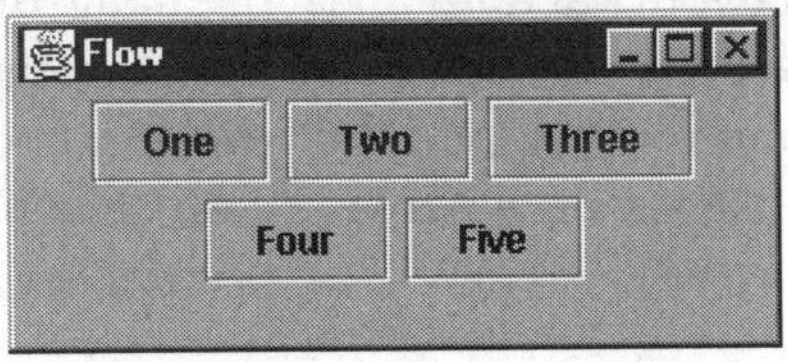

Figure 16-2. A flow layout

If the window is narrow enough, some of the buttons will spill over to a second or third row.

GridLayout

GridLayout arranges components into regularly spaced rows and columns. The components are arbitrarily resized to fit the grid; their minimum and preferred sizes are consequently ignored. GridLayout is most useful for arranging identically sized objects—perhaps a set of JPanels, each using a different layout manager.

GridLayout takes the number of rows and columns in its constructor. If you subsequently give it too many objects to manage, it adds extra columns to make the objects fit. You can also set the number of rows or columns to zero, which means that you don't care how many elements the layout manager packs in that dimension. For example, GridLayout(2,0) requests a layout with two rows and an unlimited number of columns; if you put ten components into this layout, you'll get two rows of five columns each.*

The following example sets a GridLayout with three rows and two columns as its layout manager; the results are shown in Figure 16-3.

```
//file: Grid.java
import java.awt.*;
import java.awt.event.*;
import javax.swing.*;

public class Grid extends JPanel {
```

---

* Calling new GridLayout(0, 0) causes a runtime exception; either the rows or columns parameter must be greater than zero.

```
   public Grid() {
     setLayout(new GridLayout(3, 2));
     add(new JButton("One"));
     add(new JButton("Two"));
     add(new JButton("Three"));
     add(new JButton("Four"));
     add(new JButton("Five"));
   }

   public static void main(String[] args) {
     JFrame f = new JFrame("Grid");
     f.addWindowListener(new WindowAdapter() {
       public void windowClosing(WindowEvent e) { System.exit(0); }
     });
     f.setSize(200, 200);
     f.setLocation(200, 200);
     f.setContentPane(new Grid());
     f.setVisible(true);
   }
 }
```

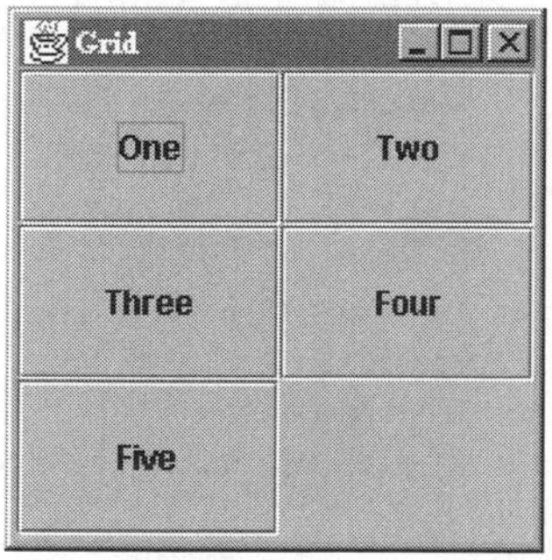

Figure 16-3. A grid layout

The five buttons are laid out, in order, from left to right, top to bottom, with one empty spot.

BorderLayout

BorderLayout is a little more interesting. It tries to arrange objects in one of five geographical locations, represented by constants in the BorderLayout class: NORTH, SOUTH, EAST, WEST, and CENTER, possibly with some padding between. BorderLayout is the default layout for the content panes of JWindow and JFrame objects. Because each component is associated with a direction, BorderLayout can manage at most five components; it squashes or stretches those components to fit its constraints. As we'll see in the second example, this means that you often want to have BorderLayout manage sets of components in their own panels.

When we add a component to a border layout, we need to specify both the component and the position at which to add it. To do so, we use an overloaded version of the add() method that takes an additional argument as a constraint. This specifies the name of a position within the BorderLayout.

The following application sets a BorderLayout layout and adds our five buttons again, named for their locations; the result is shown in Figure 16-4.

```java
//file: Border1.java
import java.awt.*;
import java.awt.event.*;
import javax.swing.*;

public class Border1 extends JPanel {

  public Border1() {
    setLayout(new BorderLayout());
    add(new JButton("North"), BorderLayout.NORTH);
    add(new JButton("South"), BorderLayout.SOUTH);
    add(new JButton("East"), BorderLayout.EAST);
    add(new JButton("West"), BorderLayout.WEST);
    add(new JButton("Center"), BorderLayout.CENTER);
  }

  public static void main(String[] args) {
    JFrame f = new JFrame("Border1");
    f.addWindowListener(new WindowAdapter() {
      public void windowClosing(WindowEvent e) { System.exit(0); }
    });
    f.setSize(300, 300);
    f.setLocation(200, 200);
    f.setContentPane(new Border1());
    f.setVisible(true);
  }
}
```

So, how exactly is the area divided up? Well, the objects at NORTH and SOUTH get their preferred height and fill the display area horizontally. EAST and WEST components, on the other hand, get their preferred width, and fill the remaining area between NORTH and SOUTH vertically. Finally, the CENTER object takes all of the rest of the space. As you can see in Figure 16-4, our buttons get distorted into interesting shapes.

What if we don't want BorderLayout messing with the sizes of our components? One option would be to put each button in its own JPanel. The default layout for

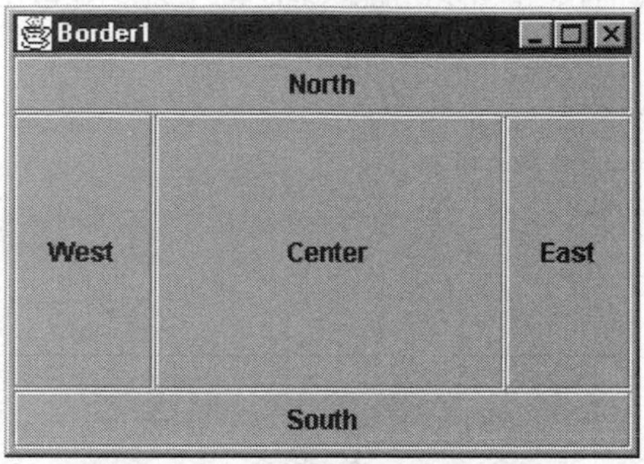

Figure 16-4. A border layout

a JPanel is FlowLayout, which respects the preferred size of components. The preferred sizes of the panels are effectively the preferred sizes of the buttons, but if the panels are stretched, they won't pull their buttons with them. The following application illustrates this approach; the result is shown in Figure 16-5.

```java
//file: Border2.java
import java.awt.*;
import java.awt.event.*;
import javax.swing.*;

public class Border2 extends JPanel {

  public Border2() {
    setLayout(new BorderLayout());
    JPanel p = new JPanel();
    p.add(new JButton("North"));
    add(p, BorderLayout.NORTH);
    p = new JPanel();
    p.add(new JButton("South"));
    add(p, BorderLayout.SOUTH);
    p = new JPanel();
    p.add(new JButton("East"));
    add(p, BorderLayout.EAST);
    p = new JPanel();
    p.add(new JButton("West"));
    add(p, BorderLayout.WEST);
    p = new JPanel();
    p.add(new JButton("Center"));
    add(p, BorderLayout.CENTER);
  }

  public static void main(String[] args) {
    JFrame f = new JFrame("Border2");
    f.addWindowListener(new WindowAdapter() {
```

```
        public void windowClosing(WindowEvent e) { System.exit(0); }
    });
    f.setSize(225, 150);
    f.setLocation(200, 200);
    f.setContentPane(new Border2());
    f.setVisible(true);
    }
}
```

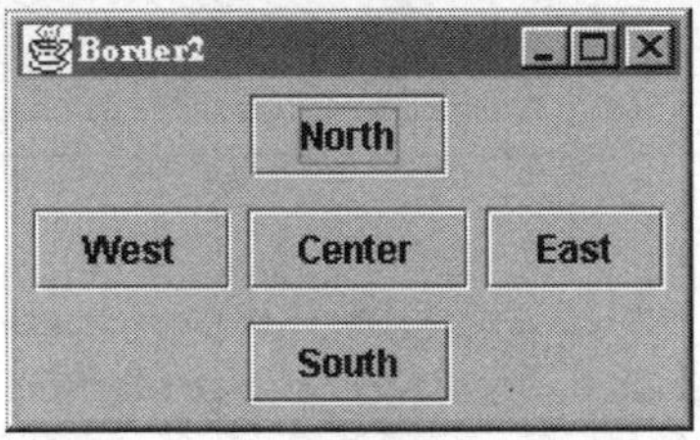

Figure 16-5. Another border layout

In this example, we create a number of panels, put our buttons inside the panels, and put the panels into the frame window, which has the BorderLayout manager. Now, the JPanel for the CENTER button soaks up the extra space that comes from the BorderLayout. Each JPanel's FlowLayout centers the button in the panel and uses the button's preferred size. In this case, it's all a bit awkward. We'll see how we could accomplish this more directly using GridBagLayout shortly.

BoxLayout

Most layout managers were defined back when Java 1.0 was first released. Swing adds only one new general-purpose layout manager, BoxLayout. This layout manager is useful for creating toolbars or vertical button bars. It lays out components in a single row or column.

Although you can use BoxLayout directly, Swing includes a handy container called Box that takes care of the details for you. Every Box uses BoxLayout, but you don't really have to worry about it; the Box class includes some very useful methods for laying out components.

You can create a horizontal or vertical box using Box's static methods.

```
Container horizontalBox = Box.createHorizontalBox();
Container verticalBox = Box.createVerticalBox();
```

Once the Box is created, you can just add() components as usual:

```
Container box = Box.createHorizontalBox();
box.add(new JButton("In the"));
```

Box includes several other static methods that create special invisible components that are handy for BoxLayout. The first of these is *glue*; glue is really space between components in the Box. When the Box is resized, glue expands or contracts as more or less space is available. The other special invisible component type is a *strut*. Like glue, a strut represents space between components, but it doesn't resize.

The following example creates a horizontal Box (shown in Figure 16-6) that includes both glue and struts. Play around by resizing the window to see the effect of the glue and the struts.

```java
//file: Boxer.java
import java.awt.*;
import java.awt.event.*;
import javax.swing.*;

public class Boxer extends JPanel {
  public static void main(String[] args) {
    JFrame f = new JFrame("Boxer");
    f.addWindowListener(new WindowAdapter() {
      public void windowClosing(WindowEvent e) { System.exit(0); }
    });
    f.setSize(250, 250);
    f.setLocation(200, 200);
    Container box = Box.createHorizontalBox();
    box.add(Box.createHorizontalGlue());
    box.add(new JButton("In the"));
    box.add(Box.createHorizontalGlue());
    box.add(new JButton("clearing"));
    box.add(Box.createHorizontalStrut(10));
    box.add(new JButton("stands"));
    box.add(Box.createHorizontalStrut(10));
    box.add(new JButton("a"));
    box.add(Box.createHorizontalGlue());
    box.add(new JButton("boxer"));
    box.add(Box.createHorizontalGlue());
    f.getContentPane().add(box, BorderLayout.CENTER);
    f.pack();
    f.setVisible(true);
  }
}
```

Figure 16-6. Using the Box class

CardLayout

CardLayout is a special layout manager for creating the effect of a stack of cards. Instead of arranging all of the container's components, it displays only one at a time. You might use this kind of layout to implement a hypercard stack or a Windows-style set of configuration screens. If CardLayout sounds interesting, you might also want to investigate the JTabbedPane component, described in Chapter 14, *Using Swing Components*.

To add a component to a CardLayout, use a two-argument version of the container's add() method; the extra argument is an arbitrary string that serves as the card's name:

```
add("netconfigscreen", myComponent);
```

To bring a particular card to the top of the stack, call the CardLayout's show() method with two arguments: the parent Container and the name of the card you want to show. There are also methods like first(), last(), next(), and previous() for working with the stack of cards. These are all CardLayout instance methods. To invoke them, you need a reference to the CardLayout object itself, not to the container it manages. Each method takes a single argument: the parent Container. Here's a simple example:

```java
//file: Card.java
import java.awt.*;
import java.awt.event.*;
import javax.swing.*;

public class Card extends JPanel {
  CardLayout cards = new CardLayout();

  public Card() {
    setLayout(cards);
    ActionListener listener = new ActionListener() {
      public void actionPerformed(ActionEvent e) {
        cards.next(Card.this);
      }
    };
    JButton button;
    button = new JButton("one");
    button.addActionListener(listener);
    add(button, "one");
    button = new JButton("two");
    button.addActionListener(listener);
    add(button, "two");
    button = new JButton("three");
    button.addActionListener(listener);
    add(button, "three");
```

```
        }

        public static void main(String[] args) {
          JFrame f = new JFrame("Card");
          f.addWindowListener(new WindowAdapter() {
            public void windowClosing(WindowEvent e) { System.exit(0); }
          });
          f.setSize(200, 200);
          f.setLocation(200, 200);
          f.setContentPane(new Card());
          f.setVisible(true);
        }
      }
```

We add three buttons to the layout and cycle through them as they are pressed. An anonymous inner class is used as an action listener for each button; it simply calls `CardLayout`'s `next()` method whenever a button is pressed. In a more realistic example, we would build a group of panels, each of which might implement some part of a complex user interface, and add those panels to the layout. Each panel would have its own layout manager. The panels would be resized to fill the entire area available (i.e., the area of the `Container` they are in), and their individual layout managers would arrange their internal components.

GridBagLayout

`GridBagLayout` is a very flexible layout manager that allows you to position components relative to one another using constraints. With `GridBagLayout` (and a fair amount of effort), you can create almost any imaginable layout. Components are arranged at logical coordinates on an abstract grid. We'll call them "logical" coordinates because they really designate positions in the space of rows and columns formed by the set of components. Rows and columns of the grid stretch to different sizes, based on the sizes and constraints of the components they hold.

A row or column in a `GridBagLayout` expands to accommodate the dimensions and constraints of the largest component it contains. Individual components may span more than one row or column. Components that aren't as large as their grid cell can be anchored within their cell. They can also be set to fill or to expand their size in either dimension. Extra area in the grid rows and columns can be parceled out according to the weight constraints of the components. In this way, you can control how various components will grow and stretch when a window is resized.

`GridBagLayout` is much easier to use in a graphical WYSIWYG GUI builder environment. That's because working with `GridBag` is kind of like messing with the "rabbit ears" antennae on your television. It's not particularly difficult to get the results that you want through trial and error, but writing out hard and fast rules for how to go about it is difficult. In short, GridBagLayout is complex and has some quirks. It is also simply a bit ugly both in model and implementation. Remember that you can do a lot with nested panels and by composing simpler layout managers within one another. If you look back through this chapter, you'll see many examples of composite layouts; it's up to you to determine how far you should go before making the break from simpler layout managers to a more complex all-in-one layout manager like GridBagLayout.

The GridBagConstraints Class

Having said that GridBagLayout is complex and a bit ugly, we're going to contradict ourselves and say that it's surprisingly simple. There is only one constructor with no arguments (GridBagLayout()), and there aren't a lot of fancy methods to control how the display works.

The appearance of a grid bag layout is controlled by sets of GridBag-Constraints, and that's where things get hairy. Each component managed by a GridBagLayout is associated with a GridBagConstraints object. GridBag-Constraints holds the following variables, which we'll describe in detail shortly:

int gridx, gridy
Controls the position of the component on the layout's grid.

int weightx, weighty
Controls how additional space in the row or column is allotted to the component.

int fill
Controls whether the component expands to fill the space alloted to it.

int gridheight, gridwidth
Controls the number of rows or columns the component spans.

int anchor
Controls the position of the component if there is extra room within the space alloted to it.

int ipadx, ipady
Controls padding between the component and the borders of its area.

Insets insets
Controls padding between the component and neighboring components.

To make a set of constraints for a component or components, create a new instance of GridBagConstraints and set these public variables to the appropriate values. There are no pretty constructors, and there's not much else to the class at all.

The easiest way to associate a set of constraints with a component is to use the version of add() that takes both a component object and a layout object as arguments. This puts the component in the container and associates the GridBagConstraints object with it:

```
Container content = getContentPane();
JComponent component = new JLabel("constrain me, please...");
GridBagConstraints constraints = new GridBagConstraints();
constraints.gridx = x;
constraints.gridy = y;
...
content.add(component, constraints);
```

You can also add a component to a GridBagLayout by using the single argument add() method, and then later calling the layout's setConstraints() method directly, to pass it the GridBagConstraints object for that component:

```
add(component);
...
myGridBagLayout.setConstraints(component, constraints);
```

In either case, the set of constraints is copied when it is applied to the component. It's the individual constraints that apply to the component, not the GridBagConstraints object. Therefore, you're free to create a single set of GridBagConstraints, modify it as needed, and apply it as needed to different objects. You might want to create a helper method that sets the constraints appropriately, then adds the component, with its constraints, to the layout. That's the approach we'll take in our examples; our helper method is called addGB(), and it takes a component plus a pair of coordinates as arguments. These coordinates become the gridx and gridy values for the constraints. We could expand upon this later and overload addGB() to take more parameters for other constraints that we often change from component to component.

Grid Coordinates

One of the biggest surprises in the GridBagLayout is that there's no way to specify the size of the grid. There doesn't have to be. The grid size is determined implicitly by the constraints of all the objects; the layout manager picks dimensions large enough so that everything fits. Thus, if you put one component in a layout and set its gridx and gridy constraints to 25, the layout manager creates a 25 × 25 grid, with rows and columns both numbered from 0 to 24. If you then add a second component with a gridx of 30 and a gridy of 13, the grid's dimensions change to 30 × 25. You don't have to worry about setting up an appropriate number of rows and columns. The layout manager does it automatically, as you add components.

With this knowledge, we're ready to create some simple displays. We'll start by arranging a group of components in a cross shape. We maintain explicit x and y local variables, setting them as we add the components to our grid. This is partly for clarity, but it can be a handy technique when you want to add a number of components in a row or column. You can simply increment gridx or gridy before adding each component. This is a simple and problem-free way to achieve relative placement. (Later, we'll describe GridBagConstraints's RELATIVE constant, which does relative placement automatically.) Here's our first layout (see Figure 16-7):

```java
//file: GridBag1.java
import java.awt.*;
import java.awt.event.*;
import javax.swing.*;

public class GridBag1 extends JPanel {
  GridBagConstraints constraints = new GridBagConstraints();

  public GridBag1() {
    setLayout(new GridBagLayout());
    int x, y;  // for clarity
    addGB(new JButton("North"),   x = 1, y = 0);
    addGB(new JButton("West"),    x = 0, y = 1);
    addGB(new JButton("Center"),  x = 1, y = 1);
    addGB(new JButton("East"),    x = 2, y = 1);
    addGB(new JButton("South"),   x = 1, y = 2);
  }

  void addGB(Component component, int x, int y) {
    constraints.gridx = x;
    constraints.gridy = y;
    add(component, constraints);
  }

  public static void main(String[] args) {
    JFrame f = new JFrame("GridBag1");
    f.addWindowListener(new WindowAdapter() {
      public void windowClosing(WindowEvent e) { System.exit(0); }
    });
    f.setSize(225, 150);
    f.setLocation(200, 200);
    f.setContentPane(new GridBag1());
    f.setVisible(true);
  }
}
```

The buttons in this example are "clumped" together in the center of their display area. Each button is displayed at its preferred size, without stretching to fill the

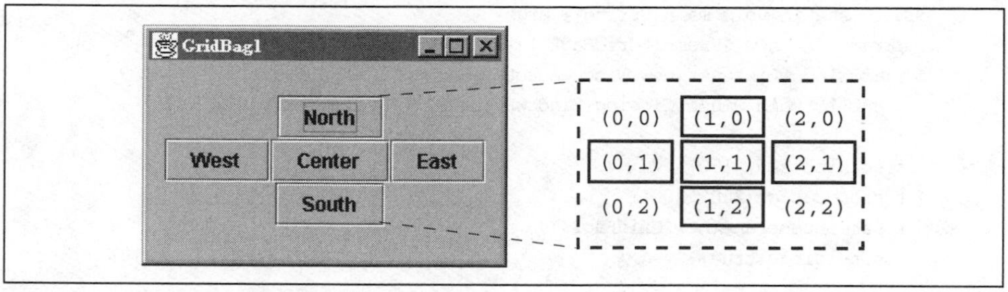

Figure 16-7. A simple GridBagLayout

available space. This is how the layout manager behaves when the "weight" constraints are left unset. We'll talk more about weights in the next two sections.

The fill Constraint

Let's make the buttons expand to fill the entire JFrame window. To do so, we must take two steps: we must set the fill constraint for each button to the value BOTH, and we must set the weightx and weighty to nonzero values, as shown in the following example. Figure 16-8 shows the resulting layout.

```java
//file: GridBag2.java
import java.awt.*;
import java.awt.event.*;
import javax.swing.*;

public class GridBag2 extends JPanel {
  GridBagConstraints constraints = new GridBagConstraints();

  public GridBag2() {
    setLayout(new GridBagLayout());
    constraints.weightx = 1.0;
    constraints.weighty = 1.0;
    constraints.fill = GridBagConstraints.BOTH;
    int x, y;  // for clarity
    addGB(new JButton("North"),  x = 1, y = 0);
    addGB(new JButton("West"),   x = 0, y = 1);
    addGB(new JButton("Center"), x = 1, y = 1);
    addGB(new JButton("East"),   x = 2, y = 1);
    addGB(new JButton("South"),  x = 1, y = 2);
  }

  void addGB(Component component, int x, int y) {
    constraints.gridx = x;
    constraints.gridy = y;
    add(component, constraints);
  }
```

```
    public static void main(String[] args) {
      JFrame f = new JFrame("GridBag2");
      f.addWindowListener(new WindowAdapter() {
        public void windowClosing(WindowEvent e) { System.exit(0); }
      });
      f.setSize(225, 150);
      f.setLocation(200, 200);
      f.setContentPane(new GridBag2());
      f.setVisible(true);
    }
  }
```

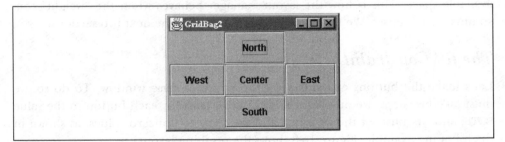

Figure 16-8. Making buttons fill the available space

BOTH is one of the constants of the GridBagConstraints class; it tells the component to fill the available space in both directions. Here are the constants you can use to set the fill field:

HORIZONTAL
    Fill the available horizontal space.

VERTICAL
    Fill the available vertical space.

BOTH
    Fill the available space in both directions.

NONE
    Don't fill the available space; display the component at its preferred size.

We set the weight constraints to 1.0; in this example it doesn't matter what they are, provided that each component has the same nonzero weight. Filling doesn't occur if the component weights in the direction you're filling are 0, which is the default value.

Spanning Rows and Columns

One of the most important features of GridBaglayout is that it lets you create arrangements in which components span two or more rows or columns. To do so, set the gridwidth and gridheight variables of the GridBagConstraints. Here's an example that creates such a display; button one spans two columns vertically, and button four spans two horizontally (see Figure 16-9):

```java
//file: GridBag3.java
import java.awt.*;
import java.awt.event.*;
import javax.swing.*;

public class GridBag3 extends JPanel {
  GridBagConstraints constraints = new GridBagConstraints();

  public GridBag3() {
    setLayout(new GridBagLayout());
    constraints.weightx = 1.0;
    constraints.weighty = 1.0;
    constraints.fill = GridBagConstraints.BOTH;
    int x, y;  // for clarity
    constraints.gridheight = 2; // span two rows
    addGB(new JButton("one"),   x = 0, y = 0);
    constraints.gridheight = 1; // set it back
    addGB(new JButton("two"),   x = 1, y = 0);
    addGB(new JButton("three"), x = 2, y = 0);
    constraints.gridwidth = 2; // span two columns
    addGB(new JButton("four"),  x = 1, y = 1);
    constraints.gridwidth = 1; // set it back
  }

  void addGB(Component component, int x, int y) {
    constraints.gridx = x;
    constraints.gridy = y;
    add(component, constraints);
  }

  public static void main(String[] args) {
    JFrame f = new JFrame("GridBag3");
    f.addWindowListener(new WindowAdapter() {
      public void windowClosing(WindowEvent e) { System.exit(0); }
    });
    f.setSize(200, 200);
    f.setLocation(200, 200);
    f.setContentPane(new GridBag3());
    f.setVisible(true);
  }
}
```

The size of each element is controlled by the gridwidth and gridheight values of its constraints. For button one, we set gridheight to 2. Therefore, it is two cells high; its gridx and gridy positions are both zero, so it occupies cell (0,0) and the

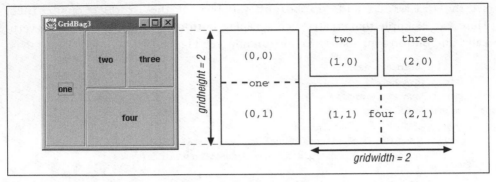

Figure 16-9. Making components span rows and columns

cell directly below it, (0,1). Likewise, button four has a `gridwidth` of 2 and a `gridheight` of 1, so it occupies two cells horizontally. We place this button in cell (1,1), so it occupies that cell and its neighbor, (2,1).

In this example, we set the `fill` to `BOTH` and `weightx` and `weighty` to 1 for all components. By doing so, we told each button to occupy all the space available. Strictly speaking, this isn't necessary. However, it makes it easier to see exactly how much space each button occupies.

Weighting

The `weightx` and `weighty` variables of a `GridBagConstraints` object determine how "extra" space in the container is distributed among the columns or rows in the layout. As long as you keep things simple, the effect these variables have is fairly intuitive: the larger the weight, the greater the amount of space allocated to the component. Figure 16-10 shows what happens if we vary the `weightx` constraint from 0.1 to 1.0 as we place three buttons in a row.

```
//file: GridBag4.java
import java.awt.*;
import java.awt.event.*;
import javax.swing.*;

public class GridBag4 extends JPanel {
  GridBagConstraints constraints = new GridBagConstraints();

  public GridBag4() {
    setLayout(new GridBagLayout());
    constraints.fill = GridBagConstraints.BOTH;
    constraints.weighty = 1.0;
    int x, y; // for clarity
    constraints.weightx = 0.1;
    addGB(new JButton("one"),    x = 0, y = 0);
    constraints.weightx = 0.5;
```

```
        addGB(new JButton("two"),    ++x,   y);
        constraints.weightx = 1.0;
        addGB(new JButton("three"), ++x,   y);
    }

    void addGB(Component component, int x, int y) {
      constraints.gridx = x;
      constraints.gridy = y;
      add(component, constraints);
    }

    public static void main(String[] args) {
      JFrame f = new JFrame("GridBag4");
      f.addWindowListener(new WindowAdapter() {
        public void windowClosing(WindowEvent e) { System.exit(0); }
      });
      f.setSize(300, 100);
      f.setLocation(200, 200);
      f.setContentPane(new GridBag4());
      f.setVisible(true);
    }
  }
```

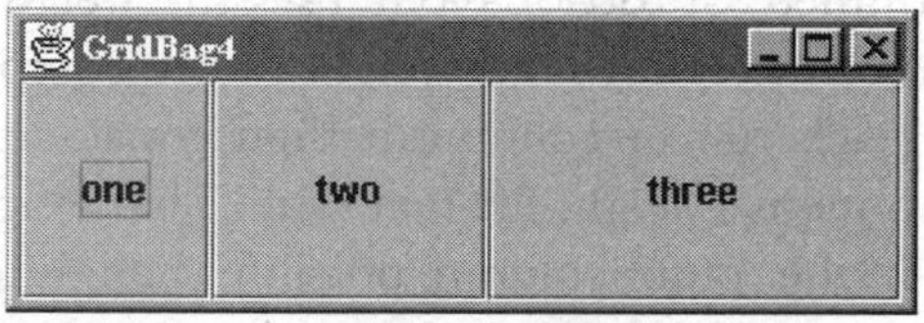

Figure 16-10. Using weight to control component size

The specific values of the weights are not meaningful; it is only their relative proportions that matter. After the preferred sizes of the components (including padding and insets—see the next section) are determined, any extra space is doled out in proportion to the component's weights. So, for example, if each of our three components had the same weight each would receive a third of the extra space. To make this more obvious, you may prefer to express the weights for a row or column as fractions totaling 1.0—for example: 0.25, 0.25, 0.50. Components with a weight of 0 receive no extra space.

The situation is a bit more complicated when there are multiple rows or columns and when there is even the possibility of components spanning more than one cell. In the general case, GridBagLayout calculates an effective overall weight for each for each row and each column and then distributes the extra space to them proportionally. Note that our single row example above is just a special case where the columns each have one component. The gory details of the calculations follow.

Calculating the weights of rows and columns

For a given row or column ("rank"), GridBagLayout first considers the weights of all of the components contained strictly within that rank—ignoring those that span more than one cell. The greatest individual weight becomes the overall weight of the row or column. Intuitively this means that GridBagLayout is trying to accommodate the needs of the weightiest component in that rank.

Next, GridBagLayout considers the components that occupy more than one cell. Here things get a little weird. GridbagLayout wants to evaluate them like the others, to see whether they affect the determination of the largest weight in a row or column. However, because these components occupy more than one cell, GridBagLayout divides their weight among the ranks (rows or columns) that they span.

GridBagLayout tries to calculate an effective weight for the portion of the component that occupies each of its rows or columns. It does this by trying to divide the weight of the component among the ranks in the same proportions that the length (or height) of the component will be shared by the ranks. But how does it know what the proportions will be before the whole grid is determined? That's what it's trying to calculate after all. It simply guesses based on the row or column weights already determined. GridbagLayout uses the weights determined by the first round of calculations to split up the weight of the component over the ranks that it occupies. For each row or column, it then considers that fraction of the weight to be the component's weight for that rank. That weight then contends for the "heaviest weight" in the row or column, possibly changing the overall weight of that row or column, as we described earlier.

Anchoring

If a component is smaller than the space available for it, it is centered by default. But centering isn't the only possibility. The anchor constraint tells a grid bag layout how to position a component within its cell in the grid. Possible values are: GridBagConstraints.CENTER, NORTH, NORTHEAST, EAST, SOUTHEAST, SOUTH, SOUTHWEST, WEST, and NORTHWEST. For example, an anchor of GridBag-Constraints.NORTH centers a component at the top of its display area; SOUTHEAST places a component at the bottom-right corner of its area.

Padding and Insets

Another way to control the behavior of a component in a grid bag layout is to use padding and insets. Padding is determined by the ipadx and ipady fields of GridBagConstraints. They specify horizontal and vertical "growth factors" for the component. In Figure 16-11, the **West** button is larger because we have set the ipadx and ipady values of its constraints to 25. Therefore, the layout manager gets the button's preferred size and adds 25 pixels in each direction to determine the button's actual size. The sizes of the other buttons are unchanged because their padding is set to 0 (the default), but their spacing is different. The **West** button is unnaturally tall, which means that the middle row of the layout must be taller than the others.

```
//file: GridBag5.java
import java.awt.*;
import java.awt.event.*;
import javax.swing.*;

public class GridBag5 extends JPanel {
  GridBagConstraints constraints = new GridBagConstraints();

  public GridBag5() {
    setLayout(new GridBagLayout());
    int x, y;  // for clarity
    addGB(new JButton("North"),  x = 1, y = 0);
    constraints.ipadx = 25;  // add padding
    constraints.ipady = 25;
    addGB(new JButton("West"),   x = 0, y = 1);
    constraints.ipadx = 0;   // remove padding
    constraints.ipady = 0;
    addGB(new JButton("Center"), x = 1, y = 1);
    addGB(new JButton("East"),   x = 2, y = 1);
    addGB(new JButton("South"),  x = 1, y = 2);
  }

  void addGB(Component component, int x, int y) {
    constraints.gridx = x;
    constraints.gridy = y;
    add(component, constraints);
  }

  public static void main(String[] args) {
    JFrame f = new JFrame("GridBag5");
    f.addWindowListener(new WindowAdapter() {
      public void windowClosing(WindowEvent e) { System.exit(0); }
    });
    f.setSize(250, 250);
    f.setLocation(200, 200);
    f.setContentPane(new GridBag5());
    f.setVisible(true);
  }
}
```

Notice that the horizontal padding, ipadx, is added on both the left and right sides of the button. Therefore, the button grows horizontally by twice the value of

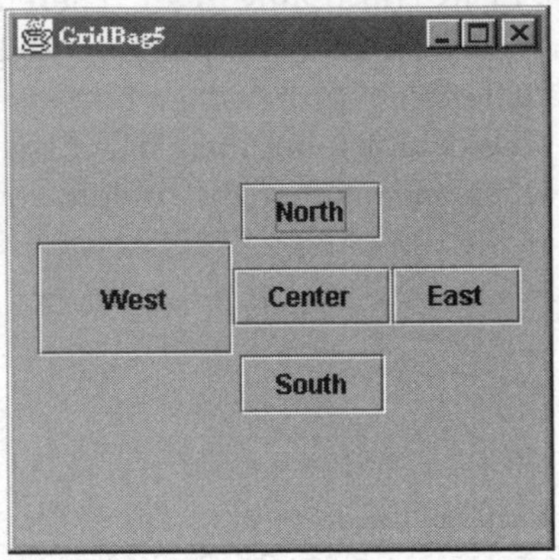

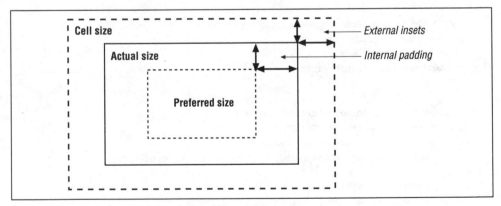

Figure 16-11. Using padding and insets in a layout

ipadx. Likewise, the vertical padding, ipady, is added on both the top and the bottom.

Insets add space between the edges of the component and its cell. They are stored in the insets field of GridBagConstraints, which is an Insets object. An Insets object has four fields, to specify the margins on the top, bottom, left, and right of the component. The relationship between insets and padding can be confusing. As shown in Figure 16-12, padding is added to the component itself, increasing its size. Insets are external to the component and represent the margin between the component and its cell.

Figure 16-12. The relationship between padding and insets

Padding and weighting have an odd interaction with each other. If you use padding, it's best to use the default weightx and weighty values for each component.

Relative Positioning

In all of our grid bag layouts so far, we have specified the `gridx` and `gridy` coordinates of each component explicitly using its constraints. Another alternative is *relative positioning*.

Conceptually, relative positioning is simple: we simply say "put this component to the left of (or below) the previous component." To do so, set `gridx` or `gridy` to the constant `GridBagConstraints.RELATIVE`. Unfortunately, it's not as simple as this. Here are a couple of warnings:

- To place a component to the right of the previous one, set `gridx` to `RELATIVE` *and* use the same value for `gridy` as you used for the previous component.

- Similarly, to place a component below the previous one, set `gridy` to `RELATIVE` *and* leave `gridx` unchanged.

- Setting both `gridx` and `gridy` to `RELATIVE` places all the components in one row, not in a diagonal line, as you would expect. (This is the default.)

In other words, if `gridx` or `gridy` is `RELATIVE`, you had better leave the other value unchanged. `RELATIVE` makes it easy to arrange a lot of components in a row or a column. That's what it was intended for; if you try to do something else, you're fighting against the layout manager, not working with it.

`GridBagLayout` allows another kind of relative positioning, in which you specify where, in a row or a column, the component should be placed. To do so, you use the `gridwidth` and `gridheight` fields of `GridBagConstraints`. Setting either of these to the constant `REMAINDER` says that the component should be the last item in its row or column, and therefore should occupy all the remaining space. Setting either `gridwidth` or `gridheight` to `RELATIVE` says that it should be the second to the last item in its row or column. Unfortunately, you can use these constants to create constraints that can't possibly be met; for example, you can say that two components must be the last component in a row. In these cases, the layout manager tries to do something reasonable—but it will almost certainly do something you don't want. Again, relative placement works well as long as you don't try to twist it into doing something it wasn't designed for.

Composite Layouts

Sometimes things don't fall neatly into little boxes. This is true of layouts as well as life. For example, if you want to use some of `GridBagLayout`'s weighting features for part of your GUI, you could create separate layouts for different parts of the GUI and combine them with yet another layout. That's how we'll build the pocket calculator interface in Figure 16-13. We will use three grid bag layouts: one for the first row of buttons (C, %, +), one for the last (0, ., =), and one for the window itself. The master layout (the window's) manages the text field we use for the display, the panels containing the first and last rows of buttons, and the twelve buttons in the middle.*

Figure 16-13. The Calculator application

Here's the code for the `Calculator` example. It implements only the user interface (i.e., the keyboard); it collects everything you type in the display field, until you press **C** (clear). Figuring out how to connect the GUI to some other code that would perform the operations is up to you. One strategy would be to send an event to the object that does the computation whenever the user presses the equals sign. That object could read the contents of the text field, parse it, do the computation, and display the results.

```
//file: Calculator.java
import java.awt.*;
import java.awt.event.*;
import javax.swing.*;

public class Calculator extends JPanel implements ActionListener {
    GridBagConstraints gbc = new GridBagConstraints();
    JTextField theDisplay = new JTextField();

    public Calculator() {
        gbc.weightx = 1.0;  gbc.weighty = 1.0;
        gbc.fill = GridBagConstraints.BOTH;
        ContainerListener listener = new ContainerAdapter() {
            public void componentAdded(ContainerEvent e) {
```

---

* If you're curious, this calculator is based on the ELORG-801, encountered in an online "calculator museum"; see *http://www.geocities.com/CapeCanaveral/6747/elorg801.jpg*.

```
            Component comp = e.getChild();
            if (comp instanceof JButton)
              ((JButton)comp).addActionListener(Calculator.this);
          }
        };
        addContainerListener(listener);
        gbc.gridwidth = 4;
        addGB(this, theDisplay, 0, 0);
        // make the top row
        JPanel topRow = new JPanel();
        topRow.addContainerListener(listener);
        gbc.gridwidth = 1;
        gbc.weightx = 1.0;
        addGB(topRow, new JButton("C"), 0, 0);
        gbc.weightx = 0.33;
        addGB(topRow, new JButton("%"), 1, 0);
        gbc.weightx = 1.0;
        addGB(topRow, new JButton("+"), 2, 0 );
        gbc.gridwidth = 4;
        addGB(this, topRow, 0, 1);
        gbc.weightx = 1.0;  gbc.gridwidth = 1;
        // make the digits
        for(int j=0; j<3; j++)
          for(int i=0; i<3; i++)
              addGB(this, new JButton("" + ((2-j)*3+i+1) ), i, j+2);
        // -, x, and divide
        addGB(this, new JButton("-"), 3, 2);
        addGB(this, new JButton("x"), 3, 3);
        addGB(this, new JButton("\u00F7"), 3, 4);
        // make the bottom row
        JPanel bottomRow = new JPanel();
        bottomRow.addContainerListener(listener);
        gbc.weightx = 1.0;
        addGB(bottomRow, new JButton("0"), 0, 0);
        gbc.weightx = 0.33;
        addGB(bottomRow, new JButton("."), 1, 0);
        gbc.weightx = 1.0;
        addGB(bottomRow, new JButton("="), 2, 0);
        gbc.gridwidth = 4;
        addGB(this, bottomRow, 0, 5);
    }

    void addGB(Container cont, Component comp, int x, int y) {
      if ((cont.getLayout() instanceof GridBagLayout) == false)
        cont.setLayout(new GridBagLayout());
      gbc.gridx = x; gbc.gridy = y;
      cont.add(comp, gbc);
    }
```

```
    public void actionPerformed(ActionEvent e) {
      if (e.getActionCommand().equals("C"))
        theDisplay.setText("");
      else
        theDisplay.setText(theDisplay.getText()
                         + e.getActionCommand());
    }

    public static void main(String[] args) {
      JFrame f = new JFrame("Calculator");
      f.addWindowListener(new WindowAdapter() {
        public void windowClosing(WindowEvent e) { System.exit(0); }
      });
      f.setSize(200, 250);
      f.setLocation(200, 200);
      f.setContentPane(new Calculator());
      f.setVisible(true);
    }
  }
```

Once again, we use an addGB() helper method to add components with their constraints to the layout. Before discussing how to build the layout, let's look at addGB(). We said earlier that three layout managers are in our user interface: one for the application panel itself, one for the panel containing the first row of buttons (topRow), and one for the panel containing the bottom row of buttons (bottomRow). We use addGB() for all three layouts; its first argument specifies the container to add the component to. Thus, when the first argument is this, we're adding an object to the content pane of the JFrame. When the first argument is topRow, we're adding a button to the first row of buttons. addGB() first checks the container's layout manager, and sets it to GridBagLayout if it isn't already set properly. It sets the object's position by modifying a set of constraints, gbc, and then uses these constraints to add the object to the container.

We use a single set of constraints throughout the example, modifying fields as we see fit. The constraints are initialized in Calculator's constructor. Before calling addGB(), we set any fields of gbc for which the defaults are inappropriate. Thus, for the answer display, we set the grid width to 4, and add the answer display directly to the application panel (this). The add() method, which is called by addGB(), makes a copy of the constraints, so we're free to reuse gbc throughout the application.

The first and last rows of buttons motivate the use of multiple GridBagLayout containers, each with its own grid. These buttons appear to straddle grid lines, but you really can't accomplish this using a single grid. Therefore, topRow has its own layout manager, with three horizontal cells, allowing each button in the row to have a grid width of 1. To control the size of the buttons, we set the weightx variables so that the clear and plus buttons take up more space than the percent button. We then add the `topRow` as a whole to the application, with a grid width of 4. The bottom row is built similarly.

To build the buttons for the digits 1 through 9, we use a doubly nested loop. There's nothing particularly interesting about this loop, except that it's probably a bit too clever for good taste. The minus, multiply, and divide buttons are also simple: we create a button with the appropriate label and use `addGB()` to place it in the application. It's worth noting that we used a Unicode constant to request a real division sign, rather than wimping out and using a slash.

That's it for the user interface; what's left is event handling. Each button generates action events; we need to register listeners for these events. We'll make the application panel, the `Calculator`, the listener for all the buttons. To register the `Calculator` as a listener, we'll be clever. Whenever a component is added to a container, the container generates a `ContainerEvent`. We use an anonymous inner `ContainerListener` to register listeners for our buttons. This means that the `Calculator` must register as a `ContainerListener` for itself, and for the two panels, `topRow` and `bottomRow`. The `componentAdded()` method is very simple. It calls `getChild()` to find out what component caused the event (i.e., what component was added). If that component is a button, it registers the `Calculator` as an `ActionListener` for that button.

`actionPerformed()` is called whenever the user presses any button. It clears the display if the user pressed the **C** button; otherwise, it appends the button's action command (in this case, its label) to the display.

Combining layout managers is an extremely useful trick. Granted, this example verges on overkill. You won't often need to create a composite layout using multiple grid bags. Composite layouts are most common with `BorderLayout`; you'll frequently use different layout managers for each of a border layout's regions. For example, the CENTER region might be a `ScrollPane`, which has its own special-purpose layout manager; the EAST and SOUTH regions might be panels managed by grid layouts or flow layouts, as appropriate.

Nonstandard Layout Managers

We've covered the basic layout managers; with them, you should be able to create just about any user interface you like.

But that's not all, folks. If you want to experiment with layout managers that are undocumented, may change, and may not be available locally on all platforms, look in the `sun.awt` classes. You'll find a `HorizBagLayout`, a `VerticalBag-Layout`, an `OrientableFlowLayout`, and a `VariableGridLayout`. Furthermore, public domain layout managers of all descriptions are on the Net; keep your eye

on Gamelan (*http://www.gamelan.com*) and the other Java archives if you need
something exotic.

Absolute Positioning

It's possible to set the layout manager to null: no layout control. You might do
this to position an object on the display at some absolute coordinates. This is
almost never the right approach. Components might have different minimum
sizes on different platforms, and your interface would not be very portable.

The following example doesn't use a layout manager and works with absolute
coordinates instead:

```java
//file: MoveButton.java
import java.awt.*;
import java.awt.event.*;
import javax.swing.*;

public class MoveButton extends JPanel {
  JButton button = new JButton("I Move");

  public MoveButton() {
    setLayout(null);
    add(button);
    button.setSize(button.getPreferredSize());
    button.setLocation(20, 20);
    addMouseListener(new MouseAdapter() {
      public void mousePressed(MouseEvent e) {
      button.setLocation(e.getX(), e.getY());
      }
    });
  }

  public static void main(String[] args) {
    JFrame f = new JFrame("MoveButton");
    f.addWindowListener(new WindowAdapter() {
      public void windowClosing(WindowEvent e) { System.exit(0); }
    });
    f.setSize(250, 200);
    f.setLocation(200, 200);
    f.setContentPane(new MoveButton());
    f.setVisible(true);
  }
}
```

Click in the window area, outside of the button, to move the button to a new location. Try resizing the window and note that the button stays at a fixed position relative to the window's upper left corner.

17

*Drawing with
the 2D API*

In the last few chapters, you've caught a glimpse of how graphics operations are performed in Java. This chapter goes into more depth about drawing techniques and the tools for working with images in Java. In the next chapter, we'll explore image-processing tools in more detail, and we'll look at the classes that let you generate images, pixel by pixel, on the fly.

The Big Picture

The classes you'll use for drawing come from six packages: `java.awt`, `java.awt.color`, `java.awt.font`, `java.awt.geom`, `java.awt.image`, and `java.awt.print`. Collectively, these classes make up most of the 2D API, a comprehensive API for drawing shapes, text, and images. Figure 17-1 shows a bird's-eye view of these classes. There's much more in the 2D API than we can cover in two chapters. For a full treatment, see Jonathan Knudsen's *Java 2D Graphics* (O'Reilly & Associates).

An instance of `java.awt.Graphics2D` is called a *graphics context*. It represents a drawing surface such as a component's display area, a page on a printer, or an off-screen image buffer. A graphics context provides methods for drawing three kinds of graphics objects: shapes, text, and images. `Graphics2D` is called a graphics context because it also holds contextual information about the drawing area. This information includes the drawing area's clipping region, painting color, transfer mode, text font, and geometric transformation. If you consider the drawing area to be a painter's canvas, you might think of a graphics context as an easel that holds a set of tools and marks off the work area.

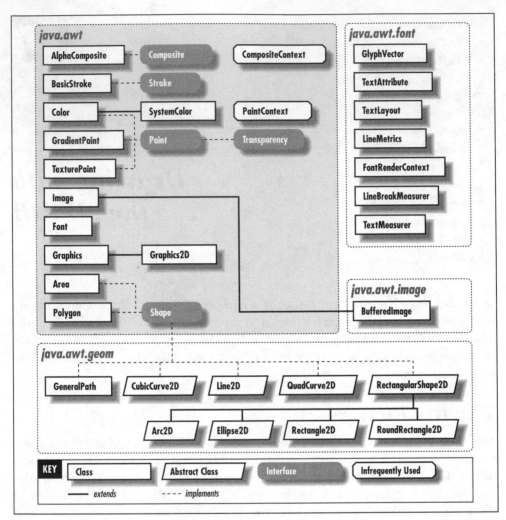

Figure 17-1. Graphics classes of the 2D API

There are four ways you normally acquire a `Graphics2D` object. Roughly, from most common to least, they are as follows:

- From AWT or Swing, as the result of a painting request on a component. In this case, a new graphics context for the appropriate area is acquired and passed to your component's `paint()` or `update()` method. (The `update()` method really applies only to AWT components, not the newer Swing components.)

- Directly from an offscreen image buffer. In this case, we ask the image buffer for a graphics context directly. We'll use this when we discuss techniques like double buffering.

- By copying an existing `Graphics2D` object. Duplicating a graphics object can be useful for more elaborate drawing operations; different copies of a `Graphics2D` object can draw on same area, but with different attributes and clipping regions. A `Graphics2D` can be copied by calling the `create()` method.

- Directly from an onscreen component. It's possible to ask a component to give you a `Graphics2D` object for its display area. However, this is almost always a mistake; if you feel tempted to do this, think about why you're trying to circumvent the normal `paint()`/`repaint()` mechanism.

Each time a component's `paint()` method is called, the windowing system provides the component with a new `Graphics2D` object for drawing in the display area. This means that attributes we set during one painting session, such as the drawing color or clipping region, are reset the next time `paint()` is called. (Each call to `paint()` starts with a tidy new easel.) For the most common attributes, like foreground color, background color, and font, we can set defaults in the component itself. Thereafter, the graphics contexts for painting in that component come with those properties initialized appropriately.

If we are working in an AWT component's `update()` method, we can assume our onscreen artwork is still intact, and we need to make only whatever changes are needed to bring the display up to date. One way to optimize drawing operations in this case is by setting a clipping region, as we'll see shortly. If our `paint()` method is called, however, we have to assume the worst and redraw the entire display.

For backwards compatibility, a graphics context is always passed to the `paint()` method as a `Graphics` object. If you want to take advantage of the nifty features in the 2D API (as you almost undoubtedly will), you will need to cast this reference to a `Graphics2D`. You'll see how this works in the upcoming examples.

The Rendering Pipeline

One of the strengths of the 2D API is that shapes, text, and images are manipulated in many of the same ways. In this section, we'll describe what happens to shapes, text, and images after you give them to a `Graphics2D`. *Rendering* is the process of taking some collection of shapes, text, and images and figuring out how to represent them by coloring pixels on a screen or printer. `Graphics2D` supports four rendering operations:

1. Draw the outline of a shape, with the `draw()` method.
2. Fill the interior of a shape, with the `fill()` method.
3. Draw some text, with the `drawString()` method.
4. Draw an image, with any of the many forms of the `drawImage()` method.

The graphics context instantiated by a `Graphics2D` object consists of the following fields, whose values are controlled by various accessor methods:

paint

The current *paint* (an object of type `java.awt.Paint`) determines what colors will be used to fill a shape. This affects shape outlines and text, as well. You can change the current paint using `Graphics2D`'s `setPaint()` method. Note that the `Color` class implements the `Paint` interface, so you can pass `Colors` to `setPaint()` if you want to use solid colors.

stroke

`Graphics2D` uses the current *stroke* for shapes that are passed to its `draw()` method. The outline of the shape is represented by another shape that is determined by the current stroke. The resulting shape (the stroked outline) is then filled. Suppose you wanted to draw the outline of a circle. If the current stroke called for a solid line, the stroked outline of a circle would look like a washer or ring. You can set the current stroke using `setStroke()`. The 2D API comes with a handy class, `java.awt.BasicStroke`, that implements different line widths, end styles, join styles, and dashing.

font

Text is rendered by creating a shape that represents the characters to be drawn. The current *font* determines what shapes are created for a given set of characters. The resulting text shape is then filled. The current font is set using `setFont()`. The 2D API gives applications access to all the TrueType and PostScript Type 1 fonts that are installed on your machine.

transformation

Shapes, text, and images are geometrically *transformed* before they are rendered. This means that they may be moved, rotated, and stretched. `Graphics2D`'s transformation converts coordinates from *user space* to *device space*. By default, `Graphics2D` uses a transformation that maps 72 units in user space to one inch on the output device. If you draw a line from point 0, 0 to point 72, 0 using the default transformation, it will be one inch long, regardless of whether it is drawn on your monitor or your printer. The current transformation can be modified using the `translate()`, `rotate()`, `scale()`, and `shear()` methods.

compositing rule

A *compositing rule* is used to determine how the colors of a primitive should be combined with existing colors on the `Graphics2D`'s drawing surface. This attribute is set using `setComposite()`, which accepts an instance of `java.awt.AlphaComposite`. Compositing allows you to make parts of a drawing or image completely or partially transparent, or to combine them in other interesting ways.

clipping shape

>All rendering operations are limited to the interior of the *clipping shape*. No pixels outside this shape will be modified. By default, the clipping shape allows rendering on the entire drawing surface (usually, the rectangular area of a Component). However, you can further limit this using any simple or complex shape, including text shapes.

rendering hints

>There are different techniques that can be used to render graphics primitives. Usually these represent a tradeoff between rendering speed and visual quality or vice versa. Rendering hints (constants defined in the RenderingHints class) specify which techniques to use.

Graphics primitives (shapes, text, and images) pass through the rendering engine in a series of operations called the *rendering pipeline*. Let's walk through the pipeline. It can be reduced to four steps, where the first step depends heavily on the rendering operation:

1. Transform the shape. For shapes that will be filled, the shape is simply transformed using the Graphics2D's current transformation. For shapes whose outlines are drawn using draw(), the current stroke is used to stroke the shape's outline. Then the stroked outline is transformed, just like any other filled shape. Text is displayed by mapping characters to shapes using the current font. The resulting text shapes are transformed, just like any other filled shape. For images, the outline of the image is transformed using the current transformation.

2. Determine the colors to be used. For a filled shape, the current *paint* object determines what colors should be used to fill the shape. For an image, the colors are taken from the image itself.

3. Combine the colors with the existing drawing surface using the current *compositing rule*.

4. Clip the results using the current *clipping shape*.

The *rendering hints* are used throughout to control the rendering quality.

A Quick Tour of Java 2D

Filling Shapes

The simplest path through the rendering pipeline is for filling shapes. For example, the following code creates an ellipse and fills it with a solid color. (This code would live inside a paint() method somewhere. We'll present a complete, ready-to-run example a little later.)

```
Shape c = new Ellipse2D.Float(50, 25, 150, 150);
g2.setPaint(Color.blue);
g2.fill(c);
```

The Ellipse2D class is abstract, but is implemented by concrete inner subclasses, called Float and Double. The Rectangle2D class, for example, has concrete subclasses Rectangle2D.Float and Rectangle2D.Double.

In the call to setPaint(), we tell the Graphics2D to use a solid color, blue, for all subsequent filling operations. Then, the call to fill() tells Graphics2D to fill the given shape.

All geometric shapes in the 2D API are represented by implementations of the java.awt.geom.Shape interface. This interface defines methods that are common to all shapes, like returning a rectangle bounding box or testing if a point is inside the shape. The java.awt.geom package is a smorgasbord of useful shape classes, including Rectangle2D, RoundRectangle2D (a rectangle with rounded corners), Arc2D, Ellipse2D, and others. In addition, a few classes in java.awt are Shapes: Rectangle, Polygon, and Area.

Drawing Shape Outlines

Drawing a shape's outline is only a little bit more complicated. Consider this example:

```
Shape r = new Rectangle2D.Float(100, 75, 100, 100);
g2.setStroke(new BasicStroke(4));
g2.setPaint(Color.yellow);
g2.draw(r);
```

Here, we tell the Graphics2D to use a stroke that is four units wide and a solid color, yellow, for filling the stroke. When we call draw(), Graphics2D uses the stroke to create a new shape, the outline, from the given rectangle. The outline shape is then filled, just as before; this effectively draws the rectangles's outline. The rectangle itself is not filled.

Convenience Methods

Graphics2D includes quite a few convenience methods for drawing and filling common shapes; these methods are actually inherited from the Graphics class. Table 17-1 summarizes these methods. It's a little easier to just call fillRect(), rather than instantiating a rectangle shape and passing it to fill().

Table 17-1. Shape-Drawing Methods in the Graphics Class

Method	Description
draw3DRect()	Draws a highlighted, 3D rectangle
drawArc()	Draws an arc

Table 17-1. Shape-Drawing Methods in the Graphics Class (continued)

Method	Description
drawLine()	Draws a line
drawOval()	Draws an oval
drawPolygon()	Draws a polygon, closing it by connecting the endpoints
drawPolyline()	Draws a line connecting a series of points, without closing it
drawRect()	Draws a rectangle
drawRoundRect()	Draws a rounded-corner rectangle
fill3DRect()	Draws a filled, highlighted, 3D rectangle
fillArc()	Draws a filled arc
fillOval()	Draws a filled oval
fillPolygon()	Draws a filled polygon
fillRect()	Draws a filled rectangle
fillRoundRect()	Draws a filled, rounded-corner rectangle

As you can see, for each of the fill() methods in the table, there is a corresponding draw() method that renders the shape as an unfilled line drawing. With the exception of fillArc() and fillPolygon(), each method takes a simple x, y specification for the top left corner of the shape and a width and height for its size.

The most flexible convenience method draws a polygon, which is specified by two arrays that contain the x and y coordinates of the vertices. Methods in the Graphics class take two such arrays and draw the polygon's outline, or fill the polygon.

The methods listed in Table 17-1 are shortcuts for more general methods in Graphics2D. The more general procedure is to first create a java.awt.geom. Shape object, and then pass it to the draw() or fill() method of Graphics2D. For example, you could create a Polygon object from coordinate arrays. Since a Polygon implements the Shape interface, you can pass it to Graphics2D's general draw() or fill() method.

The fillArc() method requires six integer arguments. The first four specify the bounding box for an oval—just like the fillOval() method. The final two arguments specify what portion of the oval we want to draw, as a starting angular position and an offset. Both the starting angular position and the offset are specified in degrees. Zero degrees is at three o'clock; a positive angle is clockwise. For example, to draw the right half of a circle, you might call:

```
g.fillArc(0, 0, radius * 2, radius * 2, -90, 180);
```

draw3DRect() automatically chooses colors by "darkening" the current color. So you should set the color to something other than black, which is the default (maybe gray or white); if you don't, you'll just get black rectangle with a thick outline.

Drawing Text

Like drawing a shape's outline, drawing text is just a simple variation on filling a shape. When you ask a `Graphics2D` to draw text, it determines the shapes that need to be drawn and fills them. The shapes that represent characters are called *glyphs*. A font is a collection of glyphs. Here's an example of drawing text:

```
g2.setFont(new Font("Times New Roman", Font.PLAIN, 64));
g2.setPaint(Color.red);
g2.drawString("Hello, 2D!", 50, 150);
```

When we call `drawString()`, the `Graphics2D` uses the current font to retrieve the glyphs that correspond to the characters in the string. Then the glyphs (which are really just `Shapes`) are filled using the current `Paint`.

Drawing Images

Images are treated a little differently than shapes. In particular, the current `Paint` is not used to render an image because the image contains its own color information. The following example loads an image from a file and displays it (you'll have to use your own file here):

```
Image i = Toolkit.getDefaultToolkit().getImage("camel.gif");
g2.drawImage(i, 75, 50, this);
```

In this case, the call to `drawImage()` tells the `Graphics2D` to place the image at the given location.

Go Crazy

Four parts of the pipeline affect every graphics operation. In particular, all rendering is transformed, composited, and clipped. Rendering hints are used to affect all of a `Graphics2D`'s rendering.

This example shows how to modify the current transformation with a translation and a rotation :

```
g2.translate(50, 0);
g2.rotate(Math.PI / 6);
```

Every graphics primitive drawn by g2 will now have this transformation applied to it. We can have a similarly global effect on compositing:

```
AlphaComposite ac = AlphaComposite.getInstance(
    AlphaComposite.SRC_OVER, (float).5);
g2.setComposite(ac);
```

Now every graphics primitive we draw will be half transparent—we'll explain more about this later.

All drawing operations are clipped by the current clipping shape, which is any object implementing the Shape interface. In the following example, the clipping shape is set to an ellipse:

```
Shape e = new Ellipse2D.Float(50, 25, 250, 150);
g2.clip(e);
```

You can obtain the current clipping shape using getClip(); this is handy if you want to restore it later using the setClip() method.

Finally, the rendering hints are used for all drawing operations. In the following example, we tell the Graphics2D to use antialiasing, a technique that smooths out the rough pixel edges of shapes and text:

```
g2.setRenderingHint(RenderingHints.KEY_ANTIALIASING,
    RenderingHints.VALUE_ANTIALIAS_ON);
```

The RenderingHints class contains other keys and values, representing other rendering hints. If you really like to fiddle with knobs and dials, this is a good class to check out.

The Whole Iguana

Let's put everything together now, just to show how graphics primitives travel through the rendering pipeline. The following example demonstrates the use of Graphics2D from the beginning to the end of the rendering pipeline. With very few lines of code, we are able to draw some pretty complicated stuff (see Figure 17-2):

```
//file: Iguana.java
import java.awt.*;
import java.awt.event.*;
import java.awt.geom.*;
import javax.swing.*;

public class Iguana extends JComponent {
  private Image image;
  private int theta;

  public Iguana() {
    image = Toolkit.getDefaultToolkit().getImage(
        "Piazza di Spagna.small.jpg");
    theta = 0;
    addMouseListener(new MouseAdapter() {
      public void mousePressed(MouseEvent me) {
        theta = (theta + 15) % 360;
```

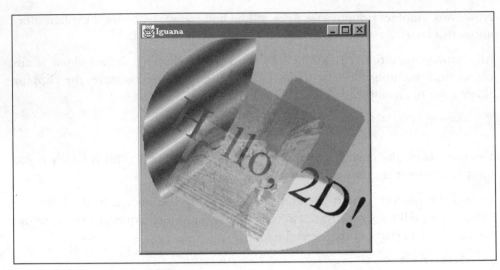

Figure 17-2. Exercising the 2D API

```
          repaint();
        }
      });
    }

    public void paint(Graphics g) {
      Graphics2D g2 = (Graphics2D)g;

      g2.setRenderingHint(RenderingHints.KEY_ANTIALIASING,
          RenderingHints.VALUE_ANTIALIAS_ON);

      int cx = getSize().width / 2;
      int cy = getSize().height / 2;

      g2.translate(cx, cy);
      g2.rotate(theta * Math.PI / 180);

      Shape oldClip = g2.getClip();
      Shape e = new Ellipse2D.Float(-cx, -cy, cx * 2, cy * 2);
      g2.clip(e);

      Shape c = new Ellipse2D.Float(-cx, -cy, cx * 3 / 4, cy * 2);
      g2.setPaint(new GradientPaint(40, 40, Color.blue,
          60, 50, Color.white, true));
      g2.fill(c);

      g2.setPaint(Color.yellow);
      g2.fillOval(cx / 4, 0, cx, cy);

      g2.setClip(oldClip);
```

```
      g2.setFont(new Font("Times New Roman", Font.PLAIN, 64));
      g2.setPaint(new GradientPaint(-cx, 0, Color.red,
          cx, 0, Color.black, false));
      g2.drawString("Hello, 2D!", -cx * 3 / 4, cy / 4);

      AlphaComposite ac = AlphaComposite.getInstance(
          AlphaComposite.SRC_OVER, (float).75);
      g2.setComposite(ac);

      Shape r = new RoundRectangle2D.Float(0, -cy * 3 / 4,
          cx * 3 / 4, cy * 3 / 4, 20, 20);
      g2.setStroke(new BasicStroke(4));
      g2.setPaint(Color.magenta);
      g2.fill(r);
      g2.setPaint(Color.green);
      g2.draw(r);

      g2.drawImage(image, -cx / 2, -cy / 2, this);
    }

    public static void main(String[] args) {
      JFrame f = new JFrame("Iguana");
      Container c = f.getContentPane();
      c.setLayout(new BorderLayout());
      c.add(new Iguana(), BorderLayout.CENTER);
      f.setSize(300, 300);
      f.setLocation(100, 100);
      f.addWindowListener(new WindowAdapter() {
        public void windowClosing(WindowEvent e) { System.exit(0); }
      });
      f.setVisible(true);
    }
  }
```

The Iguana class itself is a subclass of JComponent with a fancy paint() method. The main() method takes care of creating a JFrame that holds the Iguana component.

Iguana's constructor loads a small image (we'll talk more about this later) and sets up a mouse event handler. This handler changes a member variable, theta, and repaints the component. Each time you click, the entire drawing is rotated by 15 degrees.

Iguana's paint() method does some pretty tricky stuff, but none of it is very difficult. First, user space is transformed so that the origin is at the center of the component. Then user space is rotated by theta:

```
    g2.translate(cx, cy);
    g2.rotate(theta * Math.PI / 180);
```

Iguana saves the current (default) clipping shape before setting it to a large ellipse. Then Iguana draws two filled ellipses. The first is drawn by instantiating an Ellipse2D and filling it; the second is drawn using the fillOval() convenience method. (We'll talk about the color gradient in the first ellipse in the next section.) As you can see in Figure 17-2, both ellipses are clipped by the elliptical clipping shape. After filling the two ellipses, Iguana restores the old clipping shape.

Iguana draws some text next; we'll talk about this in more detail later. The next action is to modify the compositing rule as follows:

```
AlphaComposite ac = AlphaComposite.getInstance(
    AlphaComposite.SRC_OVER, (float).75);
g2.setComposite(ac);
```

All this means is that we want everything to be drawn with transparency. The AlphaComposite class defines constants representing different compositing rules, much the way the Color class contains constants representing different pre-defined colors. In this case, we're asking for the *source over destination* rule (SRC_OVER), but with an additional alpha multiplier of 0.75. Source over destination means that whatever we're drawing (the source) should be placed on top of whatever's already there (the destination). The alpha multiplier means that everything we draw will be treated at 0.75 or three quarters of its normal opacity, allowing the existing drawing to "show through."

You can see the effect of the new compositing rule in the rounded rectangle and the image, which both allow previously drawn elements to show through.

Filling Shapes

Iguana fills its shapes with a number of colors, using the setPaint() method of Graphics2D. setPaint() sets the current color in the graphics context, so we set it to a different color before each drawing operation. This method accepts any object that implements the Paint interface. The 2D API includes three implementations of this interface, representing solid colors, color gradients, and textures.

Solid Colors

The java.awt.Color class handles color in Java. A Color object describes a single color. You can create an arbitrary Color by specifying the red, green, and blue values, either as integers between 0 and 255 or as floating-point values between 0.0 and 1.0. You can also use getColor() to look up a named color in the system properties table, as described in Chapter 9, *Basic Utility Classes*. getColor() takes a String color property name, retrieves the integer value from the Properties list, and returns the Color object that corresponds to that color.

The `Color` class also defines a number of `static final` color values; these are what we used in the `Iguana` example. These constants, such as `Color.black` and `Color.red`, provide a convenient set of basic color objects for your drawings.

Color Gradients

A *color gradient* is a smooth blend from one color to another. The `GradientPaint` class encapsulates this idea in a handy implementation of the `Paint` interface. All you need to do is specify two points and the color at each point. The `GradientPaint` will take care of the details so that the color fades smoothly from one point to the other. For example, in the previous example, the ellipse is filled with a gradient this way:

```
g2.setPaint(new GradientPaint(40, 40, Color.blue,
    60, 50, Color.white, true));
```

The last parameter in `GradientPaint`'s constructor determines whether the gradient is *cyclic*. In a cyclic gradient, the colors keep fluctuating beyond the two points that you've specified. Otherwise, the gradient just draws a single blend from one point to the other. Beyond each endpoint, the color is solid.

Textures

A *texture* is simply an image that is repeated over and over like a floor tile. This concept is represented in the 2D API with the `TexturePaint` class. To create a texture, just specify the image to be used and the rectangle that will be used to reproduce it. But to do this, you need to know how to create and use images, which we'll get to a little later.

Desktop Colors

The `Color` class makes it easy to construct a particular color; however, that's not always what you want to do. Sometimes you want to match a preexisting color scheme. This is particularly important when you are designing a user interface; you might want your components to have the same colors as other components on that platform, and to change automatically if the user redefines his or her color scheme.

That's what the `SystemColor` class is for. A system color represents the color used by the local windowing system in a certain context. The `SystemColor` class holds lots of predefined system colors, just like the `Color` class holds some predefined basic colors. For example, the field `activeCaption` represents the color used for the background of the title bar of an active window; `activeCaptionText` represents the color used for the title itself. `menu` represents the background color of menu selections; `menuText` represents the color of a menu item's text when it is not selected; `textHighlightText` is the color used when the menu item is selected; and so on. You could use the `window` value to set the color of a `Window` to match the other windows on the user's screen—whether or not they're generated by Java programs.

```
myWindow.setBackground( SystemColor.window );
```

Because the `SystemColor` class is a subclass of `Color`, you can use it wherever you would use a `Color`. However, the `SystemColor` constants are tricky. They are constants as far as you, the programmer, are concerned; your code is not allowed to modify them. However, they can be modified at runtime. If the user changes his color scheme, the system colors are automatically updated to follow suit; as a result, anything displayed with system colors will also change color the next time it is redrawn. For example, the window `myWindow` would automatically change its background color to the new background color.

The `SystemColor` class has one noticeable shortcoming. You can't compare a system color to a `Color` directly; the `Color.equals()` method doesn't return reliable results. For example, if you want to find out whether the window background color is red, you can't call:

```
Color.red.equals(SystemColor.window);
```

Instead, you should use `getRGB()` to find the color components of both objects and compare them, rather than comparing the objects themselves.

Stroking Shape Outlines

Just as a `Graphics2D` object's current paint determines how its shapes are filled, its current stoke determines how its shapes are outlined. The current stroke includes information about line thickness, line dashing, and end styles. (If you struggled with drawing in earlier versions of Java, you'll be very grateful that there's now a way to change the line thickness.)

To set the current stroke in a `Graphics2D`, just call `setStroke()` with any implementation of the `Stroke` interface. Fortunately, the 2D API includes a `BasicStroke` class that probably does everything you need. Using `BasicStroke`, you can create dashed lines, control what decoration is added to line ends, and decide how the corners in an outline should be drawn.

By default, a `Graphics2D` uses a solid stroke with a width of 1. In the previous `Iguana` example, the line width is changed just before the outline of the rounded rectangle is drawn, like so:

```
g2.setStroke(new BasicStroke(4));
```

Using Fonts

Text fonts in Java are represented by instances of the `java.awt.Font` class. A Font object is constructed from a name, style identifier, and a point size. We can create a Font at any time, but it's meaningful only when applied to a particular component on a given display device. Here are a couple of fonts:

```
Font smallFont = new Font("Monospaced", Font.PLAIN, 10);
Font bigFont = new Font("Serif", Font.BOLD, 18);
```

Font names come in three varieties: *family* names, *face* names (also called font names), and *logical* names. Family and font names are closely related. For example, Garamond Italic is a font name for a font whose family name is Garamond.

A *logical name* is a generic name for the font family. The following logical font names should be available on all platforms:

- `Serif` (generic name for `TimesRoman`)
- `SansSerif` (generic name for `Helvetica`)
- `Monospaced` (generic name for `Courier`)
- `Dialog`
- `DialogInput`

The logical font name is mapped to an actual font on the local platform. Java's *fonts.properties* files map the font names to the available fonts, covering as much of the Unicode character set as possible. If you request a font that doesn't exist, you get the default font.

One of the big wins in the 2D API is that it can use most of the fonts you have installed on your computer. The following program prints out a full list of the fonts that are available to the 2D API:

```java
//file: ShowFonts.java
import java.awt.*;

public class ShowFonts {
  public static void main(String[] args) {
    Font[] fonts;
    fonts =
     GraphicsEnvironment.getLocalGraphicsEnvironment().getAllFonts();
    for (int i = 0; i < fonts.length; i++) {
      System.out.print(fonts[i].getFontName() + " : ");
      System.out.print(fonts[i].getFamily() + " : ");
      System.out.print(fonts[i].getName());
      System.out.println();
    }
  }
}
```

Note, however, that the fonts installed on your system may not match the fonts installed on someone else's system. For true portability, you can use one of the logical names (although your application won't look exactly the same on all platforms) or go with the defaults. You can also allow your users to configure the application by choosing fonts themselves.

The `static` method `Font.getFont()` looks up a font name in the system properties list. `getFont()` takes a `String` font property name, retrieves the font name from the `Properties` table, and returns the `Font` object that corresponds to that font. You can use this mechanism, as with `Colors`, to define fonts with properties from outside your application.

The `Font` class defines three `static` style identifiers: `PLAIN`, `BOLD`, and `ITALIC`. You can use these values on all fonts. The point size determines the size of the font on a display. If a given point size isn't available, `Font` substitutes a default size.

You can retrieve information about an existing `Font` with a number of routines. The `getName()`, `getSize()`, and `getStyle()` methods retrieve the logical name, point size, and style, respectively. You can use the `getFamily()` method to find out the family name, while `getFontName()` returns the face name of the font.

Finally, to actually use a `Font` object, you can simply specify it as an argument to the `setFont()` method of a `Component` or `Graphics` object. Subsequent text-drawing commands like `drawString()` for that component or in that graphics context use the specified font.

Font Metrics

To get detailed size and spacing information for text rendered in a font, we can ask for a `java.awt.font.LineMetrics` object. Different systems will have different real fonts available; the available fonts may not match the font you request. Furthermore, the measurements of different characters within a single font may be different, especially in multilingual text. Thus, a `LineMetrics` object presents information about a particular set of text in a particular font on a particular system, not general information about a font. For example, if you ask for the metrics of a nine-point `Monospaced` font, what you get isn't some abstract truth about `Monospaced` fonts; you get the metrics of the font that the particular system uses for nine-point `Monospaced`—which may not be exactly nine-point or even fixed-width.

Use the `getLineMetrics()` method for a `Font` to retrieve the metrics for text as it would appear for that component. This method also needs to know some information about how you plan to render the text—if you're planning to use antialiasing, for instance, which affects the text measurements. This extra information is encapsulated in the `FontRenderContext` class. Fortunately, you can just ask

Graphics2D for its current FontRenderContext rather than having to create one yourself:

```
public void paint(Graphics g) {
   Graphics2D g2 = (Graphics2D)g;
   ...
   FontRenderContext frc = g2.getFontRenderContext();
   LineMetrics metrics = font.getLineMetrics("Monkey", frc);
   ...
}
```

The Font class also has a getStringBounds() method that returns the bounding box of a piece of text:

```
public void paint(Graphics g) {
   Graphics2D g2 = (Graphics2D)g;
   ...
   FontRenderContext frc = g2.getFontRenderContext();
   float messageWidth =
       (float)font.getStringBounds("Monkey", frc).getWidth();
   ...
}
```

The following application, FontShow, displays a word and draws reference lines showing certain characteristics of its font, as shown in Figure 17-3. Clicking in the application window toggles the point size between a small and a large value.

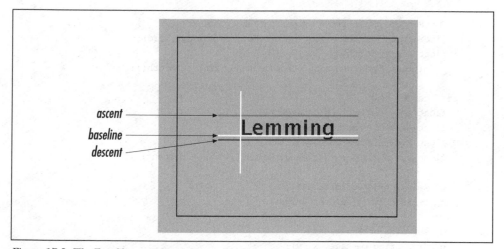

Figure 17-3. The FontShow application

```
//file: FontShow.java
import java.awt.*;
import java.awt.event.*;
import java.awt.font.*;
import javax.swing.*;
```

```java
public class FontShow extends JComponent {
  private static final int PAD = 25;    // frilly line padding
  private boolean bigFont = true;
  private String message;

  public FontShow(String message) {
    this.message = message;
    addMouseListener(new MouseAdapter() {
      public void mouseClicked(MouseEvent e) {
        bigFont = !bigFont;
        repaint();
      }
    });
  }

  public void paint(Graphics g) {
    Graphics2D g2 = (Graphics2D)g;

    g2.setRenderingHint(RenderingHints.KEY_ANTIALIASING,
        RenderingHints.VALUE_ANTIALIAS_ON);

    int size = bigFont ? 96 : 64;
    Font font = new Font("Dialog", Font.PLAIN, size);
    g2.setFont(font);
    int width = getSize().width;
    int height = getSize().height;

    FontRenderContext frc = g2.getFontRenderContext();
    LineMetrics metrics = font.getLineMetrics(message, frc);
    float messageWidth =
        (float)font.getStringBounds(message, frc).getWidth();

    // center text
    float ascent = metrics.getAscent();
    float descent = metrics.getDescent();
    float x = (width - messageWidth) / 2;
    float y = (height + metrics.getHeight()) / 2 - descent;

    g2.setPaint(getBackground());
    g2.fillRect(0, 0, width, height);

    g2.setPaint(getForeground());
    g2.drawString(message, x, y);

    g2.setPaint(Color.white);   // Base lines
    drawLine(g2, x - PAD, y, x + messageWidth + PAD, y);
    drawLine(g2, x, y + PAD, x, y - ascent - PAD);
    g2.setPaint(Color.green);   // Ascent line
    drawLine(g2, x - PAD, y - ascent,
```

```
                      x + messageWidth + PAD, y - ascent);
        g2.setPaint(Color.red);      // Descent line
        drawLine(g2, x - PAD, y + descent,
                      x + messageWidth + PAD, y + descent);
    }

    private void drawLine(Graphics2D g2,
        double x0, double y0, double x1, double y1) {
      Shape line = new java.awt.geom.Line2D.Double(x0, y0, x1, y1);
      g2.draw(line);
    }

    public static void main(String args[]) {
      String message = "Lemming";
      if (args.length > 0) message = args[0];

      JFrame f = new JFrame("FontShow");
      f.setSize(420, 300);
      f.setLocation(100, 100);
      f.addWindowListener(new WindowAdapter() {
        public void windowClosing(WindowEvent e) { System.exit(0); }
      });
      f.getContentPane().add(new FontShow(message));
      f.setVisible(true);
    }
}
```

You can specify the text to be displayed as a command-line argument:

```
java FontShow "When in the course of human events ..."
```

FontShow may look a bit complicated, but there's really not much to it. The bulk of the code is in paint(), which sets the font, draws the text, and adds a few lines to illustrate some of the font's characteristics (metrics). For fun, we also catch mouse clicks (using an event handler defined in the constructor) and alternate the font size by setting the bigFont toggle variable and repainting.

By default, text is rendered above and to the right of the coordinates specified in the drawString() method. Think of that starting point as the origin of a coordinate system; the axes are the *baselines* of the font. FontShow draws these lines in white. The greatest height the characters stretch above the baseline is called the *ascent* and is shown by a green line. Some fonts also have parts of letters that fall below the baseline. The farthest distance any character reaches below the baseline is called the *descent*. FontShow illustrates this with a red line.

We ask for the ascent and descent of our font with the LineMetrics class's getAscent() and getDescent() methods. We also ask for the width of our string (when rendered in this font) with Font's getStringBounds() method.

This information is used to center the word in the display area. To center the word vertically, we use the height and adjust with the descent to calculate the baseline location. Table 17-2 provides a short list of methods that return useful font metrics.

Table 17-2. LineMetrics Methods

Method	Description
getAscent()	Height above baseline
getDescent()	Depth below baseline
getLeading()	Standard vertical spacing between lines
getHeight()	Total line height (ascent + descent + leading)

Leading space is the padding between lines of text. The `getHeight()` method reports the total height of a line of text, including the leading space.

Displaying Images

So far, we've worked with methods for drawing simple shapes and displaying text. For more complex graphics, we'll be working with images. The 2D API has a powerful set of tools for generating and displaying image data. These tools address the problems of working in a distributed and multithreaded application environment. We'll start with the basics of the `java.awt.Image` class and see how to get an image into an applet or application and draw it on a display. This job isn't quite as simple as it sounds; the browser might have to retrieve the image from a networked source when we ask for it. Fortunately, if we're just interested in getting the image on the screen whenever it's ready, we can let the graphics system handle the details for us. In the next chapter, we'll discuss how to manage image loading manually, as well as how to create raw image data and feed it efficiently to the rest of an application.

The Image Class

The `java.awt.Image` class represents a view of an image. The view is created from an image source that produces pixel data. Images can be from a static source, such a GIF, JPEG, or PNG data file, or a dynamic one, such as a video stream or a graphics engine. The `Image` class in Java 2 also handles GIF89a animations, so that you can work with simple animations as easily as static images.

An applet can ask its viewer to retrieve an image by calling the `getImage()` method. The location of the image to be retrieved is given as a URL, either absolute or fetched from an applet's resources:

```
//file: MyApplet.java
import java.net.*;
```

```java
import java.awt.Image;

public class MyApplet extends javax.swing.JApplet {
  public void init() {
    try {
      // absolute URL
      URL monaURL =
          new URL( "http://myserver/images/mona_lisa.gif");
      Image monaImage = getImage( monaURL );
      // applet resource URL
      URL daffyURL =
          getClass().getResource("cartoons/images/daffy.gif");
      Image daffyDuckImage = getImage( daffyURL );
    }
    catch ( MalformedURLException e ) {
        // unintelligible url
    }
  }
  // ...
}
```

We usually want to package an applet's images with the applet itself, so using `getResource()` is preferred; it looks for the image in the applet's JAR file (if there is one), before looking elsewhere in the server's filesystem.

For a standalone application, where we don't have the applet's `getImage()` method available, we can use a convenience method in the `java.awt.Toolkit` class:

```java
Image dukeImage = getToolkit().getImage( url );
```

As with the previous example, this works both for URLs that we construct and for those returned by `getResource()`.

Once we have an `Image` object, we can draw it into a graphics context with the `drawImage()` method of the `Graphics2D` class. The simplest form of the `drawImage()` method takes four parameters: the `Image` object, the `x`, `y` coordinates at which to draw it, and a reference to a special *image observer* object. We'll show an example involving `drawImage()` soon, but first let's find out about image observers.

Image Observers

Images are processed asynchronously, which means that Java performs image operations like loading and scaling on its own time. For example, the `getImage()` method always returns immediately, even if the image data has to be retrieved over the network from Mars and isn't available yet. In fact, if it's a new image, Java won't even begin to fetch it until we try to try to display or manipulate it. The advantage of this technique is that Java can do the work of a powerful, multithreaded image-processing environment for us. However, it also introduces several problems. If Java is loading an image for us, how do we know when it's completely loaded? What if we want to work with the image as it arrives? What if we need to know properties of the image (like its dimensions) before we can start working with it? What if there's an error in loading the image?

These problems are handled by *image observers*—designated objects that implement the `ImageObserver` interface. All operations that draw or examine `Image` objects return immediately, but they take an image-observer object as a parameter. The `ImageObserver` monitors the image's status and can make that information available to the rest of the application. When image data is loaded from its source by the graphics system, your image observer is notified of its progress, including when new pixels are available, when a complete frame of the image is ready, and if there is an error during loading. The image observer also receives attribute information about the image, such as its dimensions and properties, as soon as they are known.

The `drawImage()` method, like other image operations, takes a reference to an `ImageObserver` object as a parameter. `drawImage()` returns a `boolean` value specifying whether or not the image was painted in its entirety. If the image data has not yet been loaded or is only partially available, `drawImage()` paints whatever fraction of the image it can and returns. In the background, the graphics system starts (or continues) loading the image data. The image-observer object is registered as being interested in information about the image. It's then called repeatedly as more pixel information is available and again when the entire image is complete. The image observer can do whatever it wants with this information. Most often it calls `repaint()` to prompt the applet to draw the image again with the updated data; a call to `repaint()` initiates a call to `paint()` to be scheduled. In this way, an applet can redraw the image as it arrives, for a progressive loading effect. Alternatively, it could wait until the entire image is loaded before displaying it.

We'll discuss creating image observers a bit later. For now, we can avoid the issue by using a prefabricated image observer. It just so happens that the `Component` class implements the `ImageObserver` interface and provides some simple repainting behavior for us. This means that every component can serve as its own default image observer; we simply pass a reference to our applet (or other component) as the image-observer parameter of a `drawImage()` call. Hence the mysterious `this` we've occasionally seen when working with graphics:

```
class MyApplet extends java.applet.Applet {
    ...
    public void paint( Graphics g ) {
        drawImage( monaImage, x, y, this );
        ...
```

Our applet serves as the image observer and calls `repaint()` for us to redraw the image as necessary. If the image arrives slowly, our applet is notified repeatedly, as new chunks become available. As a result, the image appears gradually, as it's loaded. The `awt.image.incrementaldraw` and `awt.image.redrawrate` system properties control this behavior. `redrawrate` limits how often `repaint()` is called; the default value is every 100 milliseconds. `incrementaldraw`'s default value, `true`, enables this behavior. Setting it to `false` delays drawing until the entire image has arrived.

Scaling and Size

Another version of `drawImage()` renders a scaled version of the image:

```
drawImage( monaImage, x, y, x2, y2, this );
```

This draws the entire image within the rectangle formed by the points x, y and x2, y2, scaling as necessary. (Cool, eh?) `drawImage()` behaves the same as before; the image is processed by the component as it arrives, and the image observer is notified as more pixel data and the completed image are available. Several other overloaded versions of `drawImage()` provide more complex options: you can scale, crop, and perform some simple transpositions.

If you want to actually make a scaled copy of an image (as opposed to simply painting one at draw-time), you can call `getScaledInstance()`. Here's how:

```
Image scaledDaffy =
    daffyImage.getScaledInstance(100,200,SCALE_AREA_ AVERAGING);
```

This method scales the original image to the given size; in this case, 100 by 200 pixels. It returns a new `Image` that you can draw like any other image. `SCALE_AREA_AVERAGING` is a constant that tells `getScaledImage()` what scaling algorithm to use. The algorithm used here tries to do a decent job of scaling, at the expense of time. Some alternatives that take less time are `SCALE_REPLICATE`, which scales by replicating scan lines and columns (which is fast, but probably not pretty). You can also specify either `SCALE_FAST` or `SCALE_SMOOTH` and let the implementation choose an appropriate algorithm that optimizes for time or quality. If you don't have specific requirements, you should use `SCALE_DEFAULT`, which, ideally, would be set by a preference in the user's environment.

Scaling an image before calling `drawImage()` can improve performance, because the image loading and scaling can take place before the image is actually needed. The same amount of work is required, but in most situations, prescaling will make the program appear faster, because it takes place while other things are going on; the user doesn't have to wait as long for the image to display.

The `Image getHeight()` and `getWidth()` methods retrieve the dimensions of an image. Since this information may not be available until the image data is completely loaded, both methods also take an `ImageObserver` object as a parameter. If the dimensions aren't yet available, they return values of –1 and notify the observer when the actual value is known. We'll see how to deal with these and other problems a bit later. For now, we'll use `Component` as an image observer to get by, and move on to some general painting techniques.

Using Drawing Techniques

Having learned to walk, let's try a jog. In this section, we'll look at some techniques for doing fast and flicker-free drawing and painting. If you're interested in animation or smooth updating, this is for you.

Drawing operations take time, and time spent drawing leads to delays and imperfect results. Our goal is to minimize the amount of drawing work we do and, as much as possible, to do that work away from the eyes of the user. To see how to eliminate flicker and blinking problems, we'll look at an application that animates very badly. The good news is that Swing automatically solves a lot of flicker problems.

`TerribleFlicker` illustrates some of the problems of updating a display. Like many animations, it has two parts: a constant background and a changing object in the foreground. In this case, the background is a checkerboard pattern and the object is a small, scaled image we can drag around on top of it, as shown in Figure 17-4. Our first version of `TerribleFlicker` lives up to its name, doing a very poor job of updating.

Figure 17-4. The TerribleFlicker application

```
//file: TerribleFlicker.java
import java.awt.*;
import java.awt.event.*;
```

```java
import javax.swing.*;

public class TerribleFlicker extends JComponent
                                implements MouseMotionListener {
  int grid = 10;
  int imageX, imageY;
  Image image;
  int imageWidth = 60, imageHeight = 60;

  public TerribleFlicker(Image i) {
    image = i;
    addMouseMotionListener(this);
  }

  public void mouseDragged(MouseEvent e) {
    imageX = e.getX();
    imageY = e.getY();
    repaint();
  }

  public void mouseMoved(MouseEvent e) {}

  public void paint(Graphics g) {
    Graphics2D g2 = (Graphics2D)g;

    int w = getSize().width / grid;
    int h = getSize().height / grid;
    boolean black = false;
    for (int y = 0; y <= grid; y++)
      for (int x = 0; x <= grid; x++) {
        g2.setPaint(black ? Color.black : Color.white);
        black = !black;
        g2.fillRect(x * w, y * h, w, h);
      }
    g2.drawImage(image, imageX, imageY,
                 imageWidth, imageHeight, this);
  }

  public static void main(String[] args) {
    String imageFile = "L1-Light.jpg";
    if (args.length > 0)
      imageFile = args[0];
    Image i = Toolkit.getDefaultToolkit().getImage(
        TerribleFlicker.class.getResource(imageFile));
    JFrame f = new JFrame("TerribleFlicker");
    Container content = new Panel(new BorderLayout());
    content.add(new TerribleFlicker(i), BorderLayout.CENTER);
    f.setContentPane(content);
```

```
      f.setSize(300, 300);
      f.setLocation(100, 100);
      f.addWindowListener(new WindowAdapter() {
        public void windowClosing(WindowEvent e) { System.exit(0); }
      });
      f.setVisible(true);
    }
  }
```

Run the application by specifying an image file as a command-line argument. Try dragging the image; you'll notice both the background and foreground flicker as they are repeatedly redrawn. What is TerribleFlicker doing, and what is it doing wrong?

TerribleFlicker is a custom component that is shown in the content pane of a JFrame. In the main() method, a TerribleFlicker is created and put in a Panel. The Panel is set to be the content pane of the applet. A Panel is used in place of one of the Swing containers for the purposes of illustration. At the end of this section, we'll use a JPanel, which will take care of all of our problems in one dramatic step.

As the mouse is dragged, TerribleFlicker keeps track of its position in two instance variables, imageX and imageY. On each call to mouseDragged(), the coordinates are updated, and repaint() is called to ask that the display be updated. When paint() is called, it looks at some parameters, draws the checkerboard pattern to fill the applet's area, and finally paints a small version of the image at the latest coordinates.

Our first, and biggest, problem is that we are updating, but we have neglected to implement a good strategy. The panel that contains TerribleFlicker is using the default implementation of the update() method, which looks something like this:

```
  public void update( Graphics g ) {
      setColor ( backgroundColor );
      fillRect( 0, 0, getSize().width, getSize().height );
      paint ( g );
  }
```

This method simply clears the display to the background color and calls the paint() method, which eventually calls the paint() method of Terrible-Flicker. This is almost never the best strategy, but is the only appropriate default for update(), which doesn't know how much of the screen we're really going to paint.

Our application paints its own background in its entirety, so we can provide a simpler version of update() that doesn't bother to clear the display. Here's another example that uses the `TerribleFlicker` class. This time, we create a `Panel` with a modified `update()` method:

```java
//file: UpdateFlicker.java
import java.awt.*;
import java.awt.event.*;
import javax.swing.*;

public class UpdateFlicker {
  public static void main(String[] args) {
    String imageFile = "L1-Light.jpg";
    if (args.length > 0) imageFile = args[0];
    Image i = Toolkit.getDefaultToolkit().getImage(
        TerribleFlicker.class.getResource(imageFile));
    JFrame f = new JFrame("UpdateFlicker");
    Container content = new Panel(new BorderLayout()) {
        public void update(Graphics g) { paint(g); }
    };
    content.add(new TerribleFlicker(i), BorderLayout.CENTER);
    f.setContentPane(content);
    f.setSize(300, 300);
    f.setLocation(100, 100);
    f.addWindowListener(new WindowAdapter() {
      public void windowClosing(WindowEvent e) { System.exit(0); }
    });
    f.setVisible(true);
  }
}
```

This application works better because we have eliminated one large, unnecessary, and (in fact) annoying graphics operation. However, although we have eliminated a `fillRect()` call, we're still doing a lot of wasted drawing. Most of the background stays the same each time it's drawn. You might think of trying to make `paint()` smarter, so that it wouldn't redraw these areas, but remember that `paint()` has to be able to draw the entire scene, because it might be called in situations when the display isn't intact. The solution is to draw only part of the picture whenever the mouse moves.

Limited Redrawing

Whenever the mouse is dragged, `TerribleFlicker` responds by updating its coordinates and calling `repaint()`. But `repaint()` draws the entire component. Most of this drawing is unnecessary. It turns out that there's another version of `repaint()` that lets you specify a rectangular area that should be drawn—in essence, a clipping region.

Why does it help to restrict the drawing area? Well, foremost, drawing operations that fall outside of the clipping region are not displayed. If a drawing operation overlaps the clipping region, we see only the part that's inside. A second effect is that, in a good implementation, the graphics context can recognize drawing operations that fall completely outside the clipping region and ignore them altogether. Eliminating unnecessary operations can save time if we're doing something complex, like filling a bunch of polygons. This doesn't save the time our application spends calling the drawing methods, but the overhead of calling these kinds of drawing methods is usually negligible compared to the time it takes to execute them. (If we were generating an image pixel by pixel, this would not be the case, as the calculations would be the major time sink, not the drawing.)

So we can save time in our application by redrawing only the affected portion of the display. We can pick the smallest rectangular area that includes both the old image position and the new image position, as shown in Figure 17-5. This is the only portion of the display that really needs to change; everything else stays the same.

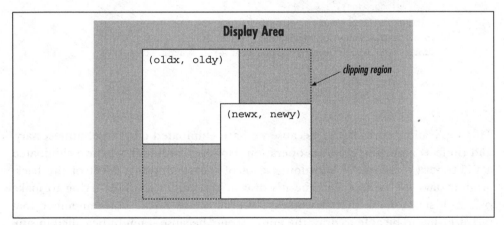

Figure 17-5. Determining the clipping region

A smarter algorithm could save even more time by redrawing only those regions that have changed. However, the simple clipping strategy we've implemented here can be applied to many kinds of drawing, and gives quite good performance, particularly if the area being changed is small.

One important thing to note is that, in addition to looking at the new position, our updating operation now has to remember the last position at which the image was drawn. Let's fix our application so it will use a specified clipping region. To keep this short and emphasize the changes, we'll take some liberties with design and make our next example a subclass of `TerribleFlicker`. Let's call it `LimitedFlicker`.

```java
//file: LimitedFlicker.java
import java.awt.*;
import java.awt.event.*;
import javax.swing.*;

public class LimitedFlicker extends TerribleFlicker {
  int oldX, oldY;

  public LimitedFlicker(Image i) { super(i); }

  public void mouseDragged(MouseEvent e) {
    imageX = e.getX();
    imageY = e.getY();
    Rectangle r = getAffectedArea(oldX, oldY, imageX, imageY,
        imageWidth, imageHeight);
    // update just the affected part of the component
    repaint(r);
    oldX = imageX;
    oldY = imageY;
  }

  private Rectangle getAffectedArea(int oldx, int oldy,
      int newx, int newy, int width, int height) {
    int x = Math.min(oldx, newx);
    int y = Math.min(oldy, newy);
    int w = (Math.max(oldx, newx) + width) - x;
    int h = (Math.max(oldy, newy) + height) - y;
    return new Rectangle(x, y, w, h);
  }

  public static void main(String[] args) {
    String imageFile = "L1-Light.jpg";
    if (args.length > 0)
      imageFile = args[0];
    Image i = Toolkit.getDefaultToolkit().getImage(
        TerribleFlicker.class.getResource(imageFile));
    JFrame f = new JFrame("LimitedFlicker");
    Container content = new Panel(new BorderLayout()) {
        public void update(Graphics g) { paint(g); }
    };
    content.add(new LimitedFlicker(i), BorderLayout.CENTER);
    f.setContentPane(content);
    f.setSize(300, 300);
    f.setLocation(100, 100);
    f.addWindowListener(new WindowAdapter() {
      public void windowClosing(WindowEvent e) { System.exit(0); }
    });
    f.setVisible(true);
  }
}
```

You may find that `LimitedFlicker` is significantly faster, though it still flickers. (You might not notice the speed-up on a fast machine.) We'll make one more change in the next section to eliminate that.

So, what have we changed? First, we've overridden `mouseDragged()` so that instead of setting the current coordinates of the image, it figures out the area that has changed. A new, `private` method helps it do this. `getAffectedArea()` takes as arguments the new and old coordinates and the width and height of the image. It determines the bounding rectangle as shown in Figure 17-6, then calls `repaint()` to draw only the affected area of the screen. `mouseDragged()` also saves the current position away, by setting the `oldX` and `oldY` variables.

Double Buffering

Now let's get to the most powerful technique in our toolbox: *double buffering*. Double buffering is a technique that fixes our flickering problems completely. It's easy to do and gives us almost flawless updates. We'll combine it with our clipping technique for better performance. In general, you can use double buffering with or without clipping.

Double buffering our display means drawing into an offscreen buffer and then copying our completed work to the display in a single painting operation, as shown in Figure 17-6. It takes the same amount of time to draw a frame, but double buffering instantaneously updates our display when it's ready.

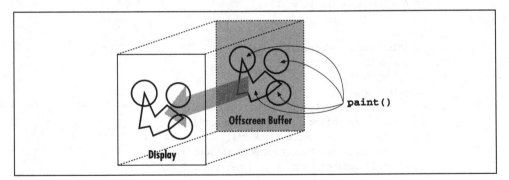

Figure 17-6. Double buffering

Although you could implement this technique yourself, there's not much point— Swing supplies double buffering for free. All you need to do is use a Swing component in a Swing container. Swing takes care of the details. Instead of using an AWT `Panel` as a container, then, let's see how it works with a Swing `JPanel`:

```
//file: Smoothie.java
import java.awt.*;
import java.awt.event.*;
```

```
import javax.swing.*;

public class Smoothie {
  public static void main(String[] args) {
    String imageFile = "L1-Light.jpg";
    if (args.length > 0)
      imageFile = args[0];
    Image i = Toolkit.getDefaultToolkit().getImage(
        TerribleFlicker.class.getResource(imageFile));
    JFrame f = new JFrame("Smoothie");
    Container content = new JPanel(new BorderLayout()) {
        public void update(Graphics g) { paint(g); }
    };
    content.add(new LimitedFlicker(i), BorderLayout.CENTER);
    f.setContentPane(content);
    f.setSize(300, 300);
    f.setLocation(100, 100);
    f.addWindowListener(new WindowAdapter() {
      public void windowClosing(WindowEvent e) { System.exit(0); }
    });
    f.setVisible(true);
  }
}
```

Now, when you drag the image, you shouldn't see any flickering. The update rate should be about the same as in the previous example (or marginally slower), but the image should move from position to position without noticeable repainting.

Note that we're still limiting repaints, because we're still using `LimitedFlicker`. You could use `TerribleFlicker` if you want. It should perform a little more slowly but you still won't see any flickering.

Offscreen Drawing

In addition to serving as buffers for double buffering, offscreen images are useful for saving complex, hard-to-produce, background information. We'll look at a simple example: the "doodle pad." `DoodlePad` is a simple drawing tool that lets us scribble by dragging the mouse, as shown in Figure 17-7. It draws into an offscreen image; its `paint()` method simply copies the image to the display area.

```
//file: DoodlePad.java
import java.awt.*;
import java.awt.event.*;
import javax.swing.*;

public class DoodlePad extends JFrame {

  public DoodlePad() {
```

Figure 17-7. The DoodlePad application

```
super("DoodlePad");
Container content = getContentPane();
content.setLayout(new BorderLayout());
final DrawPad drawPad = new DrawPad();
content.add(drawPad, BorderLayout.CENTER);
JPanel p = new JPanel();
JButton clearButton = new JButton("Clear");
clearButton.addActionListener(new ActionListener() {
  public void actionPerformed(ActionEvent e) {
    drawPad.clear();
  }
});
p.add(clearButton);
content.add(p, BorderLayout.SOUTH);
setSize(280, 300);
setLocation(100, 100);
addWindowListener(new WindowAdapter() {
  public void windowClosing(WindowEvent e) {
    System.exit(0);
  }
});
setVisible(true);
}

public static void main(String[] args) {
  new DoodlePad();
}
} // end of class DoodlePad
```

```
class DrawPad extends JComponent {
  Image image;
  Graphics2D graphics2D;
  int currentX, currentY, oldX, oldY;

  public DrawPad() {
    setDoubleBuffered(false);
    addMouseListener(new MouseAdapter() {
      public void mousePressed(MouseEvent e) {
        oldX = e.getX();
        oldY = e.getY();
      }
    });
    addMouseMotionListener(new MouseMotionAdapter() {
      public void mouseDragged(MouseEvent e) {
        currentX = e.getX();
        currentY = e.getY();
        if (graphics2D != null)
          graphics2D.drawLine(oldX, oldY, currentX, currentY);
        repaint();
        oldX = currentX;
        oldY = currentY;
      }
    });
  }

  public void paintComponent(Graphics g) {
    if (image == null) {
      image = createImage(getSize().width, getSize().height);
      graphics2D = (Graphics2D)image.getGraphics();
      graphics2D.setRenderingHint(RenderingHints.KEY_ANTIALIASING,
          RenderingHints.VALUE_ANTIALIAS_ON);
      clear();
    }
    g.drawImage(image, 0, 0, null);
  }

  public void clear() {
    graphics2D.setPaint(Color.white);
    graphics2D.fillRect(0, 0, getSize().width, getSize().height);
    graphics2D.setPaint(Color.black);
    repaint();
  }
}
```

Give it a try. Draw a nice moose, or a sunset. We just drew a lovely cartoon of Bill Gates. If you make a mistake, hit the **Clear** button and start over.

The parts should be familiar by now. We have made a type of JComponent called DrawPad. The new DrawPad component uses inner classes to supply handlers for the MouseListener and MouseMotionListener interfaces. Mouse dragging is handled by drawing lines into an offscreen image and calling repaint() to update the display. DrawPad's paint() method simply does a drawImage() to copy the offscreen drawing area to the display. In this way, DrawPad saves our sketch information.

What is unusual about DrawPad is that it does some drawing outside of paint(). In this example, we want to let the user scribble with the mouse, so we should respond to every mouse movement. Therefore, we do our work in mouseDragged() itself. As a rule, we should be careful about doing heavy work in event-handling methods because we don't want to interfere with other tasks the windowing system's painting thread is performing. In this case, our line-drawing option should not be a burden, and our primary concern is getting as close a coupling as possible between the mouse movement events and the sketch on the screen.

In addition to drawing a line as the user drags the mouse, the mouseDragged() handler maintains a set of old coordinates, to be used as a starting point for the next line segment. The mousePressed() handler resets the old coordinates to the current mouse position whenever the user moves the mouse. Finally, DrawPad provides a clear() method that clears the offscreen buffer and calls repaint() to update the display. The DoodlePad application ties the clear() method to an appropriately labeled button through another anonymous inner class.

What if we wanted to do something with the image after the user has finished scribbling on it? As we'll see in the next chapter, we could get the pixel data for the image and work with that. It wouldn't be hard to create a save facility that stores the pixel data and reproduces it later. Think about how you might go about creating a networked "bathroom wall," where people could scribble on your web pages.

Printing

Earlier in this chapter, we hinted at the possibility that you could draw the same stuff on the screen and the printer. It's true; all you really need to do is get a Graphics2D that represents a printer rather than an area of the screen. Java 2's Printing API provides the necessary plumbing. There isn't room here to describe the whole Printing API, but we will provide you with a short example that will let you get your feet wet (and your paper blackened).

The printing classes are tucked away in the java.awt.print package. You can print anything that implements the Printable interface. This interface has only one method—you guessed it, print(). This method, like the paint() methods we've already worked with, accepts a Graphics object that represents the drawing surface of the printer's page. It also accepts a PageFormat object that encapsulates information about the paper on which you're printing. Finally, print() is passed the number of the page that is being rendered.

Your print() implementation should either render the requested page or state that it doesn't exist. You can do this by returning special values from print(), either Printable.PAGE_EXISTS or Printable.NO_SUCH_PAGE.

You can control a print job, including showing print and page setup dialogs, using the PrinterJob class. The following class will enable you to get something on paper:

```java
//file: UnbelievablySimplePrint.java
import java.awt.*;
import java.awt.print.*;

public class UnbelievablySimplePrint implements Printable {
  private static Font sFont = new Font("Serif", Font.PLAIN , 64);

  public int print(Graphics g, PageFormat Pf, int pageIndex)
      throws PrinterException {
    if (pageIndex > 0) return NO_SUCH_PAGE;
    Graphics2D g2 = (Graphics2D)g;
    g2.setFont(sFont);
    g2.setPaint(Color.black);
    g2.drawString("Save a tree!", 96, 144);
    return PAGE_EXISTS;
  }

  public static void main(String[] args) {
    PrinterJob job = PrinterJob.getPrinterJob();
    job.setPrintable(new UnbelievablySimplePrint());
    if (job.printDialog()) {
      try {
        job.print();
      }
      catch (PrinterException e) {}
    }
    System.exit(0);
  }
}
```

There's not much to this example. We've created an implementation of Printable, called UnbelievablySimplePrint. It has a very simple print() method that draws some text.

The rest of the work, in the `main()` method, has to do with setting up the print job. First, we create a new `PrinterJob` and tell it what we want to print:

```
PrinterJob job = PrinterJob.getPrinterJob();
job.setPrintable(new UnbelievablySimplePrint());
```

Then we use the `printDialog()` method to show the standard print dialog. If the user presses the **OK** button, `printDialog()` returns `true` and `main()` goes ahead with the printing.

Notice, in the `print()` method, how we perform the familiar cast from `Graphics` to `Graphics2D`. The full power of the 2D API is available for printing. In a real application, you'd probably have some subclass of `Component` that was also a `Printable`. The `print()` method could simply call the component's `paint()` method, to create a component that performs the same rendering to both the screen and the printer.

18

Working with Images and Other Media

Up to this point, we've confined ourselves to working with the high-level drawing commands of the Graphics2D class, using images in a hands-off mode. In this section, we'll clear up some of the mystery surrounding images and see how they are created and used. The classes in the java.awt.image package handle images and their insides; Figure 18-1 shows the important classes in this package.*

First, we'll return to our discussion of image observers and see how we can get more control over image data as it's processed asynchronously by GUI components. Then we'll open the hood and have a look at the inside of a Buffered-Image. If you're interested in creating sophisticated graphics, such as rendered images or video streams, this will teach you about the foundations of image construction in Java.

Implementing an ImageObserver

The architects of Java realized that images might take some time to load over a slow network. Image observers implement the ImageObserver interface. They are effectively nosy neighbors of images that watch as the image data arrives.

An image is simply a rectangle of pixels. A pixel has both a color and a transparency; the transparency specifies how pixels underneath the image show through. For a static image, such as a GIF or JPEG data file, the observer is notified when the entire image is complete, and production is finished. For a video source or animation, the image observer would be notified repeatedly (at the end of each frame) as a continuous stream of pixel data was received.

---

* Before Java 2, creating and modifying images was the domain of image producers and consumers. We won't be covering these topics in this chapter; instead, we'll stick to the "new stuff," which is more capable and easier to use in some cases.

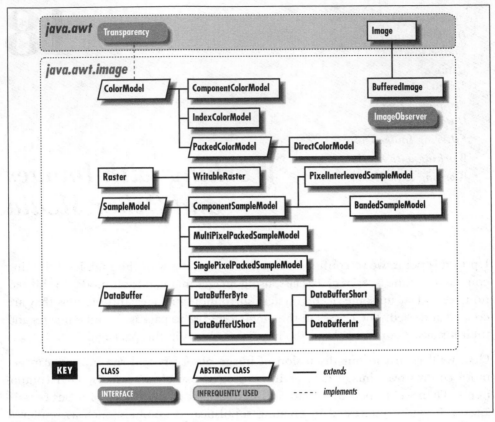

Figure 18-1. The java.awt.image package

The observer is notified as new portions of the image and new attributes are ready. Its job is to track this information and let another part of the application know its status. The image observer is essentially a callback that is notified asynchronously as the image is built. The default Component class image observer that we used in our previous examples called repaint() for us each time a new section of the image was available, so that the screen was updated more or less continuously as the data arrived. A different kind of image observer might wait for the entire image before telling the application to display it; yet another observer might update a loading meter showing how far the image loading had progressed.

To be an image observer, you have to implement the single method, image-Update(), defined by the java.awt.image.ImageObserver interface:

```
public boolean imageUpdate(Image image, int flags, int x, int y,
                           int width, int height)
```

imageUpdate() is called by the graphics system, as needed, to pass the observer information about the construction of its view of the image. Essentially, any time the image changes, the observer is notified so it can perform any necessary actions, like repainting. `image` holds a reference to the `Image` object in question. `flags` is an integer whose bits specify what information about the image is now available. The values of the flags are defined as `static` variables in the `ImageObserver` interface, as shown in Table 18-1.

Table 18-1. ImageObserver Information Flags

Flag	Description
HEIGHT	The height of the image is ready.
WIDTH	The width of the image is ready.
FRAMEBITS	A frame is complete.
SOMEBITS	Some new pixels have arrived.
ALLBITS	The image is complete.
ABORT	The image loading has been aborted.
ERROR	An error occurred during image processing; attempts to display the image will fail.

The flags determine which of the other parameters, x, y, width, and `height`, hold valid data and what that data means. To test whether a particular flag in the `flags` integer is set, we have to resort to some binary shenanigans. The following class, `MyObserver`, implements the `ImageObserver` interface; it reports on the information it receives:

```
//file: MyObserver.java
import java.awt.*;
import java.awt.image.*;

class MyObserver implements ImageObserver {

  public boolean imageUpdate( Image image, int flags, int x, int y,
                              int width, int height) {

    if ( (flags & HEIGHT) !=0 )
      System.out.println("Image height = " + height );

    if ( (flags & WIDTH ) !=0 )
      System.out.println("Image width = " + width );

    if ( (flags & FRAMEBITS) != 0 )
      System.out.println("Another frame finished.");

    if ( (flags & SOMEBITS) != 0 )
      System.out.println("Image section :"
              + new Rectangle( x, y, width, height ) );

    if ( (flags & ALLBITS) != 0 ) {
```

```
        System.out.println("Image finished!");
        return false;
      }

      if ( (flags & ABORT) != 0 ) {
        System.out.println("Image load aborted...");
        return false;
      }
      return true;
    }
  }
```

The `imageUpdate()` method of `MyObserver` is called by the consumer periodically, and prints simple status messages about the construction of the image. Notice that `width` and `height` play a dual role. If `SOMEBITS` is set, they represent the size of the chunk of the image that has just been delivered. If `HEIGHT` or `WIDTH` is set, however, they represent the overall image dimensions. Just for amusement, we have used the `java.awt.Rectangle` class to help us print the bounds of a rectangular region. (You may not want to create a new object each time you just need to report some coordinates.)

`imageUpdate()` returns a `boolean` value indicating whether or not it's interested in future updates. If the image is finished or aborted, `imageUpdate()` returns `false` to indicate it isn't interested in further updates. Otherwise, it returns `true`.

The following example uses a `MyObserver` object to generate information about an image as it is loaded. (To see the messages, enable your browser's Java console.)

```
//file: ObserveImage.java
import java.awt.*;

public class ObserveImage extends java.applet.Applet {
  Image img;

  public void init() {
    img = getImage( getClass().getResource(getParameter("img")) );
    MyObserver mo = new MyObserver();
    img.getWidth( mo );
    img.getHeight( mo );
    prepareImage( img, mo );
  }

  public void paint(Graphics g) {
    g.drawImage(img, 0, 0, null);
  }
}
```

After requesting the `Image` object with `getImage()`, we perform three operations on it to kick-start the loading process. `getWidth()` and `getHeight()` ask for the image's width and height. If the image hasn't been loaded yet, or its size can't be determined until loading is finished, our observer will be called when the data is ready. `prepareImage()` asks that the image be readied for display on the component. It's a general mechanism for starting the process of loading, converting, and possibly scaling the image. If the image hasn't been otherwise prepared or displayed, this happens asynchronously, and our image observer will be notified as the data is constructed.

You should be able to see how we could implement all sorts of sophisticated image loading and tracking schemes. The two most obvious strategies, however, are to draw an image progressively, as it's constructed, or to wait until it's complete and draw it in its entirety. We have already seen that the `Component` class implements the first scheme. Another class, `java.awt.MediaTracker`, is a general utility that tracks the loading of a number of images or other media types for us. We'll look at it next.

Using a MediaTracker

`java.awt.MediaTracker` is a utility class that simplifies life if we have to wait for one or more images to be loaded before they're displayed. A `MediaTracker` monitors the preparation of an image or a group of images and lets us check on them periodically, or wait until they are completed. `MediaTracker` uses the `Image-Observer` interface internally to receive image updates.

The following applet, `TrackImage`, uses a `MediaTracker` to wait while an image is prepared. It shows a "Loading . . ." message while it's waiting. (If you are retrieving the image from a local disk or very fast network, this message might go by quickly, so pay attention.)

```
//file: TrackImage.java
import java.awt.*;

public class TrackImage extends javax.swing.JApplet
                        implements Runnable {
  final int MAIN_IMAGE = 0;
  Image image;
  MediaTracker tracker;
  boolean loaded = false;
  Thread thread = null;
  String message = "Loading...";

  public void init() {
    image = getImage(getClass().getResource(getParameter("image")));
    tracker = new MediaTracker(this);
    tracker.addImage(image, MAIN_IMAGE);
  }
```

```
    public void start() {
        if (!tracker.checkID(MAIN_IMAGE)) {
            thread = new Thread(this);
            thread.start();
        }
    }

    public void stop() {
        thread.interrupt();
        thread = null;
    }

    public void run() {
        repaint();
        try { tracker.waitForID(MAIN_IMAGE); }
        catch(InterruptedException e) {}
        if (tracker.isErrorID(MAIN_IMAGE)) message = "Error";
        else loaded = true;
        repaint();
    }

    public void paint(Graphics g) {
        if (loaded) g.drawImage(image, 0, 0, this);
        else {
            g.drawRect(0, 0, getSize().width - 1, getSize().height - 1);
            g.drawString(message, 20, 20);
        }
    }
}
```

From its init() method, TrackImage requests its image and creates a Media-
Tracker to manage it. Later, after the applet is started, TrackImage fires up a
thread to wait while the image is loaded. Note that we do not do this in init()
because it would be rude to do anything time-consuming there; it would take up
time in a thread that we don't own. In this case, waiting in init() would be especially bad because paint() would never get called and our "loading" message
wouldn't be displayed; the applet would just hang until the image loaded. It's
often better to create a new thread for initialization and display a startup message
in the interim. (If you're not familiar with applets, you may want to take a look at
Chapter 20, *Applets*, at this point.)

When we construct a MediaTracker, we give it a reference to our component
(this). After creating a MediaTracker, we assign it images to manage. Each
image is associated with an integer identifier we'll use later for checking on its status. Multiple images can be associated with the same identifier, letting us manage
them as a group. The value of the identifier is also used to prioritize loading when
waiting on multiple sets of images; lower IDs have higher priority. In this case, we

want to manage only a single image, so we created one identifier called `MAIN_IMAGE` and passed it as the ID for our image in the call to `addImage()`.

In our applet's `start()` method, we call the `MediaTracker`'s `checkID()` routine with the ID of the image to see whether it's already been loaded. If it hasn't, the applet fires up a new thread to fetch it. The thread executes the `run()` method, which calls the `MediaTracker waitforID()` routine and blocks on the image, waiting for it to finish loading. The `loaded` flag tells `paint()` whether to display our status message or the actual image. We do a `repaint()` immediately upon entering `run()` to display the "Loading . . ." status, and again upon exiting to change the display. We test for errors during image preparation with `isErrorID()` and change the status message if we find one.[*]

This may seem like a lot of work to go through just to put up a status message while loading a single image. `MediaTracker` is more valuable when we are working with many images that have to be available before we can begin parts of our application. It saves us from implementing a custom `ImageObserver` for every application. In the future, `MediaTracker` should also be able to track the status of audio clips and other kinds of media (as its name suggests).

Producing Image Data

There are two different approaches to generating image data. The easiest way is to treat the image as a drawing surface and use the methods of `Graphics2D` to render things into the image. The second way is to twiddle the bits of the image data yourself. This is harder, but it can be useful in specific cases: loading and saving images in files or mathematically analyzing image data are two examples.

Drawing Animations

Let's begin with the simpler approach, rendering on an image. We'll throw in a twist, to make things interesting: we'll build an animation. Each frame will be rendered as we go along. This is very similar to the double buffering we examined in the last chapter, but this time we'll use a timer, instead of mouse events, as the signal to generate new frames.

Swing performs double buffering automatically, so we don't even have to worry about the animation flickering. Although it looks like we're drawing directly to the screen, we're really drawing into an image that Swing uses for double buffering. All we need to do is draw the right thing at the right time.

---

[*] In early Java 2 releases, `appletviewer` may throw an access exception when you close down the applet. The exception occurs when `TrackImage`'s `stop()` method attempts to call the `interrupt()` method on the image-loading thread. This is a problem with `appletviewer`—the example runs fine as a Java Plug-in applet. (See Chapter 20 for more information about the Java Plug-in.)

Let's look at an example, Hypnosis, that illustrates the technique. This example shows a constantly shifting shape that bounces around the inside of a component. When screen savers first came of age, this kind of thing was pretty hot stuff. Hypnosis is shown in Figure 18-2; here is its source code:

```java
//file: Hypnosis.java
import java.awt.*;
import java.awt.event.*;
import java.awt.geom.GeneralPath;
import javax.swing.*;

public class Hypnosis extends JComponent implements Runnable {
  private int[] coordinates;
  private int[] deltas;
  private Paint paint;

  public Hypnosis(int numberOfSegments) {
    int numberOfCoordinates = numberOfSegments * 4 + 2;
    coordinates = new int[numberOfCoordinates];
    deltas = new int[numberOfCoordinates];
    for (int i = 0 ; i < numberOfCoordinates; i++) {
      coordinates[i] = (int)(Math.random() * 300);
      deltas[i] = (int)(Math.random() * 4 + 3);
      if (deltas[i] > 4) deltas[i] = -(deltas[i] - 3);
    }
    paint = new GradientPaint(0, 0, Color.blue,
        20, 10, Color.red, true);

    Thread t = new Thread(this);
    t.start();
  }

  public void run() {
    try {
      while (true) {
        timeStep();
        repaint();
        Thread.sleep(1000 / 24);
      }
    }
    catch (InterruptedException ie) {}
  }

  public void paint(Graphics g) {
    Graphics2D g2 = (Graphics2D)g;
    g2.setRenderingHint(RenderingHints.KEY_ANTIALIASING,
        RenderingHints.VALUE_ANTIALIAS_ON);
    Shape s = createShape();
    g2.setPaint(paint);
```

```
      g2.fill(s);
      g2.setPaint(Color.white);
      g2.draw(s);
    }

    private void timeStep() {
      Dimension d = getSize();
      if (d.width == 0 || d.height == 0) return;
      for (int i = 0; i < coordinates.length; i++) {
        coordinates[i] += deltas[i];
        int limit = (i % 2 == 0) ? d.width : d.height;
        if (coordinates[i] < 0) {
          coordinates[i] = 0;
          deltas[i] = -deltas[i];
        }
        else if (coordinates[i] > limit) {
          coordinates[i] = limit - 1;
          deltas[i] = -deltas[i];
        }
      }
    }

    private Shape createShape() {
      GeneralPath path = new GeneralPath();
      path.moveTo(coordinates[0], coordinates[1]);
      for (int i = 2; i < coordinates.length; i += 4)
        path.quadTo(coordinates[i], coordinates[i + 1],
            coordinates[i + 2], coordinates[i + 3]);
      path.closePath();
      return path;
    }

    public static void main(String[] args) {
      JFrame f = new JFrame("Hypnosis");
      f.addWindowListener(new WindowAdapter() {
        public void windowClosing(WindowEvent we) { System.exit(0); }
      });
      Container c = f.getContentPane();
      c.setLayout(new BorderLayout());
      c.add(new Hypnosis(4));
      f.setSize(300, 300);
      f.setLocation(100, 100);
      f.setVisible(true);
    }
  }
```

The main() method does the usual grunt work of setting up a JFrame that will hold our animation component.

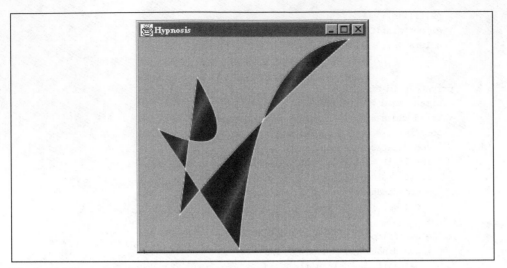

Figure 18-2. A simple animation

The Hypnosis component has a very basic strategy for animation. It holds some number of coordinate pairs in its coordinates member variable. A corresponding array, deltas, holds "delta" amounts that are added to the coordinates each time the figure is supposed to change. To render the complex shape you see in Figure 18-2, Hypnosis creates the shape from the coordinates array each time the component is drawn.

Hypnosis's constructor has two important tasks. First, it fills up the coordinates and deltas arrays with random values. The number of array elements is determined by an argument to the constructor. The constructor's second task is to start up a new thread that will drive the animation.

The animation is done in the run() method. This method calls timeStep(), which repaints the component and waits for a short time (details to follow). Each time timeStep() is called, the coordinates array is updated. Then repaint() is called. This results in a call to paint(), which creates a shape from the coordinate array and draws it.

The paint() method is relatively simple. It uses a helper method, called createShape(), to create a shape from the coordinate array. The shape is then filled, using a Paint stored as a member variable. The shape's outline is also drawn in white.

The timeStep() method updates all the elements of the coordinate array by adding the corresponding element of deltas. If any coordinates are now out of the components bounds, they are adjusted and the corresponding delta is negated. This produces the effect of bouncing off the sides of the component.

createShape() creates a shape from the coordinate array. It uses the General-Path class, a useful Shape implementation that allows you to build shapes using straight and curved line segments. In this case, we create a shape from a series of quadratic curves.

BufferedImage Anatomy

So far, we've talked about java.awt.Images and how they can be loaded and drawn. What if you really want to get inside the image to examine and update its data? Image doesn't give you access to its data. You'll need to use a more sophisticated class, java.awt.image.BufferedImage. These classes are closely related—BufferedImage, in fact, is a subclass of Image. But BufferedImage gives you all sorts of control over the actual data that makes up the image. You can think of BufferedImage as an Image on steroids. Because it's a subclass of Image, you can pass a BufferedImage to any of Graphics2D's methods that accept an Image.

To create an image from raw data arrays, you need to understand exactly how a BufferedImage is put together. It's actually quite complex—the BufferedImage class was designed to support images in nearly any storage format you could imagine. Figure 18-3 shows the elements of a BufferedImage.

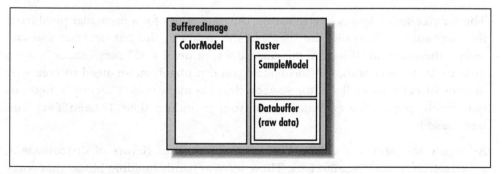

Figure 18-3. Inside a BufferedImage

An image is simply a rectangle of colored pixels, which is a simple enough concept. There's a lot of complexity underneath the BufferedImage class, because there are a lot of different ways to represent the colors of pixels. You might have, for instance, an image with RGB data where each pixel's red, green, and blue values were stored as the elements of byte arrays. Or you might have an RGB image where each pixel was represented by an integer that contained red, green, and blue values. Or you could have a 16-level grayscale image with 8 pixels stored in each element of an integer array. You get the idea—there are many different ways to store image data, and BufferedImage is designed to support all of them.

A `BufferedImage` consists of two pieces, a `Raster` and a `ColorModel`. The `Raster` contains the actual image data. You can think of it as an array of pixel values. It can answer questions like "What are the data values for the pixel at 51, 17?" The `Raster` for an RGB image would return three values, while a `Raster` for a grayscale image would return a single value. A subclass of `Raster`, `Writable-Raster`, also supports modifying pixel data values.

The `ColorModel`'s job is to interpret the image data as colors. The `ColorModel` can translate the data values that come from the `Raster` into `Color` objects. An RGB color model, for example, would know how to interpret three data values as red, green, and blue. A grayscale color model could interpret a single data value as a gray level. Conceptually, at least, this is how an image is displayed on the screen. The graphics system retrieves the data for each pixel of the image from the `Raster`. Then the `ColorModel` tells what color each pixel should be and the graphics system is able to set the color of each pixel.

The `Raster` itself is made up of two pieces, a `DataBuffer` and a `SampleModel`. A `DataBuffer` is a wrapper for the raw data arrays, which are `byte`, `short`, or `int` arrays. `DataBuffer` has handy subclasses, `DataBufferByte`, `DataBufferShort`, and `DataBufferInt`, that allow you to create a `DataBuffer` from raw data arrays. You'll see an example of this technique later, in the `StaticGenerator` example.

The `SampleModel` knows how to extract the data values for a particular pixel from the `DataBuffer`. It knows the layout of the arrays in the `DataBuffer` and can answer the question "What are the data values for pixel x, y?" `SampleModel`s are a little tricky to work with, but fortunately you'll probably never need to create or use one directly. As we'll see, the `Raster` class has many static ("factory") methods that create preconfigured `Raster`s for you, including their `DataBuffer`s and `SampleModel`s.

As Figure 18-1 shows, the 2D API comes with various flavors of `ColorModel`s, `SampleModel`s, and `DataBuffer`s. These serve as handy building blocks that cover most common image storage formats. You'll rarely need to subclass any of these classes to create a `BufferedImage`.

Color Models

Everybody wants to work with color in their application, but using color raises problems. The most important problem is simply how to represent a color. There are many different ways to encode color information: red, green, blue (RGB) values; hue, saturation, value (HSV); hue, lightness, saturation (HLS); and more. In addition, you can provide full-color information for each pixel, or you can just specify an index into a color table (palette) for each pixel. The way you represent a color is called a *color model*. The 2D API provides tools to support any color model you could imagine. Here, we'll just cover two broad groups of color models: *direct* and *indexed*.

As you might expect, you must specify a color model in order to generate pixel data; the abstract class java.awt.image.ColorModel represents a color model. By default, Java 2D uses a direct color model called ARGB. The A stands for "alpha," which is the historical name for transparency. RGB refers to the red, green, and blue color components that are combined to produce a single, composite color. In the default ARGB model, each pixel is represented by a 32-bit integer that is interpreted as four 8-bit fields; in order, the fields represent the transparency (A), red, green, and blue components of the color, as shown in Figure 18-4.

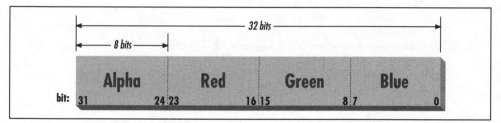

Figure 18-4. ARGB color encoding

To create an instance of the default ARGB model, call the static getRGB-default() method in ColorModel. This method returns a DirectColorModel object; DirectColorModel is a subclass of ColorModel. You can also create other direct color models by calling a DirectColorModel constructor, but you shouldn't need to unless you have a fairly exotic application.

In an indexed color model, each pixel is represented by a smaller piece of information: an index into a table of real color values. For some applications, generating data with an indexed model may be more convenient. If you have an 8-bit display or smaller, using an indexed model may be more efficient, since your hardware is internally using an indexed color model of some form.

Creating an Image

Let's take a look at producing some image data. A picture may be worth a thousand words, but fortunately, we can generate a picture in significantly fewer than a thousand words of Java. If we just want to render image frames byte by byte, you can put together a BufferedImage pretty easily.

The following application, ColorPan, creates an image from an array of integers holding RGB pixel values:

```
//file: ColorPan.java
import java.awt.*;
```

```java
import java.awt.event.*;
import java.awt.image.*;
import javax.swing.*;

public class ColorPan extends JComponent {
  BufferedImage image;

  public void initialize() {
    int width = getSize().width;
    int height = getSize().height;
    int[] data = new int [width * height];
    int i = 0;
    for (int y = 0; y < height; y++) {
      int red = (y * 255) / (height - 1);
      for (int x = 0; x < width; x++) {
        int green = (x * 255) / (width - 1);
        int blue = 128;
        data[i++] = (red << 16) | (green << 8 ) | blue;
      }
    }

    image = new BufferedImage(width, height,
        BufferedImage.TYPE_INT_RGB);
    image.setRGB(0, 0, width, height, data, 0, width);
  }

  public void paint(Graphics g) {
    if (image == null) initialize();
    g.drawImage(image, 0, 0, this);
  }

  public static void main(String[] args) {
    JFrame f = new JFrame("ColorPan");
    f.getContentPane().add(new ColorPan());
    f.setSize(300, 300);
    f.setLocation(100, 100);
    f.addWindowListener(new WindowAdapter() {
      public void windowClosing(WindowEvent e) {
        System.exit(0);
      }
    });
    f.setVisible(true);
  }
}
```

Give it a try. The size of the image is determined by the size of the application window when it starts up. You should get a very colorful box that pans from deep blue at the upper-left corner to bright yellow at the bottom right, with green and red at the other extremes.

We create a `BufferedImage` in the `initialize()` method and then display the image in `paint()`. The variable `data` is a one-dimensional array of integers that holds 32-bit RGB pixel values. In `initialize()` we loop over every pixel in the image and assign it an RGB value. The blue component is always 128, half its maximum intensity. The red component varies from 0 to 255 along the y-axis; likewise, the green component varies from 0 to 255 along the x-axis. This statement combines these components into an RGB value:

```
data[i++] = (red << 16) | (green << 8 ) | blue;
```

The bitwise left-shift operator (<<) should be familiar to C programmers. It simply shoves the bits over by the specified number of positions.

When we create the `BufferedImage`, all its data is zeroed out. All we specify in the constructor is the width and height of the image and its type. `BufferedImage` includes quite a few constants representing image storage types. We've chosen `TYPE_INT_RGB` here, which indicates we want to store the image as RGB data packed into integers. The constructor takes care of creating an appropriate `ColorModel`, `Raster`, `SampleModel`, and `DataBuffer` for us. Then we simply use a convenient method, `setRGB()`, to assign our data to the image. In this way, we've side-stepped the messy innards of `BufferedImage`. In the next example, we'll take a closer look at the details.

Once we have the image, we can draw it on the display with the familiar `drawImage()` method.

Updating a BufferedImage

`BufferedImage` can also be used to update an image dynamically. Because the image's data arrays are directly accessible, you can change the data and redraw the picture whenever you want. This is probably the easiest way to build your own low-level animation software. The following example simulates the static on a television screen. It generates successive frames of random black and white pixels and displays each frame when it is complete. Figure 18-5 shows one frame of random static; the code follows:

```
//file: StaticGenerator.java
import java.awt.*;
import java.awt.event.*;
import java.awt.image.*;
import java.util.Random;
import javax.swing.*;

public class StaticGenerator extends JComponent implements Runnable {
  byte[] data;
  BufferedImage image;
```

```
    Random random;

    public void initialize() {
        int w = getSize().width, h = getSize().height;
        int length = ((w + 7) * h) / 8;
        data = new byte[length];
        DataBuffer db = new DataBufferByte(data, length);
        WritableRaster wr = Raster.createPackedRaster(db, w, h, 1, null);
        ColorModel cm = new IndexColorModel(1, 2,
            new byte[] { (byte)0, (byte)255 },
            new byte[] { (byte)0, (byte)255 },
            new byte[] { (byte)0, (byte)255 });
        image = new BufferedImage(cm, wr, false, null);
        random = new Random();
        new Thread(this).start();
    }

    public void run() {
        while (true) {
            random.nextBytes(data);
            repaint();
            try { Thread.sleep(1000 / 24); }
            catch( InterruptedException e ) { /* die */ }
        }
    }

    public void paint(Graphics g) {
        if (image == null) initialize();
        g.drawImage(image, 0, 0, this);
    }

    public static void main(String[] args) {
        JFrame f = new JFrame("StaticGenerator");
        f.getContentPane().add(new StaticGenerator());
        f.setSize(300, 300);
        f.setLocation(100, 100);
        f.addWindowListener(new WindowAdapter() {
            public void windowClosing(WindowEvent e) {
                System.exit(0);
            }
        });
        f.setVisible(true);
    }
}
```

The initialize() method sets up the BufferedImage that produces the
sequence of images. We build this image from the bottom up, starting with the raw
data array. Since we're only displaying two colors here, black and white, we need
only one bit per pixel. We want a 0 bit to represent black and a 1 bit to represent
white. This calls for an indexed color model, which we'll create a little later.

Figure 18-5. A frame of random static

The image data is stored as a byte array, where each array element holds eight pixels. The array length, then, is calculated by multiplying the width and height of the image and dividing by eight. We also have to adjust for the fact that each image row starts on a byte boundary. For example, an image that was 13 pixels wide would actually use 2 bytes (16 bits) for each row:

```
int length = ((w + 7) * h) / 8;
```

Next, the actual byte array is created. The member variable data holds a reference to this array. Later, we'll use data to change the image data dynamically. Once we have the image data array, it's easy to create a DataBuffer from it:

```
data = new byte[length];
DataBuffer db = new DataBufferByte(data, length);
```

DataBuffer has several subclasses, like DataBufferByte, that make it easy to create a data buffer from raw arrays.

The next step, logically, is to create a SampleModel. Then we could create a Raster from the SampleModel and the DataBuffer. Lucky for us, though, the Raster class contains a bevy of useful static methods that create common types of Rasters. One of these methods creates a Raster from data that contains multiple pixels packed into array elements. We simply use this method, supplying the data buffer, the width and height, and indicating that each pixel uses one bit:

```
WritableRaster wr = Raster.createPackedRaster(db, w, h, 1, null);
```

The last argument to this method is a Point that indicates where the upper-left corner of the Raster should be. By passing null, we use the default of 0, 0.

The last piece of the puzzle is the `ColorModel`. Each pixel is either 0 or 1, but how should that be interpreted as color? In this case, we use an `IndexColorModel` with a very small palette. The palette has only two entries, one each for black and white:

```
ColorModel cm = new IndexColorModel(1, 2,
        new byte[] { (byte)0, (byte)255 },
        new byte[] { (byte)0, (byte)255 },
        new byte[] { (byte)0, (byte)255 });
```

The `IndexColorModel` constructor that we've used here accepts the number of bits per pixel (1), the number of entries in the palette(2), and three byte arrays that are the red, green, and blue components of the palette colors. Our palette consists of two colors: black $(0, 0, 0)$ and white $(255, 255, 255)$.

Now that we've got all the pieces, we just need to create a `BufferedImage`. This image is also stored in a member variable so we can draw it later. To create the `BufferedImage`, we pass the color model and writable raster we just created:

```
image = new BufferedImage(cm, wr, false, null);
```

All the hard work is done now. Our `paint()` method just draws the image, using `drawImage()`.

The `init()` method starts a thread that generates the pixel data. The `run()` method takes care of generating the pixel data. It uses a Random object to fill the data image data array with random values. Since the data array is the actual image data for our image, changing the data values changes the appearance of the image. Once we fill the array with random data, a call to `repaint()` shows the new image on the screen.

That's about all there is. It's worth noting how simple it is to create this animation. Once we have the `BufferedImage`, we treat it like any other image. The code that generates the image sequence can be arbitrarily complex. But that complexity never infects the simple task of getting the image on the screen and updating it.

Filtering Image Data

An *image filter* is an object that performs transformations on image data. The Java 2D API supports image filtering through the `BufferedImageOp` interface. An image filter takes a `BufferedImage` as input (the *source image*) and performs some processing on the image data, producing another `BufferedImage` (the *destination image*).

The 2D API comes with a handy toolbox of `BufferedImageOp` implementations, as summarized in Table 18-2.

Table 18-2. Image Operators in the 2D API

Name	Description
AffineTransformOp	Transforms an image geometrically
ColorConvertOp	Converts from one color space to another
ConvolveOp	Performs a convolution, a mathematical operation that can be used to blur, sharpen, or otherwise process an image
LookupOp	Uses one or more lookup tables to process image values
RescaleOp	Uses a multiplication to process image values

Let's take a look at two of the simpler image operators. First, try the following application. It loads an image (the first command-line argument is the filename) and processes it in different ways as you select items from the combo box. The application is shown in Figure 18-6; the source code follows:

```java
//file: ImageProcessor.java
import java.awt.*;
import java.awt.event.*;
import java.awt.geom.*;
import java.awt.image.*;
import javax.swing.*;

public class ImageProcessor extends JComponent {
  private BufferedImage source, destination;
  private JComboBox options;

  public ImageProcessor(BufferedImage image) {
    source = destination = image;
    setBackground(Color.white);
    setLayout(new BorderLayout());
    // create a panel to hold the combo box
    JPanel controls = new JPanel();
    // create the combo box with the names of the area operators
    options = new JComboBox(
      new String[] { "[source]", "brighten",
          "darken", "rotate", "scale" }
    );
    // perform some processing when the selection changes
    options.addItemListener(new ItemListener() {
      public void itemStateChanged(ItemEvent ie) {
        // retrieve the selection option from the combo box
        String option = (String)options.getSelectedItem();
        // process the image according to the selected option
        BufferedImageOp op = null;
        if (option.equals("[source]"))
          destination = source;
        else if (option.equals("brighten"))
          op = new RescaleOp(1.5f, 0, null);
```

```
        else if (option.equals("darken"))
          op = new RescaleOp(.5f, 0, null);
        else if (option.equals("rotate"))
          op = new AffineTransformOp(
              AffineTransform.getRotateInstance(Math.PI / 6), null);
        else if (option.equals("scale"))
          op = new AffineTransformOp(
              AffineTransform.getScaleInstance(.5, .5), null);
        if (op != null) destination = op.filter(source, null);
        repaint();
      }
    });
    controls.add(options);
    add(controls, BorderLayout.SOUTH);
  }

  public void paintComponent(Graphics g) {
    int imageWidth = destination.getWidth();
    int imageHeight = destination.getHeight();
    int width = getSize().width;
    int height = getSize().height;
    g.drawImage(destination,
        (width - imageWidth) / 2, (height - imageHeight) / 2, null);
  }

  public static void main(String[] args) {
    String filename = args[0];
    // load the image
    Image i = Toolkit.getDefaultToolkit().getImage(filename);
    Component c = new Component() {};
    MediaTracker tracker = new MediaTracker(c);
    tracker.addImage(i, 0);
    try { tracker.waitForID(0); }
    catch (InterruptedException ie) {}

    // draw the Image into a BufferedImage
    int w = i.getWidth(null), h = i.getHeight(null);
    BufferedImage bi = new BufferedImage(w, h,
        BufferedImage.TYPE_INT_RGB);
    Graphics2D imageGraphics = bi.createGraphics();
    imageGraphics.drawImage(i, 0, 0, null);

    // create a frame window
    JFrame f = new JFrame("ImageProcessor");
    f.addWindowListener(new WindowAdapter() {
      public void windowClosing(WindowEvent e) { System.exit(0); }
    });
    Container content = f.getContentPane();
    content.setLayout(new BorderLayout());
```

```
        content.add(new ImageProcessor(bi));
        f.setSize(bi.getWidth(), bi.getHeight());
        f.setLocation(100, 100);
        f.setVisible(true);
    }
}
```

Figure 18-6. The ImageProcessor application

There's quite a bit packed into the `ImageProcessor` application. After you've played around with it, come back and read about the details.

How ImageProcessor Works

The basic operation of `ImageProcessor` is very straightforward. It loads a source image, specified with a command-line argument, in its `main()` method. The image is displayed along with a combo box. When you select different items from the combo box, `ImageProcessor` performs some image-processing operation on the source image and displays the result (the destination image). Most of this work occurs in the `ItemListener` event handler that is created in `ImageProcessor`'s constructor. Depending on what option is selected, a `BufferedImageOp` (called op) is instantiated and used to process the source image, like this:

```
destination = op.filter(source, null);
```

The destination image is returned from the `filter()` method. If we already had a destination image of the right size, we could have passed it as the second argument to `filter()`, which would improve the performance of the application a little bit. If you just pass `null`, as we have here, an appropriate destination image is created and returned to you. Once the destination image is created, `paint()`'s job is very simple—it just draws the destination image, centered on the component.

Converting an Image to a BufferedImage

Image processing is performed on `BufferedImages`, not `Images`. This example demonstrates an important technique: how to convert an `Image` to a `Buffered-Image`. The `main()` method loads an `Image` from a file using `Toolkit`'s `getImage()` method:

```
Image i = Toolkit.getDefaultToolkit().getImage(filename);
```

Next, `main()` uses a `MediaTracker` to make sure the image data is fully loaded.

The trick of converting an `Image` to a `BufferedImage` is to draw the `Image` into the drawing surface of the `BufferedImage`. Since we know the `Image` is fully loaded, we just need to create a `BufferedImage`, get its graphics context, and draw the `Image` into it:

```
BufferedImage bi = new BufferedImage(w, h,
        BufferedImage.TYPE_INT_RGB);
Graphics2D imageGraphics = bi.createGraphics();
imageGraphics.drawImage(i, 0, 0, null);
```

Using the RescaleOp Class

Rescaling is an image operation that multiplies all the pixel values in the image by some constant. It doesn't affect the size of the image in any way (in case you thought *rescaling* meant *scaling*), but it does affect the colors of its pixels. In an RGB image, for example, each of the red, green, and blue values for each of the pixels would be multiplied by the rescaling multiplier. If you want, you can also adjust the results by adding an offset. In the 2D API, rescaling is performed by the `java.awt.image.RescaleOp` class. To create such an operator, specify the multiplier, offset, and a set of hints that control the quality of the conversion. In this case, we'll use a zero offset and not bother with the hints (by passing `null`):

```
op = new RescaleOp(1.5f, 0, null);
```

Here we've specified a multiplier of 1.5 and an offset of 0. All values in the destination image will be 1.5 times the values in the source image, which has the net result of making the image brighter. To perform the operation, we call the `filter()` method from the `BufferedImageOp` interface.

Using the AffineTransformOp Class

The `java.awt.image.AffineTransformOp` image operator geometrically transforms a source image to produce the destination image. To create an `Affine-`

TransformOp, specify the transformation you want, in the form of an `java.awt.geom.AffineTransform`. The `ImageProcessor` application includes two examples of this operator, one for rotation and one for scaling. As before, the `AffineTransformOp` constructor accepts a set of hints—we'll just pass `null` to keep things simple:

```
else if (option.equals("rotate"))
  op = new AffineTransformOp(
    AffineTransform.getRotateInstance(Math.PI / 6), null);
else if (option.equals("scale"))
  op = new AffineTransformOp(
    AffineTransform.getScaleInstance(.5, .5), null);
```

In both of these cases, we obtain an `AffineTransform` by calling one of its static methods. In the first case, we get a rotational transformation by supplying an angle. This transformation is wrapped in an `AffineTransformOp`. This operator has the effect of rotating the source image around its origin to create the destination image. In the second case, a scaling transformation is wrapped in an `AffineTransformOp`. The two scaling values, .5 and .5, specify that the image should be reduced to half its original size in both the x and y axes.

One interesting aspect of `AffineTransformOp` is that you may "lose" part of your image when it's transformed. In the rotational and image operator in the `ImageProcessor` application, the destination image has clipped some of the original image out. This has to do with how images are processed—both the source and destination need to have the same origin, so if any part of the image gets transformed into negative x or y space, it is lost. To work around this problem, you can structure your transformations such that no information will be lost. You could, for example, rotate the image around the bottom-left corner, or add a translational component to the rotation so that the entire destination image would be in positive coordinate space.

Working with Audio

So you've read all the material on drawing and image processing, and you're wondering what in the world audio has to do with images. Well, not much, actually, except that true multimedia presentations often combine image techniques such as animation with sound. So we're going to spend a few minutes here talking about audio, for lack of a better place to discuss it.

The Java Sound API is a new core API in SDK 1.3. It provides fine-grained support for the creation and manipulation of both sampled audio and MIDI music. There's space here only to scratch the surface by examining how to play sampled sound and MIDI music files.

`java.applet.AudioClip` defines an interface for objects that can play sound. An object that implements `AudioClip` can be told to `play()` its sound data, `stop()` playing the sound, or `loop()` continually.

The `Applet` class provides a handy static method, `newAudioClip()`, that retrieves sounds from files or over the network. This method takes an absolute or relative URL to specify where the audio file is located. The following application, `NoisyButton`, gives a simple example:

```java
//file: NoisyButton.java
import java.applet.*;
import java.awt.*;
import java.awt.event.*;
import javax.swing.*;

public class NoisyButton extends JFrame {

  public NoisyButton(final AudioClip sound) {
    // set up the frame
    setTitle("NoisyButton");
    addWindowListener(new WindowAdapter() {
      public void windowClosing(WindowEvent e) { System.exit(0); }
    });
    setSize(200, 200);
    setLocation(100, 100);
    // set up the button
    JButton button = new JButton("Woof!");
    button.addActionListener(new ActionListener() {
      public void actionPerformed(ActionEvent e) { sound.play(); }
    });
    getContentPane().setBackground(Color.pink);
    getContentPane().setLayout(new GridBagLayout());
    getContentPane().add(button);
    setVisible(true);
  }

  public static void main(String[] args) throws Exception {
    java.io.File file = new java.io.File("bark.aiff");
    AudioClip sound = Applet.newAudioClip(file.toURL());
    new NoisyButton(sound);
  }
}
```

`NoisyButton` retrieves an `AudioClip` from the file *bark.aiff*; we use `File` to represent the file and `toURL()` to create a URL that represents the file. (You might want to use a command-line argument to specify the file name instead.) When the button is pushed, we call the `play()` method of the `AudioClip` to start things. After that, it will play to completion unless we call the `stop()` method to interrupt it.

Playback is the limit of Java 2's built-in sound capabilities. However, you can play back a wide range of file formats: AIFF, AU, Windows WAV, standard MIDI files, and Rich Music Format (RMF) files. For a little extra zing in your applications, consider adding sound.

Working with Movies

Get some popcorn—Java can play movies, with a little work. You'll need to download and install one of Java's standard extension APIs, the Java Media Framework (JMF). The JMF defines a set of interfaces and classes in the `javax.media` and `javax.media.protocol` packages. To use the JMF, add *jmf.jar* to your class path. Depending on what version of the JMF you download, the installation program may do this for you.

We'll only scratch the surface of JMF here, by working with an important interface called `Player`. Specific implementations of `Player` deal with different media types, like Apple QuickTime (*.mov*) and Windows Video (*.avi*). `Player`s are handed out by a high-level class in the JMF called `Manager`. One way to obtain a `Player` is to specify the URL of a movie:

```
Player player = Manager.createPlayer(url);
```

Because video files are so large, and playing them requires significant system resources, `Player`s have a multi-step lifecycle from the time they're created to the time they actually play something. We'll just look at one step, *realizing*. In this step, the `Player` finds out (by looking at the media file) what system resources it will need to actually play the media file.

```
player.realize();
```

The `realize()` method returns right away; it kicks off the realizing process in a separate thread. When the player is finished realizing, it sends out an event. Once you receive this event, you can obtain a `Component` that will show the media. The `Player` has to be realized first so that it knows important information, like how big the component should be. Getting the component is easy:

```
Component c = player.getVisualComponent();
```

Now we just need to add the component to the screen somewhere. We can play the media right away (although this actually moves the `Player` through several other internal states):

```
player.start();
```

The following example displays a movie in a `JFrame` and plays it:

```
//file: MoviePlayer.java
import java.awt.*;
import java.awt.event.*;
```

```java
import java.net.URL;
import javax.swing.*;
import javax.media.*;

public class MoviePlayer extends JComponent {
  public static void main(String[] args) throws Exception {
    final JFrame f = new JFrame("MoviePlayer");
    f.addNotify();
    f.setLocation(100, 100);
    f.addWindowListener(new WindowAdapter() {
      public void windowClosing(WindowEvent we) { System.exit(0); }
    });

    URL url = new URL(args[0]);
    final Player player = Manager.createPlayer(url);
    player.realize();

    player.addControllerListener(new ControllerListener() {
      public void controllerUpdate(ControllerEvent ce) {
        if (ce instanceof RealizeCompleteEvent) {
          Component c = player.getVisualComponent();
          Container content = f.getContentPane();
          content.setLayout(new BorderLayout());
          content.add(c, BorderLayout.CENTER);
          Insets i = f.getInsets();
          Dimension d = c.getSize();
          f.setSize(d.width + i.left + i.right,
              d.height + i.top + i.bottom);
          f.setVisible(true);
          player.start();
        }
      }
    });
  }
}
```

This class creates a `JFrame` that will hold the movie. Then it creates a `Player` from the URL specified on the command line and tells the `Player` to `realize()`. There's nothing else we can do until the `Player` is realized, so the rest of the code operates inside a `ControllerListener`, after the `RealizeCompleteEvent` is received.

In the event handler, we get the `Player`'s component and add it to the `JFrame`. Then we size the `JFrame` so that it exactly fits the movie component. Finally, we play the movie.

To use this class, pass the URL of a movie in the command line. I was able to show a movie that was on another machine in my local network like this:

```
java MoviePlayer http://172.16.0.1/the.english.patient.mov
```

19

Java Beans

JavaBeans[*] is a component architecture for Java. It is a set of rules for writing highly reusable software elements that can be linked together in a "plug and play" fashion to build applications. Writing objects to the JavaBeans specification means you will have to write less custom code to glue them together. It also allows you to leverage JavaBean-aware development tools. With some graphical development environments, it is even possible to build complete applications just by connecting prefabricated Java Beans.

JavaBeans is a rich topic, and we can't give it more than a brief overview here. If this overview whets your appetite, look for *Developing Java Beans* by Robert Englander (O'Reilly & Associates).

What's a Bean?

So, what exactly is or are Java Beans? JavaBeans defines a set of rules; Java Beans are ordinary Java objects that play by these rules. That is, Java Beans are Java objects that conform to the JavaBeans API and design patterns. By doing so they can be recognized and manipulated within visual application builder environments. Beans live and work in the Java runtime system, as do all Java objects. They communicate with their neighbors using events and other normal method invocations.

For examples of Beans, we have to look no further than the javax.swing packages. All of the familiar components, like `JButton`, `JTextArea`, `JScrollpane`, etc., are not only suggestive of things suitable to be Beans, but are, in fact, Beans! Much of

---

[*] "JavaBeans" refers to the component architecture; "Java Beans" refers to components that use this architecture.

what you learned in Chapter 13, *Swing*, about the Swing components has prepared you for understanding Beans. Although most of the Swing components aren't very useful in isolation, Beans can also be large and complex application components, like spreadsheets or document editors. The `HotJavaBrowser` Bean, for example, is a complete web browser cast in the form of a Java Bean. We'll talk more about what exactly makes a Bean a Bean in a moment. For now, we want to give you a better sense of how they are used.

Java Beans are objects intended to be manipulated visually, within a graphical application builder. They will generally be chosen from a palette of tools and manipulated graphically in an application builder's workspace. In this sense, Beans are somewhat like widgets used in a traditional GUI builder: user interface components that can be assembled to make application "screens." But in traditional GUI builders, the result is usually just some automatically generated code that provides a skeleton on which you hang the meat of your application. GUI builders generally build GUIs, not entire applications.

In contrast, Java Beans can be not only simple UI components like buttons and sliders but more complex and abstract components as well. It is easy to get the impression that Beans are, themselves, always graphical objects (like the Swing components that we mentioned). But Java Beans can implement any part of an application, including "invisible" parts that perform calculations, storage, and communications. Ideally, we would like to be able to snap together a substantial application using prefabricated Beans, without ever writing a line of code! Three characteristics of the JavaBeans architecture make it possible to work with application components at this level:

Design patterns

The most important characteristic of a Java Bean is simply a layer of standardization. Design patterns (i.e., coding conventions) let tools and humans recognize the basic features of a Bean and manipulate it without knowing how it is implemented. We might say that Beans are "self-documenting." By examining a Bean, we can tell what events it can fire and receive; we can also learn about its properties (the equivalent of its public variables) and its methods. Beans can also provide information about their features that is tailored specifically for builder tools.

Reflection

Reflection is an important feature of the Java language. (It's discussed in Chapter 7, *Working with Objects and Classes*.) Reflection makes it possible for Java code to inspect and manipulate new Java objects at runtime. In the context of JavaBeans, reflection lets a development tool analyze a Bean's capabilities, examine the values of its fields, and invoke its methods. Essentially, reflection allows Java objects that meet at runtime to do all of the things that could be done if they had been put together at compile time. Even if a Bean doesn't come bundled with any "built-in" documentation, we can still gather information about its capabilities and properties by directly inspecting the class, using reflection.

Object serialization

Finally, the Java Serialization API allows us to "freeze-dry" (some prefer the word "pickle") a living, breathing application or application component and revive it later. This is a very important step; it makes it possible to piece together applications without extensive code generation. Rather than customizing and compiling large amounts of Java code to build our application on startup, we can simply paste together Beans, configure them, tweak their appearance, and then save them. Later, the Beans can be restored with all of their state and all of their interconnections intact. This makes possible a fundamentally different way of thinking about the design process. It is easy to use serialized objects from handwritten Java code as well, so we can freely mix "freeze-dried" Beans with plain old Bean classes and other Java code.

How Big Is a Bean?

Our examples of Beans have ranged from simple buttons to spreadsheets. Obviously, a button Bean would be much less complex than a spreadsheet, and would be used at a different level of the application's design. At what level are Beans intended to be used? Well, the JavaBeans architecture is supposed to scale well from small to large; simple Beans can be used to build larger Beans. A small Bean may consist of a single class; a large Bean may have many. Beans can also work together through their container to provide services to other beans.

Simple Beans are little more than ordinary Java objects. In fact, any Java class that has a default (empty) constructor could be considered a Bean. A Bean should also be serializable, although the JavaBeans specification doesn't strictly require that. These two criteria ensure that we can create an instance of the Bean dynamically, and that we can later save the Bean, as part of a group or composition of Beans. There are no other requirements. Beans are not required to inherit from a base Bean class, and they don't have to implement any special interface.

A useful Bean would want to send and receive events or expose its properties to the world. To do so, it follows the appropriate design patterns for naming the relevant methods, so that these features can be automatically recognized. Most nontrivial Beans will also provide information about themselves in the form of a `BeanInfo` class. A `BeanInfo` class implements the `BeanInfo` interface, which holds methods that can describe a Bean's features. Normally, this "bean info" is supplied by a separate class that is named for and packaged with the Bean.

The BeanBox Application

We can't have a meaningful discussion of Beans without spending a little time talking about the builder environments in which they will be used. In this book we will talk about the BeanBox container that comes with Sun's Bean Development Kit (BDK). BeanBox is by no means a real application builder environment. Its job is to provide a simple reference platform in which you can test your Beans. BeanBox reads basic Bean information, creates instances of Beans, and allows the most basic hookup of events and properties. It also comes with some interesting test Beans. Aside from that, it offers little. Its main advantage is that it is free (including source code) and universally available, because it is written in pure Java. We'll use the BeanBox fairly extensively in this chapter to demonstrate how Beans work. But keep in mind that the BeanBox isn't a real development environment, and that real development tools will do a lot more.

Some examples of real-world Java development environments that support Java Beans are:

- IBM's Visual Age for Java (*http://www7.software.ibm.com/vad.nsf/data/ document2590*). Yes, this is the real URL.

- Sun's Forte for Java (*http://www.sun.com/forte*)

- Borland/Inprise's JBuilder (*http://www.inprise.com/jbuilder*)

- WebGain's Visual Café (*http://www.webgain.com/Products/VisualCafe_Overview. html*)

- Metrowerks's CodeWarrior (*http://www.metrowerks.com*)

Running the BeanBox application

You can get the BDK from Sun at: *http://java.sun.com/beans/*. Refer to JavaSoft's directions for installing it and running the BeanBox. Figure 19-1 shows the Bean palette, BeanBox work area, and a properties sheet (or customizer window). The properties sheet or "customizer" changes its contents based on the Bean selected in the work area.

To add a Bean to the BeanBox, drag it from the palette and drop it into the work area. (If that doesn't work, try clicking on the Bean in the palette and then clicking in the work area.) Once placed in the BeanBox, a Bean can be selected by clicking on or just outside of it. You can move the Bean within the BeanBox and reshape it by dragging its corners.

Properties and Customizers

Properties represent the "state" or "data" content of a Bean. They are features that can be manipulated externally to configure the Bean. For a Bean that's a GUI

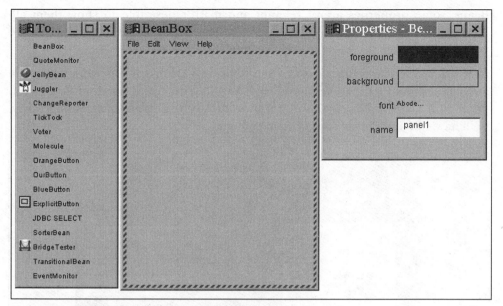

Figure 19-1. The Bean palette, the BeanBox, and a properties sheet

component, you might expect its properties to include its color, label, and other features of its basic appearance. Properties are similar to an object's public variables. Like a variable, a property can be a primitive type (like a number or boolean) or it can be a complex object type (like a `String` or a collection of spreadsheet data). Unlike variables, properties are manipulated using methods; this enables a Bean to take action whenever a property changes. By sending an event when a property changes, a Bean can notify other interested Beans of the change. (See the section "Bound Properties" later in this chapter.)

Let's pull a couple of Beans into the BeanBox and take a look at their properties. Grab a button Bean—the one called `ExplicitButton` will do—from the palette, and place it in the workspace.

When the `ExplicitButton` Bean was first loaded by the BeanBox, it was inspected to discover its properties. When we select an instance of the button, the BeanBox displays these properties in the properties sheet and allows us to modify them. As you can see in the figure, the button has four properties. `foreground` and `background` are colors; their current values are displayed in the corresponding box. `font` is the font that is used to display the label text; an example of the font is shown. And `label` is the text of the label itself. Try typing something new in the label field of the property sheet and watch the button label change.

The first three properties will become familiar to you; many GUI Beans inherit them from the base `Component` class. As you'll see when we create our own Beans, there are lots of other properties that are inherited from that class. For many

Beans, some properties aren't relevant and it isn't desirable to show them all. Later we'll show how to choose which of a Bean's properties are shown in the properties sheet.

Now place a `Juggler` Bean (one of Sun's cute test Beans) in the workspace. The animation should start: Duke should begin juggling his coffee beans as soon as you put him in the BeanBox, as shown in Figure 19-2. If he gets annoying, don't worry, we'll have him under our control soon enough.

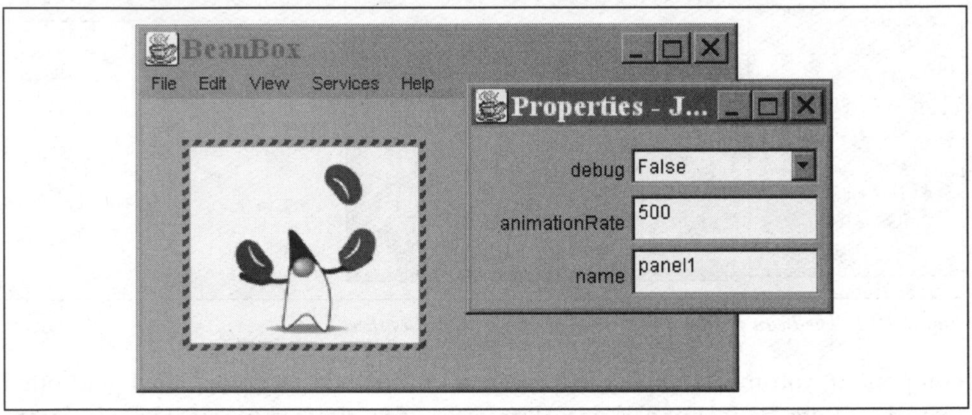

Figure 19-2. Juggling Beans

You'll see that this Bean has a different set of properties. The most interesting is the one called `animationRate`. It is an integer property that controls the interval in milliseconds between displays of the juggler's frames. Try changing its value. The juggler changes speed as you type each value. Good Beans give you immediate feedback on changes to their properties.

Notice that the property sheet understands and provides a way to display and edit each of the different property types. For the `foreground` and `background` properties, the sheet displays the color; if you click on it, a color selection dialog pops up. Similarly, if you click on the `font` property, you get a font dialog. For `integer` and `string` values, you can type a new value into the field. The BeanBox understands and can edit the most useful basic Java types.

Since the types of properties are open ended, BeanBox can't possibly anticipate them all. Beans with more complex property types can supply a *property editor*. The `Molecule` Bean that we'll play with in the next section, for example, uses a custom property editor that lets us choose the type of molecule. If it needs even more control over how its properties are displayed, a Bean can provide a *customizer*. A customizer allows a Bean to provide its own GUI for editing its properties.

Events Hookups and Adapters

Beans use events to communicate. As we mentioned in Chapter 13, events are not limited only to GUI components but can be used for signaling and passing information in more general applications. An event is simply a notification; information describing the event and other data are wrapped up in a subclass of EventObject and passed to the receiving object by a method invocation. Event sources register listeners who want to receive the events when they occur. Event receivers implement the appropriate listener interface containing the method needed to receive the events.

Sometimes it is useful to place an adapter object between an event source and a listener. An adapter can be used when an object doesn't know how to receive a particular event; it enables the object to handle the event anyway. The adapter can translate the event into some other action, like a call to a different method or an update of some data. One of the jobs of the BeanBox is to let us hook up event sources to event listeners. Another job is to provide or produce adapters that allow us to hook up events in more complex ways.

But before we get into details, let's look at Figure 19-3 and try to get our Juggler under control. Using the properties sheet, change the label of our button Bean to Start. Now while the Start button is selected, pull down the **Edit** menu of the BeanBox. Choose the submenu **Events**. You will see a menu showing the listener interfaces to which the button can send events. The names may not match the interface names that you're familiar with, but the relationship between the menu and the interfaces should be clear. (The ExplicitButton provides "friendly" names for the interfaces, rather than using the unadorned interface names. You can also see a "bound property change" event category; that's another kind of listener defined by JavaBeans, which we'll discuss soon.) Select the **button push** submenu, which corresponds to the ActionListener interface. You'll see the actual event types that can be sent. In this case, there's only one: **actionPerformed**; choose it. Recall that buttons and other GUI components generate ActionEvents when they are used; you have just chosen an event source. You should see a red line that looks like a rubber band stretching from the button. Drag the line over to the Juggler, and click on it. A dialog will appear, prompting you to choose a method to which to "hook" this event.

What does it mean to hook an event to a method? If you remember our discussion of Swing, you know that event sources signal event listeners through a very specific method, namely one defined by a listener interface. Furthermore, all the methods that can handle an ActionEvent accept an ActionEvent as an argument. Some of the methods the target dialog presents surely don't take ActionEvents as arguments. And if you take a peek at the Juggler source code, you will see that it doesn't even implement an appropriate listener interface. How can we direct events to it at all?

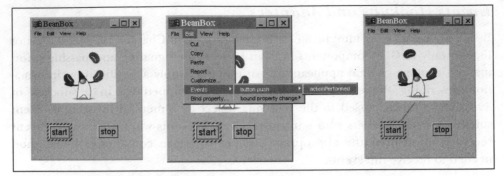

Figure 19-3. Connecting events to Beans

The answer is that the BeanBox automatically makes an adapter class for us, giving us the option of delivering an event to any method that could possibly make sense. That includes any method that could accept the `ActionEvent` object as an argument, including methods that take as an argument the type `Object`. More importantly, it includes methods that take no arguments at all. In that case, the BeanBox creates an adapter that throws away the `ActionEvent` and invokes the target method you choose whenever the event is fired.

The `Juggler` methods we're interested in targeting are `startJuggling()` and stopJuggling(). Select `startJuggling` and click **OK** to complete the hookup of our `Start` button. The BeanBox briefly displays a message saying that it is creating and compiling the necessary adapter class. Follow the same procedure to create a `Stop` button, and hook it to `stopJuggling()`. Finally, the `Juggler` will do our bidding. You should be able to start and stop him with the buttons. Choose the **Save** option from the menu to save the state of the BeanBox; we'll use the controllable `Juggler` later in another example. (There is also a **SerializeComponent** command; we'll talk about that later.)

Let's look at one more interesting example, shown in Figure 19-4, before moving on. Grab a `Molecule` Bean, and place it in the BeanBox. By dragging the mouse within the image you can rotate the model in three dimensions. Try changing the type of molecule using the properties sheet—ethane is fun. Now let's see what we can do with our molecule. Grab a `TickTock` Bean from the palette. `TickTock` is a timer. Every so many seconds, `TickTock` fires a `PropertyChangeEvent`, which is an event defined by JavaBeans that notifies Beans of a change to another Bean's properties. The timer is controlled by an integer property called `interval`, which determines the number of seconds between events. `TickTock` is an "invisible" Bean; it is not derived from a `Component` and doesn't have a graphical appearance, just as an internal timer in an application wouldn't normally have a presence on the screen. BeanBox represents invisible Beans by a simple dashed border and a label containing its name.

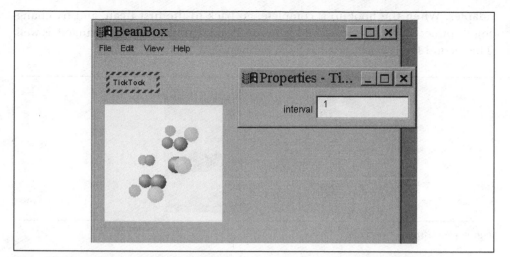

Figure 19-4. The Molecule Bean and the timer

Select the `PropertyChangeEvent` from the **Events** submenu, and click on our `Molecule` as the target for the event. Hook the event to the `rotateOnX()` method. Now the `Molecule` should turn on its own, every time it receives an event from the timer. Try changing the timer's interval. You could also hook `TickTock` to the `Molecule`'s `rotateOnY()` method, or you could use a different instance of `TickTock` and cause it to turn at different rates in each dimension, by setting different intervals. There is no end to the fun.

Bound Properties

By using a combination of events and smart adapters, we can connect Beans in many interesting ways. We can even "bind" two Beans together so that if a property changes in the first Bean, the corresponding property is automatically changed in the second Bean. In this scenario, the Beans don't necessarily have to be of the same type, but, to make sense, the properties do.

Grab two `JellyBean` Beans from the palette, drop them in the BeanBox, and select one of them, as shown in Figure 19-5. You'll notice that a `JellyBean` has the simple color and font properties of a Swing component, plus an integer property called `priceInCents`. Select the **Bind Property** option under the **Edit** menu. (This menu option may not appear for some kinds of Beans.) A dialog appears, asking which property we would like to bind. Choose `priceInCents`. Now drag the rubber band over to the other JellyBean. Another dialog appears, asking to which property you would like to bind this value. In this case, there is only one appropriate property: the corresponding `priceInCents`. However, if a `Jelly-Bean` had other integer properties, the dialog would list more options. After you choose the price property, BeanBox will say that it is creating and compiling an

adapter. When the hookup is complete, go back to the first Bean, and try changing its price. Switch to the second, and you'll see that its price has changed as well.
The second Bean's property has been bound to the first.

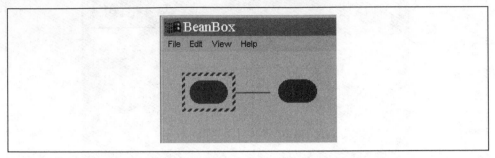

Figure 19-5. Binding properties

How does this work? It's only slightly more complicated than our previous exam-
ple, in which we hooked an event to an arbitrary method. In that case the Bean-
Box generated an adapter that received the event and, in turn, invoked the
method. Bound properties rely on the fact that the source Bean promises to fire a
PropertyChangeEvent whenever one of its "bound" properties changes. The
JellyBean supports this feature, so the **Bind property** option appears in the
menu for it. BeanBox uses the feature by generating an adapter that listens for the
PropertyChangeEvent and updates the property value in the target. Whenever
the adapter receives the event, it finds the new value and sets it in the target Bean.
Try binding the price property in the other direction as well, so that you can
change the value in either Bean, and the changes are propagated in both directions. (Some simple logic in the Beans prevents infinite loops from happening
here.)

If you look under the Events submenu for one of the JellyBeans, you'll see the
PropertyChangeEvent that we described. You can use this event like any other
event; for example, you could go ahead and hook it up to a method. Try setting
things up so that your Molecule rotates when you change the price of the
JellyBean. A more appropriate use for PropertyChangeEvent would be to connect it to the reportChange() method of an instance of the ChangeReporter
test Bean. The ChangeReporter will then display a message describing each
change event it receives.

Notice that the JellyBean has only one type of PropertyChangeEvent. How
then does the recipient know which property has changed? Well, for a simple
Bean, a PropertyChangeEvent is fired whenever any bound property changes;
information in the event (a String value) describes which property changed. A
sophisticated Bean could provide a separate type of PropertyChangeEvent for
each bindable property.

Constrained Properties

In the previous section, we discussed how Beans fire `PropertyChangeEvents` to notify other Beans (and adapters) that a property has changed. In that scenario, the object that receives the event is simply a passive listener, as far as the event's source is concerned. JavaBeans also supports constrained properties, in which the event listener gets to say whether it will allow a Bean to change the property's value. If the new value is rejected, the change is cancelled: the event source keeps its old value.

The `JellyBean` supports one constrainable property: `priceInCents`. To try this out, grab a `Voter` Bean from the palette. The `Voter` Bean listens for constrained `PropertyChangeEvents` and enforces its vote on them (`Yes` or `No`), depending on the value of its `vetoAll` property (`False` or `True`). Hook up the `vetoable-Change` event from one of your `JellyBeans` to the `vetoableChange()` method of the `Voter` Bean. By default, the `Voter` vetoes all change requests, as shown in Figure 19-6. Try changing the price of the `JellyBean`. The BeanBox should notify you that the value cannot be changed. If you set the `vetoAll` property to `False`, you will be free to change the price again. Now you can decide for yourself if price controls are warranted for jelly beans.

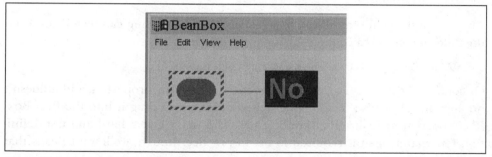

Figure 19-6. Vetoing all change requests

So how are constrained properties implemented? Normally, `PropertyChange-Events` are delivered to a `propertyChange()` method in the listener. Constrained properties are implemented by delivering `PropertyChangeEvents` to a separate listener method called `vetoableChange()`. The `vetoableChange()` method throws a `PropertyVetoException` if it doesn't like a proposed change.

Beans can handle the process of proposing changes in two ways. The first is to use a "two-phase commit" style, in which the sending Bean first issues a vetoable change. If the change passes (i.e., none of the listeners throw a `Property-VetoException`), the sending Bean issues a regular property change. Bound properties in the receiving Bean don't respond until the second phase, when the regular property change arrives.

An alternative strategy is to allow bound properties in the receiving Bean to act on the vetoable change; if the change is rejected by a receiving Bean, the sending Bean sends out a followup vetoable change to restore the property's original value. In this scenario, it would be legitimate to ignore a crazy receiving Bean that wouldn't take the old value back.

Keep in mind that binding properties and constraining properties are two separate issues. We can have either one without the other. How popular builder environments will choose to represent the two features remains to be seen. While the BeanBox does a good job of binding properties for us, it does not currently shield us from the details of hooking up constrained properties. In a real builder environment, the two processes would presumably be made to look more similar.

Building Beans

Now that you have the feel from the user's perspective, let's build some Beans. In this section we will become the Magic Beans company. We will create some Beans, package them for distribution, and use them in the BeanBox to build a very simple application. (The complete JAR file, along with all of the example code for this chapter, is on the CD-ROM that accompanies this book, and at *http://www.oreilly. com/catalog/learnjava.*)

The first thing we'll remind you of is that absolutely anything can be a Bean. Even the following class is a Bean, albeit an invisible one:

```
public class Trivial implements java.io.Serializable {}
```

Of course, this Bean isn't very useful: it doesn't have any properties, and it doesn't do anything. But it's a Bean, nonetheless and you can drag it into the BeanBox. It's important to realize that JavaBeans really doesn't give a hard and fast definition for what a Bean is required to be. In practice though, we'll want Beans that are a little more useful.

Creating a Component with Bindable Properties

We created a nifty `Dial` component in Chapter 15, *More Swing Components*. What would it take to turn it into a Bean? Well, surprise: it is already a Bean! The `Dial` has a number of properties that it exposes in the way prescribed by JavaBeans. A "get" method retrieves the value of a property; for example, `getValue()` retrieves the dial's current value. Likewise, a "set" method (`setValue()`) modifies the dial's value. The dial has two other properties, which also have "get" and "set" methods: `minimum` and `maximum`. This is all the `Dial` needs to do to inform a tool like BeanBox what properties it has and how to work with them. In addition, `Dial` is a custom Swing component, and if you look, you'll see that the `JComponent` class follows the same rules for its important properties (for example, its font).

In order to use our `Dial`, we put it in a package named `magicbeans`, and store it in a JAR file that can be loaded by the BeanBox. First, create a directory called *magicbeans* to hold our Beans, add a `package` statement to the source files *Dial. java, DialEvent.java*, and *DialListener.java*, put the source files into the *magicbeans* directory, and compile them (`javac magicbeans/Dial.java`) to create class files.

Next, we need to create a manifest file that tells the BeanBox which of the classes in the JAR file are Beans and which are support files or unrelated. At this point, we only have one Bean, *Dial.class*, so we create the following file called *magicbeans. manifest*:

```
Name: magicbeans/Dial.class
Java-Bean: True
```

The `Name:` label identifies the class file as it will appear in the JAR: `magicbeans/ Dial.class`. Specifications appearing after an item's `Name:` line and before an empty line apply to that item. (See the section on JARs and manifest files in Chapter 3, *Tools of the Trade*, for more details.) We have added the attribute `Java-Bean: True`, which flags this class as a Bean to tools that read the manifest. We will add an entry like this for each Bean in our package. We don't need to flag support classes (like `DialEvent` and `DialListener`) as Beans, because we won't want to manipulate them directly with the BeanBox; in fact, we don't need to mention them in the manifest at all. The *jar* utility will add appropriate entries for them automatically.

To create the JAR file, including our manifest information, enter the following command:

```
% jar cvmf magicbeans.manifest magicbeans.jar magicbeans/*.class
```

Now we can load our JAR into the BeanBox using the Load JAR option under the **File** menu. Use the File dialog to locate our JAR and select it. An entry for `Dial` should appear in the Bean palette. We have loaded our first Bean! Drop an instance of `Dial` Bean into the BeanBox.

As Figure 19-7 shows, the dial's properties: `value`, `minimum`, and `maximum` are on the properties sheet and can be modified by the BeanBox. (At this point, you'll see several other properties inherited from the `JComponent` class as well. This picture shows the `Dial` Bean as it will appear later in this chapter, after we've learned about the `BeanInfo` class). We're almost there. But these properties are not very useful to other Beans unless we can notify them when the dial's value changes. We need to make `value` a bound property, by firing `PropertyChangeEvents` when the value changes. (Alternately, we could have other beans that know about `DialEvents`. It really depends on how we plan to design our suite of beans.) It won't be hard to add `PropertyChangeEvents` to our Bean because the `JComponent` class already handles them for us.

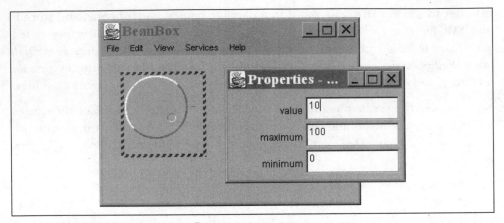

Figure 19-7. The Dial component as a Bean

We insert the `firePropertyChange` statement as the first line of the Dial's `setValue()` method:

```
public void setValue(int value) {
    firePropertyChange( "value", this.value, value );
    ...
```

That's all it takes to make `Dial` a source of `PropertyChangeEvents`. To fire an event, we use the `firePropertyChange()` method built into `JComponent`. The `JComponent` also handles all of the listener registration for us.

The `firePropertyChange()` method takes three arguments: the name of the property and the old and new values. It may seem superfluous to send both the old and new values, but there is one bonus when we do: the `firePropertyChange()` method doesn't generate an event if the value has not actually changed. This saves us the trouble of implementing "event-avoidance" logic over and over. (It also prevents looping and other bad behavior.) Various overloaded versions of `firePropertyChange()` in the `JComponent` class accept different argument types, including `Object` and all of the primitive numeric types.

Now we're ready to put the `Dial` to use. Recompile and re-JAR the classes. Next, reload the `Juggler` example that we asked you to save in the first section of this chapter. (Did you save it?) Add an instance of our new magic `Dial` Bean to the scenario, as shown in Figure 19-8.

Let's try to bind the `value` property of the `Dial` to the `animationRate` of the `Juggler`. The **Bind Property** option should now be available under the **Edit** menu because the BeanBox recognizes that we are a source of `PropertyChangeEvents`. (Note that there are a *lot* of properties listed here. Again, we'll show you later how to limit what is presented.) When you complete the hookup, you should be able to vary the speed of the juggler by turning the dial. Try changing the `maximum` and `minimum` values of the dial to change the range.

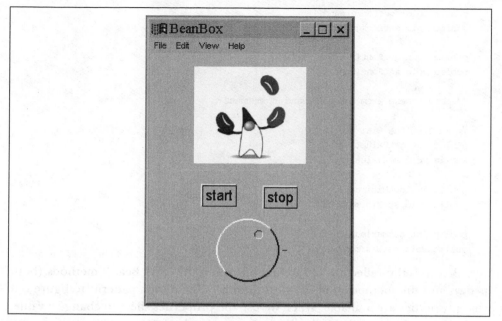

Figure 19-8. The Juggler with a dialable animation rate

Design patterns for properties

We said earlier that tools like BeanBox found out about a Bean's properties by looking at its *get* and *set* methods. The easiest way to make properties visible is to follow these simple design patterns:

- Method for getting the current value of a property:

   ```
   public propertyType getPropertyName()
   ```

- Method for setting the value of a property:

   ```
   public void setPropertyName( propertyType arg )
   ```

- Method for determining whether a boolean-valued property is currently true:

   ```
   public boolean isPropertyName()
   ```

The last method is used only for properties with boolean values, and is optional. (You could just use the *get* method in this situation.)

The appropriate *set* and *get* methods for these features of our Bean are already in the Dial class, either methods that we added or methods inherited from the java.awt.Component and javax.swing.JComponent classes:

```
// inherited from Component
public Color getForeground()
public void setForeground(Color c)
```

```
public Color getBackground()
public void setBackground(Color c)

public Font getFont()
public void setFont(Font f)

// many others from Component and JComponent

// part of the Dial itself
public int getValue()
public void setValue(int v)

public int getMinimum()
public void setMinimum(int m)

public int getMaximum()
public void setMaximum(int m)
```

BeanBox uses the reflection API to find out about the Dial Bean's methods (both its own and the methods it inherits); it then uses the design patterns to figure out what properties are available. When we use the properties sheet to change a value, the BeanBox dynamically invokes the correct *set* method to change the value.

But wait—if you look further at the JComponent class, you'll notice that other methods match the design pattern. For example, what about the setCursor() and getCursor() pair? BeanBox doesn't know how to display or edit a cursor, so it simply ignores those properties in the properties sheet.

BeanBox automatically pulls the property's name from the name of its accessor methods; it then lowercases the name for display on the properties sheet. For example, the font property is not listed as Font. Later, we'll show how to provide a BeanInfo class that overrides the way these properties are displayed, letting you provide your own friendly property names.

JavaBeans allows read-only and write-only properties, which are implemented simply by leaving out the *get* or *set* method.

A (Slightly) More Realistic Example

We now have one nifty Bean for the Magic Beans products list. Let's round out the set before we start advertising. Our goal is to build the Beans we need to make a very simple form. The application will perform a simple calculation after data is entered on the form.

A Bean for displaying text

One thing that we will need in almost any application is a plain old text label. Fortunately, Swing provides us with one for free.

We make a trivial subclass and package it as a Bean:

```
//file: TextLabel.java
package magicbeans;
import javax.swing.JLabel;

public class TextLabel extends JLabel {

    public void setText( String s ) {
        super.setText(s);

        if ( getParent() != null ) {
            invalidate();
            getParent().validate();
        }
    }
}
```

The only thing we've added here is a bit of code to make the `JLabel` behave better in the BeanBox. We override the `setText()` method to have it revalidate its container whenever the label changes. This will cause the label to snap to the correct size automatically when you change the text in the property sheet.

Recreate the JAR file and try out the label in the BeanBox. Don't forget to add *TextLabel.class* to the manifest and to specify that it's a Bean.

A Bean for validating numeric data

Another component that we're sure to need in a form is a text field that accepts numeric data. Let's build a text-entry Bean that accepts and validates numbers and makes the values available as a property. You should recognize almost all of the parts of the `NumericField` Bean:

```
//file: NumericField.java
package magicbeans;
import javax.swing.JTextField;
import java.awt.event.*;
import java.beans.*;

public class NumericField extends JTextField
                        implements ActionListener {
    private double value;

    public NumericField() {
        super(6);
        addActionListener( this );
    }

    public void actionPerformed( ActionEvent e ) {
```

```
        try {
            setValue( Double.parseDouble( getText() ) );
        } catch ( NumberFormatException ex ) {
            select(0, getText().length());
        }
    }

    public double getValue() {
        return value;
    }

    public void setValue( double newValue ) {
        double oldValue = value;
        value = newValue;
        setText( "" + newValue );
        firePropertyChange( "value", oldValue, newValue );
    }
}
```

NumericField extends the Swing JTextField component. The heart of
NumericField is in the actionPerformed() method. You'll recall that a
JTextField generates ActionEvents whenever the user presses Return to enter
the data. We catch those events and try to parse the user's entry as a number, giving it a Double value. If we succeed, we update the value property using our
setValue() method. setValue() then fires a PropertyChangeEvent to notify
any interested Beans. This event firing enables us to bind NumericField's value
property to some other property. (We'll see how in the next example.)

If the text doesn't parse properly as a number, we give feedback to the user by
selecting (highlighting) the text. The field defaults to a width of six columns, but
you can change its size by dragging it.

Verify the operation of NumericField by placing two of them in the BeanBox and
binding the value property of one to the other. You should be able to enter a new
floating point value and see the change reflected in the other.

An invisible multiplier

Finally, let's try our hand at an invisible Bean: one that performs a calculation
rather than providing part of a user interface. Multiplier is a simple invisible
Bean that multiplies the values of two of its properties (A and B) to produce the
value of a third read-only property (C). Here's the code:

```
//file: Multiplier.java
package magicbeans;
import java.beans.*;

public class Multiplier implements java.io.Serializable {
```

```
      private double a, b, c;

  synchronized public void setA( double val ) {
    a = val;
    multiply();
  }

  synchronized public double getA() {
    return a;
  }

  synchronized public void setB( double val ) {
    b = val;
    multiply();
  }

  synchronized public double getB() {
    return b;
  }

  synchronized public double getC() {
    return c;
  }

  private void multiply() {
    double oldC = c;
    c = a * b;
    propChanges.firePropertyChange(
      "c", new Double(oldC), new Double(c));
  }

  private PropertyChangeSupport propChanges =
      new PropertyChangeSupport(this);

  public void
  addPropertyChangeListener(PropertyChangeListener listener) {
    propChanges.addPropertyChangeListener(listener);
  }

  public void
  removePropertyChangeListener(PropertyChangeListener listener) {
    propChanges.removePropertyChangeListener(listener);
  }
}
```

Because a `Multiplier` is invisible, it doesn't extend the `JComponent` class. To make a `Multiplier` a source of `PropertyChangeEvents`, we enlist the help of a `PropertyChangeSupport` object. When we need to invoke `Multiplier`'s methods for registering property-change listeners, we simply call the corresponding methods in the `PropertyChangeSupport` object. Similarly, a `Multiplier` fires a property change event by calling the `PropertyChangeSupport` object's `firePropertyChange()` method. This is the easiest way to get an arbitrary class to be a source of `PropertyChangeEvents`.

The code is straightforward. Whenever the value of property A or B changes, we call `multiply()`, which multiplies their values and fires a `PropertyChangeEvent`. So we can say that `Multiplier` supports binding of any of its properties.

Putting them together

Finally, let's demonstrate that we can put our Beans together in a useful way. Arrange three `TextLabels`, three `NumericFields`, and a `Multiplier` into the scene shown in Figure 19-9.

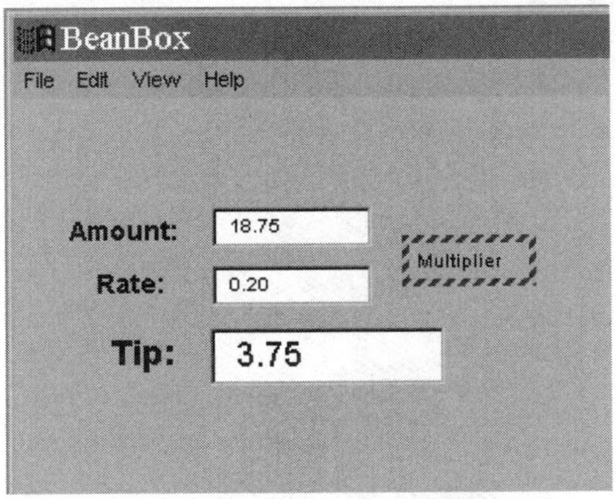

Figure 19-9. TextLabels, NumericFields, and a Multiplier

Bind the values of the first two `NumericFields` to the A and B properties of the `Multiplier`; bind the C value to the third `NumericField`. Now we have a simple calculator. You could use this as a tip calculator, but it's important to realize that much more is possible. Try some other arrangements. Can you build a calculator that squares a number? Can you see how you might build a simple spreadsheet?

Before moving on, save this work so that you can reuse it later. This time, use the BeanBox's **Serialize component** command to serialize the BeanBox container itself. To select the top-level BeanBox, click on the background of the workspace. The dashed line should appear around the entire BeanBox. Then use the **Serialize component** command to save your work. By serializing the BeanBox container, we save all of the Beans it contains and all of their interconnections. Later in this chapter, we'll show you how to put these to use. (BeanBox's **Save** command also stores the state of the BeanBox, but it may or may not use serialization to do so.)

Customizing with BeanInfo

So far, everything the BeanBox has known about our Beans has been determined by low-level reflection—that is, by looking at the methods of our classes. The `java.beans.Introspector` gathers information on a Bean using reflection, then analyzes and describes a Bean to any tool that wants to know about it. The introspection process works only if we follow design patterns that restrict what we call our methods; furthermore, it gives us little control over exactly what properties and events appear in the BeanBox menus. We have been forced to live with all of the stuff that we inherit from the base Swing components, for example. We can change all that by creating `BeanInfo` classes for our Beans. A `BeanInfo` class provides BeanBox's introspector with explicit information about the properties, methods, and events of a Bean; we can even use it to customize the text that appears in the BeanBox's menus.

A `BeanInfo` class implements the `BeanInfo` interface. That's a complicated proposition; in most situations, the introspector's default behavior is reasonable. So instead of implementing the `BeanInfo` interface, we extend the `SimpleBeanInfo` class, which implements all of `BeanInfo`'s methods. We can override specific methods to provide the information we want; when we don't override a method, we'll get the introspector's default behavior.

In the next few sections, we'll develop a `DialBeanInfo` class that provides explicit information about our `Dial` Bean.

Getting Properties information

We'll start out by describing the `Dial`'s properties. To do so, we must implement the `getPropertyDescriptors()` method. This method simply returns an array of `PropertyDescriptor` objects—one for each property we want to publicize.

To create a `PropertyDescriptor`, we call its constructor with two arguments: the property's name and the class. In the following code, we create descriptors for the `Dial`'s `value`, `minimum`, and `maximum` properties. Then we call a few methods of the `PropertyDescriptor` class to provide additional information about each property. In this example, we call the `setBound()` method to state that `minimum` and `maximum` are not bound properties but that `value` is a bound property. Our code also is prepared to catch an `IntrospectionException`, which can occur if something goes wrong while creating the property descriptors:

```
//file: DialBeanInfo.java
package magicbeans;
import java.beans.*;

public class DialBeanInfo extends SimpleBeanInfo {
```

```java
public PropertyDescriptor[] getPropertyDescriptors() {
  try {
    PropertyDescriptor value =
      new PropertyDescriptor("value", Dial.class);
    PropertyDescriptor minimum =
      new PropertyDescriptor("minimum", Dial.class);
    PropertyDescriptor maximum =
      new PropertyDescriptor("maximum", Dial.class);

    value.setBound(true);
    minimum.setBound(false);
    maximum.setBound(false);

    return new PropertyDescriptor [] { value, minimum, maximum };
  }
  catch (IntrospectionException e) {
    return null;
  }
}
```

Perhaps the most interesting thing about `DialBeanInfo` is that by providing explicit information for our properties, we automatically hide any other properties that introspection might find. If you don't provide any property information, a development tool like BeanBox will find out about all sorts of properties, including properties inherited from the superclass. When we loaded the `Dial` into the BeanBox, we saw a number of properties inherited from `Component`. If you compile `DialBeanInfo`, package it with the `Dial`, and load the resulting JAR file into the BeanBox, you'll see that the `Component` properties no longer appear in the properties sheet.

A `PropertyDescriptor` can provide a lot of other information about a property: it can provide the names of the accessor methods (if you decide not to use the design patterns); whether the property is constrained; and a class to use as a property editor (if the standard property editors aren't sufficient).

Getting Events information

The `Dial` defines its own event: the `DialEvent`. We'd like to tell development tools about this event, so that we can build applications using it. The process for telling the world about our event is similar to what we did previously: we add a method to the `DialBeanInfo` class called `getEventSetDescriptors()`, which returns an array of `EventSetDescriptors`.

Events are described in terms of their listener interfaces, not in terms of the event classes themselves, so our `getEventSetDescriptors()` method creates a descriptor for the `DialListener` interface. We also have to tell the world that we generate `PropertyChangeEvents`, so we create a descriptor for the `Property-ChangeListener`. Here's the code to add to the `DialBeanInfo` class:

```
public EventSetDescriptor[] getEventSetDescriptors() {
  try {
    EventSetDescriptor dial = new EventSetDescriptor(
      Dial.class, "dialAdjusted",
      DialListener.class, "dialAdjusted");
    dial.setDisplayName("Dial Adjusted");

    EventSetDescriptor changed = new EventSetDescriptor(
      Dial.class, "propertyChange",
      PropertyChangeListener.class, "propertyChange");
    changed.setDisplayName("Bound property change");

    return new EventSetDescriptor [] { dial, changed };
  }
  catch (IntrospectionException e) {
    return null;
  }
}
```

In this method, we create two `EventSetDescriptor` objects: `dial` and `changed`. The constructor for an `EventSetDescriptor` takes four arguments: the class that generates the event, the name of the event (the name that will be displayed, by default, by a development tool), the listener class, and the name of the method to which the event can be delivered. (Other constructors let you deal with listener interfaces that have several methods.) After creating these objects, we call the `setDisplayName()` method to provide a more friendly name to be displayed by development tools like the BeanBox. (This overrides the default name specified in the constructor.)

Just as the property descriptors we supply hide the properties that were discovered by reflection, the `EventSetDescriptors` hide the other events that are inherited from the base component classes. Therefore, when you recompile `DialBeanInfo`, package it in a JAR, and load it into the BeanBox, you'll no longer see mouse events, action events, and all the other AWT/Swing events. You will see only the two events that we have explicitly described: our own `DialEvent` and `Property-ChangeEvent` (displayed as "Dial Adjusted" and "Bound property change").

Once you have an `EventSetDescriptor`, you can provide other kinds of information about the event. In particular, you can state that the event is *unicast*, which means that it can only have one listener.

Supplying icons

Some of the Beans that come with the BeanBox are displayed on the palette with a cute icon. This makes life more pleasant for everyone. To supply an icon for the

BeanInfo object we have been developing, we have it implement the getIcon() method. You may supply as many as four icons: they may be either 16 × 16 or 32 × 32, and either color or monochrome. Here's the getIcon() method for DialBeanInfo:

```
public class DialBeanInfo extends SimpleBeanInfo {
  ...
  public java.awt.Image getIcon(int iconKind) {

    if (iconKind == BeanInfo.ICON_COLOR_16x16) {
      return loadImage("DialIconColor16.gif");
    } else
    if (iconKind == BeanInfo.ICON_COLOR_32x32) {
      return loadImage("DialIconColor32.gif");
    } else
    if (iconKind == BeanInfo.ICON_MONO_16x16) {
      return loadImage("DialIconMono16.gif");
    } else
    if (iconKind == BeanInfo.ICON_MONO_32x32) {
      return loadImage("DialIconMono32.gif");
    }
    return null;
  }
}
```

This method is called with a constant indicating what kind of icon is being requested; for example, BeanInfo.ICON_COLOR_16x16 requests a 16 × 16 color image. If an appropriate icon is available, it loads the image and returns an Image object. If the icon isn't available, it returns null. For convenience, you can package the images in the same JAR file as the Bean and its BeanInfo class.

Though we haven't used them here, you can also use a BeanInfo object to provide information about other public methods of your Bean, array-valued properties, and other features.

Creating customizers and property editors

JavaBeans also lets you provide a customizer for your Beans. Customizers are objects that do advanced customization for a Bean as a whole; they let you provide your own GUI for tweaking your Bean. (For example, the Select Bean uses a customizer rather than the standard properties sheet.) We won't show you how to write a customizer; it's not too difficult, but it's beyond the scope of this chapter. Suffice it to say that a customizer must implement the java.beans.Customizer interface, and should extend Component (or JComponent), so that it can be displayed.

A property editor isn't quite as fancy as a customizer. Property editors are a way of giving the properties sheet additional capabilities. For example, you would supply a property editor to let you edit a property type that is specific to your Bean. You could provide a property editor that would let you edit an object's price in dollars and cents. We've already seen a couple of property editors: the editor used for Color-valued properties is fundamentally no different from a property editor you might write yourself. In addition, the Molecule Bean used a property editor to specify its moleculeName property.

Again, describing how to write a property editor is beyond the scope of this chapter. Briefly, a property editor must implement the PropertyEditor interface; it usually does so by extending the PropertyEditorSupport class, which provides default implementations for most of the methods.

Hand-Coding with Beans

So far, we've seen how to create and use Beans within a Bean application builder environment. That is the primary role of a Java Bean in development. But Beans are not limited to being used by automated tools. There's no reason we can't use Beans in handwritten code. You might use a builder to assemble Beans for the user interface of your application and then load that serialized Bean collection in your own code. We'll give an example of that in a moment.

Bean Instantiation and Type Management

Beans are an abstraction over simple Java classes. They add, by convention, features that are not part of the Java language. To enable these additional capabilities of JavaBeans we have to use some special tools that take the place of basic language operations. Specifically, when working with Beans, we need replacements for three basic Java operations: creating an object with new, checking the type of an object with the instanceof operator, and casting a type with a cast expression. In place of these, use the corresponding static methods of the java. beans.Beans class, shown in Table 19-1.

Table 19-1. Methods of the java.beans.Beans Class

Operator	Equivalent
New	Beans.instantiate(classloader, name)
Instanceof	Beans.isInstanceOf(object, class)
Explicit cast	Beans.getInstanceOf(object, class)

Beans.instantiate() is the new operation for Beans. It takes a class loader and the name of a Bean class or serialized Bean as arguments. Its advantage over the new operator is that it can also load Beans from a serialized form. If you use

intantiate(), you don't have to specify in advance whether you will provide the
Bean as a class or as a serialized object. This feature will become more important
in the future; upcoming releases may allow the use of XML as an alternative serialization format for beans. If you use instantiate(), you won't care whether serialized objects are provided in the standard Java format, some new XML format, or
something even newer that we haven't heard of yet.

Beans.isInstanceOf() and Beans.getInstanceOf() do the jobs of checking
a Bean's type and casting it to a new type. In the future these methods may be
used to let Beans take control of this behavior, providing different "views" of themselves.

Working with Serialized Beans

Remember the tip calculator we developed a few sections back? We asked you to
serialize the BeanBox container and save it. As we mentioned earlier, BeanBox is a
Bean itself. We can therefore pull the serialized BeanBox along with all of our previous work into another application and use it just as we had left it. We'll assume
that you saved the serialized BeanBox in a file called *tipcalc.ser*.

Compile the following small application:

```
//file: BackFromTheDead.java
import java.awt.Component;
import javax.swing.*;
import java.beans.*;

public class BackFromTheDead extends JFrame {

  public BackFromTheDead() {
    super("Revived Beans!");
    try {
      Object bean = Beans.instantiate(
        getClass().getClassLoader(), "tipcalc" );

      if ( Beans.isInstanceOf(bean, Component.class) ) {
        Component comp = (Component)
          Beans.getInstanceOf(bean, Component.class);
        getContentPane().add("Center", comp);
      } else {
          System.out.println("Bean is not a Component...");
      }
    }

    catch ( java.io.IOException e1 ) {
      System.out.println("Error loading the serialized object");
    }
```

```
      catch ( ClassNotFoundException e2 ) {
        System.out.println(
          "Can't find the class that goes with the object");
      }
    }

    public static void main(String [] args) {
      JFrame f = new BackFromTheDead();
      f.pack();
      f.setVisible(true);
    }
  }
```

Run this program, making sure that all the BeanBox classes and associated JAR
files, including our *magicbeans.jar* file, are in your class path. (We need only those
classes since we are loading a BeanBox itself in this example—we don't need them
in general to load other serialized beans or collections of Beans.) You should see
the restored BeanBox, just as you left it, as shown in Figure 19-10.

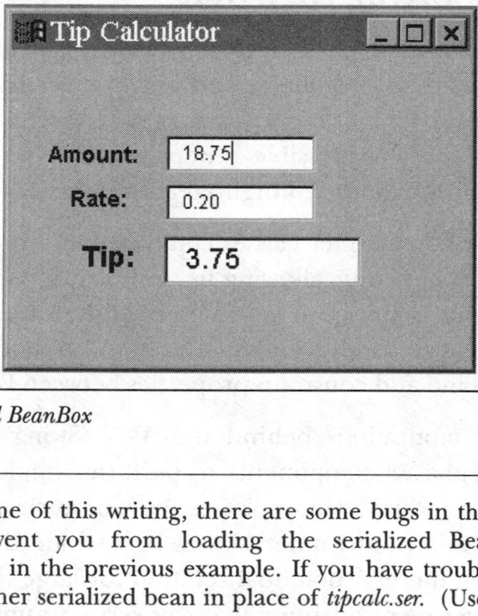

Figure 19-10. The restored BeanBox

NOTE   At the time of this writing, there are some bugs in the BDK, which
           may prevent you from loading the serialized BeanBox as we
           described in the previous example. If you have trouble, just substi-
           tute another serialized bean in place of *tipcalc.ser*. (Use the **Serialize
           Component** command in the BeanBox to save one of the other
           Beans, rather than the BeanBox itself). The example will load and
           display any serialized Bean that is a kind of Component.

In BackFromTheDead, we use Beans.instantiate() to load our serialized Bean
by name. Then we check to see whether it is a GUI component using Beans.
isInstanceOf(). (It *is,* because the BeanBox itself is a subclass of java.awt.
Panel.) Finally, we cast the instantiated object to a Component with Beans.

getInstanceOf() and add it to our application's JFrame. Notice that we still need a static Java cast to turn the Object returned by getInstanceOf() into a Component. This cast may seem gratuitous, but it is the bridge between the dynamic Beans lookup of the type and the static, compile-time view of the type.

One important question remains: how does instantiate() find a Bean using the argument tipcalc? First, it appends the extension .ser to form the filename *tipcalc.ser*. If it can find this file anywhere along the class path, it loads it as a serialized Bean. It also needs the serialized Bean's original .*class* file; the name of that file is included in the serialized object and usually doesn't have any relation to the name of the serialized object. (In this case, instantiate() would look for Bean-Box.class and the classes for the components in the BeanBox.)

If the .*ser* file doesn't exist, instantiate() appends .*class* to the name (in this case, yielding *tipcalc.class*) and looks for a class file. In this case, instantiate() instantiates the Bean like any other object—that is, with the new operator.

Putting Reflection to Work

We've discussed reflection largely in terms of how design tools use it to analyze your classes. But it would be a shame to end this discussion without showing you how to use reflection for your own purposes. It's a powerful tool that lets you do many things that wouldn't be possible otherwise. In this section, we'll build a dynamic event adapter that can be configured at runtime.

In Chapter 13, we saw how adapter classes could be built to connect event firings to arbitrary methods in our code, allowing us to cleanly separate GUI and logic in our applications. In this chapter, we have described how the BeanBox interposes adapters between Beans to do this for us. We have also described how the Bean-Box uses adapters to bind and constrain properties between Beans.

One of the primary motivations behind the AWT/Swing event model was to reduce the need to subclass components to perform simple hookups. But if we start relying heavily on special adapter classes, we can quickly end up with as many adapters as objects. Anonymous inner classes let us hide the existence of these classes, but they're still there. A potential solution for large or specialized applications is to create *generic* event adapters that can serve a number of event sources and targets simultaneously.

The following example, DynamicActionAdapter, is a generic adapter for ActionEvents. A single instance of DynamicActionAdapter can be used to hook up a number of ActionEvent sources. DynamicActionAdapter uses reflection on both the source and target objects. This enables us to direct each event on the source object to an arbitrary method of the target object.

Here's the code:

```java
//file: DynamicActionAdapter.java
import java.awt.*;
import java.util.Hashtable;
import java.lang.reflect.Method;
import java.awt.event.*;

class DynamicActionAdapter implements ActionListener {
  Hashtable actions = new Hashtable();

  public void hookup( Object sourceObject, Object targetObject,
                      String targetMethod ) {
    actions.put(sourceObject,
      new Target(targetObject, targetMethod));
    invokeReflectedMethod( sourceObject, "addActionListener",
      new Object[] {this}, new Class[] {ActionListener.class});
  }

  public void actionPerformed(ActionEvent e) {
    Target target = (Target)actions.get( e.getSource() );
    if ( target == null )
      throw new RuntimeException("unknown source");
    invokeReflectedMethod(target.object, target.methodName,
                          null, null);
  }

  private void invokeReflectedMethod(
    Object target, String methodName,
    Object [] args, Class [] argTypes ) {

    try {
      Method method =
        target.getClass().getMethod( methodName, argTypes );
      method.invoke( target, args );
    }
    catch ( Exception e ) {
      throw new RuntimeException("invocation problem: "+e);
    }
  }

  class Target {
    Object object;
    String methodName;

    Target( Object object, String methodName ) {
      this.object = object;
      this.methodName = methodName;
    }
  }
}
```

Once we have an instance of `DynamicActionAdapter`, we can use its `hookup()` method to connect an `ActionEvent` source to some method of a target object. The target object doesn't have to be an `ActionListener`—or any other particular kind of object. The following application, `DynamicHookupTest`, uses an instance of our adapter to connect a button to its own `launchTheMissiles()` method:

```java
//file: DynamicHookupTest.java
import javax.swing.*;
import java.awt.event.*;

public class DynamicHookupTest extends JFrame {
  DynamicActionAdapter actionAdapter = new DynamicActionAdapter();
  JLabel label = new JLabel( "Ready...", JLabel.CENTER );
  int count;

  public DynamicHookupTest() {
    JButton launchButton = new JButton("Launch!");
    getContentPane().add( launchButton, "South" );
    getContentPane().add( label, "Center" );
    actionAdapter.hookup(launchButton, this, "launchTheMissiles");
  }

  public void launchTheMissiles() {
    label.setText("Launched: "+ count++ );
  }

  public static void main(String[] args) {
    JFrame f = new DynamicHookupTest();
    f.addWindowListener(new WindowAdapter() {
      public void windowClosing(WindowEvent we) { System.exit(0); }
    });
    f.setSize(150, 150);
    f.setVisible( true );
  }
}
```

Here we simply call the dynamic adapter's `hookup()` method, passing it the `ActionEvent` source, the target object, and a string with the name of the method to invoke when the event arrives.

As for the code, it's pretty straightforward. `DynamicActionAdapter` implements the `ActionListener` interface. When `hookup()` is called, it registers itself with the event source, using reflection on the source object to invoke its `addAction-Listener()` method. It stores information about the target object and method in a `Target` object, using an inner class. This object is stored in a `Hashtable` called `actions`.

When an action event arrives, the dynamic adapter looks up the target for the event source in the `Hashtable`. It then uses reflection on the target object, to look up and invoke the requested method. Our adapter can invoke only a method that takes no arguments. If the method doesn't exist, the adapter throws a `Runtime-Exception`.

The heart of the adapter is the `invokeReflectedMethod()` method. This is a `private` method that uses reflection to look up and invoke an arbitrary method in an arbitrary class. First, it calls the target's `getClass()` method to get the target's `Class` object. It uses this object to call `getMethod()`, which returns a `Method` object. Once we have a `Method`, we can call `invoke()` to invoke the method.

The dynamic adapter is important because it has almost no built-in knowledge. It doesn't know what kind of object will be the event source. Likewise, it doesn't know what object will receive the event, or what method it should call to deliver the event. All this information is provided at runtime, in the call to `hookup()`. We use reflection to look up and invoke the event source's `addActionListener()` method, and to look up and invoke the target's event handler. All this is done on the fly. Therefore, you can use this adapter in almost any situation requiring an `ActionEvent`.

Safety Implications

If the target's event-handling method isn't found, the adapter throws a `RuntimeException`. Therein lies the problem with this technique. By using reflection to locate and invoke methods, we abandon Java's strong typing and head off in the direction of scripting languages. We add power at the expense of safety.

Runtime Event Hookups with Reflection

Our dynamic event adapter is limited to handling `ActionEvents`. What if we want to build something like the BeanBox that can hook up arbitrary event sources to arbitrary destinations? Can we build an adapter that can listen to any kind of event?

The answer is "yes." We can use the powerful new interface proxy reflection feature introduced in SDK 1.3. The `java.lang.reflect.Proxy` class is a factory that can generate adapters implementing any type of interface at runtime. By specifying one or more event listener interface (e.g., `ActionListener`) we get an adapter that implements those listener interfaces generated for us on the fly. The adapter is a specially created class that delegates all of the method calls on its interfaces to a designated `InvocationHandler` object. See Chapter 7 for more information about the reflection interface proxy.

We should repeat that this is a feature that was introduced in the SDK 1.3. In versions of Java prior to 1.3, there is no standard way to create an object that implements a specified interface at runtime. That is, there is no way to make a specified "kind" of event listener without creating the class yourself. The BeanBox and other utilities which generated adapters dynamically prior to the SDK 1.3 did so by creating Java byte code on the fly and loading it through a class loader.

BeanContext and BeanContextServices

So far we've talked about some sophisticated mechanisms for connecting Java Beans together at design time and runtime. However, we haven't talked at all about the environment in which JavaBeans live. To build advanced, extensible applications we need a way for Java Beans to find each other or "rendezvous" at run time. The `java.beans.beancontext` package provides this kind of container environment It also provides a generic "services" lookup mechanism for Beans that wish to advertise their capabilities.

Beans that implement the `BeanContextChild` interface (or a subinterface) are passed a reference to the container's `BeanContext`, which is the source for all container-related information. The `BeanContext` implements many useful interfaces that describe the Bean environment. (To use it, cast it to the appropriate interface.) The two interfaces that we will talk about here are `Collection` and `BeanContextServices`.

A *bean collection* is an object that implements the `java.util.Collection` interface. It can be used to enumerate the Bean instances in the container. A corresponding listener interface lets Beans find out when Beans are added or removed. The `BeanContextServices` interface provides a means for looking up Beans that provide services, either by the Bean's class type or through a list of the currently available service Beans. There is a corresponding listener interface for being informed of new services and revoked services.

Doing much with these classes is a bit beyond the scope of this chapter, but we'll show a simple example that lists the beans in the current container and the available services. Here's the code; Figure 19-11 shows what the bean looks like.

```
//file: ShowContext.java
package magicbeans;
import javax.swing.*;
import java.beans.beancontext.*;
import java.util.*;

public class ShowContext extends JTabbedPane
                      implements BeanContextProxy {
  BeanContext context;
```

```java
    BeanContextServices services;
    JList servicesList = new JList(), beansList = new JList();

    public ShowContext() {
      addTab( "Beans", new JScrollPane( beansList ) );
      addTab( "Services", new JScrollPane( servicesList ) );
    }

    private BeanContextChildSupport beanContextChild =
      new BeanContextChildSupport() {

      public void initializeBeanContextResources()  {
        context= getBeanContext();
        try {
          services = (BeanContextServices)context;
        } catch (ClassCastException ex){/*No BeanContextServices*/}

        updateBeanList();
        updateServicesList();

        context.addBeanContextMembershipListener(
          new BeanContextMembershipListener() {
            public void childrenAdded(
              BeanContextMembershipEvent e){
              updateBeanList();
            }
            public void childrenRemoved(
              BeanContextMembershipEvent e){
              updateBeanList();
            }
          } );
        services.addBeanContextServicesListener(
          new BeanContextServicesListener() {
            public void serviceAvailable(
                 BeanContextServiceAvailableEvent e ) {
              updateServicesList();
            }
            public void serviceRevoked(
                 BeanContextServiceRevokedEvent e ) {
              updateServicesList();
            }
          } );
      }
    };

    void updateServicesList() {
      if ( services == null )
        return;
      Iterator it = services.getCurrentServiceClasses();
```

```
      Vector v = new Vector();
      while( it.hasNext() )
        v.addElement( it.next() );
      servicesList.setListData( v );
  }
  void updateBeanList() {
    Iterator it = context.iterator();
    Vector v = new Vector();
    while( it.hasNext() )
      v.addElement( it.next() );
    beansList.setListData( v );
  }

  public BeanContextChild getBeanContextProxy() {
    return beanContextChild;
  }
}
```

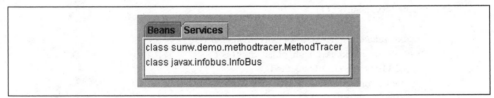

Figure 19-11. Reporting on a bean collection

The purpose of the BeanContextChild interface is to flag the bean as a child of the container and allow it to receive a reference to the BeanContext. But if you look at the code, you won't see any BeanContextChild. Instead, you see that our example implements something called BeanContextProxy. What's the story? Where is our BeanContextChild?

The easiest way to answer this question is to think about some of the design decisions that must have gone into the beancontext package. BeanContextChild isn't an extremely complicated interface, but it still has a half-dozen or so methods, and Sun's engineers didn't want to oblige Bean authors to implement all of those methods whenever they wanted an object that implements Bean-ContextChild. There's an obvious solution to this problem that has been used successfully elsewhere in Java: creating an adapter class that implements BeanContextChild, and letting the Bean author override only those methods that he or she is interested in. This adapter class is called BeanContext-ChildSupport—but it solves one problem only to create another.

If we want an object that implements BeanContextChild, we can certainly extend BeanContextChildSupport, but that's ugly: it forces all of our Beans that need to know about the context to extend a particular class, which severely limits your design flexibility.

A better solution is to introduce another interface, BeanContextProxy, with a single method, getBeanContextProxy(), that returns a BeanContextChild. If we implement BeanContextProxy, the Bean's container will call getBeanContextProxy() to get a child object for us. We can then implement getBeanContextProxy() easily, using a private anonymous inner class that extends BeanContextChildSupport, and override only the methods that are important to us. In our private instance, we override one method: initializeBeanContextResources(). This method gives us a hook on which to hang any code that needs to run after the container has given us our reference to the BeanContext. Within this method we can safely ask for the BeanContext with the getBeanContext() method and use it to look up Beans or services. There are other ways around this problem, but the one described here is as effective as any, and requires minimal work.

Once we have a BeanContext, we can use it to look at the Beans and services that are available in our container. Getting the list of Beans available is simple: we just call the iterator() method of the bean context to get an Iterator that lets us extract references to the Beans. We do this in a helper method called updateBeanList(). Likewise, getting a list of the services available requires casting the BeanContext to a BeanContextServices object, calling getCurrentServiceClasses() to retrieve an Iterator that lists the services, and extracting the services from the Iterator. Again, we use a helper method called updateServicesList() to do most of this work. Finally, the Beans and services available can change at any time, so we register with the BeanContext as a BeanContextMembershipListener to find out about changes to the Beans, and as a BeanContextServicesListener to find out about changes to the services. BeanContextMembershipListener requires two methods, childrenAdded() and childrenRemoved(), both of which handle a BeanContextMembershipEvent. Likewise, BeanContextServicesListener requires the methods serviceAvailable() and serviceRevoked(), which handle (respectively) BeanContextServiceAvailableEvents and BeanContextServiceRevokedEvents.

Whew! That was a dense example. But there's really not much to it when you pick it apart. Next we'll move on a bit and talk about some additional JavaBeans-related APIs.

The Java Activation Framework

The Java Activation Framework (JAF) is a standard extension that can be used by Beans that work with many external data types, such as media retrieved from files and streams. It is essentially a generalized content/protocol handler mechanism for Java Beans. The JAF is an extensible set of classes that wrap arbitrary, raw data sources to provide access to their data as streams or objects, identify the MIME type of the data, and enumerate a registered set of "commands" for operating on the data.

The JAF provides two primary interfaces: `DataSource` and `DataHandler`. The `DataSource` acts something like the protocol handlers we discussed in Chapter 12, *Programming for the Web*. It wraps the data source and determines a MIME type for the data stream. The `DataHandler` acts something like a content handler, except that it provides a great deal more than access to the data. A `DataHandler` is constructed to wrap a `DataSource` and interpret the data in different forms. It also provides a list of command operations that can be used to access the data. `DataHandler` also implements the `java.awt.datatransfer.Transferable` interface, allowing data to be passed among application components in a well defined way.

You can grab the latest JAF from Sun at *http://java.sun.com/beans/glasgow/jaf.html.*

Enterprise JavaBeans

Enterprise JavaBeans is a very big topic, and we can't do more than provide a few paragraphs to whet your appetite. If you want more information, see *Enterprise JavaBeans* by Richard Monson-Haefel (O'Reilly & Associates). The thrust of EJB is to take the JavaBeans philosophy of portable, pluggable, components and extend it to accommodate the sorts of things that three-tiered networked and database-centric applications require. Although EJB is built on the basic JavaBeans concepts, it is much larger and more "special-purpose." It doesn't have a lot in common with the kinds of things we've been talking about in this chapter. EJBs are primarily server-side components for networked applications. Sun's Forte development environment, among others, provides some support for working with Enterprise JavaBeans.

EJB ties together a number of other Java "enterprise"-oriented APIs, including database access, transactions, and name services, into a single component model for server applications. EJB imposes a lot more structure on how you write code than plain old JavaBeans. But it does so in order to allow the server-side EJB container to take on a lot of responsibility for you and to optimize your application's activities without you having to write a lot of code. Here are a few of the things that Enterprise JavaBeans tackles:

- Object lifecycle and name service lookup
- Container-managed persistence
- Transaction management

- Server resource pooling and management
- Deployment configuration

EJB divides the world into two camps: *Entity Beans*, which represent data objects, and *Session Beans*, which implement services and operations over entity beans. These correspond well to the second and third tiers in a three-tiered business application. "Business Logic" is represented by Session Bean services and database access is made transparent through automated object mapping by Entity Beans.

Many aspects of EJB behavior can be controlled through "deployment descriptors" that customize bean behavior for the local environment. The result is a high level of abstraction over ordinary business-specific code. It allows powerful, networked business application components to be packaged and reused in the sort of way that ordinary Beans are reused to build client-side applications.

Sun has created a reference EJB platform as part of Java 2 Enterprise Edition (J2EE); currently, the most robust EJB implementations are provided by third-party companies. Usually the EJB "container" is packaged as part of a more general "application server" that performs other duties such as providing a web server. There are many vendors of commercial EJB servers. Two extremes: Weblogic makes a very popular one with many high-end features; Valto's Ejipt is a very small (embeddable) EJB container.

20

In this chapter:
- *The JApplet Class*
- *The APPLET Tag*
- *Using the Java Plug-in*
- *Using Digital Signatures*

Applets

One of the original tenets of Java was that applications would be delivered over the network to your computer. Instead of buying a shrink-wrapped box containing a word processor, you would pay per use for a program available over the Internet. This revolutionary idea has been temporarily shelved by the realities of a slow Internet. But small downloadable applications called *applets* are practical and interesting.

An applet is part of a web page, just like an image or hyperlink. It "owns" some rectangular area of the user's screen. It can draw whatever it wants and respond to keyboard and mouse events in that area. When the web browser loads a page that contains a Java applet, it knows how to load the classes of the applet and run them.

This chapter describes how applets work and how to put them in web pages. You'll learn how to use Sun's Java Plug-In to take advantage of the latest Java features. Finally, we'll cover the details of creating signed applets, which can step outside the typical applet security restrictions to do useful things, like reading and writing files.

The JApplet Class

If you've been waiting for a more detailed discussion of the applet class, here it is. A JApplet is something like a Panel with a mission. It is a GUI container that has some extra structure to allow it to be used in an "alien" environment, such as a Web browser. Applets also have a lifecycle that lets them act more like an application than a static component, such as a paragraph of text or an image. Although applets tend to be relatively simple, there's no inherent restriction on their complexity. There's no reason you couldn't write an air traffic control system (well, let's be less ambitious—a word processor) as an applet.

Originally, the `java.applet.Applet` class defined the functionality of an applet. The `javax.swing.JApplet` class is a simple extension of `Applet` that adds the plumbing necessary for Swing.

Structurally, an applet is a sort of wrapper for your Java code. In contrast to a standalone graphical Java application, which starts up from a `main()` method and creates a GUI, an applet is itself a component that expects to be dropped into someone else's GUI. Thus, an applet can't run by itself; it runs in the context of a web browser or a special applet viewer program (which is described later). Instead of having your application create a `JFrame` to hold your GUI, you stuff your application inside a `JApplet` (which is itself a `Container`), and let someone else add the applet to their GUI.

Applets are placed on web pages with the `<APPLET>` HTML tag, which we'll discuss later in this chapter. At its simplest, you just specify the name of the applet class and a size for the applet:

```
<APPLET code=AnalogClock width=100 height=100></APPLET>
```

Pragmatically, an applet is an intruder into someone else's environment, and therefore has to be treated with suspicion. The web browsers that run applets impose restrictions on what the applet is allowed to do. The restrictions are enforced by an applet security manager, which unsigned applets are not allowed to change. The browser also provides an "applet context," which is additional support that helps the applet live within its restrictions.

Aside from that top-level structure and the security restrictions, there is no difference between an applet and an application. If your application can live within the restrictions imposed by a browser's security manager, you can easily structure it to function as an applet and a standalone application. (We'll show an example of an applet that can also be run as a standalone shortly.) Conversely, if you can supply all of the things that an applet requires from its environment, you can use applets within your standalone applications and within other applets (though this requires a bit of work).

As we said a moment ago, a `JApplet` expects to be embedded in GUI (perhaps a document) and used in a viewing environment that provides it with special resources. In all other respects, however, applets are just ordinary `Panel` objects. As Figure 20-1 shows, an applet is a kind of `Panel`. Like any other `Panel`, a `JApplet` can contain user interface components and use all the basic drawing and event-handling capabilities of the `Component` class. We draw on a `JApplet` by overriding its `paint()` method; we respond to events in the `JApplet`'s display area by providing the appropriate event listeners. Applets have additional structure that helps them interact with the viewer environment.

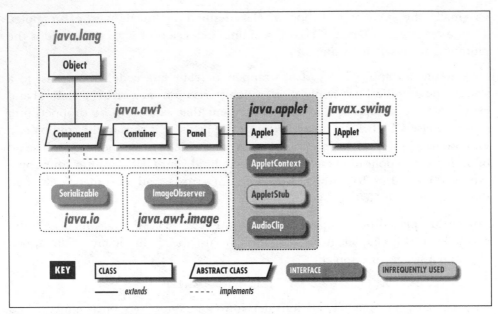

Figure 20-1. The java.applet package

Applet Control

The Applet class contains four methods an applet can override to guide it through its lifecycle. The init(), start(), stop(), and destroy() methods are called by the appletviewer or a web browser to direct the applet's behavior. init() is called once, after the applet is created. The init() method is where you perform basic setup like parsing parameters, building a user interface, and loading resources. Given what we've said about objects, you might expect the applet's constructor would be the right place for such initialization. However, the constructor is meant to be called by the applet's environment, for simple creation of the applet. This might happen before the applet has access to certain resources, like information about its environment. Therefore, an applet doesn't normally do any work in its constructor; it relies on the default constructor for the JApplet class and does its initialization in the init() method.

The start() method is called whenever the applet becomes visible; it shouldn't be a surprise then that the stop() method is called whenever the applet becomes invisible. init() is only called once in the life of an applet, but start() and stop() can be called any number of times (but always in the logical sequence). For example, start() is called when the applet is displayed, such as when it scrolls onto the screen; stop() is called if the applet scrolls off the screen or the viewer leaves the document. start() tells the applet it should be active. The applet may want to create threads, animate, or otherwise perform useful (or annoying) activity. `stop()` is called to let the applet know it should go dormant. Applets should cease CPU-intensive or wasteful activity when they are stopped and resume it when (and if) they are restarted. However, there's no requirement that an invisible applet stop computing; in some applications, it may be useful for the applet to continue running in the background. Just be considerate of your user, who doesn't want an invisible applet dragging down system performance. There are user tools that help to monitor and squash rogue applets in a web browser.

Finally, the `destroy()` method is called to give the applet a last chance to clean up before it's removed—some time after the call to `stop()`. For example, an applet might want to close down suspended communications channels or remove graphics frames. Exactly when `destroy()` is called depends on the browser; Netscape calls `destroy()` just prior to deleting the applet from its cache. This means that although an applet can cling to life after being told to `stop()`, how long it can go on is unpredictable. If you want to maintain your applet as the user progresses through other activities, consider putting it in an HTML frame, so that it remains visible and won't be told to `stop()`.

The Applet Security Sandbox

Applets are quarantined within the browser by an applet `SecurityManager`. The `SecurityManager` is part of the web browser or applet viewer. It is installed before the browser loads any applets and implements the basic restrictions that let the user run untrusted applets safely. Remember, aside from basic language robustness, there are no inherent security restrictions on a standalone Java application. It is the browser's responsibility to install a special security manager and limit what applets are allowed to do.

Most browsers impose the following restrictions on untrusted applets:

- Untrusted applets cannot read or write files on the local host.

- Untrusted applets can open network connections (sockets) only to the server from which they originated.

- Untrusted applets cannot start other processes on the local host.

- Untrusted applets cannot have native methods.

The motivation for these restrictions should be fairly obvious: you clearly wouldn't want a program coming from some random Internet site to access your files or run arbitrary programs. Although untrusted applets cannot directly read and write files on the client side or talk to arbitrary hosts on the network, applets can work with servers to store data and communicate. For example, an applet can use Java's RMI (Remote Method Invocation) facility to do processing on its server. An applet can communicate with other applets on the Net by proxy through its server.

Trusted applets

Newer versions of Java make it possible to *sign* archive files that contain applets. Because a signature identifies the applet's origin unambiguously, we can now distinguish between "trusted" applets (i.e., applets that come from a site or person you trust not to do anything harmful) and run-of-the-mill "untrusted" applets. In browser environments that support signing, trusted applets can be granted permission to "go outside" of the applet security sandbox. Trusted applets can be allowed to do most of the things that standalone Java applications can do: read and write files, open network connections to arbitrary machines, and interact with the local operating system by starting processes. Trusted applets still can't have native methods, but including native methods in an applet would make it unportable, and would therefore be a bad idea.

Chapter 3, *Tools of the Trade*, discussed how to package your applet's class files and resources into a JAR file. Later in this chapter, I'll show you how to sign an applet with your digital signature.

Getting Applet Resources

An applet must communicate with its browser or applet viewer. For example, it must get its parameters from the HTML document in which it appears. An applet may also need to load images, audio clips, and other items. It may also want to ask the viewer about other applets on the same HTML page in order to communicate with them. To get resources from the environment, applets use the `AppletStub` and `AppletContext` interfaces. Unless you're writing a browser or some other application that loads and runs applets, you won't have to implement these interfaces, but you do use them within your applet.

Applet parameters

An applet gets its parameters from the <PARAM> tags placed inside the <APPLET> tag in the HTML document, as we'll describe later. Inside the applet, you can retrieve these parameters using `Applet`'s `getParameter()` method. For example, the following code reads the `imageName` and `sheep` parameters from its HTML page:

```
String imageName = getParameter( "imageName" );
try {
    int numberOfSheep = Integer.parseInt(getParameter( "sheep" ));
} catch ( NumberFormatException e ) { /* use default */ }
```

A friendly applet will provide information about the parameters it accepts through its `getParameterInfo()` method. `getParameterInfo()` returns an array of string arrays, listing and describing the applet's parameters. For each parameter, three strings are provided: the parameter name, its possible values or value types, and a verbose description. For example:

```
public String [][] getParameterInfo() {
  String [][] appletInfo = {
      {"logo",   "url",  "Main logo image"},
      {"timer", "int",   "Time to wait before becoming annoying"},
      {"flashing", "constant|intermittant", "Flag for how to flash"}
  };
  return appletInfo;
}
```

Applet resources

An applet can find where it lives by calling the `getDocumentBase()` and `getCodeBase()` methods. `getDocumentBase()` returns the base URL of the document in which the applet appears; `getCodeBase()` returns the base URL of the Applet's class files. An applet can use these to construct relative URLs from which to load other resources like images, sounds, and other data. The `getImage()` method takes a URL and asks for an image from the viewer environment. The image may be pulled from a cache or loaded asynchronously when later used. The `getAudioClip()` method, similarly, retrieves sound clips.

The following example uses `getCodeBase()` to construct a URL and load a properties configuration file, located in the same remote directory as the applet's class file:

```
Properties props = new Properties();
try {
  URL url = new URL(getCodeBase(), "appletConfig.props");
  props.load( url.openStream() );
} catch ( IOException e ) { /* failed */ }
```

A better way to load resources is by calling the `getResource()` and `getResourceAsStream()` methods of the `Class` class, which search the applet's JAR files (if any) as well as its codebase. The following code loads the properties file `appletConfig.props`:

```
Properties props = new Properties();
try {
  props.load( getClass().getResourceAsStream("appletConfig.props") );
} catch ( IOException e ) { /* failed */ }
```

Driving the browser

The status line is a blurb of text that usually appears somewhere in the viewer's display, indicating a current activity. An applet can request that some text be placed in the status line with the showStatus() method. (The browser isn't required to do anything in response to this call, but most browsers will oblige you.)

An applet can also ask the browser to show a new document. To do this, the applet makes a call to the showDocument(url) method of the AppletContext. You can get a reference to the AppletContext with the applet's getAppletContext() method. Calling showDocument(url) replaces the currently showing document, which means that your currently running applet will be stopped.

Another version of showDocument() takes an additional String argument to tell the browser where to display the new URL:

```
getAppletContext().showDocument( url, name );
```

The name argument can be the name of an existing labeled HTML frame; the document referenced by the URL will be displayed in that frame. You can use this method to create an applet that "drives" the browser to new locations dynamically, but keeps itself active on the screen in a separate frame. If the named frame doesn't exist, the browser will create a new top-level window to hold it. Alternatively, name can have one of the following special values:

self
    Show in the current frame

_parent
    Show in the parent of our frame

_top
    Show in outermost (top-level) frame

_blank
    Show in a new top-level browser window

Both showStatus() and showDocument() requests may be ignored by a cold-hearted viewer or web browser.

Inter-applet communication

Applets that are embedded in documents loaded from the same location on a web site can use a simple mechanism to locate one another (rendezvous). Once an applet has a reference to another applet, it can communicate with it, just as with any other object, by invoking methods and sending events. The getApplet() method of the applet context looks for an applet by name:

```
Applet clock = getAppletContext().getApplet("theClock");
```

Give an applet a name within your HTML document using the name attribute of the <APPLET> tag. Alternatively, you can use the getApplets() method to enumerate all of the available applets in the pages.

The tricky thing with applet communications is that applets run inside of the security sandbox. An untrusted applet can only "see" and communicate with objects that were loaded by the same class loader. Currently, the only reliable criterion for when applets share a class loader is when they share a common base URL. For example, all of the applets contained in web pages loaded from the base URL of *http://foo.bar.com/mypages/* should share a class loader and should be able to see each other. This would include documents such as *mypages/foo.html* and *mypages/bar.html*, but not *mypages/morestuff/foo.html*.

When applets do share a class loader, other techniques are possible too. As with any other class, you can call static methods in applets by name. So you could use static methods in one of your applets as a "registry" to coordinate your activities. There are also proposals that would allow you to have more control over when applets share a class loader and how their life cycles are managed.

Applets versus standalone applications

The following lists summarize the methods of the applet API. From the `Applet-Stub` interface:

```
boolean isActive();
URL getDocumentBase();
URL getCodeBase();
String getParameter(String name);
AppletContext getAppletContext();
void appletResize(int width, int height);
```

From the `AppletContext` interface:

```
AudioClip getAudioClip(URL url);
Image getImage(URL url);
Applet getApplet(String name);
Enumeration getApplets();
void showDocument(URL url);
public void showDocument(URL url, String target);
void showStatus(String status);
```

These are the methods that are provided by the applet viewer environment. If your applet doesn't happen to use any of them, or if you can provide alternatives to handle special cases (such as loading images), then your applet could be made able to function as a standalone application as well as an applet. The basic idea is to add a `main()` method that provides a window (`JFrame`) in which the applet can run. Here's an outline of the strategy:

```
//file: MySuperApplet.java
import java.applet.Applet;
import java.awt.*;
import javax.swing.*;
```

```
public class MySuperApplet extends JApplet {

    // applet's own code, including constructor
    // and init() and start() methods

    public static void main( String [] args ) {
        // instantiate the applet
        JApplet theApplet = new MySuperApplet();

        // create a window for the applet to run in
        JFrame theFrame = new JFrame();
        theFrame.setSize(200,200);

        // place the applet in the window
        theFrame.getContentPane().add("Center", theApplet);

        // start the applet
        theApplet.init();
        theApplet.start();

        // display the window
        theFrame.setVisible(true);
    }
}
```

Here we get to play "applet viewer" for a change. We have created an instance of the class, MySuperApplet, using its constructor—something we don't normally do—and added it to our own JFrame. We call its init() method to give the applet a chance to wake up and then call its start() method. In this example, MySuperApplet doesn't implement init() and start(), so we're calling methods inherited from the Applet class. This is the procedure that an applet viewer would use to run an applet.(If we wanted to go further, we could implement our own AppletContext and AppletStub and set them in the JApplet before startup.)

Trying to make your applets into applications as well often doesn't make sense and is not always trivial. We show this example only to get you thinking about the real differences between applets and applications. It is probably best to think in terms of the applet API until you have a need to go outside it. Remember that trusted applets can do almost all of the things that applications can. It may be wiser to make an applet that requires trusted permissions than an application.

The <APPLET> Tag

Applets are embedded in HTML documents with the <APPLET> tag. The <APPLET> tag resembles the HTML <IMG> image tag. It contains attributes that identify the applet to be displayed and, optionally, give the web browser hints about how it should be displayed.* The standard image tag sizing and alignment attributes, such as height and width, can be used inside the applet tag. However, unlike images, applets have both an opening <APPLET> and a closing </APPLET> tag. Sandwiched between these can be any number of <PARAM> tags that contain data to be passed to the applet:

```
<APPLET attribute attribute ... >
    <PARAM parameter >
    <PARAM parameter >
    ...
</APPLET>
```

Attributes

Attributes are name/value pairs that are interpreted by a web browser or appletviewer. (Many HTML tags besides <APPLET> have attributes.) Attributes of the <APPLET> tag specify general features that apply to all applets, such as size and alignment. The definition of the <APPLET> tag lists a fixed set of recognized attributes; specifying an incorrect or nonexistent attribute should be considered an HTML error.

Three attributes are required in the <APPLET> tag. Two of these attributes, width and height, specify the space the applet occupies on the screen. The third required attribute may be either code or object; you must supply one of these attributes, and you can't specify both. The code attribute specifies the class file from which the applet is loaded; the object attribute specifies a serialized representation of an applet. Most often, you'll use the code attribute; the tools for creating serialized applets aren't quite there yet.

The following is an HTML fragment for a hypothetical simple clock applet that takes no parameters and requires no special HTML layout:

```
<APPLET code=AnalogClock width=100 height=100></APPLET>
```

The HTML file that contains this <APPLET> tag must be stored in the same directory as the AnalogClock.class class file. The applet tag is not sensitive to spacing, so the previous code is therefore equivalent to:

```
<APPLET
    code=AnalogClock
    width=100
    height=100>
</APPLET>
```

You can use whatever form seems appropriate.

---

* If you are not familiar with HTML or other markup languages, you may want to refer to *HTML: The Definitive Guide*, by Chuck Musciano and Bill Kennedy (O'Reilly & Associates), for a complete reference on HTML and structured web documents.

Parameters

Parameters are analogous to command-line arguments; they provide a way to pass information to an applet. Each <PARAM> tag contains a name and a value that are passed as strings to the applet:

```
<PARAM name = parameter_name value = parameter_value>
```

Parameters provide a means of embedding application-specific data and configuration information within an HTML document.* Our AnalogClock applet, for example, might accept a parameter that selects between local and universal time:

```
<APPLET code=AnalogClock width=100 height=100>
    <PARAM name=zone value=GMT>
</APPLET>
```

Presumably, this AnalogClock applet is designed to look for a parameter named zone with a possible value of GMT.

Parameter names and values can be quoted to contain spaces and other special characters. We could therefore be more verbose and use a parameter value like the following:

```
<PARAM name=zone value="Greenwich Mean Time">
```

The parameters a given applet expects are determined by the developer of that applet. There is no fixed set of parameter names or values; it's up to the applet to interpret the parameter name/value pairs that are passed to it. Any number of parameters can be specified, and the applet may choose to use or ignore them as it sees fit. The applet might also consider parameters to be either optional or required, and act accordingly.

¿Habla Applet?

Web browsers ignore tags they don't understand; if the web browser doesn't interpret the <APPLET> or <PARAM> tags, they should disappear and any HTML between the <APPLET> and </APPLET> tags should appear normally.

By convention, Java-enabled web browsers do the opposite and ignore any extra HTML between the <APPLET> and </APPLET> tags. This means we can place some alternative HTML inside the <APPLET> tag, which is displayed only by web browsers that can't run the applet.

---

* If you are wondering why the applet's parameters are specified in yet another type of tag, here's the reason. In the original alpha release of Java, applet parameters were included inside of a single <app> tag along with formatting attributes. However, this format was not SGML-compliant, so the <PARAM> tag was added.

For our `AnalogClock` example, we could display a small text explanation and an image of the clock applet as a teaser:

```
<APPLET code=AnalogClock width=100 height=100>
    <PARAM name=zone value=GMT>
    <strong>If you see this you don't have a Java-enabled Web
    browser. Here's a picture of what you are missing.</strong>
    <img src="clockface.gif">
</APPLET>
```

The Complete <APPLET> Tag

We can now spell out the syntax for the full-blown <APPLET> tag:

```
<APPLET
    code = class_name
```

or:

```
    object = serialized_applet_name

    width = pixels_high
    height = pixels_wide

    [ codebase = location_URL ]
    [ archive = comma_separated_list_of_archive_files ]
    [ name = applet_instance_name ]
    [ alt = alternate_text ]
    [ align = style ]
    [ vspace = vertical pad pixels ]
    [ hspace = horizontal pad pixels ]
>
    [ <PARAM name = parameter_name value = parameter_value> ] ...

... [ HTML code for non-Java-aware browsers ]
</APPLET>
```

Either the `code` attribute or the `object` attribute must be present to specify the applet to run. The `code` attribute specifies the applet's class file; you'll see this most frequently. The `object` attribute specifies a serialized (pickled) representation of an applet. When you use the `object` attribute to load an applet, the applet's `init()` method is not called. However, the serialized applet's `start()` method is called.

The `width`, `height`, `align`, `vspace`, and `hspace` attributes deterine the preferred size, alignment, and padding, respectively. The `width` and `height` attributes are required.

The `codebase` attribute specifies the directory to be searched for the applet's class file (or archive file). If this attribute isn't present, the browser looks in the same directory as the HTML file. The `archive` attribute specifies a list of JAR or ZIP files in which the applet's class file is located. To put two or more files in the list, separate the filenames by commas; for example, the following attribute tells the browser to search three archives for the applet:

```
archive=Part1.jar,Part2.jar,Utilities.jar
```

The `archive` attribute must be present if you have packaged your applet in an archive. When searching for classes, a browser checks the files listed in the `archives` attribute before searching any other locations on the server.

The `alt` attribute specifies alternate text that is displayed by browsers that understand the `<APPLET>` tag and its attributes, but can't actually run applets. This attribute can also describe the applet, since in this case any alternate HTML between `<APPLET>` and `</APPLET>` is, by convention, ignored by Java-enabled browsers.

The `name` attribute specifies an instance name for the executing applet. This is a name specified as a unique label for each copy of an applet on a particular HTML page. For example, if we include our clock twice on the same page (using two applet tags), we should give each instance a unique name to differentiate them:

```
<APPLET code=AnalogClock name="bigClock" width=300 height=300></APPLET>
<APPLET code=AnalogClock name="smallClock" width=50 height=50></APPLET>
```

Applets use instance names to recognize and communicate with other applets on the same page. We could, for instance, create a "clock setter" applet that knows how to set the time on an `AnalogClock` applet and pass it the instance name of a particular target clock on this page as a parameter. This might look something like:

```
<APPLET code=ClockSetter>
    <PARAM name=clockToSet value="bigClock">
</APPLET>
```

Loading Class Files

The `code` attribute of the `<APPLET>` tag should specify the name of an applet. This is either a simple class name, or a package path and class name. For now, let's look at simple class names; we'll discuss packages in a moment. By default, the Java runtime system looks for the class file in the same location as the HTML document that contains it. This location is known as the *base URL* for the document.

Consider an HTML document, *clock.html*, that contains our clock applet example:

```
<APPLET code=AnalogClock width=100 height=100></APPLET>
```

Let's say we retrieve the document at the following URL:

```
http://www.time.ch/documents/clock.html
```

Java tries to retrieve the applet class file from the same base location:

```
http://www.time.ch/documents/AnalogClock.class
```

The `codebase` attribute of the `<APPLET>` tag can be used to specify an alternative base URL for the class file search. Let's say our HTML document now specifies `codebase`, as in the following example:

```
<APPLET
    codebase=http://www.joes.ch/stuff/
    code=AnalogClock
    width=100
    height=100>
</APPLET>
```

Java now looks for the applet class file at:

```
http://www.joes.ch/stuff/AnalogClock.class
```

Packages

Packages are groups of Java classes. A package name is a little like a URL, in that they both use a hierarchical, dot-separated naming convention. The full name of a Java class file is formed by prefixing the class name with the package name.

In addition to providing a naming scheme, packages determine the storage locations of class files. Before a class file is retrieved from a server, its package-name component is translated by the client into a relative path name under the base URL of the document. The components of a class package name are turned into the directory components of a pathname, just as with classes on your local system.

Let's suppose that our `AnalogClock` has been placed into a package called `time.clock` (a subordinate package for clock-related classes, within a package for time-related classes). The fully qualified name of our class is `time.clock.AnalogClock`. Our simple `<APPLET>` tag would now look like:

```
<APPLET code=time.clock.AnalogClock width=100 height=100></APPLET>
```

Let's say the *clock.html* document is once again retrieved from:

```
http://www.time.ch/documents/clock.html
```

Java now looks for the class file in the following location:

```
http://www.time.ch/documents/time/clock/AnalogClock.class
```

The same is true when specifying an alternative `codebase`:

```
<APPLET
    codebase=http://www.joes.ch/stuff/
    code=time.clock.AnalogClock
    width=100
```

```
        height=100>
    </APPLET>
```

Java now tries to find the class in the corresponding path under this base URL:

```
http://www.joes.ch/stuff/time/clock/AnalogClock.class
```

One possible package-naming convention proposes that Internet host and domain names be incorporated as part of package names to form a unique identifier for classes produced by a given organization. If a company with the domain name foobar.com produced our AnalogClock class, they might distribute it in a package called com.foobar.time.clock. The fully qualified name of the Analog-Clock class would then be com.foobar.time.clock.AnalogClock. This would presumably be a unique name stored on an arbitrary server. A future version of the Java class loader might use this to automatically search for classes on remote hosts. Perhaps soon we'll run Sun's latest and greatest web browser directly from its source with:

```
% java com.sun.java.hotjava.HotJava
```

Viewing Applets

Sun's SDK comes with an applet-viewer program, aptly called appletviewer. To use appletviewer, specify the URL of the document on the command line. For example, to view our AnalogClock at the URL shown ealier, use the following command:

```
% appletviewer http://www.time.ch/documents/clock.html
```

appletviewer retrieves all applets in the specified document and displays each one in a separate window. appletviewer is not a web browser; it doesn't attempt to display HTML. It's primarily a convenience for testing and debugging applets. If the document doesn't contain <APPLET> tags, appletviewer does nothing.

Using the Java Plug-in

The disadvantage of the <APPLET> tag is that you have to rely on the browser's Java interpreter. This is bad for two reasons:

- The version of Java that is included in popular browsers lags the current version of the SDK. It was a painfully long time, for instance, between the release of SDK 1.1 and the time that SDK 1.1 was supported in Netscape and Internet Explorer. As a matter of fact, it hasn't ever been fully supported in Internet Explorer—Microsoft has its own agenda, which may not match up with your "write once, run anywhere" aspirations.

- The browser's Java implementation has its own bugs and idiosyncrasies, which are different from the bugs and idiosyncrasies of Sun's SDK. If you are hoping to run your applet on both Netscape and Internet Explorer, you will have to test it on both platforms to make sure you don't run into any trouble. This is tedious and frustrating.

At the time of this writing, both browsers are moderately stable for SDK 1.1 development. As a developer, though, you're probably itching to use all of those cool Java 2 features. What can you do? In light of the lawsuits brought by Sun and the Department of Justice, it is unlikely that Microsoft will ever support Java 2 in Internet Explorer. Netscape's Java support in Navigator is likewise questionable, though for different reasons. In the foreseeable future, you can't rely on Java 2 support in Navigator or Internet Explorer.

What Is the Java Plug-in?

Does that mean applets are dead? Heck no! A clever technology called the Java Plug-in saves the day. Both Navigator and Internet Explorer have a *plug-in* mechanism that allows the browser to be extended to handle new types of data.* For example, you can view movies in your browser using Apple's QuickTime plug-in. You can view interactive multimedia with Macromedia's Shockwave plug-in. The idea is strikingly similar to applets; basically the browser hands off responsibility for some rectangular area on the screen to someone else's code. The Java Plug-in is simply a Java runtime environment implemented as a browser plug-in.

Applets that use the Java Plug-in can take advantage of the very latest Java platform features. Furthermore, applets should run exactly the same in any browser. The browser isn't even really running the applet anymore—the Plug-in takes care of it.

This is nifty technology, but it does come at a price. Users who want to use the Java Plug-in to run applets will have to download and install it first. While this is not a huge deal, it is a barrier to universal acceptance. (It's conceivable that America Online, which owns Netscape now, will package the Plug-in with future versions of Navigator. But it's unlikely that Microsoft would make the same move with Internet Explorer.)

Messy Tags

The HTML for web pages that contain Plug-in applets is much messier than the <APPLET> tag you've already seen. Part of the problem is that you have to use

---

* Microsoft calls this technique ActiveX custom controls. But it's exactly the same concept: the browser gives control for some part of a web page to another piece of code.

separate tags for Internet Explorer and Navigator. Navigator recognizes the `<EMBED>` tag, while Internet Explorer recognizes the `<OBJECT>` tag. If you are clever about fitting the `<EMBED>` tag inside the `<OBJECT>` tag, you'll end up with some HTML that both browsers will recognize and run correctly.

These tags have their own little syntax, but basically you're still providing the same information to the browser. You specify the size of the applet, the class name to use, where to find additional classes, and parameters that should be passed to the applet itself. Fortunately, you don't have to worry too much about the details. Sun provides a handy utility, the *HTML Converter*, that converts `<APPLET>` tags to the appropriate `<EMBED>` and `<OBJECT>` tags. Assuming you've set up your `<APPLET>` tag correctly, you should have no trouble converting your HTML page to use the Java Plug-in. This utility is available for download at *http://java.sun.com/products/plugin/1.2/converter.html*.

Suppose, for example, that you create a web page called *ShowOff.html*. Once you have the `<APPLET>` tag set up the way you want (you can test it with `appletviewer`), you can use the HTML Converter to set up your web page to use the Plug-in. The HTML Converter runs as a Swing application. To run it, navigate to the directory where you installed the HTML Converter and type the following:

```
C:\> java HTMLConverter
```

The window is pretty self-explanatory. You can convert all HTML files in a directory or just convert a single HTML file. The conversion is done "in-place," which means that your original HTML is overwritten with the new stuff. The Converter will automatically back up your old files unless you tell it otherwise.

You can perform different kinds of conversions, represented by different *templates*. By default, the HTML Converter uses a template that produces a page that will work with Navigator and Internet Explorer. If you want it to work with other browsers that support Java 2, you'll need to specify the "Extended" template rather than the "Standard" template.* In addition to adding the `<EMBED>` and `<OBJECT>` tags, the "Extended" template will preserve the original `<APPLET>` tag. This has the added benefit that you'll still be able to test your applet with `appletviewer`.

Viewing Plug-in Applets

What actually happens when users browse to a page with a Plug-in applet? It depends, of course, on which browser you're using. Internet Explorer asks the user for permission to download and run the Java Plug-in in order to display the applet. Netscape Navigator directs the user to the Java Runtime Environment

---

* At this writing, no browsers support Java 2. But it seems likely that Sun will release a new version of HotJava soon.

(JRE) download page. The Java Plug-in is distributed as part of the JRE. In either case, the download and installation times vary, depending on network speed and user expertise. You can expect that most Internet users will have to spend ten or more minutes downloading and installing the JRE.

The good news is that the installation only needs to be done once. Once you have JRE installed and running, you can view Plug-in applets immediately (at least as soon as the browser loads the plug-in). The only time you'll need to install a new Plug-in is when a new version of Java comes out.

Despite the price of installation and HTML tag messiness, the Plug-in is powerful medicine indeed. No longer do you have to wait for browser vendors to implement the latest Java platform features—the Plug-in makes the latest Java releases available to applets immediately, and it provides a more hospitable environment for applets, regardless of what browser displays them.

Using Digital Signatures

Digital signatures provide a way to authenticate documents and other data. They solve one of the Internet's biggest problems: given that you've received a message from Ms. X, how do you know that the message really came from Ms. X and not an imposter? Just as important for Java, let's say that you've downloaded a great new applet written by your favorite author, Jonathan Knudsen, and you'd like to grant it some additional privileges, so that it can do something cool for you. You trust that this particular author wouldn't intentionally distribute something harmful. But how do you know that the author really is who he says he is? And what if you downloaded the applet from a third-party location, like an archive? How can you be sure that someone hasn't modified the applet since the author wrote it? With Java's default security manager, such an applet can't do anything serious, but when we're talking about configuring your browser to grant additional privileges to applets coming from trusted sites, you would be in for trouble—if it weren't for digital signatures.

Like their inky analogs, digital signatures associate a name with an item in a way that is difficult to forge. In reality, a digital signature is much more difficult to forge than a traditional signature. Furthermore, digital signatures provide another benefit: they allow you to authenticate a document, proving that it hasn't been altered in transit. In other words, you know who the sender is, and that the data you received is exactly what the sender sent. Some malicious person can't clip out a digital signature, modify the original document (or applet), and attach the old signature to the result. And he can't generate a new signature—at least, he can't generate a signature claiming that the document came from its original sender.

(He could, of course, attach his own signature—but that would be like signing the stick up note you hand to the bank teller.)

Digital signatures are based on public-key cryptography, which is beyond the scope of this book. However, the basics are important and interesting.* In a public-key system, there are two pieces of information: a public key and a private one. They have a special, asymmetric relationship, such that a message encrypted with one key can only be decrypted with the other key. Furthermore, if you know only one key, it is very difficult to compute the other. Therefore, if I give you my public key, you can use it to create an encrypted message that only I can read. No one else, including you, has enough information to go through the process of decrypting the encoded message, so it's safe to send it over untrusted networks. Furthermore, I can (and probably will) give my public key to anyone in the world, since the public key only lets people send me messages; it doesn't let them read my messages.

Digital signatures are based on the reverse process. If I encrypt something with my private key, anyone can use my public key to read the message. That may not sound very useful, since I already said that I'd give my public key away to anyone who wants it. But in this case, we're not trying to keep the message secret, we're trying to prove that I'm the only one who could have sent the message. And that's exactly what we've done. No one else has my private key, so no one else can send a message that can be decrypted with my public key. Therefore, only the real me could have sent the message.

We've simplified the process in one crucial way. Encrypting a large message with complex algorithms takes a long time, even with fast computers. And some public key algorithms just aren't suitable for encrypting large amounts of data for other reasons, as well. For digital signatures, then, we don't usually encrypt the entire message. First, we use a standard algorithm to create a "hash" or "message digest." To produce the signature, we then encrypt the (relatively small) message digest with the private key. The recipient can then decrypt the signature with the public key and check whether the resulting message digest matches the message he received. If it does, the recipient knows that the message hasn't been altered and that the sender is who he claims to be.

Digital signatures can be used to authenticate Java class files and other types of data sent over the network. The author of an object signs the data with his or her digital signature, and we use the author's public key to authenticate that signature after we retrieve it. We don't have to communicate with anyone in order to verify the authenticity of the data. We don't even have to make sure that the communications by which we received the data are secure. We simply check the signature

---

* See Bruce Schneier's encyclopedic *Applied Cryptography* (John Wiley & Sons) or Jonathan Knudsen's *Java Cryptography* (O'Reilly & Associates).

after the data arrives. If it is valid, we know that we have the authentic data and that it has not been tampered with . . . or do we?

Well, there is a larger problem that digital signatures alone don't solve: verifying identity. If the signature checks out, we know that only the person (or entity) that published the public key could have sent the data. But how do we know that the public key really belongs to whomever we think it does? How do we associate an identity with that public key in the first place? We've made it more difficult to counterfeit a message, but it's not impossible. A forger could conceivably create a counterfeit Java class, sign it with his own private key, and try to trick you into believing that his public key is that of the real author or the trusted web site. In this case, you'll download the bad applet, then use the wrong public key to verify the applet, and be tricked into thinking that there's nothing wrong. This is where *certificates* and *certificate authorities* come into play.

Certificates

A certificate is a document that lists a name and a public key. By a name, we mean some real world information describing a person or entity. For example, a certificate might contain your full name and address, or the name of a company and the location of its headquarters. We'll consider the combination of a name and a public key in this way to make up an *identity*. If we have valid information for a particular identity, we can verify data that the identity has signed.

A certificate is signed with the digital signature of a certificate authority—the entity that issued the certificate. The certificate is, in effect, a proclamation by the certificate authority that the identity listed is valid—in other words, that the listed public key really does belong to the entity named. If we decide to trust the certificate authority, we can then believe the identities contained in the certificates it issues are valid. The certificate acts as a sort of electronic ID card, backed up by the credentials of the certificate authority. Of course, we no longer issue certificates on fancy vellum scrolls, as shown in Figure 20-2; the format for modern certificates is described by a standard called X.509.

Certificate authority (CA) certificates

This is all well and good, but the original problem remains: in order to verify the authenticity of a certificate, we need to verify its signature. Now, to do that, we need to know the certificate authority's public key; rather than solving the problem, we simply seem to have shifted the problem to a new front. If a counterfeiter could substitute her public key for the public key of one entity, she might be able to do the same for the certificate authority. But shifting the problem helps quite a bit. We have reduced the number of public keys that we need to know from an unlimited number (all of the identities we might ever encounter) to a very small

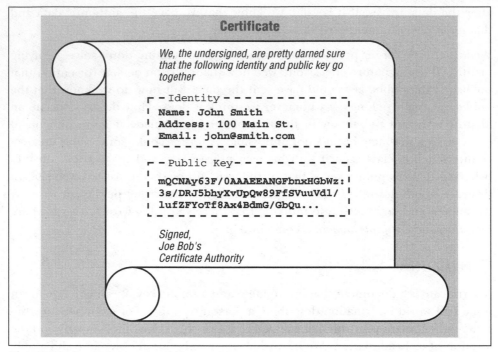

Figure 20-2. An old-fashioned certificate

number: one for each certificate authority. We have chained our trust of the identity to the trust of the certificate authority's identity. Chaining can be allowed to extend further, to an arbitrary depth, allowing certificate authorities to back up lower certificate authorities, and so on. At some point, of course, the chain has to stop, and that usually happens with a "self-signed" or *certificate authority certificate*, that is, a certificate that is issued by the certificate authority for itself, containing its own public key. "What good is that?" you might ask.

As for the authenticity of the top-level certificate authorities themselves, we will have to rely on very strong, well-known certificates that we have acquired by very secure or perhaps very tangible means. Web browsers, like Netscape Navigator and Microsoft Internet Explorer, come with CA certificates for several popular certificate authorities. Netscape Navigator and MSIE are, for example, shipped with a CA certificate for Verisign (*http://www.verisign.com*), so that you can safely verify any certificates signed by Verisign, wherever you encounter them. So, if all is working, we've reduced the problem to just that of your getting your copy of the web browser software securely the first time. As far as maintenance goes, browsers like Netscape Navigator let you download new CA certificates dynamically, using secure transports.

Site certificates

Certificates are presented to your web browser for verification when you encounter signed objects (signed JAR files). They are also issued by web servers when you make a secure connection using the HTTPS (HTTP Secure Socket Layer) protocol. Browsers like HotJava, Netscape, and Internet Explorer may save these certificates encountered from third-party locations, so that you can assign privileges or attributes to those identities and so that they can be recognized again. We'll call these certificates *site certificates*—though they may belong to any third party, like a person or an organization. For example, you might declare that objects signed by a certain site are allowed to write local files. The browser then saves that site's certificate, marking it with the privileges (writing local files) that it should grant.

User (signer) certificates

Finally, you, the user, can have your own identity and your own certificates to validate your identity. Browsers like Netscape Navigator store *user certificates* that can be used to identify you to third parties. A user certificate is associated with a private key—the private key that goes with the public key in the certificate. When you use a private key to sign an object, the corresponding certificate is shipped as part of the signature. Remember, the recipient needs the public key in your certificate to validate your signature. The certificate says on whose authority the recipient should trust that public key.

So, where do you get private keys, public keys, and certificates validating your public keys? Well, as for the keys, you generate those yourself. No other party should ever have access to your private key, much less generate it for you. After you generate a public and private key pair, you send your public key to the certificate authority to request that they certify you. The CA can make you jump through whatever hoops are necessary; when they are satisfied that you are who you say you are, they grant you a certificate.

In Netscape Navigator, this entire process can be accomplished by the user, within the browser, using the KEYGEN extension to HTML. You can then use Netscape tools to sign JAR files, send secure email, etc. HotJava is not quite as slick. The SDK supplies a utility called `keytool` for managing keys and certificates. Another utility, `jarsigner`, is used for signing JAR files. We'll discuss these utilities in detail in the next section.

Signed JAR Files: The keytool and jarsigner Utilities

`keytool` is a utility for managing a database of identities. With it, you can generate or import key pairs and certificates. You can then use these keys and certificates to sign JAR files.

For a variety of reasons, including antiquated cryptography export control laws in the U.S. and patents on various cryptographic algorithms, Sun was forced to separate the security API itself from the packages that actually implement encryption algorithms.* The packages that implement cryptography are called "provider" packages; Sun's security provider package comes with the SDK by default. Other packages can be installed to provide additional or alternate implementations of the cryptographic algorithms. By default, `keytool` uses the implementations found in Sun's provider package, though it can use other packages if any are available.

The user interface to `keytool` is awkward. It's a good bet that someone will implement a key management utility with a more friendly graphical interface; maybe it will be built into a future version of HotJava. Therefore, we won't spend a great deal of time discussing the details of `keytool`; it's more important to understand the concepts.

What about Netscape and Internet Explorer?

Before the debut of the Java Plug-in, Netscape and Microsoft both invented their own code-signing schemes. As a result, signed applets in the SDK 1.1 world were a disaster—there were three different ways to sign and deploy code, one each for Netscape Navigator, Sun's HotJava, and Microsoft's Internet Explorer. Unless you knew in advance that you had only one kind of browser worry about, you were pretty much out of luck.

The Plug-in levels the field for signed applets, because the packaging and deployment strategy is the same for Navigator and Internet Explorer.

The TestWrite example

Before we dive into the muck, let's take a look at an example, just to prove that you can actually sign objects with the current releases of the SDK and the Java Plug-in. In the process of discussing the example, we'll point out some things that are lacking.

Use your browser to navigate to *http://www.oreilly.com/catalog/learnjava/TestWrite/Unsigned.html.* You'll see the applet shown in Figure 20-3. When you push the button, this applet attempts to write a harmless file on the local host. Give it a try. The applet should fail with a security exception and display a message.

At this point, load a web page that displays the same applet: *http://www.oreilly.com/catalog/learnjava/TestWrite/Signed.html.* The only difference is that I've wrapped the

---

* See the JCE (Java Cryptography Extension), which is available to U.S. and Canadian citizens from *http://java.sun.com/products/jce.*

Figure 20-3. An unsigned applet violating security policy

applet in a JAR file that I have signed, with a key and certificate that I generated using `keytool`. When it loads the applet's JAR file, the Java Plug-in also retrieves the signature. However, nothing has changed for the applet just yet. When you click the button, you still get a security exception when the applet tries to write a file.

But now that an identity is associated with the applet, we can do more. You can download my certificate from *http://www.oreilly.com/catalog/learnjava/TestWrite/ Jonathan.cer*. Enabling the signed applet to write a file takes two steps. First, you'll have to import this certificate file into a *keystore*, which is simply a collection of keys and certificates. The second step is to create a *policy file* that tells the Java Plug-in that this applet is allowed to write a file.

To import the certificate file, use the `keytool` utility that comes with the SDK. For this example, we'll create an entirely new keystore. The following command imports the *Jonathan.cer* certificate file and puts it in a keystore called *client.keystore*. If the keystore file doesn't exist, it will be created.

```
C:\> keytool -import -file Jonathan.cer -alias Jonathan
      -keystore client.keystore -storepass buendia
```

The `-alias` option tells `keytool` what alias to use for the imported certificate. This is just a name you can use to refer to the keys in the certificate. The integrity of the keystore is protected using a password, specified with the `-storepass` option. Whenever you access the keystore, you'll need to supply the same password to verify that the keystore hasn't been tampered with.

After you type this command, `keytool` prints out some information about the certificate you are about to import. Then it asks if this certificate should be trusted. This is an important question, as anyone can generate this kind of self-signed certificate. (I've decided to be my own certificate authority of one, for now.)

```
Owner: CN=Jonathan Knudsen
Issuer: CN=Jonathan Knudsen
Serial number: 3804d2c1
Valid from: Wed Oct 13 14:43:13 EDT 1999 until:
    Tue Jan 11 13:43:13 EST 2000
```

```
Certificate fingerprints:
     MD5:  A6:56:C2:52:2B:20:69:26:67:A2:0B:78:D3:3C:AC:45
     SHA1: A3:AF:41:93:73:1F:48:EE:6E:F5:8B:93:66:3E:73:F5:99:5D:54:AF
Trust this certificate? [no]:  yes
Certificate was added to keystore
```

```
C:\>
```

What can we do? We might simply get a certificate signed by a more popular authority than myself. But you would still have to register the CA's certificate somehow, following this same process.

For now, you can verify this certificate by hand. We'll do this not only to get through this example, but because it presents a useful analogy to the process of certification. The SHA1 "thumbprint" that `keytool` displays should match this:

```
A3:AF:41:93:73:1F:48:EE:6E:F5:8B:93:66:3E:73:F5:99:5D:54:AF
```

If everything looks good, you can type "yes" to accept this certificate. By doing so, you are saying that you accept my identity, and believe that I have in fact signed certificates that match this thumbprint. You have effectively chained your trust to this printed page rather than an online certificate authority. You can be reasonably sure that no one has gone to the effort of issuing counterfeit O'Reilly books.

You are now ready to assign greater privileges to this applet. For example, you can allow it to write files. To grant privileges in this way, you need to create a security policy. Use the SDK's `policytool` utility (which we introduced in Chapter 3). Start the utility from a command line:

```
C:\> policytool
```

The `policytool` interface isn't pretty, but it gets the job done. When you first run `policytool`, you may get a message that it can't find the default policy file. Just click **OK**. (If you don't get this message, choose **New** from the **File** menu to start with a clean slate.)

Our eventual goal is to tell the Plug-in that any applet we have signed is allowed to write a file on your computer. The policy file needs to reference the certificate in the keystore we just created. The first thing we need to do, therefore, is tell `policytool` where to find the keystore. Select the **Change KeyStore** option from the **Edit** method. Type the URL of the keystore file you just created. (On a Windows system, it looks something like this: *file:/c:/SignTest/client.keystore.*) You can leave the keystore type blank. Then click **OK**.

Now that we're pointed at the right keystore, we need to add a permission for file writing. Click on the **Add Policy Entry** button. In the window that comes up, leave the CodeBase field blank. Fill in the SignedBy field with `Jonathan`. This means that we're setting a policy for all code signed by Jonathan. (Remember, Jonathan is the alias we used for the certificate when it was imported to the keystore.)

To give code signed by Jonathan permission to write files, click on the **Add Permission** button. In the next dialog, choose **FilePermission** from the top combo box. In the second combo box, choose **<<ALL FILES>>**. In the third combo box, choose **write**. Finally, click on **OK** to finish creating the permission. Then click on **Done** to finish creating the policy.

Having set this up, you now need to save the policy file. Choose **Save** from the **File** menu; save this policy file as *client.policy*. You can exit the `policytool` utility now.

The last thing you need to do is tell the Java Plug-in to use the policy file we've just so laboriously created. To do this, use a text editor to edit the *java.security* file. This file is found underneath the installation directory for the JRE, in the *lib/security* subdirectory. (If you have both the SDK and the JRE installed, you will actually have two copies of this file in different locations. For example, you might have one JRE installed in *C:\sdk1.3\jre* and another in *C:\Program Files\JavaSoft\JRE*. Make sure you edit the `java.security` file that is used by the Plug-in, which is probably the one that's not in the SDK installation directory.)

Once you've found the right *java.security* file, you need to find the section that contains entries for `policy.url`. Add a line to reference the policy file we just created, like this:

```
policy.url.3=file:/c:/SignTest/client.policy
```

Finally, you're ready to test the signed applet. (You may need to restart your browser.) Navigate to the signed applet page. When you press the button, the file is written successfully.

So, how did we create this certificate and sign the JAR file? Let's move on.

Keystores, Keys, and Certificates

The SDK supports *keystores* that hold identities along with their public keys, private keys, and certificates. It includes a utility called `keytool` that manages keystores. You just saw how Jonathan's certificate could be contained in a keystore. The identities in keystores are visible to Java. We'll discuss what that means in a bit, but for the most part, we'll only use this database as a repository while we create and work with our identity locally.

An identity can be a person, an organization, or perhaps a logical part of an organization. Before it can be used, an identity must have a public key and at least one certificate validating its public key. `keytool` refers to entities in the local database by IDs or aliases. These names are arbitrary and are not used outside of the keystore and any policy files that reference it. Identities that have a private key stored locally in the keystore, along with their public key, can be used to sign JAR files. These identities are also called *signers*.

The default location for a keystore is the file *.keystore* in the user's home directory. On a single user system, the Java installation directory is used instead of the user's home directory.* The default keystore location is used by keytool unless you specify another keystore with the –keystore option.

If you are going to maintain any private keys in a keystore (if you will have any signers), you must take special care to keep the keystore file safe (and not publicly readable). Private keys must be kept private.

Public and private keys

We can create a new entry in the default keystore, complete with a key pair, with the following keytool command:

```
C:\> keytool –genkey –alias Jonathan –keyalg DSA –keysize 1024 –dname "CN=Jonathan
Knudsen, OU=Technical Publications, O=O'Reilly & Associates, C=US" –keypass gianni
–storepass buendia
```

There are a lot of options to explain. The most important one is –genkey, which tells keytool to create a new key pair for this entry. A key pair enables this entry to sign code. The –alias options supplies an alias for this entry, Jonathan. The –keyalg argument, DSA, is the algorithm for which we are going to generate the keys. The current release of Java only supports one: DSA, the Digital Signature Algorithm, which is a U.S. government standard for signing. The –keysize argument is the key length in bits. For most algorithms, larger key sizes provide stronger encryption. DSA supports keys of either 512 or 1024 bits. You should use the latter, unless you have a specific reason to do otherwise.

keytool generates the keys and places them in the default keystore. Private keys are specially protected using the –keypass option. To retrieve Jonathan's private key, you will have to know the correct key password. The integrity of the keystore as a whole is protected by the –storepass option. You need to supply the same keystore password to retrieve data from this keystore later.

Once we've created a keystore entry, we can display it with the command:

```
C:\> keytool -list -alias Jonathan -storepass buendia
```

To see more detail, add the –v option (for "verbose"):

```
C:\> keytool -list -alias Jonathan -v -storepass buendia
```

---

* Beware if you have both the SDK and HotJava installed in separate locations on a single user system, such as a PC running Windows. You will have to inform HotJava where to find the SDK package using the JDK_HOME environment variable.

Or we can list the entire contents of the database:

```
C:\> keytool -list -storepass buendia
```

Certificates

Now that we have keys, we want a certificate in which to wrap our public key for distribution. Ideally, at this point, we'd send a public key to a trusted certificate authority and receive a certificate in return. keytool can generate such a request, called a Certificate Signing Request (CSR). To generate a signing request for the entry we just created, you would do this:

```
C:\> keytool -csr -alias Jonathan -file Jonathan.csr -keypass firenze -storepass
buendia
```

You need to specify the alias for the entry you want, a filename where the CSR will be written, and the password for the private key. Once you've generated the CSR file, you can send it off to your favorite Certificate Authority. Once they've performed some identity checks on you, and once you pay them, they will send a certificate back to you. Suppose they send it back in a file called *Jonathan.x509*. You can use keytool to import this certificate as follows:

```
C:\> keytool -import -alias Jonathan -file Jonathan.x509 -keypass firenze
-storepass buendia
```

To demonstrate the features of keytool, we will serve as our own authority (as we did in the example) and use our own self-signed certificate. It turns out that keytool already did this for us when we created keys! A self-signed certificate already exists in the keystore; all we have to do is export it as follows:

```
C:\> keytool -export -alias Jonathan -file Jonathan.cer -storepass buendia
```

Signing JARs

If we have a signer keystore entry, initialized with its private and public keys, we are ready to sign JAR files. This is accomplished using another command-line utility, jarsigner. All we need to do is specify which keystore entry should do the signing, which JAR needs to be signed, and the keystore password.

```
C:\> jarsigner -storepass buendia testwrite.jar Jonathan
```

If we now list the archive, we will see that jarsigner has added two files to the *META-INF* directory: *JONATHAN.SF* and *JONATHAN.DSA*. *JONATHAN.SF* is the signature file—it is like the manifest file for this particular signature. It lists the objects that were signed and the signature algorithms. *JONATHAN.DSA* is the actual binary signature.

Where We've Been

We've covered a lot of territory in the past few pages. Here's a summary of what we can and can't do. We can:

- Use keytool to create a keystore entry, including public and private keys.

- Use keytool to create a self-signed certificate, or import a certificate that has been issued by a certificate authority.

- Use jarsigner to sign a JAR file.

- Tell the Java Plug-in (by hand) what certificates it should trust and what permissions to grant to each identity.

Unfortunately, we can't do any of this automatically. We can't just tell the Plug-in, "I trust John Doe" and have it try to look up a verifiable certificate for John Doe. Furthermore, we are personally responsible for the security of our keystores. It's important that private keys remain private; but anyone who walks up to my computer can use keytool to retrieve information about any identity that I have issued. The keystore password provides some protection, but it won't foil a determined attacker. The fundamental problem, keeping secrets secret, will always be difficult.

A

Content and Protocol Handlers

Content and protocol handlers represent one of the most interesting ideas from the original Java vision. Unfortunately, as far as we can tell, no one has taken up the challenge of using this intriguing facility. We considered dropping them from the book entirely, but that decision just felt bad. Instead, we banished the discussion of how to write content and protocol handlers to an appendix. If you let us know that this material is important to you, we'll keep it in the next edition. If you feel "yes, this is interesting, but why do I care?" we'll drop them from the book. (You can send us comments through the book's web page at *http://www.oreilly.com/ catalog/learnjava.*)

This appendix picks up where we left our discussion of content and protocol handlers in Chapter 12. We'll show you how to write your own handlers, which can be used in any Java application, including the HotJava web browser. In this section, we'll write a content handler that reads Unix tar files and a protocol handler that implements a pluggable encryption scheme. You should be able to drop both into your class path and start using them in the HotJava web browser right away.

Writing a Content Handler

The URL class's `getContent()` method invokes a content handler whenever it's called to retrieve an object at some URL. The content handler must read the flat stream of data produced by the URL's protocol handler (the data read from the remote source), and construct a well-defined Java object from it. By "flat," we mean that the data stream the content handler receives has no artifacts left over from retrieving the data and processing the protocol. It's the protocol handler's job to fetch and decode the data before passing it along. The protocol handler's output is your data, pure and simple.

The roles of content and protocol handlers do not overlap. The content handler doesn't care how the data arrives, or what form it takes. It's concerned only with what kind of object it's supposed to create. For example, if a particular protocol involves sending an object over the network in a compressed format, the protocol handler should do whatever is necessary to unpack it before passing the data on to the content handler. The same content handler can then be used again with a completely different protocol handler to construct the *same* type of object received via a *different* transport mechanism.

Let's look at an example. The following lines construct a URL that points to a GIF file on an FTP archive and attempt to retrieve its contents:

```
try {
  URL url =
      new URL ("ftp://ftp.wustl.edu/graphics/gif/a/apple.gif");
  ImageProducer imgsrc = (ImageProducer)url.getContent();
  ...
```

When we construct the URL object, Java looks at the first part of the URL string (everything prior to the colon) to determine the protocol and locate a protocol handler. In this case, it locates the FTP protocol handler, which is used to open a connection to the host and transfer data for the specified file.

After making the connection, the URL object asks the protocol handler to identify the resource's MIME type. The handler can try to resolve the MIME type through a variety of means, but in this case, it might just look at the filename extension (*.gif*) and determine that the MIME type of the data is `image/gif`. Here, `image/gif` is a string that denotes that the content falls into the category of images and is, more specifically, a GIF image. The protocol handler then looks for the content handler responsible for the `image/gif` type and uses it to construct the right kind of object from the data. The content handler returns an `ImageProducer` object, which `getContent()` returns to us as an `Object`. As we've seen before, we cast this `Object` back to its real type so we can work with it.

In an upcoming section, we'll build a simple content handler. To keep things as simple as possible, our example will produce text as output; the URL's `get-Content()` method will return this as a `String` object.

Locating Content Handlers

When Java searches for a class, it translates package names into filesystem path-names. (The classes may also be in a JAR file in the class path, but we'll refer to them as files and directories anyway.) This applies to locating content-handler classes as well as other kinds of classes. For example, a class in a package named `foo.bar.handlers` would live in a directory with *foo/bar/handlers/* as part of its pathname. To allow Java to find handler classes for arbitrary new MIME types, content handlers are organized into packages corresponding to the basic MIME type categories. The handler classes themselves are then named after the specific MIME type. This allows Java to map MIME types directly to class names. The only remaining piece of information Java needs is a list of packages in which the handlers might reside. To supply this information, use the system properties `java.content.handler.pkgs` and `java.protocol.handler.pkgs`. In these properties, you can use a vertical bar (|) to separate different packages in a list.

We'll put our content handlers in the `learningjava.contenthandlers` package. According to the scheme for naming content handlers, a handler for the `image/gif` MIME type is called `gif` and placed in a package that is called `learningjava.contenthandlers.image`. The fully qualified name of the class would then be `learningjava.contenthandlers.image.gif`, and it would be located in the file *learningjava/contenthandlers/image/gif.class*, somewhere in the local class path, or, perhaps someday, on a server. Likewise, a content handler for the `video/mpeg` MIME type would be called `mpeg`, and an *mpeg.class* file would be located in a *learningjava/contenthandlers/video/* directory somewhere in the class path.

Many MIME type names include a dash (-), which is illegal in a class name. You should convert dashes and other illegal characters into underscores (_) when building Java class and package names. Also note that there are no capital letters in the class names. This violates the coding convention used in most Java source files, in which class names start with capital letters. However, capitalization is not significant in MIME type names, so it is simpler to name the handler classes accordingly.

The application/x-tar Handler

In this section, we'll build a simple content handler that reads and interprets tar (tape archive) files. tar is an archival format widely used in the Unix-world to hold collections of files, along with their basic type and attribute information.[*] A *tar* file is similar to a *JAR* file, except that it's not compressed. Files in the archive are stored sequentially, in flat text or binary with no special encoding. In practice, tar files are usually compressed for storage using an application like Unix *compress* or GNU *gzip* and then named with a filename extension like *.tar.gz* or *.tgz*.

Most web browsers, upon retrieving a tar file, prompt the user with a File Save dialog. The assumption is that if you are retrieving an archive, you probably want to save it for later unpacking and use. We would like to implement a *tar* content

---

[*] There are several slightly different versions of the tar format. This content handler understands the most widely used variant.

handler that allows an application to read the contents of the archive and give us a
listing of the files that it contains. In itself, this would not be the most useful thing
in the world, because we would be left with the dilemma of how to get at the
archive's contents. However, a more complete implementation of our content
handler, used in conjunction with an application like a web browser, could generate HTML output or pop up a dialog that lets us select and save individual files
within the archive.

Some code that fetches a tar file and lists its contents might look like this:

```
try {
    URL listing =
        new URL("http://somewhere.an.edu/lynx/lynx2html.tar");
    String s = (String)listing.getContents();
    System.out.println( s );
    ...
```

Our handler will produce a listing similar to the Unix *tar* application's output:

```
Tape Archive Listing:

0       Tue Sep 28 18:12:47 CDT 1993 lynx2html/
14773 Tue Sep 28 18:01:55 CDT 1993 lynx2html/lynx2html.c
470     Tue Sep 28 18:13:24 CDT 1993 lynx2html/Makefile
172     Thu Apr 01 15:05:43 CST 1993 lynx2html/lynxgate
3656   Wed Mar 03 15:40:20 CST 1993 lynx2html/install.csh
490     Thu Apr 01 14:55:04 CST 1993 lynx2html/new_globals.c
    ...
```

Our handler will dissect the file to read the contents and generate the listing. The
URL's getContent() method will return that information to an application as a
String object.

First we must decide what to call our content handler and where to put it. The
MIME-type hierarchy classifies the tar format as an *application type extension*. Its
proper MIME type is then application/x-tar. Therefore, our handler belongs in
the learningjava.contenthandlers.application package and goes into the
class file *learningjava/contenthandlers/application/x_tar.class*. Note that the name of
our class is x_tar, rather than x-tar; you'll remember the dash is illegal in a class
name so, by convention, we convert it to an underscore.

Here's the code for the content handler; compile it and put it in *learningjava/con-
tenthandlers/application/*, somewhere in your class path:

```
//file: x_tar.java
package learningjava.contenthandlers.application;

import java.net.*;
import java.io.*;
```

```
import java.util.Date;

public class x_tar extends ContentHandler {
  static int
    RECORDLEN = 512,
    NAMEOFF = 0, NAMELEN = 100,
    SIZEOFF = 124, SIZELEN = 12,
    MTIMEOFF = 136, MTIMELEN = 12;

  public Object getContent(URLConnection uc) throws IOException {
    InputStream is = uc.getInputStream();
    StringBuffer output =
        new StringBuffer( "Tape Archive Listing:\n\n" );
    byte [] header = new byte[RECORDLEN];
    int count = 0;

    while ( (is.read(header) == RECORDLEN)
            && (header[NAMEOFF] != 0) ) {
      String name =
          new String(header, NAMEOFF, NAMELEN, "8859_1"). trim();
      String s =
          new String(header, SIZEOFF, SIZELEN, "8859_1").trim();
      int size = Integer.parseInt(s, 8);
      s = new String(header, MTIMEOFF, MTIMELEN, "8859_1").trim();
      long l = Integer.parseInt(s, 8);
      Date mtime = new Date( l*1000 );

      output.append( size + " " + mtime + " " + name + "\n" );

      count += is.skip( size ) + RECORDLEN;
      if ( count % RECORDLEN != 0 )
        count += is.skip ( RECORDLEN - count % RECORDLEN);
    }

    if ( count == 0 )
      output.append("Not a valid TAR file\n");

    return( output.toString() );
  }
}
```

The ContentHandler class

Our x_tar handler is a subclass of the abstract class java.net.ContentHandler. Its job is to implement one method: getContent(), which takes as an argument a special "protocol connection" object and returns a constructed Java Object. The getContent() method of the URL class ultimately uses this getContent() method when we ask for the contents of the URL.

The code looks formidable, but most of it's involved with processing the details of the tar format. If we remove these details, there isn't much left:

```
public class x_tar extends ContentHandler {

    public Object getContent( URLConnection uc ) throws IOException {
        // get input stream
        InputStream is = uc.getInputStream();

        // read stream and construct object
        // ...

        // return the constructed object
        return( output.toString() );
    }
}
```

That's really all there is to a content handler; it's relatively simple.

The URLConnection

The java.net.URLConnection object that getContent() receives represents the protocol handler's connection to the remote resource. It provides a number of methods for examining information about the URL resource, such as header and type fields, and for determining the kinds of operations the protocol supports. However, its most important method is getInputStream(), which returns an InputStream from the protocol handler. Reading this InputStream gives you the raw data for the object the URL addresses. In our case, reading the InputStream feeds x_tar the bytes of the tar file it's to process.

Constructing the object

The majority of our getContent() method is devoted to interpreting the stream of bytes of the tar file and building our output object: the String that lists the contents of the tar file. Again, this means that this example involves the particulars of reading tar files, so you shouldn't fret too much about the details.

After requesting an InputStream from the URLConnection, x_tar loops, gathering information about each file. Each archived item is preceded by a header that contains attribute and length fields. x_tar interprets each header and then skips over the remaining portion of the item. To parse the header, we use the String constructor to read a fixed number of characters from the byte array header[]. To convert these bytes into a Java String properly, we specify the character encoding used by web servers: 8859_1, which (for the most part) is equivalent to ASCII. Once we have a file's name, size, and time stamp, we accumulate the results (the file listings) in a StringBuffer—one line per file. When the listing is complete, getContent() returns the StringBuffer as a String object.

The main while loop continues as long as it's able to read another header record, and as long as the record's "name" field isn't full of ASCII null values. (The tar file format calls for the end of the archive to be padded with an empty header record, although most tar implementations don't seem to do this.) The while loop retrieves the name, size, and modification times as character strings from fields in the header. The most common tar format stores its numeric values in octal, as fixed-length ASCII strings. We extract the strings and use Integer.parseInt() to parse them.

After reading and parsing the header, x_tar skips over the data portion of the file and updates the variable count, which keeps track of the offset into the archive. The two lines following the initial skip account for tar's "blocking" of the data records. In other words, if the data portion of a file doesn't fit precisely into an integral number of blocks of RECORDLEN bytes, tar adds padding to make it fit.

As we said, the details of parsing tar files are not really our main concern here. But x_tar does illustrate a few tricks of data manipulation in Java.

It may surprise you that we didn't have to provide a constructor; our content handler relies on its default constructor. We don't need to provide a constructor because there isn't anything for it to do. Java doesn't pass the class any argument information when it creates an instance of it. You might suspect that the URLConnection object would be a natural thing to provide at that point. However, when you are calling the constructor of a class that is loaded at runtime, you can't easily pass it any arguments.

Using our new handler

When we began this discussion of content handlers, we showed a brief example of how our x_tar content handler would work for us. You can try that code snippet now with your favorite tar file by setting the java.content.handler.pkgs system property to learningjava.contenthandlers and making sure that package is in your class path.

To make things more exciting, try setting the property in your HotJava properties file. (The HotJava properties file usually resides in a *.hotjava* directory in your home directory or in the HotJava installation directory on a Windows machine.) Make sure that the class path is set before you start HotJava. Once HotJava is running, go to the **Preferences** menu, and select **Viewer Applications**. Find the type **TAR archive**, and set its **Action** to **View in HotJava**. This tells HotJava to try to use a content handler to display the data in the browser. Now, drive HotJava to a URL that contains a tar file. The result should look something like that shown in Figure A-1.

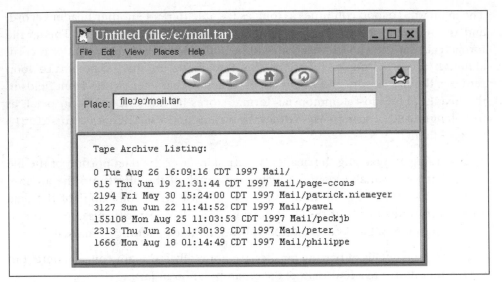

Figure A-1. Using a content handler to display data in a browser

We've just extended our copy of HotJava to understand tar files! In the next section, we'll turn the tables and look at protocol handlers. There we'll be building URLConnection objects; someone else will have the pleasure of reconstituting the data.

Writing a Protocol Handler

A URL object uses a protocol handler to establish a connection with a server and perform whatever protocol is necessary to retrieve data. For example, an HTTP protocol handler knows how to talk to an HTTP server and retrieve a document; an FTP protocol handler knows how to talk to an FTP server and retrieve a file. All types of URLs use protocol handlers to access their objects. Even the lowly "file" type URLs use a special "file" protocol handler that retrieves files from the local filesystem. The data a protocol handler retrieves is then fed to an appropriate content handler for interpretation.

While we refer to a protocol handler as a single entity, it really has two parts: a java.net.URLStreamHandler and a java.net.URLConnection. These are both abstract classes that we will subclass to create our protocol handler. (Note that these are abstract classes, not interfaces. Although they contain abstract methods we are required to implement, they also contain many utility methods we can use or override.) The URL looks up an appropriate URLStreamHandler, based on the protocol component of the URL. The URLStreamHandler then finishes parsing the URL and creates a URLConnection when it's time to communicate with the server. The URLConnection represents a single connection with a server, and implements the communication protocol itself.

Locating Protocol Handlers

Protocol handlers are organized in a package hierarchy similar to content handlers. But unlike content handlers, which are grouped into packages by the MIME types of the objects that they handle, protocol handlers are given individual packages. Both parts of the protocol handler (the URLStreamHandler class and the URLConnection class) are located in a package named for the protocol they support.

For example, if we wrote an FTP protocol handler, we might put it in an learningjava.protocolhandlers.ftp package. The URLStreamHandler is placed in this package and given the name Handler; all URLStreamHandlers are named Handler and distinguished by the package in which they reside. The URLConnection portion of the protocol handler is placed in the same package and can be given any name. There is no need for a naming convention because the corresponding URLStreamHandler is responsible for creating the URLConnection objects it uses.

As with content handlers, Java locates packages containing protocol handlers using the java.protocol.handler.pkgs system property. The value of this property is a list of package names; if more than one package is in the list, use a vertical bar (|) to separate them. For our example, we will set this property to include learningjava.protocolhandlers.

URLs, Stream Handlers, and Connections

The URL, URLStreamHandler, URLConnection, and ContentHandler classes work together closely. Before diving into an example, let's take a step back, look at the parts a little more, and see how these things communicate. Figure A-2 shows how these components relate to each other.

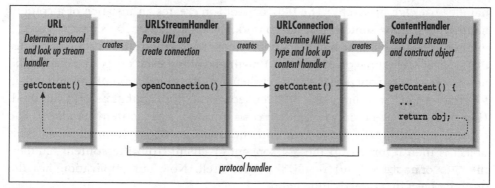

Figure A-2. The protocol handler machinery

We begin with the URL object, which points to the resource we'd like to retrieve. The URLStreamHandler helps the URL class parse the URL specification string for its particular protocol. For example, consider the following call to the URL constructor:

```
URL url = new URL("protocol://foo.bar.com/file.ext");
```

The URL class parses only the protocol component; later, a call to the URL class's getContent() or openStream() method starts the machinery in motion. The URL class locates the appropriate protocol handler by looking in the protocol-package hierarchy. It then creates an instance of the appropriate URLStream-Handler class.

The URLStreamHandler is responsible for parsing the rest of the URL string, including hostname and filename, and possibly an alternative port designation. This allows different protocols to have their own variations on the format of the URL specification string. Note that this step is skipped when a URL is constructed with the "protocol," "host," and "file" components specified explicitly. If the protocol is straightforward, its URLStreamHandler class can let Java do the parsing and accept the default behavior. For this illustration, we'll assume that the URL string requires no special parsing. (If we use a nonstandard URL with a strange format, we're responsible for parsing it ourselves, as we'll show shortly.)

The URL object next invokes the handler's openConnection() method, prompting the handler to create a new URLConnection to the resource. The URL-Connection performs whatever communications are necessary to talk to the resource and begins to fetch data for the object. At that time, it also determines the MIME type of the incoming object data and prepares an InputStream to hand to the appropriate content handler. This InputStream must send "pure" data with all traces of the protocol removed.

The URLConnection also locates an appropriate content handler in the content-handler package hierarchy. The URLConnection creates an instance of a content handler; to put the content handler to work, the URLConnection's getContent() method calls the content handler's getContent() method. If this sounds confusing, it is: we have three getContent() methods calling each other in a chain. The newly created ContentHandler object then acquires the stream of incoming data for the object by calling the URLConnection's getInputStream() method. (Recall that we acquired an InputStream in our x_tar content handler.) The content handler reads the stream and constructs an object from the data. This object is then returned up the getContent() chain: from the content handler, the URLConnection, and finally the URL itself. Now our application has the desired object in its greedy little hands.

To summarize, we create a protocol handler by implementing a URLStream-Handler class that creates specialized URLConnection objects to handle our protocol. The URLConnection objects implement the getInputStream() method, which provides data to a content handler for construction of an object. The base URLConnection class implements many of the methods we need; therefore, our URLConnection needs to provide only the methods that generate the data stream and return the MIME type of the object data.

If you're not thoroughly confused by all that terminology (or even if you are), let's move on to the example. It should help to pin down what all these classes are doing.

The crypt Handler

In this section, we'll build a *crypt* protocol handler. It parses URLs of the form:

```
crypt:type://hostname[:port]/location/item
```

type is an identifier that specifies what kind of encryption to use. The protocol itself is a simplified version of HTTP; we'll implement the GET command and no more. We added the *type* identifier to the URL to show how to parse a nonstandard URL specification. Once the handler has figured out the encryption type, it dynamically loads a class that implements the chosen encryption algorithm and uses it to retrieve the data. Obviously, we don't have room to implement a full-blown public-key encryption algorithm, so we'll use the rot13InputStream class from Chapter 10, *Input/Output Facilities*. It should be apparent how the example can be extended by plugging in a more powerful encryption class.

The Encryption class

First, we'll lay out our plug-in encryption class. We'll define an abstract class called CryptInputStream that provides some essentials for our plug-in encrypted protocol. From the CryptInputStream we'll create a subclass called rot13Crypt-InputStream, that implements our particular kind of encryption:

```java
//file: rot13CryptInputStream.java
package learningjava.protocolhandlers.crypt;
import java.io.*;

abstract class CryptInputStream extends InputStream {
    InputStream in;
    OutputStream out;
    abstract public void set( InputStream in, OutputStream out );
} // end of class CryptInputStream

class rot13CryptInputStream extends CryptInputStream {
```

```
        public void set( InputStream in, OutputStream out ) {
            this.in = new learningjava.io.rot13InputStream( in );
        }
        public int read() throws IOException {
            return in.read();
        }
    }
```

Our `CryptInputStream` class defines a method called `set()` that passes in the `InputStream` it's to translate. Our `URLConnection` calls `set()` after creating an instance of the encryption class. We need a `set()` method because we want to load the encryption class dynamically, and we aren't allowed to pass arguments to the constructor of a class when it's dynamically loaded. (We noticed this same issue in our content handler previously.) In the encryption class, we also provide for the possibility of an `OutputStream`. A more complex kind of encryption might use the `OutputStream` to transfer public-key information. Needless to say, *rot13* doesn't, so we'll ignore the `OutputStream` here.

The implementation of `rot13CryptInputStream` is very simple. `set()` takes the `InputStream` it receives and wraps it with the `rot13InputStream` filter. `read()` reads filtered data from the `InputStream`, throwing an exception if `set()` hasn't been called.

The URLStreamHandler

Next we'll build our `URLStreamHandler` class. The class name is `Handler`; it extends the abstract `URLStreamHandler` class. This is the class the Java URL looks up by converting the protocol name (*crypt*) into a package name. Remember that Java expects this class to be named `Handler`, and to live in a package named for the protocol type.

```
//file: Handler.java
package learningjava.protocolhandlers.crypt;
import java.io.*;
import java.net.*;

public class Handler extends URLStreamHandler {

    protected void parseURL(URL url, String spec,
                            int start, int end) {
        int slash = spec.indexOf('/');
        String crypType = spec.substring(start, slash-1);
        super.parseURL(url, spec, slash, end);
        setURL( url, "crypt:"+crypType, url.getHost(),
            url.getPort(), url.getFile(), url.getRef() );
    }
```

```
        protected URLConnection openConnection(URL url)
          throws IOException {
            String crypType = url.getProtocol().substring(6);
            return new CryptURLConnection( url, crypType );
        }
    }
```

Java creates an instance of our URLStreamHandler when we create a URL specifying the *crypt* protocol. Handler has two jobs: to assist in parsing the URL specification strings and to create CryptURLConnection objects when it's time to open a connection to the host.

Our parseURL() method overrides the parseURL() method in the URLStreamHandler class. It's called whenever the URL constructor sees a URL requesting the *crypt* protocol. For example:

```
    URL url = new URL("crypt:rot13://foo.bar.com/file.txt");
```

parseURL() is passed a reference to the URL object, the URL specification string, and starting and ending indexes that show what portion of the URL string we're expected to parse. The URL class has already identified the simple protocol name; otherwise, it wouldn't have found our protocol handler. Our version of parseURL() retrieves our *type* identifier from the specification and stores it temporarily in the variable crypType. To find the encryption type, we take everything between the starting index we were given and the character preceding the first slash in the URL string (i.e., everything up to the colon in ://). We then defer to the superclass parseURL() method to complete the job of parsing the URL after that point. We call super.parseURL() with the new start index, so that it points to the character just after the type specifier. This tells the superclass parseURL() that we've already parsed everything prior to the first slash, and it's responsible for the rest. Finally we use the utility method setURL() to put together the final URL. Almost everything has already been set correctly for us, but we need to call setURL() to add our special type to the protocol identifier. We'll need this information later when someone wants to open the URL connection.

Before going on, we'll note two other possibilities. If we hadn't hacked the URL string for our own purposes by adding a type specifier, we'd be dealing with a standard URL specification. In this case, we wouldn't need to override parseURL(); the default implementation would have been sufficient. It could have sliced the URL into host, port, and filename components normally. On the other hand, if we had created a completely bizarre URL format, we would need to parse the entire string. There would be no point calling super.parseURL(); instead, we'd have called the URLStreamHandler's protected method setURL() to pass the URL's components back to the URL object.

The other method in our Handler class is openConnection(). After the URL has been completely parsed, the URL object calls openConnection() to set up the data transfer. openConnection() calls the constructor for our URLConnection with appropriate arguments. In this case, our URLConnection object is named CryptURLConnection, and the constructor requires the URL and the encryption type as arguments. parseURL() put the encryption type in the protocol identifier of the URL. We recognize it and pass the information along. openConnection() returns the reference to our URLConnection, which the URL object uses to drive the rest of the process.

The URLConnection

Finally, we reach the real guts of our protocol handler, the URLConnection class. This is the class that opens the socket, talks to the server on the remote host, and implements the protocol itself. This class doesn't have to be public, so you can put it in the same file as the Handler class we just defined. We call our class CryptURLConnection; it extends the abstract URLConnection class. Unlike ContentHandler and StreamURLConnection, whose names are defined by convention, we can call this class anything we want; the only class that needs to know about the URLConnection is the URLStreamHandler, which we wrote ourselves:

```java
//file: CryptURLConnection.java
   import java.io.*;
   import java.net.*;

class CryptURLConnection extends URLConnection {
    static int defaultPort = 80;
    CryptInputStream cis;

    public String getContentType() {
        return guessContentTypeFromName( url.getFile() );
    }

    CryptURLConnection ( URL url, String crypType )
      throws IOException {
        super( url );
        try {
            String classname = "learningjava.protocolhandlers.crypt."
                + crypType + "CryptInputStream";
            cis = (CryptInputStream)
                    Class.forName(classname).newInstance();
        } catch ( Exception e ) {
            throw new IOException("Crypt Class Not Found: "+e);
        }
    }

    public void connect() throws IOException {
        int port = ( url.getPort() == -1 ) ?
```

```
                        defaultPort : url.getPort();
        Socket s = new Socket( url.getHost(), port );

        // Send the filename in plaintext
        OutputStream server = s.getOutputStream();
        new PrintWriter( new OutputStreamWriter( server, "8859_1" ),
                    true).println( "GET " + url.getFile() );

        // Initialize the CryptInputStream
        cis.set( s.getInputStream(), server );
        connected = true;
    }

    public InputStream getInputStream() throws IOException {
        if (!connected)
            connect();
        return ( cis );
    }
}
```

The constructor for our CryptURLConnection class takes as arguments the destination URL and the name of an encryption type. We pass the URL on to the constructor of our superclass, which saves it in a protected url instance variable. We could have saved the URL ourselves, but calling our parent's constructor shields us from possible changes or enhancements to the base class. We use crypType to construct the name of an encryption class, using the convention that the encryption class is in the same package as the protocol handler (i.e., learningjava. protocolhandlers.crypt); its name is the encryption type followed by the suffix CryptInputStream.

Once we have a name, we need to create an instance of the encryption class. To do so, we use the static method Class.forName() to turn the name into a Class object and newInstance() to load and instantiate the class. (This is how Java loads the content and protocol handlers themselves.) newInstance() returns an Object; we need to cast it to something more specific before we can work with it. Therefore, we cast it to our CryptInputStream class, the abstract class that rot13CryptInputStream extends. If we implement any additional encryption types as extensions to CryptInputStream and name them appropriately, they will fit into our protocol handler without modification.

We do the rest of our setup in the connect() method of the URLConnection. There, we make sure we have an encryption class and open a Socket to the appropriate port on the remote host. getPort() returns -1 if the URL doesn't specify a port explicitly; in that case we use the default port for an HTTP connection (port 80). We ask for an OutputStream on the socket, assemble a GET command using the getFile() method to discover the filename specified by the URL, and send our request by writing it into the OutputStream. (For convenience, we wrap the

`OutputStream` with a `PrintWriter` and call `println()` to send the message.) We then initialize the `CryptInputStream` class by calling its `set()` method and passing it an `InputStream` from the `Socket` and the `OutputStream`.

The last thing `connect()` does is set the boolean variable `connected` to `true`. `connected` is a `protected` variable inherited from the `URLConnection` class. We need to track the state of our connection because `connect()` is a `public` method. It's called by the `URLConnection`'s `getInputStream()` method, but it could also be called by other classes. Since we don't want to start a connection if one already exists, we check `connected` first.

In a more sophisticated protocol handler, `connect()` would also be responsible for dealing with any protocol headers that come back from the server. In particular, it would probably stash any important information it can deduce from the headers (e.g., MIME type, content length, time stamp) in instance variables, where it's available to other methods. At a minimum, `connect()` strips the headers from the data so the content handler won't see them. I'm being lazy and assuming that we'll connect to a minimal server, like the modified `TinyHttpd` daemon we discuss below, which doesn't bother with any headers.

The bulk of the work has been done; a few details remain. The `URLConnection`'s `getContent()` method needs to figure out which content handler to invoke for this `URL`. In order to compute the content handler's name, `getContent()` needs to know the resource's MIME type. To find out, it calls the `URLConnection`'s `getContentType()` method, which returns the MIME type as a `String`. Our protocol handler overrides `getContentType()`, providing our own implementation.

The `URLConnection` class provides a number of tools to help determine the MIME type. It's possible that the MIME type is conveyed explicitly in a protocol header; in this case, a more sophisticated version of `connect()` would have stored the MIME type in a convenient location for us. Some servers don't bother to insert the appropriate headers, though, so you can use the method `guess-ContentTypeFromName()` to examine filename extensions, like *.gif* or *.html*, and map them to MIME types. In the worst case, you can use `guessContent-TypeFromStream()` to intuit the MIME type from the raw data. The Java developers call this method "a disgusting hack" that shouldn't be needed, but that is unfortunately necessary in a world where HTTP servers lie about content types and extensions are often nonstandard. We'll take the easy way out and use the `guessContentTypeFromName()` utility of the `URLConnection` class to determine the MIME type from the filename extension of the URL we are retrieving.

Once the `URLConnection` has found a content handler, it calls the content handler's `getContent()` method. The content handler then needs to get an `InputStream` from which to read the data. To find an `InputStream`, it calls the

URLConnection's getInputStream() method. getInputStream() returns an
InputStream from which its caller can read the data after protocol processing is
finished. It checks whether a connection is already established; if not, it calls
connect() to make the connection. Then it returns a reference to our
CryptInputStream.

A final note on getting the content type: the URLConnection's default
getContentType() calls getHeaderField(), which is presumably supposed to
extract the named field from the protocol headers (it would probably spit back
information connect() had stored away). But the default implementation of
getHeaderField() just returns null; we would have to override it to make it do
anything interesting. Several other connection attributes use this mechanism, so in
a more general implementation, we'd probably override getHeaderField()
rather than getContentType() directly.

Trying it out

Let's try out our new protocol! Compile all of the classes and put them in the
learningjava.protocolhandlers package somewhere in your class path. Now
set the java.protocol.handler.pkgs system property in HotJava to include
learningjava.protocolhandlers. Type a "crypt" style URL for a text document; you should see something like that shown in Figure A-3.

Figure A-3. The crypt protocol handler at work

This example would be more interesting if we had a *rot13* server. Since the *crypt* protocol is nothing more than HTTP with some encryption added, we can make a *rot13* server by modifying one line of the TinyHttpd server we developed earlier, so that it spews its files in *rot13*. Just change the line that reads the data from the file—replace this line:

```
f.read( data );
```

with a line that reads through a rot13InputStream:

```
new learningjava.io.rot13InputStream( f ).read( data );
```

We'll assume you placed the rot13InputStream example in a package called learningjava.io, and that it's somewhere in your class path. Now recompile and run the server. It automatically encodes the files before sending them; our sample application decodes them on the other end.

We hope that this example has given you some food for thought. Content and protocol handlers are among the most exciting ideas in Java. It's unfortunate that we have to wait for future releases of HotJava and Netscape to take full advantage of them. But in the meantime, you can experiment and implement your own applications.

B

BeanShell: Simple Java Scripting

In this book, I (Pat Niemeyer) have tried to avoid talking about specific software products or tools, other than those that are part of the standard JDK. However I'm going to make a small exception here to mention a nifty, free Java tool called *Bean-Shell*. As its name suggests, BeanShell can be used as a Java "shell." It allows you to type standard Java syntax—statements and expressions—on the command line and see the results immediately. With BeanShell, you can try out bits of code as you work through the book. You can access all Java APIs and even create graphical user interface components and manipulate them "live". BeanShell uses only reflection, so there is no need to compile class files.

I wrote BeanShell while developing the examples for this book, and I think it makes a good companion to have along on your journey through Java. BeanShell is a free software project, so the source code is included on the CD-ROM that accompanies this book. And you can always find the latest updates and more information at its official home: *http://www.beanshell.org*. BeanShell is also distributed with Emacs as part of Paul Kinnucan's Java Development Environment (the JDE). I hope you find it both useful and fun!

Running BeanShell

All you need to run BeanShell is the Java runtime system. Under Windows, with SDK 1.2 or greater, you may simply double-click the JAR file icon to start the Bean-Shell desktop. More generally, you can simply add the JAR to your class path:

```
Unix:      export CLASSPATH=$CLASSPATH:bsh.jar
Windows:   set classpath %classpath%;bsh.jar
```

and run BeanShell in one of its two basic modes: GUI or on the command line.

```
java bsh.Console       // run the graphical desktop
java bsh.Interpreter   // run as text-only on the command line
```

Running BeanShell with the GUI Console brings up a simple desktop that allows you to open multiple shell windows with basic command history, line editing, and cut-and-paste capability. There are some other GUI tools available, as well, including a simple text editor and class browser. Alternately, you can run BeanShell on the command line, in text-only mode.

Java Statements and Expressions

At the prompt, you can type standard Java statements and expressions. Statements and expressions are all of the normal things that you'd say inside a Java method: e.g., variable declarations and assignments, method calls, loops, and conditionals.

You can type these exactly as they would appear in Java. You also have the option of working with "loosely typed" variables and arguments. That is, you can simply be lazy and not declare the types of variables that you use (both primitives and objects). BeanShell will still give you an error if you attempt to misuse the actual contents of the variable. If you do declare types of variables or primitives, Bean-Shell will enforce them.

Here are some examples:

```
foo = "Foo";
four = (2 + 2)*2/2;
print( foo + " = " + four );    // print() is a bsh command

// do a loop
for (i=0; i<5; i++)
    print(i);

// pop up an AWT frame with a button in it
b = new JButton("My Button");
f = new JFrame("My Frame");
f.getContentPane().add(b, "Center");
f.pack();
f.setVisible(true);
```

BeanShell Commands

BeanShell comes with a number of useful built-in commands (methods). These commands are implemented as BeanShell scripts, and are supplied in the *bsh* JAR file. You can make your own commands by defining new methods or adding scripts to your class path. See the BeanShell user's manual for more information.

One important BeanShell command is print(), which displays values. print() does pretty much the same thing as System.out.println() except that it insures that the ouput always goes to the command line (if you have multiple windows open). print() also displays some types of objects (such as arrays) more verbosely than Java would. Another very useful command is show(), which toggles on and off automatic print()ing of the result of every line you type. (Turn this on if you want to see every result.)

Here are a few other examples of BeanShell commands:

source(), run()
    Read a *bsh* script into this interpreter, or run it in a new interpreter

frame()
    Display an AWT or Swing component in a frame

load(), save()
    Load or save serializable objects (such as Java Beans)

cd(), cat(), dir(), pwd(), etc.
    Unix-like shell commands

exec()
    Run a native application

See the BeanShell user's manual for a full list of commands.

Scripted Methods and Objects

You can declare and use methods in BeanShell, just as you would inside a Java class:

```
int addTwoNumbers( int a, int b ) {
    return a + b;
}

sum = addTwoNumbers( 5, 7 );   // 12

BeanShell methods may also have dynamic (loose) argument and return types.
add( a, b ) {
    return a + b;
}

foo = add(1, 2);               // 3
foo = add("Hello ", "Kitty");  // "Hello Kitty"
```

In BeanShell, as in JavaScript and Perl, method closures take the place of scripted objects. You can turn the results of a method call into an object reference by having the method return the special value this. You can then use the this reference to refer to any variables which were set during the method call. An object is useful only if it has methods; so in BeanShell, methods may also contain methods at any level. Here is a simple example:

```
foo() {
    print("foo");
    x=5;

    bar() {
        print("bar");
    }

    return this;
}

myfoo = foo();      // "foo"
print( myfoo.x );  // "5"
myfoo.bar();       // "bar"
```

Learning More . . .

BeanShell has many more features than I've described here. With BeanShell, you can script event handling and threads. You can embed BeanShell into your applications as a lightweight scripting engine; passing live Java objects into and out of scripts. You can even run BeanShell in a remote server mode, which lets you work in a shell inside of your running application, for debugging and experimentation.

BeanShell is small (only about 175KB) and it's free, under the GNU Library Public License. You can learn more by checking out the full user's manual and FAQ on the web site. If you have ideas, bug fixes, or improvements, please consider joining the developer's mailing list.

As a final caveat, I should say that you do get what you pay for and BeanShell is still somewhat experimental. So you will certainly find bugs. Please feel free to send feedback, using the book's web page, *http://www.oreilly.com/catalog/learnjava*. Enjoy!

Glossary

abstract

The abstract keyword is used to declare abstract methods and classes. An abstract method has no implementation defined; it is declared with arguments and a return type as usual, but the body enclosed in curly braces is replaced with a semicolon. The implementation of an abstract method is provided by a subclass of the class in which it is defined. If an abstract method appears in a class, the class is also abstract.

API (Application Programming Interface)

An API consists of the functions and variables programmers use in their applications. The Java API consists of all `public` and `protected` methods of all `public` classes in the `java.applet`, `java.awt`, `java.awt.image`, `java.awt.peer`, `java.io`, `java.lang`, `java.net`, and `java.util` packages.

applet

An embedded Java application that runs in the context of an applet viewer, such as a web browser.

<APPLET> tag

An HTML tag that specifies an applet run within a web document.

appletviewer

Sun's application that implements the additional structure needed to run and display Java applets.

application

A Java program that runs standalone; i.e., it doesn't require an applet viewer.

AWT (Abstract Window Toolkit)

Java's platform-independent windowing, graphics, and user interface toolkit.

boolean

A primitive Java data type that contains a truth value. The two possible values of a boolean variable are `true` and `false`.

byte

A primitive Java data type that's an eight-bit two's-complement signed number (in all implementations).

callback

A behavior that is defined by one object and then later invoked by another object when a particular event occurs.

cast

A technique that explicitly converts one data type to another.

catch

The `catch` statement introduces an exception-handling block of code following a `try` statement. The `catch` keyword is followed by an exception type and argument name in parentheses and a block of code within curly braces.

certificate

An electronic document used to verify the identity of a person, group, or organization. Certificates attest to the identity of a person or group and contain that organization's public key. A certificate is signed by a certificate authority.

certificate authority (CA)

An organization that is entrusted to issue certificates, taking whatever steps are necessary to verify the identity for which it is issuing the certificate.

char

A primitive Java data type; a variable of type `char` holds a single 16-bit Unicode character.

class

a) An encapsulated collection of data and methods to operate on the data. A class may be instantiated to produce an object that's an instance of the class.

b) The `class` keyword is used to declare a class, thereby defining a new object type. Its syntax is similar to the `struct` keyword in C.

class loader

An object in the Java security model that is responsible for loading Java binary classes from the network into the local interpreter. A class loader keeps its classes in a separate namespace, so that loaded classes cannot interact with system classes and breach system security.

class method

A method declared `static`. Methods of this type are not passed implicit `this` references and may refer only to class variables and invoke other class methods of the current class. A class method may be invoked through the class name, rather than through an instance of the class.

class path

The directory path specifying the location of compiled Java class files on the local system.

class variable

A variable declared `static`. Variables of this type are associated with the class, rather than with a particular instance of the class. There is only one copy of a static variable, regardless of the number of instances of the class that are created.

client

The application that initiates a conversation as part of a networked client/server application. See also *server*.

compilation unit

The source code for a Java class. A compilation unit normally contains a single class definition and, in most current development environments, is simply a file with a *.java* extension.

compiler

A program that translates source code into executable code.

component

Any of the GUI primitives implemented in the `java.awt` package as subclasses of `Component`. The classes `Button`, `Choice`, and `TextField` (among many others) are components.

component architecture

A methodology for building parts of an application. It is a way to build reusable objects that can be easily assembled to form applications.

composition

Using objects as part of another, more complex object. When you compose a new object, you create complex behavior by delegating tasks to the internal objects. Composition is different from inheritance, which defines a new object by changing or refining the behavior of an old object. See also *inheritance*.

constructor

A method that is invoked automatically when a new instance of a class is created. Constructors are used to initialize the variables of the newly created object. The constructor method has the same name as the class.

container

One of the `java.awt` classes that "contain" GUI components. Components in a container appear within the boundaries of the container. The classes `Dialog`, `Frame`, `Panel`, and `Window` are containers.

content handler

A class that is called to parse a particular type of data and that converts it to an appropriate object.

datagram

A packet of data sent to a receiving computer without warning, error checking, or other control information.

data hiding

See *encapsulation*.

double

A Java primitive data type; a `double` value is a 64-bit (double-precision) floating-point number.

encapsulation

An object-oriented programming technique that makes an object's data `private` or `protected` (i.e., hidden) and allows programmers to access and manipulate that data only through method calls. Done well, encapsulation reduces bugs and promotes reusability and modularity of classes. This technique is also known as *data hiding*.

event

A user's action, such as a mouse-click or key press.

event model

The overall design of the mechanism for sending and receiving events. The Java event model changed between the 1.0 and 1.1 releases in order to allow more explicit control over how and when events are delivered from sources to listeners.

exception

A signal that some unexpected condition has occurred in the program. In Java, exceptions are objects that are subclasses of `Exception` or `Error` (which themselves are subclasses of `Throwable`). Exceptions in Java are "raised" with the `throw` keyword and received with the `catch` keyword. See also *catch, throw,* and *throws*.

extends

A keyword used in a `class` declaration to specify the superclass of the class being defined. The class being defined has access to all the `public` and `protected` variables and methods of the superclass (or, if the class being defined is in the same package, it has access to all non-`private` variables and methods). If a class definition omits the `extends` clause, its superclass is taken to be `java.lang.Object`.

final

A keyword modifier that may be applied to classes, methods, and variables. It has a similar, but not identical, meaning in each case. When `final` is applied to a class, it means that the class may never be subclassed. `java.lang.System` is an example of a `final` class. When `final` is applied to a variable, the variable is a constant; i.e., it can't be modified.

finalize

A reserved method name. The `finalize()` method is called when an object is no longer being used (i.e., when there are no further references to it), but before the object's memory is actually reclaimed by the system. A finalizer should perform cleanup tasks and free system resources not handled by Java's garbage-collection system.

finally

A keyword that introduces the `finally` block of a `try/catch/finally` construct. `catch` and `finally` blocks provide exception handling and routine cleanup for code in a `try` block. The `finally` block is optional, and appears after the `try` block, and after zero or more `catch` blocks. The code in a `finally` block is executed once, regardless of how the code in the `try` block executes. In normal execution, control reaches the end of the `try` block and proceeds to the `finally` block, which generally performs any necessary cleanup.

float

A Java primitive data type; a `float` value is a 32-bit (single-precision) floating-point number represented in IEEE 754 format.

garbage collection

The process of reclaiming the memory of objects no longer in use. An object is no longer in use when there are no references to it from other objects in the system and no references in any local variables on the method call stack.

GC

An abbreviation for garbage collection or garbage collector (or occasionally "graphics context").

graphics context

A drawable surface represented by the `java.awt.Graphics` class. A graphics context contains contextual information about the drawing area and provides methods for performing drawing operations in it.

GUI (graphical user interface)

A GUI is a user interface constructed from graphical push buttons, text fields, pull-down menus, dialog boxes, and other standard interface components. In Java, GUIs are implemented with the classes in the `java.awt` package.

hashcode

An arbitrary-looking identifying number used as a kind of signature for an object. A hashcode stores an object in a hashtable. See also *hashtable*.

hashtable

An object that is like a dictionary or an associative array. A hashtable stores and retrieves elements using key values called hashcodes. See also *hashcode*.

hostname

The name given to an individual computer attached to the Internet.

HotJava

A web browser written in Java, capable of downloading and running Java applets.

ImageConsumer

An interface for receiving image data from an image source. Image consumers are usually implemented by the `awt.peer` interface, so they are largely invisible to programmers.

ImageObserver

An interface in the `java.awt.image` package that receives information about the status of an image being constructed by a particular `ImageConsumer`.

ImageProducer

An interface in the `java.awt.image` package that represents an image source (i.e., a source of pixel data).

implements

A keyword used in class declarations to indicate that the class implements the named interface or interfaces. The `implements` clause is optional in class declarations; if it appears, it must follow the `extends` clause (if any). If an `implements` clause appears in the declaration of a non-`abstract` class, every method from each specified interface must be implemented by the class or by one of its superclasses.

import

The `import` statement makes Java classes available to the current class under an abbreviated name. (Java classes are always available by their fully qualified name, assuming the appropriate class file can be found relative to the `CLASSPATH` environment variable and that the class file is readable. `import` doesn't make the class available; it just saves typing and makes your code more legible.) Any number of `import` statements may appear in a Java program. They must appear, however, after the optional `package` statement at the top of the file, and before the first class or interface definition in the file.

inheritance

An important feature of object-oriented programming that involves defining a new object by changing or refining the behavior of an existing object. That is, an object implicitly contains all the non-`private` variables of its superclass and can invoke all the non-`private` methods of its superclass. Java supports single inheritance of classes and multiple inheritance of interfaces.

inner class

A class definition that is nested within another class. An inner class functions within the lexical scope of another class.

instance

An object. When a class is instantiated to produce an object, we say the object is an instance of the class.

instance method

A non-static method of a class. Such a method is passed an implicit this reference to the object that invoked it. See also *class method* and *static.*

instanceof

A Java operator that returns true if the object on its left-hand side is an instance of the class (or implements the interface) specified on its right-hand side. instanceof returns false if the object is not an instance of the specified class or does not implement the specified interface. It also returns false if the specified object is null.

instance variable

A non-static variable of a class. Copies of such variables occur in every instance of the created class. See also *class variable* and *static.*

int

A primitive Java data type that's a 32-bit two's-complement signed number (in all implementations).

interface

A keyword used to declare an interface. More generally, an interface defines a list of methods that enables a class to implement the interface itself.

internationalization

The process of making an application accessible to people who speak a variety of languages. Sometimes abbreviated I18N.

interpreter

The module that decodes and executes Java byte-code.

introspection

The process by which a Java Bean provides additional information about itself, supplementing information learned by reflection.

ISO 8859-1

An eight-bit character encoding standardized by the ISO. This encoding is also known as Latin-1 and contains characters from the Latin alphabet suitable for English and most languages of western Europe.

ISO 10646

A four-byte character encoding that includes all of the world's national standard character encodings. Also known as UCS. The 2-byte Unicode character set maps to the range 0x00000000 to 0x0000FFFF of ISO 10646.

JavaBeans

A component architecture for Java. It is a way to build interoperable Java objects that can be manipulated easily in a visual application builder environment.

Java Beans

Individual Java Beans are Java classes that are built using certain design patterns and naming conventions.

JavaScript

A language developed by Netscape for creating dynamic web pages. From a programmer's point of view, it's unrelated to Java, although some of its capabilities are similar. Internally, there may be a relationship, but even that is unclear.

Java WorkShop

Sun's web browser-based tool written in Java for the development of Java applications.

JDBC

The standard Java API for talking to an SQL (structural query language) database.

JDK (Java Development Kit)

A package of software distributed by Sun Microsystems for Java developers. It includes the Java interpreter, Java classes, and Java development tools: compiler, debugger, disassembler, applet viewer, stub file generator, and documentation generator.

layout manager

An object that controls the arrangement of components within the display area of a container. The `java.awt` package contains a number of layout managers that provide different layout styles.

Latin-1

A nickname for ISO 8859-1.

lightweight component

A Java component that has no native peer in the AWT.

local variable

A variable that is declared inside a single method. A local variable can be seen only by code within that method.

long

A primitive Java data type that's a 64-bit two's-complement signed number (in all implementations).

message digest

A long number computed from a message, used to determine whether the message's contents have been changed in any way. A change to a message's contents will change its message digest. It is almost impossible to create two similar messages with the same digest.

method

The object-oriented programming term for a function or procedure.

method overloading

Providing definitions of more than one method with the same name but with different argument lists or return values. When an overloaded method is called, the compiler determines which one is intended by examining the supplied argument types.

method overriding

Defining a method that exactly matches (i.e., same name, same argument types, and same return type) a method defined in a superclass. When an overridden method is invoked, the interpreter uses "dynamic method lookup" to determine which method definition is applicable to the current object.

Model-View-Controller (MVC) framework

A user-interface design that originated in Smalltalk. In MVC, the data for a display item is called the "model." A "view" displays a particular representation of the model, and a "controller" provides user interaction with both. Java incorporates many MVC concepts.

modifier

A keyword placed before a class, variable, or method that alters the item's accessibility, behavior, or semantics. See also *abstract, final, native, private, protected, public, static,* and *synchronized.*

NaN (not-a-number)

This is a special value of the `double` and `float` data types that represents an undefined result of a mathematical operation, such as zero divided by zero.

native

A modifier that may be applied to method declarations. It indicates that the method is implemented (elsewhere) in C, or in some other platform-dependent fashion. A `native` method declaration should end with a semicolon instead of a brace-enclosed code block. A `native` method cannot be `abstract`, but all other method modifiers may be used with `native` methods.

native method

A method that is implemented in a native language on a host platform, rather than being implemented in Java. Native methods provide access to such resources as the network, the windowing system, and the host filesystem.

new

`new` is a unary operator that creates a new object or array (or raises an `OutOfMemoryException` if there is not enough memory available).

null

> `null` is a special value that indicates a variable doesn't refer to any object. The value `null` may be assigned to any class or interface variable. It cannot be cast to any integral type, and should not be considered equal to zero, as in C.

object

> An instance of a class. A class models a group of things; an object models a particular member of that group.

<OBJECT> tag

> A proposed HTML tag that may replace the widely used but nonstandard `<APPLET>` tag.

package

> The `package` statement specifies which package the code in the file is part of. Java code that is part of a particular package has access to all classes (`public` and non-`public`) in the package, and all non-`private` methods and fields in all those classes. When Java code is part of a named package, the compiled class file must be placed at the appropriate position in the `CLASSPATH` directory hierarchy before it can be accessed by the Java interpreter or other utilities. If the `package` statement is omitted from a file, the code in that file is part of an unnamed default package. This is convenient for small test programs, or during development because it means the code can be interpreted from the current directory.

<PARAM> tag

> An HTML tag used within `<applet>` ... `</applet>` to specify a named parameter and string value to an applet within a web page.

peer

> The actual implementation of a GUI component on a specific platform. Peer components reside within a `Toolkit` object. See also *toolkit*.

primitive type

> One of the Java data types: `boolean`, `char`, `byte`, `short`, `int`, `long`, `float`, `double`. Primitive types are manipulated, assigned, and passed to methods "by value" (i.e., the actual bytes of the data are copied). See also *reference type*.

private

> The `private` keyword is a visibility modifier that can be applied to method and field variables of classes. A `private` field is not visible outside its class definition.

protected

> A keyword that is a visibility modifier; it can be applied to method and field variables of classes. A `protected` field is visible only within its class, within subclasses, or within the package of which its class is a part. Note that subclasses in

different packages can access only `protected` fields within themselves or within other objects that are subclasses; they cannot access protected fields within instances of the superclass.

protocol handler

Software that describes and enables the use of a new protocol. A protocol handler consists of two classes: a `StreamHandler` and a `URLConnection`.

public

A keyword that is a visibility modifier; it can be applied to classes and interfaces and to the method and field variables of classes and interfaces. A `public` class or interface is visible everywhere. A non-`public` class or interface is visible only within its package. A `public` method or variable is visible everywhere its class is visible. When none of the `private`, `protected`, or `public` modifiers are specified, a field is visible only within the package of which its class is a part.

public key cryptography

A cryptographic system that requires two keys, a public key and a private key. The private key can be used to decrypt messages encrypted with the corresponding public key, and vice versa. The public key can be made available to the public without compromising cryptographic security.

reference type

Any object or array. Reference types are manipulated, assigned, and passed to methods "by reference." In other words, the underlying value is not copied; only a reference to it is. See also *primitive type*.

reflection

The ability of a programming language to interact with structures of the language itself. Reflection in Java allows a Java program to examine class files at runtime to find out about their methods and variables, and to invoke methods or modify variables dynamically.

Remote Method Invocation (RMI)

RMI is a native Java distributed object system. With RMI you can pass references to objects on remote hosts and invoke methods in them just as if they were local objects.

root

The base of a hierarchy, such as a root class, whose descendants are subclasses. The `java.lang.Object` class serves as the root of the Java class hierarchy.

SecurityManager

The Java class that defines the methods the system calls to check whether a certain operation is permitted in the current environment.

serialize

To serialize means to put in order or make sequential. A serialized object is an object that has been packaged so that it can be stored or transmitted over the network. Serialized methods are methods that have been synchronized so that only one may be executing at a given time.

server

The application that accepts a request for a conversation as part of a networked client/server application. See also *client*.

shadow

To declare a variable with the same name as a variable defined in a superclass. We say the variable "shadows" the superclass's variable. Use the super keyword to refer to the shadowed variable, or refer to it by casting the object to the type of the superclass.

signature

A combination of a message's message digest, encrypted with the signer's private key, and the signer's certificate, attesting to the signer's identity. Someone receiving a signed message can get the signer's public key from the certificate, decrypt the encrypted message digest, and compare that result with the message digest computed from the signed message. If the two message digests agree, the recipient knows that the message has not been modified and that the signer is who he or she claims to be.

signed class

A Java class (or Java archive) that has a signature attached. The signature allows the recipient to verify the class's origin and that it is unmodified. The recipient can therefore grant the class greater runtime privileges.

short

A primitive Java data type that's a 16-bit two's-complement signed number (in all implementations).

socket

An interface that listens for connections from clients on a data port and connects the client data stream with the receiving application.

static

A keyword that is a modifier applied to method and variable declarations within a class. A static variable is also known as a class variable as opposed to non-static instance variables. While each instance of a class has a full set of its own instance variables, there is only one copy of each static class variable, regardless of the number of instances of the class (perhaps zero) that are created. static variables may be accessed by class name or through an instance. Non-static variables can be accessed only through an instance.

stream

A flow of data, or a channel of communication. All fundamental I/O in Java is based on streams.

String

A class used to represent textual information. The `String` class includes many methods for operating on string objects. Java overloads the + operator for string concatenation.

subclass

A class that extends another. The subclass inherits the `public` and `protected` methods and variables of its superclass. See also *extends*.

super

A keyword that refers to the same value as `this`: the instance of the class for which the current method (these keywords are valid only within non-`static` methods) was invoked. While the type of `this` is the type of the class in which the method appears, the type of `super` is the type of the superclass of the class in which the method appears. `super` is usually used to refer to superclass variables shadowed by variables in the current class. Using `super` in this way is equivalent to casting `this` to the type of the superclass.

superclass

A class extended by some other class. The superclass's `public` and `protected` methods and variables are available to the subclass. See also *extends*.

synchronized

A keyword used in two related ways in Java: as a modifier and as a statement. First, it is a modifier applied to class or instance methods. It indicates that the method modifies the internal state of the class or the internal state of an instance of the class in a way that is not thread-safe. Before running a `synchronized` class method, Java obtains a lock on the class, to ensure that no other threads can modify the class concurrently. Before running a `synchronized` instance method, Java obtains a lock on the instance that invoked the method, ensuring that no other threads can modify the object at the same time.

Java also supports a `synchronized` statement that serves to specify a "critical section" of code. The `synchronized` keyword is followed by an expression in parentheses, and a statement or block of statements. The expression must evaluate to an object or array. Java obtains a lock on the specified object or array before executing the statements.

TCP (Transmission Control Protocol)

A connection-oriented, reliable protocol. One of the protocols on which the Internet is based.

this

Within an instance method or constructor of a class, this refers to "this object"—the instance currently being operated on. It is useful to refer to an instance variable of the class that has been shadowed by a local variable or method argument. It is also useful to pass the current object as an argument to static methods or methods of other classes.

There is one additional use of this: when it appears as the first statement in a constructor method, it refers to one of the other constructors of the class.

thread

A single, independent stream of execution within a program. Since Java is a multithreaded programming language, more than one thread may be running within the Java interpreter at a time. Threads in Java are represented and controlled through the Thread object.

throw

The throw statement signals that an exceptional condition has occurred by throwing a specified exception object. This statement stops program execution and resumes it at the nearest containing catch statement that can handle the specified exception object. Note that the throw keyword must be followed by an exception object, not an exception class.

throws

The throws keyword is used in a method declaration to list the exceptions the method can throw. Any exceptions a method can raise that are not subclasses of Error or RuntimeException must either be caught within the method or declared in the method's throws clause.

toolkit

The property of the Java API that defines the look and feel of the user interface on a specific platform.

try

The try keyword indicates a block of code to which subsequent catch and finally clauses apply. The try statement itself performs no special action. See also *catch* and *finally* for more information on the try/catch/finally construct.

UCS (universal character set)

A synonym for ISO 10646.

UDP (User Datagram Protocol)

A connectionless unreliable protocol. UDP describes a network data connection based on datagrams with little packet control.

Unicode

A 16-bit character encoding that includes all of the world's commonly used alphabets and ideographic character sets in a "unified" form (i.e., a form from which duplications among national standards have been removed). ASCII and Latin-1 characters may be trivially mapped to Unicode characters. Java uses Unicode for its `char` and `String` types.

UTF-8 (UCS transformation format 8-bit form)

An encoding for Unicode characters (and more generally, UCS characters) commonly used for transmission and storage. It is a multibyte format in which different characters require different numbers of bytes to be represented.

vector

A dynamic array of elements.

verifier

A theorem prover that steps through the Java byte-code before it is run and makes sure that it is well-behaved. The byte-code verifier is the first line of defense in Java's security model.

Index

About the Authors

Patrick Niemeyer (*pat@pat.net*) became involved with Oak (Java's predecessor) while working at Southwestern Bell Technology Resources. He is currently an independent consultant and author in the areas of networking and distributed applications. Most recently, Pat developed components for the client/server migration at Edward Jones & Co. and communications software for Strata-Group, Inc. Pat is the author of BeanShell, an embeddable Java scripting language, and various other free goodies available on the Internet. He currently lives in the Central West End area of St. Louis with some cats and other creatures.

Jonathan B. Knudsen (*jonathan@oreilly.com*) is an editor for O'Reilly & Associates, a job that allows him to exercise the right and left sides of his brain but little of his body. In 1977, when Jonathan was knee-high to a grasshopper, he began his computer career by programming in BASIC on a TRS-80. In 1993, he graduated cum laude from Princeton with a degree in mechanical engineering. Jonathan is still unsure what mechanical engineers do for a living. He is author of *Java Cryptography*, *Java 2D Graphics*, and *The Unofficial Guide to LEGO™ MINDSTORMS® Robots*. He writes a monthly online column called "Bite-Size Java" and has authored articles about LEGO robotics for the O'Reilly Network.

Jonathan lives in New Jersey with his wife and technical advisor, Kristen, his children, Daphne, Luke, and Andrew, and two black and white cats. In his spare time, he enjoys playing the piano and bicycling.

Colophon

Our look is the result of reader comments, our own experimentation, and feedback from distribution channels. Distinctive covers complement our distinctive approach to technical topics, breathing personality and life into potentially dry subjects.

The cover of *Learning Java* features a suitcase covered in luggage labels. Labels such as these were popular during the "Golden Age of Travel," a time that can roughly be placed between the 1880s and 1950s. The labels, which were given out by hotels, ocean-liners, railroads, and, after World War I, airlines, served two purposes. For the companies that gave them away, they were a portable and inexpensive way to advertise themselves around the world. For the travelers who affixed the labels to their luggage, they were also a form of advertisement; the colorful and exotic-looking labels told all who saw them that the person carrying that suitcase was well-traveled and adventurous and, of course, wealthy. With the introduction of the jet engine in the 1950s, traveling became less expensive and more convenient, and, therefore, more accessible to all. As being well-traveled became less a mark of distinction and as the world began to seem a smaller and smaller place, luggage labels became obsolete.

Nicole Arigo was the production editor for *Learning Java*. Nancy Kotary was the copyeditor, and Norma Emory proofread the book. Darren Kelly, Colleen Gorman, and Jane Ellin provided quality control. Ellen Troutman wrote the index. The colophon was written by Clairemarie O'Leary.

Edie Freedman designed the cover of this book, using an image from the CMCD PhotoCD Collection that she manipulated in Adobe Photoshop. The cover layout was produced by Emma Colby with Quark XPress 3.3 using the Bodoni Black font from URW Software. The CD label was designed by Emma Colby.

Alicia Cech designed the interior layout based on a series design by Nancy Priest. The heading font is Bodoni BT; the text font is New Baskerville. Mike Sierra implemented the design in FrameMaker 5.5. The illustrations that appear in the book were produced by Robert Romano and Rhon Porter using Macromedia FreeHand 8 and Adobe Photoshop 5.

Whenever possible, our books use RepKover™, a durable and flexible lay-flat binding. If the page count exceeds RepKover's limit, perfect binding is used.

How to stay in touch with O'Reilly

1. Visit Our Award-Winning Web Site

http://www.oreilly.com/

★ "Top 100 Sites on the Web" —*PC Magazine*
★ "Top 5% Web sites" —*Point Communications*
★ "3-Star site" —*The McKinley Group*

Our web site contains a library of comprehensive product information (including book excerpts and tables of contents), downloadable software, background articles, interviews with technology leaders, links to relevant sites, book cover art, and more. File us in your Bookmarks or Hotlist!

2. Join Our Email Mailing Lists

New Product Releases

To receive automatic email with brief descriptions of all new O'Reilly products as they are released, send email to:
listproc@online.oreilly.com
Put the following information in the first line of your message (*not* in the Subject field):
subscribe oreilly-news

O'Reilly Events

If you'd also like us to send information about trade show events, special promotions, and other O'Reilly events, send email to:
listproc@online.oreilly.com
Put the following information in the first line of your message (*not* in the Subject field):
subscribe oreilly-events

3. Get Examples from Our Books via FTP

There are two ways to access an archive of example files from our books:

Regular FTP

- ftp to:
  ftp.oreilly.com
  (login: anonymous
  password: your email address)
- Point your web browser to:
  ftp://ftp.oreilly.com/

FTPMAIL

- Send an email message to:
  ftpmail@online.oreilly.com
  (Write "help" in the message body)

4. Contact Us via Email

order@oreilly.com
To place a book or software order online. Good for North American and international customers.

subscriptions@oreilly.com
To place an order for any of our newsletters or periodicals.

books@oreilly.com
General questions about any of our books.

software@oreilly.com
For general questions and product information about our software. Check out O'Reilly Software Online at **http://software.oreilly.com/** for software and technical support information. Registered O'Reilly software users send your questions to: **website-support@oreilly.com**

cs@oreilly.com
For answers to problems regarding your order or our products.

booktech@oreilly.com
For book content technical questions or corrections.

proposals@oreilly.com
To submit new book or software proposals to our editors and product managers.

international@oreilly.com
For information about our international distributors or translation queries. For a list of our distributors outside of North America check out:
http://www.oreilly.com/www/order/country.html

5. Work with Us

Check out our website for current employment opportunites:
www.jobs@oreilly.com
Click on "Work with Us"

O'Reilly & Associates, Inc.
101 Morris Street, Sebastopol, CA 95472 USA
TEL   707-829-0515 or 800-998-9938
          (6am to 5pm PST)
FAX   707-829-0104

International Distributors

UK, EUROPE, MIDDLE EAST AND AFRICA (EXCEPT FRANCE, GERMANY, AUSTRIA, SWITZERLAND, LUXEMBOURG, LIECHTENSTEIN, AND EASTERN EUROPE)

INQUIRIES
O'Reilly UK Limited
4 Castle Street
Farnham
Surrey, GU9 7HS
United Kingdom
Telephone: 44-1252-711776
Fax: 44-1252-734211
Email: information@oreilly.co.uk

ORDERS
Wiley Distribution Services Ltd.
1 Oldlands Way
Bognor Regis
West Sussex PO22 9SA
United Kingdom
Telephone: 44-1243-779777
Fax: 44-1243-820250
Email: cs-books@wiley.co.uk

FRANCE

INQUIRIES
Éditions O'Reilly
18 rue Séguier
75006 Paris, France
Tel: 33-1-40-51-52-30
Fax: 33-1-40-51-52-31
Email: france@editions-oreilly.fr

ORDERS
GEODIF
61, Bd Saint-Germain
75240 Paris Cedex 05, France
Tel: 33-1-44-41-46-16 (French books)
Tel: 33-1-44-41-11-87 (English books)
Fax: 33-1-44-41-11-44
Email: distribution@eyrolles.com

GERMANY, SWITZERLAND, AUSTRIA, EASTERN EUROPE, LUXEMBOURG, AND LIECHTENSTEIN

INQUIRIES & ORDERS
O'Reilly Verlag
Balthasarstr. 81
D-50670 Köln
Germany
Telephone: 49-221-973160-91
Fax: 49-221-973160-8
Email: anfragen@oreilly.de (inquiries)
Email: order@oreilly.de (orders)

CANADA (FRENCH LANGUAGE BOOKS)

Les Éditions Flammarion ltée
375, Avenue Laurier Ouest
Montréal (Québec) H2V 2K3
Tel: 00-1-514-277-8807
Fax: 00-1-514-278-2085
Email: info@flammarion.qc.ca

HONG KONG

City Discount Subscription Service, Ltd.
Unit D, 3rd Floor, Yan's Tower
27 Wong Chuk Hang Road
Aberdeen, Hong Kong
Tel: 852-2580-3539
Fax: 852-2580-6463
Email: citydis@ppn.com.hk

KOREA

Hanbit Media, Inc.
Chungmu Bldg. 201
Yonnam-dong 568-33
Mapo-gu
Seoul, Korea
Tel: 822-325-0397
Fax: 822-325-9697
Email: hant93@chollian.dacom.co.kr

PHILIPPINES

Global Publishing
G/F Benavides Garden
1186 Benavides Street
Manila, Philippines
Tel: 632-254-8949/637-252-2582
Fax: 632-734-5060/632-252-2733
Email: globalp@pacific.net.ph

TAIWAN

O'Reilly Taiwan
No. 3, Lane 131
Hang-Chow South Road
Section 1, Taipei, Taiwan
Tel: 886-2-23968990
Fax: 886-2-23968916
Email: taiwan@oreilly.com

CHINA

O'Reilly Beijing
Room 2410
160, FuXingMenNeiDaJie
XiCheng District
Beijing, China PR 100031
Tel: 86-10-66412305
Fax: 86-10-86631007
Email: beijing@oreilly.com

INDIA

Computer Bookshop (India) Pvt. Ltd.
190 Dr. D.N. Road, Fort
Bombay 400 001 India
Tel: 91-22-207-0989
Fax: 91-22-262-3551
Email: cbsbom@giasbm01.vsnl.net.in

JAPAN

O'Reilly Japan, Inc.
Yotsuya Y's Building
7 Banch 6, Honshio-cho
Shinjuku-ku
Tokyo 160-0003 Japan
Tel: 81-3-3356-5227
Fax: 81-3-3356-5261
Email: japan@oreilly.com

ALL OTHER ASIAN COUNTRIES

O'Reilly & Associates, Inc.
101 Morris Street
Sebastopol, CA 95472 USA
Tel: 707-829-0515
Fax: 707-829-0104
Email: order@oreilly.com

AUSTRALIA

Woodslane Pty., Ltd.
7/5 Vuko Place
Warriewood NSW 2102
Australia
Tel: 61-2-9970-5111
Fax: 61-2-9970-5002
Email: info@woodslane.com.au

NEW ZEALAND

Woodslane New Zealand, Ltd.
21 Cooks Street (P.O. Box 575)
Waganui, New Zealand
Tel: 64-6-347-6543
Fax: 64-6-345-4840
Email: info@woodslane.com.au

LATIN AMERICA

McGraw-Hill Interamericana
Editores, S.A. de C.V.
Cedro No. 512
Col. Atlampa
06450, Mexico, D.F.
Tel: 52-5-547-6777
Fax: 52-5-547-3336
Email: mcgraw-hill@infosel.net.mx

O'REILLY®

TO ORDER: **800-998-9938** • **order@oreilly.com** • **http://www.oreilly.com/**

OUR PRODUCTS ARE AVAILABLE AT A BOOKSTORE OR SOFTWARE STORE NEAR YOU.

FOR INFORMATION: **800-998-9938** • **707-829-0515** • **info@oreilly.com**

O'REILLY™

O'Reilly & Associates, Inc.
101 Morris Street
Sebastopol, CA 95472-9902
1-800-998-9938

Visit us online at:
**http://www.ora.com/
orders@ora.com**

O'REILLY WOULD LIKE TO HEAR FROM YOU

Which book did this card come from?

_____

Where did you buy this book?
- ❑ Bookstore
- ❑ Direct from O'Reilly
- ❑ Bundled with hardware/software
- ❑ Other _____
- ❑ Computer Store
- ❑ Class/seminar

What operating system do you use?
- ❑ UNIX
- ❑ Windows NT
- ❑ Other _____
- ❑ Macintosh
- ❑ PC(Windows/DOS)

What is your job description?
- ❑ System Administrator
- ❑ Network Administrator
- ❑ Web Developer
- ❑ Programmer
- ❑ Educator/Teacher
- ❑ Other _____

❑ Please send me O'Reilly's catalog, containing a complete listing of O'Reilly books and software.

Name _____   Company/Organization _____

Address _____

City _____   State _____   Zip/Postal Code _____   Country _____

Telephone _____   Internet or other email address (specify network)

Nineteenth century wood engraving
of a bear from the O'Reilly &
Associates Nutshell Handbook®
Using & Managing UUCP.

POST CARD

NO POSTAGE
NECESSARY IF
MAILED IN THE
UNITED STATES

BUSINESS REPLY MAIL

FIRST CLASS MAIL   PERMIT NO. 80   SEBASTOPOL, CA

Postage will be paid by addressee

O'Reilly & Associates, Inc.
101 Morris Street
Sebastopol, CA 95472-9902